Educational Media and Technology Yearbook

For further volumes:
http://www.springer.com/series/8617

Michael Orey · Stephanie A. Jones
Robert Maribe Branch

Editors

Educational Media and Technology Yearbook

Volume 36, 2011

 Springer

LB
1028. 3
. E 37
2011

Editors

Michael Orey
Learning, Design, and Technology Program
The University of Georgia
Athens, GA, USA
mikeorey@uga.edu

Stephanie A. Jones
Instructional Technology
Georgia Southern University
Statesboro, GA, USA
sjones@georgiasouthern.edu

Robert Maribe Branch
Learning, Design, and Technology Program
University of Georgia
Athens, GA, USA
rbranch@uga.edu

ISSN 8755-2094
ISBN 978-1-4614-1304-2   e-ISBN 978-1-4614-1305-9
DOI 10.1007/978-1-4614-1305-9
Springer New York Dordrecht Heidelberg London

© Springer Science+Business Media, LLC 2012
All rights reserved. This work may not be translated or copied in whole or in part without the written permission of the publisher (Springer Science+Business Media, LLC, 233 Spring Street, New York, NY 10013, USA), except for brief excerpts in connection with reviews or scholarly analysis. Use in connection with any form of information storage and retrieval, electronic adaptation, computer software, or by similar or dissimilar methodology now known or hereafter developed is forbidden.
The use in this publication of trade names, trademarks, service marks, and similar terms, even if they are not identified as such, is not to be taken as an expression of opinion as to whether or not they are subject to proprietary rights.

Printed on acid-free paper

Springer is part of Springer Science+Business Media (www.springer.com)

Preface

The audience for the *Yearbook* consists of media and technology professionals in schools, higher education, and business contexts. Topics of interest to professionals practicing in these areas are broad, as the Table of Contents demonstrates. The theme unifying each of the following chapters is the use of technology to enable or enhance education. Forms of technology represented in this volume vary from traditional tools such as the book to the latest advancements in digital technology, while areas of education encompass widely ranging situations involving learning and teaching which are idea technologies.

As in prior volumes, the assumptions underlying the chapters presented here are as follows:

1. Technology represents tools that act as extensions of the educator.
2. Media serve as delivery systems for educational communications.
3. Technology is *not* restricted to machines and hardware, but includes techniques and procedures derived from scientific research about ways to promote change in human performance.
4. The fundamental tenet is that educational media and technology should be used to:

    (a) Achieve authentic learning objectives
    (b) Situate learning tasks
    (c) Negotiate the complexities of guided learning
    (d) Facilitate the construction of knowledge
    (e) Aid in the assessment/documenting of learning
    (f) Support skill acquisition
    (g) Manage diversity

The *Educational Media and Technology Yearbook* (EMTY) has become a standard reference in many libraries and professional collections. Examined in relation to its companion volumes of the past, it provides a valuable historical record of current ideas and developments in the field. Part One, "Trends and Issues," presents an array of chapters that develop some of the current themes listed above, in addition to others. Part Two, "Library and Information Science," concentrates upon chapters of special relevance to K-12 education, library science education, school learning resources, and various types of library and media centers – school, public, and academic among others. In Part Three, "Leadership Profiles," authors provide biographical sketches of the careers of instructional technology leaders. Part Four, "Organizations and Associations in North America," and Part Five, "Graduate Programs in North America," are, respectively, directories of instructional technology-related organizations and institutions of higher learning offering degrees in related fields. Finally, Part Six, the "Mediagraphy," presents an annotated listing of selected current publications related to the field.

The Editors of the *Yearbook* invite media and technology professionals to submit manuscripts for consideration for publication. Contact Michael Orey (mikeorey@ uga.edu) for submission guidelines.

For a number of years we have worked together as editors and the eighth with Dr. Michael Orey as the senior editor. Within each volume of the EMTY we try to list all the graduate programs, journals, and organizations that are related to both Learning, Design, and Technology (LDT) and Information and Library Science (ILS). We also include a section on trends in LDT, trends in ILS, and we have a section profiling some of the leaders in the field. Beginning with the 2007 volume, we have attempted to generate a list of leading programs in the combined areas of LDT and ILS. One year, we were able to compose an alphabetical list of 30 of the programs that people told us were among the best. However, each year we have worked on being more systematic. Instead of following the *US News and World Report* model and have one top program list, we decided to use some of the same numbers that they use and generate a collection of top-20 lists, rather than attempt to generate a statistical model to generate the rankings list. One thought was to rank programs according to the number of publications that were produced; however, deciding which journals to include was an issue. We decided to use 2007 through 2009 as the years to count (since at the time of writing, it is still 2010 and so we do not have a complete year). Furthermore, we decided to only count actual research reports that appeared in one of two journals, *Educational Technology Research and Development* and the *Journal of the Learning Sciences*. These two journals were primarily selected based on the general sense that they are the leading journals in the area of LDT. Noticeably absent is the area of information and library science. So, while these numbers are pretty absolute, choosing to only count these journals is somewhat arbitrary.

The other top-20 lists are based on self-report data collected as part of the program information in the EMTY. Every year, we collect general information about programs in LDT and ILS and publish this information in the Yearbook. This year we opted to collect some additional data. We asked the representatives of each of the institutions to enter the US dollar amount of grants and contracts, the number of PhD graduates, the number of Masters graduates, and the number of other graduates from their programs. We also asked them for the number of full-time and part-time faculty. We then generated a top-20 list for some of these categories. The limitation in this case is that it is self-report data and there is no real way of verifying that the

Table 1 Top 20 Graduate Programs in the area of Learning, Design, and Technology as measured by the number of publications in *Educational Technology Research and Development* and the *Journal of the Learning Sciences*

Rank	Institution	Pubs
1	University of Georgia	7.65
2	Indiana University	6.66
3	Arizona State University	5.32
4	Nanyang Technological University	4.33
5	University of Wisconsin	4.1
6	University of Colorado	2.83
7	Stanford University	2.5
7	University of New Mexico	2.5
9	University of Toronto	2.3
10	Sultan Qaboos University	2
10	SUNY-Buffalo	2
10	University of Hong Kong	2
10	Wayne State University	2
10	Florida State University	2
10	Open University of the Netherlands	2
16	Brigham Young University	1.83
16	UCLA	1.83
18	SRI International	1.81
19	University of Northern Colorado	1.75
20	University of Memphis	1.7

data is accurate. So, while the list of the 30 top programs from the first year lacked hard data, and the lists this year are based on numbers, those numbers may be just as unreliable. In the end, we have a collection of lists that we hope will be of use to our readers. Many of the universities that appeared in the list last year are here again, in addition to many others. More information about many of these universities can be found in part five of this edition.

There are six top-20 lists in this preface. The first of these top-20 lists is based on a count of publications. We used every issue from the 2007 through 2009 volume years of the *Educational Technology Research and Development* journal and the *Journal of the Learning Sciences*. We eliminated all book reviews and letters-to-the-editor and such. We only used the primary academic articles of these journals. Each publication counted 1 point. If the article had two authors, then each authors' institution received 0.5 points. If there were three authors, then 0.33 was spread across the institutions. Also, as an additional example, if there were three authors and two of them were from the same institution, then that institution received 0.66 points and the institution of the remaining author received 0.33. Finally, the unit receiving the points was the University. So, in the case of Indiana University where they have both a Learning Sciences and an Instructional Technology program, all of the points for IT and LS were aggregated into one variable called Indiana University. Table 1 shows our results. The University of Georgia came out as the top LDT program in the world. They were not in the top 5 last year; they were tied for sixth. Moving to the top program moved the University of Colorado to the sixth position. Since we are now counting publications across 3 years, we are getting a bit more variance. Last year, we had a 28-way tie for twentieth. This year we still have a large number of institutions in a tie (six tied for tenth), but we do have a list of just 20 schools. Even with large number of ties last year, we had the University of Toronto not make last year's list and come out as the ninth-ranked LDT program this year. Others that made the top 20 this year that were not in last year's top 20 included Florida State University, SRI International, and the University of Northern Colorado. While we did this list to rate universities, it is interesting that a research center comes in eighteenth place on the list even though they are not a university. We included them because of the way we counted the data.

We would love to hear your feedback on this approach for the future. Are there other journals that ought to be included? Is it unfair that there are more publications in ETRD than IJLS? What about recent graduates publishing with their new institution when the work was done at their previous institution? I am certain there are many other issues, and we welcome constructive feedback.

The two primary measures of research achievement are publications and grants. While choosing ETRD and IJLS was somewhat arbitrary, the numbers are verifiable. In Table 2, we present the top-20 programs according to the dollar amount of grants and contracts for that program over the academic year of 2009–10. While Table 1 was constrained to LDT, Table 2 has both LDT programs and ILS programs which resulted in the University of Calgary being number one in the grants and contracts list, but not appearing at all in the publication list. In fact, the only institutions that are both on the list for publications and grants are the University of Wisconsin (five for publications and ten for grants) and Wayne State University (ten for publications and fourteen for grants).

Tables 1 and 2 are measures of research productivity. The remaining four tables are more related to teaching than research. The first, Table 3, shows the top-20 programs in terms of the number of fulltime faculty. You will notice that the list is ordered by the number of full-time faculty (FT), but number five, The University of Hong Kong has 102 total faculty members. We decided that full-time faculty was more important than part time as a measure and so only generated one list for number of faculty. We just thought it would be interesting to see the total number of faculty as well. For example, it is interesting to see The University of Hong Kong and the University of Calgary with very large numbers (102 and 83, respectively), while the University of North Carolina has 31 full-time and only one part-time faculty members.

Table 2 Top-20 LDT and ILS programs by the amount of grant and contract monies

Rank	University	Department/Program	Monies
1	University of Calgary	Office of Graduate Programs, Faculty of Education	$20,000,000.00
2	University of North Carolina	School of Information and Library Science	$6,843,136.00
3	George Mason University	Instructional Technology Programs	$2,500,000.00
4	University of Massachusetts, Amherst	Learning, Media and Technology Masters Program/Math Science and Learning Technology Doctoral Program	$2,300,000.00
5	Virginia Tech	College of Liberal Arts and Human Sciences	$1,800,000.00
6	Georgia State University	Middle-Secondary Education and Instructional Technology	$1,600,000.00
7	University of Missouri-Columbia	School of Information Science & Learning Technologies	$1,585,885.00
8	New York University	Educational Communication and Technology Program, Steinhardt School of Culture, Education, and Human Development	$1,500,000.00
9	The Ohio State University	Cultural Foundations, Technology, & Qualitative Inquiry	$1,200,000.00
10	University of Wisconsin-Madison	Curriculum and Instruction, School of Education	$1,000,000.00
10	Lehigh University	Teaching, Learning, and Technology	$1,000,000.00
10	California State University Monterey Bay	Master of Science in Instructional Science and Technology (IST)	$1,000,000.00
13	Texas A&M University	Educational Technology Program, Department of Educational psychology	$876,000.00
14	Wayne State University	Instructional Technology	$750,000.00
15	Utah State University	Department of Instructional Technology & Learning Sciences, Emma Eccles Jones College of Education and Human Services	$642,000.00
16	University of Virginia	Department of Curriculum, Instruction and Special Education, Curry School of Education	$500,000.00
16	University of Geneva	Master of Science in Learning and Teaching Technologies	$500,000.00
16	Rutgers-The State University of New Jersey	School of Communication and Information	$500,000.00
16	Ohio University	Instructional Technology	$500,000.00
20	Valley City State University	School of Education and Graduate Studies	$450,000.00

Table 3 Top-20 LDT and ILS programs by the number of fulltime faculty (also shown is the total faculty which includes both full and part-time faculty)

Rank	University	Department/Program	FT	Total
1	University of North Carolina	School of Information and Library Science	31	32
2	Rutgers-The State University of New Jersey	School of Communication and Information	22	37
3	Valdosta State University	Curriculum, Leadership, & Technology	20	30
4	University of Bridgeport	Instructional Technology	14	35
5	Anadolu University	Computer Education and Instructional Technology	12	21
5	Valley City State University	School of Education and Graduate Studies	12	17
5	The University of Hong Kong	Faculty of Education	12	102
5	Fordham University	MA Program in Public Communications in the Department of Communication and Media Studies	12	16
9	University of Georgia	Department of Educational Psychology and Instructional Technology, College of Education	11	11
9	University of Louisville	College of Education and Human Development	11	25
9	The University of Oklahoma	Instructional Psychology and Technology, Department of Educational Psychology	11	11
12	Taganrog State Pedagogical Institute	Media Education (Social Pedagogic Faculty)	10	30
12	University of West Georgia	Department of Media and Instructional Technology	10	14
12	California State University Monterey Bay (CSUMB)	Master of Science in Instructional Science and Technology (IST)	10	22
12	Indiana University	School of Education	10	14
12	Utah State University	Department of Instructional Technology & Learning Sciences, Emma Eccles Jones College of Education and Human Services	10	11
12	University of Missouri-Columbia	School of Information Science & Learning Technologies	10	18
18	Hacettepe University	Computer Education and Instructional Technology	9	19
19	Western Illinois University	Instructional Technology and Telecommunications	8	11
19	University of Calgary	Office of Graduate Programs, Faculty of Education	8	83
19	Ball State University	Masters of Arts in Curriculum and Educational Technology	8	12

The next top-20 list is the number of PhD graduates. This list might be a good measure of research productivity as well as teaching productivity. The number of graduates is self-reported. The number of publications is verifiable, so it is interesting to compare who is on both lists. None of the top four are on the top-20 publications list, but there are six institutions on both lists. Wayne State, Florida State, Indiana, Northern Colorado, Georgia, and Memphis are on both of these lists. The top school in terms of PhD graduates is also on the list for the top grant-awarded institutions, George Mason (Table 4).

Our next top-20 list is based on the number of master's graduates. In our mind, we might consider this an indication of whether the program is more practitioner-oriented than say the number of PhD graduates. Interestingly, George Mason comes in fifth here whereas they were number one in PhD graduates. So, this differentiation may be meaningless. It is interesting to note that schools like University of Bridgeport, University of Calgary, Rutgers, NYIT, George Mason, and North Carolina are all producing more than 100 graduates per year. It appears that for profit institutions such as Walden University and the University of Phoenix are very active; however, neither of these two schools chose to complete the form. We are not implying that the large numbers are necessarily because these programs are online, but online degree programs certainly allow many more people to further their education (Table 5).

The final top-20 list is the combined degree graduate list. It is very similar to the master's list, but since the online form only had entries for PhD graduates, masters graduates, and other graduates, I thought it might be most useful to just show the total number of graduates from each of the programs who chose to update their information in our database. It is very interesting to see the University of Bridgeport come out on top here with 426°! This is nearly double the number of second place University of Calgary with 261 graduates (Table 6).

We acknowledge that any kind of rankings of programs is problematic. We hope you find our lists useful. If you have suggestions, please let us know and we will try to accommodate those changes in future publications of the *Yearbook*. If your program is not represented, please contact one of us and we can add you to the database so that you can be included in future issues.

Athens, GA, USA	Michael Orey
Statesboro, GA, USA	Stephanie A. Jones
Athens, GA, USA	Robert Maribe Branch

Table 4 Top 20 LDT and ILS programs by the number of PhD graduates

Rank	University	Department/Program	PhD Grads
1	George Mason University	Instructional Technology Programs	15
1	University of Bridgeport	Instructional Technology	15
3	University of Central Florida	College of Education - ERTL	12
4	University of Calgary	Office of Graduate Programs, Faculty of Education	11
4	Wayne State University	Instructional Technology	11
6	University of Missouri-Columbia	School of Information Science & Learning Technologies	10
6	Florida State University	Educational Psychology and Learning Systems	10
6	Illinois State University	Curriculum and Instruction	10
6	Ohio University	Instructional Technology	10
10	Indiana University	School of Education	7
10	Virginia Tech	College of Liberal Arts and Human Sciences	7
12	The Ohio State University	Cultural Foundations, Technology, & Qualitative Inquiry	5
12	The University of Texas at Austin	Curriculum & Instruction	5
12	Kent State University	Instructional Technology	5
12	University of Louisville	College of Education and Human Development	5
16	Utah State University	Department of Instructional Technology & Learning Sciences, Emma Eccles Jones College of Education and Human Services	4
16	University of Northern Colorado	Educational Technology	4
16	Texas A&M University	Educational Technology Program, Dept. of Educational psychology	4
16	University of Toledo	Curriculum & Instruction	4
20	Rutgers-The State University of New Jersey	School of Communication and Information	3
20	University of Georgia	Department of Educational Psychology and Instructional Technology, College of Education	3
20	University of North Carolina	School of Information and Library Science	3
20	University of Memphis	Instructional Design and Technology	3
20	University of Virginia	Department of Curriculum, Instruction and Special Education, Curry School of Education	3
20	Georgia State University	Middle-Secondary Education and Instructional Technology	3

Table 5 Top 20 LDT and ILS programs by the number of master's graduates

Rank	University	Department/Program	Masters
1	University of Bridgeport	Instructional Technology	294
2	University of Calgary	Office of Graduate Programs, Faculty of Education	235
3	Rutgers-The State University of New Jersey	School of Communication and Information	144
4	New York Institute of Technology	Department of Instructional Technology and Educational Leadership	130
5	George Mason University	Instructional Technology Programs	130
6	University of North Carolina	School of Information and Library Science	111
7	University of Colorado Denver	School of Education and Human Development	84
8	The University of Rhode Island	Graduate School of Library and Information Studies	80
9	University of Central Florida	College of Education - ERTL	65
10	University of Missouri-Columbia	School of Information Science & Learning Technologies	59
11	San Francisco State University	College of Education, Department of Instructional Technology	50
11	Buffalo State College	Computer Information Systems Department	50
11	Illinois State University	Curriculum and Instruction	50
14	Wayne State University	Instructional Technology	48
14	Emporia State University	Instructional Design and Technology	48
16	University of Nebraska-Omaha	Department of Teacher Education	41
17	University of Georgia	Department of Educational Psychology and Instructional Technology, College of Education	40
17	Georgia Southern University	College of Education	40
17	Lehigh University	Teaching, Learning, and Technology	40
17	University of West Georgia	Department of Media and Instructional Technology	40
17	University of Central Arkansas	Leadership Studies	40
17	Bloomsburg University	Instructional Technology & Institute for Interactive Technologies	40
17	University of Nebraska at Kearney	Teacher Education	40
17	Michigan State University	College of Education	40

Table 6 Top 20 LDT and ILS programs by the overall total number of graduates

Rank	University	Department/Program	Total Degrees
1	University of Bridgeport	Instructional Technology	426
2	University of Calgary	Office of Graduate Programs, Faculty of Education	261
3	Illinois State University	Curriculum and Instruction	260
4	Valley City State University	School of Education and Graduate Studies	191
5	Rutgers-The State University of New Jersey	School of Communication and Information	147
6	George Mason University	Instructional Technology Programs	145
7	University of North Carolina	School of Information and Library Science	136
8	New York Institute of Technology	Department of Instructional Technology and Educational Leadership	130
9	University of Missouri-Columbia	School of Information Science & Learning Technologies	87
10	University of West Georgia	Department of Media and Instructional Technology	85
10	University of Colorado Denver	School of Education and Human Development	85
12	University of Central Florida	College of Education - ERTL	84
13	California State University Monterey Bay (CSUMB)	Master of Science in Instructional Science and Technology (IST)	80
13	The University of Rhode Island	Graduate School of Library and Information Studies	80
15	Wayne State University	Instructional Technology	67
16	University of Central Arkansas	Leadership Studies	60
17	University of Nebraska-Omaha	Department of Teacher Education	54
18	University of Georgia	Department of Educational Psychology and Instructional Technology, College of Education	53
19	San Francisco State University	College of Education, Department of Instructional Technology	50
19	Buffalo State College	Computer Information Systems Department	50

Contents

Part I   Trends and Issues in Learning, Design, and Technology

Introduction 3
Liz May and Michael Orey

Storytelling Among Israeli and Palestinian Children in the Era
of Mobile Innovation 7
Elizabeth Buckner and Paul Kim

Self-regulated Learning as a Foundational Principle for a Successful
Strategy in Teaching Educational Research Methods to Doctor
of Philosophy Students 23
Tonia A. Dousay, Diane Igoche, and Robert Maribe Branch

Fostering Student Cognition in Computer-Supported Online
Collaborative Learning Environment 37
Khe Foon Hew, Seng Chee Tan, and Wing Sum Cheung

A Two-Dimensional Framework for Evaluating Teachers'
Technology Adoption 49
Manuel Gerardo Saldivar, Keith E. Maull, Benjamin R. Kirshner,
and Tamara R. Sumner

Issues and Trends in Instructional Technology: Lean Times, Shifts
in Online Learning, and Increased Attention to Mobile Devices 67
Abbie Brown and Tim Green

Enlisting the Collaboration of the Educational Technology
Professional Community to Develop a Knowledge Management
System of the Field: edu-techKNOWiki 81
Anne K. Bednar and Nancy L. Copeland

The Vital Role(s) of School Librarians in Literacy Learning 91
Nancy Flanagan Knapp

An Analysis of Educational Technology-Related Doctoral Programs
in the United States 99
Heng-Yu Ku, Shari Plantz-Masters, Kim Hosler, Watsatree Diteeyont,
Chatchada Akarasriworn, and Tzong-Yih Lin

Examining the Design of Media-Rich Cognitive Tools as Scaffolds
in a Multimedia Problem-Based Learning Environment 113
Min Liu, Lucas Horton, Paul Toprac, and Timothy T. Yuen

An Instructional Design Approach to Effective Instructional
Game Design and Assessment 127
Debbie Denise Reese

PowerPoint and the Pedagogy of Digital Media Technologies 139
Catherine Adams

Part II   Trends and Issues in Library and Information Science

Introduction 157
Stephanie A. Jones

Culturally Sensitive Learning Practices 161
Lesley S.J. Farmer

In the District and on the Desktop: School Libraries as Essential
Elements of Effective Broadband Use in Schools 173
Nancy Everhart and Marcia Mardis

ACCESS Issues in School Library Media Centers: Examining
Library Schedules, Library Closures, and Poverty 187
Karen Gavigan, Gail Dickinson, and Shana Pribesh

School Counselors and School Media Specialists: Innovative Leaders
in Partnerships Promoting Student Mental Health with Online
Resources 199
Kylie P. Dotson-Blake and Kaye B. Dotson

Towards an Understanding of Professional Dispositions
of Exemplary School Librarians 209
Jami L. Jones and Gail Bush

Revised Library Media Standards Adopted by the National Board
for Professional Teaching Standards 219
Delia Neuman

Part III   Leadership Profiles

Introduction... 229
Robert Maribe Branch

**Tillman (Tim) James Ragan: Celebrating Four Decades
of Excellent Scholarship** 231
Diane Igoche

Thomas Reeves 235
Diane Igoche

Glenn Snelbecker 239
Diane Igoche

Ron Zemke: A Leader on the Other Side of the Fence.............................. 243

Part IV   Organizations and Associations in North America

Introduction... 247
Michael Orey

Organizations and Associations in the US and Canada 249

Part V   Graduate Programs

Introduction... 333
Michael Orey

Organizations and Associations in the US and Canada 335

Part VI   Mediagraphy: Print and Non-print Resources

Introduction... 481
Jinn-Wei Tsao

Mediagraphy 485

Index.. 507

Contributors

Catherine Adams Department of Secondary Education, Faculty of Education, University of Alberta, Edmonton, AB, Canada
cathy.adams@ualberta.ca

Chatchada Akarasriworn Educational Technology Program, College of Education and Behavioral Sciences, University of Northern Colorado, Greeley, CO, USA

Anne K. Bednar Educational Media & Technology, Eastern Michigan University, Ypsilanti, MI, USA
abednar@emich.edu

Robert Maribe Branch Learning, Design, and Technology Program, University of Georgia, Athens, GA, USA
rbranch@uga.edu

Abbie Brown Department of Mathematics, Science Instructional Technology Education, East Carolina University, Greenville, NC, USA
brownab@ecu.edu

Elizabeth Buckner Stanford University, Palo Alto, CA, USA
ebuckner@stanford.edu

Gail Bush Department of Reading and Language, National-Louis University, Skokie, IL, USA

Wing Sum Cheung Learning Sciences and Technologies, National Institute of Education, Nanyang Technological University, Singapore, Singapore
wingsum.cheung@nie.edu.sg

Nancy L. Copeland Educational Media & Technology, Eastern Michigan University, Ypsilanti, MI, USA
ncopeland@emich.edu

Gail Dickinson Darden College of Education, Old Dominion University, Norfolk, VA, USA
gdickins@odu.edu

Watsatree Diteeyont Educational Technology Program, College of Education and Behavioral Sciences, University of Northern Colorado, Greeley, CO, USA

Kaye B. Dotson Department of Library Science, East Carolina University, Greenville, NC, USA
dotsonl@ecu.edu

Kylie P. Dotson-Blake Department of Higher, Adult and Counselor Education, East Carolina University, Greenville, NC, USA
blakek@ecu.edu

Tonia A. Dousay Department of Educational Psychology and Instructional Technology, University of Georgia, Athens, GA, USA
teedee@uga.edu

Nancy Everhart Partnerships for Advancing Library Media (PALM) Center, School of Library and Information Studies, College of Communication & Information, The Florida State University, Tallahassee, FL, USA
everhart@fsu.edu

Lesley S.J. Farmer CSULB/EdPAC, California State University Long Beach, Long Beach, CA, USA
lfarmer@csulb.edu

Karen Gaviganssor School of Library and Information Science, University of South Carolina, Columbia, SC, USA
kgavigan@mailbox.sc.edu

Tim Green Department of Elementary and Bilingual Education, California State University, Fullerton, CA, USA
timdgreen@gmail.com

Khe Foon Hew Learning Sciences and Technologies, National Institute of Education, Nanyang Technological University, Singapore, Singapore
khefoon.hew@nie.edu.sg

Lucas Horton Instructional Technology Program, Department of Curriculum and Instruction, The University of Texas at Austin, Austin, TX, USA

Kim Hosler Educational Technology Program, College of Education and Behavioral Sciences, University of Northern Colorado, Greeley, CO, USA

Diane Igoche Department of Educational Psychology and Instructional Technology, University of Georgia, Athens, GA, USA
dai011@uga.edu

Jami L. Jones Department of Library Science, East Carolina University, Greenville, NC, USA
jonesj@ecu.edu

Stephanie A. Jones Instructional Technology, Georgia Southern University, Statesboro, GA, USA
sjones@georgiasouthern.edu

Paul Kim Stanford University, Palo Alto, CA, USA
phkim@stanford.edu

Benjamin R. Kirshner Institute of Cognitive Science, University of Colorado at Boulder, Boulder, CO, USA
Ben.kirshner@colorado.edu

Nancy Flanagan Knapp Applied Cognition and Development Program, University of Georgia, Athens, GA, USA
nfknapp@uga.edu

Heng-Yu Ku Educational Technology Program, College of Education and Behavioral Sciences, University of Northern Colorado, Greeley, CO, USA
heng-yu.ku@unco.edu

Tzong-Yih Lin Educational Technology Program, College of Education and Behavioral Sciences, University of Northern Colorado, Greeley, CO, USA

Min Liu Instructional Technology Program, Department of Curriculum and Instruction, The University of Texas at Austin, Austin, TX, USA
MLiu@mail.utexas.edu

Marcia Mardis Partnerships for Advancing Library Media (PALM) Center, School of Library and Information Studies, College of Communication & Information, The Florida State University, Tallahassee, FL, USA
mardis@fsu.edu

Keith E. Maull Institute of Cognitive Science, University of Colorado at Boulder, Boulder, CO, USA

Liz May Learning, Design, and Technology Program, The University of Georgia, Athens, GA, USA
lizmay3@hotmail.com

Delia Neuman College of Information Science and Technology, Drexel University, Philadelphia, PA, USA
dneuman@drexel.edu

Michael Orey Learning, Design, and Technology Program, The University of Georgia, Athens, GA, USA
mikeorey@uga.edu

Shari Plantz-Masters Educational Technology Program, College of Education and Behavioral Sciences, University of Northern Colorado, Greeley, CO, USA

Shana Pribesh Darden College of Education, Old Dominion University, Norfolk, VA, USA
spribesh@odu.edu

Debbie Denise Reese Center for Educational Technologies, Wheeling Jesuit University, Wheeling, WV, USA
debbie@cet.edu

Manuel Gerardo Saldivar Institute of Cognitive Science, University of Colorado at Boulder, Boulder, CO, USA
saldivar@colorado.edu

Tamara R. Sumner Institute of Cognitive Science, University of Colorado at Boulder, Boulder, CO, USA
tamara.sumner@gmail.com

Seng Chee Tan Learning Sciences and Technologies, National Institute of Education, Nanyang Technological University, Singapore, Singapore
sengchee.tan@nie.edu.sg

Paul Toprac Southern Methodist University, Dallas, TX, USA

Jinn-Wei Tsao Learning, Design, and Technology Program, The University of Georgia, Athens, GA, USA
miketsao@uga.edu

Timothy T. Yuen The University of Texas at San Antonio, San Antonio, TX, USA

Part I
Trends and Issues in Learning, Design, and Technology

Introduction

Liz May and Michael Orey

Storytelling is not a new phenomenon; nor is using education as a way of fostering socialization and identity. However, pairing storytelling with technology as a way to solve social problems is new, and therefore *Storytelling among Israeli and Palestinian Children in the Era of Mobile Innovation* by Buckner and Kim provides us with a glimpse into an innovative way to enhance peace education. This Stanford University project provided *TeacherMate* handheld devices to 185 Palestinian children to record their own stories. Having access to firsthand accounts from children in a war-torn area provides a way to enter their perceptions and experiences into the record, bypassing the nation-state political, religious, or military rhetoric that is often the only information available. Such accounts may increase understanding of the Other, also help both sides to establish a global identity that acknowledges the dignity and worth of all individuals. Peace education has many challenges; perhaps innovative technology can overcome some of them, as it opens up avenues for collaboration across cultures that have long held conflicts.

The next article explains a project that was collaborative across cultures, and across levels of expertise. In *Self-regulated Learning as a Foundational Principle for a Successful Strategy in Teaching Educational Research Methods to Doctor of Philosophy Students*, Dousay, Igoche, and Branch share the particulars of their project-based research model in a way that may inspire other faculty to follow suit. Even though those pursuing doctoral studies are often self-motivated and self-regulated, it could be that some teaching methods do not exploit these qualities. Research classes, for example, that teach students about research without affording them opportunities to conduct it leave much to be desired. With a commitment to learning by doing, the Sentence Period Spacing (SPS) project members became involved in self-regulated learning, as well as mentoring, and practicing all aspects of the research process. With the aid of a tenured faculty who provided support and advice,

L. May (✉) • M. Orey
Learning, Design, and Technology Program, The University of Georgia, Athens, GA, USA
e-mail: lizmay3@hotmail.com; mikeorey@uga.edu

M. Orey et al. (eds.), *Educational Media and Technology Yearbook: Volume 36, 2011*,
Educational Media and Technology Yearbook 36, DOI 10.1007/978-1-4614-1305-9_1,
© Springer Science+Business Media, LLC 2012

the SPS team was able to take ownership of the project from its conception all the way to publication of findings. Surveys of past participants of this ongoing project have indicated that it helped them to be adequately prepared for their faculty positions as they learned how to do something by actually doing it.

No matter whether one is a novice or expert faculty member, facilitating meaningful class discussions can be a challenge. In *Fostering Student Cognition in Computer Supported Online Collaborative Learning Environment*, Hew, Tan, and Cheung tackle the formidable task of fostering more robust online discussions. As anyone who has facilitated such discussions knows, it is often a challenge to get students to post comments beyond polite exchanges or surface knowledge sharing onto more critical knowledge building. With this goal in mind, the authors reviewed two vignettes that provide guidelines and techniques to develop deeper discussion levels, as well as an examination of how levels of knowledge building are influenced by the nature of assigned tasks. Their thorough review would be helpful for those who have wondered how to raise the level of online discussions (or perhaps even face-to-face discussions). Since discussions will most likely continue to be an integral part of online learning, this article would be a useful for both novice and expert faculty.

As they have done in previous years, Brown and Green reviewed the current state of instructional technology across three sectors: corporate, K-12, and higher education. In *Issues and Trends in Instructional Technology: Lean Times, Shifts in Online Learning, and Increased Attention to Mobile Devices*, one finds some good news and some bad news. The bad news is that all sectors have had to tighten their fiscal belts, although the corporate sector had a slight increase in spending. The good news is that even in difficult financial times the internet affords enough low-cost options to still be used effectively. In higher education, for example, mobile devices are now owned by virtually all students, and now have broader capabilities and applications. Brown and Green's thorough review provides areas to watch for future growth, namely cloud computing, and collaborative learning platforms, but of course both of these tools have privacy and security issues that must be successfully managed. They also mention growth in digital textbooks as a way to cut costs, but these also will come with new problems to be managed. It will be interesting to see if future trends will include development of innovative ways to deal with the new issues that arise from the new technologies.

Web 2.0 tools have already been mentioned as a useful collaborative learning tool; but how can faculty use them for their own professional development? Although instructional technology is a relatively young field, the internet has made it a field that is difficult to keep up with. Therefore, the faculty of Eastern Michigan University have developed a knowledge management wiki for professionals to share, interact, and collaborate with each other. In their article *Enlisting the Collaboration of the Educational Technology Professional Community to Develop a Knowledge Management System of the Field: edu-teKNOWiki*, Bednar and Copeland explain how the wiki came about, its theoretical foundation, and its potential for connecting those interested in all facets of educational technology. The project is an open source that is not connected to any vendor, but welcomes links to organizations such as

AECT and ISTE as way to foster mutually beneficial dialogue. Due to its nationwide contributors, the wiki was designed to serve a broad audience, and is even open to an evolving design as user practices are permitted to influence its functionality. It is easy to see how such a tool would help anyone interested in educational technology, and we should not be surprised to see this helpful resource expand to international contributors as well.

While virtual resources will continue to grow, and libraries will follow suit as they digitize, Knapp makes a very good case for the importance of onsite librarians in *Concierges, Sherpas, and Cruise Directors: The Vital Role(s) of School Librarians in Literacy Learning.* She skillfully demonstrates a correlation between literacy and school librarians who maintain a full service facility, and an active, collaborative role with faculty and students. For example, librarians are often the gateway to selection of quality books that hook young readers, and even challenge them to eventually branch out. They also function as guides for those who need help navigating the vast amount of resources that can overwhelm today's students. Finally they can foster a social component into literacy as they plan with teachers how to get students collaboratively involved in reading. Knapp concludes with relevant suggestions for both schools and library education programs that will bring the promotion of literacy to the forefront of librarianship.

Sorting through vast stores of information is not limited to school librarians. Ku, Plantz-Masters, Hosler, Diteeyont, Akarasriworn, and Lin have undertaken a daunting task in their article *An Analysis of Educational Technology Related Doctoral Programs in the United States.* The fact that programs differ in name, emphasis, and curriculum makes the analysis a bit difficult, but Ku and his team have managed to wade through these somewhat murky waters to aid those who are interested in pursuing a doctoral degree in the field. This very informative article includes information about number of programs, as well as variation in titles, credit hours, delivery method, and dissertation requirements. It also offers explanations on why the variations exist, such as marketing, and economic necessities that impact when, where and how programs are offered. Anyone who is reviewing programs will find much helpful and relevant information in this article.

While evaluating doctoral programs is an authentic problem-based learning scenario, it is not nearly as much fun as using the *Alien Rescue* program to learn middle-school science. In their article *Examining the Design of Media Rich Cognitive Tools as Scaffolds in a Multimedia Problem-Based Learning Environment*, Liu, Horton, Toprac, and Yuen set out to examine technology-enhanced scaffolding. Using a series of studies, the authors examined how and when the cognitive tools were used in the problem-solving process, as well as the effect of group use of cognitive tools on individual performance. Apparently there was a connection between the use of cognitive tools and high performance on problem-solving tasks. Since both problem solving and technology use are important in today's schools, it is important to know how to design multimedia programs that assist students in problem solving, but that are also fun enough to keep students engaged.

Keeping games both fun and educationally sound is not easy, as Reese points out in *An Instructional Design Approach to Effective Instructional Game Design and Assessment*. She proposes that instructional designers need to work with content experts for sound game design, but notes that challenges exist. Some of these challenges have to do with budgetary concerns, and some have to do with insufficient interaction of game design with education theory. Using the CyGaMEs research game *Selena* as an example, she proposes the use of instructional design principles to build a repository of similar games that can aid in the development of future educational games. Reese also calls for the field of instructional technology to continue to develop instructional game design since the use of educational games will continue to grow.

Storytelling Among Israeli and Palestinian Children in the Era of Mobile Innovation

Elizabeth Buckner and Paul Kim

Introduction

Research in the field of educational media and technology has tended to focus on the intersection of technology and learning. Some of the major themes in the field include: how to improve technological design; how to expand access to technology for disadvantaged populations; and how to use technology to improve instructional design and promote learning objectives (AECT, 2009; Kozma, 2000). These are important areas of research; however, promoting academic learning is only one of the many roles educational institutions play in our societies. We must recognize that formal education is an incredibly powerful institution in every society, which not only educates children, but also socializes them and instills them with national identities and values (Dewey, 1938; Meyer, 1977; Ramirez & Boli, 1987). Just as we do not limit our definition of technology to mere computers or connectivity, neither can we limit our definition of education so narrowly as academic achievement – or even learning.

This study emerged out of a desire to understand how educational technology can not only promote academic achievement, but also improve other social problems through its impact on education. Prior research has shown that schools are powerful socializing agents, and that educational media and technology, namely television, can influence children's attitudes, beliefs, and behaviors (Sanders, Montgomery, & Brechman-Toussaint, 2000; Zimmerman, 1996). Building off of this literature, we advocate a research agenda that investigates the role that newer educational technologies can play in socializing young people and shaping their identities, values, and characters, as well as their knowledge about the issues that shape their lives. Recognizing that technological innovation is re-defining the social

E. Buckner (✉) • P. Kim
Stanford University, Palo Alto, CA, USA
e-mail: ebuckner@stanford.edu; phkim@stanford.edu

M. Orey et al. (eds.), *Educational Media and Technology Yearbook: Volume 36, 2011,*
Educational Media and Technology Yearbook 36, DOI 10.1007/978-1-4614-1305-9_2,
© Springer Science+Business Media, LLC 2012

world, condensing the time-space continuum and altering traditional boundaries, in this article, we explore how educational technology might be utilized to improve entrenched social problems, such as poverty, political conflict, and oppression by altering the way that young people think about, learn about, and experience these phenomena.

Prior literature is complete with myriad ways that technology is contributing to improving larger social problems, including by promoting small loans and entrepreneurship (Yunus, 1998), improving access to information about health (Istepanian, Laxminarayan, & Pattichis, 2005; Kaplan, 2006; Vilella et al., 2004), improving women's safety in regions of conflict, encouraging citizen journalism (Palen & Liu, 2007), and promoting cross-border dialogue among individuals (Austin et al., 2009). However, very little literature focuses on how these technologies can be combined with educational initiatives to improve the future of generations of children. With this in mind, we narrowed in on one specific social problem – entrenched political conflict – and questioned: how can we use educational technology in the service of peace education?

This paper presents a model for how educational technologies can be leveraged to promote peace education, by traversing national boundaries and encouraging the development of mutual understanding and a global sense of identity through storytelling. It presents initial findings from fieldwork conducted in Palestine in March 2010 and offers theoretical contributions to future studies on the role educational media and technology can play in supporting other intersections between education and social movements, including health education and financial literacy.

Borders and Conflict: The Case of Israel and Palestine

The idea that technology can link people across borders has become a platitude in the popular media today; but the focus on how technology can connect individuals across borders tends to obscure the fact that borders of all kinds still shape our social world and our lived experiences (Evans, 1997). In fact, for most of the world, movement across political boundaries is still highly restricted, and even accurate information about others beyond one's borders is difficult to obtain.

Moreover, in a world where the prevalence of inter-state conflict is largely declining (Sarkees, Wayman, & Singer, 2003), certain decades-long cross-border conflicts stand out as particularly glaring examples of where real and imagined categories between "us" and "them" are clearly delineated. The border between Israel and Palestine is one such border – a striking example of a political, cultural, religious, and militarized border. It is also the site of an ongoing, decades-long inter-state conflict, and as a result, its borders are laden with violence and struggle.

In such conflicts, violence becomes a constant part of young people's lives. For example, the Palestinian Ministry of Health reports that in the violent clashes in late 2008 and early 2009, more than 400 children in Gaza were killed by violence and 1,800 were wounded (UNICEF, 2009). As the victims and witnesses of violence, adolescents in the West Bank and Gaza suffer long-term psychological damage from constant exposure to violence. A 2004 survey of 2,100 Palestinian youth aged 14–17 found that 99% of surveyed youth had experienced exposure to violence and that 35% of Gaza youth report suffering from symptoms characteristic of full post-traumatic stress disorder (PTSD) and 11% reported symptoms characteristic of partial PTSD. Nearly 60% of both boys and girls exposed to violence in both the West Bank and Gaza report having functional impairment in school (Abdeen, Qasrawi, Nabil, & Shaheen, 2008).

Israeli youth have also suffered. Between when the Second (al-Asqa) Intifada broke out in September 2000 and the summer of 2001, reports that 20 Israeli youth under the age of 18 were killed and many more injured. Their research also finds that approximately 28% of youth in Jewish settlements outside the cities suffered from PTSD. A lower, but still substantial number of Israeli youth in Jerusalem (12.4%) and Gili (11.2%) also showed symptoms of moderate to severe post-traumatic stress (Solomon & Lavi, 2005).

When students grow up surrounded by violence, the goal of a lasting peace becomes ever more elusive. A Congressional Sub-Committee hearing in 2003 cites Palestinian polls that show that "72 to 80 percent of Palestinian children desire death [as religious martyrs]" (The US Senate, 2003). Similarly, Solomon and Lavi (2005) found that two-thirds of children living in the Israeli settlements, aged 11.5–15, rejected the idea of peace talks entirely, while approximately half of Israeli youth living in the cities of Jerusalem and Gili supported continued peace talks (Solomon & Lavi). These findings are simply striking because of how young the surveyed youth are, and how entrenched their views are concerning the potential for peace. With this in mind, we wondered what impact technology could have to traverse boundaries and promote mutual understandings among children, before their political views and perceptions of the conflict have become entirely entrenched.

Technology and Peace Education

Numerous types of peace education have been proposed to break the cycle of violence in Israel and Palestine, with varying levels of success. Recently, many researchers have begun to incorporate technology into their design to provide more authentic opportunities for connections between Israelis and Palestinians. This study aimed to investigate the impact that technology can have on peace education – however, even defining "peace education" is value-laden.

The definition, focus, and implementation of peace-related curricula vary tremendously across different national contexts in terms of ideology, curricular focus, practices, and objectives (Burns & Aspelagh, 1996). In fact, peace education worldwide ranges from focus on de-militarization and conflict resolution, to emphases on structural violence, economic inequality, environmental issues, and human rights. Despite these differences, Bar Tal (2002) explains that a shared objective is to make the world a better and more humane place, "by reducing a variety of human ills such as injustice, inequality, prejudice and intolerance, the abuse of human rights, environmental destruction, violent conflict, war and other evils" (28).

Despite a deep and rich body of research on peace education initiatives, effective peace education is incredibly difficult to accomplish in places with deep-seated fears and prejudices born out of historical conflict, as it requires a fundamental re-definition of "us" and "them" and potentially, a re-conceptualization of personal and collective identities. Nonetheless, some empirical research suggests that peace education, and specifically, long, open, and honest encounters with individuals from the other side of the conflict, can have an impact on individual perceptions of the conflict and begin a process of understanding the other side (Feuerverger, 1997). For example, Feuerverger (1998) quotes a Palestinian student in stating: "I never really appreciated how afraid they were and that they had a right to that fear" (715). Although this re-conceptualization is the true foundation for a lasting peace in the region, Tomlinson and Benefield (2005) remind us that the impacted youth of such programs are few and far between (Tomlinson & Benefield).

In addition, others criticize the real efficacy of short encounter programs as an effective means to peace (Abu-Nimer, 1999; Bekerman, 2007; Halabi & Sonnenshein, 2000). For example, Bekerman (2007) argues that encounter programs developed between Israelis and Palestinians are based on a naïve acceptance of the "contact hypothesis,"(Amir, 1969) which argues that encounters between opposing sides can come together in trusting environments to overcome prejudices. He argues that most intergroup experiences adopt an essentialist understanding of identity, while simultaneously failing to account for the fact that group identities are formed within larger national and political contexts, namely the nation-state (Bekerman, 2002, 2007). Building off of the successes of encounter programs, while seeking to address such critiques, Bekerman has argued that future peace education initiatives must question the hegemony of nation-state in creating identities.

Recently, researchers and practitioners have looked to technology to do just that. Given the long, highly polarized conflict between Israel and Palestine, which has often left both sides feeling at an impasse, some have argued that virtual peace education is the "only feasible way to practice peace education in an open violent conflict as is the current Israeli/Palestinians one" (Firer, 2008). In a recent article, entitled *Virtual Peace Education*, Roger Firer argues that virtual learning offers a number of benefits as a platform for promoting peace education. Specifically, the major benefits of virtual peace education are that it can be carried out even during times of conflict and can be used to promote a more substantive positive peace by promoting extended contact between different groups. Other research on the influence of educational media has shown positive effects of certain media, such as television, on youth socialization (Sanders et al., 2000; Zimmerman, 1996). Building off of Firer's insights and a belief in the power of educational media and technology to shape youth attitudes and beliefs, we wondered how technology might be used to scale-up peace education initiatives, particularly those that can create space for mutual understanding and re-defining individual and group identities without relying on inherently biased national ideologies.

Global and Mobile Stories: A New Model for Peace Education

One way that we can conceive of peace education is as promoting a universal vision of shared humanity – by promoting a conception of identity that traverses national borders. While national identities are still incredibly powerful identity markers, and by far the most dominant method of organization of individuals throughout the world (Evans, 1997), new media and interactive technology are allowing for increasing levels of cross-border connections. This approach to peace education is in line with Bekerman's recommendations for peace education curricular that do not simply perpetuate national identity hegemonies.

A wide body of literature in institutional theory has shown the rise of a common world culture of humanism, which promotes a belief in individual human rights, the rise of child-centered pedagogies and an expansive view of rights, including cultural, linguistic, peace, environmental rights (Meyer, Boli, Thomas, & Ramirez, 1997; Ramirez, Suarez, & Meyer, 2007; Suarez, 2006). In this body of literature, scholars are increasingly interested in whether individuals are beginning to identify not only with others within their own national boundaries, but also with a global sense of common humanity. Indeed, this may be the most basic premise of peace education initiatives – a belief in the fundamental worth and dignity of all humanity, regardless of nationality, race, or religion. We wondered how advances in technology could promote the development of this ideal by promoting the development of global identities.

Global Stories and Global Identities

Although researchers have pointed out the possible existence of a world culture at the global level – we wondered how technology might promote this sense of a global identity among individuals. Digital cross-border storytelling and story sharing offered a promising avenue to investigate, as it allows for contact between individuals and the promotion of certain ideals. Prior studies show that storytelling confers a wide range of social and emotional benefits, ranging from developing a sense of self, identity, and wellbeing fostering a moral and ethical value system (Friedberg, 1994; Palmer, Harshbarger, & Koch, 2001; Peck, 1989).

Building off of these findings, researchers have suggested models of digital storytelling for a variety of goals. For example, advocate a digital storytelling model for writing public histories (Klaebe, Foth, Burgess, & Bilandzic, 2009). Additionally, a growing body of research has investigated the power of digital stories and other types of youth-created media as a means to youth empowerment (Barrett, 2006).

Specifically, researchers have investigated how youth-created media can serve as empowering tools for young people to express their personal experiences amidst conflict, to counter dominant media narratives, and offer a vision of peace. Researchers in Israel and Palestine have argued that a peace education model built on storytelling can help individuals overcome perceived barriers amidst intractable conflict (Bar-On & Kassem, 2004). Similarly, Norman (2009) explains why youth storytelling is a particularly compelling form of peace education, stating, "Youth media provide opportunities for creative expression and civic engagement in spaces in which youth participation is often marginalized" (1). She adds that, "youth media offer alternative information sources to potentially challenge dominant discourses of the Israeli–Palestinian conflict generally and the roles of Palestinian youth specifically" (Norman).

Moreover, digital stories are also a type of creative content, which can bridge both global and local communities. In this way, the digital nature of mobile stories allows students to share their narratives with a larger, global community. The idea of "local–global stories" builds off of the idea of a "glocal" community, which is simultaneously based in local experiences and interactions, but extends to global audiences (Klaebe et al., 2009; Robertson, 1995). Specifically, we see the potential for students' stories to be shared on digital platforms, incorporating them into the larger peace movement. By providing the digital infrastructure to youth affected by violence to discuss the realities of living through war, digital storytelling allows children to not only bear witness to the experience of childhood amidst conflict and develop an awareness of life on the other side of the conflict, but also helps build international awareness of the realities of conflict generally and the Israeli–Palestinian conflict specifically.

Mobile Learning Devices

Despite the many advantages that virtual peace efforts offer over traditional peace educational curricula, access to stable electricity, functioning computers, and the Internet, are certainly not ubiquitous in many parts of the developing world. In fact, the most isolated and impoverished communities, including those in areas ravished by war, do not have steady access to the Internet, electricity, or even schools. Consequently, the benefits of Internet-based virtual peace education programs cannot reach these populations. Mobile technologies, on the other hand, are more economical, portable, and flexible than traditional computers.

Many researchers have pointed out the distinct benefits that mobile devices offer as educational tools (Cabrero, 2002; Chinnery, 2006; Joseph, Binsted, & Suthers, 2005; Kadyte, 2004; Kiernan & Aizawa, 2004; Levy & Kennedy, 2005; Norbrook, English, & Scott, 2003; Ogata & Yano, 2004; Paredes et al., 2005; Thornton & Houser, 2005). Today's mobile devices can store and deliver a vast amount of information, including a wide variety of curricula materials targeted to appropriate ages. The rapid innovations and advances in information and communication technology (ICT), specifically, increases in processing power, memory, and connectivity for mobile, handheld devices have made mobile devices more interactive and media-rich than ever before (Pea and Maldonado 2006), offering a fun and engaging context in which to promote peace education.

Fig. 1 Mobile storytelling application

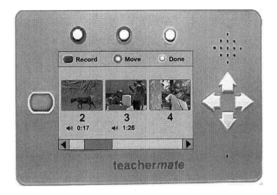

Moreover, unlike desktop computers, mobile devices require substantially less infrastructure and electricity, which gives them many advantages over traditional computers. Most importantly, mobile devices are capable of reaching even the most isolated audiences (Attewell, 2005; Kim, 2009), and research has shown mobile learning devices have the potential to widen access and supplement education in remote and underserved areas of the world (Zurita & Nussbaum, 2004). Many have noted that this makes them more apt tools for large-scale impact (Kim, Miranda, & Olaciregui, 2008). For these reasons, mobile devices offer an important alternative to computer-based virtual peace education initiatives, particularly for youth in Palestine, given the lack of fully resourced schools in many parts of the West Bank and Gaza (UNICEF, 2008).

Other research suggests that prepackaged content on a light and inexpensive mobile device is a better option than downloadable computer-based modules (Kim, 2009). Consequently, part of our future strategizing process will be to consider how to develop mobile technology applications relevant to peace education and human rights education, and specifically examining how the storytelling process can be integrated into units prepared by the UN Human Rights Education curriculum currently being implemented in refugee schools.[1]

A Model for Global-Mobile Stories

This study aimed to understand how mobile technology could be utilized to promote peace in resource-deprived areas of the world. To investigate this question, researchers at Stanford initiated a cross-border storytelling project in Israel and Palestine. This project utilized the *TeacherMate Handheld Computer System (TeacherMate)* mobile learning devices (see Fig. 1). These devices were developed by the nonprofit Innovations for Learning (IFL), a US-based NGO that focuses on developing

---

[1] See UNICEF Human Rights Curriculum: http://www.unrwa.org/etemplate.php?id=92.

Fig. 2 Optional language settings

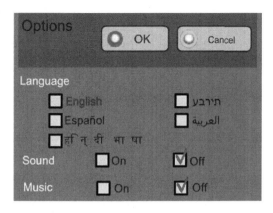

innovative technology to improve early elementary education for students and teachers in particularly difficult learning environments.

TeacherMate is a relatively affordable means to provide computer-assisted instruction for all students in the classroom. This mobile device consists of a color screen (11 cm by 7.5 cm), four direction arrow buttons, three control buttons, one execution button, a built-in microphone, an integrated speaker, and a headphone output jack. A headphone set is included for individual use.

The devices use a Linux operating system, and programs can be developed in open-source Flash (GNASH), allowing open-access and easy development for further interactive learning contents with little knowledge of Flash programming. The manufacturing cost of a single device is $50 USD.

Each mobile device can be loaded with a number of mobile e-books aligned with age-appropriate curriculum, e-books, storytelling software, and activities to assess student performance. For example, the e-book software includes a text-to-audio feature, allowing for students to interact with the devices, by looking at the images associated with the stories, hearing corresponding narrations, and reading the text of the stories by following each word as it was highlighted and narrated with either a male or female voice.

Stanford University School of Education (SUSE) has also developed a storytelling program that allows students to record their own narration through the built-in microphone. Images can be uploaded so that students can personalize their stories with cartoon images or pictures from their daily life.

The TeacherMate is now in use in nearly 300 schools throughout the United States. Currently, the creators of the TeacherMate have begun collaborating with Stanford University's School of Education to bring TeacherMates to disadvantaged communities around the globe. Pilot programs already have commenced in Costa Rica, El Salvador, Mexico, the Philippines, Rwanda, and Uganda (Fig. 2).

Figure 3, below, shows a story from Uganda translated, packaged, and made available on iPhone App store to raise funds to provide educational resources to underserved communities while helping a child from a hard-to-reach village reach the global content economy.

Fig. 3 Mobile story
from Uganda as an iPhone
App

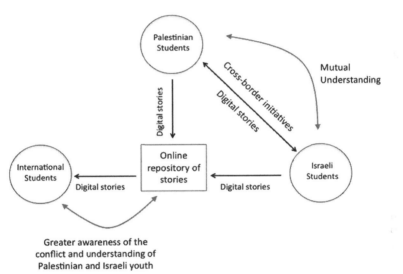

Fig. 4 Model for global-mobile stories to promote mutual understanding

Figure 4 depicts the proposed model for how mobile technology can link Israeli and Palestinian students through digital stories to promote mutual understanding, while also creating a repository of stories for students around the world to learn about Palestinian and Israeli lives, and gain a better understanding of the conflict.

Project Implementation

In 2010, a team of researchers, programmers, students, and professors at Stanford University began translating stories into Arabic and Hebrew, and developing content in both languages. At this point, approximately 14 stories (second-grade reading level)

Fig. 5 Palestinian students
playing with the mobile
devices

have been collected from students in the United States and Uganda and translated
into Hebrew and Arabic.

In March 2010, a delegation of two researchers from SUSE visited Palestinian
schools and after-school centers and implemented workshops using mobile devices
with approximately 185 Palestinian youth. In these workshops, we used inquiry-
based learning methods to promote curiosity and peak interest, by simply entering
classrooms and asking students to be the "scientists," by discovering how to turn on
the devices and play games. This method of teaching is uncommon in Palestine, but
represents an important way of encouraging students to learn without teachers to
mediate their understanding, which we believe constitutes a crucial element of
story-based peace education. The devices were well-received by primary-age
students, and we found that students were able to quickly manipulate the devices
and play critical-thinking activities, regardless of their prior level of exposure to
technology (Fig. 5).

During our trip, we visited seven different groups of students and carried out
workshops with approximately 185 students in total, ranging in age from 8 to 15.
Our sample was not designed to be representative, but rather constituted the preliminary step of an action-research design targeted to serve disadvantaged populations
(see Kim, 2009). With this aim, we sought out a wide variety of situations in which
to collect stories from children. In total, we visited seven institutions, including:
public and private schools, after-school programs run by the UN Relief and Works
Agency for Palestine Refugees (UNRWA), private English language centers, and
non-governmental organizations (NGOs). Students came from a variety of backgrounds, including those studying in prestigious bilingual private schools in
Ramallah, as well as students in rural villages and those cut off from the rest of
Palestine by the separation wall between Israel and Palestine. For students in these
isolated schools, children did not have access to home computers, and electricity
was often restricted to 2 h a day. Given the wide diversity of students and schools
we visited, we are confident that we captured the experiences and stories from a
wide range of Palestinian students.

Fig. 6 A Palestinian boy listens to his recorded story

We asked students to both narrate stories to be collected orally on the mobile devices, while also collecting written stories from students' lives. Many students used the storytelling application to record stories from their imagination, or reflect on stories shared by students in other countries. Others chose to write stories from their imaginations or daily lives. Findings from the data-collection process and initial implementation process are reported below (Fig. 6).

Findings and Future Possibilities

One of the most striking observations from our trip was the constant presence of political tension – the conflict was ubiquitous, and we witnessed it through our own experiences crossing through checkpoints, as well as through students' stories of violence, the graffiti on the walls which stated "Stop Killing Children," or just the sight of soldiers and guns everywhere. The effects of the conflict were palpable and we left Palestine still concerned over both Israeli and Palestinian children's mental and physical health. For example, Fig. 7 below comes from an NGO organization in Nablus, and depicts students' drawings of local buildings, one of which is depicted with a rocket hitting it. The pervasive images of Palestinian victims, depicted as martyrs carrying machineguns, were similarly disturbing. These visible signs of conflict only reinforced our commitment to action-research that twin mobile technologies and innovative peace education initiatives.

A number of noteworthy findings emerged from our data collection and analysis of student stories. First, we found that students living in conflict regions have personal stories to share with the world, many of which draw on their own experiences growing up in conflict, while also recalling common themes of friendship, justice, and hope. We believe these themes must be at the core of any peace education curriculum based on storytelling. However, students' stories also included frequent references to violence, killing, and injustice, suggesting that many have already

Fig. 7 Children's drawing of
a house with a rocket

experienced the negative effects of conflict firsthand. For example, students' stories included narratives of having been confronted by Israeli soldiers or settlers, difficulties crossing the border, or experiencing the death of a family member. These were particularly striking, as students were not asked directly to discuss their experiences with the conflict or to mention any difficult experiences they have had; to the contrary, they were simply asked to share a story with children from other countries.

Second, we found that even at relatively young ages, students have developed distinct identities and have developed an affiliation with their respective national group, forged from both personal experiences and political rhetoric. This finding aligns with Bekerman's claim that future peace efforts must promote a type of transnational, counter-hegemonic, or an individual-humanistic conception of identity, as national identities tend to be conflated with national ideologies about the conflict. In practical terms, this suggests the importance to reach children at younger ages to promote a sense of commonality outside national identities.

Third, we found that in many of our sites, particularly those with few resources, or those serving disadvantaged populations, we found that the major barrier to both storytelling, and peace education initiatives generally, appears to be low levels of academic proficiency. Specifically, we found that many students suffered from low levels of literacy and could not express themselves in written form. Many others had difficulty reading basic stories, even into fourth and fifth grade. Our site visits suggest that literacy still remains a significant barrier to students' ability to read, write, and share their stories with the world.

However, when students were asked to narrate their stories, rather than write, they eagerly raised their hands and formed a line to tell their stories, which we were captured as short videos using mobile devices. One young Palestinian boy, who could not write his story, eagerly narrated a story from his life about playing soccer with friends when he was approached by Israeli settlers and had to run and hide behind a rock. As is clear from this student's story, the negative effects of political conflict constantly surround children and make it difficult for them to imagine a peaceful solution to the conflict. Yet at the same time, if they cannot read, they certainly cannot learn about life on both sides of conflict, or learn about the complex political economy that makes a peaceful solution so difficult. Indeed, a literacy barrier will necessarily prevent youth from engaging in any type of peace education. It is in this context that we think multimedia technology offers distinct advantages, which could allow young people to connect through audio–video media, before or while they are developing their literacy skills. Given the rapid rise of mobile devices able to capture movies or pictures and recordings, we believe that mobile technologies or smartphones could be the next wave of innovative peace education, which could reach even pre-literate children. Reaching pre-literate children may be necessary, if by the time children can already read and write well, they have already adopted a highly nationalist account of the conflict.

Conclusions

Digital storytelling offers an innovative method for young people to share their narratives about peace and conflict with others, while also reading and learning from others' experiences in conflict. Through a lived-experience approach to narrative storytelling, we believe children can begin to develop cross-border awareness and a sense of commonality through universal themes of hope and compassion. Through an initial action-research project of a storytelling model for mobile learning devices, we believe that multimedia stories have the distinct advantage of making students' narratives come alive, while also overcoming the traditional barrier of literacy.

However, our initial study revealed that while mobile technology offers many possibilities, a number of challenges remain. It remains quite difficult to keep the mobile learning devices affordable, while also making them durable and functional, particularly if we want to include advanced features such as cameras and voice recorders. In addition, more studies are needed to maximize the usability of mobile learning devices for children of all ages while also ensuring the sustainability of the education model (e.g., structure, funding, resources, etc.). These obstacles, however, if overcome, could prepare many young children, whose access to technology is currently limited, to leverage digital tools of the twenty-first century to confront the many obstacles they will face in their futures, a peaceful solution to political conflict being only one such problem.

At the same time, we must not forget that the devices themselves are simply vehicles for content and pedagogy. They must be filled with meaningful content and integrated in proven pedagogy, which promotes the higher values of shared peace and prosperity. Any content that is not integrated in pedagogy does not support our larger mission of educating and nurturing our children, and perhaps more importantly, any pedagogies purposefully nullifying or disrupting shared peace and prosperity must be identified and stopped.

Lastly, this study argues that mobile applications can be incorporated into educational initiatives in myriad ways, many of which are yet unexplored. At the present time, we are investigating opportunities for incorporating health education and financial literacy programs into mobile devices and applications. The opportunities are limitless, but they require us to go beyond the traditional boundaries of the classroom to examine the role technology and media can play when placed at the intersection of society and schooling.

References

Abdeen, Z., Qasrawi, R., Nabil, S., & Shaheen, M. (2008). Psychological reactions to Israeli occupation: Findings from the national study of school-based screening in Palestine. *International Journal of Behavioral Development, 32*(4), 290.

Abu-Nimer, M. (1999). *Dialogue, conflict resolution, and change: Arab-Jewish encounters in Israel.* Albany, NY: State University of New York Press.

AECT. (2009). *32nd Annual proceedings of selected papers on the practice of educational communications and technology.* Paper presented at the annual convention of the AECT, Louisville, KY.

Amir, Y. (1969). Contact hypothesis in ethnic relations. *Psychological Bulletin, 71*(5), 319–342.

Attewell, J. (2005). *Mobile technologies and learning.* London: Learning and Skills Development Agency.

Austin, R., Smyth, J., Mallon, M., Rickard, A., Flynn, P., & Metcalfe, N. (2009). *Cross-border digital school partnerships: Dissolving Boundaries 1999–2009.*

Bar-On, D., & Kassem, F. (2004). Storytelling as a way to work through intractable conflicts: The German-Jewish experience and its relevance to the Palestinian-Israeli context. *Journal of Social Issues, 60*(2), 289–306.

Barrett, H. (2006). Researching and evaluating digital storytelling as a deep learning tool. *Technology and Teacher Education Annual, 1*, 647.

Bekerman, Z. (2002). The discourse of nation and culture: Its impact on Palestinian–Jewish encounters in Israel* 1. *International Journal of Intercultural Relations, 26*(4), 409–427.

Bekerman, Z. (2007). Rethinking intergroup encounters: Rescuing praxis from theory, activity from education, and peace/co-existence from identity and culture. *Journal of Peace Education, 4*(1), 21–37.

Burns, R., & Aspelagh, R. (1996). Approaching peace through education: Background, concepts and theoretical issues. In *Three decades of peace education around the world: An anthology* (pp. 25–69). New York, NY: Garland Publishing.

Cabrero, J. (2002). Third generation telephony: New technological support for computer assisted language learning. *International Journal of English Studies, 2*(1), 167–178.

Chinnery, G. (2006). Emerging technologies going to the MALL: Mobile assisted language learning. *Language Learning & Technology, 10*(1), 9–16.

Dewey, J. (1938). *Education and experience.* New York: Touchstone.

Evans, P. (1997). The eclipse of the state? Reflections on stateness in an era of globalization. *World Politics, 50*(1), 62–87.

Feuerverger, G. (1997). An educational program for peace: Jewish-Arab conflict resolution in Israel. *Theory into Practice, 36*(1), 17–25.

Firer, R. (2008). Virtual peace education. *Journal of Peace Education, 5*(2), 193–207.

Friedberg, R. (1994). Storytelling and cognitive therapy with children. *Journal of Cognitive Psychotherapy, 8*(3), 209–217.

Halabi, R., & Sonnenshein, N. (2000). Consciousness, identity, and challenge to reality: Educational approaches at the Neveh Shalom School for peace. In A. Halabi (Ed.), *Identities in dialogue* (pp. 16–27). Tel Aviv, Israel: Hakibbutz Hameuchad Publishing House.

Istepanian, R., Laxminarayan, S., & Pattichis, C. (2005). *M-health: Emerging mobile health systems.* New York: Springer.

Joseph, S., Binsted, K., & Suthers, D. (2005). *PhotoStudy: Vocabulary learning and collaboration on fixed and mobile devices*. Paper presented at the IEEE International WMTE.

Kadyte, V. (2004). Learning can happen anywhere: A mobile system for language learning. In J. Attewell & C. Savill-Smith (Eds.), *Learning with mobile devices* (pp. 73–78). London: Learning and Skills Development Agency.

Kaplan, W. (2006). Can the ubiquitous power of mobile phones be used to improve health outcomes in developing countries? *Globalization and Health, 2*(1), 9.

Kiernan, P., & Aizawa, K. (2004). Cell phones in task based learning. Are cell phones useful language learning tools? *ReCALL, 16*(1), 71–84.

Kim, P. (2009). Action research approach on mobile learning design for the underserved. *Educational Technology Research and Development, 57*(3), 415–435.

Kim, P., Miranda, T., & Olaciregui, C. (2008). Pocket School: Exploring mobile technology as a sustainable literacy education option for underserved indigenous children in Latin America. *International Journal of Educational Development, 28*(4), 435–445.

Klaebe, H., Foth, M., Burgess, J., & Bilandzic, M. (2009). Digital storytelling and history lines: Community engagement in a master-planned development.

Kozma, R. (2000). Reflections on the state of educational technology research and development. *Educational Technology Research and Development, 48*(1), 5–15.

Levy, M., & Kennedy, C. (2005). Learning Italian via mobile SMS. In A. Kukulska-Hulme & J. Traxler (Eds.), *Mobile learning: A handbook for educators and trainers* (pp. 76–83). London: Routledge.

Meyer, J. (1977). The effects of education as an institution. *American Journal of Sociology, 83*(1), 55–77.

Meyer, J., Boli, J., Thomas, G., & Ramirez, F. (1997). World society and the nation-state. *American Journal of Sociology, 103*(1), 144–181.

Norbrook, H., English, B., & Scott, P. (2003). Motivation in mobile modern foreign language learning. *Further information, 50.*

Norman, J. (2009). Creative activism: Youth media in Palestine. *Middle East Journal of Culture and Communication, 2*(2), 251–274.

Ogata, H., & Yano, Y. (2004). *Knowledge awareness map for computer-supported ubiquitous language-learning.*

Palen, L., & Liu, S. (2007). *Citizen communications in crisis: Anticipating a future of ICT-supported public participation.*

Palmer, B., Harshbarger, S., & Koch, C. (2001). Storytelling as a constructivist model for developing language and literacy. *Journal of Poetry Therapy, 14*(4), 199–212.

Paredes, R., Ogata, H., Saito, N., Yin, C., Yno, Y., Oishi, Y., et al. (2005). *LOCH: Supporting informal language learning outside the classroom with handhelds.*

Peck, J. (1989). Using storytelling to promote language and literacy development. *The Reading Teacher, 43*(2), 138–141.

Ramirez, & Boli, J. (1987). The political construction of mass schooling: European origins and worldwide institutionalization. *Sociology of Education, 60*(1), 2–17.

Ramirez, F., Suarez, D., & Meyer, J. (2007). The worldwide rise of human rights education. In *School knowledge in comparative and historical perspective* (pp. 35–52).

Robertson, R. (1995). Glocalization: Time-space and homogeneity-heterogeneity. In *Global modernities* (pp. 25–44).

Sanders, M., Montgomery, D., & Brechman-Toussaint, M. (2000). The mass media and the prevention of child behavior problems: The evaluation of a television series to promote positive outcomes for parents and their children. *The Journal of Child Psychology and Psychiatry and Allied Disciplines, 41*(7), 939–948.

Sarkees, M., Wayman, F., & Singer, J. (2003). Inter-state, intra-state, and extra-state wars: A comprehensive look at their distribution over time, 1816–1997. *International Studies Quarterly, 47*, 49–70.

Solomon, Z., & Lavi, T. (2005). Israeli youth in the second Intifada: PTSD and future orientation. *Journal of American Academy of Child & Adolescent Psychiatry, 44*(11), 1167.

Suarez, D. (2006). Education professionals and the construction of human rights education. *Comparative Education Review, 51*(1), 48–70.

The US Senate. (2003). *Palestinian education – Teaching peace or war*. Retrieved from http://www.access.gpo.gov/congress/senate.

Thornton, P., & Houser, C. (2005). Using mobile phones in English education in Japan. *Journal of Computer Assisted Learning, 21*(3), 217–228.

Tomlinson, K., & Benefield, P. (2005). Education and conflict: Research and research possibilities. *Slough: National Foundation for Educational Research*. Retrieved January 24, 2005.

UNICEF. (2008). Students return to Gaza schools still suffering from lack of heat and electricity. Retrieved May 5, 2010, from http://www.unicef.org/infobycountry/oPt_42766.html.

UNICEF. (2009). Displaced families in Gaza face public health crisis. Retrieved May 5, 2010, from http://www.unicef.org/emerg/index_47466.html.

Vilella, A., Bayas, J., Diaz, M., Guinovart, C., Diez, C., SimÛ, D., et al. (2004). The role of mobile phones in improving vaccination rates in travelers. *Preventive medicine, 38*(4), 503–509.

Yunus, M. (1998). Essays on science and society: Alleviating poverty through technology. *Science, 282*(5388), 409.

Zimmerman, J. (1996). A prosocial media strategy: "Youth against violence: choose to de-fuse." *American Journal of Orthopsychiatry, 66*(3), 354–362.

Zurita, G., & Nussbaum, M. (2004). A constructivist mobile learning environment supported by a wireless handheld network. *Journal of Computer Assisted Learning, 20*(4), 235–243.

Self-regulated Learning as a Foundational Principle for a Successful Strategy in Teaching Educational Research Methods to Doctor of Philosophy Students

Tonia A. Dousay, Diane Igoche, and Robert Maribe Branch

Introduction

There is a gap that exists between a novice scholar's intent to conduct research and the actual effort of conducting research, regardless of academic discipline. Students describe research methods as "too abstract" or "irrelevant" (Rushing & Winfield, 1999). Research methods refer to the knowledge, skills, and techniques needed to efficiently conduct academic research. While there is extensive literature regarding what should be taught in a research methods course (Birbili 2002), Deem and Lucas (2006) note that there is less emphasis on doing research than on learning about how to do research. This comes as no surprise as institutions continue to acknowledge that many students find courses in research methods difficult and challenging (Edwards & Thatcher, 2004). Since active learning in the classroom is an effective way to develop skills (Meyers & Jones, 1993), using such a concept could be an effective means of teaching research methods. The question then becomes how to incorporate active learning effectively teach research methods to graduate students.

While the skills and techniques needed to conduct academic research should be explained in theory, students are more effectively transformed into researchers in instances where instructors have engaged students in individual projects that provide hands-on methodological experience and application of statistical concepts (Smith, 2002). According to Lundahl (2008), many adages convey the essence of active learning, including the maxim that practice makes perfect. The debate about the teaching objectives of a research methods course revolves around a distinction between providing students with the ability to be critical consumers of research and enabling them to become research practitioners (Burgess & Bulmer, 1981;

T.A. Dousay (✉) • D. Igoche • R.M. Branch
Department of Educational Psychology and Instructional Technology,
University of Georgia, Athens, GA, USA
e-mail: teedee@uga.edu; dai011@uga.edu; rbranch@uga.edu

M. Orey et al. (eds.), *Educational Media and Technology Yearbook: Volume 36, 2011,*
Educational Media and Technology Yearbook 36, DOI 10.1007/978-1-4614-1305-9_3,
© Springer Science+Business Media, LLC 2012

Rose, 1981; Schutt, Blalock, & Wagenaar, 1984). Thus, an effective solution to teaching research methods combines knowledge, skills, and practice in an authentic learning experience.

There has been a growing interest in the use of team-based learning in education. Forman (1994) suggests emphasizing cognitive performance to consider social or group contexts as an environment for the indivdualistic approach. This context allows for learners to become integrated into a community of practice, extending the authentic learning experience into the group environment. Livingstone and Lynch (2000) further promote this view by stating that, "team-based learning can be a method of increasing complexity in the learning experience, which thus strengthens students' preparedness for the complex environments into which they move after completing their degrees" (p. 326). The intention of a team-based approach for authentic learning environments is to encourage active learning.

Actively involving students in learning to become independent researchers through opportunities for self-regulated practice is consistent with student-centered learning environments. Continuing the trend to move towards more student-centered approaches to teaching (Spronken-Smith, 2005) and as an alternative to classroom-based training, a professor at a Research Extensive university in the United States of America has spent the past 7 years working with a group of doctoral students in a student-centered, active learning research project where the purpose of the project is to focus on the process. The alternative training project is known as Sentence Period Spacing (SPS).

Sentence Period Spacing

The SPS research team has evolved from an informal research group into an authentic research project that allows novice researchers to experience all the aspects involved in academic research. A group of students working under the supervision of a tenured faculty member identified a set of conversations that had been associated with proper layout as a means for achieving optimal readability (Clinton, Branch, Holschuh, & Shewanown, 2003). Attempting to align accepted practice with the number of spaces between sentences in printed documents, the team identified two main ways of thinking about sentence-period spacing. Initially, the group of students considered individuals who are accustomed to pressing the space bar of the typewriter twice after entering a period. Next, the team addressed individuals who feel the extra space on the printed page is unnecessary. Additionally, the team began to search out information regarding the readability of text in an onscreen environment. Unable to identify studies of this nature, the group turned to analyzing style guides such as the American Psychological Association (APA). While guidelines did recommend a single space after periods in their 5th Edition, there was no clear reasoning for this decision. The students concluded that APA's recommendation was based on current software practice of using a default of one space after the period. The SPS Project was launched in an effort to research the topic with due diligence.

However, at the conclusion of the first year of study, the SPS team found that they had not completely answered their initial research questions.

Over the past 7 years, student-led research teams have continued the original mission and transformed the project into an ongoing authentic learning experience for teaching research methods. A list of recommendations for future research was generated from the conclusions of the first informal study. The team transitioned leadership in the following years to a student at the end of their first year on the team. First-year students were initiated to the project with an overview presentation of the study's goal, purpose, and objectives. The cycle has continued annually in this manner, encouraging second-year students to guide the study and mentor first-year students in understanding the research process. Team members work collaboratively throughout the year on the core task as well as drafting a research proposal, seeking institutional review board (IRB) approval, participant recruitment, data collection, and data analysis. The faculty advisor further compliments these efforts by encouraging team members to write up the results of the study, submit the manuscript for publication in a peer-reviewed academic journal, and seek out a relative industry conference in which to present the research results. Team members are provided with a number of tools, including a guide to constructing an initial draft of a research proposal and a matrix of types of data collection tools (Appendix A) in order to prepare them for project tasks.

During the 2009–2010 academic year, the Sentence Period Research team members included an evaluation of the effectiveness of the project as a means for teaching research methods as well as expand the basic mission of the project. The students' decision to undertake an effectiveness study further illustrates the autonomy of the SPS project. Students set the yearly project agenda under the guidance, but not direct involvement, of their faculty advisor. Team members plan to seek grants to support future research efforts and opening the research to outside institutions in order to expand the project mission. An expanded project mission will add to the responsibilities of the team members as well as encourage collaborative work with other institutions. As this is an expectation of academic faculty, the task fits appropriately into the current framework of intended applications of the project.

Cognitive Learning Processes and Sentence Period Spacing

Motivation and Metacognition

How motivation and metacognition affect learning processes plays a key role in engaging students. Studying motivation often begins with the question of why behavior occurs (Deci & Ryan, 1985; McClelland, 1985; Weiner, 1992). Considering Deci and Ryan's self-determination theory, reasons for engaging in certain behaviors are driven by needs for autonomy, competence, and relatedness. Liu, Wang, Tan, Koh, and Ee (2009) point out, "learners are motivated to satisfy these needs because they are considered essential for personal growth and well-being" (p. 139).

As beginning scholars, doctoral students are constantly faced with information that stresses upon them the importance to grow academically throughout the course of their studies. This importance may well be a motivation trigger for some team members to complete coursework and conduct academic research. Considering that research has indicated a positive association between metacognitive strategies and motivational constructs (Bartels & Magun-Jackson 2009), SPS capitalizes on cognitive learning processes to engage students in a research project that fosters an authentic research experience with meaningful outcomes.

Metacognition refers to the deliberate conscious control of cognitive activity. Student performance can be positively affected by metacognition and self. Zimmerman (2000) notes that educators have long recognized that students' beliefs about their academic capabilities play an essential role in their motivation for scholastic achievement. Furthermore, researchers such as Zimmerman posit that self-efficacy measures offer predictive advantages when a task is familiar and can be specified precisely. Therefore, the SPS project creates a cyclical model where first-year students are promoted in the second year of the project. As a result, second-year team members generally have an advantage over first-year team members. Students' familiarity with the project and knowledge of expectations lends to a greater chance of success in learning appropriate research methods and the tasks involved therein.

Self-regulated Learning

Metacognition is central to the self-regulatory cycle. Students metacognitively monitor their progress against standards and adjust metacognitive thoughts and strategies accordingly (Hadwin, Wozney, & Pontin, 2005). Bembenutty (2009) is quick to point out that metacognitive processes involved in self-regulated learning (SRL) include comparing one's judgment of learning to one's actual performance. The calibration between judgment of learning and judgment of actual performance is an essential feature of SRL. SPS team members' participation in the research project provides ample opportunity to work collaboratively with team members and adjust one's own perception of abilities versus performance. Furthermore, an annual debriefing of the project highlights strengths and weaknesses exhibited throughout the course of the year. First-year students are provided a chance to compare relative task difficulty with their ability to learn and complete the tasks.

Looking at the bigger picture of how SPS engages students, researchers must further look at self-regulation and control. Self-regulated learners engage in planning activities by setting goals and effective time management. This includes tactically selecting and using strategies such as elaboration, organization, and rehearsal. As active learners, they also allocate resources, time, and engage in effort regulation to attain goals and acquire knowledge (Bembenutty, 2009). The very nature of the SPS project requires team members to set all agendas and timelines for the year. This process creates an active learning environment that fosters SRL, tapping into the team members' intrinsic motivation to succeed.

SRL allows learners to plan or set their learning goals, monitor the progress of the goals, and regulate their learning according to the success or failure of their goals. SRL is a self-initiated action involving goal setting and monitoring the process of reaching the set goals (Zimmerman & Risemberg, 1997). The SPS project involves goal setting, team members set goals that must be achieved prior to the end of each semester. Planning, monitoring, and regulating goals are important tenets of SRL; each tenet is accompanied by other components that are important in transitioning from one to the other.

1. Planning – Goals or learning objectives are mapped out by learners to meet an objective that is centered on individual learning.
2. Monitoring – Once a goal has been planned, steps outlined during the planning stage are implemented and monitored. This phase requires learners to practice time management and manage outside influences to ensure that they will meet their goals.
3. Regulating – End results are assessed to decide on the success of the goals. Students learn how to regulate their learning by adjusting goals to meet objectives (if not met) or begin planning to meet other objectives, sometimes related to previous goals.

Goal setting and monitoring of set goals are important characteristics to possess in becoming a successful, independent researcher and learner; as stated above, this is the main mission of the SPS project. The originators of the SPS project believed that introducing students to a student-centered style of learning environment would further aid the students' abilities to conduct scholarly research. The concept of student-centered learning supports a learner's ability to regulate one's learning goals with individual approach to their learning goals. Integrating SRL into a student-centered learning approach such as the SPS project allows students to become better aware of their learning; Chen (2003) believes that this makes the student a better learner overall. A learner who is prepared to take control of their experiences is more likely to be successful.

Rationale

The SPS Project, as an authentic learning experience, exposes doctoral students to the practical aspects of research methodology that is taught in their research methods courses. As previously noted, project members participate in all phases of academic research including, identifying a problem area, drafting a proposal to address the research problem, designing the research study and compiling a final report on the findings of the study. Final reports have been presented at academic conferences and submitted as manuscripts for publication. As a result of these presentations, project team members encountered criticism regarding the project and nature of the research being conducted. Due to this feedback, it became apparent that a study to examine the effectiveness of SPS to teach research methods was necessary to support continuation of the project.

Creating a stronger appreciation for how research is conducted is one intended outcome of teaching research methods. Lundahl (2008) suggests that active learning is a successful method of teaching research methodology and students view this approach favorably. However, there has not been an exclusive focus on doctoral students' (Deem & Lucas, 2006) perception of active learning methods used for teaching research methods. The purpose of this study is to summarize perceptions, successes, and failures of the efforts of project members who have transitioned from the SPS project to their respective research agenda. Some of the project members are in the final stages of their dissertation study and others have become faculty members actively contributing to global research communities. This study also provides a framework for future researchers and their mentors to possibly adopt similiar authentic learning experiences for their students.

Conceptually, this style of teaching research methods promotes effective learning transfer. Theoretically, the project members gain genuine knowledge when involved in an authentic context. Practically, this project-based approach is effective in transferring the knowledge and abilities required to conduct independent research.

Research Questions

This study sought to determine if participation in the SPS project improved past project members' ability to conduct independent research at the dissertation level and as faculty members of their respective institutions. The following questions guided the data collection, analysis, and summaries:

1. How did participation in SPS impact your perception of conducting research?
2. How did participation in SPS prepare you to conduct research independently as a graduate student?
3. How did participation in SPS prepare you to conduct research as a new faculty member?

Research Design

Participants. In order to compile data, the researchers solicited the assistance of all past project members who participated on SPS between Fall semester 2002 and Spring semester 2009.

Context. Given the geographical disbursement of past project members, the researcher used an online survey tool to distribute the study questions and collect responses.

Data Collection Procedures. Upon receiving IRB approval to conduct the study, the researchers contacted past project members via email. This communication included

Cognitive Tools for Research Method Selection			
Research Questions	Data Type	Collection Tools	Analysis Procedures
1. How did participation in the Sentence Period Spacing project impact your perception of conducting research?	Statistical (Descriptive statistics)	Survey	Distribution of data (Descriptive Statistics)
2. Does participation in the Sentence Period Spacing project prepare doctoral students to conduct research independently?	Statistical (Descriptive statistics)	Survey	Distribution of data (Descriptive Statistics)
3. Does participation in the Sentence Period Spacing project prepare doctoral students to conduct research independently?	Statistical (Descriptive statistics)	Survey	Distribution of data (Descriptive Statistics)

Fig. 1 Data collection tools

a brief introduction about the study, consent form, and a URL link to the online survey tool. Participants were asked to complete the survey within 1 week. At the conclusion of the week, the respondents were thanked for their participation and the survey collection was closed.

Data Collection Tools. As previously mentioned, an online survey tool will be the primary source of data collection. Refer to Fig. 1 for more information.

Data Analysis Plan. Descriptive statistics were used to report the results of each research question.

Results

How Did Participation in SPS Impact Your Perception of Conducting Research?

Seeking to determine how participation in SPS impacted past team members' perception of conducting research, the respondents were asked to identify how much research experience they had prior to beginning the project. As seen in Fig. 2, 62.5% of the responses indicated some prior research experience, or 1–3 years. Only 12.5% of respondents stated that they had more experience, or 3–5 years, and 25% of respondents noted that they had no prior experience. Taking this prior experience into consideration, respondents were asked how their participation in SPS impacted their perception of academic research. For respondents with little or no prior experience, 62.5% indicated that participation improved their perception of academic research.

Fig. 2 Participants' years
of prior research experience
before joining Sentence
Period Spacing

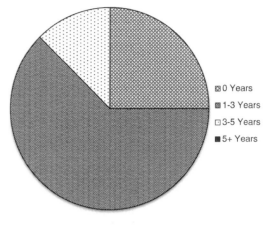

Fig. 3 Participants'
perception of academic
research as affected by
participation in Sentence
Period Spacing

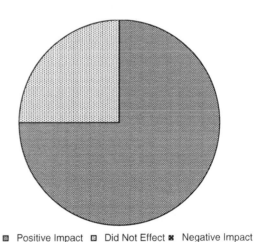

For respondents with more prior experience, 25% noted that participation improved their perception of academic research. Figure 3 summarizes all of these responses collectively. Not surprisingly, all of the respondents with prior research experience indicated that their background helped them work on the project.

How Did Participation in SPS Prepare You to Conduct Research Independently as a Graduate Student?

Respondents were asked a series of three questions to gauge how participation on the project prepared team members to conduct research independently as a graduate student. The first question asked about SPS participation in relation to preparing team members for the dissertation process. Exactly 100% of respondents noted that their participation in SPS somewhat prepared them for the dissertation process.

Fig. 4 Participants'
perception of project
participation effect on
preparing them for completing
the dissertation

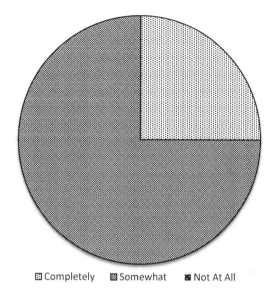

☒ Completely   ☒ Somewhat   ☒ Not At All

Specific break down of these responses are shown in Fig. 4. The second question addressed SPS participation in relation to building their own personal publication and conference presentation portfolio. While only 12.5% of respondents indicated no relationship at all, 62.5% felt that it somewhat helped, and 12.5% felt that it competely helped. Lastly, respondents were asked to indicate how strongly they agreed or disagreed that working as a team was most helpful in preparing them to conduct research as a graduate student. Responses to this question were equally distributed between completely agree (37.5%), somewhat agree (37.5%), and neither agree or disagree (25%).

How Did Participation in SPS Prepare You to Conduct Research as a New Faculty Member?

The study also sought to identify if participation in SPS prepared past team members who are now faculty members at academic institutions to conduct research as a new faculty member. This demographic made up 50% of the respondent base. While 25% of these respondents indicated that participation in SPS did not prepare them for the hiring process, 75% felt that it somewhat prepared them. Similar to a previous question, respondents were asked to indicate how strongly they agreed or disagreed that working as a team was most helpful in preparing them to conduct research as a new faculty member. Again, responses were equally distributed between completely agree (25%), somewhat agree (25%), neither agree or disagree (25%), and somewhat disagree (25%). Lastly, respondents were asked if they had considered making a similar avenue available for their own students to prepare them to conduct research. Overwhelmingly, 75% of the respondents indicated that they had considered this possibility.

Discussion

Given that not all students complete a master's degree prior to beginning doctoral studies, and those who do may or may not have completed a master's thesis, it was not surprising to find an array of previous research experience ranging from 0 to 5 years. Furthermore, all of the respondents with prior experience noted that this helped their SPS experience. Combine this with the fact that most of the respondents indicated that SPS participation improved their perception of academic research, the researchers extrapolated that the two-year cyclical process had a positive impact on self-efficacy.

Examining the impact of project participation on conducting research as a graduate student, it is particularly of interest that all respondents felt that participation somewhat prepared them for the dissertation process. Sachs (2002) noted that "the most daunting task facing senior undergraduate and graduate students is writing a thesis." While the dissertation is specifically reserved for doctoral students, the concept behind the two is the same. Sachs further states:

> Unlike other degree requirements, such as coursework, where the knowledge content domain to be mastered is well prescribed, as are the assessment criteria, a thesis has no predefined content domain or assessment criteria. Rather, the student selects a topic for independent research and demonstrates his/her degree of topic mastery in the written thesis, which, in essence, is a reflection of the students academic and intellectual maturity. (p. 99)

This perspective translates to a strong positive relationship between SPS participation and preparation for the dissertation process. By providing an opportunity well in advance of the dissertation timeline to learn and conduct academic research, participants are better equipped to complete the process. Having successfully mastered the individual steps involved, both self-effifacy and motivation related to academic research is positively impacted. Related to this, doctoral students are well aware of the importance of buliding a personal portfolio of publications and conference presentations. We were not surprised to see that a majority of respondents felt like SPS participation either completely or somewhat guided respondents through building their own academic portfolio. The task of concluding each year with a manuscript and planned presentation provides a scaffold for team members in preparation for the research tasks in their graduate school careers. Consider that the first-year student is engaged in observational learning or modeling at the end of their first year. This role transitions into practiced behavior as second-year student are able to fully participate in the study and possibly mentor the newer team members. From Schunk's (2001) perspective, this is the very essence of self-regulatory activities, and is perhaps explanation for the team members' perceived success.

Some of the most useful responses related to impact came from the respondents who are current faculty members. As previously noted, SPS provides a scaffold for preparing research studies for publication and presentation. This is also true of preparing team members for the academic hiring process. Presenting at conferences, engaging in discussions with peers and faculty, and completing the sometimes long publication process is an expectation of academic faculty. As SPS team members are expected, and encouraged, to engage in the data collection, analysis, publication, and presentation activities as part of the project, it can be inferred that sucessful completion of the project is directly related to conducting the same tasks as an independent researcher or new faculty member. Once again, self-efficacy is called into consideration as team members feel mentally prepared to undertake these tasks and regulate their own success. Perhaps the most significant finding of the study was 75% of respondents indicating that they had considered creating a similar avenue for their current students to use for learning and conducting research. If an overwhelming majority of past team members felt the project had such a profound effect on their own abiliities that they are willing to use the same means of teaching for their own students, then the message is clear. This without a doubt confirms the consensus in the literature that competence in conducting research can only be gained through the actual experience (Burgess & Bulmer, 1981; Rose, 1981). Furthermore, the results reinforce that students appreciate a "learning by doing" approach to research methods (Winn, 1995).

Recommendations

The study was very informative for the researchers and a wonderful opportunity for self-reflection for the past team members and initiator of the project. Research methods courses are very important in every research-oriented program of study; however students have indicated that they find it difficult to connect the concepts learned in the classroom to their individual research projects (Barraket, 2005). Teaching research methods using SPS or any other student-led project can be successful when it incorporates tenets of SRL and a student-centered learning approach.

Implementation of a "learning by doing" research methods course has the potential to become a tedious effort for the course facilitator and an overwhelming endeavor for students that are new to conducting research methods. We suggest using a similar team-based approach used in the SPS project to allow students to work in a group environment with goals that can be successfully achieved with the division of tasks to each team member. Not only does this make the project more manageable, but it also facilitates SRL for each student.

Lastly, future research studies on student perception of teaching research methods should include interviews as a source of data collection. Interviews will further reveal student perception of teaching research methods and possibly improve approaches to teaching research methods to students with diverse needs and experiences.

Professional Development Aid for Educational Researchers

Components of a Research Proposal[1]

Title Page
> Title (maximum of 12 words)
> Your name with middle initial (no titles)
> Institutional affiliation
> Date

"A title should summarize the main idea of the paper simply and, if possible, with style. It should be a concise statement of the main topic and should identify the actual variables or theoretical issues under investigation and the relationship between them" (American Psychological Association, 2010, p. 23). "A title should be fully explanatory when standing alone" (APA, p. 23).

Introduction
Gain reader's attention, and share your motivation for proposing the study. State the explicit purpose of the study early within this section. Identify a single problem, idea or a specific perspective[2]. Focus on unanswered questions as implied by literature relevant to the problem. Avoid presenting an answer or solution at this point. Cite published empirically supported research studies throughout the proposal to support your contentions. Indicate any assumptions or other biases. Identify the information void that will be filled as a result of this investigation. Present the preliminary evidence that support the need for this study (a comprehensive summary of the relevant literature is presented in another section). Explain who will benefit from this study.

Conceptual Framework
The purpose of presenting a *Conceptual Framework* is to share the mental scheme that will be used to guide the thinking for the actions that occur in the study. Concept is defined as a phenomenon that is conceived in the mind such as a thought, notion and idea. A concept is covert, idiosyncratic and socially constructed. An example of a concept is the idea of a visual language. The conceptual framework of a visual language is based upon the idea that a message composed exclusively of images is bound by the juxtaposition of symbols in time and space, which can be learned, used, and integrated simultaneously into various forms of communication.

Theoretical Framework
The purpose of presenting a *Theoretical Framework* is to identify the primary theory that will be tested during the study. Theory is defined as a set of facts, and their relation to one another. A theory is overt, represents a concise systematic view of a subject, and shares frames of references that are testable. An example of a theory is that image only messages are fundamental to complex cognitive processing. The theoretical framework image only messages should provide data, information and knowledge for analysis that is relevant for educational communications.

Practical Framework
The purpose of presenting a *Practical Framework* is to illustrate specific applications directly related to any aforementioned concepts and theories. Practice is defined as putting something into use. A practical application is the performance work based on principles and processes or implementing something that functions as intended. An example of practice is utilizing effective applications of typography, layout, elements and color to design messages for teaching and learning situations. The practical framework provides a space for making theoretical and empirical observations.

Research Questions
The research questions are the focal point for the entire study and should seek to answer the unknown. Therefore, research questions should state exactly what you want to know. The study's *delimitations*, which are the self-imposed limits for keeping the study manageable, can be presented in the prose preceding the itemized list of research questions. (*Limitations*, such as inherent weaknesses discovered during the study as well as variables that were uncontrolled will be identified elsewhere.) Explain any perspectives that will substantively influence the research design. The Research Questions section should end with an itemized list of actual questions [that end with question marks.]

---

[1] Primary reference: *Publication Manual of the American Psychological Association* 6th ed. (2001).
[2] You are encouraged to include a sentence in this section that begins: "The problem is . . ."

Robert Maribe Branch, Ed.D.
The University of Georgia
4 March 2010

References

Barraket, J. (2005). Teaching research methods using a student-centred approach? Critical reflections on practice. *Journal of University Teaching and Learning in Practice, 2*(2), 65–74.

Bartels, J. M., & Magun-Jackson, S. (2009). Approach–avoidance motivation and metacognitive self-regulation: The role of need for achievement and fear of failure. *Learning and Individual Differences, 19*(4), 459–463.

Bembenutty, H. (2009). Three essential components of college teaching: Achievement calibration, self-efficacy, and self-regulation. *College Student Journal, 43*(2), 562–570.

Birbili, M. (2002). Teaching educational research methods. In *The Higher Education Academy Education Subject Centre*. Retrieved from http://escalate.ac.uk/resources/teachingresearchmethods/.

Burgess, R. G., & Bulmer, M. (1981). Research methodology teaching: Trends and developments. *Sociology, 15*, 477–489.

Chen, P. P. (2003). Exploring the accuracy and predictability of the self-efficiacy beliefs of seventh-grade mathematics students. *Learning and Individual Differences, 14*(1), 79–92.

Clinton, G., Branch, R. M., Holschuh, D., & Shewanown, S. (2003). *Online reading performance time as a function of text layout*. Roundtable paper presented at the 2003 AECT Leadership & Technology International Convention, Anaheim, CA.

Deci, E. L., & Ryan, R. M. (1985). *Intrinsic motivation and self-determination in human behavior*. New York: Plenum Press.

Deem, R., & Lucas, L. (2006). Learning about research: Exploring the learning and teaching/research relationship amongst educational practitioners studying in higher education. *Teaching in Higher Education, 11*(1), 1–18.

Edwards, D. F., & Thatcher, J. (2004). A student-centered tutor-led approach to teaching research methods. *Journal of Further and Higher Education, 28*(2), 195–206.

Forman, F. (1994). Peer collaboration as situated activity: Examples from research on scientic problem solving. In H. C. Foote, C. J. Howe, A. Anderson, A. K. Tolmie, & D. A. Warden (Eds.), *Group and interactive learning* (pp. 3–8). Southampton: Computational Mechanics Publications.

Hadwin, A., Wozney, L., & Pontin, O. (2005). Scaffolding the appropriation of self-regulatory activity: A socio-cultural analysis of changes in teacher–student discourse about a graduate research portfolio. *Instructional Science, 33*(5–6), 413–450.

Liu, W. C., Wang, C. J., Tan, O. S., Koh, C., & Ee, J. (2009). A self-determination approach to understanding students' motivation in project work. *Learning and Individual Differences, 19*(1), 139–145.

Livingstone, D., & Lynch, K. (2000). Group project work and student-centred active learning: Two different experiences. *Studies in Higher Education, 25*(3), 325–425.

Lundahl, B. (2008). Teaching research methodology through active learning. *Journal of Teaching in Social Work, 28*(1/2), 273–288.

McClelland, D. C. (1985). *Human motivation*. New York: Scott, Foresman.

Meyers, C., & Jones, T. B. (1993). *Promoting active learning: Strategies for the college classroom*. San Francisco: Jossey-Bass.

Rose, D. (1981). Methods for whom? *Sociology, 15*, 512–519.

Rushing, B., & Winfield, I. (1999). Learning about sampling and measurement by doing content analysis of personal advertisements. *Teaching Sociology, 27*(2), 159–166.

Sachs, J. (2002). A path model for students' attitude to writing a thesis. *Scandinavian Journal of Educational Research, 46*(1), 99–108.

Schunk, D. H. (2001). Social cognitive theory and self-regulation. In B. J. Zimmerman & D. H. Schunk (Eds.), *Self-regulated learning and academic achievement* (pp. 119–144). Mahwah, NJ: Lawrence Erlbaum Associates.

Schutt, R., Blalock, H. M., & Wagenaar, T. C. (1984). Goals and means for research methods courses. *Teaching Sociology, 11*, 235–258.

Smith, R.A. (2002). Learning science in a junior colleague model. In R.A. Smith (Chair), *Introducing students to research: Variations on a theme*. Symposium conducted at the 14th annual convention of the American Psychological Society, New Orleans, LA.

Spronken-Smith, R. (2005). Implementing a problem-based learning approach for teaching research methods in geography. *Journal of Geography in Higher Education, 29*(2), 203–221.

Weiner, B. (1992). *Human motivation: Metaphors, theories, and research*. Newbury Park, CA: Sage.

Winn, S. (1995). Learning by doing: Teaching research methods through student participation in a commissioned research project. *Studies in Higher Education, 20*(2), 203–214.

Zimmerman, B. J. (2000). Self-efficacy: An essential motive to learn. *Contemporary Educational Psychology, 25*(1), 82–91.

Zimmerman, B. J., & Risemberg, R. (1997). Self-regulatory dimensions of academic learning and motivation. In G. D. Phye (Ed.), *Handbook of academic learning: Construction of knowledge* (pp. 105–125). San Diego, CA: Academic Press.

Fostering Student Cognition in Computer-Supported Online Collaborative Learning Environment

Khe Foon Hew, Seng Chee Tan, and Wing Sum Cheung

Introduction

The use of computer tools to support online collaboration, or commonly known as Computer Supported Collaborative Learning (CSCL), is increasingly becoming widespread in many education institutes throughout the world (De Wever, Schellens, Valcke, & Van Keer, 2006). Central to CSCL environments is the notion of discussion, in particular asynchronous online discussion, which enables students to exchange messages through computers with one another without the constraint of time and place (De Wever et al., 2006). Asynchronous online discussion has been identified as one of the key activities that students found most beneficial to their learning (Ertmer et al., 2007; Richardson & Swan, 2003). Researchers seem to agree that online discussions can promote both student critical thinking and knowledge building (De Wever et al., 2006; Lazonder, Wilhelm, & Ootes, 2003). This is mainly due to the premise that asynchronous discussions present several unique advantages over face-to-face synchronous discussions: students having greater opportunities to exchange information with one another, students having the ability to revisit earlier exchanges for reflection purposes, and students having more time to think before contributing to the discussions (Pena-Shaff & Nicholls, 2004; Thomas, 2002).

It is important to note, however, that in-depth critical thinking and higher levels of knowledge building do not happen naturally or automatically in students' online discussions. Many previous research studies have suggested that limited student critical thinking or knowledge building to be a persistent and widespread problem. Khine, Yeap, and Lok (2003), for example, found that many students exhibited surface-level critical thinking in their discussions. Burt, Grady, and McMann (1994) examined the level of information processing in critical thinking among graduate

K.F. Hew (✉) • S.C. Tan • W.S. Cheung
Learning Sciences and Technologies, National Institute of Education,
Nanyang Technological University, 1 Nanyang Walk, Singapore, Singapore
e-mail: khefoon.hew@nie.edu.sg; sengchee.tan@nie.edu.sg; wingsum.cheung@nie.edu.sg

M. Orey et al. (eds.), *Educational Media and Technology Yearbook: Volume 36, 2011*,   37
Educational Media and Technology Yearbook 36, DOI 10.1007/978-1-4614-1305-9_4,
© Springer Science+Business Media, LLC 2012

students in computer-mediated discussions. The researchers found very few instances of in-depth level of information processing in critical thinking. Cheong and Cheung (2008) found that close to two-fifths of critical thinking skills exhibited by students were surface levels. This was corroborated by Hew and Cheung (2003) who found that more than 40% of all critical thinking instances exhibited by students were of surface-level information processing.

Similarly with regard to knowledge building, many previous studies have found that students rarely go beyond the information sharing level to higher levels where ideas are argued, challenged, negotiated, or tested against existing literature, data or personal experiences (Cheung & Hew, 2006; Gunawardena, Lowe, & Anderson, 1997; Kanuka & Anderson, 1998; Maor, 2010; McLoughlin & Luca, 2000; Jamaludin & Quek, 2006; Schellens, Keer, & Valcke, 2005). Maor (2010), for example, in her analysis of about 2,000 online postings of a postgraduate course in an Australian university, found that sharing information (71%) was most frequently exhibited by the students.

In the next section, we provide two vignettes of studies that we conducted at the National Institute of Education, Nanyang Technological University in Singapore. These studies examined student cognition in CSCL environment, in particular asynchronous online discussions. We define student cognition as students exhibited critical thinking skills and knowledge building. In the first vignette, we describe certain discussion guidelines, as well as student facilitation techniques, and how these may foster in-depth levels of critical thinking in discussion forums. In the second vignette, we examine what levels of knowledge building were demonstrated by participants in an online forum, as well as how the nature of the task or activity undertaken by the participants might influence these levels.

Vignette 1: Fostering In-depth Critical Thinking

Case Example 1: Discussion Guidelines

One approach to eliminating or at the very least minimizing the occurrences of surface-level critical thinking is to understand why surface-level critical thinking occurs in the first place. Knowing the reasons for its occurrence have practical significance because it can help formulate some possible guidelines to facilitate students' in-depth thinking. In one of our studies (Cheung & Hew, 2006), we attempted to uncover some of these reasons. Thirty-eight students enrolled in a hypermedia design course that required them to plan, design, and develop instructional hypermedia materials for use in actual classroom contexts. The hypermedia design course was a blended class, involving both face-to-face and online components.

In the face-to-face component, the instructor shared certain instructional design principles and guidelines with the students. In the online component, students participated in online discussions lasting 8 weeks in total using the threaded forum available in BlackBoard. The students utilized the online forums to discuss their

Table 1 Surface- and in-depth levels of critical thinking

Surface-level critical thinking	In-depth-level critical thinking
Does not justify conclusions or judgments made	Justifies conclusions or judgments made
Merely stating that one agrees or disagrees with the conclusions or judgments made by others without taking these further	Stating that one shares/disagrees with the conclusions or judgments made by others and supporting them with relevant facts, experience, or personal comments, build on each other's ideas
Does not spell out the advantages or disadvantages of a suggestion, conclusion, or judgment	Identifying the advantages or disadvantages of a suggestion, conclusion, or judgment
Sticking to prejudices or assumptions	Making valid assumptions based on the available indicators

hypermedia design projects. Specifically, the students identified design problems of their classmates' hypermedia materials, gave suggestions to overcome the problems, and responded to the ideas and suggestions raised. At the end of the course, students' discussion posts were analyzed for evidence of critical thinking using a dichotomy of surface or in-depth level of information processing.

Surface-level critical thinking includes the following (Cheung & Hew, 2006, p. 5), as summarized in Table 1: (a) making conclusions or judgments without offering justification, (b) sticking to prejudices or assumptions, (c) stating that one shares the conclusions or judgments made by others without taking these further, and (d) failure to state the advantages or disadvantages of a suggestion, conclusion, or judgment. In-depth-level critical thinking, on the other hand, involves (Cheung & Hew, p. 6): (a) making conclusions or judgments supported by justification, (b) setting out the advantages or disadvantages of a suggestion, conclusion, or judgment, (c) stating that one shares the conclusions or judgments made by others and supporting them with relevant facts, experience, or personal comments, and (d) making valid assumptions based on the available indicators.

Results suggested that a majority of the surface-level critical thinking instances occurred due to the following three main reasons: (a) students failing to justify their judgments or comments, (b) proposing a suggestion with little details or explanations, or (c) merely repeating a previously mentioned idea (e.g., ideas or comments beginning to sound alike). To overcome these problems, certain discussion guidelines could be implemented prior to the commencement of the actual discussions. First, students are required to strive for quality by furnishing additional information such as insights based on personal experiences or knowledge to either support or refute somebody else's ideas, rather than merely stating "I agree" or "I disagree." Second, students need to justify all their judgments or conclusions made. This would enable students to progressively sharpen their understanding as they reflect on their conclusions and refine their initial conceptions. Third, students need to clarify all suggestions made with the appropriate details or relevant examples.

To test the efficacy of some of these guidelines, another study was conducted (Cheung & Hew, 2007). This latter study involved 22 students enrolled in a postgraduate diploma in education course at the National Institute of Education, Singapore.

These students were put into four groups, where each group had one or two student facilitators. The online discussions on BlackBoard forums lasted for 3 weeks. Subsequent analysis of the entire participants' postings showed that the use of these guidelines (in particular the first guideline) were effective in helping pre-empt the problem of little new insights in students' contributions.

Case Study 2: Facilitation Techniques

Besides the use of certain discussion guidelines, what other ways or methods that could be employed to foster in-depth critical thinking in online discussions? We posit that certain facilitation techniques may help enhance students' critical thinking since a facilitator is typically seen as playing an instrumental role in shaping or influencing the discourse (Duphorne & Gunawardena, 2005; Yang, Newby, & Bill, 2005, 2008).

In recent years, we have been concentrating our efforts to investigating student facilitation techniques and how these may foster in-depth critical thinking in online discussions. In one of our case studies (Hew, Cheung, & Jumain, 2010), we examined the online discussion forums of a graduate "multimedia design" course. Ten students (six males and four females) participated in the study. Before the start of the online discussion, the instructor created a forum for each student, thus yielding a total of ten discussion forums.

As part of the course requirement, each student had to design and develop a instructional software. After the students had drafted their projects, they uploaded the materials into their individual discussion forums in BlackBoard. Each student then facilitated the discussions in his or her own forum, without any involvement from the instructor, to critique each other's instructional project. Students could choose to participate in whichever discussion forum they wanted. Overall, the duration of the online discussions was about four weeks. At the end of the course, the students' postings were analyzed to determine the quality of critical thinking manifested in the discussions, using the surface- and in-depth-level indicators illustrated in Table 1. We then identified the top 30% of forums in terms of the most number of in-depth critical thinking incidences, hereafter referred to as the higher-level group. Next, the bottom 30% forums were identified as the lower-level critical thinking group.

Our analysis of these two critical thinking groups revealed some important and interesting differences. First, in the higher-level group, the student facilitators were focused in helping the participants build on or develop each other's ideas, either by agreeing or disagreeing with the ideas or bringing in new different perspectives of examining the ideas. Participants in the higher-level group were also asked to either justify their earlier stand or to think deeper about the issues or questions raised. Such facilitation, however, was missing in the lower-level group. The facilitators in this group seemed to take a no-action attitude towards the discussion occurring in their forums. Each participant would post a different idea to the same issue or question and no one bothered to further elaborate on the idea or question the idea. Consequently, the ideas in the lower-level group forums were not well developed and at times seemed disjointed.

Second, student facilitators in the higher-level group tended to pose more questions as well as a wider variety of questions than those in the lower-level group. Six types of questions were employed (Hew et al. 2010): (a) questions that focus on specific areas (e.g., how can the specific media used in the storyboard be improved further?); (b) questions of comparison (e.g., Your suggestion seems to be more suited for face-to-face classroom environments. Do you think this also applies for an online learning session?); (c) questions that require learners to explore other options (e.g., what do you think of the color used for the five tabs that link to the five sections? If I were to use a different color for each tab, as a learner, would you find it very cluttered or distracting?); (d) questions that require justification (e.g., do you think your material would be able to engage your students' interest and entice them to progress through the course after a heavy day of work? If yes, which are the activities do you think the students would find motivating and interesting? If not, what type of activities will motivate them as a learner?); (e) questions of reflection (e.g., I get confused at times about how many colors should be used per slide and that if too many colors are used in a slide will it be too cluttered and distracting. Do you have the same problem also?); and (f) questions on assumptions (e.g., In my opinion, colors are more visual things, hence, I thought it will be more appropriate to do away with narration. But then again, am I too narrow minded in making that assumption?).

Third, facilitators in the higher-level group demonstrated persistency and perseverance in the use of questions in their forums. Questions were posted throughout the entire discussion, unlike their counterparts in the lower-level groups who posted questions only at the start of the discussion. For example, in one of the lower-level forums, the facilitator had posted five questions at the start of the discussion and did not follow up with further questions or comment on the participants' response. However, in the higher-level group, the facilitators used questioning techniques throughout the discussion. The facilitators would pose follow-up questions to encourage the participants to think deeper on their earlier comments.

Fourth, student facilitators in the higher-level group created follow-up activities in the discussions. All online discussions, after a while, will inevitably be saturated – meaning that comments or ideas being posted would begin to sound alike to one another. If nothing further is done, the discussion would die. It was noted that facilitators in the higher-level group made the effort of putting together all the ideas brought up by the participants and make revisions to their projects that they had posted earlier in the forum. The revisions were made after receiving the comments and ideas from the participants. Such an effort made by the facilitators, not only made the participants felt that their ideas were valued, but also helped in the further development of the earlier ideas and recharged the discussion. Participants were invited by the facilitators to compare the revised projects from the earlier original ones. This provided new room for the discussions to develop. Participants could evaluate the fruit of their ideas that were implemented in the revised projects, and offer further suggestions for improvement.

Vignette 2: Fostering Collaborative Knowing Through Knowledge Building

Besides the use of discussion guidelines and student facilitation techniques to encourage in-depth critical thinking among students engaging in online discussions, another strand that we have been studying is knowledge building, which is succinctly defined by Scardamalia and Bereiter (2003) as "the production and continual improvement of ideas of value to a community, through means that increase the likelihood that what the community accomplishes will be greater than the sum of individual contributions and part of broader cultural efforts" (p. 1370). In this case example, a group of graduate students who were full-time teachers participated in a knowledge-building community, which involved both face-to-face interactions and discussion using Knowledge Forum, an asynchronous online forum. Our goal was to develop knowledge-building capacity among these participants so that they could collaboratively advance their understanding about theories of learning and critically reflect on their practices. This case example focuses on the analysis of data from the Knowledge Forum, a CSCL tool.

Characteristics of Knowledge Building

Knowledge-building approach is influenced by socio-cultural theories of learning and focuses on learning in a community (Bielaczyc & Collins, 1999). Social interaction between a student and surrounding people is an important means for developing higher mental functions or cognition (Vygotsky, 1986). Through the support of an instructor or more capable peers, a student can accomplish tasks that otherwise could not be achieved independently. Cultural tools, like language, are important mediating tools for the interactions, through which a student makes meaning of the signs, symbols, and language of a particular discipline. The knowledge gained through the interactions represents the shared knowledge of the community.

Premised on Popper's (1972) ontological constructs of World 3 objects (cognitive artifacts), Bereiter (1994) further suggested the importance of reifying what is in our mind (cognitive artifacts) as concrete ideas (e.g., notes) in a public forum, so that the ideas can be worked on and improved through social interactions like questioning, clarifying, or elaboration. Thus, when using knowledge-building approach, students are encouraged to work on real and authentic ideas (Scardamalia, 2002), put forth these ideas in a public forum (e.g., Knowledge Forum), so that there can be continual idea improvement through social collaborative process like knowledge-building discourse, which is a type of discourse characterized by epistemic moves of improving the ideas under discussion. As the discussion progresses, the students are encouraged to rise above to a higher level of understanding, for example, from discussion of pieces of evidence to the use of a more inclusive principle to explain the evidence.

In this study, we focused on the two key characteristics of knowledge building: social collaboration and idea improvement. This study was guided by two research questions: (1) what levels of collaborative advancement of understanding were demonstrated by the participants? (2) Is there a relationship between the nature of activity related and the levels of collaborative advancement of understanding? The first research question examined the level of idea improvement (i.e., knowledge building) that occurred among the students in this study. The second research question examined the relationships between the level of idea improvement and the type of tasks set by the instructor or student facilitators. Answers to these research questions could provide guidance to instructors on designing a learning environment that is conducive to knowledge building.

Participants

The participants consisted of 11 adult students, aged between 27 and 50 years old, who were full-time teachers in elementary schools or high schools. They enrolled in a Master-level program that was sponsored by the Ministry of Education.

Intervention

The course consisted of 13 sessions, each lasted for about three hours, excluding online discussion that the participants did out of the formal curriculum hours. The course aimed to develop deep understanding among the participants about knowledge-building approach through experiential learning. The design of the course was informed by the knowledge-building principles (Scardamalia, 2002). The participants' discussions were guided by the following big questions: "What is knowledge building?", "What are the theoretical underpinnings of knowledge building?", "What are the principles of knowledge building?", "How to design for knowledge building?", and "Why knowledge building?" To initiate the students into the knowledge building community, the instructor (second author) guided the discussion for the first big question. To foster epistemic agency among the participants, they were asked to form four groups; each group was responsible to scaffold the discussion for the other four big questions. A forum was set up for each of these big questions. Half way through the course, a forum called "What I want to know" was set up by the instructor to encourage the students to discuss pertinent issues they would like to pursue and near the end of the course, a forum called "Rise Above" was set up for the participants to consolidate their understanding.

Data Analysis

In this study, the content of the notes in the Knowledge Forum were analyzed following Gunawardena et al.'s (1997) Interaction Analysis Model (IAM).

Table 2 The five phases of Interaction Analysis Model (IAM)

Phase 1: Sharing/comparing of Information
Phase 2: Discovering dissonance, gaps in understanding or areas for improvements among ideas or
            concepts
Phase 3: Negotiation of meaning/co-construction of knowledge
Phase 4: Testing and modification of proposed synthesis or co-construction
Phase 5: Agreement statements/application of newly constructed knowledge

Table 3 Summary of IAM level of notes in Knowledge Forum

| | IAM level | | | | | No. of | Average |
Forum	1	2	3	4	5	notes	level per note
1. What is KB?	26	3	3	0	0	32	1.3
2. Principles of KB	25	1	0	0	0	26	1.0
3. What I want to know	2	4	15	6	0	27	2.9
4. KB and collaborative	13	1	3	0	0	17	1.4
knowing							
5. Designing for KB	15	6	1	0	0	22	1.4
6. Rationales for KB	14	2	0	0	0	16	1.1
7. Rise Above	5	0	3	5	0	13	2.6
Total	100	17	25	11	0	153	1.7

Initially developed to analysis students' online debate, the IAM model consisted of
five levels of meaning negotiation and co-construction of knowledge (see Table 2).

The IAM is applicable for this study because it is premised on social constructivist
theory of learning and it represents collaborative negotiation of meaning and co-
construction of knowledge. It has been used in similar study (Chai & Tan, 2009) to
analyze teacher's discussion using Knowledge Forum. IAM was also recommended
by several researchers (e.g., Marra, Moore, & Klimczak, 2004) for its reliability and
ease of use. In our study, each note is taken as a unit of analysis. Notes that were not
relevant to collaborative knowing (e.g., notes giving instructions) were excluded.

Results and Discussions

The results are summarized in Table 3, which contains the frequency counts of the
IAM level of the notes, the total number of the notes, and the average IAM level
per note.

Level of collaborative advancement. From the results in Table 3, it is evident that
Level 1 notes occurred the most frequently in the discussions. Frequency of Level 3
note was higher than Level 2 note because in the third forum (What I want to know),
each issue raised by a student received several comments on how it can be resolved.
Within the 13 sessions, some students revised their views (Level 4) after few rounds
of exchanges but there was no explicit discussion on their agreement to the rise
above notes. There was thus no Level 5 note coded.

Relationship between nature of task and level of collaborative advancement. Forums 1, 3, and 7 were set up with the following purposes: Exploring knowledge building, Raising issues and clarifying doubts, and Consolidating understanding. It is evident that this continuity of the topic of discussion generated higher-level notes. In Forum 3, the students referred to the notes posted in earlier forum and in Forum 7, the students explicitly identified the earlier notes in their Rise Above notes. Thus, to encourage higher level of collaborative advancement of understanding, it is important to provide opportunities for the students to revisit, discuss, debate, and supersede their ideas through iterative negotiation.

Forum 2, 4, 5, and 6 were facilitated by the students. It was likely that the students perceived them as "assignments" rather than opportunities to explore and advance ideas related to knowledge building. This is evident from the observation that the facilitating students were very active in each forum, whereas the "audience" was more passive. Compared to Forum 2 and 6, Forum 4 and 5 have more higher-level notes. Examining the ways the students facilitated the discussion shed some lights into this outcome. In Forum 2, the facilitators focused on getting the participants to summarize their understanding of a few papers. In Forum 6, the facilitators asked the participants to discuss several issues without connecting the issues, e.g. "Discuss whether knowledge building facilitates effective communication skills", "Discuss how knowledge building enables high productivity in students". In contrast, facilitators for Forum 4 organized a synchronous chat session among the participants and asked them to reflect on their experience. This was followed by a discussion on the theory of collaborative knowing (Stahl, 2004) with explicit link to their personal experience. In Forum 5, the facilitators asked a number of probing questions like "how do we recognize advancement in ideas?" The findings illuminate the importance of facilitation skills. Asking probing questions and making theory–practice connection seem to encourage the students to engage in higher-level discussion.

Conclusion

In this chapter, we described our effort in studying student cognition in CSCL environment. Specifically, the aforementioned two vignettes illustrate several possible strategies to foster deeper student cognition in an online forum environment. First, with regard to promoting in-depth critical thinking levels, certain discussion guidelines, especially ones that require students to furnish additional information based on personal experiences, knowledge, relevant literature, or justify all suggestions and judgments made, should be implemented prior to the start of the actual discussions. Student facilitators should also be trained to build on the participants' ideas and suggestions by either agreeing or disagreeing with the ideas and bringing new perspectives to examine these ideas. Student facilitators should also use a wider variety of questions and employ them consistently throughout the discussion.

Second, with regard to encouraging higher levels of knowledge building among students in an online forum, provide opportunities and explicit guidance for the participants to reflect on their understanding and their gaps in knowledge, as well as opportunities to consolidate their understanding. In addition, facilitation strategies such as asking probing questions or connecting theory to practice are more effective than activities than focus on summarizing reading materials or discussing disparate topics.

We are currently conducting further research involving larger samples of participants to empirically verify the findings reported in this chapter. We are also exploring if other factors (e.g., group size or the duration of the online discussion) may affect the levels of knowledge building among students in an online forum. Answers to these research efforts would provide additional insights as to how deeper level of student cognition can be fostered.

References

Bereiter, C. (1994). Constructivism, socioculturalism, and Popper's World 3. *Educational Researcher, 23*(7), 21–23.

Bielaczyc, K., & Collins, A. (1999). Learning communities in classrooms: A reconceptualization of educational practice. In C. M. Reigeluth (Ed.), *Instructional design theories and models* (Vol. II, pp. 269–291). Mahwah, NJ: Lawrence Erlbaum Associates.

Burt, M. T., Grady, M., & McMann, G. (1994). *Interaction analysis of an inter-university computer conference.* Paper presented at the distance learning research conference, College Station, TX.

Chai, C. S., & Tan, S. C. (2009). Professional development of teachers for computer-supported collaborative learning (CSCL) through knowledge building. *Teacher College Records, 111*(5), 1296–1327.

Cheong, M. C., & Cheung, W. S. (2008). Online discussion and critical thinking skills: A case study in a Singapore secondary school. *Australasian Journal of Educational Technology, 24*(5), 556–573.

Cheung, W. S., & Hew, K. F. (2006). Examining students' creative and critical thinking and student to student interactions in an asynchronous online discussion environment: A Singapore case study. *Asia-Pacific Cybereducation Journal, 2*(2). Retrieved June 11, 2010, from http://www.acecjournal.org/current_issue_current_issue.php.

Cheung, W., & Hew, K. (2007). Use of ground rules and guidelines in online discussion: A case study. In C. Montgomerie & J. Seale (Eds.), *Proceedings of world conference on educational multimedia, hypermedia and telecommunications 2007* (pp. 2753–2758). Chesapeake, VA: AACE.

De Wever, B., Schellens, T., Valcke, M., & Van Keer, H. (2006). Content analysis schemes to analyze transcripts of online asynchronous discussion groups: A review. *Computers and Education, 46*, 6–28.

Duphorne, P. L., & Gunawardena, C. N. (2005). The effect of three computer conferencing designs on critical thinking skills of nursing students. *The American Journal of Distance Education, 19*(1), 37–50.

Ertmer, P. A., Richardson, J. C., Belland, B., Camin, D., Connolly, P., Coulthard, G., et al. (2007). Using peer feedback to enhance the quality of student online postings: An exploratory study. *Journal of Computer-Mediated Communication, 12*(2), 412–433. Retrieved March 20, 2007, from http://jcmc.indiana.edu/vol12/issue2/ertmer.html.

Gunawardena, C., Lowe, C., & Anderson, T. (1997). Analysis of a global online debate and the development of an interaction analysis model for examining social construction of knowledge in computer conferencing. *Journal of Educational Computing Research, 17*(4), 397–431.

Hew, K. F., & Cheung, W. S. (2003). Evaluating the participation and quality of thinking of pre-service teachers in an asynchronous online discussion environment: Part II. *International Journal of Instructional Media, 30*(4), 355–366.

Hew, K. F., Cheung, W. S., & Jumain, S. N. (2010). Critical thinking in asynchronous online discussions: Examining the role of the student facilitator. In Z. Abas et al. (Eds.), *Proceedings of Global Learn Asia Pacific 2010* (pp. 4210–4215). Chesapeake, VA: Association for the Advancement of Computing in Education.

Jamaludin, A., & Quek, C. L. (2006). Using asynchronous online discussions in primary school project work. *Australasian Journal of Educational Technology, 22*(1), 64–87.

Kanuka, H., & Anderson, T. (1998). Online social interchange, discord, and knowledge construction. *The Journal of Distance Education, 13*(1), 57–74. Retrieved September 30, 2008, from http://www.jofde.ca/index.php/jde/article/view/137/412.

Khine, M. S., Yeap, L. L., & Lok, A. T. C. (2003). The quality of message ideas, thinking and interaction in an asynchronous CMC environment. *Educational Media International, 40*(1/2), 115–125.

Lazonder, A. W., Wilhelm, P., & Ootes, S. A. W. (2003). Using sentence openers to foster student interaction in computer-mediated learning environments. *Computers and Education, 41*, 291–308.

Maor, D. (2010). Examining cognitive attributes in student-teacher and student-student online interactions. In Z. Abas et al. (Eds.), *Proceedings of Global Learn Asia Pacific 2010* (pp. 4247–4252). Chesapeake, VA: AACE.

Marra, R., Moore, J., & Klimczak, A. (2004). Content analysis of online discussion forums: A comparative analysis of protocols. *Educational Technology Research and Development, 52*, 23–40.

McLoughlin, C., & Luca, J. (2000). Cognitive engagement and higher order thinking through computer conferencing: We know why but do we know how? In A. Herrmann & M. M. Kulski (Eds.), *Flexible futures in tertiary teaching*. Proceedings of the 9th annual teaching learning forum, 2–4 February 2000. Perth: Curtin University of Technology. Retrieved June 11, 2010, from http://lsn.curtin.edu.au/tlf/tlf2000/mcloughlin.html.

Pena-Shaff, J. B., & Nicolls, C. (2004). Analyzing student interactions and meaning construction in computer bulletin board discussions. *Computer and Education, 42*, 243–265.

Popper, K. R. (1972). *Objective knowledge: An evolutionary approach*. Oxford: Clarendon Press.

Richardson, J. C., & Swan, K. (2003). Examining social presence in online courses in relation to students' perceived learning and satisfaction. *Journal of Asynchronous Learning Networks, 7*(1), 68–88.

Scardamalia, M. (2002). Collective cognitive responsibility for the advancement of knowledge. In B. Smith (Ed.), *Liberal education in a knowledge society* (pp. 76–98). Chicago: Open Court.

Scardamalia, M., & Bereiter, C. (2003). Knowledge building. In J. W. Guthrie (Ed.), *Encyclopedia of education* (2nd ed., pp. 1370–1373). New York: Macmillan Reference.

Schellens, T., Keer, H. V., & Valcke, M. (2005). The impact of role assignment on knowledge construction in asynchronous discussion groups. *Small Group Research, 36*(6), 704–745.

Stahl, G. (2004). Building collaborative knowing: Elements of a social theory of CSCL. In J. W. Strijbos, P. A. Kirschner, & R. L. Martens (Eds.), *What we know about CSCL: And implementing it in higher education* (pp. 53–86). The Netherlands: Kluwer Academic Publishers.

Thomas, J. (2002). Smart E-classrooms, traditional classrooms and critical thinking. In G. Richards (Ed.), *Proceedings of world conference on e-learning in corporate, government, healthcare, and higher education 2002* (pp. 2288–2291). Chesapeake, VA: AACE.

Vygotsky, L. S. (1986). *Thought and language*. Cambridge, MA: MIT Press.

Yang, Y. T. C., Newby, T. J., & Bill, R. L. (2005). Using Socratic questioning to promote critical thinking skills through asynchronous discussion forums in distance learning environments. *American Journal of Distance Education, 19*(3), 163–181.

Yang, Y. T. C., Newby, T., & Bill, R. (2008). Facilitating interactions through structured web-based bulletin boards: A quasi-experimental study on promoting learners' critical thinking skills. *Computers and Education, 50*(4), 1572–1585.

A Two-Dimensional Framework for Evaluating Teachers' Technology Adoption

Manuel Gerardo Saldivar, Keith E. Maull, Benjamin R. Kirshner, and Tamara R. Sumner

A Two-Dimensional Framework for Evaluating Teachers' Technology Adoption

A large body of research suggests that teachers' instructional practices are the most important factor influencing students' academic achievement (Brophy & Good, 1986; Fraser, Walberg, Welch, & Hattie, 1987). Further, a consensus has emerged among teacher educators, accreditation agencies, and education researchers that effective use of technology[1] in classrooms can have a positive impact on teacher practice (International Society for Technology in Education, 2008; National Council for Accreditation of Teacher Education, 1997; U.S. Department of Education, 2000, 2004; Zhao, 2003). Before technology can have an impact, however, it must first be adopted. *Technology adoption* occurs when an individual determines that a given technological innovation has utility and can add value to his or her activities – such as teaching – *if* that innovation is somehow incorporated into those activities (cf. Straub, 2009 for an excellent review of the literature in this area). Technology adoption among teachers is the focus of our chapter.

We describe our mixed-methods study of the Curriculum Customization Service, a new Web-based system developed for use by Earth science teachers in the Denver Public Schools district. Our research objective was to determine how and why this new technological system was adopted by the teachers in our sample. Using qualitative techniques including classroom observations and semistructured interviews, we

---

[1] For the purposes of our study, we use the term "technology" to refer specifically to information and communication technology (ICT) – desktop and laptop computer systems, peripheral components such as computer projectors, and the networks and related software that connect all of these systems and components together.

M.G. Saldivar (✉) • K.E. Maull • B.R. Kirshner • T.R. Sumner
Institute of Cognitive Science, University of Colorado at Boulder,
1777 Exposition, Room 180, Boulder, CO 80301, USA
e-mail: saldivar@colorado.edu; Ben.kirshner@colorado.edu; tamara.sumner@gmail.com

M. Orey et al. (eds.), *Educational Media and Technology Yearbook: Volume 36, 2011*,
Educational Media and Technology Yearbook 36, DOI 10.1007/978-1-4614-1305-9_5,
© Springer Science+Business Media, LLC 2012

developed descriptive case studies of the ways in which teachers adopted the new system, as well as the ways in which adopting the Curriculum Customization Service influenced teachers' instructional practices and beliefs about teaching. Further, we analyzed quantitative data from surveys of teachers and from Web server logs that recorded teachers' behaviors within the system. These quantitative data informed our understanding of how many teachers used the system, how much time each teacher spent logged into the system, and what parts of the system were most frequently accessed by users. Finally, we applied a novel conceptual framework to these data to develop a detailed portrait of teachers' use of the Curriculum Customization Service.

A Review of the Literature

Prior research tends to apply two major criteria to the study of technology adoption. The first criterion is a quantitative description of the amount or frequency of adoption of a technology by the population of interest. This notion, first introduced by Everett Rogers in the 1960s (Rogers, 2003) and extended by Geoffrey Moore in the 1990s (Moore, 2002), has influenced many subsequent technology adoption frameworks. Researchers who apply this quantitative criterion consider a technology to have been adopted by a population if it is used by some specified percentage of individuals within the population. For instance, Rogers segmented the population of interest according to a normal distribution curve and deemed the first 2.5% of technology adopters to be "innovators," the next 13.5% of technology adopters to be "early adopters," and so forth until a technology had been adopted by 85% of consumers in a market, thus achieving "mass market" status. Because this criterion has a quantitative focus – in this case, how many people have adopted a technology – neither Rogers nor Moore considered qualitative differences in how individuals use the technology they have adopted. In their writings, Rogers, Moore, and theorists with similar quantitative outlooks appear to accept the notion that adopting new technology can influence many parts of an individual's life. For example, Rogers describes how farmers in the American Midwest enjoyed larger crop yields after adopting new farming techniques taught to them by agricultural scientists during the 1940s and 1950s. On the specific issue of how an individual uses a technology after he or she has adopted it, however, researches in the tradition of Rogers and Moore seem implicitly to assume that all users of a given technology behave in essentially the same way vis-à-vis that technology.

In some contexts, inattention to how technology is used after it is adopted may be reasonable. For example, a business that sells television sets earns its revenue when it sells a television to a customer; the business probably is not concerned about whether the buyer will use the television to watch educational documentaries or horror movies – the customer's television viewing habits may not have any direct impact on the television store's future sales. Indeed, many quantitatively oriented technology adoption theorists, like Moore, explicitly concern themselves with the commercial and economic implications of technology adoption, hence their focus on quantitative questions like *How many people are now using this technology?* (the more people who already are using a technology, the smaller the market for that technology becomes) and *How frequently do they use it?* (more frequent use may lead to a shorter product life cycle and thus the need to replace the technology sooner rather than later).

A growing number of educational researchers reject the application of purely quantitative technology adoption models to K-12 learning settings (cf. Hooper & Rieber, 1995) because they view quantitative models developed to analyze commercial or economic activities as insufficient to describe the phenomena taking place in schools. Instead, these education researchers call for those investigating technology use in K-12 to apply a qualitative criterion – *In what way, or for what purpose, is the technology being used in the K-12 classroom?* These researchers have developed a large body of evidence indicating that, first, the presence or availability of a technology does not guarantee that it will be used at all by teachers (Cuban, 1997, 2001) and, second, a given technology, regardless of its intended purpose, can in fact be used in very different ways by different educators based upon a teacher's experience level (Meskill, Mossop, DiAngelo, & Pasquale, 2002), his or her knowledge of how to integrate technology with the subject matter being taught (Mishra & Koehler, 2006), his or her access to technological infrastructure in the classroom (Hanson & Carlson, 2005), or some combination of these and other variables. Whereas quantitatively oriented researchers such as Rogers and Moore believe technology is best viewed as a consumable product that is acquired and used by some number of people, qualitatively oriented educational technology researchers instead focus on technology as a tool that can mediate teaching and learning in K-12 classrooms. A brief overview of Hooper and Rieber's (1995) model, which purposely was developed to give educational technologists insights into qualitative approaches to teacher technology adoption, illustrates qualitative models' orientation towards the *How?* rather than the *How much?* or *How frequently?* of technology use.

Hooper and Rieber's model is composed of a hierarchy of five stages. At the first stage, *familiarization*, a teacher has a basic "how to" knowledge of a given technology, but this familiarity does not lead the teacher to integrate the technology into his or her teaching practice at all. At the *utilization* stage, a teacher incorporates a technology into his or her teaching, but the teacher is not committed to the technology. For instance, the teacher may abandon the technology at the first sign of difficulty because the technology is merely an adjunct to the teacher's pedagogy – that is, it could be removed from one day to the next without impacting instruction. Hooper and Rieber argue that most teachers never advance beyond the utilization stage, if they ever reach it at all.

Next is the *integration* stage, which Hooper and Rieber call a "breakthrough phase" (p. 155) in teachers' technology adoption. At this stage, a teacher has integrated technology into his or her practice to such a degree that if the technology was removed, there would be a substantial impact on the teacher's instruction. For many teachers who are avid adopters of technology, this is as far as they progress through Hooper and Rieber's hierarchy. The fourth stage of the hierarchy is *reorientation*. At this stage, teachers begin to use technology in extremely constructivist ways, such that their students engage with technology as much as, if not more than, their teachers.

For example, teachers in the reorientation stage often assign students projects that cannot be completed without the use of technology; further, this technology use often takes place during class, replacing, rather than supplementing, traditional teacher-centric class activities. Teachers at this stage do not view technology primarily as a tool that mediates their teaching practice, but rather as a tool that mediates their students' learning. "In this phase, the learner becomes the subject rather than the object of education" (Hooper & Rieber, p. 157). The final stage of the hierarchy, *evolution*, "serves as a reminder that the educational system must continue to evolve and adapt to remain effective. There will never be a final solution or conclusion" to the challenges of teaching (p. 158). In other words, Hooper and Rieber conceive of this final stage as a sort of perpetually unreachable "promised land" that nonetheless serves as a reminder that teachers' use of technology must always be dynamic and responsive to students' learning needs as well as to the instructional requirements a teacher must meet, such as state standards.

Qualitative stage models can be useful in describing and classifying the technology adoption behaviors of teachers, but are limited by their tendency to pay little attention to quantitative factors that may influence the adoption process. Hooper and Reiber, for instance, focus primarily on a teacher's current stage of technology adoption. This allows one to understand how the teacher is using technology at present and what support can be provided by researchers, administrators, fellow teachers, and others to foster the transition to a more advanced stage of technology adoption. Qualitative stage models, however, tend not to consider how a teacher arrived at a given stage in the first place. For instance, if two teachers are both at the utilization stage – Stage Two in Hooper and Reiber's model – have they been at Stage Two for an equal amount of time? Were they both in Stage One for an equal amount of time? Will they remain at Stage Two for a comparable period? These kinds of questions can only be answered by quantitative data.

In the 1995 book chapter in which they describe their model, Hooper and Reiber cite Everett Rogers in their list of references but do not refer to him at all within the body of their chapter. Although the reader cannot know precisely why Rogers was not cited within the body of the manuscript, the omission of any specific mention of Rogers' work in Hooper and Reibert's piece symbolizes the relationship between quantitatively and qualitatively oriented technology researchers – anecdotal evidence suggests each side is aware of the other but in practice the two groups do not appear to build upon each other's work. It is for this reason that we propose our new two-dimensional framework.

A Two-Dimensional Conceptual Framework of Technology Adoption

As we have illustrated, a framework that focuses on quantitative descriptions of technology adoption can answer research questions such as *How many individuals have adopted this technology?* and *How frequently do these individuals use the technology?* but does not give us insights into qualitative aspects of technology use. Are individuals using the technology as intended by the designers? Is a new technology used the same way by individuals who share characteristics (such as years of teaching experience) or who share attitudes or behaviors (such as a positive, or negative, opinion of computer technology)? Will an individual use a technology he or she adopts today in the same way next month or next year? These kinds of questions require qualitative data to answer because a conceptual model of technology use that accounts only for frequency or amount of use may not provide insights into precisely how teachers are using technology and how their posttechnology adoption practices differ from their pretechnology adoption practices. Thus, our conceptual framework incorporates two dimensions: a *quantitative description* and a *qualitative description* of technology adoption.

Quantitative Description of Technology Adoption

Our quantitative dimension is based on the two fundamental questions addressed by existing quantitatively oriented models – how many users have adopted the new technology (in this case, the Curriculum Customization Service) and how frequently do they use this new technology? *How many?* is measured by a simple count of system users while *How frequently?* is measured by the number of times an individual teacher has logged into the system (i.e., how many *sessions* per user), the average length of each session, the average number of minutes per day that a teacher uses the system, and the total number of minutes that a teacher has used the Curriculum Customization Service over the entire lifetime of the system. These quantitative data are available for every teacher in our sample who has ever used the system.

Qualitative Description of Technology Adoption

Our qualitative dimension is inspired by the kinds of questions that frameworks like Hooper and Reiber's seek to answer – How does a teacher integrate new technology into his or her teaching practices? Does the new technology make the teacher more effective? Do any teacher characteristics, attitudes, and behaviors influence the way in which the new technology is adopted, or the way in which the technology is used for planning and teaching?

The Curriculum Customization Service

To place our method and findings into context, we must describe the Curriculum Customization Service (hereafter "CCS"), the technological system at the heart of our study. We begin with an overview of the digital libraries from which the CCS draws instructional resources. Then, we briefly describe Investigating Earth Systems (IES) and EarthComm, the Earth science curricula used by Denver Public Schools, the district where our research study was carried out. Finally, we explain the structure and features of the CCS system itself.

The Digital Library Concept

A digital library, like a traditional physical library, is a repository for information resources that are gathered and organized by librarians and subject matter experts (Greenstein & Thorin, 2002). While physical libraries often contain digital resources, physical libraries traditionally tend to focus on printed materials such as books and periodicals. In contrast, digital libraries focus on materials that exist primarily in digital form, such as Web sites, video clips, animated images, and electronic files such as PDF documents. Unlike the unmanaged repositories of information that can be accessed through the World Wide Web, digital libraries offer their patrons the same kinds of services provided by physical libraries. These services include not only making materials available but also organizing and evaluating materials in order to maximize the utility of the library for its users.

For example, entering the phrase *Earth science*[2] into an Internet search engine like Google will result in a set of search results determined by an algorithm whose primary criterion is the popularity of a given Web site. An Earth science Web site need not be accurate or legitimate in order to appear near the top of a set of search results – it need only be linked to by numerous other Web sites. In contrast, digital libraries use vetting processes comparable to those that traditional physical libraries use – librarians and other experts with both subject matter knowledge and knowledge of information management apply their expertise to develop resource collections that serve "the needs of one or more communities of users" (Institute of Museum and Library Services, 2007, p. 1). Thus, a digital library can combine the convenience and ready access of the World Wide Web with a standard of quality control that may be difficult, if not impossible, to achieve with an Internet search engine.

NDSL and DLESE

The National Science Digital Library (NSDL) was developed by the National Science Foundation to "provide organized access to high quality resources and tools that support innovations in teaching and learning at all levels of science, technology, engineering, and mathematics (STEM) education" (National Science Digital Library, n.d.). NSDL's repository of over two million resources is divided into over

---

[2] The American Geological Institute describes Earth science as the study of "Earth's physical composition, structure, history, [and] natural processes" such as tides and weather systems (American Geological Institute, 1997).

154 collections, one of which is the Digital Library for Earth System Education (DLESE). DLESE aggregates "a wide variety of pedagogically sound, technologically robust, and scientifically accurate resources, collections of resources, datasets, services, and communications to support inquiry-based, active, student-centered learning about the Earth system" (Digital Library for Earth System Education, n.d.). DLESE has been developed with a specific focus on K-12 Earth science education. Because DLESE's digital resources, unlike those of the World Wide Web, are managed by scientists and librarians, DLESE users have assurance that resources accessed through DLESE are of a quality comparable to that found in the Earth science section of a traditional physical library.

Denver Public Schools Earth Science Curricula

Denver Public Schools (hereafter "DPS") teaches Earth science to its students in Grade 6 and Grade 9. DPS uses two curricula developed by the American Geological Institute: Investigating Earth Systems (IES) in Grade 6 and EarthComm in Grade 9. Both IES and EarthComm embrace a vision of inquiry learning that calls for students to develop an understanding of Earth science concepts not by acting as passive recipients of knowledge transmitted by their teachers but rather by actively engaging in hands-on activities and projects. Unlike more programmatic approaches to instruction, which stress adherence to scripted lessons and rote activities, the DPS Earth science curricula – and the school district – encourage teachers to be innovative in their teaching and to differentiate their instructional methods and activities to meet the needs of their specific students. In pedagogical terms, DPS Earth science teachers have autonomy in their day-to-day teaching but their instruction must focus on the key Earth science concepts outlined in the IES/EarthComm curricula. These concepts, in turn, meet Colorado state standards for Earth science. Thus, while students must learn the concepts covered by the curricula and are tested on their knowledge of those concepts, teachers can tailor their instructional approaches so that individual students are engaged in learning in a personally meaningful way.

Overview of CCS Features

The Curriculum Customization Service is a National Science Foundation-funded[3] program overseen by the Digital Learning Sciences (DLS) organization.[4] Beginning

---

[3] NSF award numbers 0734875, 0734872, and 0926398.

[4] Digital Learning Sciences is a joint center of the University of Colorado at Boulder Institute of Cognitive Science (ICS) and the University Corporation for Atmospheric Research (UCAR), a Boulder-based consortium of 75 major research universities.

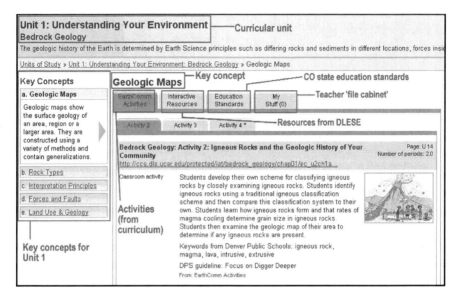

Fig. 1 A screen capture illustrating the curricular unit home screen of the Curriculum Customization Service.

This screen shows Unit 1 of the 9th Grade EarthComm curriculum. The workspace displays the following information:

1. Unit's key concepts.
2. For each key concept:
   a. EarthComm activities developed as part of the curriculum. This figure shows Activity 2, on igneous rocks, which is part of Unit 1 – bedrock geology.
   b. Interactive digital resources (from DLESE).
   c. State of Colorado education standards (for a given topic or concept).
   d. "My Stuff" – a virtual "file cabinet" where teachers can save links to digital resources or upload their own materials, which can then be shared with other CCS users. The CCS includes social networking functionality, such as the ability to give resources a "star rating" and the ability to label resources with searchable tags

in 2008, DLS designed and developed the CCS in cooperation with Denver Public Schools and Herff Jones Publishing, the publisher of the IES and EarthComm curricula. A group of ten Earth science teachers who were identified as exemplary educators by DPS pilot tested the CCS during the 2008–2009 school year, and in July 2009, the CCS was made available to all Earth science teachers in DPS for use in 2009–2010 and beyond.

The CCS incorporates three major features (see Fig. 1). First, it provides users with Web-based access to digital versions of the paper-based student textbooks, teacher manuals, and curriculum guides that comprise the DPS Earth science curricula for both Grade 6 and Grade 9. The manuals and guides outline the Colorado state standards that must be met, explain how the various units in the Earth science curricula are connected to state standards, and provide various supplementary materials for teacher use, such as prefabricated activities, extension resources, and student assessments. These materials are all grouped under a CCS component, or tab, labeled *Activities* and are organized by key concept, which allows teachers to organize their lessons in a manner that best meets the learning needs of their students rather than simply proceeding linearly through the student text. The digital versions of these curricular materials are identical to what was already available to teachers in paper form but can now be accessed from any computer with a Web connection. Colorado state standards that correspond to key concepts are listed under the *Education Standards* tab.

Second, the CCS integrates the digitized curricular content with digital resources available from DLESE. By clicking on the *Digital Resources* tab, a CCS user can see the system's recommendations for animations, video clips, classroom activities, and other digital resources that pertain to the given key concept. Unlike digital resources that might be found using an Internet search engine such as Google, the digital resources available via the CCS have been vetted by the experts who manage the DLESE collection. Moreover, these digital resources are filtered by the system to ensure that the resources align with the DPS Earth science curricula.

The final major feature of CCS is an interactive "Web 2.0" capability. Teachers can save digital resources recommended to them via the *Digital Resources* tab or they can upload their own resources to a private "filing cabinet" called *My Stuff*, found under its own CCS tab, thus storing teacher-developed materials in the same space as digital resources from DLESE or from the curriculum for easy access. Once a resource is saved to *My Stuff*, teachers have the option to upload a copy of the resource to an area of the CCS called *Shared Stuff*, which is accessible to any CCS user who clicks on the *Shared Stuff* tab associated with a given key concept. When a digital resource is added to *Shared Stuff*, the teacher who originally uploaded the resource, as well as other CCS users, can add searchable tags or keywords to the resource so that any search of the CCS system for those tags will list all digital resources tagged with the same keyword or phrase.[5] Finally, CCS users can add "star ratings" to resources so that other users can determine how their colleagues rate a given resource. A resource that many users rate highly – four or five stars – might be more likely to capture the attention of system users than a resource with a low rating. Hew and Hara argue that this kind of "informal knowledge sharing... [via] informal social networks can be powerful catalysts for enabling teachers to improve their practice" (2007, p. 574) because such knowledge sharing tends to be tied to shared, situated instructional goals and challenges and is thus more likely to be relevant to a teacher's immediate, short-term needs. In other words, a resource uploaded by or at least highly rated by a fellow educator in the same district using the same curriculum is more likely to "make sense" to a teacher than a resource developed in a different milieu.

In summary, the CCS brings together Denver Public Schools' Earth science curricular materials, digital resources housed by DLESE, and digital resources uploaded by users themselves, providing a single portal that assists DPS Earth

---

[5] Note that adding a resource to the CCS system, as in this example, does not mean that the resource will be added to the DLESE collection, merely that it will be available to all CCS users.

science teachers in the planning and delivery of instruction by offering "one stop" access to a broad range of Earth science materials, thus facilitating the differentiation of instruction – the development of pedagogical approaches customized to the needs of specific learners or groups of learners (cf. Tomlinson & McTighe, 2006).

Method

Due to space constraints, we present here an abbreviated description of our method. Readers who desire more information can refer to Saldivar (2011) [available from the first author of this chapter] and Maull, Saldivar, and Sumner (2010). Saldivar (2011) in particular expands upon the specific instruments and protocols we used, details the analysis performed, and discusses the various limitations of our study.

Setting

The Denver Public Schools district is located in Denver, Colorado and serves approximately 75,000 students distributed among 152 schools. Fifty-five percent of DPS students are Latino, 23% are white, and 18% are African-American. Less than 5% of students are Asian-American or Native American. Approximately two-thirds of DPS students qualify for free or reduced lunch, and approximately one in five students are English language learners. The district calculates its graduation rate to be 52%. DPS employs approximately 13,000 personnel, of whom about 4,500 are teachers (Denver Public Schools, n.d.). As of 2007–2008 (the last year for which data are available), approximately 95% of DPS teachers were rated "highly qualified" as per No Child Left Behind Act standards, but the majority of DPS schools did not make adequate yearly progress (AYP) that school year (Colorado Department of Education, 2009). The students in the Earth science classes we studied had demographic characteristics generally representative of the DPS student population as a whole.

Sample and Data Collection

There are roughly 124 Earth science teachers in the Denver Public Schools district. This figure is approximate because, during the course of the 2009–2010 school year when the study was conducted, some teachers left the district or were reassigned from teaching Earth science to teaching other subjects.

Quantitative Data

All DPS Earth science teachers were invited (but not required) to use the CCS, and 98 teachers logged into the system at least once. The Web server where the CCS

Table 1 Summary of data sources and data analysis techniques

Data source	Sample size	Primary data analysis technique
Web server usage log	98	Counts and frequencies and cluster analysis
Presurvey	84	Quantitative items: Counts and frequencies
		Qualitative items: Content analysis
Mid-year survey	80	Quantitative items: Counts and frequencies
		Qualitative items: Content analysis
Postsurvey	83	Quantitative items: Counts and frequencies
		Qualitative items: Content analysis
Adoption interviews	24	Content analysis
Classroom observation cycles	8	Content analysis

Note: The samples for our various data sources are not mutually exclusive. For example, all of the teachers who participated in the classroom observation cycles and adoption interviews also responded to the three surveys

resides was programmed to capture the quantitative data described in our two-dimensional conceptual framework. In addition to the Web server logs of CCS usage, we also collected quantitative data in the form of three surveys (see Table 1). The three surveys were administered to all DPS Earth science teachers. The presurvey, intended to establish a baseline of pre-CCS instructional behaviors and attitudes, was administered at the beginning of the school year from September 8 through October 17. At approximately 65 questions (including both quantitative and qualitative), the first survey was the longest administered to Earth science teachers. The final two surveys were composed of approximately 40 questions each.

The mid-year survey was administered during the end of the fall semester from December 14 through January 28; this survey focused on teachers' use of and attitudes toward educational technology in general and digital resources in particular. The post final survey was administered in the last weeks of the school year from May 10 to June 14 and contained slightly modified versions of items from the first two surveys so that we could conduct a longitudinal analysis. The quantitative survey data, along with the Web server logs, helped us establish broad patterns of how much and how frequently DPS Earth science teachers used the CCS. Given our conceptual framework, however, these quantitative data represent only one of the two dimensions we used to analyze our findings.

Qualitative Data

Table 1 lists all of our qualitative data sources.

Surveys (Qualitative Items)

Each of the surveys contained qualitative items, mostly open-ended short answer questions that asked respondents to describe their attitudes and behaviors vis-à-vis educational technology, instructional planning, and teaching.

Technology Adoption Interviews

These semi structured telephone interviews were conducted from November 2009 through February 2010. The sample of 24 teachers was interviewed regarding their adoption and use of the CCS. All the teachers approached to participate in these adoption interviews were recruited because the Web server logs indicated that they were mostly moderate to heavy CCS users. We defined *moderate users* as individuals who used the CCS for at least 30 min per month during the period from September 1, 2009 through November 30, 2009 (the first period for which we had usage data). We classified a *CCS nonuser* as someone who has only logged into the system once or twice for less than 15 min during this same period. Of the 24 teachers interviewed, two were nonusers and the rest were moderate-to-heavy users.

Classroom Observation Cycles

Out of the total population of 124 Earth science teachers in Denver Public Schools, the eight teachers recruited to participate in classroom observation cycles were the smallest sample but, in many ways, the most fruitful. These eight teachers each agreed to several hours of interviews and classroom observations during the course of the school year. The five Grade 6 and three Grade 9 teachers each sat for pre-interviews that asked them to describe their approach to instructional planning and teaching before the CCS was made available to them. Then, each teacher went through two classroom observations cycles 2–3 months apart. Each observation cycle consisted of a think-aloud interview where a researcher observed the teacher using the CCS system in real time to complete a lesson planning task; then, the researcher visited the teacher's class to observe him or her teach the lesson that had been planned using the CCS. After the classroom visit, each observation cycle concluded when the researched debriefed the teacher to learn how the teacher himself or herself evaluated the lesson. At the end of the school year, each teacher wrote a short essay describing the role of the CCS in their instructional planning and teaching. Finally, each teacher sat for a post-interview where he or she reflected on their experiences using the CCS during the 2009–2010 school year in a "big picture" manner.

Data Analysis

We analyzed quantitative data from both Web server logs and surveys to determine counts and frequencies that described user behaviors, such as *What percentage of CCS users logged into the system?* and *How often did users log in?* Further, an analytical technique called cluster analysis was applied to Web server log data to determine how usage patterns recorded by the CCS system compared to system usage as reported by study participants (see Saldivar, Maull, and Sumner (2011) for more information on cluster analysis and its application to the CCS study). Qualitative data were analyzed using a content analysis approach. A common set of codes based on the study's major research questions of was devised and multiple raters applied these codes to all the qualitative data, allowing us to determine how often themes of interest appeared across multiple data sources.

Findings and Discussion

Quantitative Findings

Table 2 summarizes the number of hours users spent logged into the system, by quartile, from September 1, 2009, when the school year began, through the end of February 2010, the most recent period for which Web server log data are available. Each quartile was comprised of 22 teachers. A total of 98, or 79%, of the 124 Earth science teachers in DPS logged into the system at least once. During this 6-month period, teachers in the bottom-most quartile spent less than 1 h using the CCS, so we considered those teachers to be nonusers. This left the 63 teachers in the top three quartiles as our population of CCS users, which meant that approximately half of the total Earth science teachers in DPS used the CCS regularly.

As Table 2 illustrates, CCS usage varied greatly among quartiles, but the quantitative data recorded by the CCS Web server indicate that usage behaviors also varied within a given quartile. Refer to Table 3, which lists the top 10 users by number

Table 2 Quantitative summary of CCS usage from September 2009 through February 2010

Quartile	Usage in hours	
	Minimum	Maximum
1	13	45
2	5	13
3	2.5	4
4	<0.1	2

Note: Each quartile is comprised of 21 teachers

Table 3 Top 10 CCS users by frequency and amount of usage

User	Grade	Quartile	Total no. of sessions	Avg minutes		Total lifetime Minutes
				Per session	Per day	
1	9	1	115	23.12	88.62	2658.45
2	9	1	105	22.29	78.02	2340.62
3	6	1	71	32.63	77.22	2316.63
4	6	1	86	25.36	72.71	2181.18
5	9	1	59	32.39	63.70	1911.07
6	9	1	91	19.22	58.30	1749.12
7	6	1	62	26.20	54.15	1624.53
8	6	1	84	17.41	48.75	1462.48
9	9	1	73	19.92	48.47	1454.00
10	9	1	50	28.36	47.27	1418.07

of total minutes of CCS usage during the period from September 1 to February 28 – these 10 users are at the top of the first quartile. Note, for instance, User 2 and User 3, both of whom spent approximately 2,300 min (38 h) logged into the CCS during the period in question. Although their total minutes of usage were comparable, User 2 logged into the system 34 more times than did User 3 (105 sessions versus 71 sessions). If our analysis relied on a coarse quantitative measure – *How much time did each user spend logged into the CCS?* – these two teachers would appear to be comparable. By digging more deeply in the quantitative data, we find that, at least in terms of number of CCS sessions, the two teachers are not comparable. But what is the significance, if any, of this difference? Quantitative data alone cannot shed any insights into this question, but by triangulating our quantitative findings with the qualitative data we gathered, can offer a possible answer.

Qualitative Findings

As we discussed earlier, the CCS was intended to support teachers' instructional planning and encourage them to differentiate their teaching to best meet the learning needs of their students. The reasons why this differentiation occurred among CCS users, and how it occurred, shed light on the different usage patterns revealed by the quantitative data.

The overarching reason teachers reported via interviews and open-ended survey items for *why* they used the CCS was to supplement the Earth science curriculum. Teachers reported that they needed to supplement the textbook and other curricular materials provided by the publisher and by DPS for two major reasons. First, teachers with students who were English language learners or who otherwise had below-grade level reading skills reported that such students often had difficulty learning course material directly from the text. In such cases, teachers reported using the CCS to find alternative representations of Earth science phenomena that went beyond the simple graphic or textual descriptions in the text, such as animations of volcanoes erupting or diagrams of geologic structures. These alternative representations also were helpful for students who had adequate reading skills but who nonetheless struggled to comprehend the course material. Thus, the CCS helped teachers differentiate their instruction by providing access to digital resources that supplemented and extended the content available in the existing Earth science curricula.

The second major reason why teachers used the CCS was to leverage their fellow teachers' knowledge and experience by downloading instructional materials shared by others in the *Shared Stuff* component of the system. Teachers reported that they perceived these teacher-developed materials to be useful and valuable because they came from others engaged in a similar endeavor in the same district. Many teachers reasoned along the following lines: *If I find it challenging to teach this concept, perhaps other teachers also have found it challenging, and perhaps the materials they have uploaded to* Shared Stuff *can offer me guidance.* Indeed, many teachers reported that their own thinking about or perspective on a certain Earth science concept evolved as they reviewed instructional materials developed by their colleagues. As with the digital resources available from DLESE, teachers differentiated their instruction by reviewing materials uploaded by colleagues and selecting materials that they believed would best supplement the curriculum for their own population of students.

We have described *why* teachers used the CCS but it is the qualitative description of *how* teachers used the system that helps us understand the quantitative differences in usage that were revealed by the Web server logs. Recall that User 2 and User 3 spent comparable amounts of time in the system overall but User 2 logged in more frequently for shorter periods of time compared to User 3, who logged in less frequently for longer periods of time. Qualitative data collected from these two teachers suggests that they fall on opposite ends of a spectrum.

User 2 relies heavily on existing curricular materials in his teaching. He acknowledges the utility of the CCS but views differentiation as primarily a matter of supplementing the student text and other materials provided by the publisher and the school district. He logs into the CCS frequently for relatively short periods of time because his intent in using the system is to find materials that fit into an instructional plan he already has developed – a plan based on the existing curricular materials. In contrast, User 3 reports that he often builds lessons entirely from scratch, developing PowerPoint slide shows, handouts, and classroom activities that are entirely based on digital resources he found using the CCS. User 3 logs into the CCS less frequently but for longer periods of time than User 2 because User 3 is searching not for materials that fit into an existing lesson but rather for materials that will inspire and inform his development of a new lesson. To User 3, the process of differentiation requires him to include digital resources at the beginning, not at the end, of his planning process. User 3's sessions are longer and thus less numerous because the time he spends logged into the system is spent closely reviewing and learning from digital resources from DLESE and from his fellow Earth science teachers. User 2's sessions are shorter and more frequent because he logs into the system with a specific goal in mind (e.g., *Find a diagram of the water cycle*) and then exits the system as soon as he finds the material he logged into the CCS to find.

User 2 and User 3 are representative of the spectrum of CCS use we found. On one end of the spectrum are teachers like User 2 whose use of the CCS is characterized by a desire to supplement an instructional plan they already have developed. These teachers seem to value the notion of differentiated instruction but their teaching appears to rely heavily on the one-size-fits-all curricular materials available to them before the CCS was developed. On the other end of the spectrum are teachers who make more expansive use of the CCS; they are much more likely to spend their time within the CCS reviewing materials not available before the CCS was introduced and using those materials to develop lessons specifically targeted at their own students' learning needs. Thus, teachers' use of the CCS appears to be at least partly influenced by how teachers approach the differentiation of instruction. Why this is the case is a matter of ongoing analysis; we will report those findings in a separate manuscript.

Conclusion

In this chapter, our goal was to argue that applying a conceptual framework incorporating both qualitative and quantitative dimensions would allow us to develop a more detailed description of CCS use than would be possible if we had applied only a quantitatively or a qualitatively focused framework. Our quantitative data indicated that CCS usage among DPS Earth science teachers varied in terms of how much time they spent logged into the system as well as how often they logged in relative to other users. The qualitative data we collected allowed us to determine one possible reason for this variance – the specific instructional planning and teaching goals held by teachers also varied and appeared to influence how they used the system. Our continued analysis of the data collected during this study will allow us to investigate the possible reasons why teachers approach instructional planning and teaching in different ways, but already our two-dimensional framework has proved useful by demonstrating that teachers who spent comparable amounts of time logged into the CCS can nonetheless exhibit different behaviors and motivations as they use the system.

References

American Geological Institute. (1997). Geoscience career frequently asked questions. Retrieved June 20, 2009, from http://www.agiweb.org/workforce/faqs/index.html.

Brophy, J., & Good, T. L. (1986). Teacher behavior and student achievement. In M. C. Wittrock (Ed.), *Handbook of research on teaching* (3rd ed., pp. 328–375). New York: McMillan.

Colorado Department of Education. (2009, July 1). School district data: Denver County 1. Retrieved July 1, 2009, from http://www.cde.state.co.us/scripts/districtprofiles/DistInfo.asp?DistCode=0880.

Cuban, L. (1997). High-tech schools and low-tech teaching. *Education Week, 16*(34), 38–41.

Cuban, L. (2001). *Oversold and underused: Computers in the classroom.* Cambridge, MA: Harvard University Press.

Denver Public Schools. (n.d.). About Denver public schools. Retrieved June 28, 2009, from http://communications.dpsk12.org/newsroom/73/55/.

Digital Library for Earth System Education. (n.d.). DLESE and NSDL. Retrieved June 17, 2009, from http://www.dlese.org/about/dlese_nsdl.php.

Fraser, B. J., Walberg, H. J., Welch, W. W., & Hattie, J. A. (1987). Syntheses of educational productivity research. *International Journal of Educational Research, 11*, 145–252.

Greenstein, D., & Thorin, S. E. (2002). *The digital library: A biography.* Washington, DC: Digital Library Federation & Council on Library and Information Resources.

Hanson, K., & Carlson, B. (2005). *Effective access: Teachers' use of digital resources in STEM teaching.* Newton, MA: Education Development Center, Inc.

Hew, K., & Hara, N. (2007). Empirical study of motivators and barriers of teacher online knowledge sharing. *Educational Technology Research & Development, 55*(6), 573–595.

Hooper, S., & Rieber, L. P. (1995). Teaching with technology. In A. C. Ornstein (Ed.), *Teaching: Theory into practice* (pp. 154–170). Needham Heights, MA: Allyn and Bacon.

Institute of Museum and Library Services. (2007, December). *A framework of guidance for building good digital collections* (3rd ed.). Retrieved June 14, 2009, from http://framework.niso.org/.

International Society for Technology in Education. (2008). *National educational technology standards for teachers* (2nd ed.). Eugene, OR: ISTE.

Maull, K. E., Saldivar, M. G., & Sumner, T. R. (2010). Online curriculum planning behavior of teachers. In R. S. Jd. Baker, A. Merceron, & P. I. Pavlik Jr. (Eds.), *Proceedings of the 3 rd international conference on educational data mining* (pp. 121–130). Pittsburgh, PA: International Working Group on Educational Data Mining.

Meskill, C., Mossop, J., DiAngelo, S., & Pasquale, R. K. (2002). Expert and novice teachers talking technology: Precepts, concepts, and misconcepts. *Language Learning & Technology, 6*(3), 46–57.

Mishra, P., & Koehler, M. J. (2006). Technological pedagogical content knowledge: A framework for teacher knowledge. *Teachers College Record, 108*(6), 1017–1054.

Moore, G. A. (2002). *Crossing the chasm: Marketing and selling high-tech products to mainstream customers*. New York: HarperCollins.

National Council for Accreditation of Teacher Education. (1997). *Technology and the new professional teacher: Preparing for the 21st century classroom*. Washington, DC: NCATE.

National Science Digital Library. (n.d.). About NSDL. Retrieved June 18, 2009, from http://nsdl.org/about/.

Rogers, E. M. (2003). *Diffusion of innovations* (5th ed.). New York: The Free Press.

Saldivar, M. G. (2011). *Earth science teachers' adoption of a web-based instructional planning system*. Doctoral dissertation. Boulder, CO: University of Colorado.

Saldivar, M. G., Maull, K. E. and Sumner, T. R. (2011, June 13). *Understanding digital libran, adoption:* A use-diffusion approach Joint Conferance on Digital Library, Ottawa, Canada.

Straub, E. T. (2009). Understanding technology adoption: Theory and future directions for informal learning. *Review of Educational Research, 79*(2), 625–649.

Tomlinson, C. A., & McTighe, J. (2006). *Integrating differentiated instruction and understanding by design: Connecting content and kids*. Alexandria, VA: Association for Supervision and Curriculum Development.

U. S. Department of Education. (2000). *Teachers' tools for the 21st century: A report on teachers' use of technology*. Washington, DC: NCES.

U.S. Department of Education. (2004). *Toward a new golden age in American education: How the Internet, the law and today's students are revolutionizing expectations*. Washington, D.C.: Office of Educational Technology.

Zhao, Y. (Ed.). (2003). *What teachers should know about technology: Perspectives and practices*. Greenwich, CT: Information Age.

Issues and Trends in Instructional Technology: Lean Times, Shifts in Online Learning, and Increased Attention to Mobile Devices

Abbie Brown and Tim Green

We continue the tradition of reporting the issues and trends of instructional technology that have continued or arisen within the past year. This chapter is comprised of four sections: overall developments; corporate training and development; higher education; and K-12 settings.

Overall Developments

While there were signs that pointed to an improvement of the nation's economy, a full economic recovery was not evident. Higher than expected unemployment and decreases in tax revenues continued to play a significant role in how various sectors approached technology spending. Similar to the previous year, funding for K-12 and higher education was less than robust. Technology spending in the private sector, however, did seem to pick up from the previous review, though it remained conservative and cautious. Despite the issue of funding, all sectors continued to explore innovative uses of instructional technology. Online learning, Web-based collaborative tools, and the use of mobile devices are this year's significant trends to watch.

A. Brown (✉)
Department of Mathematics, Science Instructional Technology Education,
East Carolina University, Flanagan Hall, Greenville, NC 27858, USA
e-mail: brownab@ecu.edu

T. Green
Department of Elementary and Bilingual Education, California State University,
Fullerton, CA, USA
e-mail: timdgreen@gmail.com

M. Orey et al. (eds.), *Educational Media and Technology Yearbook: Volume 36, 2011*,
Educational Media and Technology Yearbook 36, DOI 10.1007/978-1-4614-1305-9_6,
© Springer Science+Business Media, LLC 2012

Interest in Mobile Computing Devices

This year's ECAR study examines closely the use of mobile devices on campus (Smith, Salaway, & Borreson Caruso, 2009), noting that nearly every undergraduate now owns a cell phone and engages regularly in text messaging. The Horizon Report mentions Mobiles as a "technology to watch" (Johnson, Levine, & Smith, 2009). As mobile devices become more versatile, incorporating functions like global positioning, Web browsing, and video capture, they show greater promise as learning tools.

The Current State of Online Learning

Online learning continues to expand in higher education and K-12, but not in corporate training and development. The Sloan Consortium's report on online education in the United States indicates that online enrollments in higher education settings have increased 17% from the previous year (Allen & Seaman, 2010). The ASTD state of the industry report, however, indicates a slight decrease in business and industry's use of e-learning.

Corporate Training and Development

As we have done in previous issues and trends chapters of the yearbook (e.g., Brown & Green, 2009, 2010), we continue to track corporate application of instructional technologies primarily by referring to the American Society for Training and Development's (ASTDs), *State of the Industry Report,* (Paradise & Patel, 2009). The current ASTD annual report is based on data collected from the Benchmarking Forum (BMF) organizations, ASTD BEST award winners, and responses from users of ASTD's WLP (Workforce Learning and Performance) Scorecard. The report describes the activities of organizations recognized as exemplary in their approach to workplace learning and performance as represented by the BEST award winners; larger, global organizations typically represented by BMF members; and data collected from users of ASTD's WLP Scorecard benchmarking and decision support tool.

Expenditure for Learning

ASTD reports organizational expenditures for learning remained relatively stable over that past year (Paradise & Patel, 2009). The average annual learning expenditure per employee fell slightly (3.8%) from $1,110 in 2007 to $1,068 in 2008. Paradise and Patel observe the decrease in spending on workplace learning was similar to spending reductions in all aspects of business and industry. Paradise and

Patel also point out the consolidated average learning expenditure as a percentage of payroll *increased* 0.09% (from 2.15 to 2.24) between 2007 and 2008, and direct learning expenditures increased 0.03% (from 5.6 to 5.9), indicating business and industry's continued commitment to workplace learning.

The trend in spending on internal learning operations (as opposed to external training providers and instructional media producers) continues (Paradise & Patel, 2009). Internal learning departments continue to take on greater importance in corporate training and development.

The ASTD report also indicates that learning professionals are increasing their productivity: the average number of employees per learning staff member increased from 227 in 2007 to 253 in 2008, suggesting the average learning department is serving a relatively larger population (Paradise & Patel, 2009).

Instructional Content

ASTD reported no major changes in instructional content emphasis between 2007 and 2008 (Paradise & Patel, 2009). Paradise and Patel suggest this indicates that business and industry did not engage in radical restructuring during this period despite economic uncertainties.

Corporate instructional content remains focused on profession and industry-specific subject matter (Paradise & Patel, 2009). The second largest content area over the past year was information technology knowledge; Paradise and Patel suggest this can be attributed to greater focus on organizational efficiency. Other top content areas such as managerial and supervisory training, mandatory and compliance training, and processes procedures and business practices remained similar to previous years (Paradise & Patel). Though it accounts for a small percentage of instructional content overall, sales-oriented instruction increased significantly (from 5.4 to 6.1%) as did instruction for interpersonal skills, which is peripherally related to sales (from 5.6 to 7.4%) (Paradise & Patel).

Use of Technology: A Surprising Emphasis on Face-to-Face Instruction

The 2009 ASTD report reveals a surprising reduction in the use of e-learning.

After a consistent rise over several years, e-learning approaches diminished between 2007 and 2008. Instructor-led classroom learning accounted for almost two-thirds of the learning hours employed in 2008 (Paradise & Patel, 2009). Self-paced online learning declined in use for the second consecutive year.

Paradise and Patel (2009) suggest the use of e-learning approaches for formal learning will rebound; that its flexibility and efficiency (particularly the ability to reuse technology-based instruction) make it an increasingly important platform, and we are inclined to agree. Furthermore, Paradise and Patel observe that e-learning used for informal education is increasing rapidly; Web 2.0 technologies, including social networking, are changing the ways people share information and collaborate (Paradise & Patel).

Higher Education

We examine higher education's information technology use and instructional technology application primarily by referring to the *EDUCAUSE Core Data Service Fiscal Year 2008 Summary Report* (Arroway & Sharma, 2009), *The ECAR Study of Undergraduate Students and Information Technology, 2009* (Smith et al., 2009), and *The Horizon Report* (Johnson et al., 2009). Trends in online learning are further examined by referring to The Sloan Consortium's report, *Learning on Demand: Online Education in the United States* (Allen & Seaman, 2010). Each of these is a large, ongoing study with significant resources allocated to measuring the technological climate of higher education. *The EDUCAUSE Core Data Service Fiscal Year 2008 Summary Report* is drawn from information supplied by over 900 participating institutions (Arroway & Sharma); *The ECAR Study of Undergraduate Students and Information Technology, 2009* compiles and summarizes responses provided by over 30,000 undergraduate students (Smith et al.); *The Horizon Report* is a qualitative analysis that examines the use of emerging technologies in learning-focused organizations, produced in collaboration between the EDUCAUSE Learning Initiative and the New Media Consortium (Johnson et al.); and the Sloan Consortium's report on online learning is based on the responses provided by over 2,500 colleges and universities.

According to Allen and Seaman (2010), the economic downturn has increased demand for both traditional "face-to-face" courses and courses presented entirely online. Over half of the institutions surveyed for the Sloan Consortium's report confirmed an increased demand for face-to-face courses (Allen & Seaman). The demand for online courses was even higher: 66% of reporting institutions saw increased demand for new courses and programs, and 73% saw increased demand for existing online offerings.

Information Technology on Campus: Staffing and Compensation

The top three functional areas for information technology (IT) staff on college and university campuses are "administrative/enterprise information systems," "desktop computing, user support services, training, computer store," and "instructional technology, multimedia services and student computing" (Arroway & Sharma, 2009). Campus IT leaders (the administrative head of IT) typically report directly to the institution's highest academic or administrative officer (Arroway & Sharma).

Eight-seven percent of the institutions providing information have a technology advisory committee that provides feedback and direction for strategic IT planning (Arroway & Sharma).

Instructional Technology (IT) employee compensation remains consistent (modest or no increase in salary over the past 2 years) for full-time staff. Student worker compensation in IT has dropped considerably in past years (Arroway & Sharma, 2009). Although the EDUCUASE report makes no mention of this specifically, it is reasonable to assume that a majority of students in instructional technology/educational technology graduate programs who work for IT services while attending school are receiving lower wages than in the past.

Campus Technology Support and Use of Technology for Instruction

Bandwidth continues to increase on most campuses (Arroway & Sharma, 2009). Remote access for students and faculty off campus is largely supported, as is on-campus Wireless (WiFi) access, and most campuses have videoconferencing facilities, though videoconferencing support varies widely by institution type (Arroway & Sharma).

Course management systems (CMS) are currently supported by the vast majority of institutions, virtually all of which are commercial (e.g., Blackboard) or open-source (e.g., Moodle) applications, as opposed to "home-grown" applications developed by and at the institution (Arroway & Sharma). Smith et al. (2009) report an increase in undergraduate CMS use from 79.7% in 2006 to 91% in 2009.

Undergraduate students report making regular use of their college or university library Web site as well as a CMS (Smith et al., 2009). A majority of undergraduates further report making regular use of presentation software (e.g., PowerPoint) and spreadsheet software regularly for course work; about 25% of these students report using Wikis for course work as well (Smith et al.). Just over 25% of undergraduates reporting state they use social networking sites such as Facebook or Ning for course work, and roughly 15% report using blogging, graphics software, Internet messaging, and programming languages (e.g., Java) regularly in their studies (Smith et al.).

Learning Online. According to the Sloan Consortium report, over 4.6 million students took at least one online course in the fall 2008 term; this is a 17% increase over the previous year's reported number (Allen & Seaman, 2010).

Technology Support for Faculty

Arroway and Sharma (2009) report the three most common methods of providing faculty support for integrating technology into teaching are opportunities for successful technology users to share their experiences, seminars on technology-oriented topics, and training on request. Arroway and Sharma also note a downward trend in college/university support for centralized instructional technology centers, while the use of student technology assistants is on the rise (2009).

Undergraduate students continue to find faculty use of information technology (IT) to be mediocre at best (Smith et al., 2009); 45% reported that most of their instructors use IT effectively in their courses. The past year's ECAR report continues to report a preference among students for only a moderate amount of IT in any of their courses: undergraduates on campus continue to appreciate the face-to-face learning experience (Smith et al.).

Support for Online Instruction. Although undergraduate students on campus tend to prefer face-to-face or relatively "low-tech" instruction, there is a rising demand for online course delivery. According to Allen and Seaman (2010), institutions differ widely in the support they provide for developing skill with online instruction: 19% of reporting institutions provide no training of any sort; over half of those institutions offering online courses provide training courses and informal mentoring; a smaller group (15%) provides training from external sources.

Student Computing

Undergraduates are bringing their own, relatively new laptops with them to campus (Smith et al., 2009). In 2009, 88.3% of students responding to the ECAR study reported owning their own laptops, while 44% reported owning desktop systems (Smith et al.). Arroway and Sharma (2009) point out a difference in student computer ownership depending upon the type of institution: students attending DR (doctoral degree granting) institutions tend to own their own computers far more often than students attending AA (associates degree granting) institutions. Arroway and Sharma also report that all responding BA, MA, and DR (doctoral degree granting) institutions with residence halls provide high-speed network connections (2009).

The vast majority (over 90%) of undergraduate students are using social networking sites and instant messaging and text messaging to communicate (Smith et al., 2009).

Mobile Devices. This year's ECAR report focuses attention on student use of mobile devices. It is generally assumed that cell phone ownership and use among undergraduates is ubiquitous, and over half the study's respondents report owning an Internet-capable mobile device (Smith et al., 2009). Mobile devices are also a "technology to watch" in this year's Horizon Report (Johnson et al., 2009).

K-12 Education

In reporting the trends and issues for the K-12 education section, the following reports were predominantly used: *Technology Counts 2010*, *The 2010 Horizon Report: K-12 Edition*, *Learning in the 21st Century: 2009 Trends Update*, and *Generation M2: Media in the Lives of 8- to 18-Year-Olds*. *Technology Counts 2010* is the 11th annual report published by *Education Week.* This report focuses on the overall state of educational technology in K-12 schools. *The Horizon Report*, produced by the New Media Consortium and the Consortium for School Networking (CoSN), focuses on emerging technologies or practices that are likely to gain use within K-12 over the next year to 5 years. *Learning in the 21st Century* is part of a series of reports published by Project Tomorrow in conjunction with Blackboard Inc. This report examined data collected from over 335,000 U.S. K-12 students, teachers, administrators, and parents regarding technology use. The *Generation M2* report was sponsored by The Kaiser Family Foundation. This report is the third in a series of studies that focused on the media use of approximately 2,200 3 rd–12th grade students throughout the United States.

When reflecting on the previous reviews, many of the major issues regarding instructional technology use in K-12 have remained relatively consistent. Issues that were key holdovers from previous reviews are online learning, mobile devices, and the use of Web 2.0 tools (Brown & Green, 2009, 2010). A major issue from the last review, STEM education, continues to be pushed in K-12 despite evidence that funding for many of these federally funded projects was never received (Robelen, 2010). Funding for overall K-12 continued to be a major issue that, not surprisingly, had a direct effect on instructional technology use.

The Overall State of K-12 Technology

Previous *Technology Counts* reports provided an overall view of technology use in schools broken down state by state and the District of Columbia. Data for last year's report was collected on 10 indicators covering state technology policy and practice – specifically, technology use and technology capacity. Technology use was based on the following policy indicators: student technology standards, student testing on technology, virtual schools, and computer-based student assessment. Technology capacity focused on technology standards for teachers and administrators, course work or a test for initial professional licensure, and technology training or a technology test for professional recertification. Last year's report provided letter grades in technology use and technology capacity for the USA as a whole. The nation earned a B in technology use and a C + in technology capacity for use. Nine states received A grades for technology use while 11 received D + grades and the District of Columbia received an F. Three states earned A grades in technology capacity for use while seven earned D grades and five earned F grades (Hightower, 2009).

Due to a lack of sufficient state-level data, the recent *Technology Counts* shifted its focus to how public school districts are using technology to enhance and improve teaching and learning (data from this report will be discussed in various sections that follow). Thus, letter grades were not provided in the report for states or the nation. Based on the trends from previous reviews and based on the level of available funds for K-12 during this review, we believe that the overall grade for technology use and technology capacity for the nation as a whole would have most likely remained the same.

Funding

The overall funding for K-12 dropped – significantly in many states – as state budget deficits rose. Market analysts predict large deficits for states to continue for another 2–3 years (Devaney, 2010). As with previous reviews, specific numbers on how much money states spent on K-12 technology remains difficult to obtain. Despite the specifics, there is evidence that spending was down. According to a report published by the American Association of School Administrators, administrators (435 from 45 states; 92% superintendents) who responded to a survey school funding indicated that technology purchases are increasingly being delayed due to lack of available funds. "While 13% made delays in 2008–2009, 29% and 57% report delays in 2009–2010 and 2010–2011, respectively" (Elerson, 2010).

Despite the lower reported funds available for technology, federal funds for educational technology seemed to be available (e.g., $650 million from the Enhancing Education Through Technology initiative; other monies are available; albeit, buried in various federal education programs such as Title 1 and IDEA). The president requested an increase of $4 billion for education in the federal budget plan for the fiscal year 2011. The administration, however, proposed moving to a greater percentage of federal dollars from "formula-based grants to competitive grants—a move that school leaders fear will further squeeze their limited resources" ("Survey: School budget cuts," 2010).

Teacher Technology Availability and Use

The "Tracking Trends" section of *Technology Counts 2010* provided a snapshot of the technology resources public school districts made available to their teachers and students (Education Week, 2010). The data was gathered from a federal study conducted by the U.S. Department of Education (Gray, Lewis, & Tice, 2009). The data points to teachers having relatively good access to various technology tools. Access to electronic tools was 95% for all secondary teachers and 87% for all elementary teachers. Eighty-two percent of secondary teachers and 83% of elementary teachers had server space for posting a Web page and class materials. Online student assessment tools access was 72% (secondary teachers) and 73% (elementary teachers). Online curricula access were 66% for both elementary and secondary teachers. Opportunity for distance learning was 65% (secondary) and 64% (elementary). Access to course-management and course-delivery software was 57% for all teachers. Finally, 44% (secondary) and 46% (elementary) have remote access to school or district software.

According to the seventh annual PBS national survey of teachers' (1,212 K-12 public schools; 206 pre-K in public and private schools) use of media and technology, *Digitally Inclined,* teachers' attitudes toward and use of digital media and social networking tools have increased (PBS, 2010). Some key findings from the survey regarding K-12 teachers were:

- 76% use digital media in their classroom (33% pre-K)
- 44% reported being frequent users (everyday to two times a week)
- 93% indicated that their schools have computers with Internet access
- 81% have computers with Internet access in their classroom
- 61% have DVD players or computer DVD drives in their classroom
- 72% stream or download digital content from the Internet
- 58% indicated use digital media for games and activities for students
- 51% access digital images

The survey indicated that the trend of teachers' use of games is on the rise as is teachers valuing student-produced multimedia, student-created Web sites, and Web sites for student work submission (the use of games in K-12 is also supported by *The Horizon Report: 2010 K-12 Edition*).

The *Digitally Inclined* report also indicates, "Teachers report that their students prefer digital media over other types of instruction and that digital media increases student motivation and stimulates discussions. Teachers also believe digital media supports their own creativity and student creativity" (PBS, 2010, p. 5). More teachers are using video than in previous years. The use of video is different, however; 42% of teachers indicated that they were more likely to use partial segments (5–10 min) of videos rather than an entire video (PBS). Finally, the survey indicated that 29% of teachers report using social networking sites or social media community for instructional purposes. Twenty-six percent reported belonging to an online community specifically for teachers. These percentages are up from the previous year's survey (PBS). The data points to a key trend for teachers' use of instructional technology, which is the use of digital content. We believe that teachers' use of digital content – especially from the Internet – will continue to rise.

Teacher Technology Training, Certification, and Professional Development

During the previous three reviews (Brown & Green, 2008, 2009, 2010), we were optimistic that the number of states with technology standards for teachers would increase (46 states had teacher technology standards, as of the last review). We were also hopeful that additional states would implement technology requirements for teacher licensure. We predicted that the number of states requiring technology course work or the passing of a test to demonstrate competency would slightly increase (Brown & Green, 2010). As of the last review (Brown & Green, 2010), only 21 states required either technology course work or the passing of a test to demonstrate competency. Ten states required course work or a test for initial licensure for administrators (Hightower, 2009).

Table 1 Data from Education Week (2010)

Teacher professional development topics	% of Districts *offered*	% of Districts *required*
Integrating technology into instruction	95	39
Using Internet resources and communication tools for instruction	91	15
Internet safety	89	55
Using content-specific software tools for instruction	86	16
Using multimedia digital content for instruction	86	14
Developing curriculum plans that include using technology to address content standards	85	37
Using technology to access or manipulate data to guide instruction	83	32
Applying technology in assessing student achievement with respect to state curriculum standards	82	40
Using technology to support collaboration	80	16
Intellectual property and copyright rules	77	45
Using student-assessment and student-evaluation strategies that involve technology	74	27
Using technology to promote dialogue on student-performance indicators and related data	72	20
Creating or using digital portfolios	51	5
Teaching via distance learning	47	4

Although data are not readily available to support our predictions from our previous review, what we can report is the percentage of public school districts that *offer* teacher professional development and the percent that *require* teacher professional development in various technology topics. This provides a glimpse into what teachers are being asked to know and to do regarding instructional technology use. *Technology Counts 2010* reported data on 14 technology topics (Education Week, 2010). The data they provided is presented in Table 1.

Student Use and Ownership of Technology

Our last review reported that 8- to 18-year-olds' use of media in and out of school averaged 6½ h a day according to a 2005 Kaiser Foundation Study (Rideout, Roberts, & Foehr, 2005). Of these 6½ h, this group was actually exposed to the equivalent of 8½ h of media. The media ranged from watching television to reading print-based materials. The largest percentage of time was spent using digital media (e.g., watching live or recorded television 4 h a day). A new Kaiser Foundation Study (Rideout, Roberts, & Foeher, 2010) on media use of 8- to 18-year-olds found that since the last study the amount of time this group spends with media has increased an hour and 17 min to a total of 7 h, 38 min a day. This translates into the equivalent of 10 h, 45 min of media content. All media use increased except for movies (which remained at 25 min a day) and print-based (which dropped 5 min a day to 38 min). Music and audio had the greatest increase at 47 min a day for a total of 2 h and 31 min a day (Rideout et al., 2010).

Related to media use there are some interesting findings that we believe are important to highlight. The 8- to 18-year-olds who spent more time with media (indicated being "heavy users") reported lower grades and lower levels of personal contentment than those who considered themselves to be "moderate" or "light users" of media (Rideout et al., 2010, p. 4).

Mobile Devices. In our previous review (Brown & Green, 2010) we provided data from the *Speak Up 2008* survey indicating that approximately half of the students surveyed had access to a cell phone, while approximately 65% had access to an MP3 player, and half had access to a laptop (Project Tomorrow, 2009). According to the *Generation M2: Media in the Lives of 8- to 18-Year-Olds*, the percentages of ownership are 66% for cell phones, 76% for iPod/MP3 players, and 29% for laptops (Rideout et al., 2010). *Technology Counts 2010* reported 71% of teens owned a cell phone (Manzo 2010a, b). The key point here is that student ownership to mobile devices – especially cell phones – continues to rise. Rideout et al. (2010) indicated the use of cell phones "morphed from a way to hold a conversation with someone into a way to consume more media" (p. 3). The 8- to 18-year-olds surveyed reported using their phones the following ways on average per day:

- 30 min talking
- 17 min listening to music
- 17 min playing games
- 15 min watching TV

Those in 7th through 12th grades reported spending an average of 1½h text-messaging.

We predict that more K-12 students will have access to mobile devices and the use of these devices will continue to increase. As a result, students will continue to put pressure on schools to allow use of these devices as learning tools in and out of the classroom.

Online Learning. Our last review (Brown & Green, 2010) reported that according to the Sloan Consortium the growth of K-12 students using online courses significantly rose (more than one million public school students) from 2008 to 2009. The total number of students using online courses increased 47% from 2005. We predicted that the number of students taking online courses would increase during this review period. Although there is no new data available to indicate whether this number has increased over the review period, we believe that the numbers have indeed increased and will continue to increase. There is speculation (Christensen & Horn, 2008) based on current data regarding student growth that by 2019 about 50% of high school courses will be delivered online. We predict that school districts that do not provide online learning opportunities for their students will find their students seeking these opportunities outside of their school (e.g., for-profit institutions).

Innovative and Emerging Technologies and Practices Used in K-12

The use of mobile devices and online learning were two innovative and emerging technologies and practices used in K-12 that persisted during this review period. We predict, based on past data trends, mobile devices and online learning will most continue to gain popularity. Schools, however, will need to overcome challenges (e.g., network infrastructure, teacher professional development, safety and security) in order to realize the full potential for mobile devices and online learning.

In addition to these trends, there is evidence of other innovative and emerging technologies being used in K-12. *The 2010 Horizon Report: K-12 Edition* reported on "emerging technologies for their potential impact on and use in teaching, learning, and creative expression within the environment of pre-college education" (Johnson, Smith, & Levine, 2010, p. 3). This report focused on technologies or practices that are likely to gain use within K-12 over the next year to 5 years. The six they identified as ones to watch are cloud computing, collaborative environments, game-based learning, mobiles, augmented reality, and flexible displays. Of these, we predict that cloud computing, collaborative environments, game-based learning, and, as we previously mentioned, mobile devices, will have the greatest near-term effects on K-12.

In previous reviews (Brown & Green, 2009, 2010), we predicted that as Web 2.0 tools continued to become more sophisticated their use in K-12 would increase. *The Horizon Report: 2010 K-12 Edition* lends support to our predictions by pointing to two emerging technologies – cloud computing and collaborative environments – that the report states have 1 year or less time to adoption. These two technologies both support Web 2.0 tools. Schools have begun to adopt cloud-based tools mostly for productivity and administrative purposes (Johnson et al., 2010, p. 9). We predict that as schools become more familiar and comfortable with using these types of tools other cloud-based tools (e.g., Google docs) will increase in use for teaching and learning. We also predict the use of collaborative environments (e.g., Ning, VoiceThread, Wikis) will continue to increase for teaching and learning, if schools are able to manage security and safety issues while providing adequate access to these tools for teachers and students (Robinson, Brown, & Green, 2010).

Our final prediction regarding innovative and emerging technologies is that we believe digital textbooks will gain more attention as schools continue to try and lower costs while at the same time provide teachers and students with access to the most current and useful content (e.g., Rich, 2010). Digital textbooks could find a great deal of traction if publishers provided content in ways that could be accessed on the various mobile devices students use.

Conclusion

We predict that spending on instructional technology will remain at the same level with the possibility of a decrease in the K-12 sector until a full economic recovery has been realized. As reported in our previous review, state budgets tend to take

18–24 months to recover after an economic downturn (Griffiths, 2008). With this in mind, increased spending on instructional technology in K-12 (and possibly public higher education) could be as far off as 2012.

Based on the trends observed online learning will no doubt continue to increase in higher education and K-12. Although corporate use of e-learning was slightly down, we predict its continued use, and its increase as the economy improves and as mobile devices become more popular and versatile to the point where instruction delivered through them becomes practically *de rigueur*.

Overall, we continue to anticipate financially lean times for all sectors. However, this will not stop innovative uses of instructional technology and opportunities being available for instructional technology specialists in corporate, higher education, and K-12 environments.

References

Allen, I. A., & Seaman, J. (2010). *Learning on demand: Online education in the United States*. Babson Park, MA: Babson Survey Research Group.

Arroway, P., & Sharma, B. (2009). *EDUCAUSE core data service fiscal year 2008 summary report*. Retrieved from http://net.educause.edu/ir/library/pdf/PUB8006.pdf.

Brown, A., & Green, T. (2009). Issues and trends in instructional technology: Web 2.0, second life, and STEM share the spotlight. In M. Orey, V. J. McClendon, & R. M. Branch (Eds.), *Educational media and technology yearbook* (Vol. 34, pp. 7–23). Springer.

Brown, A., & Green, T. (2010). Issues and trends in instructional technology: Growth and maturation of web-based tools in a challenging climate; social networks gain educators' attention. In M. Orey, S. A. Jones, & R. M. Branch, (Eds.), *Educational media and technology yearbook* (Vol. 35, pp. 29–44). Springer.

Brown, A., & Green, T. (2008). Issues and trends in instructional technology: Making the most of mobility and ubiquity. In M. Orey, V. J. McClendon, & R. Branch (Eds.), *Educational media and technology yearbook* (Vol. 33). Westport, CT: Greenwood Publishing Group Libraries Unlimited.

Christensen, C. M., & Horn, M. B. (2008). How do we transform our schools. *Educationnet, 8*(3), 13–19. Retrieved from http://educationnext.org/how-do-we-transform-our-schools/.

Devaney, L. (2010, February). Economy continues to batter schools. *eSchool News, 13*(2), 1, 38.

Education Week. (2010). Ed-tech states. *Technology Counts 2010, 29*(26), 36–37.

Elerson, N. (2010). Cliff hanger: How America's public schools continue to feel the impact of the economic downturn. American Association for School Administrators. Retrieved from http://www.aasa.org/uploadedFiles/Policy_and_Advocacy/files/CliffHangerFINAL(1).pdf.

Gray, L., Lewis, L., & Tice, P. (2009). *Educational technology in public schools: Fall 2008*. National Center for Education Statistics: U.S. Department of Education. Retrieved from http://nces.ed.gov/pubs2010/2010003.pdf.

Griffith, M. (2008). Education policy fellowship program leadership forum. Retrieved from http://ww.ads2008.org/ads/index.php.

Hightower, A. M. (2009). Tracking U.S. trends: States earn B average for policies supporting educational technology use. *Technology Counts, 28*(26), 20–33.

Johnson, L., Levine, A., & Smith, R. (2009). *The 2009 Horizon Report*. Austin, TX: The New Media Consortium.

Johnson, L., Smith, R., Levine, A., & Haywood, K. (2010). *The 2010 Horizon Report: K-12 Edition*. Austin, TX: The New Media Consortium.

Manzo, K. K. (2010a). Tracking trends: Ed-tech stats. *Technology Counts 2010, 29*(26), 36–37.

Manzo, K. K. (2010b). Tracking trends: Mobilizing the research. *Technology Counts 2010, 29*(26), 34–36.

Paradise, A., & Patel, L. (2009). *2009 state of the industry report: ASTD's annual review of trends in workplace learning and performance.* Alexandria, VA: American Society for Training & Development.

PBS. (2010). *Digitally inclined.* Retrieved from http://www.pbs.org/teachers/_files/pdf/annual-pbs-survey-report.pdf.

Project Tomorrow. (2009). *Speak up 2008.* Retrieved from http://www.tomorrow.org/SpeakUp/.

Rich, M. (February, 2010). Textbooks that professors can rewrite digitally. *The New York Times.* Retrieved from http://www.nytimes.com/2010/02/22/business/media/22textbook.html.

Rideout, V. J., Foehr, U. G., & Roberts, D. F. (2005). *Generation M: Media in the lives of 8- to 18-year-olds.* Menlo Park, CA: Henry J. Kaiser Family Foundation.

Rideout, V. J., Foehr, U. G., & Roberts, D. F. (2010). *Generation M2: Media in the lives of 8- to 18-year-olds.* Menlo Park, CA: Henry J. Kaiser Family Foundation.

Robelen, E. K. (2010). Talk bigger than federal funding for STEM projects. *Education Week, 29*(22), 8.

Robinson, L. K., Brown, A. H., & Green, T. D. (2010). *Security vs. access: Balancing safety and productivity in the digital school.* International Society for Technology in Education (ISTE): Eugene, OR.

Smith, S. D., Salaway, G., & Borreson Caruso, J. (2009). *The ECAR study of undergraduate students and information technology, 2009.* Boulder, CO: EDUCAUSE.

Staff Reporters. (2010, April 9). Survey: School budget cuts even worse next year. *eSchool News.* Retrieved from http://www.eschoolnews.com/2010/04/09/survey-school-budget-cuts-even-worse-next-year/.

Enlisting the Collaboration of the Educational Technology Professional Community to Develop a Knowledge Management System of the Field: edu-techKNOWiki

Anne K. Bednar and Nancy L. Copeland

Overview

The field of educational technology presents a conundrum to educators because it evolves so rapidly, constantly increasing in complexity and sophistication. University faculty, K-12 teachers, and trainers in corporate, military, or health organizations are constantly confronted with new developments in technology that challenge the currency of their expertise. Moreover, while the development of the Internet as a resource in education has focused on its roles in electronic communications and as a content library, the current direction of development of the Internet is in its capabilities as a means of collaboration and information sharing, commonly referred to as Web 2.0. Web 2.0 is an umbrella term which describes a trend toward development of open architecture World Wide Web technologies which aim to enhance creativity, and facilitate information sharing and collaborative knowledge building; it includes such technologies as blogs, wikis, podcasts, twitter, and social networking. While some developments in the field of educational technology have been marked by rapid evolution, Web 2.0 concepts represent more of a paradigm shift in the ways in which the Internet is used, away from a depository of content information and toward a means of collaboration for knowledge sharing and building that is challenging teachers, administrators, university faculty and staffs, and trainers worldwide to adapt. The goal of the edu-techKNOWiki project is to mobilize professionals in the field of educational technology as a collaborative professional development learning community to apply one of the Web 2.0 tools, a wiki, as an online environment to develop a knowledge management system organizing content related to educational technology.

A.K. Bednar (✉) • N.L. Copeland
Educational Media & Technology, Eastern Michigan University, Ypsilanti, MI, USA
e-mail: abednar@emich.edu; ncopeland@emich.edu

M. Orey et al. (eds.), *Educational Media and Technology Yearbook: Volume 36, 2011*,   81
Educational Media and Technology Yearbook 36, DOI 10.1007/978-1-4614-1305-9_7,
© Springer Science+Business Media, LLC 2012

Wikis are online knowledge structures that can be modified by everyone who accesses them so that they continue to grow their content and remain on the cutting edge of current information. The edu-techKNOWiki allows sharing of theoretical, pedagogical, and technical information about educational technology from the perspectives of classroom teacher, technology mentor, curriculum developer, technology coordinator, professor, student, and corporate trainer; thereby contributing to the ability of those groups to remain current in technological innovations and their uses in education. The discussion pages in the wiki provide a vehicle for the development of communities of practice to engage professionals at all levels in open conversation. In addition, both the process of development of the wiki and its later uses present scholarly opportunities.

Recent literature about wikis reports research in a variety of areas including learning from wikis and knowledge building. Much of it reports isolated learning projects involving writing or language development goals. At a more general level, Wheeler, Yeomans, and Wheeler (2008) examined the potential for open architecture software to promote and support collaborative learning through student-generated content, identifying strengths and weaknesses of the tool for collaborative learning. In the area of knowledge building, Cress and Kimmerle (2008) propose a theoretical framework for the process of collaborative learning and knowledge building, grounded in part in Piaget's theory of equilibration, which provides a structure for examining both the social and cognitive processes involved in using a wiki as a learning tool. Reports also include the public launch of knowledge management systems in the form of wikis in various content areas, including nursing, music, and medicine. Looking at knowledge management systems more broadly, a 2006 issue of Performance Improvement Quarterly (Schwen, 2006) looks at theoretical underpinnings and analysis for the development of knowledge management tools, focusing on the need to extend processes which have been part of the instructional development model to include sociocultural factors.

Conceptual Framework

The ease of use of the knowledge system will depend on the interfaces that include the categorization and tagging of the information nodes and the structure of the nodes themselves. The name edu-techKNOWiki was chosen to emphasize the intersection of learning, as the focus of educational technology, and knowledge (KNOW), as the focus of the wiki. In addition, the word NOW, taken from the last three letters of KNOW, calls attention to the cutting edge nature of the information (see Fig. 1).

A variety of approaches are built into the edu-techKNOWiki to facilitate access to the knowledge by professionals. The Association for Educational Communications and Technology (AECT) has sponsored development of a definition of educational technology, updating that definition several times across the decades. This series of evolving definitions (Januszewski & Molenda, 2007) serves as the structural

Fig. 1 Graphic representation
of concepts embedded in the
edu-techKNOWiki name

foundation for the knowledge base: "Educational technology is the study and ethical practice of facilitating learning and improving performance by creating, using, and managing appropriate technological processes and resources." While there are many published definitions, the AECT definition was built through a collaborative process including a committee of AECT members, participants in an annual retreat of the Professors of Instructional Design and Technology (PIDT), and many readers; this collaborative process reflects the collaboration goal of the edu-techKNOWiki project. The words that form the definition also form the portals in the edu-techKNOWiki.

As a field, educational technology is only slightly older than its current conceptual leaders. That is to say developmentally it is a seedling. Using the analogy of a growing body of knowledge, the additional dimensions of history (roots), personality (gardeners – leaders who plant the seeds in the field), and future trends/emerging technologies (buds) permeate the nodes of the wiki. Through documenting the growth of ideas and their influences, future directions for research and reflection open. "Roots" is a category of information that appears in many of the nodes of information to document the evolution that results from many cycles of research. Often the pieces of history carry the names of pioneers in the field, and current theories are named for leaders. Even more important, a goal of the edu-techKNOWiki project is ongoing professional development supported by communities of practice; personality and social networking are an integral element in that goal. "Gardeners" is a category of information parallel to "roots" as it identifies the people related to each node of information. Further, a distinct element of the wiki is the sociogram of educational technology professionals. It identifies relationships among individuals based on characteristics such as university affiliation, collaborative projects, and research interests. The sociogram also encourages peer and mentoring interactions. An additional element of each node draws the user into the future; "buds" reveal innovations and new directions related to each part of the knowledge system.

Educational technology is practiced in a variety of contexts: K-12 education, higher education, business/industry, health sciences, military, and international contexts. The models of educational technology adopted in each context vary to customize the application of the knowledge and skills to suit the needs of the environment. While the AECT definition cuts across contexts, more specialized concepts of the field are enacted in such organizations as the International Society for Technology in Education (ISTE) for K-12 Education. To assist practitioners in the K-12 context to access information in the wiki, the wiki developers expanded

subject	the activity being investigated
object	the thing that is changed as a result of the activity
outcome	the goal of the activity
community	the stakeholders and context in which the activity is performed
instrument	the tools used in performance of the activity
rules	the cultural norms governing performance of the activity
division of labor	the roles related to performance of the activity

Fig. 2 Elements of activity

the descriptors supported by the basic structure of the AECT definition by overlaying the ISTE National Educational Technology Standards for Teachers (NETS-T). Development of this K-12 context is the first step. As the wiki continues to develop, participants will expand the descriptors to include common practice in additional contexts; for example, addition of the performance model practiced in business/industry and military contexts would be appropriate.

In addition to the knowledge structure, the ease of use of the edu-techKNOWiki for K-12 educators was increased through development of a problem-based interface that reflects professional practice in the K-12 context. Research in technology infusion in K-12 environments has shown that training teachers through workshops and short interventions is not effective (Wells, 2007). Teachers need immediately accessible support at the time that they are trying new technologies in their classrooms. School-based mentoring and on-site technical support help, but are difficult to provide because of budget constraints. The concept of just-in-time learning (Jackson, 1999) is common in performance improvement approaches to instructional design; learners may perform tasks which benefit from the availability of a database of information, but their performance is not improved through long and diligent memorization of that information, or, perhaps, the information changes so rapidly that it is obsolete by the time it is memorized; instead they need easy access to the information exactly at the moment it is needed in the performance of the task. The route to improved performance is through structuring of an information system and/or immediate access to an expert (Stigler & Thompson, 2009). In the K-12 context, edu-techKNOWiki can be a source of just-in-time support in the form of information and access to colleagues through communities of practice. The development of the problem-based K-12 interface began with an analysis of tasks related to educational technology performed by K-12 teachers and educational technology specialists. Participants generated a list of tasks (activities they perform involving educational technology in schools) through a Delphi technique. Then each participant was interviewed using an application of Finnish researcher Yrjö Engeström's activity theory (Marken, 2006; Schwen, Kalman, & Evans, 2006) to tease out the Elements of Activity which include the following: subject, object, outcome, community, instrument, rules, division of labor (Fig. 2).

The analysis revealed the following types of contradictions among the elements: primary contradictions – when an element contradicts itself; secondary contradictions – when any element conflicts with any other element; and tertiary contradictions – when a new process conflicts with an older process for accomplishing the activity.

The analysis process was used to design an interface to the system for educators based on the tasks that are performed in schools using educational technology and the sociocultural patterns that surround problem solving on those tasks. The interface provides access to supporting information from the wiki and also to a collaborative environment for the development of communities of practice and ongoing professional development.

Wenger (2006) defines communities of practice as: "groups of people who share a concern or a passion for something they do and learn how to do it better as they interact regularly." He further contrasts communities of practice to clubs or networks between people, indicating that a community of practice centers around a commitment to a "domain of interest" through which members "build relationships that enable them to learn from each other." Physical proximity is not necessary, but opportunities to problem solve together, share information, experiences, and assets are. Teachers using technology in their classrooms and educational technologists in specialized roles in the schools may work in slightly different roles in distinct states and districts, but share concerns, ideas, and solutions with colleagues around the country in a community of practice. Enactment of the concept in the form of the edu-techKNOWiki takes advantage of the functions of multimedia information display together with open discussion pages for peer discussion, sharing, and mentoring. Future development of similar interfaces is anticipated for educational technologists across other practice contexts such as business and industry, higher education, military, health, and international arenas.

Contributors

The ongoing development process proceeded in stages involving waves of faculty and graduate students in educational technology programs nationwide. In addition, professional organizations were invited to cosponsor the edu-techKNOWiki project. Guided by the tenets of a loosely structured task, the first invited contributors are being asked to develop nodes of information related to diverse content and post it in the nearly empty wiki. As part of the task, they are including roots, gardeners, buds, and frequently asked questions (faqs) where appropriate in their nodes of information. Using and expanding the list of descriptors related initially to the terms from the 2007 AECT definition of educational technology (technology, study, ethics, practice, facilitating, learning, improving, performance, creating, using, managing, appropriate, processes, and resources) and augmented with concepts from the 2008 ISTE NETS-T, the initial contributors are selecting descriptors for their nodes. Once the individual nodes are posted, these contributors are reviewing all of the material and, through collaboration, assisting with the development of the style guidelines for information nodes on the wiki. The broader call for contributions and the launch of the sociogram is being made through presentations at national meetings and conferences and additionally through contacts among faculty at educational technology graduate programs nationwide.

The edu-techKNOWiki includes "Keynoters" – leaders in the field who are identified to be honored; their contributions to the field are captured in audio/video interviews, writings, and multimedia presentations. While their contributions are linked into the wiki knowledge base, they are not editable. Various other models have been developed for contribution; for example, university faculty may design graduate course projects that involved generating content for the wiki.

Usability

In the spirit of open access to knowledge resources, the edu-techKNOWiki provides open access to the knowledge of the field of educational technology in a collaborative venue which can be used by professors and university students, teachers, and educational technology specialists, trainers, designers, and researchers – to name but a few. Its two main functions, to creatively display current information and provide an interactive environment for discussion, are an open invitation to participants to develop their own strategies to make the resource suit their needs. Rather than enact the vision of its creators or sponsors, the wiki enacts the evolving vision of the audience that uses it – as textbook, reference, venue for publication, or source of professional interaction.

Technical Elements

Technically the wiki is served from a virtual server and uses MediaWiki, the same software engine that drives Wikipedia, arguably the most successful online collaboration project (http://en.wikipedia.org) in the world. The development of the content of a wiki is by definition a collaborative enterprise of the community that uses it. Wiki is a word in Hawaiian that means fast; its usage in the lexicon of electronics applies because an electronic wiki enables rapid development of content material, based on a "What I Know Is…" collaboration. Wikis are based on an open software architecture system, commonly used for collaborative community Web pages, that encourages collective development. Such a system in professional development would benefit everyone who used it either to access or to contribute to the development of its knowledge system. Parallel to developing the conceptual framework, technical elements of the system were constructed, including selecting the server, installing and configuring the software to interface with the university network, implementing the wiki interface, and developing the policies for user interaction. Technical decisions emanated from a clear understanding of various audience requirements (e.g., system administrator, contributor, end user) and have been implemented to facilitate usability and support of proactive learning by the community.

Determining the technical logistics of the edu-techKNOWiki was an important consideration; for example, choosing to use an external or internal system to host the site would impact the remaining development process. Numerous commercial wiki applications are available for personal, educational, or entrepreneurial use. Commercial sites such as Wikispaces (http://www.wikispaces.com) and PB Works (http://www.pbworks.com) are popular systems used by many in the educational community, particularly K-12, because of the ease with which wikis can be created. Registered users choose between free and fee-based options. These systems are marketed as "powerful, reliable, and secure" (PB Works), which are attractive to those users looking for an easy way to produce and administer their own wiki without requiring extensive technical skills. Free systems include basic functionality for groups to create, edit, share, and discuss information online (McPherson, Wang, Hsu, & Tsuei, 2007); however, basic wikis are often interspersed with banner and pop-up advertisements that detract from the user experience. Alternatively, fee-based versions of these commercial systems eliminate distracting elements from the Web site, exclude vendor identification within the domain name, and provide access to increased functionality and greater technical support. Organizations may choose an external service rather than hosting their own wiki when considering cost, flexibility, personnel, and control. Open source wiki engines such as MediaWiki are freely available and are distributed under the GNU General Public License (GPL) that "guarantees freedom to share and change all versions of a program--to make sure it remains free software for all its users" (http:// http://www.gnu.org/). The MediaWiki software contains substantial functionality that can be hosted on virtually any server; the application is relatively easy to administer and supports the need for future scalability of the knowledge system. It is important to the edu-techKNOWiki's mission of content creation and collaboration that the wiki is free of association with any particular vendor. Affiliations with international educational technology professional organizations such as AECT and ISTE have the potential to foster mutually beneficial relationships among community members. Although hosted on an Eastern Michigan University (EMU) server, the knowledge management system reflects shared ownership by the collective participants and contributors.

Very early in the planning process, technical requirements for the knowledge management system were explored in consult with the IT department at EMU. As more faculty began using wikis for student collaboration, this project provided IT a beta system, a type of experimental sandbox, for technical analysis to help inform their decisions while considering offering Web 2.0 resources for administrative staff, academic personnel, and various students. Dedicated IT personnel assigned to the project provide ongoing administrative assistance by maintaining the integrity of the system, including security and software updates, all of which are critical given the wiki's open architecture and interface with the university's network; project staff are responsible for the day-to-day operations and user technical support. The popularity of MediaWiki makes it an attractive target for spam, hacks, and other security breaches. Thus long-term growth of the edu-techKNOWiki, from a technical perspective, will benefit from continued IT support to address security, maintenance, and scalability issues related to successful management of the system.

Initial configurations for the wiki have been modified to provide differing levels of accessibility. For example, edits to keynoter articles are prevented by everyone except the author and system administrator. Other user levels include viewer, discussant, and contributor. Without registration, the edu-techKNOWiki is open for viewing only.

Sustainability

In the culture of the collaborative Internet, the wiki community expects contributors to act responsibly; it typically does not tolerate abuse of the freedom it extends to editors of its material and self-regulates its content. To facilitate negotiation of controversial or sensitive content, each content entry, called an "article," has an accompanying discussion, called a "talk page." Written guidelines, which are being developed during the initial invited contributions phase, inform users of expectations related to the etiquette of creating new content or changing material submitted by others. Models of content articles also being developed during that phase, together with a style sheet, show contributors the style guidelines.

As part of the faculty at the hosting school, Educational Media and Technology faculty at Eastern Michigan University are integrating maintenance of the wiki into their teaching, service, and scholarship roles. In the future, if it serves the needs of the wiki and the educational technology community, a board will be formed to monitor the system.

References

Cress, U., & Kimmerle, J. (2008). A systemic and cognitive view on collaborative knowledge building with wikis. *International Journal of Computer-Supported Collaborative Learning, 3*(2), 105–122.

Jackson, R. (1999). Just in time: Web delivered professional development. *THE Journal, 26*(5), 26–28.

Januszewsk, A., & Molenda, M. (Eds.). (2007). *Educational technology: A definition with commentary.* New York: Lawrence Erlbaum Associates.

Marken, J. A. (2006). *Activity theory as a lens for considering culture: A descriptive case study of a multinational company developing and supporting training around the world.* Doctoral dissertation, Indiana University.

McPherson, S., Wang, S.-K., Hsu, H.-Y., & Tsuei, M. (2007). New literacies instruction in teacher education. *TechTrends, 51*(5), 24–31.

Schwen, T. M. (2006). Editorial: Special issue on new frameworks for HPT scholarship. *Performance Improvement Quarterly, 19*(2), 3–4.

Schwen, T. M., Kalman, H. K., & Evans, M. A. (2006). A framework for new scholarship in human performance technology. *Performance Improvement Quarterly, 19*(2), 5–26.

Stigler, J. W., & Thompson, B. J. (2009). Thoughts on creating, accumulating, and utilizing sharable knowledge to improve teaching. *The Elementary School Journal, 109*(5), 442–458.

Wells, J. (2007). Key design factors in durable instructional technology professional development. *Journal of Technology and Teacher Education, 15*(1), 101–122.

Wenger, E. (2006). Communities of practice: A brief introduction. Retrieved February, 2010, from http://www.ewenger.com/theory/.

Wheeler, S., Yeomans, P., & Wheeler, D. (2008). The good, the bad and the wiki: Evaluating student-generated content for collaborative learning. *British Journal of Educational Technology, 39*(6), 987–995.

The Vital Role(s) of School Librarians in Literacy Learning

Nancy Flanagan Knapp

As a child in elementary school, I learned to be literate in the library. Most of the textbooks I read in class, like many textbooks even today, were both poorly and boringly written (Armbruster & Anderson, 1988), and even more likely to be out of date (I distinctly remember reading a history text in eighth grade that ended its final chapter on the wonders of modern science with the startling prediction that "someday, people will fly in airplanes as routinely as they take trains, and may even venture into the uncharted realms of space!"). Our "readers," what I guess today would be called basals, contained only made-to-order stories with carefully limited vocabularies about Tip and Mitten and Jack, Janet, and Penny (McKee, 1957); even then, I think, I recognized that these were not "real stories," not the kind anyone outside of school would ever read. It was in the school library that I found books that enticed me, enthralled me, and seduced me into learning to read because I wanted so much to read them. I passed quickly from the *Cat in the Hat* (Seuss, 1957) to more ambitious books; the *Wizard of Oz* (Baum, 1900) was the first "chapter book" I made it through, at the end of third grade. Shortly thereafter, I discovered the nonfiction section, reading *All About Dinosaurs* (Andrews, 1953), which inspired a brief ambition to become a fossil hunter, and later innumerable books about horses.

Even today, as I do research on struggling readers in schools, I eventually migrate towards the library and often end up borrowing a book to read with my lunch. For me, still, the library is the spiritual "home" of literacy in the school.

Yet, current literacy research has concerned itself very little with the role(s) libraries and librarians play in the literacy learning of students in schools. For example, in the 2009 program for the National Reading Conference, the annual meeting of the premier literacy researchers in the United States, not one presentation used the words *library* or *librarians* in its title. Likewise, the recommendations put forth by panels of experts over the past decade to deal with the "literacy crisis" in our

N.F. Knapp (✉)
Applied Cognition and Development Program, University of Georgia, Athens, GA, USA
e-mail: nfknapp@uga.edu

M. Orey et al. (eds.), *Educational Media and Technology Yearbook: Volume 36, 2011*,
Educational Media and Technology Yearbook 36, DOI 10.1007/978-1-4614-1305-9_8,
© Springer Science+Business Media, LLC 2012

schools (e.g., NICHD, 2000) have paid scant, if any, attention to changes needed in the staffing or function of typical school libraries. Even at most universities, including my own, the preparation of teachers to teach literacy and the preparation of school librarians are done by different departments, sometimes even in different schools or colleges.

Surely this is a strange state of affairs! School libraries contain or manage by far the majority of literacy resources, both print and digital, available in most schools. The American Association of School Librarians, the branch of the American Library Association most focused on schools and education, has for many years advocated for school librarians to become more involved not only in developing in children a love of literacy, but also in teaching and working with teachers to promote literacy and critical thinking skills (AASL, 2009). In fact, the AASL has just this past January voted to abandon the less obviously literacy-related title of "school media specialist" to return to the traditional designation of their members as "school librarians" (Staino, 2010). Most importantly, research done in school library science has repeatedly confirmed the strong influence of the school library and the library staff on students' reading achievement in schools. For example, Lance, Rodney, and colleagues have done a number of statewide studies showing that students scored significantly higher on state reading tests in schools with more library staff per 100 students, greater funding for collections and digital access, and more hours of collaborative work by the librarian with teachers and administrators, even when students' SES, overall school funding, and community education levels were factored into the study (e.g., Hamilton-Pennell, Lance, Rodney, & Hainer, 2000). A survey of 13,123 elementary and secondary students in Ohio found that an amazing 99.4% of them indicated that the school library had helped them learn better in school, especially by helping them "work out questions" and find, use, and evaluate information (Todd & Kuhlthau, 2005, p. 69). Achterman (2009) recently published analyses of state testing in California, in which he found that "the strength of the relationship between library services and test scores" was significant at all grade levels and "increased with grade level." In addition, "the number of hours the library is open is significantly related to test [scores] at all… levels" (p. 26), again, irrespective of overall school SES or funding.

I am not suggesting that school librarians should start teaching phonics or composition, or even English literature. Librarians need not imitate classroom teachers; they have their own unique role(s) *to* play in students' literacy learning. What follows is a closer look at three of these roles that are best supported by research in the field.

The Roles

The Concierge

An effective school librarian is much like the concierge at a five-star hotel. He not only "knows the territory," in that he knows the good and the bad of children's and adolescent literature and both print and digital resources, but he is also gifted in suggesting the specific book or website that will meet a specific "patron's" (student's) needs or interests at the time. Literacy research has repeatedly demonstrated that out of school, voluntary reading is a major discriminator between high- and low-achieving students in literacy at all levels (Baker & Wigfield, 1999; Brozo, 2008; Guthrie & Wigfield, 2000), and it is often the school librarian who can help a student find that "first book" that "hooks" them on recreational reading (Foster & Knapp, 2008; Roberts, 2006). In this role, the school librarian can also be a vital resource for teachers, searching out materials to complement lessons and collaborating in lesson construction as well (AASL, 2009; Kitain, 2009; Moreillan, 2009). Finally, a good librarian, like a good concierge, encourages students to be adventurous, to move beyond their first, beloved serial books or to try a new genre, thus expanding their literate horizons and tastes (Green, 2010; Wyatt, 2008).

National Board Certified Teacher Steve Gardiner (2007) writes about two librarians at his high school, Lyn McKinney and Jan Allen, who have become expert and enthusiastic *literacy concierges.* As part of a partnership with teachers to promote recreational reading through Sustained Silent Reading (SSR), Lyn and Jan have revolutionized their once-staid high school library to focus on helping students find books they want to read and getting those books into their hands. To get students excited about books, they do booktalks in classrooms and work with two fellow teachers who designed a *Read it Forward* Web site for the school (http://senior. billings.k12.mt.us/readitforward/) which currently houses hundreds of student book reviews and comment. They have greatly expanded the variety of their library holdings, venturing, as Jan says, into "books [far] outside our own areas of interest," (p. 16) to add more nonfiction books (often favored by boys even for recreational reading), popular series books, a new section of graphic novels, and up to a dozen copies of the most popular books, so friends can read the same book together. They partner effectively with district elementary schools to access engaging reading materials for special education students and other struggling readers. All these efforts have not come close to meeting the increased student demand, however, so Lyn and Jan have instituted a "hold" list for readers in waiting, integrated their library catalog into the school district's online catalog (which offers access to over 100,000 books), and connected their library to OCLC's World Cat (http://www. worldcat.org/), which allows students to access over one million items through interlibrary loan. Finally, although, "it's pretty rare that we can't find the book a student wants," Jan says, "if we can't find, we'll buy it" (p. 17).

The results? Where students used to come into the library saying, "I don't like to read," or even, "I never read," they now declare, "My friend said I need to read this book!" SSR has spread from a few English classrooms to become "part of the routine of the school"; students read books of their own choosing for the first 15 minutes of every period in a biology class, a study hall, and, with support from specially assembled classroom libraries, in three Spanish classes (in Spanish!) and a Special Education resource room. Most important, Jan and Lyn feel they are "creating a culture at the school" that encourages and supports reading for all students; "Our entire school has been affected by SSR, and it is a very positive thing" (p. 18).

The Sherpa

But literacy in schools, as in life, is not all for recreation or pure enjoyment. John Hubbard (2006) first used the term "Sherpa" to describe his work helping college students' access and use information, and the metaphor is very apt. A Sherpa is traditionally a knowledgeable native who guides mountain climbers on their most difficult and risky ascents. Sherpas, from long experience, know the safe paths and the dangerous zones; they give advice, point out the best routes, and often accompany a party of climbers in their attempt, yet the climbers must still climb the mountain for themselves. Similarly, a good librarian can help students to locate, analyze, and appropriately use the growing "mountain" of information, both print and digital, now available to them. She points out the safe, useful resources, and guides them away from the treacherous byways of unreliable websites (Arnone, Reynolds, & Marshall, 2009; Anderson, 2009). She teaches them how to navigate the best routes to the information they need and how to analyze, summarize, and use it once they have found it. She also performs similar services for her school faculty, sharing her expertise and helping them become better finders and consumers of information as well (NAIS, 2008).

Eric Oatman (2006) writes about a project at Gill Saint Bernard's School in Gladstone, New Jersey in which the librarians epitomize the Sherpa role. At Gill Saint Bernard's (GSB), after completing a series of shorter research projects in various subject areas each year since seventh grade, every junior does a scientific literature review on a personally chosen science topic. Librarians and science teachers collaborate 50/50 on the design, implementation, and even the grading of this project. Science teachers help students develop and bound meaningful topics, consult on scientific issues, and grade the final projects for content, while librarians help students find, evaluate, and synthesize sources, often working as much as five hours one on one with a single student, and grade each final project for quality of the research process and sources found. Again, the results have been outstanding. Last spring, after spending a typical 40 or more hours each locating, reading, and understanding peer-reviewed articles and writing up their results, GSB students completed college-level reviews on a variety of cutting edge science topics, including superstring theory, auxins (a type of plant hormone), and recent trends in teenage sexual behavior. There is little doubt that climbing these "mountains" of research has greatly helped prepare GSB students for college and even graduate-level work. Educators from countries as distant as Australia and Scotland come regularly to learn about the GSB model, and in 2005, the New Jersey Association of School Librarians named the GSB eleventh-grade project the "Library Media Program of the Year."

The Cruise Director

Finally, we know that literacy and literacy learning are social activities. Again, research in the field recognizes the importance of "creating a welcoming and inviting environment" in the library (Tilley, 2009), but the "cruise director" role goes far beyond this. Good librarians help students connect with other people around books.

Just like cruise directors, they structure inviting activities and encourage struggling readers to "join the group." They run book clubs, coordinate volunteers, sponsor contests, and even raise funds by, for, and through reading, writing, and information literacy (Arnone et al., 2009; Moreillan, 2009; Roberts, 2006; Whelan, 2007), and in this way play a vital role in inviting the novice reader into the "literate talk" that research shows is such an important part of becoming a fully literate person (Heath, 1991).

A study done by Elizabeth Foster (Foster & Knapp, 2008), a school librarian in a remote rural Georgia elementary school, shows the potential power of this role for helping struggling readers join the "Literacy Club" (Smith, 1988). Elizabeth was looking for some way to help a sizable group of third graders at her school identified as likely to fail the state-mandated third-grade CRCT test because they currently read at a second-grade level or less. She contacted me about offering at her school the Reading Apprenticeship (RA) program, an intervention I had developed and tested to help struggling readers improve both their reading skills and their desire to read through supported, engaged reading of personally chosen texts with parents or other adults (Knapp, 2000, 2005; Knapp & Winsor, 1998). Unfortunately, with her school more than 90 minutes away from the University, I could neither provide the undergraduate volunteers I had used in previous projects, nor commit the time necessary to supervise them 2–3 days a week.

Elizabeth was undaunted; she spoke at a small church only a couple miles from the school and recruited over 20 committed adult volunteers. I conducted the initial, hour-long volunteer training in the RA intervention, but she set up the reading schedules (no mean feat, with children from four different classrooms and 20 adults, all with different available times), supervised, helped, consulted, and encouraged participants, and then analyzed the results, using tests already given by the school to measure students' progress. Again, the results were good beyond anyone's expectations. Reading with adults just two days a week for 12 weeks, these struggling readers gained an average of 24.8 WPM on the DIBELS, exceeding the standardized expected gain of 18 WPM during that time by 38%. Even more impressive was the average gain of 9.1 months of reading comprehension skill as measured by the STAR test during the 12 weeks of the intervention; this average gain is triple the expected rate for regular, not struggling, readers. Evidence that it was the reading sessions that made the difference was confirmed by a clear correlation between the number of reading sessions a child attended and the gains he or she made in fluency and comprehension, and also by teachers' reports describing greater enjoyment of reading and changed reading behaviors in the classroom.

Conclusions

An understanding of the scope and potential of the many roles of the school librarian in literacy learning suggests needed change in at least three areas:

First, schools need to rethink their traditional casting of librarians in the roles of "Book Warehouse Manager" and/or "Museum Curator." Resources spent staffing and equipping the school library, and policies enabling and encouraging its use, are not "extras" that can be easily cut when finances get tight (as they are now being at in many states and districts). Rather, time and money that schools spend wisely on library resources and staff will pay undoubted dividends in higher literacy achievement now, and later lifelong learning, for their students.

But none of this will happen unless school librarians are prepared to assume these roles. Right now, few library science degrees require any courses in the psychology or teaching of reading; a quick search of Peterson's Guide (https://www.petersons.com/) for major state universities offering School Library Science programs in various regions of the country shows no courses in reading or writing required in the school library certification programs at the University of Illinois (http://www.lis.illinois.edu/academics/programs/k12/course-summary), San Jose State in California (http://slisweb.sjsu.edu/classes/teacherlibrarian.htm), Syracuse University in New York (http://ischool.syr.edu/academics/graduate/mls/mediaprogram/curriculum.aspx), the University of Texas at Austin (http://www.ischool.utexas.edu/programs/specializations/sslc.php#1), and many others. At my own university, the program coordinator for School Library Media is just now designing a new course called "Supporting Literacy in School Libraries," to fill this need. In addition to a better understanding of literacy acquisition and difficulties, to better fulfill their various roles, librarians could also use coursework in consulting and group processes.

Finally, more research needs to be done on how school libraries and librarians do and can help children become literate. Researchers in other areas of literacy need to pay much more attention to the role of school libraries and librarians in students' literacy achievement; school-based literacy studies should routinely include measures of library access and resources, as well as librarian activities and expertise. Indeed, researchers in literacy and in school library science need to develop truly collaborative projects and to include librarians, reading specialists, and teachers in their work. If we can combine the knowledge and insights of all the professionals involved in school literacy, then we may finally begin to make better progress in helping children learn and love to read.

References

Achterman, D. (2009). A new California study: School libraries give students a better chance at success. *CSLA Journal, 33*(1), 26–27.

American Association of School Librarians (AASL). (2009). *The library media specialist's role in reading.* Retrieved August 3, 2010, from http://www.ala.org/aasl/positionstatements.

Anderson, C. (2009). The five pillars of reading. *Library Media Connection, 28*, 22–25.

Andrews, R. C. (1953). *All about Dinosaurs.* New York: Random House.

Armbruster, B. B., & Anderson, T. H. (1988). On selecting "considerate" content area textbooks. *Remedial and Special Education, 9*(1), 47–52.

Arnone, M. P., Reynolds, R., & Marshall, T. (2009). The effect of early adolescent's psychological needs satisfaction upon their perceived competence in information skills and intrinsic motivation for research. *School Libraries Worldwide, 15*(2), 115–134.

Baker, L., & Wigfield, A. (1999). Dimensions of children's motivation for reading and their relations to reading activity and reading achievement. *Reading Research Quarterly, 34*, 452–477.

Baum, L. F. (1900). *The wonderful wizard of Oz*. Chicago, IL: George M. Hill.

Brozo, W. G. (2008). Engagement in reading: Lessons learned from three PISA countries. *Journal of Adolescent and Adult Literacy, 51*, 304–315.

Foster, E., & Knapp, N. F. (2008*). Cougar readers: A pilot scale-up study of the reading apprenticeship intervention*. Paper presented at the annual meeting of the National Reading Conference, Orlando, FL.

Gardiner, S. (2007). Librarians provide strongest support for sustained silent reading. *Library Media Connection, 25*(5), 16–18.

Green, J. (2010). The future of reading. *School Library Journal, 56*(1), 24–28.

Guthrie, J. T., & Wigfield, A. (2000). Engagement and motivation in reading. In M. L. Kamil, P. B. Mosenthal, P. D. Pearson, & R. Barr (Eds.), *Handbook of reading research* (Vol. 3, pp. 403–422). Mahwah, NJ: Erlbaum.

Hamilton-Pennell, C., Lance, K. C., Rodney, M. J., & Hainer, E. (2000). Dick and Jane go the head of the class. *School Library Journal, 46*, 44–47.

Heath, S. B. (1991). The sense of being literate: Historical and cross-cultural features. In R. Barr, M. L. Kamil, P. Mosenthal, & P. David Pearson (Eds.), *Handbook of reading research* (Vol. II, pp. 3–25). New York: Longman Publishing Group.

Hubbard, J. (2006). Technological Sherpa. *Library Journal, 131*, 50.

Kitain, S. (2009). Crafting literacy lessons one article at a time. *Library Media Connection, 28*(3), 28–29.

Knapp, N. F. (2000, November). *From the parent's perspective: A summer family reading apprenticeship program for delayed and novice readers*. Paper presented at the annual meeting of the National Reading Conference, Scottsdale, AZ.

Knapp, N. F. (2005, April). *Learning together: Struggling readers and pre-service teachers in a reading apprenticeship project*. Paper presented at the annual conference of the American Educational Research Association, Montreal, Canada.

Knapp, N. F., & Winsor, A. P. (1998). A reading apprenticeship for delayed primary readers. *Reading Research and Instruction, 38*(1), 13–29.

McKee, P. M. (1957). *Tip and Mitten* (revised ed.). Boston, MA: Houghton Mifflin.

Moreillan, J. (2009). Reading4Life @ your library. *School Library Monthly, 26*, 17–20.

National Association of Independent Schools (NAIS). (2008). *NAIS guidelines of professional practice for librarians*. Retrieved August 3, 2010, from http://www.nais.org/about/sereisdoc.efm?ItemNumber=151374.

National Institute of Child Health and Human Development (NICHD). (2000). *Report of the National Reading Panel. Teaching children to read: An evidence-based assessment of the scientific research literature on reading and its implications for reading instruction* (NIH Publication No. 00–4769). Washington, DC: U.S. Government Printing Office.

Oatman, E. (2006). Overwhelming evidence. *School Library Journal, 52*(1), 56–59.

Roberts, J. (2006). Building a community of high school readers. *Knowledge Quest, 35*(1), 24–29.

Seuss, Dr. (1957). *The cat in the hat*. New York: Random House.

Smith, F. (1988). *Joining the literacy club: Further essays into education*. Portsmouth, NH: Heinemann.

Staino, R. (2010). AASL adopts 'school librarian' as official term for the profession. *School Library Journal*. Retrieved August 3, 2010, from http://www.schoollibraryjournal.com/article/CA6715763.html.

Tilley, C. L. (2009). Reading motivation and engagement. *School Library Monthly, 26*, 39–42.

Todd, R. J., & Kuhlthau, C. C. (2005). Student learning through Ohio school Libraries, part 1: How effective school libraries help students. *School Libraries Worldwide, 11*(1), 63–88.

Whelan, D. L. (2007). Like a rock. *School Library Journal, 53*(5), 41–43.

Wyatt, N. (2008). The RA tool kit. *Library Journal, 133*(1), 42–45.

An Analysis of Educational Technology-Related Doctoral Programs in the United States

Heng-Yu Ku, Shari Plantz-Masters, Kim Hosler, Watsatree Diteeyont, Chatchada Akarasriworn, and Tzong-Yih Lin

Introduction

Potential graduate students face a plethora of challenges when trying to find and decide upon a doctoral studies program in educational technology. What exactly is educational technology? According to the Definition and Terminology Committee of the Association for Educational Communications and Technology (2007), "Educational technology is the study and ethical practice of facilitating learning and improving performance by creating, using, and managing appropriate technological processes and resources" (p. 1). However, the definition of the field of practice continues to evolve and change in tandem with changes in education and technology. Reiser (2007) believes that it is unlikely that professionals will ever reach a consensus through thoughts or actions on a single definition.

Coupled with the elusive definition of the field, prospective doctoral students and potential employers often are confounded by the myriad of naming conventions for higher educational programs in our field. When searching for doctoral programs, students typically find the names of educational technology, learning sciences, instructional technology, curriculum and instruction, or instructional design and technology (IDT). According to Persichitte (2007), these titles represent responses to the changes in the field, and it is perhaps impossible to separate the application of the field from the systemic changes that are intrinsic to it. Nonetheless, individuals seeking doctoral degrees in the field of educational technology face challenges.

One of the challenges is that students must try to wade through differing program and degree titles to find the curriculum within an educational technology doctoral degree program. They evaluate the core requirements as well as investigate the extent of the research curriculum and the intensity of the dissertation. One way to

H.-Y. Ku (✉) • S. Plantz-Masters • K. Hosler • W. Diteeyont • C. Akarasriworn • T.-Y. Lin
Educational Technology Program, College of Education and Behavioral Sciences,
University of Northern Colorado, Greeley, CO, USA
e-mail: heng-yu.ku@unco.edu

M. Orey et al. (eds.), *Educational Media and Technology Yearbook: Volume 36, 2011*,
Educational Media and Technology Yearbook 36, DOI 10.1007/978-1-4614-1305-9_9,
© Springer Science+Business Media, LLC 2012

consider a meaningful educational technology curriculum is to place it in a professional competency-based framework, such as those offered by the International Board of Standards for Training, Performance and Instruction (IBSTPI), International Society for Performance Improvement (ISPI), the American Society for Training and Development (ASTD), and the Association for Educational Communications and Technology (AECT). Davidson-Shiver and Rasmussen (2007) suggest,

> Competencies for IDT can be used as follows: …To provide academic programs with information to develop and evaluate curriculum, courses, internships, and program requirements. To provide academic programs with a basis for program evaluation and planning. …To provide IDT academicians with a direction for forming a research agenda (p. 279).

However, they also pointed out that the lack of common titles for programs at colleges and universities make it difficult for potential students to match their goals with a specific professional competency framework. Caffarella (1999) reported that universities offered doctoral degrees with a variety of titles encompassing the field of educational technology. The titles of degrees vary from educational technology to instructional design to information and learning sciences, and there is considerable debate over which terms are more appropriate to use in identifying the field (Carr-Chellman, 2006). For example, in a debate with Merrill about the future of the field, Wilson argued that the growth of graduate programs in the field is in both instructional design and technology, and in learning sciences (Merrill & Wilson, 2007).

Another challenge faced by those seeking advanced degrees in the field is deciding which type of degree to pursue; the Ph.D. or the Ed.D., and understanding the differences. Some institutions offer both doctoral degrees (Ph.D. – Doctor of Philosophy and Ed.D. – Doctor of Education) while most offer one or the other. In their Carnegie Initiative on the Doctorate study, Shulman, Golde, Bueschel, and Grabedian (2006) explained that the goal of the Ed.D. is to train leaders, managers, and evaluators in education as differentiated from the Ph.D., which trains researchers in the academic field. They argue that even though overlap between the degrees is expected and necessary, the distinction between the degrees has blurred, and the Ed.D. is widely considered a "Ph.D. – Lite" (p. 27).

Over the past 10 years, the number of institutions offering doctoral degree programs in educational technology-related fields has fluctuated. Lowenthal and Wilson (2008) evaluated the field by looking at the titles of programs and degrees, job titles, and professional organizations, concluding that the variety of different labels impact the confusion of identity in the field. Davidson-Shiver and Rasmussen (2007) claimed, "A lack of easily identified, common titles makes the field difficult to distinguish from other professions in education and training. The lack of common titles for IDT programs at college and universities makes it difficult for prospective students to match professional goals to programs." (p. 283).

The effort to define the field of educational technology is not new. Gentry (1995) wrote, "Regardless of how well this collection of interpretations of educational technology clarifies or confuses matters, it is safe to assume that some time will pass before precise meanings are accepted across the field" (p. 8). Reiser (2007) added that the definition of the field changed over the years and there are no universally accepted answers to questions about the nature of the field and its definition. Persichitte (2007) further reiterated that the lack of consensus extends to the name used to identify the field.

While there are sources to find listings of doctoral programs in educational technology and related fields, there is a lack of comprehensive studies to categorize and evaluate the requirements for those programs. This study provided an analysis of those programs and their curriculum. By taking an in-depth look at the similarities and differences among the programs, this study benefits potential doctoral students seeking appropriate doctoral degree programs that best fit their needs. It also helps current doctoral students identify potential universities with doctoral degree programs in educational technology-related fields for their future employment. In addition, the study also sought to shed light on the growth in doctoral education in the field of educational technology while at the same time evaluating the focus of the programs.

The purpose of this study was to analyze the doctoral programs in educational technology-related fields in the United States. The research addressed the following questions:

1. What was the growth of educational technology doctoral programs over the last 30 years?
2. How many institutions (both campus-based and online programs) offer doctoral degrees in educational technology?
3. What is the variation of doctoral program degree titles?
4. What is the range of credit hours required to earn a doctoral degree?
5. What are the varying dissertation requirements?
6. How do the requirements for the Ed.D. differ from those for the Ph.D. among universities who offer both degrees?

Method

Data Sources

A document analysis method was implemented for this study, which provided key information about the universities, their program requirements, and curricula central to addressing the research questions. By collecting data from five different data sources, a group of prospective doctoral programs at varying universities were identified, including campus-based and online programs.

The initial data source included the *Educational Media and Technology Yearbook* (Branch, 2008), which identified instructional technology-related organizations and graduate programs across North America. The second source was the *Curricula Data of Degree Programs in Educational Communications and Technology*, an online database provided by the Association for Educational Communications and Technology (n.d.). This source contained self-reported curricula data of degree programs in the educational communications and technology field offered by universities around the world. Information provided in the database included program and degree titles, degrees offered, program requirements, lists of faculty, and contact information for the programs.

In addition to these two educational technology graduate program-related resources, a third data source, *GradSchools.com* (2009) was utilized. This online resource provided a search engine that allowed us to discover educational technology graduate programs from universities in the United States. A fourth data source consulted for the selection of potential programs was the online version of *The College Blue Book* (2007). This electronic resource included lists of degrees offered by universities in the United States. The online version of *The College Blue Book* provided summaries and general information including contact information, entrance requirements, and website addresses of each college and university around the country. The doctoral programs that had educational technology-related titles were selected and added to the master list for further analysis. Finally, to evaluate each doctoral program more completely, we consulted the fifth data source – the university's website for each of the doctoral programs offered.

Procedures

We paired into three groups for the first step in the data gathering process, which was to identify which universities in the United States offered a Ph.D. or Ed.D. program in educational technology-related fields. One team focused on the *Educational Media and Technology Yearbook*, the second team reviewed the AECT's *Curricula Data of Degree Programs in Educational Communications and Technology* database, and the third team collected data from *Gradschools.com* and *The College Blue Book*. Once collected, we combined these data into a matrix that listed all the universities offering doctoral programs in educational technology and related fields. For each listed program, we compiled program names and degree titles along with website addresses and contact information.

The goal of using multiple sources was to triangulate the program data. Once we collected the data, we compiled a master list and removed duplications to ensure accuracy. We then summarized and created an updated master university list that included 93 school names, program website addresses, degree titles, doctoral curriculum website addresses, type of degrees (Ed.D. or Ph.D.), degree completion requirements (total credit hours and dissertation hours), and contact information from all four different sources. Next, we alphabetized the university list by state.

Following this step, we divided the list so each pair of team members researched 31 universities in greater detail. For each university, we identified the website addresses of the curriculum for each program or its doctoral program handbook for later referencing and cross-checking. To insure validity and accuracy of these data, we again paired up to validate the collected data. Following this step, we compiled the curriculum data for each program. At this point, we evaluated each program to determine if the curricula offered supported educational technology-related programs.

To conduct this evaluation, we compared the course names and curriculum requirements from five well-known educational technology-related doctoral programs in the United States: Arizona State University, Florida State University, Indiana University, Pennsylvania State University, and University of Georgia (Ku, 2009). We analyzed the curricula from these five universities and developed a set of curriculum criteria. The curriculum criteria included (a) foundational courses in instructional or educational technology (e.g., Introduction to Instructional Systems or Instructional Design and Technology), (b) educational practice and design courses (e.g., Instructional Media Design or Design of Distance Educational Environments), (c) cognitive learning and instructional theory courses (e.g., Theories of Learning and Instruction or Theoretical Views of Learning), (d) instructional systems research methods or research design applied to education-type courses (e.g., Research in Technology, Quantitative Data Analysis, Qualitative Data Analysis, or Mixed Methods), and (e) the dissertation. We then used these criteria to evaluate and categorize the universities' curricula with respect to educational technology. We engaged in many conversations to come to a consensus regarding which universities had educational technology or closely related programs. The range of disciplines from instructional design to the trends toward learning sciences perplexed us as we assessed each individual program.

Once we created a list of potential university programs, we evaluated each program's curriculum for the required core courses and content to assess if the university's Ph.D. or Ed.D. curriculum was substantially educational technology-focused. We repeated this process three times, as we developed a common understanding of the scope of the field. After a final comparison of the degree titles, course names, and curriculum requirements from the principle universities, we discussed and decided on which of the 93 universities that offered doctoral programs in educational technology-related fields met the curriculum criteria and should be included in the study.

Data Analysis

In order to explore the growth of educational technology doctoral programs over the last 30 years, the records of educational technology programs offered by universities in the United States from five issues of the *Educational Media and Technology Yearbooks* (Witt, 1980; Logan, 1985; Branyan-Broadbent & Ward, 1990; Ely & Minor, 1995/1996; Branch, 2000; McClendon, 2005) were analyzed. A descriptive analysis of all degree titles (Ph.D. and Ed.D.) for both campus-based and online programs was conducted with the goal of examining the variation and frequency of the different degree titles. We used the degree titles exactly as they appeared on the universities' website for greater accuracy in the variation and frequency analysis.

Additionally, the range of credit hours required for the degree and the varying dissertation hours required were clarified by examining the specific curricula from each university. For programs using the quarter hour system, quarter credit hours were converted to semester hours assuming every three-quarter hours is equivalent to two semester hours. We used the semester hour equivalents for the comparison of both course and dissertation requirements. Lastly, we compared and evaluated the total credit hour and dissertation hour requirements among ten universities that offered both Ph.D. and Ed.D. degree programs in the educational technology-related fields.

Results

The Growth of the Educational Technology Doctoral Programs

According to the data regarding the growth of educational technology doctoral programs, the number of universities and institutions that offer doctoral degree programs has expanded over the past 30 years. The findings show that the number of doctoral programs in educational technology-related fields fluctuated from 1980 to 2009.

A total of 42 universities offered doctoral programs in educational technology-related fields in 1980, 62 in 1985, 64 in 1990, 47 in 1995, 49 in 2000, 54 in 2005, and 59 in 2009, respectively. After an initial increase of over 52% (from 42 to 64) between 1980 and 1990, the number decreased by 23% (from 64 to 49) in 2000. Then, the number of institutions offering relevant degrees rose over 20% (from 49 to 59) between 2000 and 2009.

Numbers of Institutions Offer Doctoral Degrees

The results from the study show that 59 institutions in the Unites States offer doctoral programs in educational technology and related fields in 2009 as presented in Appendix A. Among those institutions, 55 offer campus-based degree programs and 4 offer online degree programs in educational technology and related fields. Among the 55 campus-based degree programs, 30 institutions offer only Ph.D. degree programs, 16 institutions offer only Ed.D. degree programs, and 9 institutions offer both Ph.D. and Ed.D. degree programs. In terms of the four online degree programs, two institutions offer Ph.D. degree programs (Capella University and Walden University), one institution (University of Phoenix) offers an Ed.D. degree program, and one institution (Northcentral University) offers both Ph.D. and Ed.D. degrees in educational technology. The states with the most institutions offering educational technology-related doctoral programs are Florida (6 institutions), Pennsylvania (4 institutions), Texas (4 institutions), and Virginia (4 institutions).

The Variation and Frequency of Doctoral Program Degree Titles

The results show that there are 29 different degree titles across 55 campus-based universities, resulting in 53% of the universities examined offering different degree titles in the field of study called educational technology. The three most common degree titles are Instructional Technology, Educational Technology, and Instructional Design and Technology.

Results for the four online university doctoral degree programs were also investigated and the names of the degree titles are Instructional Design for Online Learning, Educational Leadership/Educational Technology, Educational Technology and e-Learning, and Educational Technology. No common program degree titles were found among the four online educational technology doctoral degree programs reviewed. However, the title "Educational Technology" is included in three (75%) of the four titles. As a result, 33 different degree titles represented 59 campus-based and online institutions who offered doctoral degrees.

Furthermore, a keyword analysis of both campus-based and online university degree titles revealed five most commonly occurring words or word pairs. These terms by rank order are Instructional Technology, Educational Technology, Instructional Systems, Curriculum & Instruction, and Instructional Design.

The Range of Total Credit Hours Required

For the 55 campus-based universities, the total credit hours for the Ph.D. programs range from a minimum of 48 credit hours (Lehigh University and University of Northern Texas) to a maximum of 113 credit hours (Wayne State University). For Ed.D. programs, the total credit hours range from 42 credit hours (University of Kentucky and West Virginia University) to 113 credit hours (Wayne State University). Two campus-based programs did not publish their total credit hour requirements. For the four online programs, the total credit hours range from 62 (University of Phoenix) to 89 (Walden University). Overall, the most common requirements for total credit hours ranged from 56 to 65 among 59 institutions.

The Range of Dissertation Hours Required

Dissertation hours for the Ph.D. programs range from a minimum of 1 credit hour (University of Hawaii at Manoa) to a maximum of 30 credit hours (University of South Florida, Kansas State University, Wayne State University, Kent State University, and Virginia Tech University) with 15 credit hours being the most common. For Ed.D. programs, dissertation hours range from 4 credit hours (Boston University) to 45 credit hours (University of Cincinnati). Six campus-based programs did not publish their requirements on dissertation hours. The range of required dissertation hours for the four online programs ranged from 11 to 30 credit hours. Overall, the most common requirements for dissertation hours ranged from 7 to 12 among 59 institutions.

Differences in Degree Requirements Between Ed.D. and Ph.D.

Of the 59 institutions, 10 institutions (17%) offered both the Ph.D. and Ed.D. degrees in educational technology-related programs. Nine are campus-based (University of Central Florida, University of Florida, Kansas State University, Wayne State University, Pennsylvania State University, University of North Texas, The College of William & Mary, University of Virginia, and Virginia Tech University) while one is an online-based university (Northcentral University).

However, only nine universities were compared due to unavailable data from Pennsylvania State University regarding the requirements of the total credit hour and dissertation hours. Of these nine universities, three (33%) require their Ph.D. students to complete more total credit hours than Ed.D. students. These three universities are University of North Texas (72 vs. 69), The College of William & Mary (69 vs. 48), and Virginia Tech University (96 vs. 90). In contrast, three universities (33%) require their Ed.D. students to complete more total credit hours than Ph.D. students. These three universities are University of Central Florida (108 vs. 99), Kansas State University (94 vs. 90), and University of Virginia (84 vs. 72). Another three universities (33%) require both the Ph.D. and Ed.D. students to take the same amount of total credit hours. These three universities are University of Florida (90 vs. 90), Wayne State University (113 vs. 113), and Northcentral University (51 vs. 51).

Furthermore, the comparison of dissertation hours revealed that five out of nine universities (56%) require more dissertation hours for the Ph.D. program than for the Ed.D. program. These five universities are University of Central Florida (24 vs. 21), Kansas State University (30 vs. 16), Wayne State University (30 vs. 20), The College of William & Mary (9 vs. 6), and Virginia Tech University (30 vs. 24). Four universities (44%) require the same dissertation hours for both degrees. These four universities are University of Florida (12 vs. 12), University of North Texas (12 vs. 12), University of Virginia (12 vs. 12), and Northcentral University (9 vs. 9).

Discussion

According to our findings, educational technology doctoral programs increased from 42 in 1980 to 64 in 1990. This increase parallels the development of advanced technologies in the United States after 1980. As Senese (1983) stated, the beginning of the technological revolution in 1980 affected both worlds of work and education. Technology became a significant component for improving the educational system. Many teachers and instructors were encouraged to include technology within their instruction to facilitate student learning. Teachers and instructors were required to have basic skills in technology usage. Therefore, the increasing need for combining teaching and technology in education became a major influence on the number of educational technology-related programs offered from 1980 to 1990. However, the number of institutions offering educational technology doctoral degrees declined from 64 in 1990 to 49 in 2000. This phenomenon may have paralleled a significant economic downturn in the United States where budgets for improving and expanding programs were limited in both public and private universities in the 1990s. Therefore, several programs within institutions were closed, which led to a decreasing number of programs in the field.

As the economy improved and significant advances were made in technology, within a few years, the number of institutions offering educational technology and related degrees increased from 49 in 2000 to 59 in 2009. One major impetus to support this increase may be the rising numbers of distance learning courses offered by various institutions. Leonard and Guha (2001) shared that online courses presented flexible options allowing students to access classes anytime and anywhere, which responded to the needs of students with busy lifestyles and second-career college students who previously faced a barrier to attending regular classes on campus. Dobbs, Waid, and Carman (2009) also pointed out that the affordability and accessibility of technology for students, especially computer and Internet accessibility, led to an exponentially growing demand for online courses.

There is a dramatic difference between the number of campus-based degree programs and online degree programs. Fifty-five institutions (93%) are campus-based programs while four (7%) institutions offer online doctoral degrees. This may indicate that the demand for online doctoral degree programs is not as strong as for campus-based programs. It may also point to issues around meeting residency doctoral degree requirements and the challenges of pursuing a doctoral degree with limited face-to-face instructor contact and cohort contact. Furthermore, students and faculty may perceive the quality of learning found in campus-based programs to be better than online-based degree programs. In addition, Adams and DeFleur (2006) indicated that employers prefer traditional degree programs to online degree programs. This may also have an impact on the demand for online programs.

The variance and frequency of the 33 different degree titles serve to underpin the lack of a clear definition and consistency within the field of educational or instructional technology. However, it seems logical that as the field has varied definitions and interpretations, so do the programs and degree titles that prepare professionals for entry into the field. The fact that the degree title *Instructional Technology* occurs 12 times among the 59 doctoral programs supports what Reiser (2007) claimed to be the term used most frequently to describe our field.

One explanation for the variety of program titles in our field is that the program degree titles may be driven by a university's marketing initiatives. In an effort to attract students, universities need to differentiate themselves to make themselves stand out and appear unique in the eyes of prospective students. One way to do that is to create a program name that is different, catchy, or sounds innovative, such as learning sciences or learning design and technology. Conversely, the absence of the words instructional design from a program title may mean that a key component of our field, instructional design, is not as heavily emphasized by that particular curriculum. As Merrill pointed out in his debate with Wilson (Merrill & Wilson, 2007), down the broad road of instructional technology, it may be more and more difficult to determine if there is an academic field of instructional design (p. 349). Either way, how a university positions and markets its educational or instructional technology doctoral program may influence the degree title and program curricula.

This study provided an overall view of the credit hour range for completing a Ph.D. or Ed.D. degree in educational technology-related fields in the United States. According to Wellman (2005), institutions have a high degree of flexibility to vary credit hour requirements to meet internal institutional standards. The variation of the credit hours for the Ph.D. (48–113 semester hours) and Ed.D. programs (42–113 semester hours) in the educational technology field is extensive. In terms of dissertation hours, the range and variability for the number of dissertation hours required by various programs reflects the range and variability found in degree titles. One reason for this variability could be due to the challenges faced by doctoral education in the United States in general. According to Nerad (2008), one of the challenges faced by U.S. doctoral education includes managing the intricate link between doctoral education and the institutional research mission of the university. Similar to the total credit hours, the range of the total dissertation hours varies depending on the program's goals and mission.

Finally, this study addressed the different requirements for the Ph.D. and Ed.D. programs in the educational technology-related fields. Several sources indicated that both the Ph.D. and Ed.D. programs were designed for different purposes and, therefore, prepared students differently (Shulman et al. 2006; Deering, 1998). Of the nine programs that offer both Ph.D. and Ed.D. degrees, three programs require more total credit hours for the Ph.D. than the Ed.D. degrees, three universities require the same number of total credit hours for both degrees, and three programs require less total credit hours for the Ph.D. than the Ed.D. degrees. Therefore, there is no significant relationship between total credit hours required of the Ph.D. and the Ed.D. programs. Although Shulman et al. (2006) declared that the Ed.D. is often viewed as a Ph.D. Lite, "with fewer requirements than the Ph.D., much less emphasis on fulltime study and residency…" (p. 27), our findings did not demonstrate a disparity of effort between degree types.

Even though the Ph.D. and the Ed.D. programs serve different theoretical goals, they are "similar in programmatic requirements, knowledge bases, competency standards, and in employment expectancies" (Andersen, 1983, p. 5). In terms of dissertation hours, the results revealed that the Ph.D. degree required more dissertation hours than the Ed.D. degree. Deering (1998) stated that the Ph.D. dissertation illustrated scholarly and high quality research and the Ed.D. dissertation was more applied but not theoretical in nature. Redden (2007) also implied that a Ph.D. dissertation is more research-oriented while an Ed.D. dissertation is more applied and practitioner-oriented. Therefore, institutions who offer both Ph.D. and Ed.D. degrees in the same field might demand more dissertation hours for Ph.D. than Ed.D. degrees.

As with many studies, there are limitations as well as areas for future investigation. This study does not explain or detail what the degree program fluctuations represented beyond the growth or decline of numbers. Further investigation may shed light about which degree titles have remained stable, which are in decline and which are new. In addition, future research can focus on in-depth curriculum analysis among these doctoral programs to help clarify the core competencies in the field of educational technology.

Appendix A

Educational Technology-Related Doctoral Programs

Degree Program	States	Institutions	Ph.D.	Ed.D.	Ph.D.& Ed.D.
Campus-Based Degree Programs	Alabama	University of South Alabama	x		
	Arizona	Arizona State University	x		
	California	California State Polytechnic, Pomona		x	
	Colorado	University of Northern Colorado	x		
	Cincinnati	University of Cincinnati		x	
	Connecticut	University of Connecticut	x		
	Florida	Florida State University	x		
		Nova Southeastern University		x	
		University of Central Florida			x
		University of Florida			x
		University of South Florida	x		
		University of West Florida		x	
	Hawaii	University of Hawaii at Manoa	x		
	Georgia	Georgia State University	x		
		University of Georgia	x		
	Illinois	Northern Illinois University		x	
		Southern Illinois University	x		
	Indiana	Indiana University	x		
		Indiana State University	x		
		Purdue University	x		
	Iowa	Iowa State University	x		
	Kansas	Kansas State University			x
	Kentucky	University of Kentucky		x	
	Louisiana	Louisiana State University	x		
	Maryland	Towson University		x	
	Massachusetts	Boston University		x	
	Michigan	Wayne State University			x
	Minnesota	University of Minnesota	x		
	Missouri	University of Missouri	x		
	New Mexico	University of New Mexico	x		
	Nevada	University of Nevada, Las Vegas	x		

(continued)

(continued)

Degree Program	States	Institutions	Ph.D.	Ed.D.	Ph.D.& Ed.D.
	New York	Columbia University- Teacher's College		x	
		New York University	x		
		Syracuse University	x		
	Ohio	Kent State University	x		
		Ohio University	x		
	Oklahoma	University of Oklahoma	x		
	Pennsylvania	Dusquensne University		x	
		Lehigh University	x		
		Pennsylvania State University			x
		Widener University		x	
	Tennessee	University of Memphis		x	
		University of Tennessee	x		
	Texas	Texas Tech		x	
		University of Houston		x	
		University of North Texas			x
		University of Texas Austin	x		
	Utah	Brigham Young University	x		
		Utah State University	x		
	Virginia	Old Dominion University	x		
		The College of William & Mary			x
		University of Virginia			x
		Virginia Tech University			x
	West Virginia	West Virginia University		x	
	Wyoming	University of Wyoming		x	
		Sub-Total	30	16	9
		Total Campus-Based Programs	55		
Online Degree Programs	Arizona	Northcentral University			x
		University of Phoenix		x	
	Minnesota	Capella University	x		
		Walden University	x		
		Sub-Total	2	1	1
		Total Online Degree Programs	4		

References

Adams, J., & DeFleur, M. H. (2006). The acceptability of a doctoral degree earned online as a credential for obtaining employment. *Communication Education, 55*(1), 32–45.

Andersen, D. G. (1983). Differential of the Ed.D. and the Ph.D in education. *Journal of Teacher Education, 34*, 55–58.

Association for Educational Communications and Technology. (n.d.) *Curricula data of degree programs in educational communications and technology*. Retrieved March 28, 2009, from http://www.aect.org.

Branch, O. M. (2000). Graduate programs in instructional technology (IT). In R. M. Branch & M. A. Fitzgerald (Eds.), *Educational media and technology yearbook* (pp. 230–273). Englewood, CO: Libraries Unlimited, Inc.

Branch, R. M. (2008). Graduate programs in North America. In M. Orey, V. J. McClendon, & R. M. Branch (Eds.), *Educational media and technology yearbook* (pp. 269–321). Westport, CT: Libraries Unlimited, Inc.

Branyan-Broadbent, B., & Ward, L. A. (1990). Doctoral programs in instructional technology. In B. Branyan-Broadbent & R. K. Wood (Eds.), *Educational media and technology yearbook* (pp. 273–292). Littleton, CO: Libraries Unlimited, Inc.

Caffarella, E. P. (1999). *Major themes and trends in doctoral dissertation research in educational technology from 1977 through 1998.* Paper presented at the national convention of the Association for Educational Communications and Technology, Houston, TX.

Carr-Chellman, A. A. (2006). Where do educational technologists really publish? An examination of successful emerging scholars' publication outlets. *British Journal of Educational Technology, 37*(1), 5–15.

Davidson-Shiver, G. V., & Rasmussen, K. L. (2007). Competencies for instructional design and technology professionals. In R. A. Reiser & J. V. Dempsey (Eds.), *Trends and issues in instructional design and technology* (pp. 271–286). Upper Saddle River, NJ: Pearson Education, Inc.

Deering, T. E. (1998). Eliminating the doctor of education degree: It's the right thing to do. *The Educational Forum, 37*(1), 5–15.

Definition and Terminology Committee of the Association for Educational Communications and Technology. (2007). Definition. In A. Januszewski & M. Molenda (Eds.), *Educational technology: A definition with commentary* (pp. 1–14). New York: Routledge/Taylor & Francis Group.

Dobbs, R. R., Waid, C. A., & Carmen, A. D. (2009). Students' perceptions of online courses: The effect of online course experience. *The Quarterly Review of Distance Education, 10*(1), 9–26.

Ely, D. P., & Minor, B. B. (1995/1996). Doctoral programs in instructional technology. In D. P. Ely & B. B. Minor (Eds.), *Educational media and technology yearbook* (pp. 246–261). Englewood, CO: Libraries Unlimited, Inc.

Gentry, C. G. (1995). Educational technology: A question of meaning. In G. J. Anglin (Ed.), *Instructional technology: Past, present, future* (pp. 1–10). Englewood, CO: Libraries Unlimited.

GradSchool.com. (n.d.). *Find a program: Educational/instructional media and technology graduate programs in USA.* Retrieved March 12, 2009, from http://www.gradschools.com.

Ku, H. Y. (2009). Twenty years of productivity in ETR&D by institutions and authors. *Educational Technology Research and Development, 57*(6), 801–805.

Leonard, J., & Guha, S. (2001). Education at the crossroads: Online teaching and students' perspective on distance learning. *Journal of Research on Technology in Education, 34*(1), 52–57.

Logan, E. N. (1985). Doctoral programs in instructional technology. In E. E. Miller & M. L. Mosley (Eds.), *Educational media and technology yearbook* (pp. 181–201). Littleton, CO: Libraries Unlimited, Inc.

Lowenthal, P., & Wilson, B. G. (2008). Labels DO matter: A critique of AECT's redefinition of the field. In M. Simonson (Ed.), 31st annual proceedings: Selected research and development papers presented at the annual convention of the Association for Educational Communications and Technology (Vol. 2, pp. 297–306). Washington D. C.: Association for Educational Communications and Technology.

McClendon, J. (2005). Graduate programs in instructional technology. In M. Orey, J. McClendon, & R. M. Branch (Eds.), *Educational media and technology yearbook* (pp. 331–395). Westport, CT: Libraries Unlimited, Inc.

Merrill, D. M., & Wilson, B. (2007). The future of instructional design point/counterpoint. In R. A. Reiser & J. V. Dempsey (Eds.), *Trends and issues in instructional design and technology* (pp. 335–351). Upper Saddle River, NJ: Pearson.

Nerad, M. (2008). Doctoral education in the United States of America. In M. Nerad & M. Heggelund (Eds.), *Toward a global PhD?* (pp. 278–297). Seattle, WA: University of Washington Press.

Persichitte, K. A. (2007). Implications for academic programs. In A. Januszewski & M. Molenda (Eds.), *Educational technology: A definition of the field* (pp. 327–338). New York: Lawrence Erlbaum Associates.

Redden, E. (2007). Envisioning a new Ed.D. *Inside Higher Ed.* Retrieved July 18, 2009, from http://www.insidehighered.com/news/2007/04/10/education.

Reiser, R. A. (2007). What field did you say you were in? In R. A. Reiser & J. V. Dempsey (Eds.), *Trends and issues in instructional design and technology* (pp. 2–9). Upper Saddle River, NJ: Pearson.

Senese, D. J. (1983). The challenge of excellence in education through technology. Paper presented at the Microfest '83. Retrieved March 8, 2009, from http://eric.ed.gov/ERICWebPortal/contentdelivery/servlet/ERICServlet?accno=ED297695.

Shulman, L. S., Golde, C. M., Bueschel, A. C., & Grabedian, K. J. (2006). Reclaiming education's doctorates: A critique and a proposal. *Educational Researcher, 35,* 25–32.

The College Blue Book. (2007). (34th ed.). Detroit, MI: Macmillan Reference.

Wellman, J. (2005). The student credit hour. *Change, 37*(4), 18–23.

Witt, P. W. F. (1980). Doctoral programs in instructional technology. In J. W. Brown & S. N. Brown (Eds.), *Educational media yearbook* (pp. 307–318). Littleton, CO: Libraries Unlimited, Inc.

Biography

Heng-Yu Ku is an Associate Professor in the Educational Technology Program, College of Education and Behavioral Sciences at the University of Northern Colorado, Greeley, CO, 80639.

Email: heng-yu.ku@unco.edu. Phone: 970-351-2935. Fax: 970-351-1622

Shari Plantz-Masters, Kim Hosler, Watsatree Diteeyont, Chatchada Akarasriworn, and Tzong-Yih Lin are doctoral students in the Educational Technology Program at the University of Northern Colorado.

Examining the Design of Media-Rich Cognitive Tools as Scaffolds in a Multimedia Problem-Based Learning Environment

Min Liu, Lucas Horton, Paul Toprac, and Timothy T. Yuen

Learner acquisition of problem-solving skills is an important education goal, especially as those skills relate to complex problems. Solving complex problems, however, proves to be especially challenging for young learners. Problem-based learning (PBL) is an effective instructional approach that promotes the development of problem-solving skills (Hmelo-Silver, 2004). When complex, student-centered learning environments such as PBL are implemented, the inclusion of embedded scaffolds can boost motivation and facilitate learning (Guthrie, Wigfield, & Perencevich, 2004). Technology-based scaffolds within these environments are often called cognitive tools: instruments that can enhance the cognitive powers of learners during their thinking, problem solving, and learning (Harper, Hedberg, Corderoy, & Wright, 2000).

Research Framework

Our research is based on a theoretical framework that draws upon literature on the use of technology as cognitive tools (e.g. Jonassen & Reeves, 1996; Iiyoshi, Hannifin, & Wang, 2005; Kim & Reeves, 2007; Lajoie, 1993, 2000; Pea, 1985; Salomon, Perkins, & Globerson, 1991). The overall emphasis is to design effective cognitive tools to assist students' problem solving in student-centered learning environments. The context of the research reported here is *Alien Rescue*.

M. Liu(✉) • L. Horton
Instructional Technology Program, Department of Curriculum and Instruction,
The University of Texas at Austin, Austin, TX, USA
e-mail: MLiu@mail.utexas.edu

P. Toprac
Southern Methodist University, Dallas, TX, USA

T.T. Yuen
The University of Texas at San Antonio, San Antonio, TX, USA

M. Orey et al. (eds.), *Educational Media and Technology Yearbook: Volume 36, 2011*, 113
Educational Media and Technology Yearbook 36, DOI 10.1007/978-1-4614-1305-9_10,
© Springer Science+Business Media, LLC 2012

Alien Rescue is a technology-enriched problem-based-learning (PBL) program (Liu, Williams, & Pedersen, 2002). *Alien Rescue*'s goal is to engage sixth-grade students in solving a complex problem that requires them to gain specific knowledge about our solar system and the tools and procedures scientists use to study it.

Problem-based learning is an instructional approach that exemplifies authentic learning and emphasizes solving problems in richly contextualized settings. PBL emphasizes the importance of active, self-directed learning from the learners and of everyday relevance of the problems under investigation (Schmidt, 1995). The aspect of anchoring learning in real world contexts in PBL has been found to provide opportunities for transferring knowledge and skills from the classroom to authentic settings more easily (Stepien, Gallagher, & Workman, 1993). PBL has been shown to result in better long-term content retention than lecture-based instruction, and supports the development of problem-solving skills (Hmelo & Ferrari, 1997; Norman & Schmidt, 1992).

The benefits of PBL, however, are accompanied by specific implementation challenges (Hoffman & Richie, 1997). Complex student-centered learning environments, such as PBL, need scaffolds embedded within them to facilitate learning (Pellegrino, 2004). Technological tools often are designed to serve as these scaffolds, and when they are used in such learning environments, they are often referred to as cognitive tools. According to Jonassen (1996), cognitive tools are: "Computer-based tools and learning environments that have been adapted or developed to function as intellectual partners with the learner in order to engage and facilitate critical thinking and higher order learning" (p. 9). Cognitive tools are instruments that can enhance learners' cognitive powers during their thinking, problem solving, and learning processes (Jonassen & Reeves, 1996; Pea, 1985; Salomon et al., 1991). As such, cognitive tools should be of particular use in supporting students' accomplishment of complex cognitive tasks (Kozma, 1987).

Multimedia technology can enhance the PBL delivery through its video, audio, graphics, and animation capabilities as well as its interactive affordances to allow students to access information according to their own learning needs and present multiple related problems in one cohesive environment (Hoffman & Richie, 1997). Multimedia-enhanced PBL environments provide a new and different means that can assist students to develop problem-solving skills, to reflect on their own learning, and to develop a deep understanding of the content domain (Cognition and Technology Group at Vanderbilt, 1997). In *Alien Rescue,* various media were used to enrich the designs of cognitive tools in creating an immersive multimedia environment and to scaffold conceptual understanding and complex problem solving of young learners.

Designing Media-Rich Cognitive Tools

Alien Rescue Environment

Alien Rescue begins with a video presentation, which shows that a group of six alien species, each with different characteristics, have traveled to Earth because their solar system has been destroyed. Students take on the role of scientists who are tasked with the mission of finding new homes that can support these aliens, thereby ensuring their survival. To accomplish this goal, students engage in a variety of problem-solving activities; these activities include researching the aliens' requirements for life and analyzing species-related factors, such as habitable temperature ranges, and the basic atmospheric composition needed for survival. To identify a suitable home for the aliens, students must discover critical scientific characteristics of the planets and moons in our solar system by querying provided databases and collecting direct observations using simulated probes.

Students must also engage in planning and decision-making as they determine how to use the provided resources efficiently and then recommend an appropriate choice for relocating each alien species, supporting each choice with a justification. Critical aspects of the program design include an intentional lack of definitive outcomes and a range of locations with suitable characteristics for placing each of the six alien species. The program is designed according to the National Science Standards and the Texas Essential Knowledge and Skills (TEKS) for science and as a science curriculum unit for approximately fifteen 45-minute class sessions. More information about *Alien Rescue* can be found at http://alienrescue.edb.utexas.edu.

Media-Rich Cognitive Tools

To support middle school students in solving the complex problem, *Alien Rescue* includes a set of 14 cognitive tools (see Table 1). These cognitive tools are multimedia-based, interactive, and found to be highly engaging for students (Liu, Toprac, & Yuen, 2009). These tools are described in terms of their primary function(s) using Lajoie's (1993) four conceptual categories: Tools (a) share cognitive load, (b) support cognitive processes, (c) support cognitive activities that would otherwise be out of reach, and (d) support hypothesis generation and testing.

First, in order to *share cognitive load*, the four databases (i.e., Alien Database, Solar System Database, Mission Database, and Concept Database) provide access to highly organized information stores that contain textual, visual, and animated media. These databases are essential to students, providing important information for use during the problem-solving process. Additionally, these tools can help learners manage their cognitive load by reducing memory burdens and by providing structured ways of storing, accessing, and understanding information. As an example, a student wishing to obtain information on the Akona alien species could access the Alien Database and receive data on the alien's appearance, habitat, diet, and behavior. Audio narration accompanies the text in both Alien and Solar Databases. Students can select to listen the audio narration if they want. PBL environments typically involve a substantial amount of reading. Audio narration is provided with the intention of helping slow readers or ESL students, in particular.

Table 1 Descriptions of fourteen cognitive tools provided in *Alien Rescue*

Tool categories	Tool functions
Tools sharing cognitive overload	
Alien database	Provides information on the aliens' home worlds, their story, and their characteristics and habitat requirements
Solar system database	Provides limited information on the characteristics of selected worlds within the solar system
Missions database	Provides information on selected NASA missions
Concepts database	Provides instructional modules on various scientific concepts
Spectral database	Allows students to interpret spectra found in the Alien Database
Periodic table	Allows students to look up information on the elements
Spanish/English glossary	Provides Spanish translations of selected English words found within the program
Tools supporting cognitive process	
Notebook	Allows students to generate and store notes on their research findings
Notebook comparison tool	Supports students in comparing information contained in multiple notebook entries
Tools supporting otherwise out-of-reach activities	
Probe Design Center	Provides information on real scientific equipment used in both past and future probe missions. Students construct probes by deciding probe type, communication, power source, and instruments
Launch Center	Provides an interface for launching probes. Students review the probes built in Probe Design, and decide which probe(s) to actually launch considering the budget
Tools supporting hypothesis testing	
Mission Status Center	Allows students to view data retrieved by probes. Students must interpret these data in order to turn it into information that the students can use in developing the solution. Malfunctions are possible, and poor planning can result in mission failure and wasted budgetary expenditures
Message tool	Serves as a repository of text messages sent to the student during problem solving
Solution form	Allows students to submit solutions and rationales for the problem that can be reviewed and critiqued by the teacher

Second, the Notebook and Notebook Comparison tools are examples of tools that *support cognitive processes*. The key characteristic of these tools is that they serve to augment the learners' existing problem-solving capabilities. To illustrate, the Notebook tool assists the learner in organizing, storing, and retrieving information that can be used throughout the problem-solving processes. The Notebook Comparison tool allows students to compare information contained in multiple notebook entries and assists students in identifying forms of critical information needed to solve the problem.

Third, despite the data-richness of the database tools, the information they contain is not sufficient for the learners to completely justify a solution. Probe Design and Probe Launch centers are provided to *support cognitive activities that would be out of reach otherwise.* These tools allow the collection of additional data that are unavailable anywhere else within the program. Using the Probe Design and Probe Launch centers, learners are able to equip exploratory space probes with numerous measurement instruments, such as thermometers, seismographs, and cameras, and then direct those probes to collect data on specific worlds of interest.

The Mission Status Center, Solution Form, and Message tools represent a fourth type of tool that *allows hypothesis testing.* The Mission Status Center provides an interface for the learners to observe data that the probes have captured, and the Solution Form provides a space for the learners to generate and submit their completed solutions and rationales. The Message tool serves as a repository of text messages sent to the student during problem solving.

Cognitive tools can guide conceptualization and interpretation of a problem through the use of internal and external representations to express relationships among concepts and attributes (Zhang & Norman, 1994). Cognitive tools such as the Alien Database and the Solar System Database use multimedia to provide forms of external representations. Other tools such as the Notebook and Solution Forms provide ways in which the students can develop and articulate internal representations of the problem itself, and their interpretations and understandings of the information presented within the program. The design of these tools integrates certain principles from Mayer's Cognitive Theory of Multimedia Learning (2009). Many of the tools are multi-modal and provide representations of content through the use of text, images, animation, video, and sound. Information within the program is segmented in ways that promote student comprehension and facilitate knowledge building, while, at the same time, further problematizing the learning task. For example, the Solar System Database provides structured multimedia content on the planets and moons of the solar system, but is intentionally incomplete. While the tool encourages students to hypothesize on potential solutions, a good solution can only be found by supplementing the information found within the Solar System Database through the use of other cognitive tools. That is, each of the 14 tools has its unique function. Together they provide necessary scaffolding to support students' problem solving. In all, the design of these cognitive tools can allow the elements of a problem to productively interact with one another and, hence, facilitate learners' processing of the problem (Sweller & Chandler, 1994). Although these tools are provided and available at any time, the decision on which tool to use at what point of the problem-solving process is entirely up to the students. Figure 1 provides screenshots of a few tools.

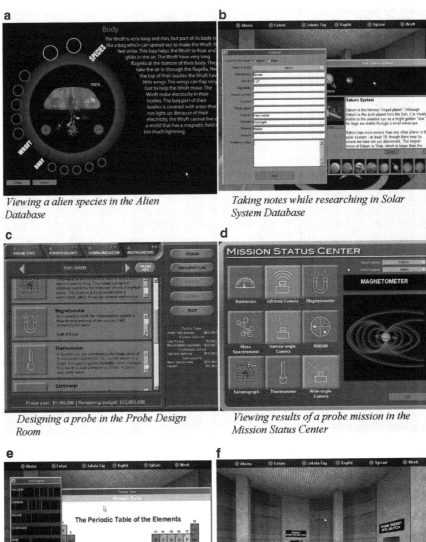

Viewing a alien species in the Alien
Database

Taking notes while researching in Solar
System Database

Designing a probe in the Probe Design
Room

Viewing results of a probe mission in the
Mission Status Center

Using the Periodic Table & Spectra to
interpret database information

Navigating the 3D environment, in
Communication Center

Fig. 1 Screen shots showing some cognitive tools provided in *Alien Rescue*

Research on Use of Cognitive Tools

Use of Cognitive Tools in Facilitating Students' Problem Solving

It is important to find out empirically how these cognitive tools can offer scaffolding and support the theoretical notion that technology-based cognitive tools play an important role in assisting students' problem-solving (Jonassen & Reeves, 1996). A series of studies was conducted with each study building upon the previous. The research context of each study consisted of the same problem-solving environment, *Alien Rescue*.

Study 1

In this study ($n = 110$), sixth-graders' log data were used to examine their tool use patterns while navigating the PBL environment to see which tools were used and at what stages of their problem-solving process (Liu & Bera, 2005). All student actions performed while using the program were logged to a data file. The log file consisted of time and date stamped entries for each student. The data set consisted of the number of times a student accessed each of the cognitive tools and the amount of time the student stayed in each tool. Descriptive statistics and cluster analyses were performed on the log data.

The results showed that tools supporting cognitive processing and tools sharing cognitive load played a more central role early in the problem-solving process whereas tools supporting cognitive activities that would be out of students' reach otherwise and tools supporting hypothesis generation and testing were used more in the later stages of problem-solving. The findings also indicated that the students increasingly used multiple tools in the later stages of the problem-solving process. The various tools, performing different functions, appeared to enable students to coordinate multiple cognitive skills in a seamless way and, therefore, facilitated their information processing. Results also suggested that students with higher performance scores seemed to exercise more productive use of the tools than students with lower performance scores.

Study 2

In Study 2 ($n = 164$), patterns of cognitive tool use among collaborative groups of sixth-graders to determine the ways in which group tool use patterns may affect students' individual performance and their experience of the problem-solving process were examined (Bera & Liu, 2006).

Cluster analysis of log data was used to identify the types of tool use groups. The results revealed that cognitive tools interacted with group members to create different types of tool-using groups, and that students with similar characteristics (i.e. students with a low level of need for cognition) functioned differently depending on the type of work group with which they were associated. The findings of this study offered some empirical evidence to show that cognitive tools, individual differences, and group processing can interact for sixth-graders during their problem solving. Group tool use patterns seemed to support a more contextual approach to individual cognition and learning.

Study 3

Although the log data provided an objective and unobtrusive way to examine students' actual use of tools, the thinking processes that students were engaged in while selecting the tools could only be inferred. In this study ($n = 161$), the connection between sixth-graders' tool use and their cognitive processes was investigated by using self-reported data from a questionnaire asking sixth-graders to report the cognitive tool(s) used for each of their problem-solving steps (Liu, Bera, Corliss, Svinicki, & Beth, 2004).

Using chi-square analyses and MANOVA, it was found that different cognitive tools were used for different cognitive processes and that students' degree of engagement in cognitive processing was positively related to the frequency of tool use. These results indicated that there was a connection between cognitive tool use and cognitive processing. In addition, tool use patterns reflected different learner characteristics. Students, who were more metacognitively or information processing-oriented, exhibited different characteristics in the consistency and activeness of their tool use. However, there was no difference in the diversity of tool use or in the performance scores between the groups of students. The findings from this study also confirmed the tool use patterns revealed by the log data in the first and second studies.

Study 4

As a follow-up step in our investigation (Liu, Horton et al., 2009), log data were matched with self-reported surveys for a more explicit investigation of students' thinking processes as reflected by their tool use. Stimulated recall interviews were also added as a data source to elicit information on students' cognitive processes at specific points in the problem-solving process. Our goal was to further examine the cognitive tool use patterns using multiple data sources and to investigate whether students with high and low performance scores used cognitive tools similarly.

This study ($n=61$) was conducted in a more "laboratory" setting with undergraduate students using the same problem-solving environment as in previous studies with sixth-graders. It is believed that college students, as compared to sixth-graders, would be able to articulate their thinking more easily and clearly. Three data sources were used: (1) log files to find out the overall tool use patterns, as in Studies 1 and 2; (2) a self-reported survey to understand which cognitive tools were used for which cognitive processes (as in Study 3), and (3) stimulated recall interviews for insight into why students used a particular tool at a particular time.

With multiple data sources, both objective and subjective, the results of this study with college students confirmed the findings from previous two studies with sixth-graders (Liu & Bera, 2005; Liu et al., 2004). The descriptive analysis, based on the log data, provided a visual representation of tool use patterns, indicating certain categories of tools were more dominant in use during different stages of problem solving (e.g. tools sharing cognitive load and supporting cognitive processes were more heavily used earlier), and there were indications that students simultaneously used multiple tools while engaged in integrating and evaluating information. Results from the chi-square analyses based upon the self-reported data showed strong connections between cognitive processes and cognitive tool use. Moreover, the stimulated recall data confirmed the findings from these two analyses and showed deliberate and careful use of tools by the students.

The MANOVA revealed no overall significant differences in the diversity, consistency, and activeness of tool use by the three performance groups (low, intermediate, and high). This finding suggested that different types of tools were needed and used by the college students in this study, as they were by sixth-graders in the previous research (Liu & Bera, 2005; Liu et al., 2004), but did not provide evidence that students with higher performance reported using the tools more consistently or actively than the other groups as in a previous study.

Study 5

Currently, the researchers are examining tool use patterns of 15 advanced learners (graduate students majoring in science, learning and cognition, and instructional technology) and investigate how they use the tools to assist their problem-solving using stimulated recall interviews and log files as data sources. The goal is to gain further insights on how experienced learners use the tools and how cognitive tools can be designed to assist novice learners (i.e. sixth-graders) to problem solve.

Students' and Teachers' Motivation in Using the Cognitive Tools

Since motivation is often considered to be a necessary antecedent for learning (Gottfried, 1985; Lepper, Corpus, & Iyengar, 2005), two studies were also conducted examining students' and teachers' motivation in using the student-centered learning environment. Fifty-seven sixth-graders were interviewed to find out in what ways students considered *Alien Rescue* motivating to learn science (Liu, Toprac et al., 2009). Analysis of the interviews using the constant comparative method showed that students were intrinsically motivated and that there were 11 key elements of *Alien Rescue* that helped evoke students' motivation: authenticity, challenge, cognitive engagement, competence, choice, fantasy, identity, interactivity, novelty, sensory engagement, and social relations. These elements reflect the five sources of intrinsic motivation: problem solving, playing, socializing, information processing, and voluntary acting (Lepper & Malone, 1987), with problem solving and playing contributing the highest level of intrinsic motivation. Analyses showed that the use of media-rich cognitive tools within the immersive multimedia environment contributed to ten of the eleven elements that correspond to the five sources of intrinsic motivation.

The analyses showed the following features made the learning environment more compelling and engaging for these sixth-graders: (1) situating the central problem within a science fiction premise, (2) using video by newscasts to announce the arrival of the aliens, (3) placing students in the role of a scientist, (4) providing a 3D environment for students to explore and discover, and (5) providing numerous databases of information enriched with videos, graphics, 3D images, and animation.

Students in the study repeatedly described their experience of using *Alien Rescue* as fun, interesting, and enjoyable, with the two strongest sources of intrinsic motivation being their engagement in problem solving and playing. That is, these students enjoyed the cognitive challenge of problem solving and the feeling of playing that the learning environment provided. The findings suggested that *Alien Rescue*'s cognitive tools played an important role in help enhance intrinsic motivation by providing interaction, fantasy support, and sensory engagement. Furthermore, students valued the use of authentic and "adult world" processes and tools, such as the Notebook, Probe Design and Probe Launch Centers, and informational databases about NASA missions, and our solar system. Collectively, *Alien Rescue*'s cognitive tools provided students with both cognitive scaffolding to assist in the development of their solution to a complex problem, and motivational scaffolding to attempt to prevent students from feeling overwhelmed or helpless.

Liu, Wivagg, Geurtz, Lee, and Chang (2010) conducted in-depth interviews and classroom observations with a group of 10 teachers, who have used *Alien Rescue* for a number of years, to examine teachers' motivation and implementation techniques in using *Alien Rescue* as a PBL environment. Findings showed that teachers used both "soft" and "hard" scaffolding to support their students' problem solving. According to Saye and Brush (2002), "soft" scaffolds are dynamic and just-in-time guidance teachers provide as they "continuously diagnose the understandings of learners" (p. 82) and "hard" scaffolds refer to "static supports that can be anticipated and planned in advance based on typical student difficulties with a task" (p. 81). The "hard" scaffolding embedded within *Alien Rescue* in the form of cognitive tools is an important contributor to teachers' motivation in adopting *Alien Rescue* as a part of their curriculum. The teachers pointed out the media-rich environment (specifically with characteristics such as multimedia, students acting as scientists, authentic learning, and game-like look and feel) helped them address different learning needs of students and provided teaching tools their students found enjoyable and challenging. More importantly, because these cognitive tools provide scaffolds to students, teachers can make best use of their time during their teaching to help individual students who are most in need.

What We have Learned and Future Research

The findings of the series of studies on tool use patterns suggested that the built-in cognitive tools in *Alien Rescue* assisted the students' understanding of the problem and facilitated their strategic problem solving. The tools appeared to activate problem-solving processes that the students may not have otherwise performed without having quick access to the cognitive tools. Apparently, embedding a diverse range of cognitive tools in the problem space helped the young learners conceptualize the problem and conceive a solution process. Using the tools in various categories over the entire problem-solving process, students are provided an opportunity to apply higher-level thinking skills. Together, the results from this line of research provide some empirical evidence that multimedia-based cognitive tools play an important role in assisting sixth-graders' problem solving, and facilitate the internal and external representations of a complex problem.

Preliminary findings suggested that there was some connection between more effective and strategic use of tools and better performance (in Study 1). The findings in Studies 2 and 3 suggested that students with different characteristics appeared to have used tools differently, indicating that other factors may influence tool use. Yet, the inconclusive finding from Study 4 calls for further studies examining the relationship between tool use and performance, and on strategies to support learners' productive use of tools in their problem-solving process.

Literature has indicated both "soft and "hard" scaffolds are necessary in supporting students' learning (Ertmer & Simons, 2006; Saye & Brush, 2002). The cognitive tools as "hard" scaffolds in this case contributed significantly to students' and teachers' motivation in using *Alien Rescue*. Intrinsic motivation is shown to be highly correlated with the academic success of students, and is thought to be the antecedent to learning. Thus, designers of multimedia learning environments need to consider incorporating elements that promote the sources of intrinsic motivation such as problem solving, playing, information processing, voluntary acting, and socializing.

Given what has been learned so far in this process, research and development continues in several ways with the ultimate goal of designing effective media-rich cognitive tools to support learning. Current design and development work surrounding *Alien Rescue* emphasizes the development of a research platform for future inquiry on the design and implementation of cognitive tools, issues of student motivation, and strategies for classroom implementation. A new version of *Alien Rescue* is in currently under development. Guided by the emerging paradigm of design-based research, this new iteration of *Alien Rescue* will provide a modular architecture that enables frequent revisions, the ability to integrate experimental features, and an adaptable design that enables research from a variety of perspectives. A key feature is the use of real-time 3D graphics to create an even more immersive environment that augment the authenticity and contextualization of the problem-solving tasks with new technology tools. A 3D immersive environment has the potential to impact student motivation and is an important element in potential lines of research that investigate the intersection of digital game-based learning and problem-based learning.

Ongoing research into the cognitive tools will utilize the new features of the program to implement new tool designs, modify existing designs, and manipulate the ways in which cognitive tools are presented within the environment. For example, since the articulation of well-reasoned solution rationales is of key importance to the students' problem-solving process, one area of research might investigate ways to enhance the solution form tool with various forms of scaffolding. Audio is an important element in multimedia and yet, is often overlooked. Audio can provide signal to cue students to certain important aspects of the environment that students miss. Understanding how audio can serve as a scaffolding tool by incorporating layers of audio effects, music, and background sound into *Alien Rescue* represents a new research dimension for the project.

The overall goal is to improve learner acquisition of problem-solving skills to solve complex problems. Development of *Alien Rescue* will continue using an iterative design-based research approach, to learn more about how to design better tools to promote motivation and learning. Future research trajectories include enhancing cognitive tools, implementing communication and collaboration features, and integrating digital game-based learning techniques. The goal of such research studies is to not only improve student learning and motivation, but also inform multimedia design and PBL theories.

References

Bera, S., & Liu, M. (2006). Cognitive tools, individual differences, and group processing as mediating factors in a hypermedia environment. *Computers in Human Behavior, 22*(2), 295–319.

Cognition and Technology Group at Vanderbilt. (1997). *The Jasper project: Lessons in curriculum, instruction, assessment, and professional development*. Mahwah, NJ: Erlbaum.

Ertmer, P. A., & Simons, K. D. (2006). Jumping the implementation hurdle: Supporting PBL in K-12 classrooms. *The Interdisciplinary Journal of Problem-Based Learning, 1*(1), 41–56.

Gottfried, A. E. (1985). Academic intrinsic motivation in elementary and junior high school students. *Journal of Educational Psychology, 77*(6), 631–645.

Guthrie, J. T., Wigfield, A., & Perencevich, K. C. (2004). Scaffolding for motivation and engagement in reading. In J. T. Guthrie, A. Wigfield, & K. C. Perencevich (Eds.), *Motivating reading comprehension: Concept oriented reading instruction* (pp. 55–86). Mahwah, NJ: Erlbaum.

Harper, B., Hedberg, J., Corderoy, B., & Wright, R. (2000). Employing cognitive tools within interactive multimedia applications. In S. P. Lajoie (Ed.), *Computers as cognitive tools: The next generation* (pp. 227–245). Mahwah, NJ: Lawrence Erlbaun Publishers.

Hmelo, C. E., & Ferrari, M. (1997). The problem-based learning tutorial: Cultivating higher order thinking skills. *Journal for the Education of the Gifted, 20*(4), 401–422.

Hmelo-Silver, C. (2004). Problem-based learning: What and how do students learn? *Educational Psychology Review, 16*(3), 235–266.

Hoffman, B., & Richie, D. (1997). Using multimedia to overcome the problems with problem based learning. *Instructional Science, 25*, 97–115.

Iiyoshi, T., Hannifin, M. J., & Wang, F. (2005). Cognitive tools and student-centered learning: Rethinking tools, functions, and applications. *Educational Media International, 42*, 281–296.

Jonassen, D. H. (1996). *Computers in the classroom: Mindtools for critical thinking*. Englewood Cliffs, NJ: Prentice Hall, Inc.

Jonassen, D. H., & Reeves, T. C. (1996). Learning with technology: Using computers as cognitive tools. In D. H. Jonassen (Ed.), *Handbook of research for educational communications and technology* (pp. 693–719). New York: Macmillan.

Kim, B., & Reeves, T. (2007). Reframing research on learning with technology: In search of the meaning of cognitive tools. *Instructional Science, 35*, 207–256.

Kozma, R. B. (1987). The implications of cognitive psychology for computer-based learning tools. *Educational Technology, 27*, 20–25.

Lajoie, S. P. (2000). Computers as cognitive tools: No more walls, Vol. II. Hillsdale, NJ: Lawrence Erlbaum Associates, Inc.

Lajoie, S. P. (1993). Computer environments as cognitive tools for enhancing learning. In S. P. Lajoie & S. J. Derry (Eds.), *Computers as cognitive tools* (pp. 261–288). Hillsdale, NJ: Lawrence Erlbaum Associates, Inc.

Lepper, M. R., & Malone, T. W. (1987). Intrinsic motivation and instructional effectiveness in computer based education. In R. E. Snow & M. J. Farr (Eds.), Aptitude, learning and instruction: Cognitive and affective process analysis (Vol. 3, pp. 255–287). Hillsdale, NJ: Lawrence Erlbaum Associates.

Lepper, M. R., Corpus, J. H., & Iyengar, S. S. (2005). Intrinsic and extrinsic motivational orientations in the classroom: Age differences and academic correlates. *Journal of Educational Psychology, 97*(2), 184–196.

Liu, M., & Bera, S. (2005). An analysis of cognitive tool use patterns in a hypermedia learning environment. *Educational Technology Research and Development, 53*(1), 5–21.

Liu, M., Bera, S., Corliss, S. B., Svinicki, M. D., & Beth, A. D. (2004). Understanding the connection between cognitive tool use and cognitive processes as used by sixth graders in a problem-based hypermedia learning environment. *Journal of Educational Computing Research, 31*(3), 309–334.

Liu, M., Horton, L., Corliss, S. B., Svinicki, M. D., Bogard, T., Kim, J., et al. (2009). Students' problem-solving as mediated by their cognitive tool use: A study of tool use patterns. *Journal of Educational Computing Research, 40*(1), 111–139.

Liu, M., Toprac, P., & Yuen, T. (2009). What factors make a multimedia learning environment engaging: A case study. In R. Zheng (Ed.), *Cognitive effects of multimedia learning* (pp. 173–192). Hershey, PA: Idea Group Inc.

Liu, M., Williams, D., & Pedersen, S. (2002). *Alien Rescue*: A problem-based hypermedia learning environment for middle school Science. *Journal of Educational Technology Systems, 30*(3), 255–270.

Liu, M., Wivagg, J., Geurtz, R., Lee, S. T. & Chang. M. (2010). *Examining how middle school science teachers implement a multimedia enriched problem-based learning environment.* Interdisciplinary Journal of Problem-Based Learning.

Mayer, R. E. (2009). *Multimedia learning.* Cambridge, UK: Cambridge University Press.

Norman, G. R., & Schmidt, H. G. (1992). The psychological basis of problem-based learning: A review of the evidence. *Academic Medicine, 67*, 557–565.

Pea, R. D. (1985). Beyond amplification: Using the computer to reorganize mental functioning. *Educational Psychologist, 20*, 167–182.

Pellegrino, J. (2004). Complex learning environments: Connecting learning theories, instructional design, and technology. In N. M. Seel, S. Dijkstra, & R. Marra (Eds.), *Curriculum, plans, and processes in instructional design: International perspectives* (pp. 25–48). Mahwah, NJ: Lawrence Erlbaum.

Salomon, G., Perkins, D. N., & Globerson, T. (1991). Partners in cognition: Extending human intelligent technologies. *Educational Researcher, 20*, 2–9.

Saye, J. W., & Brush, T. (2002). Scaffolding critical reasoning about history and social issues in multimedia-supported learning environments. *Educational Technology Research and Development, 50*(3), 77–96.

Schmidt, H. (1995). Problem-based learning: An introduction. *Instructional Science, 22*, 247–250.

Stepien, W. J., Gallagher, S. A., & Workman, D. (1993). Problem-based learning for traditional and interdisciplinary classrooms. *Journal for the Education of the Gifted, 16*(4), 338–357.

Sweller, J., & Chandler, P. (1994). Why some material is difficult to learn. *Cognition and Instruction, 12*(3), 185–233.

Zhang, J., & Norman, D. A. (1994). Representations in distributed cognitive tasks. *Cognitive Science, 18*, 87–122.

An Instructional Design Approach to Effective Instructional Game Design and Assessment

Debbie Denise Reese

A native learning technology is one in which learner participation during instruction and/or assessment mimics the natural processes through which people learn in everyday life. Current advances in hardware, software, cyber-infrastructure, and human learning technologies conjoin as unprecedented opportunity to design, develop, and implement native educational environments that assess while they instruct. CyGaMEs is an approach to instructional game design and assessment for producing native learning objects that are ready for learners with sound intuitions (i.e., prior knowledge) for acquisition of targeted concepts. CyGaMEs learning objects are native learning technologies for two reasons. First, they pragmatically guide learners through an inquiry process to construct conceptual knowledge (see Jonassen, 2006, for an inquiry model of conceptual learning). Second, the CyGaMEs approach specializes in the application of human analogical reasoning theory as a guide and constraint for development of game-based technologies. An analogically derived instructional game is native because analogical reasoning is ubiquitous in human cognition (Holyoak & Thagard, 1995; Hummel & Holyoak, 1997; Lakoff & Johnson, 1980). Design and development of games that entertain is an exacting (Schell, 2008), expensive (Langhoff et al., 2009), and risk-filled investment (Fullerton, Swain, & Hoffman, 2004). The demands of *instructional* game design and development are equal (Schell, 2008), if not greater, and should require equal investment. The stake of enabling humans to achieve their conceptual potential is profound; instructional game design should not be left to intuition and chance. To ensure that instructional games enhance learning while assessing knowledge growth, it is important to develop, understand, and implement formal methodologies derived from well-substantiated instructional design, game design, learning science, and cognitive science theories.

D.D. Reese (✉)
Center for Educational Technologies, Wheeling Jesuit University,
316 Washington Avenue, Wheeling, WV 26003, USA
e-mail: debbie@cet.edu

M. Orey et al. (eds.), *Educational Media and Technology Yearbook: Volume 36, 2011*,   127
Educational Media and Technology Yearbook 36, DOI 10.1007/978-1-4614-1305-9_11,
© Springer Science+Business Media, LLC 2012

Due to pioneering advocates like James Gee (e.g., Gee, 2003, 2005a, 2005b) and Henry Jenkins (Jenkins, 2002; Jenkins, Klopfer, Squire, & Tan, 2003), there is national and even global investment to harness the power of game-based technologies for educational and instructional aims. Although recognition and appreciation of the instructional promise inherent in game-based technologies are good starts, they do not provide theories and methods for effective design and assessment. When specialists and experts from diverse fields aspire to produce games that support instructional objectives, it seems expedient that the perspective and expertise from the field of instructional design and technology inform design, development, and assessment efforts.

An Instructional Design Perspective for Instructional Game Design

The CyGaMEs formalism for instructional game design and embedded assessment developed from the perspective of instructional design with focus on alignment, task analysis, and prior knowledge.

Alignment

One fundamental instructional design practice is aligning learning outcome/ objectives, instructional strategies, and assessment. Alignment is just as essential to effective instructional *game* design: The instructional game world, gameplay, game goals, and any embedded assessment must align with targeted instructional objectives and goals. Without alignment, there is no way to ensure an instructional game will produce or assess targeted learning. An effective instructional design formalism for ensuring alignment provides guidance and oversight during design, development, and evaluation.

Task Analysis: First Step in CyGaMEs Application of Analogy Theory

CyGaMEs (Reese, 2009b) uses the structure mapping theory of analogical reasoning (Gentner, 1983) to specify and align a targeted conceptual domain and its instructional game specification. The first step is a conceptual task analysis: specify the subconcepts and the relationships that connect them. Then design a game world as a concrete analog of the targeted knowledge domain, as specified in the task analysis. The relational structure that connects subconcepts in the target domain is retained and a game world (a concrete source domain) is selected, designed, constrained, and developed over it. In the game world, the relational structure connects game components.

The game goal is designed (and constrained) as an analog of the targeted learning goal, and it motivates and guides player transactions (i.e., gameplay) within the game world. This component of CyGaMEs design follows from the principle that goal structures guide and constrain analogical reasoning (e.g., Holyoak & Thagard, 1997; Spellman & Holyoak, 1996). In order to attain the game goal/sub-goals, the CyGaMEs player must use gameplay to discover and conquer the relational structure connecting game components. The CyGaMEs approach produces alignment from target conceptual domain to game world, game goals, and game play.

Prior Knowledge: Preparing Learners for Knowledge Acquisition

Instructional designers activate learners' relevant prior knowledge as an initial event of instruction (e.g., Gagné, Briggs, & Wager, 1992; Smith & Ragan, 2005). When learners lack relevant prior knowledge, an instructional designer must engage the learner in experiences to build prior knowledge (Merrill, 2002). The CyGaMEs approach specializes in design and development of games through which learners construct viable prior knowledge. However, I maintain and have argued elsewhere (Reese, 2010) that all instructional games must ensure robust and coherent alignment between the to-be-learned and the instructional game by formally mapping the targ et domain to the game world.

The CyGaMEs player constructs a mental model of the game world's relational structure through a cycle of inquiry (hypothesizing, testing, and revising). This process corresponds to contemporary models of concept development (Jonassen, 2006).

Analogical reasoning works as a cognitive process of structural alignment (Gentner, 1983). People align the source (a concrete or relatively familiar domain) and target (the to-be-learned or relatively unfamiliar domain), and then reply on the source domain's relational structure to project *inferences* from the source to the target. Inferences are intuitions. Because the CyGaMEs game world is an analog of the target domain, the player's mental model of the game world is a preconceptual mental model for targeted learning. This means that the player has constructed viable intuitions, and these prepare the learner for future knowledge acquisition within the target domain. The CyGaMEs type of gameplay functions as one means to prepare learners for future learning (see Schwartz & Martin, 2004, to learn more about the preparation for future learning paradigm). CyGaMEs preparation is learning through *doing*.

Seymour Papert (1980) coined the term body syntonic (i.e., referring to a child's sense of his or her own body) to explain the experience and effect of learning geometric concepts through LOGO turtle programming. A CyGaMEs gameworld engages a player in "virtual" transactions that provide body syntonic experience. The CyGaMEs approach translates abstract concepts (what experts think) into analogous gameplay (what a learner does). In other words, the CyGaMEs approach enables players to construct *embodied* prior knowledge.

The Transition from Game-based Entertainment to Game-based Instruction

Renowned game designer Will Wright's approach to game design parallels the CyGaMEs approach[1]. This is neither accident nor coincidence; CyGaMEs derived from the confluence of Wright's methodologies with first principles of instructional design, learning science theory, and cognitive science (analogical reasoning) theory (Reese, 2006, 2007, 2008). Unfortunately, CyGaMEs design is not an intuitive process for game designers—even talented, industrious, and successful game developers invested in the success of their instructional projects and mentored by a CyGaMEs specialist. Wright was quoted to say that theory-based methods that seem intuitive to him, such as "game worlds as analogs of targeted concepts that scaffold player's emergent mental models through discovery" (Langhoff et al., 2009, p. 16) are far from intuitive to most game designers. He explains this is because game design is a young field.

Klopfer, Osterweil, and Salen (2009) identified sets of barriers and challenges to successful integration of game-based technologies into education. I have encountered three that interact during instructional game design and development: (a) Game developers typically do not collaborate with learning scientists, (b) "Bottom-line market concerns" may compromise educational facets, and (c) Development costs are high (p. 19). A CyGaMEs approach is a steep learning curve for a game production house. Programmers, designers, animators, and graphic designers do not realize or accept the degree to which they must collaborate with the CyGaMEs specialist. They do not realize or accept the degree to which they must rigorously adhere to the specified structural alignment and specification for assessment tools. This means the CyGaMEs personnel must vigilantly review game prototypes and builds. If deviations are discovered, they cost in revisions that strain production budgets.

Within the field of instructional technology, instructional designers already interface with media production specialists to develop effective instruction. It seems expedient to develop an instructional technology specialty that leverages game-based technologies for instructional goals. As these instructional technology specialists build their skill sets and tools, the CyGaMEs approach is one theory-rich and empirically supported method they can add to their toolkits.

Selene: A Lunar Construction GaME

Selene Classic, the first fully produced CyGaMEs learning environment, has been online, available to the public, and collecting player data since May 2007. Originally developed in Java and set within a Flash backbone, CyGaMEs released a 100% Flash version as *Selene II* during summer, 2010 (see Fig. 1). The *Selene* game world is a concrete source domain for the introductory and basic concepts of lunar and planetary science. Four superordinate concepts (accretion, differentiation, impact

---

[1] The methods diverge when entertainment games privilege gameplay over authenticity.

Fig. 1 (**a**) A screen capture from the *Selene II* instructional videogame 2010. Copyright 2010 by Debbie Denise Reese. Used with permission. (**b**) A second screen capture from the *Selene II* instructional videogame. Copyright 2010 by Debbie Denise Reese. Used with permission

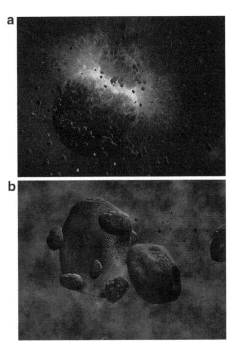

cratering, and volcanism) and their subconcepts are organized into a concept map of 101 conceptual nodes. The relational structure of the domain is the relational structure of the source domain, which instantiates as the *Selene* game world, gameplay, and game goals. *Selene* players construct the Earth's early Moon, then pepper it with impact craters and flood it with lava. *Selene* is both a learning object and a research environment for studying game-based learning and assessment. The environment uses a backend that allows investigators to arrange modules into conditions of instruction, gameplay, and scaffolds idiosyncratic to study specifications. The CyGaMEs backend is programmed to randomly assign players to conditions.

Situating Assessment within Authentic Contexts

Schwartz and Martin (2004) have argued "preparing [students] for future learning requires the development of new instructional methods and the development of assessments that can evaluate whether students have been prepared to learn" (p. 130). CyGaMEs provides both a new method of instruction and an aligned method of assessment.

There are education scholars who claim that all learning is situated (e.g., Greeno, 1997; Greeno, Collins, & Resnick, 1996). If so, valid assessment should measure knowledge as situated within authentic performance. By 1990, medical education had begun to implement performance-based assessment. The late George E. Miller – a founding father of research-based medical education—counseled that tests of medical students' knowledge base are, by themselves, inadequate measures of readiness for professional practice. Instead, it is essential to assess medical knowledge as it might be applied during authentic performance in real-world medical practice (1990). Reform-based medical educators like Miller wanted to certify that graduates could satisfactorily apply knowledge within professional practice; that is, they wanted to measure what pre-practitioners could *do*. During the same time period, reform-based K-12 education scholars also proposed situated cognition and authentic assessment (e.g., Archald & Newmann, 1988; Newmann, Ron, & Wiggins, 1998). Newmann's approach fosters "authentic intellectual work," defined as "construction of knowledge through disciplined inquiry to produce discourse, products, or performance that have value beyond school" (Newmann, King, & Carmichael, 2007, p. 3). In 2001, the National Research Council established the Committee on the Foundations of Assessment to synthesize advances in measurement with cognitive science advances in human learning and "consider the implications for reshaping education assessment" (2001, p. xii). The committee stressed that "technology-based assessment embedded in instructional settings" (p. 10) holds promised for assessment based upon models of cognition and learning. These assessments should report information from statistical analysis of formative and summative measures in accessible formats that could easily incorporate into instructional practice. Today, scholars and leaders anticipate that cyberlearning and game-based environments will automate learner-centered, performance-based assessment across many educational contexts (Borgman et al., 2008). Game-based environments, especially, hold promise for authentic assessment because assessment might be embedded within gameplay. That is, eventually and ideally, a game-based instructional technology should have the capacity to measure learning as it occurs through endogenous measures of player transactions within the game world.

This expectation appears reasonable, given that entertainment software and technology companies already collect embedded data collections of players' gameplay to inform marketing, research, design, and development. For example, prior to 2006 Valve[2] collected written evaluation data from players. Today Valve's Steam digital delivery system doubles as a reporting mechanism for collecting statistics profiling players, gameplay, and users' computer systems (http://www.steampowered.com/status/ep2/ep2_stats.php#).

CyGaMEs Embedded Assessment

The CyGaMEs approach specifies how to design three embedded assessment tools: gesture reports, timed reports, and flowometer reports.

Gesture reports. A gesture occurs at the level of player interaction with the game world. It is the level at which the player (or the game itself) change the state of the game. Most *Selene* gestures derive from a core gameplay mechanic named

---

[2] Valve's portfolio includes Half-Life,® and Valve games "account for over 80% of the PC online action market" (http://www.valvesoftware.com/about.html).

the slingshot. Players click on objects (analogs for planetesimals and debris), then drag to impart velocities (direction and speed). Each gesture has parameters such as player identification and the time and location of the gesture. Gesture reports are embedded within gameplay, so players are unaware that gesture report postings occur. Each instructional game will have its own set of gestures and parameters.

Timed report. The timed report is a measure of player progress toward the game goal/subgoals, calculated every 10 s of gameplay. The game goal is an analog of the targeted learning goal, so player progress toward the game goal is a performance measure analogous to growth in player's preconceptual knowledge growth. Timed reports are embedded within gameplay, so players are unaware that they occur. Essential timed report parameters include player identification and the time and location of the timed report, and the value of the report. Using the CyGaMEs approach, each instructional game will design idiosyncratic algorithms to determine progress toward the goal.

Flowometer. The flow literature defines flow, flow measurement tools and techniques, and flow data analysis (e.g., Csikszentmihalyi & Csikszentmihalyi, 1988; Csikszentmihalyi & Larson, 1987; Hektner, Schmidt, & Csikszentmihalyi, 2007). Flow experience is intrinsically rewarding, productive, and concentrated attention that occurs when an individual's self-perception of skill and challenge are high and balanced. Quantitatively, flow and other states of experience are measured by self-reports of skill and challenge level. The CyGaMEs players rate their level of skill and challenge on a scale from 0 to 100 using the flowometer (Reese, 2010). The flowometer interrupts gameplay within every 5-min interval at a preselected, but random time. Using the CyGaMEs approach, each instructional game will retain the CyGaMEs flowometer as specified; however the flow prompt interval may be longer or slightly shorter, depending on game characteristics.

Overview of Data Analysis

Timed report, gesture, and flowometer data can be profiled individually or aggregated. Profiling of *Selene* individual players has included triangulation of gameplay behavior over video data, slingshot velocity data, and timed reports. Triangulation identified a prototypical learning moment labeled accretionLM. AccretionLM is the target domain accretion concept: high energy collisions fragment and low energy collisions accrete. AccretionLM player behavior begins with high-velocity slingshot gestures that later persistently attenuate to lower velocities. Statistical analyses of timed reports for players exhibiting accretionLM indicate the timed report is a sensitive measure of player learning. CyGaMEs has also worked with project partners Larry V. Hedges and James Pustejovsky, who replicated the analyses by algorithmically determining the accretionLM.

Using the CyGaMEs *Selene* environment and assessment suit tools, we have gathered evidence that the tools function reliably and produce valid measures (Reese, 2009a; Reese & Tabachnick, 2010). We have found that the game produces

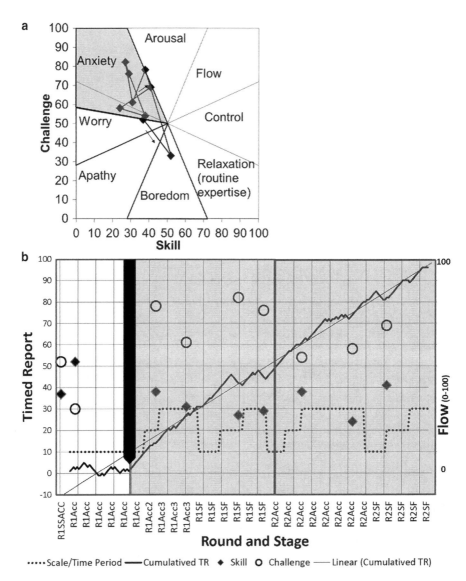

Fig. 2 (**a**) Eight-channel flow model and one player's flow trace collected during round 1 while the player watched a solar system accretion animation and during rounds 1 and 2 gameplay. This player reported a state of worry while watching the solar system accretion gameplay, boredom before learning (accretionLM), and sustained anxiety for the next half hour of round 1 and round 2 gameplay. (**b**) Cumulative timed report trace of the moment of learning (accretionLM) for case study participant over two rounds of gameplay, including flowometer reports (skill and challenge) for initial instructional section and subsequent two rounds of gameplay. The dark arrow points to the time of the accretionLM, as identified by the velocity data analysis. *Note:* R1SSACC=Round 1 solar system accretion, R1Acc=Round 1 accretion scale 1, R1Acc2=Round 1 accretion scale 2, R1Acc3=Round 1 accretion scale 3, R1SF=Round 1 surfaces features (time periods 1–3), R2Acc=Round 2 accretion (scales 1–3), R2SF=Round 2 surfaces features (time periods 1–3) (Reese & Tabachnick, 2010). Copyright 2010 by Debbie Denise Reese. Used with permission

significant gains in learner understanding and behavioral application of targeted domain content (e.g., Reese, Diehl, & Lurquin, 2009).

Looking Ahead: Assessment Aspirations

In addition to the proximal use of CyGaMEs assessment to measure individual and cohort achievement, the fact that embedded assessments are time stamped affords rich opportunity to expand knowledge about learning and states of experience. Mihaly Csikszentmihalyi and his colleagues have identified eight channels of experience: apathy, boredom, relaxation (more appropriately identified as routine expertise, see, for example, Bransford, 2005; Hatano & Inagaki, 1986), control, flow, arousal, anxiety, and worry (see Fig. 2). Flow is a coveted state characterized by high productivity and intrinsic reward, but are people typically in a state of flow when they learn? Perhaps not. Mihaly Csikszentmihalyi advised that "arousal is the area where most people learn from because that's where they are pushed beyond their comfort zone and that to enter going back to flow then they develop higher skills. [sic] (transcript of audio, 2008, 16 m 48 s). Figure 2 illustrates flow states for one participant before and after the accretionLM. The case study participant swung from pre-learning boredom to post-learning anxiety. Generalized conclusions about learning and flow, even within the context of *Selene* gameplay, will require a great deal of data. For this reason, we are building a robust, optimized, and graphically compelling version of *Selene* to support data-gathering from thousands of players and generalizable conclusions about learning and flow states.

Conclusion

CyGaMEs provides one of the first-generation models for instructional videogame design and assessment. The CyGaMEs vision is an integrated content management system repository of CyGaMEs learning objects across domains, metatagged for critical entry-level concepts represented many cognitive levels, available 24/7, available to scaffold learning when and as needed by each individual learner. One research team is not enough to build the science to support this effort. One research game, like *Selene*, shared by many research teams, is a start. But it is just a beginning. Scholars must use formal instructional game design approaches to develop other research games, accrue knowledge, and create that repository of CyGaMEs-like learning objects across the curriculum. Game-based learning is a powerful technology. Using *Selene* as a test case, I have demonstrated that a virtual environment can be designed as a viable analog to scaffold knowledge of a targeted conceptual domain, and the game goal can lead and reinforce student discovery and application of targeted concept. With or without large-scale support, the field of instructional technology should develop and refine principled methods and formalisms for instructional game design and assessment to ensure that today's investment in game-based technologies results in tomorrow's advances in human achievement.

Acknowledgments Debbie Denise Reese, Research and Evaluation, Center for Educational Technologies, Wheeling Jesuit University.

This research was supported in part by National Science Foundation grant DRL-0814512 awarded to the author and National Aeronautics and Space Association NCC5-451, NNX06AB09G-Basic, NNX06AB09G-Supplement #1, NNX06AB09G-Supplement #2, NNX08AJ71A-Basic and No. NAG-13782 awarded to the NASA-sponsored Classroom of the Future.

Any opinions, findings, and conclusions or recommendations expressed in this material are those of the author and do not necessarily reflect the views of the National Science Foundation or the National Aeronautics and Space Association.

Correspondence regarding this article should be sent to Debbie Denise Reese, Center for Educational Technologies, Wheeling Jesuit University, 316 Washington Ave, Wheeling, WV 26003. E-mail: debbie@cet.edu.

References

Archald, D. A., & Newmann, F. M. (1988). *Beyond standardized testing: Assessing authentic academic achievement in the secondary school*. Reston: VA: National Association of Secondary School Principals. Retrieved from http://www.eric.ed.gov/ERICDocs/data/ericdocs2sql/content_storage_01/0000019b/80/1e/2b/75.pdf.

Borgman, C. L., Abelson, H., Johnson, R., Koedinger, K. R., Linn, M. C., Lynch, C. A. et al. (2008). *Fostering learning in the networked world: The cyberlearning opportunity and challenge: A 21st century agenda for the National Science Foundation*. Arlington, VA: National Science Foundation. Retrieved from http://www.nsf.gov/pubs/2008/nsf08204/nsf08204.pdf?govDel=USNSF_124.

Bransford, J. D. (2005). Benjamin Cluff Lecture. Provo, UT: David O. McKay School of Education, Brigham Young University. Retrieved from http://education.byu.edu/media/index.html?video=50.

Csikszentmihalyi, M. (2008). Creativity, fulfillment, and flow. *TED: Ideas worth spreading*. Retrieved from http://www.youtube.com/watch?v=fXIeFJCqsPs.

Csikszentmihalyi, M., & Csikszentmihalyi, I. S. (Eds.). (1988). *Optimal experience: Psychological studies of flow in consciousness*. New York: Cambridge University Press.

Csikszentmihalyi, M., & Larson, R. (1987). Validity and reliability of the experience sampling method. *The Journal of Nervous and Mental Disease, 175*(9), 526–536.

Fullerton, T., Swain, C., & Hoffman, S. (2004). *Game design workshop: Designing, prototyping, and playtesting games*. San Francisco: CMP Books.

Gagné, R. M., Briggs, L. J., & Wager, W. W. (1992). *Principles of instructional design* (4th ed.). Belmont, CA: Wadsworth/Thomson Learning.

Gee, J. P. (2003). *What video games have to teach us about learning and literacy*. New York: Palgrave Macmillan.

Gee, J. P. (2005a). Learning by design: Good video games as learning machines. *e-Learning, 2*(1), 5–16.

Gee, J. P. (2005b). What would a state of the art instructional video game look like? *Innovate, 1*(6). Retrieved from http://www.innovateonline.info/index.php?view=article&id=80.

Gentner, D. (1983). Structure mapping: A theoretical framework for analogy. *Cognitive Science, 7*, 155–170.

Greeno, J. G. (1997). On claims that answer the wrong question. *Educational Researcher, 26*(1), 5–17.

Greeno, J. G., Collins, A., & Resnick, L. B. (1996). Cognition and learning. In D. C. Berlinger & R. C. Calfee (Eds.), *Handbook of educational psychology* (pp. 15–46). New York: Macmillan.

Hatano, G., & Inagaki, K. (1986). Two courses of expertise. In H. Stevenson, H. Azuma, & K. Hakuta (Eds.), *Child development and education in Japan* (pp. 262–272). New York: W. H. Freeman and Company.

Hektner, J. M., Schmidt, J. A., & Csikszentmihalyi, M. (2007). *Experience sampling method: Measuring the quality of everyday life*. Thousand Oaks, CA: Sage.

Holyoak, K. J., & Thagard, P. (1995). *Mental leaps: Analogy in creative thought*. Cambridge, MA: MIT Press.

Holyoak, K. J., & Thagard, P. (1997). The analogical mind. *American Psychologist, 52*(1), 35–44.

Hummel, J. E., & Holyoak, K. J. (1997). Distributed representations of structure: A theory of analogical access and mapping. *Psychological Review, 104*(3), 427–466.

Jenkins, H. (2002). Game theory. *Technology Review*. Retrieved from http://web.mit.edu/cms/People/henry3/publications.htm.

Jenkins, H., Klopfer, E., Squire, K., & Tan, P. (2003). Entering the education arcade. *ACM Computers in Entertainment, 1*(1), 1–17.

Jonassen, D. H. (2006). On the role of concepts in learning and instructional design. *Educational Technology, Research, & Development, 54*(2), 177–196.

Klopfer, E., Osterweil, S., & Salen, K. (2009). *Moving learning games forward: Obstacles, opportunities, and openness*. Boston, MA: The Education Arcade, MIT.

Lakoff, G., & Johnson, M. (1980). *Metaphors we live by*. Chicago: The University of Chicago Press.

Langhoff, S., Cowan-Sharp, J., Dodson, E., Damer, B., Ketner, B., & Reese, D. D. (2009). *Workshop report: Virtual worlds and immersive environments*. (NASA/CP–2009-214598). Moffett Field, CA: NASA Ames Research Center.

Merrill, M. D. (2002). First principles of instruction. *Educational Technology Research and Development, 50*(3), 43–59.

Miller, G. E. (1990). The assessment of clinical skills/competence/performance. *Academic Medicine: Supplement, 65*(9), S63–S67.

National Research Council. (2001). *Knowing what students know: The science and design of educational assessment*. Committee on the Foundations of Assessment. J. Pelligrino, N. Chudowsky, R. Glaser (Eds.). Board on Testing and Assessment, Center for Education. Division of Behavioral and Social Sciences and Education. Washington, DC: National Academy Press.

Newmann, F. M., King, M. B., & Carmichael, D. L. (2007). *Authentic instruction and assesssment: Common standards or rigor and relevance in teaching academic subjects*. Des Moines, IA: Iowa Department of Education. Retrieved from http://www.smallschoolsproject.org/PDFS/meetings/auth_instr_assess.pdf.

Newmann, F. M., Ron, B., & Wiggins, G. (1998). An exchange of views on "semantics, psychometrics, and assessment reform: A close look at 'authentic' assessments". *Educational Researcher, 27*(6), 19–22.

Papert, S. (1980). *Mindstorms: Children, computers, and powerful ideas*. New York: Basic Books.

Reese, D. D. (2006). *Foundations of serious games design and assessment*. (COTF/LVP/Sep-2006). Wheeling, WV: Center for Educational Technologies, Wheeling Jesuit University.

Reese, D. D. (2007). First steps and beyond: Serious games as preparation for future learning. *Journal of Educational Media and Hypermedia, 16*(3), 283–300.

Reese, D. D. (2008). GaME design for intuitive concept knowledge. In R. E. Ferdig (Ed.), *Handbook of research on effective electronic gaming in education* (Vol. 3, pp. 1104–1126). Hershey, PA: Idea Group.

Reese, D. D. (2009a). *Replication supports Flowometer: Advancing cyberlearning through game-based assessment technologies*. Paper presented at the 2009 international conference of the Association for Educational Communications and Technology, Louisville, KY.

Reese, D. D. (2009b). Structure mapping theory as a formalism for instructional game design and assessment. In D. Gentner, K. Holyoak, & B. Kokinov (Eds.), *New frontiers in analogy research: Proceedings of the 2nd international conference on analogy (Analogy '09)* (pp. 394–403). Sofia, Bulgaria: New Bulgarian University Press.

Reese, D. D., Diehl, V. A., & Lurquin, J. L. (2009). *Metaphor enhanced instructional video game causes conceptual gains in lunar science knowledge.* Poster presented at the Association for Psychological Science 21st Annual Convention, San Francisco, CA.

Reese, D. D. (2010). Introducing flowometer: A CyGaMEs assessment suite tool. In R. V. Eck (Ed.), *Gaming & cognition: Theories and perspectives from the learning sciences.* (pp. 227–254). Hershey, PA: IGI Global.

Reese, D. D., & Tabachnick, B. G. (2010). *The moment of learning: Quantitative analysis of exemplar gameplay supports CyGaMEs approach to embedded assessment* [structured abstract]. Paper to be presented at the Society for Research on Educational Effectiveness 2010 Annual Research Conference, Washington, DC. Retrieved from http://www.sree.org/conferences/2010/program/abstracts/191.pdf.

Schell, J. (2008). *The art of game design: A book of lenses.* New York: Elsevier.

Schwartz, D. L., & Martin, T. (2004). Inventing to prepare for future learning: The hidden efficiency of encouraging original student production in statistics instruction. *Cognition and Instruction, 22*(2), 129–184.

Smith, P. L., & Ragan, T. J. (2005). *Instructional design* (3rd ed.). Hoboken, NJ: John Wiley & Sons.

Spellman, B. A., & Holyoak, K. J. (1996). Pragmatics in analogical mapping. *Cognitive Psychology, 31*(3), 307–346.

PowerPoint and the Pedagogy
of Digital Media Technologies

Catherine Adams

*With the ever-increasing importance of technologies
as what orients us in the practical lifeworld, our extensive
dependence on them has never been more central or more
deserving of sustained critical attention. Indeed, since this
dependence forms the very basis of our agency in the
technologically mediated lifeworld, developing some
understanding of and command over it forms the prerequisite
for any subsequent practical project and must accordingly
be considered the central concern of contemporary
technocultural criticism. (Hansen, 2000, p. 258)*

Background

The Internet, iPods, gaming systems, and smart phones are changing the way we work, play, and interact in the digital age. Similarly new media, Virtual Learning Environments, electronic whiteboards, and new software tools are significantly altering processes of teaching and learning in primary, secondary, and postsecondary education settings. Few are surprised that in virtually every classroom in schools, training institutions and universities, computers are commonplace. Students supplement textbooks by accessing their assignments and readings online, they wordprocess their course papers, download PowerPoint presentations and class notes, keep in touch via Learning Management System discussion boards and online social networks, all the while texting and twittering on their smart phones. New technological tools are changing how we learn, what we know, and how we understand and live in the world around us. Yet, we have barely begun to grasp the profoundly co-constitutive

C. Adams (✉)
Department of Secondary Education, Faculty of Education,
University of Alberta, Edmonton, AB, Canada
e-mail: cathy.adams@ualberta.ca

M. Orey et al. (eds.), *Educational Media and Technology Yearbook: Volume 36, 2011*,
Educational Media and Technology Yearbook 36, DOI 10.1007/978-1-4614-1305-9_12,
© Springer Science+Business Media, LLC 2012

relationships we share with our digital technologies, relationships that simultaneously open new worlds of possibilities while silently foreclosing others.

My research investigates this over-riding question: How are new media technologies, (re)shaping knowledge,[1] altering how it is represented, presented, and subsequently comprehended? The unique issue underlying this inquiry is captured in Marshall McLuhan's notion of the invisible "lines of force" (1964, p. 15) that digital media technologies seem to be exerting in the educational context. To narrow the scope of my investigation I elected to study a now ubiquitous, relatively simple-to-use, software presentation tool: PowerPoint. In particular, my research explores how PowerPoint may extend but also serve to constrain what a student sees, experiences and has access to. I examine how teachers are not only aided and "enhanced" by this software presentation tool, they are also enmeshed, restrained by and relinquished to the language, imagery, framing, at-handedness, and sensuality of its materiality and design.

As Merleau-Ponty observes, "our existence changes with the appropriation of a fresh instrument" (1962/2002, p. 143). We might wonder then, what transformations of perception occur, what translations of action manifest as teachers adopt a "fresh instrument" like PowerPoint in the lived space of the classroom? What is it like for students to learn via PowerPoint presentation? Does PowerPoint affect habits of mind? What is the nature of the vocative appeal digital technologies like PowerPoint seem to exercise in the lived space of the classroom? Can we catch glimpse of the new lifeworlds opened as teachers and students respond to the invitational quality[2] of these new media technologies?

The PowerPoint Literature So Far

Much of the educational literature on PowerPoint has focused on how-to advice and providing practical exemplars (e.g. Buchholz & Ullman, 2004). Some survey data suggest students have an overall positive attitude toward PowerPoint (Atkins-Sayre,

---

[1] My use of the term knowledge is intended to be inclusive of the passions, skills, attitudes, and emotions that inhere in teachers' knowing.

[2] The "invitational quality" of a thing is very similar to J. J. Gibson's original term "affordance" (now popularized in human–computer interaction and design literature, cf. Donald Norman). Gibson (1979) claimed affordance as "a radical hypothesis, for it implies that the 'values' and 'meanings' of things in the environment can be directly perceived" (p. 127). He credited his coinage of the term to Kurt Lewin's description of the *Aufforderunscharakter* of environments and objects. Lewin (1926) illustrates:

> The beautiful weather, a certain landscape invites one to go for a walk. A staircase entices the two-year old child to climb up and jump down; doors entice one to open and shut them, little crumbs to pick them up, a dog to pet it; the sandbox to play in it; chocolate or a piece of cake to be eaten, etc. (p. 350)

Around that time, American philosopher George Herbert Mead (1934/62) similarly wrote of armchairs "calling out" for us to sit in them (p. 278–80). Phenomenologically speaking, we often "hear" objects and aspects of the environment as invitations to partake of and participate in the world in particular ways.

Hopkins, Mohundro, & Sayre, 1998; Apperson, Laws, & Scepansky, 2006; Daniels, 1999; Frey & Birnbaum, 2002; Kask, 2000; Lowry, 1999; Mantei, 2000; Nowaczyk, Santos, & Patton, 1998; Szabo & Hastings, 2000). Students report PowerPoint is a useful cognitive tool, especially when the electronic files or slide printouts are made available for review. They describe teachers using presentation software as generally more organized. On the other hand, a recent poll of 4,500 American undergraduates reveals significant student unhappiness with the way technology is being employed in lecture halls, most particularly PowerPoint (Kvavik, Caruso, & Morgan, 2004).

Studies aimed at determining the efficacy of PowerPoint relative to other teaching methods have yielded mixed results. Lowry (1999), Mantei (2000), and Szabo and Hastings (2000) report PowerPoint-enhanced lectures increased levels of academic performance among college students, whereas Daniels (1999), Rankin and Hoaas (2001) report no effect. Kask (2000) found female, but not male, college students achieved better grades in a microeconomics course using PowerPoint. However, Susskind (2005) questions the results of some of these early studies, citing research design flaws. Apperson, Laws and Scepansky (2006), also in an attempt to overcome previous research design flaws, measured student satisfaction and test performance in ten classes across four disciplines. One semester was taught with PowerPoint, one without, with each pair given by the same professor. This study concludes PowerPoint does not impact academic achievement, but does develop an overall positive impression of the professor including likeability, organization, and a host of other "good" teaching behaviors not directly attributable to PowerPoint. Levasseur and Sawyer (2006), offering the most comprehensive review of the educational literature on PowerPoint to-date, similarly conclude that "the majority of studies comparing computer-generated slide-based instruction against other instructional methods have failed to find significant differences in learning outcomes" (p. 116).

Critical analyses of PowerPoint have also been forwarded. Most notably, visual communications expert Edward Tufte (2003) claims PowerPoint supports a cognitive style that is inconsistent with both the development of higher analytical thinking skills and the acquisition of rich narrative and interpretive understanding. Some geography scholars, whose discipline is embedded in visual representation practices, worry PowerPoint is commanding an "epistemological monopoly [that] reinforces the interchangeability of content within the single (re)presentational system" (Crang, 2003, p. 239) and carries unfortunate corporate undertones (Matless, 2003; Rose, 2004). In this way, PowerPoint may prove to be a "killer app" superseding a variety of classroom practices and potentially rendering obsolete valuable, perhaps critical, knowledge forms (Adams, 2006).

Sherry Turkle (2004) suggests productivity software like PowerPoint "constitute a particular aesthetic in educational computing" (p. 101). PowerPoint promotes a particular way of thinking, one that "does not encourage students to make an argument [but rather] to make a point" (p. 101). Digital media researcher Jamie O'Neil (2005) uses Bourriaud's theory of relational esthetics to examine "how the medium of PowerPoint effects (or affects) the message" (p. 84). His intent is to dislodge the common instrumental, effective view of PowerPoint and install a critical, affective, experiential one. O'Neil concurs with artist David Byrne's claim that PowerPoint "tells you how to think as it helps you accomplish your task" (Byrne, 2003, p. 3) and welcomes the arrival of "critical PowerPoint artworks (or covert interventions) as a mode of resistance to groupthink" (O'Neil, 2005, p. 84).

> What does all this mean for educators using PowerPoint in their classrooms? Studies show no significant gains in academic performance. At the same time, there is an appreciable increase in positive feelings toward instructors using PowerPoint. Finally, critical analyses are aligned on this point: PowerPoint tends to encourage a particular way of thinking, a way that may have questionable – or at least limited – merit in academic environments. Meanwhile, we still do not know how students or teachers actually experience PowerPoint-mediated lessons and lectures. We are missing what Turkle (2004) calls "the phenomenology of the digital experience" (p. 102).

Methodology

Mindful of Turkle's suggestion that we may be missing a phenomenology of the digital experience, this is precisely the approach I take for my research methodology. The main focus and aim of phenomenological inquiry is the description of lived experience, that is, the description of phenomena as they present themselves or as they are given in experience. Phenomenology is concerned with how we experience our world *prereflectively*, *preverbally* in its lived immediacy; it is the practice of fidelity to lived experience. As well as describing experience, *hermeneutic* phenomenology seeks to draw out the meaning or significance of our practical involvements in the world. Such research formulates questions of the type, "What is this or that human experience like?" It is an attempt to return "to the things themselves", and further, to let these things (phenomena) speak for themselves (Heidegger, 1962). Phenomenology is not interested in conceptualizing, theorizing or idealizing experience, but rather in describing and interpreting experience as it is lived.

Phenomenological inquiry explicitly positions the researcher to comprehend information and communication technologies, not as solely objective *or* subjective phenomena, but as *lived*. A central feature of phenomenological method is the gathering of a field of descriptive evidence from which underlying patterns and structures of experience can be drawn (van Manen, 1997). My study addresses three distinct modes of PowerPoint engagement: (1) how PowerPoint presentation is experienced by students; (2) how teachers experience constructing a presentation with PowerPoint; and (3) how teachers experience teaching through PowerPoint presentation.

The phenomenological study involved in-depth interviews with 14 college students and 12 instructors at two different academic, postsecondary institutions; observation of large university lecture classes where PowerPoint was being employed as a primary means of teaching; and reflection on my own use of PowerPoint as an instructor in postsecondary settings. I used hermeneutic phenomenological methodology to capture the particularities of the PowerPoint experience in the form of lived experience descriptions (LEDs). Methods employed include thematic analysis, linguistic interpretations, honing of exemplary or anecdotal narratives through eidetic reduction. Phenomenological method also requires a systematic scholarly "reading" of relevant philosophical literature and phenomenological studies. Using techniques such as comparing pedagogical styles of classroom discussions and presentations with and without PowerPoint I examine how the experiences of software-mediated presentations are uniquely sponsoring and providing for modes of teaching and learning that are always and inevitably embodied and situated in particular temporal, spatial and relational contexts.

Theoretical Framework

The totality of the immediate environment that we inhabit, our lifeworld, is best described as "a *milieu* – a field of intensive forces, vibrant according to their own inner codes" (Lingis, 2004, p. 278). Ivan Illich (1997) coins the phrase *le milieu technique* to refer to the irresistible embrace of the high technology lifeworlds we find ourselves dwelling in today. The technological milieu is shaping substantially – insinuating itself, habituating us and simultaneously reinterpreting – how we act in and perceive the world. Mark Hansen suggests that new media technologies are "poised on the cusp between phenomenology and materiality" and as such have introduced "a theoretical oscillation that promises to displace the empirical-transcendental divide" (2006, p. 297) that has long structured western thinking.

This research is situated in the midst of this difficult theoretical divide, and attempts to make visible some of the tight intimacies, primordial interminglings, and, at times, acute dependencies teachers and students find themselves living with their educational technologies every day. To this end, this research project draws on four phenomenologically informed traditions: curriculum and pedagogy studies (e.g. Max van Manen, Iain Thomson), philosophy of technology (e.g. Martin Heidegger, Don Ihde), human environmental esthetics (e.g. Berleant, & Carlson, Pauline von Bonsdorff), and media studies (e.g. Hansen, Marshall McLuhan). For example, in the section below, I frame participants' lived experience descriptions in light of Martin Heidegger's foundational insights about human–technology relations. Heidegger, one of the earliest philosophers of technology, shows that each thing (or place) opens a new world to us, revealing novel structures of experience and meaning; every technology discloses a new horizon of possibilities to us. Human beings are "the be-thinged" (Heidegger, 1971, p. 181), that is, we are prereflectively inhabited, conditioned, and creatively provoked by the things of our world.

In the remaining pages, I provide an excerpt of the final phase of my project, which attempts a phenomenology of university teachers' everyday experiences of PowerPoint.

Inhabiting PowerPoint: Constructing a Lesson with PowerPoint

The vocative appeal of PowerPoint to the teacher is at once a linguistic gesture: "Click to add title," "• Click to add text". It is also a promisingly familiar and easy-to-use digital environment; a hermeneutic horizon of previous PowerPoint design and teaching experiences; entrance to an architected form intending persuasive presentation; a windowed milieu that the teacher traverses with her eyes upon screen, fingertips on keyboard, hand shuffling a mouse. As Heidegger (1972) tells us, "When we handle a thing, for example, our hand must fit itself to the thing. Use implies a fitting response" (p. 187). Reaching out with anticipation of PowerPoint's promise to help her point powerfully, the teacher orients herself toward her windowed environment; her being is drawn in and gently caught up in the "draft" of PowerPoint, the unique horizon of possibilities it brightly frames for her. She responds fittingly.

One teacher describes how she constructs a lesson using PowerPoint:

I insert an image, add some text, then try them in different positions on the slide. I'm looking for balance. I like using compelling images, with minimal, carefully chosen text for impact. As I work, I do not, cannot separate the composition of slides themselves from the subject matter at hand, the vision of my students, and the appeal I am trying to make. I sit back and look (perhaps trying to see the slide as my students might), then adjust, and adjust things again. I try out different fonts, sample background colors from my images, wanting to give the whole presentation a sense of visual cohesion. I take a certain pleasure and satisfaction in this. I move to Slide Sorter View [where all the slide thumbprints are laid out across the window] to grasp the whole so far, to visualize the general flow of the presentation. From here, I move a few slides to a different place in the sequence to see how that flows, then return to Normal view. I find I am variously engaged with trying to represent the content, the purpose of this teaching presentation, visually, in text, or both, and thinking about, imagining presenting the slides to my class.[3]

Within the PowerPoint environment or milieu, the teacher's work materializes as an accumulating series of slides. The basic elements of each slide are text, images, color, and animation. She composes, adjusts, tries out new fonts, samples colors, switches "views," plays with order. She is wholly engaged, representing content as slides then imagining their presentation in the immediacy of a classroom with her students. Slides, subject matter, the vision of her students, and her presentational and teacherly intentions intermingle.

In performing this preparatory work, the teacher is sitting in her office with computer, screen, keyboard and mouse; texts and papers litter the desk. Her screen shows numerous windows open: a web browser, email, a Word document, as well as

---

[3] The italicized text represents phenomenological research material drawn from interviews conducted with 12 university and college instructors regarding their everyday, "lived" experiences of PowerPoint. Individual participants are identified only as "the teacher", "the instructor", "he" or "she".

PowerPoint. Occasionally her eyes wander from the screen, and stare thoughtfully out her office window into the distance. She turns back to the PowerPoint window, pulls her keyboard a little closer, nudges her mouse and continues work. Once the teacher is engaged in her preparation work, her office, desk, screen, keyboard and mouse recede into the background. PowerPoint too withdraws from full view, fading to a transparent framework, a sophisticated but peripherally present set of tools that she may variously call upon to perform her presentation design activities in this digital world.

Phenomenologically speaking, we do not usually engage a tool as a discrete, obvious object, that is, in what Heidegger calls its present-at-hand mode (*vorhandenheit*). Rather we tend to encounter a tool through using it, in its handiness (*zuhandenheit*). In this handy encounter, the tool is essentially invisible to us, taken-for-granted. It is, as Sartre says about the everyday experience of our own bodies, passed over in silence – "*passé sous silence*" (Sartre in Bleeker & Mulderij, 1990).

> Consider the example (used by Wittgenstein, Polyani, and Merleau-Ponty) of the blind man's cane. We hand the blind man a cane and ask him to tell us what properties it has. After hefting and feeling it, he tells us that it is light, smooth, about three feet long, and so on; it is occurrent for him. But when the man starts to manipulate the cane, he loses his awareness of the cane itself; he is aware only of the curb (or whatever object the cane touches); or, if all is going well, he is not even aware of that....Precisely when it is most genuinely appropriated equipment becomes transparent. (Dreyfus, 1991, p. 65)

Hammering a nail in the wall to hang a picture, we are focused on the picture-hanging, the project we are engaged in, not on the hammer. When we are writing a scholarly paper or an email, we are barely aware of our typing fingers or the keyboard. Our fingers serve us silently, tapping transparently on the vaguely present keyboard, while we are primarily engaged in the higher-level business at hand: writing thoughtfully. Only when we accidentally hit our finger with the hammer do we suddenly awaken to our throbbing finger and to the hammer as an obvious object. Too, until our fingers know how to type, the keyboard stands as an insurmountable obstacle. But, as Heidegger (1962) describes, "the less we just stare at the [tool], and the more we seize hold of it and use it, the more primordial does our relationship to it become" (p. 98). To be what it is, a tool must recede from visibility.

The work-object or focal project of our instructor is thus not PowerPoint. Her project is the classroom situation she will find herself in a few days hence. As teacher, her primary intention is to creatively assist her students in learning the particular subject matter at-hand. For this purpose, for this subject matter, she has chosen to use PowerPoint. Thus while the presentation software expertly frames and facilitates her activity of planning a lesson, PowerPoint is not the main objective and intention, anymore than canvas and paint palette are the objective and intention of the artist. Nonetheless, we must also notice how the instructor's activity patterns and meaning structures are also being quietly *in-formed* – conformed, deformed, and reformed – by the architecture of the particular software she finds herself *inhabiting*.

The PowerPoint Habit

Another teacher relates simply: *"Sitting down to prepare a PowerPoint, I can't help but think in bullets."* Parker (2001) humorously notes how PowerPoint seems to promote a certain kind of thinking: "Last week I caught myself planning out (in my head) the slides I would need to explain to my wife why we couldn't afford a vacation this year" (p. 78). As the teacher seizes hold of PowerPoint as a tool of teaching, he or she necessarily begins to think in terms of the form it suggests. At minimum the teacher must think in slides, reconfiguring his or her knowledge in the new 4:3 rectangular landscape delineated by PowerPoint. The software readily assists in this project by inviting the teacher to consider certain formats: to title each slide, to reform subject material as abbreviated, bulleted points.

In PowerPoint, the teacher sees and understands her teaching world in terms of the sphere of possibilities this software discloses to her as she works: slides, menus, animations, Slide Sorter View, Normal View. Her lesson planning world unfolds in the context of a bright, spacious rectangular "window," a bright-screened facade framing and containing explicit text and iconic invitations. Ihde (1990) suggests, "technologies, by providing a framework for action,…form intentionalities and inclinations within which use-patterns take dominant shape" (p. 141). In PowerPoint, the teacher "does not, cannot separate" the software's possibilities and designs from her own: the aims and inscriptions of the Microsoft programming team and the teacher intentionalities and inclinations intertwine, enmesh and reorient. The teacher's world is translated into new vocabularies and presentation genres, expanding her possibilities of action while simultaneously framing and constraining the world as a screenic succession of 4:3 slides.

Having responded to the vocative appeals of PowerPoint – its invitational qualities or affordances – the teacher enters a mode of human–technology engagement Chesher (in Suchman, 2007) describes as "managed indeterminacy" or *invocation*. "Invocation involves those actions that define the terms of engagement written into the design script or discovered by the participating user" (Suchman, p. 282). The teacher is now conversationally engaged, enfolded into, and intertwined with PowerPoint. The teacher–technology relational boundaries blur and a hermeneutically rich but "silent" corporeal rapport sets in. What sorts of conversations seem to unfold between teacher and PowerPoint?

Yet another instructor describes a somewhat different approach and concern when creating her PowerPoint slides:

> Composing this slide, there was a particular aesthetic I was striving for: thoughtful use of color, thematic cohesiveness, consistency between the slides (not sameness!), but also movement, meaningful movement through and among the slides. There is clearly an art to this.

This teacher is preoccupied with visual appeal and attaining thematic integrity with the subject matter. Movement achieved "through and among" her slides has significance to her. The teacher is trying to be sensitive to the atmospheric quality of the PowerPoint media on her students. This raises the question of how atmosphere is usually anticipated in the planning of a lesson and how the esthetic of PowerPoint slides may be seen as an evocative tool for establishing a sphere.

"PowerPointing": Teaching by and with PowerPoint

Enter teacher with trolley replete with laptop, mouse, and data projector. Untangling the garage-band knot of electrical cords and connector cables, the teacher connects, plugs in, and turns on laptop and projector. This process is sometimes accompanied by palpable anxiety surrounding the stages of equipment hook-up, and worries about self-competence in the face of difficulties or breakdown and the implications of "no PowerPoint" to the fate of the class. The projector hums at last, the slides are cued up, the teacher breathes a quiet sigh of relief.

The simple act of drawing the blinds or switching off the light darkens perceptibly the hue of the wall, softens the faces of students. The teacher becomes less visible; the projected slide shines brighter. The mood changes, the classroom atmosphere shifts. PowerPoint reconfigures the classroom as a cinematic space: the students settle in as spectators, the teacher as orator, narrates the slides from the side. When the teacher turns to the opening slide, the students are cued to sit back, get comfortable and hopefully enjoy and learn from the PowerPoint presentation with a certain sense of (inter)passivity. A subtle change occurs in the students' attitude and orientation. The large, bright slideshow reminds students they may become a particular kind of audience, "invigorated or drowsy, [but] a generally passive audience that is rarely called upon to really interrogate the images" (Crang, 2003, p. 242). But what does the projected PowerPoint slide evoke for the teacher?

The Vocal Rhythm of PowerPoint

I notice when I turn to begin my PowerPoint, I shift my role slightly – I'm less conversational, more oratorical. PowerPoint locks you into a gait in your speech, a kind of vocal rhythm.

The teacher with-PowerPoint finds himself standing somewhat differently in relationship to his class: less dialogic, more monologic; less open to interruption and discussion, fastening to a vocal pattern that rhythmically signals oration not conversation. Vocal rhythm may also establish a kind of synchrony with the slide rhythm.

The arrival of a new slide is the occasion to take a breath, a momentary pause to look at the slide, allow its meaning to prompt me: a reminder of what to say next, what direction to pursue. But too, I must somehow find connection with what I have just said. Or not. It tells me what comes next. I feel I must press on.

Like walking and talking with a good friend, footfalls – narrative breaths and slidefalls – find a mutually comfortable rhythm and pace. Here a special kind of pathic relation is hosted, not between teacher and students, but between teacher and projected slides. This human–technology dialogue appears more determined and rigid than the comparably flexible, nuanced relation engaged during the planning and design phase. More specifically, the slides are no longer in the midst of being created and manipulated. In "View Show" mode, the teacher cannot change the slides themselves, he can only control the direction of movement between the slides and animation moments – forward, backward – as well as access preset links and buttons. This predicament of being instructionally captivated in a slide set seems too to be a consequence of the teacher planning the lesson with a series of headlines or points, as we saw above.

In the lived moment of the class, as each new slide appears, it "speaks" prereflectively to both students and teachers alike. That is, before we are even aware of it, we have already seen the new slide and begun to read and make sense of it; the teacher finds himself or herself speaking to the slide. When the next slide is summoned, it "speaks" again, and the teacher must now speak to it.

> *"I am committed to do this PowerPoint"*
> *As soon as I clicked to the next slide, I knew immediately it was the wrong thing. Seeing their eyes, I felt: I simply can't go on. It was the same sinking feeling you get realizing the person you are having a conversation with isn't listening to you. I had spent all this time preparing this PowerPoint presentation and then the problem with PowerPoint is you just can't simply jump ahead, be extemporaneous – "just ignore this and this while I find the right slide." I was stuck with my plan.*

This college instructor recalls a time when he suddenly felt that, in the lived context of his class, his choice of using PowerPoint to address a particular topic was misjudged. Of course, any lesson plan or teaching approach can go awry or fall flat. In such moments, the teacher may decide to "stick with the plan" or diverge and improvise. The seasoned teacher usually has a few other "tricks" at-hand. Yet, is there something about PowerPoint that complicates the move to diverge in response to one's felt sensibilities? One teacher describes her PowerPoint dilemma like this:

> *PowerPoint is a finished product. It is hard for me to loose myself from the slides in the context of my class. The story has, so to speak, already been decided.*

But perhaps, the problem is precisely that the story had not been decided. The teacher did not prepare a story but a series of points, stops on the way to some cognitive end point. She goes on to describe the resistance she feels in deviating from the slide set she herself has constructed: "If I answer a question, how will I go back to the slides?" In planning and carefully constructing the lecture beforehand, she tried to imagine her students there before her, tried to anticipate their questions. But now, in the context of her actual class, the world looks different.

> *In the classroom, PowerPoint is a representation of my anticipated presentation – an imagining of what my presentation would be, could be. But in the actual moment of teaching, things are often otherwise. In the midst of teaching, my slides and I sometimes come into conflict with one another. Then I feel fragmented, forced to choose this particular outcome – what is represented up there on the slides – over the felt relation with my students – what seems to present itself to me in the moment. I am committed to do this PowerPoint. I cannot now easily choose to do something else.*

When a teacher uses PowerPoint in her classroom, she commits to the unfolding of a particular form of teaching and learning, a predetermined story wending its reckoned path to a decided conclusion. A PowerPoint presentation prepared beforehand is also an investment, visible proof of preparation and organization in the face of the contingent, indeterminate lifeworld of the classroom. To abandon such obvious evidence of competence may strike as fool-hearty, exposing oneself to an uncertain, unprepared-for future. As Howell (2007) laments

> From the moment I walk into the lecture theatre I feel the pressure from my students to line up my thinking with their PowerPoint notes, without which they seem to be lost. I usually succumb by connecting them to the screen rather than to myself, each other, and the subject matter. In giving precedence to the object of PowerPoint, where the slides take on a language and world of their own, …students may subconsciously be encouraged to zoom out of the teacher's presence in favor of the rectangle on the screen. (p. 139)

The Times-Square-like surround of slick and easy possibilities is so appealing and omnipresent, our inner compass as teachers may be quietly lifted from us and replaced by the veneer of "powerful" solutions. As sociologist Daniel Bell prophetically wrote in the early 1970s, the new "intellectual technologies" – tools that specifically extend our cognitive reach – substitute "algorithms (problem-solving rules) for intuitive judgments" (1973, p. 29). A digital technology is given default proxy for professional knowing.

Ready, set, teach!
Not so long ago, I gave a lecture for a PowerPoint-loving colleague of mine who had to be away. Standing before his students, I opened his PowerPoint file on my laptop, the whole system struggling to cope with the gigantic file. While we are waiting, I tell his students that their professor has left me 143 slides to cover today. "That means," I calculate, "one slide every 21 seconds. So we better hurry up and get started!"

PowerPoint exhibits the tendency toward or certainly the desire to achieve maximum efficiency in teaching. Contemporary technologies are both the product of as well as the increasingly complex scaffold supporting and reifying a particular technological frame of mind, "a mode of revealing," which Heidegger calls "enframing" (*das Gestell*). In today's ubiquitous surround of technologies

> we increasingly think and act in accordance with the world picture [modern technology] provides…The technological mode of revealing is a fixation of things by categorizing them and representing them to ourselves in thought through abstract categories, thus making manageable and capable of being efficiently manipulated – a demand to which the fluid and the ill-defined remains inconveniently resistant….We "enframe" things by turning them into instances – understanding them in terms of the objective properties attributed to members of the category to which they have been allocated. (Bonnett, 2002, p. 234)

This technological way of apprehending things – wherein all things, including human beings, increasingly show up to us as resources to be enhanced and optimized for maximal efficiency – is radically restructuring our daily lives, along with contemporary learning experiences and teaching practices. To put it another way and perhaps a little more forcefully, postmodern technology engenders a totalizing style of practices that, according to Dreyfus and Spinosa (2003) threaten to: "restrict our openness to people and things by driving out all other styles of practice that enable us to be receptive to reality. This threat is not a problem for which we must find a solution but an ontological condition that requires a transformation of our understanding of being. For that, we need to understand technicity as our current mode of revealing things and people" (p. 341).

The demand to "have" the PowerPoint
   On the first day of class, a student asks, "Will you be making your PowerPoint slides
   available?" I reply, "I haven't yet read all of Plato's dialogues, nor have I learned yet how
   to put slides up on the web. Given a choice between taking the time to read another dia-
   logue and putting my PowerPoint files on the web, I think I'd choose the former." At the
   back of the lecture hall, a young woman snaps her book shut, gathers her things and
   promptly leaves my classroom.

The PowerPoint slide deck is a lecture product that students are increasingly expecting to procure from their teacher. In becoming a product, the teacher's work may seem less a matter of developing pedagogic relations and the sharing of understanding, skill and expertise, and more a matter of commodity and consumption. Here the young woman expresses her disgruntlement that the new covenant of entitled student-consumer has been broken. She has nothing to gain from the philosopher in his person, only his PowerPoint. Another example:

   At a conference recently, where PowerPoint is the norm, I am speaking before a fairly large
   group. As I begin, I am surprised to notice someone, several rows back, raise their hand as
   if for a question. But then I see the hand is holding a camera, and it quickly goes back down
   again. Next slide. The same digital-camera-hand goes up then down, and now, off to my
   right, some ways back, I see another camera-touting hand shoot up. I feel taken aback.
   Surely my PowerPoint slides are not so compelling that each slide should warrant photo-
   graphing. No: I, or rather, my work, is being consumed, commoditized and owned…and all
   without my consent.

Borgmann (1984) claims modern technology is decisively separating means from ends. The activities or processes of creating things are progressively being hidden from view and replaced with the more singular activity of procuring end-products or commodities. "What distinguishes a [modern] device is its sharp internal division into a machinery and a commodity procured by that machinery" (p. 33). As a result, some of the practices associated traditionally with creative teaching activities are ostensibly disappearing in the wake of sophisticated technologies.

As illustrated above, the PowerPoint slide deck is essentially a product of a teacher's knowing and thinking in conversation with the PowerPoint software, now inscribed as single framed, sequential snapshots. Thus with PowerPoint, students witness more often the projected knowledge product, and less the teacher's knowing-in-action. Then again, each slide has the potential to trigger the embodied insights of an experienced practitioner in the immediacy of the now. This *punctum* or evocative capacity can "save" a PowerPoint presentation from being merely a product.

Yet it may be that "the ultimate success of teaching actually may rely importantly on the 'knowledge' forms that inhere in practical actions, in an embodied thoughtfulness, and in the personal space, mood and relational atmosphere in which teachers find themselves with their students" (van Manen, 1995, p. 48). Thus, a primary concern here is a bypassing of the experiential dimensions of practical knowledge, both in the discipline of the subject as well as in teaching practice. When educators try to capture and translate aspects of their tacit understandings to a series of slides, there is the danger of "short-circuiting" the normally contingent enactments of their ordinary teaching and professional actions. Of course, "shortening the circuit" is precisely what devices of expedience, like PowerPoint, are designed to do: eliminate "unnecessary" sub-steps (via hardware or software solutions) to allow the most efficient path to an end.

Overview of Findings

Our corporeal being – our lived body – is increasingly and intimately enhanced by, enmeshed with and enfolded into new digital technologies. These paratextual[4] machines mediate our lived experience with startling immediacy and complexity, lending us novel sensory worlds, and prescribed ways of knowing and doing that are increasingly shared globally. The moniker "digital" is signaling a radical change in our material world, but also in our human selves. Techno-utopian thinkers like Hans Moravec and Ray Kurzweil predict human–technology fusions where the "software" of our minds will one day be uploadable to more durable, faster hardware, thus rendering our "mere jelly" (Moravec, 1988, p. 117) bodies – the "old slow carbon-based neural-computing machinery" (Kurzweil, 1999, p. 129) – obsolete. In the wake of such euphoric claims of transcendence, philosopher N. Katherine Hayles (1999) reminds us that the "human mind without human body is not human mind. More to the point, it doesn't exist" (p. 246). Our human self is intimately tethered to the possibilities as well as the limits of our flesh-and-blood, human body. Thus, as the "mere jelly" body is gradually being relinquished in these technology turf wars, a new version of human being has been conceived: the posthuman, "whose basic capabilities so radically exceed those of present humans as to be no longer human by our current standards" (Bostrom, 2003, p. 5).

What does all this mean for educators employing new media technologies? Foremost, we must begin to discern and "focus on our own embodiment as the material site – the bearer – of technology's otherwise wholly inhuman impact" (Hansen, 2000, p. 263). Digital technologies are locally deployed "mimetic vehicles" (Benjamin, 1978) that prereflectively shape our embodied agency. "Software quite literally conditions existence" (Thrift, 2005, p. 241) by scaffolding a habituation process that occurs primarily outside of the phenomenal field of subjectivity. One of the difficulties in grasping the mediating influence of software is that its texts do not fit the usual model of representation, wherein humans and objects represent each other via words and images. Instead, software texts concern words *doing* things in particular contexts: the language of the machine has immediate material effects.

---

[4] The term "paratextual" is used by Gerard Genette in his book *Palimpsestes* (1997) to describe "accompanying productions" that bind the text and the reader together. He lists the following as examples of paratexts: "title, subtitle, intertitles; prefaces, postfaces, notices, forewords, etc; marginal, infrapaginal, terminal notes; epigraphs; illustrations; blurbs, book covers, dust jackets, and many other kinds of secondary signals."

Our interactions with software, often via a screen and keyboard/mouse/controller, are direct, sensuous and mimetic. Software "affects our experience first and foremost through its infrastructural role, its import occurs prior to and independently of our production of representations" (Hansen, 2000, p. 4). PowerPoint sponsors a style of thinking and presenting, a normative framework for staging knowledge: headings and bullet points for teachers to "talk to." This scaffolding of abbreviation, built into the software as default signage, implicitly informs how some teachers visualize and subsequently present their knowledge in the lived space of the classroom. The projected PowerPoint slide presentation, regardless of the kind of knowledge it is serving to frame, exercises a powerful sway over the teacher in the moments of teaching, at times appearing as impenetrable obstacle, rather than a generative support to the teacher desiring to pursue her pedagogical sense of tact. In this way, our lived experience is being radically, prereflectively re-habilitated; our intentional involvements perturbed and re-inscribed via the constraints and dispensations of prefabricated digital architectures. We are now well into an era of technological-becoming, our sensible bodies quietly adapting to the inhuman rhythms of an evolving, digitally coded and intensifying mechanosphere.

It is imperative that we attend mindfully to the material, hermeneutic, and existential shifts that are transpiring as our worlds are daily extended, intensified, and complicated by digital technologies. The continued promotion of digital technologies as neutral agents – a foundational belief or "posit" of our current ontological epoch – imperils the normative project of pedagogy by concealing the instrumental constructs they materialize. Rather, these paratextual machines must be recognized as effective and affective *mimetic interventions* that prereflectively shape our being, knowing and doing in the world. Such a view necessarily burdens tomorrow's teachers with a renewed sense of professional responsibility, one sensitive to the uncertain ecology of today's classrooms in the wake of digital technology integration, but more importantly, for the well-being of our posthuman children living this brave new world.

Finally, this research provides argument, ground, and example of how educational scholars must qualitatively document and critically theorize media technology's "hidden" curriculum, that is, the material effects, activity patterns and meaning structures ICTs are mobilizing at a startling speed in education. Educational technologists have spent much energy in trying to assist teachers to use these new media tools, but through this research I show how we must also concern ourselves with how these tools may be using us.

References

Adams, C. (2006). PowerPoint, habits of mind, and classroom culture. *Journal of Curriculum Studies, 38*(4), 389–411.

Apperson, J. M., Laws, E. L., & Scepansky, J. A. (2006). The impact of presentation graphics on students' experience in the classroom. *Computers and Education, 47*, 116–126.

Atkins-Sayre, W., Hopkins, S., Mohundro, S., & Sayre, W. (1998). *Rewards and liabilities of presentation software as an ancillary tool: Prison or paradise?* Corpus Christi, TX: Del Mar College (ERIC Document Reproduction Service No. ED430260).

Bell, D. (1973). *The coming of post-industrial society: A venture in social forecasting*. New York: Basic Books.

Benjamin, W. (1978). On the mimetic faculty. In P. Demetz (ed.) *Reflections: Essays, aphorisms, autobiographical writings* (E. Jephcott, Trans.), (pp. 333–336). New York: Random House.

Bleeker, H., & Mulderij, K. J. (1990). The experience of motor disability. *Phenomenology + Pedagogy*. Retrieved March 18, 2008, from http://www.phenomenologyonline.com/articles/bleeker.html.

Bonnett, M. (2002). Education as a form of the poetic: A Heideggerian approach to learning and the teacher-pupil relationship. In M. A. Peters (Ed.), *Heidegger, education and modernity* (pp. 229–243). Lanham, MD: Rowman & Littlefield.

Borgmann, A. (1984). *Technology and the character of contemporary life: A philosophical inquiry*. Chicago: University of Chicago Press.

Bostrom, N. (2003). *The transhumanist FAQ: A general introduction*. Retrieved August 5, 2008, from http://www.transhumanism.org/resources/FAQv21.pdf.

Buchholz, S., & Ullman, J. (2004). 12 commandments for PowerPoint. *The Teaching Professor, 18*(6), 4.

Byrne, D. (2003). Learning to love PowerPoint. *Wired, 11*(09). Retrieved October 13, 2011, from http://www.wired.com/wired/archive/11.09/ppt1.html.

Crang, M. (2003). The hair in the gate: Visuality and geographical knowledge. *Antipode, 35*, 238–243.

Daniels, L. (1999). Introducing technology in the classroom: PowerPoint as a first step. *Journal of Computing in Higher Education, 10*, 42–56.

Dreyfus, H. (1991). *Being-in-the-world: A commentary on Heidegger's Being and Time, division 1*. Cambridge, MA: MIT Press.

Dreyfus, H. L., & Spinosa, C. (2003). Further reflections on Heidegger, technology, and the everyday. *Bulletin of Science, Technology and Society, 23*(5), 339–349.

Frey, B. A. and Birnbaum, D. J. (2002). Learners' perceptions on the value of PowerPoint in lectures. ERIC ED 467 192.

Genette, G. (1997) *Palimpsests: Literature in the second degree* (C. Newman & C. Doubinsky, Trans.). Lincoln: University of Nebraska Press.

Gibson, J. J. (1979). *The ecological approach to visual perception*. Boston: Houghton Mifflin Company.

Hansen, M. (2000). *Embodying technesis: Technology beyond writing*. Ann Arbor: University of Michigan Press.

Hansen, M. (2006). Media theory. *Theory, Culture & Society, 23*(2–3), 297–306.

Hayles, N. K. (1999). *How we became posthuman: Virtual bodies in cybernetics, literature, and informatics*. Chicago: University of Chicago Press.

Heidegger, M. (1962). *Being and time*. New York: Harper and Row.

Heidegger, M. (1971). *Poetry, language, and thought* (A. Hofstadter, Trans.). New York: Harper Colophon Books.

Heidegger, M. (1972). *What is called thinking* (F. D. Wieck and J. Grey, Trans.). New York: Harper and Row.

Howells, K. (2007). PowerPoint: Friend or foe? In J. Sigafoos & V. Green (Eds.), *Technology and teaching* (pp. 137–146). New York: Nova Science Publishers.

Ihde, D. (1990). *Technology and the lifeworld: From garden to earth*. Bloomington: Indiana University Press.

Illich, I. (1997). Philosophy … artifacts … friendship – And the history of the gaze. In T.-A. Druart (Ed.), *Philosophy of technology: Proceedings of the American Catholic Philosophical Association, 70* (pp. 61–82). Washington, DC: National Office of the American Catholic Philosophical Association, Catholic University of America.

Kask, S. (2000, January). *The impact of using computer presentations (CAP) on student learning in the microeconomics principles course*. Paper presented at the meeting of the American Economic Association, Boston.

Kvavik, R. B., Caruso, J. B., & Morgan, G. (2004). *ECAR study of students and information technology, 2004: Convenience, connection and control*. Boulder, CO: EDUCAUSE Center for Applied Research. Retrieved October 13, 2011, from http://www.educause.edu/ir/library/pdf/ers0405/rs/ers0405w.pdf.

Kurzweil, R. (1999). *The age of spiritual machines: When computers exceed human intelligence.* New York: Penguin.

Levasseur, D. G., & Sawyer, J. K. (2006). Pedagogy meets PowerPoint: A research review of the effects of computer-generated slides in the classroom. *The Review of Communication, 6*(1–2), 101–123.

Lewin, K. (1926). Vorsatz, Wille und Bedürfnis. *Psychologische Forschung, 7*(4), 330–385.

Lingis, A. (2004). The music of space. In B. V. Foltz & R. Frodeman (Eds.), *Rethinking nature: Essays in environmental philosophy* (pp. 273–288). Bloomington, IN: Indiana University Press.

Lowry, R. B. (1999). Electronic presentation of lectures effect upon student performance. *University Chemistry Education, 3*, 18–21.

Mantei, E. J. (2000). Using internet class notes and PowerPoint in physical geology lecture: Comparing the success of computer technology with traditional teaching techniques. *Journal of College Science Teaching, 29*, 301–305.

Matless, D. (2003). Gestures around the visual. *Antipode, 35*(2), 222–226.

McLuhan, M. (1964). *Understanding media: The extensions of man.* New York: McGraw Hill.

Mead, G. H. (1934/62) *Mind, Self, and Society: From the Standpoint of a Social Behaviorist.* Chicago, IL: University of Chicago Press.

Merleau-Ponty, M. (1962/2002). *Phenomenology of perception* (C. Smith, Trans.). New York: Routledge.

Moravec, H. (1988). *Mind children: The future of robot and human intelligence.* Cambridge, MA: Harvard University Press.

Nowaczyk, R. H., Santos, L. T., & Patton, C. (1998). Student perception of multimedia in the undergraduate classroom. *International Journal of Instructional Media, 25*, 367–382.

O'Neil, J. (2005). The relational aesthetics of PowerPoint: Affective/not effective communication. *International Journal of Technology Knowledge and Society, 1*(1), 84–91.

Parker, I. (2001). Absolute PowerPoint: Can a software package edit our thoughts? *The New Yorker, 77*(13), 76–87.

Rankin, E. L., & Hoaas, D. J. (2001). The use of PowerPoint and student performance. *Atlantic Economic Journal, 29*, 113.

Rose, G. (2004). On the importance of asking the right questions, or what is the power of PowerPoint, exactly? *Antipode, 36*(5), 795–797.

Suchman, L. A. (2007). *Human-machine reconfigurations: Plans and situated actions* (2nd ed.). New York, NY: Cambridge University Press.

Susskind, J. E. (2005). PowerPoint's power in the classroom: Enhancing students' self-efficacy and attitudes. *Computers and Education, 45*(2), 203–215.

Szabo, A., & Hastings, N. (2000). Using IT in the undergraduate classroom: Should we replace the blackboard with PowerPoint? *Computers and Education, 35*, 175–187.

Thrift, N. (2005). Beyond mediation: Three new material registers and their consequences. In D. Miller (Ed.), *Materiality* (pp. 231–256). Durham, NC: Duke University Press.

Tufte, E. R. (2003). *The cognitive style of PowerPoint.* Cheshire, CT: Graphics Press LLC.

Turkle, S. (2004). The fellowship of the microchip: Global technologies as evocative objects. In M. M. Suárez-Orozco & D. B. Qin-Hilliard (Eds.), *Globalization: Culture and education in the new millennium* (pp. 97–113). Berkeley, CA: University of California Press.

Van Manen, M. (1995). On the epistemology of reflective practice. *Teachers and Teaching: Theory and Practice, 1*(1), 33–50.

Van Manen, M. (1997). *Researching lived experience: Human science for an action sensitive pedagogy* (2nd ed.). London, ON: The Althouse Press.

Part II
Trends and Issues in Library and Information Science

Introduction

Stephanie A. Jones

Possibly the most startling event to occur in 2010 was the decision by the American Association of School Librarians (AASL) to adopt school librarian as the official name for our profession. The announcement, which came at the ALA Midwinter Conference held in Boston, has been received with mixed reactions (Staino, 2010). Some people lauded the decision, while others thought that the name change was a step backwards for the profession (Bunn, 2010; Nelson, 2010). While AASL is a guiding light for our profession, it is not the only organization with an interest in this issue. Both the Association for Educational Communications and Technology (AECT) and the International Society for Technology in Education (ISTE), who are both more technologically oriented than AASL, still include "media" in the job title. This is especially important to AECT, which wrote a letter supporting the continued use of the title 'Library media specialist' (D. Neuman, personal communication, July 8, 2010). Nevertheless, despite the continued debate about what our job title should be called, it is only through employing improved and innovative ways of educating twenty-first-century learners that we will transform our profession. Gail Dickinson (2010) stated this belief well:

> It's time to keep the name, but lose the job and the image that goes with it, recreating the vibrancy of the school librarian positions our students need....Each time that we are in touch with the school community, we have the chance to change the profession (p. 6).

The six chapters in this section of the yearbook provide insights into a variety of approaches that school librarians can adopt to achieve the goal of renewing our vital place in the educational system. Four of the chapters deal with issues of access to library resources and services as they relate to student learning. The remaining two chapters pertain to aspects of the professional role of the school librarian.

S.A. Jones (✉)
Instructional Technology, Georgia Southern University, Statesboro, GA, USA
e-mail: sjones@georgiasouthern.edu

M. Orey et al. (eds.), *Educational Media and Technology Yearbook: Volume 36, 2011*,   157
Educational Media and Technology Yearbook 36, DOI 10.1007/978-1-4614-1305-9_13,
© Springer Science+Business Media, LLC 2012

Given the increasingly diversified student population in contemporary schools, Farmer contends that cultural sensitivity is an essential consideration in instructional design. Using Hofsted's model of cultural dimensions as a framework, Farmer delineates the various cultural differences that affect the way people from different cultures learn. These include language, gender, age, and cultural norms. Farmer asserts that teacher librarians need to become culturally competent in order to work in a cross-cultural environment and describes the variables for them to consider when designing learning experiences for individuals from different cultural backgrounds. She explicates a variety of strategies which teacher librarians should employ concerning student–teacher relations, topics of discussion, choice of resources, level of learner participation, and learning activities. Farmer concludes by highlighting the advantages of the e-learning environment for all learners, but stresses that unreliable physical and intellectual access to technology may be an impediment to learning.

The chapter by Everhart and Mardis supports Farmer's assessment of technological barriers to learning. In order to successfully integrate technology into the curriculum, schools must have the necessary infrastructure to support that integration. Although 98% of schools in the U.S. have a connection to the Internet, that connection may not be the high-speed, high-capacity transmission medium, commonly referred to as broadband, which is widely regarded as the standard for today's information-rich environment. Broadband permits schools to take advantage of a wide range of new and rich educational tools and resources which can lead to innovative teaching and learning. However, as Everhart and Mardis explain, many schools do not have adequate connectivity to meet current usage needs, much less anticipate future needs. Additionally, these schools are often located in rural and poor counties where students without rapid, reliable internet access in their homes rely on getting that access at school. This digital divide can be detrimental to the students' educational prospects and even to their future employability. The authors remind us that as school librarians we are charged with providing equitable access to library resources and services, and offer several steps that we can take to facilitate that access including developing policies, providing technology coordination, support and leadership in addressing access issues at both the school and district level.

The issue of equitable access is also addressed by Gavigan, Pribesh, and Dickinson who conducted a study of school libraries in North Carolina and Virginia to examine the effects that various school library characteristics might have on accessibility to library resources and services. Some of the factors they looked at were the type of library schedule (i.e., flexible, fixed, or a combination schedule), the number of hours the library was open daily, the number of days per year the library was closed, and the percentage of students eligible for free and reduced price lunch (FRPL). Among their most significant finding was the relationship between poverty and school library accessibility. Schools with the greatest percentage of FRPL students (which is a common indicator of lower SES) were characterized by several factors which correlated with reduced access to library services and resources, including more frequent library closures. The unfortunate effect of this is that students who may most need access to print and technological resources because they do not have them at home, are the ones least likely to have access to such resources at school. The authors emphasize that school librarians must take up the challenge to provide equitable access to information and resources to all students; especially given the research that supports that access to school libraries improves student achievement.

There is little doubt that the preferred mode of information seeking for young adults is digitally via the internet. School counselors who anticipate meeting the social and emotional needs of middle- and high-school students may desire to make appropriate information available through a digital portal. However, school counselors may lack the time or the skills to do so. Dotson-Blake and Dotson detail a possible solution to this dilemma in the form of a collaborative partnership between school librarians and school counselors. They describe a case study in which the skills and strengths of each of the professionals are employed to best advantage. The goal of the partnership is the development of a counseling program website with resources and educational materials focused on positive mental and social/emotional health for teens. In this example, the school librarian leverages her technological and information literacy skills to guide a group of involved students as they locate and evaluate suitable resources both in print and online. Those resources are then vetted by the school counselor; subsequently the school librarian facilitates student development of the website. The result is a counseling website that provides relevant and authoritative materials to students in the digital environment that they prefer.

When the AASL released the *Standards for the 21st-Century Learner* in 2007, there was both anticipation and anxiety among the library community over implementation of the standards, particularly in regard to the dispositions in action. Not only did school librarians wonder how they were going to teach dispositions, there was confusion over exactly what dispositions were. Are dispositions the same as attitudes, habits, or values? How can they be taught? How can they be assessed? Happily, Jones and Bush stepped in to address several of these questions. Their chapter begins with an explanation of how dispositions have come to be regarded as a significant factor in educator effectiveness. Next, they tackle the topics of how dispositions have been defined by prominent educators such as Dewey, how dispositions are developed, and whether dispositions can be taught and measured. The authors emphasize that in order for school librarians to teach dispositions to their students, they must first model those dispositions themselves. Concurrently, library educators must display and model appropriate dispositions to school library candidates. Finally, Jones and Bush challenge the profession to design effective assessments to measure the dispositions of exemplary school librarians with the goal of developing school librarians capable of transforming the profession.

Neuman, who was on the committee responsible for revising the standards, reports on the recent changes in the National Board for Professional Teaching Standards (NBPTS) Library Media Standards. The revisions, the first such since the Standards debuted in 2001, consider the myriad advances in the role of the media profession, especially the leadership component. Although all ten standards underwent modifications to reflect the transformation of the profession, six of them have substantially new content. Neuman summarizes both the changes and the rationale behind them. She concludes by saying that the committee's final step is the revision of the corollary assessment instruments for candidates to use to document their achievement of the revised Library Media Standards.

References

Bunn, A. (2010). Name change from media specialist to school librarian-moving forward? [Web log post]. Retrieved from February 20, 2010, from http://librarygarden.net/2010/02/20/name-change-media-specialist-to-school-librarian/.

Dickinson, G. (2010, May). The true joy in life. *Library Media Connection*, 6. Retrieved from Academic Search Complete database.

Nelson, C. (2010, January 21). School librarian: Is the name change a step backwards? [Web log post]. Retrieved from Techno Tuesday, Cathy Nelson's Professional thoughts at http://blog.cathyjonelson.com/?p=1124.

Staino, R. (2010, January 21). AASL adopts 'school librarian' as official term for the profession. *School Library Journal*. Retrieved from http://www.schoollibraryjournal.com/article/CA6715763.html?industryid=47074.

Culturally Sensitive Learning Practices

Lesley S.J. Farmer

Introduction

Globalization impacts people's lives – and the preparation for those life choices. People are more likely to migrate so that schools have become more diverse. Concurrently, learners are seeking distance education delivery options in order to get the training needed from experts who may reside continents away. In either case, learners bring their cultural experiences and expectations to the educational experience, and interact with others having potentially much different cultural backgrounds, which impact their education significantly. Particularly as Western educational philosophies do not reflect the preponderance of educational approaches worldwide, it behooves teacher librarians to address cultural nuances as they seek to help their students learn optimally.

Background About Culture

Culture may be defined as "the customary beliefs, social forms, and material traits of a racial, religious, or social group" and "the set of shared attitudes, values, goals, and practices that characterizes an institution or organization" (Merriam-Webster, 1985, p. 314). In education, cultural issues apply to the learner, the instructor, the intended learning environment, and the content of learning itself.

L.S.J. Farmer (✉)
CSULB/EdPAC, California State University Long Beach, Long Beach, CA, USA
e-mail: lfarmer@csulb.edu

M. Orey et al. (eds.), *Educational Media and Technology Yearbook: Volume 36, 2011*,
Educational Media and Technology Yearbook 36, DOI 10.1007/978-1-4614-1305-9_14,
© Springer Science+Business Media, LLC 2012

As teacher librarians work in cross-cultural settings, or at the very least work with learners from different cultures, they should strive for cultural competence. Kalyanpur and Harry (1999) list several benchmarks that note progress in this endeavor.

1. *Cultural knowledge.* one becomes familiar with cultural characteristics, history, behaviors, and values of people of another cultural group.
2. *Cultural awareness.* understanding of another culture, changing attitudes about culture, and open flexibility in relating to people of another culture.
3. *Cultural sensitivity.* realization that cultural similarities and differences exist, without assigning relative value to those differences.
4. *Cultural competence.* congruent set of behaviors, attitudes, and policies to enable one to work effectively in cross-cultural situation.
5. *Cultural proficiency.* a way of being that enables people to interact with others who are different from them.

Hofstede's (1980) model of cultural dimensions and Biggs' (1978) 3P model of teaching and learning provide useful frameworks for examining culturally sensitive library instruction implications (*noted in italics*).

- *Power distance.* What is the degree of equality between people? How equitable is the power distribution as defined from low-status people? In low-power distance societies, status is less important. *Power distance affects teacher–student relations. In high-power distance cultures, the teacher is omnipotent, and the student never questions the teacher; conversely, in low-power distance cultures, little hierarchy exists so that teacher and student are considered co-learners with equal status.*
- *Individualism vs. collectivism.* People in individualistic societies tend to belong to several groups, each of which is loosely knit, while collectivist societies tend to have a few, well-defined groups who are highly loyal. In-group refers to a collective in which members are highly interdependent and have a sense of common fate; groups to which they do not belong are out-groups. *Learners and teachers have preconceived attitudes about individual vs. cooperative efforts. In the U.S., individual effort is usually promoted, while in Indian culture, the caste is the central identity.*
- *Masculinity.* To what degree are genders differentiated? Are traditional gendered roles supported in terms of achievement, control, and power? How are women valued relative to men? *In instruction, males in some cultures might be more competitive or need more praise. Some educational roles are sex-linked in some cultures; only males can be doctors and only women can be nurses.*
- *Uncertainty avoidance.* How tolerant is society of uncertainty and ambiguity? Are different options acceptable or are strict rules the norm? *How structured should learning activities be? Does assessment ask for one right answer or does it encourage new answers? Do learning activities focus on accuracy or on different perspectives? In the traditional Chinese culture, students are expected to parrot back the single right answer. In some theocratic societies, dogma is absolute and to be obeyed without question. In contrast, parts of the U.S. culture encourage open-mindedness and intellectual exploration such as in scientific research.*

More specifically, different cultures tend to reinforce different learning styles. For example, collective societies tend to reinforce field-dependent and non-linear learning where the specific location and people present determine the meaning of a concept. In contrast, other cultures emphasize essential truths or step-by-step learning. Instructors need to start a unit by giving the Big Picture, and they provide such learners with more guidance along the way (Chen & Macredie, 2002).

The impact of culture may be analyzed using Biggs' (1978) 3P model of teaching and learning. Presage deals with experiences before learning takes place. This includes learning characteristics, prior knowledge, and experience. Process occurs during learning and concerns learning conditions and activities. Products focus on the outcomes of learning such as assessments, application, and context. Thus, learner experiences are interdependent with situational elements such as teaching factors (e.g., style, institutional procedures, and assessment) and the learning environment (e.g., learning activities and social climate). Biggs also differentiates surface approaches to learning (i.e., reproducing information), deep approaches (thorough understanding), and achievement orientation (i.e., focus on grades). Biggs, Kember, & Leung (2001) emphasize the importance of identifying which factors are universal and which are culturally defined. Most significant are those practices that are imposed as if universal such as outlining a report, that actually reflect specific cultural norms, particularly those of North America; learners outside that teacher-centric culture may feel discounted or under-prepared.

Examination of the learner specifically leads to several contributing cultural factors that can impact teaching effectiveness:

- Language (idioms): native/primary language skills of reading and writing; the quality and quantity of second language experience and skill; formal vs. informal language usage; vocabulary and idiomatic knowledge
- Educational philosophy and experiences: role of education; curriculum and instruction practices; student behavior norms (which might differ from the institution's expectations); learner-specific experiences
- Gender issues: sex-linked educational, career, and workplace expectations/norms that are culturally defined
- Age-linked cultural norms: generation-specific roles and expectations; familial roles and norms; roles and expectations impacted by global/social realities (e.g., digital natives)
- Knowledge of content: transmission of information patterns (e.g., family, academic counseling, libraries); cultural expectations and norms relative to specific disciplines; community needs and practices (e.g., local agricultural economy vs. globalized knowledge economy) (McMahon & Bruce, 2002).

Connecting Learning to the Larger Environment

Learning occurs in a setting, be it physical or virtual, that involves people (peers and instructor), curriculum (content information and resources), and instructional design. Within that environment, learners interact with the content and individuals.

An e-learning environment incorporates technology as a communications and storage vehicle.

Regardless of content, the student population is increasingly diversified in cultural background and experience. All too often, cultural sensitivity is overlooked when designing curriculum and delivery. Not only should teacher librarians be aware of the impact of culture in their instruction, but also they should leverage those cultural differences to provide a richer educational experience.

Teacher librarian instructors of diverse students need to help those learners navigate within the educational culture and their family culture successfully. These skills might include learning social expectations and norms, identifying the cultural assumptions being made about presented (and missing) content, and communicating in socially acceptable ways (e.g., avoiding jargon, understanding social space). For instance, "school" talk might be more formal than discussions at home. At school, females might be taught to speak up but at home be expected to be passively quiet. Furthermore, educational practice itself reflects culturally defined philosophies. For example, a belief in the professor as the all-wise transmitter of knowledge opposes the idea of the instructor as a manager of a learning environment that is co-constructed with students. The student who is used to rote memorization may well feel uncomfortable with inquiry-based learning.

As learners straddle two (or more) cultures, they need to interpret information in light of differing perspectives, and negotiate the relevant application of such information to their daily life. Particularly if the school ethos contradicts familial values, learners might artificially separate those two worlds, try to integrate the two, or reject one set of values. Instructors should take care to respect each student's cultural stance while noting the importance of learning about the social climate to be experienced as a potential employee. Furthermore, teacher librarians would do well to contextualize content in terms of students' local reality or at least build on those realities as students need to assimilate new cultural understandings (McMahon & Bruce, 2002).

In an e-learning environment, technology significantly impacts student learning, and is subject to cultural influence. For instance, learners might have different degrees of access due to cultural attitudes about technology, socially constructed gender role expectations, and socio-economic values. World experience and knowledge impacts learners' ability to locate and evaluate online information. Even social attitudes about language acquisition and attitudes about English can impact online use.

Solutions to Language Problems

Language remains the main means of interacting and communicating, and thus can pose significant problems in culturally sensitive learning. International students may have taken English courses, but that instruction is typically provided by teachers whose primary language is not English. British English (with a British accent) is more likely to be taught than American English, which can also impact the meaning of common terms, such as "bonnet" for car hood. Additionally, the English taught is unlikely to address technical educational vocabulary. On the other hand, as more content is being created in non-English speaking cultures, teacher librarians may encounter more difficulties in evaluating the content's quality.

The following language-related tips, largely from Sarkodie-Manash (2000), apply across the board in instruction across cultures.

- Make the structure of the class explicit.
- In all communication, use plain English and short sentences, and avoid idioms. Rephrase and simplify statements. Define new terms. Use meaningful gestures.
- If using audio files or online speech, speak clearly and slowly without accent.
- Make documents comprehensible through simpler vocabulary and grammar as well as visual cues.
- Use repetition, paraphrasing, and summaries.
- Focus attention on essential vocabulary needed for the specific training or profession. Provide bilingual glossaries and visual references.
- Use visual aids and graphic organizers to help learners understand content organization and relationships.
- Include frequent comprehension checks and clarification questions.
- If you cannot understand a student, do not pretend to.
- If possible, instruct in the learner's primary language (unless learners represent several native languages). Pair students linguistically. Consider providing resources in primary languages. Check the readability of written sources, and locate materials that include visual or aural cues. It should be noted that some images may be unrecognizable, demeaning, or have different meanings to difference cultures.

Technology-based instruction can ameliorate language problems significantly. E-learning tends to be text-based (with some visual support), which enables learners to consult dictionaries and peers to understand concepts. Additionally, asynchronous discussion enables learners to take their time crafting their responses in their primary language and then translating their words with less time stress. The anonymity of online communication can also make females from masculine-dominated cultures feel more comfortable voicing their opinion.

Instructional Design Factors

In the global society, people come into contact with other cultures more frequently and deeply. In some cases, those interactions may be characterized as clashes. Misunderstandings occur because of tacit assumptions and cultural perceptions. Thus, the need for understanding different cultures is more important than ever. Hofstede's (1980) model of cultural differences can aid teacher librarians in creating culturally sensitive learning environments. Domer and Gorman (2006) offer several useful suggestions, which largely apply to all types of learning settings.

Student–Teacher Relations

Learners from high power-distance cultures expect formal, hierarchical relationships with their teachers; in such cultures, the teacher has high status and his judgment should never be questioned by students. To ease their stress in more egalitarian or constructivist courses, teacher librarians can clearly and explicitly define their roles, and work with students to make clear decisions about learning expectations. Personal acknowledgment rituals and relationships can also counterbalance power distance formality (Gurubatham, 2005). They can also tell students the appropriate term of address to use (e.g., Mrs. Ramirez, Mrs. R, Paula). Traditional males may feel uncomfortable having a female teacher librarian, although e-learning environments tend to mitigate this issue. Providing information about the teacher librarian's expertise and status, along with testimonials from high-status males, can further elevate a female librarian's credibility. Students who are shy about asking for help should have several options available: confidential email, intermediation by a course student representative/spokesperson, peer assistance, referrals to resources such as online tutorials. Teacher librarians can pre-emptively help this situation by frequently checking for understanding (e.g., short online quizzes and quick writes) and giving all students immediate feedback.

Topics of Discussion

Teacher librarians should be aware of possible taboo subjects. This issue might emerge in health issues where gendered practices might inhibit practice, such as attitudes towards family planning in cultures where males are expected to make such decisions or are praised for impregnating women. Teacher librarians would do well to consult their peers in relevant countries to find out ahead of time what topics might be sensitive to their learners. Accommodations for alternative topics, resources, or ways of learning should be provided so as to not disadvantage affected learners. In almost all cases, connecting course concepts with real-world context and applications helps all learners, not just field-dependent ones.

Choice of Resources

In most cases, teacher librarians choose the material to be covered in a lesson, or they select in collaboration with classroom teachers. That selection or filtering process may reflect cultural bias that might disadvantage some international students; specific ideas might be supported and other omitted, thus shutting down opposing viewpoints. Even a simple factor of choosing examples reflecting only urban practice might ignore the needs of students working in rural areas. At the least, teacher librarians should enable students to choose from a wide spectrum of reading materials reflecting a variety of perspectives. It should be noted that students tend to find and understand web-based information more quickly when the content is created by designers from their own cultures (Faiola & Matei, 2005). Alternatively, teacher librarians should permit students to seek self-relevant sources. This latter approach might trouble classroom teachers who want to control students' reading materials, which, in itself, reflects a certain cultural value. Likewise, in some cultures, such as China, students typically read only what the instructor chooses, so self-determination of materials can be uncomfortable for them at first. Furthermore, as they seek relevant resources, many non-U.S. students have little experience using school libraries and may hesitate before asking librarians for assistance (U.S. Citizenship and Immigration Services, 2006).

Learner Participation

Again, clear expectations and course norms from the first contact will help reduce learner confusion and distress. If the student population includes a mix of cultures, then a corresponding combination of individual and collaborative activities would be appropriate. Likewise, a mix of cooperative and competitive activities allows learners from different backgrounds to excel at different points. Alternatively, teacher librarians can provide students with options to do work independently or with others. To accommodate learners from collective cultures, teacher librarians may need to initiate discussion or start groups off when introducing problem-based learning; step-by-step guidelines also facilitate field-dependent learners. Web 2.0 technology should also be incorporated in order to provide learners with opportunities to interact with each other, collaborate, and produce creative work for authentic audiences. In any case, the e-learning environment should be safe and comfortable for all learners.

Learning Activities

Probably the best solution for culturally sensitive activities is inclusive of instructional design that accommodates *all* students. Here are some other specific suggestions.

- Some students are not used to self-directed learning. Rather than telling students the answer, the teacher librarian can model the process required to find it.
- Students may be accustomed to rote learning facts, rather than applying skills; teacher librarians can help students apply general principles to a variety of research situations.
- Students might not be used to critically evaluating information; teacher librarians can provide checklists or criteria for students to use in evaluating sources.
- Many students are only interested in what is needed to pass exams (achievement orientation); teacher librarians can emphasize the importance of knowledge and skills for lifelong success as well as immediate career advancement.

Assessment Issues

Culture impacts student performance when information literacy skills are required. In terms of language, even simple tasks such as following directions can disadvantage some students. Some of the measures that can be taken to mitigate cultural discrepancies include: giving shorter tests and recall items rather than tasks that require language and literacy skills (Teresi, Holmes, Ramirez, Gurland, & Lantiqua, 2001), provide accurate translations in those cases where language ability is not the element being tested, provide bilingual glossaries, consider the option of having students demonstrate their skill kinesthetically (e.g., video recording their performance or having a local expert verify their ability).

Teacher librarians also need to make sure that the test is not culturally biased, that is, one cultural group does not outperform others systemically. Bias usually occurs when cultural knowledge is assumed (e.g., use of bidets, knowledge of July 4, eating habits). Images too may have culturally defined meanings or connotations (for example, owls connote different attributes in different cultures). The easiest approach is to check with students via non-test activities about their understanding of textual and visual information.

The writing process is another area of possible cultural misunderstanding. While U.S. students are taught to write sequentially, often relying on an outline, other cultures prefer that writers build arguments starting with a general stance and arriving at the specific issue only at the end, and still other cultures use an argument/counter-argument structure. Therefore, teacher librarians need to focus on the content more than the presentation, or they need to specify how a report is to be written – and provide the support needed for students to succeed in writing in a particular style. Furthermore, non-U.S. cultures sometimes have a different attitude about intellectual property. Many students are not used to crediting their sources, and do not know about citation styles. A blanket punishment for plagiarism is obstructive without explicit instruction and support to help student comply with U.S. copyright laws.

Assessment also needs to take into consideration affective elements. For instance, non-cognitive variables accounted for about a quarter of the variance in grade point averages for African Americans at predominately white universities; at black universities, non-cognitive variables accounted for about 18 percent of grade average variation (Lockett & Harrell, 2003). The author concluded that the relationship between students and faculty influence self-confidence and self-efficacy. Even though e-learning might mitigate such differences in perception, language use in written and oral communication may indicate a person's cultural background, and might influence some party's perceptions either of the instructor or the interaction. Zhang (2000) found that deep understanding correlated significantly with achievement (as opposed to surface reproduction of information), and therefore recommended that instructors assess accordingly.

Technology Issues

On one hand, technology enables learners from around the world to get information at the click of a button. On the other hand, physical and intellectual access to technology remains uneven in different countries. Some areas still lack electricity, and some nations lack a stable Internet infrastructure. While cell phones have become ubiquitous, desktops and software programs may be less common. Hardware still is too costly for many people, and educational institutions may have little equipment. Particularly with the increased use of multimedia, which drains broadband signaling power, learners in developing countries may be severely disadvantaged. Even time zone differences can be a challenge for students who have to log in at 3 am in order to participate in live chat.

Furthermore, learners reflect a vast spectrum of technological experience and expertise. Some millennials may be used to the Internet since childhood, but other peers may still have problems navigating with a mouse. Additionally, learners may have an unrealistic idea of their own technical ability; instant messaging does not constitute technological fluency. The deeper issue of evaluating online information also poses an issue, particularly for learners who are not world-savvy.

Therefore, teacher librarians need to find out what technological access their students have at school and at home, and aim for the lowest common denominator, which might consist of a frameless set of text-based web pages that are accessible via cell phone. In a couple of cases, schools have developed partnerships so that equipment could be loaned to the other country. Application programs should be free and web-based as well, such as Google's suite. Learners should be able to get technical assistance at any time, hopefully, in a language that they can understand. Teacher librarians should also be sure to show learners how to navigate the online training, and use the required technology tools. Additional support may be in the form of a list of online tutorials, tech buddies, local tech center help, and alternative ways to demonstrate competence such as phoning in responses.

One interesting recent development is localization service. Private businesses are making differentiated online documents that will be culturally acceptable at the local level in terms of language, measurement units, geographic representations, gender role, color connotations, and so on. Even metatagging (i.e., describing an item using subject headings, labels, etc.) can be localized to facilitate culturally defined retrieval patterns. "Intelligent" tutoring systems are also being developed to offer different content and media based on the user's demographic profile. While an attractive idea, localization services tend to offer a content-neutral solution, they may lack of deep domain knowledge, and they certainly do not know the learners. So, at best, this service can be used to provide a draft course look, but it needs to be customized by teacher librarians instructing the specific learner.

With the convergence and miniaturization of technology, teacher librarians can leverage emerging technologies engage today's students, and foster active, collaborative learning.

- *Podcasting* and *videocasting* compress audio and video files for portable, flexible consumption. In a study of podcast lectures, Evans (2007) found that adult learners thought podcasts were more useful than textbooks or notetaking for reinforcing learning. English-language learners find 'casts especially attractive because they can review the 'casts repeatedly until the information is well comprehended. Instructors are also designing learning activities that require learners to create their own 'casts to share with their peers or other authentic audiences.
- *Mobile learning, or m-learning* uses handheld devices to help collect observation data and to facilitate quick in-class quizzes to check for understanding. Stripped-down application programs such as word processing and concept mapping enable learners to brainstorm and journal their learning experiences easily, and then share those ideas with their peers. *"Smart" phones* have ratcheted up m-learning because of their many features: two-way communication, text messaging, photo capture, calendaring, calculating, Internet access, online reading, application downloading and operating options, geographic information system (GIS) or global positioning system (GPS) functions, and language support.
- On a grander scale, *virtual worlds* enable learners to experience situated learning in three dimensions, or a facsimile thereof. Visual immersion systems, from head-mounted visual systems to 3D "caves," enable learners to experience a visual simulated environment. These systems can sense the learners' movements, and adjust the visual components accordingly.

Conclusion

The following strategies summarize the key points for teacher librarians to follow in designing culturally sensitive learning.

- Provide clear information and expectations about learning activities, including content, technical aspects, procedures, participation, assessment, and available support.
- Get to know the students, and help them learn about each other. Obtain and share demographic information. Provide opportunities for students to share their perspectives and experiences, thus enriching curriculum content.
- Create a positive learning climate. Make learning safe and comfortable so that students who are not used to voicing opinions or do not want to take intellectual risks will be supported in their efforts.
- Structure learning for meaning. Bring in cultural differences rather than masking them. Help students to connect training content to their own environments.
- Provide access to resources, and give students choices about the types of resources to use. Offer instruction or other kinds of support if students are not used to locating resources independently.
- Provide support and scaffolding for students as needed: online tutorials, local expertise, peer assistants, translation tools, technical help, time management, etc.

- Give students time to process and evaluate information. Foster critical thinking by modeling analytical information processing.
- Help students clarify and justify their understanding. Encourage study groups and study buddies as a way to refine their knowledge.
- Give timely and specific feedback throughout instruction.
- Help students self-monitor and express their learning. Give them opportunities to demonstrate competencies in several ways: written, visual, orally.

In any case, in order to provide meaningful and culturally sensitive learning experiences, both teacher librarians and their students need to become culturally competent: open to learning about other cultures and sharing one's own culture, able to change personal perspectives, and able to communicate effectively across cultures (Liaw, 2006).

Ideally, teacher librarians around the world should work more closely with each other and their institutions in order to provide culturally sensitive content and instructional design. Imagine a team of teacher librarians offering anytime training around the globe to learners as they need the information and skills. Now that would signal true global, culturally proficient information literacy.

References

Biggs, J. (1978). Individual and group differences in study processes. *British Journal of Educational Psychology, 48*, 266–279.

Biggs, J., Kember, D., & Leung, D. (2001). The revised 2-factor study process questionnaire R-SP2-2 F. *British Journal of Educational Research, 71*, 133–149.

Chen, S., & Macredie, R. (2002). Cognitive styles and hypermedia navigation: Development of a learning model. *Journal of the American Society for Information Science and Technology, 53*(1), 3–15.

Domer, D., & Gorman, G. (2006). Information literacy education in Asian developing countries: Cultural factors affecting curriculum development and programme delivery. *IFLA Journal, 32*(4), 281–293.

Evans, C. (2007). The effectiveness of m-learning in the form of podcast revision lecturers in higher education. *Computers and Education, 50*, 491–498.

Faiola, A., & Fatei, S. (2005). Cultural cognitive style and web design. *Journal of Computer-Mediated Communication, 11*(1). Retrieved February 13, 2010, from http://jcmc.indiana.edu/vol11/faiola.html.

Gurubatham, M. (2005). Cognition, culture and effective e-praxis guiding principles. In P. Nicholson et al. (Eds.), *E-training practices for professional organizations* (pp. 121–128). Boston: Kluwer Academic Publishers.

Hofstede, J. (1980). *Culture's consequences: International differences in work-related values.* Newbury Park, CA: Sage Publications.

Kalyanpur, M., & Harry, B. (1999). *Culture in special education: Building a posture of reciprocity in parent-professional relationships.* Baltimore: Paul Bookes.

Liaw, S. (2006). E-learning and the development of intercultural competence. *Language Learning and Technology, 10*(3), 49–64.

Lockett, C., & Harrell, J. (2003). Racial identity, self-esteem, and academic achievement. *Journal of Black Psychology, 29*(3), 325–336.

McMahon, C., & Bruce, C. (2002). Information literacy needs of local staff in cross-cultural development projects. *Journal of International Development, 14*(1), 113–137.

Sarkodie-Manash, K. (Ed.). (2000). *Reference services for the adult learner*. New York: Haworth Press.

Teresi, J., Holmes, D., Ramirez, M., Gurland, B., & Lantiqua, R. (2001). Performance of cognitive tests among different racial/ethnic and education groups: Findings of differential item functioning and possible item bias. *Journal of Mental Health & Aging, 7*(1), 79–89.

U.S. Citizenship and Immigration Services. (2006). *Library services to immigrants: A report on current practices*. Washington, DC: U.S. Citizenship and Immigration Services.

Webster's ninth new collegiate dictionary. (1985). Springfield, MA: Merriam-Webster.

Zhang, L. F. (2000). University students' learning approaches in three cultures. *Journal of Psychology, 134*(1), 37–56.

In the District and on the Desktop: School Libraries as Essential Elements of Effective Broadband Use in Schools

Nancy Everhart and Marcia Mardis

Introduction

Internet use has increased dramatically in schools since the adoption of the federal E-Rate connectivity assistance program 10 years ago. School administrators estimate that their bandwidth needs will multiply five times in the upcoming 5 years; other researchers have estimated that those needs will likely reflect nine times the current usage (Greaves & Hayes, 2008).

The upswing in demand is not surprising since infusing robust broadband throughout the learning process has garnered some impressive results:

- Improved student achievement, attendance, and graduation rates, and decreased dropout rates
- Gains on high-stakes tests that enable schools to meet AYP (Adequate Yearly Progress) and performance benchmarks under No Child Left Behind
- Heightened school efficiency, productivity, and decision-making
- Advances in teachers meeting state-mandated curriculum requirements
- Improved student learning skills
- Assistance in meeting the needs of all students, including those with special needs
- Promotion of equity and access
- Improved workforce skills
- Increased parent involvement (Ed Tech Action Network, 2008)

N. Everhart, Ph.D. (✉) • M. Mardis, Ed.D.
Partnerships for Advancing Library Media (PALM) Center, School of Library and Information Studies, College of Communication & Information, The Florida State University, 106 Collegiate Way, Tallahassee, FL 32306-2100, USA
e-mail: everhart@fsu.edu; mardis@fsu.edu

M. Orey et al. (eds.), *Educational Media and Technology Yearbook: Volume 36, 2011*,   173
Educational Media and Technology Yearbook 36, DOI 10.1007/978-1-4614-1305-9_15,
© Springer Science+Business Media, LLC 2012

If all students are to realize these outcomes, equitable high-speed Internet and broadband access is critical. Although national statistics boast almost 98% connectivity in U.S. schools, myriad problems prevent educators and learners from receiving the maximum benefit of broadband connectivity (National Center for Technology Innovation, 2008).

Broadband Connectivity Is Important for Schools

For Americans to engage in a global information society, it is critical that they have access to high-speed, high-bandwidth Internet, meaning broadband. The *Free Press* has called broadband "the essential communications infrastructure of the 21st century" (Turner, 2009, p. 83). In many communities, public libraries and schools provide the only free public Internet and computer access to millions of Americans. For public schools to remain vital community Internet access points, they need to be connected to high-speed broadband (at least 100 Mbps).

Representatives from the National Telecommunications and Information Administration (NTIA) have stated that public schools and libraries have a critical role to fill in Internet access. In the 1995 report, *Falling Through the Net*, NTIA concluded that "[C]onnectivity to…households will not occur instantaneously; rather, there is a pivotal role to be assumed in the new electronic age by the traditional providers of information access for the general public – the public schools and libraries" (National Telecommunications & Information Administration [NTIA], 2000, p. 17).

In addition to providing free public access to computers and the Internet, schools can serve as anchor tenants on broadband networks, providing the impetus for Internet service providers (ISPs) to build networks into American communities. Indeed, studies have demonstrated the symbiotic relationship between home and school Internet access: a fast connection at home raises the demand for more bandwidth at school and vice versa. Once a local school has gained access to higher connectivity speeds and greater bandwidth, that access infrastructure also has been brought into the community where last-mile connections can expand this high-speed Internet into private homes and businesses (Charytan et al., 2009; Gupta, Berejka, Griffin, & Boyd, 2009; Oblinger, Van Houweling, & Semer, 2009; Sheketoff, 2009).

Despite the known benefits of broadband Internet access, most district administrators feel that the cost of bandwidth is quickly outstripping their available financial resources. In their Greaves & Hayes, 2008 report, educational researchers from The Greaves Group and The Hayes Connection asked school administrators in the United States if they anticipated problems with affording bandwidth. Though many administrators reported that the availability of bandwidth was a concern, most administrators surveyed felt that bandwidth cost was a more pressing challenge Greaves & Hayes, 2008 (Fig. 1).

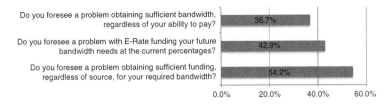

Fig. 1 School administrators' responses to the question, "Do you foresee problems with band-width funding?" (ADS, 2008, p. 111)

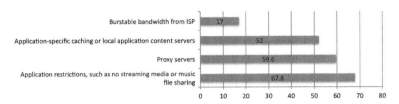

Fig. 2 Frequency of bandwidth leverage techniques used as reported by district technology staff (ADS, 2008, p. 110)

Connectivity speeds are disparate, and often desperate, situations in many public schools. Most often, the slowest bandwidth speeds are in rural and poor counties where rapid, reliable access to web-based learning resources benefits students without access and resource alternatives.

To address capacity limitations, many school technology staff leverage capacity through various means. Some of these methods involve copying Internet-hosted files and data to local servers, but some of these means are restrictions on types of activities and/or times during which they can be conducted. Figure 2 illustrates the prevalence of various bandwidth control measures.

Even more alarming is the realization that should bandwidth management techniques fail and the Internet connection become overloaded and go down, only 20% of public school districts have a backup Internet connection (Gray & Lewis, 2009).

Insufficient Broadband Impacts Learning Environments

In so many ways, inadequate bandwidth shapes the quality of learning. Even when all members of a school community are skilled in teaching with digital technologies and students are excited about using a variety of technologies to learn, a lack of bandwidth can bring all innovation to a halt.

In this scenario, broadband connectivity can enrich learning for students:

In Ms. Sanchez's third-grade classroom, technology is an integral part of the learning process. Ms. Sanchez begins the school day by playing a streaming video from the Internet to engage students and introduce the topic of weather. After a class discussion, she explains that to learn about the weather from various regions of the United States she has arranged a Skype video conference with three other third-grade classes around the country to share and discuss weather in their area. As a part of this project Ms. Sanchez's students will create a presentation on the weather in their state to share with students across the country. Students are split up into groups according to the seasons of weather in their state and begin researching online. Before the online presentation to the other classes, students use digital cameras to take pictures outside, upload them to Flickr, and create a slideshow to share with the students in the other states as a part of their presentation.

With robust bandwidth, Ms. Sanchez is able to engage all of the learners in her classroom. She excites the visual learners with video and digital photography; engages the auditory learners with Skype; and enhances all learners' abilities to use technology appropriate for learning, synthesis, and connecting to the world beyond the classroom. The resources she uses are web-based and free, but depend on reliable, high-speed access to the Internet.

In contrast, consider this scenario:

In Mr. Davis' third-grade classroom the Internet connection is slow and unpredictable. Mr. Davis would like to use the Internet more in his teaching and with his students, but has found that it cannot be relied upon. Mr. Davis begins the school day by asking students to follow along in their textbook as he reads the chapter about weather. He explains that they will be working on a project about weather in different regions around the country. Each group researches facts about the weather in their region and creates a visual aid to present to the class and students work in groups using encyclopedias, almanacs, and other nonfiction books to learn about the weather in their areas. One student mentions that his book does not have pictures and seems out of date. Children fight over volumes of the encyclopedia and complain that the project is too hard to complete with so few books. Many students grumble about their better computers and Internet access at home.

Without reliable Internet access, Mr. Davis struggles to engage students in the relevance of the project and allow them to connect the topic of weather to phenomena outside of the school. He cannot rely on out-of-date and insufficient book sources, so he has lost vital instructional impetus and student focus. The lesson dissolves into behavior issues and leaves the children discouraged.

These two scenarios represent just a few of the effects broadband investment can have on learners; broadband impacts students, teachers, administrators, and equity. The provocative report *High-Speed Broadband Access for All Kids: Breaking through the Barriers* (State Educational Technology Directors Association [SETDA], 2008) frames the issues affecting these four key groups and emphasizes the need to focus on broadband in schools.

Issue 1

Students need high-speed broadband access in their schools to take advantage of a wide range of new and rich educational tools and resources available for anytime, anywhere learning.

Innovative learning technologies have become more diverse and more bandwidth intensive. Activities such as podcasting, media streaming, and videoconferencing require a robust network. For example, a connectivity-rich district, Palm Beach County, Florida, uses a multitude of web-based, bandwidth-intensive applications to support curricular goals, career exploration, research, and science learning. The district's lists of "Learning Tools" for learners in each grade span consists of a range of web-based and bandwidth intensive media.

Other connectivity-rich districts use web-based applications to differentiate learning in Alaska; engage English Language Learners in California; provide opportunities not previously available in rural Hawaii and Maine and poor communities in Nevada; use video to increase parent participation in Kentucky; support mathematics learning in West Virginia, diagnose and remediate reading difficulties in Texas, and support children with special education needs in Massachusetts. As the number of English Language Learners and children with Individualized Education Plans (IEPs) continues to increase, districts are turning to online solutions to serve these students (Education & Libraries Networks Coalition [EdLiNC], 2007). The barriers to all districts using applications to support these pressing needs are not necessarily the finances to subscribe to or purchase the services; rather, all too often, the district's network and connectivity cannot support intensive usage (Project & PASCO Scientific, 2008).

This situation can exact a toll on teachers' abilities to prepare students for the most essential elements of learning as one teacher described:

> *It makes no sense to me that so much money is poured into technology and online programs for our students yet it seems our server is often not capable of handling our district's usage. Our school often has issues with slow Internet speed even though we supposedly have a "fast" connection. Teachers use online programs such as Accelerated Reader, Compass Odyssey, [and] Discovery Streaming daily during reading and math center time or during instruction. We have grown to rely on these programs to supplement our curriculum. We even cite these programs as interventions for low achieving students. They should be supported by a server/Internet connection that is the most reliable.*
>
> –Third-Grade Teacher, Polk County, Florida

A lack of access to web-based learning applications and reliable network access has the effect of stifling technology use in the classroom overall. In 2009, 17% of teachers in the U.S. are not interested in using technology in the classroom, partially because only 58% of them have access to the skills and tools they need to effective integrate technology into their teaching and confidently facilitate student use of it (Gray & Lewis, 2009).

When students have access to technology tools mediated by robust bandwidth, powerful learning occurs. Across the country, the possibilities afforded to in-person and online learning enabled by fast, reliable networks and applications are boundless. In addition to using bandwidth-intensive applications to conduct research, manage information, and create learning products, online learning provides access to high-school courses for credit recovery, scheduling conflicts, AP courses, and other reasons (Project Tomorrow, 2010; Sloan Consortium, 2009). Since its debut less than a decade ago, high-school student enrollment in online courses has grown exponentially. As children enter high school with a greater variety of learning wants, needs, and challenges, demand for options and flexibility with completion will only continue to grow. A recent report from Project Tomorrow warns that bandwidth limitations not only decrease the options for student learning within the classroom, a lack of high-speed connectivity may also mean the difference between high-school completion or college entry (Project Tomorrow, 2010).

Issue 2

Teachers need high-speed broadband access for professional development, and engaging in professional learning communities as well as accessing new educational resources such as curriculum cadres and education portals.

Ensuring that children have access to high-speed connectivity in school is merely a part of improving their learning experiences. Teachers who have the up-to-date content knowledge and pedagogical strategies necessary to create an equitable learning environment for all children must facilitate these experiences.

A substantial and well-established body of research conducted across the country has demonstrated that when teachers are not comfortable integrating new techniques and tools in their practice, they tend to avoid embracing innovation (Adams & Krockover, 1997; Apple & Jungck, 1992; BellSouth Foundation, 2003; Bolliger, 2006; Cooper & Bull, 1997; Cornelius-White, 2007; Engel & Randall, 2009; Smerdon et al., 2000; Trotter, 1999; Willis & Mehlinger, 1996; Zeichner & Tabachnick, 1981). Indeed, many teachers do not exit their preservice education with technology fluency (Gibson, 2009), so it is essential that their first experiences with it in the classroom be seamless and support rapid integration into their teaching. Unfortunately, for students in high needs urban and rural schools, bandwidth paucity is often coupled with low levels of teacher skill and preparedness to make best use of broadband (Chapman, Masters, & Pedulla, 2009).

Therefore, it is essential that any strategy to increase connectivity in schools contain a component that encourages administrators to ensure that all teachers have access to professional learning opportunities. Teacher resources like education portals deliver courses and provide discussion forums for educators. In addition to professional development resources, most universities offer online degrees and coursework in library and information science, technology integration, reading instruction, and a variety of advanced educational opportunities. All of this professional learning is best delivered through robust, high-speed connectivity (Hansen & Zambo, 2009).

Yet, even the most excited and engaged children and innovative and technology-savvy teachers cannot change the bandwidth environments in their schools. Administrators must see the need to invest in high-speed connectivity.

Issue 3

Administrators need high-speed broadband access to conduct online assessments and to access data for effective decision-making.

School administrators tend to have a high degree of awareness about the importance of broadband, but relatively little awareness of the specifics of the implementation landscapes in their schools and classrooms. Most administrators do not know what their teachers and students are unable to do as a result of inadequate bandwidth and restrictive management policies (Anderson & Christiansen, 2006). Yet, administrators carry a lot of responsibility in the ground-level implementation bandwidth. Among their priorities should be ensuring that student data are accurate and secure, and that parents have mechanisms to communicate with teachers and school administrators.

In addition to facilitating a climate of constant professional improvement, district and building-level administrators must monitor student achievement and ensure that students are assessed in a timely and accurate fashion. Many of the tools that school administrators need to accomplish important tasks like tracking enrollment, IEP, health, and student achievement data are available online and require secure, reliable, robust network infrastructure. In 2009, 100% of public school districts in the United States reported keeping student data in online systems (Gray & Lewis, 2009).

While many parents remain skeptical about the use of mobile devices and social networking in student learning, 90% of the parents surveyed as part of Project Tomorrow's *Speak Up 2009* survey reported that school websites, blogs, and other digital means of getting school news, achievement data, and other school-related information were very important (Project Tomorrow, 2010). In order to keep parents involved with and informed about their children's education, administrators must ensure that all of the school's bandwidth-mediated channels be functional, dynamic, and easy to access.

Children experience a wide variety of connectivity situations depending on their geographical locations and family financial situations. Rural areas are hit hardest by a lack of connectivity, and this rural-to-urban variation has perpetuated a digital divide that once fell solely along economic lines (Gray & Lewis, 2009). About half of the middle-school and high-school students surveyed as part of Project Tomorrow's *Speak Up 2009* felt that their Internet access at school needed to be expanded (Project Tomorrow, 2010). Unfortunately, a lack of bandwidth tends to disproportionately affect the most diverse schools and the highest-need students (Hsu, 2009);

less than half of schools with a large percentage of students in poverty or located in rural areas reported district-wide bandwidth speeds of T1, T3, or district fiber, thus meeting broadband standards (Gray & Lewis, 2009).

Students in U.S. schools expect bandwidth to support their learning needs whether they are in school or out. In many instances, even when bandwidth might be adequate to support the school's teaching and administrative uses, it falls short of supporting student-led applications. In this instance, students disengage from school as a source of learning they feel is relevant, and a digital disconnect occurs. Middle-school and high-school students overwhelmingly prefer digital media and applications for test preparation and taking, completing assignments, performing research, and learning classroom concepts through other means (Project Tomorrow, 2010). However, student point to the constant hindrance of school network filtering software in their learning experiences (Project & PASCO Scientific, 2008) and a lack of school-provided information about virtual and informal learning opportunities as major barriers to their further use of the Internet in their own educations. As a result, students are seeing school as an increasingly irrelevant source of the kinds of learning in which they feel valuable (Project Tomorrow).

The toll of inadequate bandwidth is just not in stifling student enthusiasm for learning in school, but also their exposure to learning applications delivered over robust bandwidth that are essential to their future careers. As the National Science Board stated in 2007, "Jobs in the 21st century…will increasingly demand a technologically literate workforce…all students must…be full and active participants in our increasingly technology-based democracy" (National Science Board, 2007, p. 22). Denying student adequate bandwidth not only impacts their learning during their school years, it has the potential to shape the rest of their lives.

Going the Last Mile for Broadband in Schools

A solution to these situations is on-site support to streamline and enable effective use of broadband-enabled technology. For most schools, the school librarian can expertly direct this "last mile" implementation in broadband access, skill, policy, and motivation.

In their roles as school leaders, school librarians provide tech coordination, support, and leadership necessary to address access issues from desktop to district. As one of the only faculty members who works across curriculum areas and grade levels, the school librarian has unique knowledge of classroom activities throughout the schools and places in which technology would enhance learning. Moreover, it is the school librarian who often provides desktop-level technology support and liaises with district-level technology staff to identify the needs of teachers and students.

The school librarian's role encompasses integrating technology into the teaching and learning process for both teachers and students. School librarians develop and facilitate professional development with technology equipment and instructional resources to help teachers make the best use of the district's investments in these areas.

The school librarian also uses the principles of *Standards for the 21st Century Student Learner* (AASL, 2007) to help teachers bring new technology, interdisciplinary skills, and learning resources to students through class instruction and one-on-one learning. Such standards highlight the importance of integrating technology within schools and reinforce the institutional roles played by school librarian at the K-12 level in facilitating high levels of overall student educational achievement. Students see the school library as a digitally enriched place where information can be located and used, projects can be designed and created, and knowledge can be expressed within and beyond school walls. The school librarian is often the guide to these technology-mediated experiences and ensures that students are learning essential skills and dispositions of twenty-first-century learners.

Because the school librarian sees the use of technology and connectivity at both the desktop and district levels and has knowledge of not only the issues inherent in instructional integration but also technology infrastructure, this person is in a unique position to anticipate and articulate needs for policy creation and revision. Experienced in developing policies for the school library, the school librarian is knowledgeable about ensuring equal and safe access to learning for all members of the school community in policies that support the district's mission and goals.

Finally, because school librarians connect work across grades and subjects, they have the ability to help students and teachers make interdisciplinary connections that increase the relevance of classroom content. They also have the resources, technology, and knowledge to ensure that learning is appropriately infused with inspiring techniques and ideas that motivate learning and teaching. School librarians know when simulations or other learning objects may be able to express a concept in a more interesting or direct fashion and engage student interest. School librarians also know when the creation of a digital video, podcast, or mash-up might illustrate student learning in a way that will be exciting to create and compelling to experience. Table 1 depicts the ways in which school librarians are very involved in supporting effective use of broadband in all areas in all of their roles to education stakeholders.

Concluding Thoughts and Recommendations

The current draft of the National Educational Technology Plan, *Transforming American education: Learning powered by technology* (Office of Educational Technology, 2010), challenges all stakeholders to work to ensure that educators and students:

- …have engaging and empowering learning experiences both in and outside of school that prepare them to be active, creative, knowledgeable, and ethical participants in our globally networked society (p. 9)
- …leverage the power of technology to measure what matters and use assessment data for continuous improvement (p. 25)

Table 1 School librarian leadership roles as they pertain to the four areas of broadband implementation in schools

	Teacher	Instructional partner	Resource specialist	Program leader	Even further
Access	• Promote awareness of Web 2.0 and other broadband-enabled applications available in the school and school library • Support e-portfolio creation by students	• Co-plan, co-teach, and co-assess assignments that make effective use of broadband-enabled applications and digital resources • Ensure equal access for all students, subject areas, and grade levels via curriculum mapping and sharing connections and overlap with teachers • Develop unique electronic resources to supplement curriculum	• Maintain school library website to allow 24–7 access to catalog and databases from home and other locations • Locate sources of free, downloadable digital video, learning objects and e-books to integrate objects into catalog • Correlate physical and digital resources to school textbook series in OPAC	• Determine match between desktop and district connectivity speeds as well as desktop computer adequacy as part of technology planning process • Maintain extended hours in the school library • Facilitate the integration of online course offerings • Serve as an advocate for student access • Develop partnerships to obtain funding and free resources	• Use RSS and push technologies to make teachers aware of new learning resources • Help teachers to develop and tailor online learning options • Design and facilitate online interactions with students, faculty and experts in remote locations
Skill	• Design professional development using latest research about professional development for technology • Facilitate after school clubs for students to create media and participate in online learning experiences	• Co-teach aspects of revamped lessons that include digital resources, broadband applications, and 21st Century Skills • Provide support and professional development for integration of streaming video • Serve as a model for broadband enabled applications in your own instruction	• Collect a variety of tutorials and just-in-time PD resources • Work with student assistants to create step-by-step "job aids" for innovative technology activities like video creation	• Survey teachers on professional development needs • Seek own professional development for network administration and new application use • Educate parents on copyright, safety, and implications of broadband	• Promote a collection of "just in time" professional learning digital videos and resources • Incorporate digital media into school television production
Policy	• Educate students and teachers on capacity limitations, copyright and safety implications of broadband applications • Promote digital citizenship	• Collect information about instructional events that make use of broadband and present in annual or quarterly reports to administration and school board • Participate on technology-planning committees that make decisions about bandwidth, equipment, and resources	• Ensure that collection policy pertains to collecting and describing digital resources • Develop Acceptable Use Policies that include Web 2.0 applications	• Determine future bandwidth-intensive application needs and communicate those to district personnel • Review compatibility between filtering policies and use of bandwidth-intensive applications	• Perform ongoing measurements of policy impact and adjust on an ongoing basis
Motivation	• Promote Web 2.0 applications that make good use of bandwidth and are engaging for learners	• Share co-teaching successes with digital resources and broadband applications with other teachers • Facilitate digital field trips	• Create an online repository of student-created digital work • Set up stations in the library for student creations	• Share research on student learning with technology • Collect and share school-based data on student success with technology	• Facilitate an online community for student learners to share ideas and projects

- …be supported individually and in teams by technology that connects them to data, content, resources, expertise, and learning experiences that can empower and inspire them to provide more effective teaching for all learners (p. 37)
- …have access to a comprehensive infrastructure for learning when and where they need it (p. 51)

And finally, that "[o]ur education system at all levels…redesign processes and structures to take advantage of the power of technology to improve learning outcomes while making more efficient use of time, money, and staff." (Office of Educational Technology, 2010, p. 63). Essential to realizing this vision for national technology expertise is the connectivity to ensure that all applications perform smoothly and seamlessly integrate into the learning experience.

Network connectivity opens up a wealth of possibilities to K-12 educators. While it has the potential to result in fundamental changes in teaching methods, it can definitely be used to enhance already effective teaching methods.

However, schools must have confidence in their network infrastructure before network connectivity will be integrated into the classroom. Networks must be reliable and quick; and, if they do not function as expected and technical support is not readily available, then teachers will not use them. Last mile support is essential and all stakeholders must work together to address the main issues facing the improvement of broadband in schools. Table 2 includes some possible approaches to and actors for addressing the main issues facing broadband in schools in light of these six recommendations:

1. Develop a Return-on-Investment (ROI) calculator so that administrators can easily see the benefits of broadband investment.
2. Assemble a national advisory panel of "last mile" personnel including school librarians, school administrators, and technology personnel to interface with state-level educational technology policymakers.
3. Undertake a vigorous and thorough measurement of current bandwidth capacities and applications at the classroom level.
4. Collect quantitative and qualitative data about the impact of broadband on student learning.
5. Survey educators on a state-by-state about their skills with and needs for broadband.
6. Select exemplar schools for in-depth professional development, classroom support, and student achievement study.

All schools face challenges to the integration of broadband in teaching and learning in the areas of access, skills, policy, and motivation. While it is possible for a school to be connectivity-rich but integration-poor; conversely a school can experience the thwarting effect of inadequate connectivity on instructional innovation. School librarians have a vital role to play in helping broadband and school technology work together to maximize teaching and learning for all education stakeholders.

Table 2 Recommended actors and actions for issues facing broadband in schools

Issue	Actor	Related recommendations
Issue 1: Students need high-speed broadband to access in their schools to take advantage of a wide range of new and rich educational resources available for anytime, anywhere learning	Researchers School librarians Teachers Students	• Undertake a vigorous and thorough measurement of current bandwidth capacities and applications *at the classroom level* • Select exemplar schools for in-depth professional development, classroom support, and student achievement study
Issue 2: Teachers need high-speed broadband access for professional development and engaging in professional learning communities as well as accessing new educational resources	Researchers School librarians Teachers Students	• Survey educators about their skills with and needs for broadband • Select exemplar schools for in-depth professional development, classroom support, and student achievement study
Issue 3: Administrators need high-speed broadband to conduct online assessments and access data for effective decision-making	Researchers Administrators	• Develop a Return-on-Investment (ROI) calculator so that administrators can easily see the benefits of broadband investment • Collect quantitative and qualitative data about the impact of broadband on student learning
Issue 4: Students need high-speed broadband to overcome the digital divide in rural areas	Researchers School librarians Teachers Students	• Assemble an advisory panel of "last mile" personnel including school librarians, school administrators, and technology personnel to interface with state-level educational technology policymakers • Collect quantitative and qualitative data about the impact of broadband on student learning

Acknowledgments Many thanks Dr. Charles McClure, Lauren Mandel, Melissa Johnston and Daniella Smith for their contributions to this chapter.

References

AASL. (2007, November 17). Standards for the 21st-Century Learner. Retrieved January 1, 2008, from http://www.ala.org/ala/aasl/aaslproftools/learningstandards/standards.cfm.

Adams, P. E., & Krockover, G. H. (1997). Concerns and perceptions of beginning secondary science and mathematics teachers. *Science Education, 81*, 29–50.

Anderson, T., & Christiansen, J. (2006). Perceptions on the ground: Principals' perception of government interventions in high-speed educational networking. *Electronic Journal for the Integration of Technology in Education, 5*, 3–16.

Apple, M. W., & Jungck, S. (1992). You don't have to be a teacher to teach this unit: Teaching, technology and control in the classroom. In A. Hargreaves & M. G. Fullan (Eds.), *Understanding teacher development* (pp. 20–42). New York: Teachers College.

BellSouth Foundation. (2003). *The growing technology gap between schools and students: Findings from the bellsouth power to teach program.* Retrieved February 20, 2004, from http://www.bellsouthfoundation.org/pdfs/pttreport03.pdf.

Bolliger, D. U. (2006). Creating constructivist learning environments. In M. Orey, V. J. McClendon, & R. M. Branch (Eds.), *Educational and media technology yearbook 2006.* Westport, CT: Libraries Unlimited.

Chapman, L., Masters, J., & Pedulla, J. (2009). *Do digital divisions still persist in our schools? Access to technology and technical skills of teachers in high-needs schools.* Paper presented at the World conference on e-learning in corporate, government, healthcare, and higher education (E-LEARN) 2009, Vancouver, Canada.

Charytan, L. R., Zachary, H. M., DeVries, W. T., Sherwood, A. H., Zinman, J. S., & Phillips, G. L. (2009). Comments of AT&T Inc. before the Federal Communications Commission in the matter of a national broadband plan for our future. Retrieved June 15, 2009, from http://fjallfoss.fcc.gov/prod/ecfs/retrieve.cgi?native-or-pdf=pdf&id=6520220047.

Cooper, J. M., & Bull, G. L. (1997). Technology and teacher education: PAST practice and recommended directions. *Action in Teacher Education, XIX*(2), 97–106.

Cornelius-White, J. (2007). Learner-centered teacher-student relationships are effective: A meta-analysis. *Review of Educational Research, 77*(1), 113–143.

Ed Tech Action Network. (2008). Why technology in schools? Retrieved July 6, 2009, from http://www.edtechactionnetwork.org/why-technology-in-schools.

Education and Libraries Networks Coalition [EdLiNC]. (2007). E-rate: 10 years of connecting kids and community. Retrieved March 22, 2010, from http://www.edlinc.org/pdf/NCTETReport_212.pdf.

Engel, S., & Randall, K. (2009). How teachers respond the children's inquiry. *American Educational Research Journal, 46*(1), 183–202.

Gibson, S. (2009). *Are our preservice teachers prepared to teach in a digital age?* Paper presented at the proceedings of World conference on e-learning in corporate, government, healthcare, and higher education (E-LEARN) 2009, Vancouver, Canada.

Gray, L., & Lewis, L. (2009). *Educational technology in public school districts: Fall 2008 (First Look) (No. NCES 2010003).* Washington, DC: National Center for Education Statistics [NCES].

Greaves, T. W., & Hayes, J. (2008). America's Digital Schools 2008: Six trends to watch. Shelton, CT: Market Data Research [MDR].

Gupta, A., Berejka, M., Griffin, T., & Boyd, P. (2009). Comments of Microsoft Corporation before the Federal Communications Commission in the matter of a national broadband plan for our future. Retrieved June 15, 2009, from http://fjallfoss.fcc.gov/prod/ecfs/retrieve.cgi?native-or-pdf=pdf&id=6520220228.

Hansen, C., & Zambo, R. (2009). *Increasing teacher efficacy through technology-based professional development.* Paper presented at the World Conference on E-Learning in Corporate, Government, Healthcare, and Higher Education 2009, Vancouver, Canada.

Hsu, H.-Y. (2009). *Preparing teachers to teach literacy to diverse students.* Paper presented at the World Conference on E-Learning in Corporate, Government, Healthcare, and Higher Education 2009, Vancouver, Canada.

National Center for Technology Innovation. (2008). Need for high-speed broadband in schools. Retrieved July 2, 2009, from http://www.nationaltechcenter.org/index.php/2008/06/19/need-for-broadband-in-schools/.

National Science Board. (2007). A national action plan for addressing the critical needs of the U.S. science, technology, engineering, and mathematics education system. Retrieved January 10, 2010, from http://www.nsf.gov/nsb/documents/2007/stem_action.pdf.

National Telecommunications and Information Administration [NTIA]. (2000). Falling through the net: Toward digital inclusion. Retrieved April 10, 2009, from http://www.ntia.doc.gov/ntiahome/fttn00/falling.htm.

Oblinger, D., Van Houweling, D., & Semer, J. (2009). Comments by EDUCAUSE, Internet2 and ACUTA before the Federal Communications Commission in the matter of a national broadband plan for our future. Retrieved June 15, 2009, from http://net.educause.edu/ir/library/pdf/EPO0917.pdf.

Office of Educational Technology. (2010). *Transforming American education: Learning powered by technology. Draft national educational technology plan 2010.* Washington, DC: U.S. Department of Education.

Project Tomorrow. (2010, March). Speak Up 2009: Creating our future: Students speak up about their vision for 21st learning. Retrieved April 10, 2010, from http://www.tomorrow.org/speakup/pdfs/SUNationalFindings2009.pdf.

Project Tomorrow, & PASCO Scientific. (2008, July). Inspiring the next generation of innovators: Students, parents, and educators speak up about science education. Retrieved April 1, 2010, from http://www.tomorrow.org/speakup/pdfs/Inspiring_the_next_generation_of_innovators.pdf.

Sheketoff, E. (2009). Stimulate your library: How libraries can benefit from the American Recovery and Reinvestment Act. Retrieved May 6, 2009, from http://www.ala.org/ala/alaonline/resources/selectedarticles/arrastimulus.cfm.

Sloan Consortium. (2009). K-12 online learning: A 2008 follow-up of the survey of U.S. school district administrators. Retrieved from http://www.sloanconsortium.org/publications/survey/pdf/k-12_online_learning_2008.pdf.

Smerdon, B., Cronen, S., Lanahan, L., Anderson, J., Iannotti, N., & Angeles, J. (2000). *Teachers' tools for the 21st century: A report on teachers' use of technology.* Washington, DC: National Center for Educational Statistics, U.S. Department of Education.

State Educational Technology Directors Association [SETDA]. (2008). High-speed broadband access for all kids: Breaking through the barriers. Retrieved from http://www.setda.org/c/document_library/get_file?folderId=270&name=DLFE-211.pdf.

Trotter, A. (1999). Preparing teachers for the digital age. *Education Week, 19*, 37–43.

Turner, S. D. (2009). Dismantling digital deregulation: Toward a national broadband strategy. Retrieved May 13, 2009, from http://www.freepress.net/files/Dismantling_Digital_Deregulation.pdf.

Willis, J. W., & Mehlinger, H. D. (1996). Information technology and teacher education. In J. Sikula (Ed.), *Handbook of research on teacher education* (pp. 978–1030). New York, NY: Macmillan Library Reference USA/Simon & Schuster Macmillan.

Zeichner, K. M., & Tabachnick, B. R. (1981). Are the effects of university teacher education 'washed out' by School experience? *Journal of Teacher Education, 32*(3), 7–11.

ACCESS Issues in School Library Media Centers: Examining Library Schedules, Library Closures, and Poverty

Karen Gavigan, Gail Dickinson, and Shana Pribesh

Introduction

As stated in *School Libraries Count!* (AASL, 2007b), "The value of a school library media center to its students and teachers is determined largely by the extent to which it is available" (p. 8). The concept of providing equal and open access across school libraries is further endorsed in the following AASL documents:

- *Access to Resources and Services in the School Library Media Program, an Interpretation of the Library Bill of Rights* (AASL, 2005)
- *Empowering Learners: Guidelines for School Library Media Centers* (AASL, 2009)
- *Information Power* (AASL, 1998)
- *Position statement on Flexible Scheduling* (AASL, 1991)
- *Position Statement on the Value of Library Media Programs in Education* (AASL, 2006)

It is evident from these and other documents that school librarians play a key role in providing learners with opportunities to access print, video, and electronic resources. This role is constantly evolving, however, since twenty-first-century learners have information needs that are increasingly sophisticated. As digital resources have grown exponentially, and information access has become more dependent upon online resources, school librarians are challenged with providing

K. Gavigan (✉)
School of Library and Information Science, University of South Carolina, Columbia, SC, USA
e-mail: kgavigan@mailbox.sc.edu

G. Dickinson • S. Pribesh
Darden College of Education, Old Dominion University, Norfolk, VA, USA
e-mail: gdickins@odu.edu; spribesh@odu.edu

M. Orey et al. (eds.), *Educational Media and Technology Yearbook: Volume 36, 2011*, 187
Educational Media and Technology Yearbook 36, DOI 10.1007/978-1-4614-1305-9_16,
© Springer Science+Business Media, LLC 2012

maximum access to technology. Finally, the controversy regarding flexible versus fixed scheduling has yet to be resolved, which also has an impact on students' access to library collections and services. The purpose of this study was to examine the ways in which library scheduling, library closures, and poverty affect access to resources and services across school libraries in North Carolina and Virginia.

Review of Literature

The theoretical framework for this study is based on the concept of equitable access to library resources and services. Keith Curry Lance and peers addressed issues of access when they published *The Colorado Study: Impact of School Library Media Centers on Academic Achievement* (Lance, 1994). Lance's research has been replicated in fourteen other states: Alaska, Arkansas, Florida, Iowa, Illinois, Massachusetts, Missouri, Minnesota, Michigan, New Mexico, North Carolina, Oregon, Pennsylvania, and Texas. Findings from these studies indicate that access to school libraries improves student achievement (Lance, 1994, 2002a, 2002b, Lance, Rodney, & Hamilton-Pennell, 2003a, 2003b, Lance, Wellburn, & Hamilton-Pennell, 1993). In several of these studies, Lance specifically addresses access issues when referring to variables such as funding, the correlation between longer library media center hours, higher student usage and, consequently, test scores.

Although there is a growing body of research examining access to school libraries and student achievement, there are currently few studies that examine the correlation between school library scheduling and access to materials and services. There are generally three types of schedules utilized in school library settings: fixed, flexible, and partially flexible schedules. For the purpose of this study, flexible scheduling was defined as a scheduling arrangement in which hours are available for library use that are not regularly scheduled for fixed activities such as class visits and study halls. Fixed scheduling was defined as a scheduling arrangement in which there are prescribed class visits to the media center. Partially flexible scheduling was defined as a combination of fixed and flexible scheduling.

The American Association of School Librarians included several questions regarding flexible versus fixed scheduling in its longitudinal survey, *School Libraries Count! The Second National Survey of School Library Media Programs 2008* (AASL, 2008). Findings from the study revealed that the hours available for flexible scheduling were associated with grade level. Specifically, it was found that the median hours available for flexible scheduling were 8 h for elementary schools, 35 h for middle school schools, and 37 h for high schools. The results from the AASL study build on findings from previous work documenting that, when comparing by grade level, elementary schools have the lowest percentage of school libraries implementing flexible scheduling (AASL, 2007a, 2007b, McCracken, 2001; Michie & Chaney, 2000). The majority of empirical studies investigating flexible access in school library media centers have focused on collaboration and implementation rather than issues regarding access to resources and services (Haycock, 1998;

McGregor, 2006; Miller & Shontz, 2003; Shannon, 1996; Van Deusen, 1996; Van Deusen & Tallman, 1994, Zweizig, 1999). Findings from these studies support the theory that flexible scheduling resulted in improved library services in schools.

In their *Position Statement on Flexible Scheduling*, the American Association of School Libraries (AASL) endorses flexible scheduling as a means of ensuring equitable access to school libraries. They state, "The integrated library media program philosophy requires that an open schedule must be maintained. Classes cannot be scheduled in the library media center to provide teacher release or preparation time. Students and teachers must be able to come to the center throughout the day to use information sources, to read for pleasure, and to meet and work with other students and teachers." (AASL, 1991, para. 2). Yet, there is currently a gap in the literature regarding the correlation between school library scheduling and physical access issues. Similarly, there are a limited number of studies that examine the correlation between library closures and access to resources and services. The few studies that do examine the hours that libraries are open and closed focused on student achievement. The findings from these studies demonstrate a correlation between the number of hours a school library is open, higher student usage, and, consequently, student achievement (Burgin & Bracy, 2003; Lance, 1994, 2002a, 2002b; Lance, Rodney et al., 2003a, 2003b, Lance, Wellburn et al., 1993).

Studies by Lance and his colleagues have contributed significantly to advancing knowledge in the field of school librarianship; however, there is currently limited research articulating the correlation between poverty and accessibility issues in school libraries. Although the American Library Association (ALA)'s policy statement, *Library Services to the Poor* (ALA, 2011), articulates the need to serve patrons living in poverty, literature in the field has focused more on public library services than on services in school libraries. For example, only two books are known to have been written regarding library services to the poor, and both pertain to public library services (Holt & Holt, 2010; Venturella, 1998). Furthermore, there is only one known study pertaining to school libraries and issues of poverty. In the study, Neuman and Celano (2001) examined the relationship between school library media closings and poverty. The authors found that school libraries in low-income neighborhoods were open fewer days per week than those in middle-income neighborhoods.

Methodology

The purpose of this study was to examine the ways in which school library schedules, school library closings, and poverty affect access to school library resources and services. The following research questions guided this study:

- How do school library schedules correlate with access to library resources and services?
- How do school library closings correlate with access to library resources and services?
- How does student poverty correlate with access to library resources and services?

In order to address these questions, we used a non-experimental research design. Specifically, we developed and administered an online survey to a random sample of over 600 public school librarians in North Carolina and Virginia. The sample was drawn from members of the North Carolina School Library Media Association (NCSLMA) and the Virginia Educational Media Association (VEMA) who were school library practitioners at the time of the survey. Each organization has approximately 1,000 members and, together, the organizations represent approximately 1/3 of all school library media specialists employed in North Carolina and Virginia. Partial funding for the study was provided by NCSLMA and VEMA. Although the sample was not nationally representative, it was representative of the memberships of the two large school library organizations. Thirty percent of the 600-person sample responded for a total of 181 respondents. The records were removed for two respondents who indicated that they did not want to participate and three who entered blanks throughout the survey. The result was a 29.3% response rate (176 respondents in the analysis file).

The 22 questions used in the survey were designed to determine, among other things, the following information:

- Type of schedule utilized (fixed, flexible, or partially flexible) in the school library
- How many days the school library was closed in the previous year
- Percentage of students eligible for free and reduced price lunch (FRPL)

Findings

In this section we present the results of our examination of school library characteristics, and how they affect the accessibility of resources and services. First, we describe the findings as they relate to school library scheduling. Next, we present the findings related to school library closures. We then present the findings that determine if poverty and accessibility issues are correlated. Finally, we present a summary of the findings and their implications for future research.

School Library Schedules

As shown in previous studies, middle schools and high schools predominantly use flexible scheduling in their school libraries (AASL, 2007a, 2007b; McCracken, 2001; Michie & Chaney, 2000). Therefore, in order to determine how flexible versus fixed scheduling affected access to school library resources and services, this analysis focused on elementary school libraries. In particular, we sought to determine whether or not flexible scheduling provided greater access to library collections and an increase in book circulation per pupil.

Altogether, 62% of elementary school libraries in this study used some sort of flexible schedule, while 38% of the elementary school libraries maintained a fixed schedule.

Table 1 Estimated means of book circulation by schedule type

Schedule	Mean	Adjusted mean	SD	Lower bound	Upper bound	N
Fixed	50.6	56.7*	13.78	28	85	18
Partially flexible	46.1	68.3	12.41	42	94	26
Totally flexible	71.4	102.0*	19.71	61	143	9

*Significantly different from each other, $p = 0.03$

The following factors were taken into account in order to determine the correlation between schedule and per pupil circulation: type of school, location, socioeconomic status, funding, staffing, collection size, loss, rules about circulation restrictions, and total days closed. An ANCOVA was conducted and, after all of these factors were considered, it was found that schedule was significantly related to circulation per pupil ($F = 2.734$, d$f = 2$, $p = 0.089$).[1] Specifically, it was found that students who attended schools whose libraries used a totally flexible schedule checked out an average of 102 books per year when other factors influencing circulation were accounted for (Table 1). However, students who attended schools with libraries using fixed schedules checked out 56.7 books per year after other factors were accounted for.

The findings from this study revealed that flexible scheduling in elementary schools provided greater access to resources and, ultimately, higher circulation per pupil than fixed scheduling (Gavigan, Dickinson, & Pribesh, 2010). The results of this study are not generalizable; however, they support the premise that students who attend schools with totally flexible schedules are likely to check out a significantly larger number of books per academic year than students who attend schools with fixed schedules. This finding is important since, as stated in the *Common Beliefs of the American Association of School Librarians* (AASL), "All children deserve equitable access to books and reading, to information, and to information technology in an environment that is safe and conducive to learning" (AASL, 2007a).

School Library Closures

This study also examined the reasons that school libraries close during the academic year and the effect that library closures had on access to resources and services (Dickinson, Gavigan, & Pribesh, 2008). On average, it was found that school libraries were closed almost 15 full days and 9 partial days per academic year. If one prorates partial days as a half-day, then the total time school library media centers are closed for resources and services, on average, is 17 full days in an academic year (Table 2). The number of days closed varied by type of school. Elementary schools

---

[1] We used the critical alpha threshold of $p < 0.10$ for testing statistical significance.

Table 2 Description of full and partial days school libraries are closed

Types of closures	Full days closed					Partial days closed				
	N	Mean	SD	Min	Max	N	Mean	SD	Min	Max
Beginning of the school year	69	4.4	2.53	1	14	10	4.7	3.23	1	10
End of the school year	120	7.2	3.53	2	15	26	5.2	3.66	1	10
Due to absence of librarian	19	3.7	4.45	1	20	15	3.9	3.35	1	10
Student picture or senior portraits	15	1.8	0.77	1	4	11	1.7	1.27	1	5
Health screenings (speech, hearing, or other)	20	1.9	0.88	1	4	17	1.3	0.59	1	3
School or district staff meetings	24	2.7	2.16	1	10	30	2.8	2.45	1	10
PTA/PTO meetings	0	0.0	0.00	0	0	6	2.5	1.22	1	4
Book fairs or other special events	52	7.2	3.63	1	14	25	4.5	4.30	0	18
Testing	69	7.0	5.12	1	23	87	6.7	5.24	1	27
Other	15	4.9	3.00	1	12	8	2.5	1.07	2	5
Total	156	14.8	9.95	1	48	121	9.1	7.81	1	32
Combined Total	168	17.0	11.07	1	58					

Table 3 ANCOVA of school type on total days closed

School type	Mean	Std. Error	95% Confidence interval	
			Lower bound	Upper bound
Elementary	18.2	1.19	15.83	20.53
Middle	16.6	1.51	13.61	19.60
High	13.9	2.12	9.75	18.14

were closed an average of 18.2 days, whereas middle schools closed an average of 16.6 days. High schools closed 13.9 days a year, on average (Table 3). The differences in days closed by school type were not statistically significant.

Since there are typically 185 days in a school year, this means that, on average, school libraries are closed 9% of the time students are in school. It is important to note that this is an average. Of the 168 schools reporting closures, the range was from one to 48 full days. Similarly, schools reported closing for partial days for anywhere from one to 32 days. Although it is disconcerting to learn that the school libraries were closed an average of 9% of the time, it was even more troubling to learn that school libraries frequently closed for purposes other than for which they are designed. For example, the findings indicated that the three most commonly reported reasons for closure of the school library were book fairs, standardized testing, and end of the school year. Other reasons for school library closings included student pictures, health screenings, PTO meetings, and the absence of the librarian (Table 2). The mission of the school library program may be impaired when students are denied access to resources and services due to school library closings.

Poverty and Its Effect on School Library Accessibility

To investigate the ways in which poverty affected accessibility to library collections and services, a question on the survey was included to determine the percentage of students in each school who were eligible for FRPL. Eligibility for FPRL is widely considered an indicator of poverty. Our concern was that the concentration of poverty at the school and the number of days that students are able to access resources and services were related. In fact, we found a significant difference in the amount of school library closures in schools with differing FRPL percentages ($F_{(1513,5)} = 2.580$, $p = 0.028$) (Table 4).

The findings revealed that as FRPL percentages increased the number of days that the school libraries were closed increased as well (Pribesh & Gavigan, 2009). In other words, the poorest schools closed school libraries the most days. This builds on a study by the American Association of School Librarians, in which it was found that schools with a larger number of students receiving FRPL were found to have a lower number of flexibly scheduled hours (19) than schools with a lower percentage of FRPL students (23 h) (AASL, 2008).

In the *Power of Reading*, Krashen (2004) writes about the "overwhelming evidence that children of poverty have far less access to reading material than do children

Table 4 ANCOVA of school FRPL eligibility on total days closed

School FRPL eligible	Mean	Std. Error	95% Confidence interval		Sig Dif
			Lower bound	Upper bound	
Less than 10%	12.21	1.990	8.278	16.138	a, b
11–20%	14.04	2.273	9.555	18.532	
21–30%	17.57	2.273	13.077	22.054	
31–40%	18.11	2.569	13.037	23.185	
41–50%	20.26	2.379	15.565	24.959	a
More than 50%	18.99	1.526	15.976	22.004	b
	Type III Sum of Squares	df	Mean Square	F	Sig.	Partial Eta Squared
Intercept	42,116.87	1	42,116.87	354.506	0.000	0.69
School FRPL eligible	1,344.40	5	268.88	2.263	0.051	0.07
Error	19,008.68	160	118.80			
Total	68,030.08	166				

R Squared = 0.066 (Adjusted R Squared = 0.037)

from higher-income families" (p. 68). There is reason for concern when marginalized students, who stand to benefit the most from access to school library resources and services, are the ones who have the fewest days of access compared with those in schools with a lower percentage of students receiving FRPL. The differences in access to print resources may have significant implications for students' literacy development.

As Krashen (2004) states, "While it is true that students of poverty have less access to books, given two groups of such children, the group provided with more access to books will show more literacy development" (p. 71). Furthermore, students of poverty are less likely to have computers and other technological resources in their homes, which results in a "digital divide" in public schools. Unfortunately, this divide may only widen when students are denied access to digital and information technology because of limited library hours.

Conclusion

Addressing the issues relating to students' access to resources and services may be one of school librarians' toughest challenges, especially given the research indicating that equitable access to physical and intellectual resources is a key component for academic achievement (Lance, 1994, 2002a, 2002b; Lance, Rodney et al., 2003a, 2003b, Lance, Wellburn et al., 1993). As stated in the American Association of School Librarians' *Position Statement on the Value of Library Media Programs in Education*, "In today's information age, an individual's success, even existence, depends largely on the ability to access, evaluate, and utilize information" (AASL, 2006).

The quest to provide equitable physical and intellectual access for all students must examine the effects that library scheduling, library closures, and poverty have on twenty-first-century learners. The findings from this study shed new light on access issues relating to school libraries. Further studies are needed to address school-based inequities that pertain to school library accessibility. Finally, school library stakeholders must use the results of such studies to help "implement district policies and procedures to ensure equitable access to resources and services for all students" (AASL, 2005).

References

American Association of School Librarians. (1991). *Position statement on flexible scheduling.* Chicago: American Association of School Librarians. Retrieved April 10, 2010, from http://www.ala.org/ala/mgrps/divs/aasl/aaslproftools/positionstatements/ALA_print_layout_1_202360_202360.cfm.

American Association of School Librarians. (2005). *Access to resources and services in the school library media program, an interpretation of the library bill of rights.* Chicago: American

Library Association. Retrieved April 10, 2010, from http://www.ala.org/ala/issuesadvocacy/librarybill/interpretations/accessresources.cfm.

American Association of School Librarians. (2006). *Position statement on the value of library media programs in education.* Chicago: American Library Association. Retrieved April 10, 2010, from http://www.ala.org/ala/aasl/aaslproftools/positionstatements/aaslpositionstatementvalue.cfm.

American Association of School Librarians. (2007). *Standards for the 21st – Century learner.* Retrieved April 10, 2010, from http://www.ala.org/ala/mgrps/divs/aasl/guidelinesandstandards/learningstandards/AASL_Learning_Standards_2007.pdf.

American Association of School Librarians. (2007). *School libraries count! A national survey of school library media programs. 2007.* Chicago, IL. Retrieved April 14, 2010, from http://www.ala.org/ala/aasl/school_libraries_count07_report.pdf.

American Association of School Librarians. (2008). *School libraries count! The second national survey of school library media programs. 2008.* Chicago, IL. Retrieved on April 14, 2010, from http://www.btsb.com/brochures/SLCreport2008.pdf.

American Association of School Librarians. (2009). *Empowering learners: Guidelines for school library media programs.* Chicago: American Library Association.

American Association of School Librarians and Association for Educational Communications and Technology. (1998). *Information power: Building partnerships for learning.* Chicago: American Library Association.

American Library Association. (2011). *Policy statement on library services to the poor.* Chicago: American Library Association. Retrieved April 11, 2010, from http://www.ala.org/ala/aboutala/governance/policymanual/servicespoor.cfm.

Burgin, R., & Bracy, P. B. (2003). *An essential connection: How quality school library media programs improve student achievement in North Carolina.* Spring, TX: Hi Willow Research and Publishing.

Dickinson, G, Gavigan, K., & Pribesh, S. (2008). Open and accessible: The relationship between closures and circulation in school library media centers. *School Library Media Research, 11.* American Library Association. Retrieved August 26, 2008, from http://www.ala.org/ala/mgrps/divs/aasl/aaslpubsandjournals/slmrb/slmrcontents/volume11.

Gavigan, K., Pribesh, S., & Dickinson, G. (2010). Fixed or flexible schedule? Schedule impacts and school library circulation. *Library & Information Science Research, 32,* 131–137.

Haycock, K. (1998). The impact of scheduling on cooperative program planning and teaching (CPPT) and information skills instruction. *School Libraries in Canada, 18*(3), 20–23.

Holt, L. E., & Holt, G. E. (2010). *Public library services for the poor: Doing all we can.* Chicago: American Library Association.

Krashen, S. (2004). *Power of reading: Insights from the research* (2nd ed.). Portsmouth, NH: Heinemann.

Lance, K. C. (1994). The impact of school library media centers on academic achievement. *School Library Media Quarterly, 22,* 167–170. {in Colorado}.

Lance, K. C. (2002a). The impact of school library media centers on academic achievement. *Teacher Librarian, 29*(3), 29–34.

Lance, K. C. (2002b). What research tells us about the importance of school libraries. *Teacher Librarian: The Journal for School Library Professionals, 30*(1), 76–78.

Lance, K. C., Rodney, M., & Hamilton-Pennell, C. (2003a). *How school libraries improve outcomes for children: The New Mexico study.* San Jose, CA: Hi Willow Press.

Lance, K. C., Rodney, M., & Hamilton-Pennell, C. (2003b). *The impact of Michigan school librarians on academic achievement: Kids who have libraries succeed.* Lansing, MI: Library of Michigan.

Lance, K. C., Welllburn, L., & Hamilton-Pennell, C. (1993). *The impact of school library media centers on academic achievement.* Castle Rock, CO: Hi Willow Research & Publishing.

McCracken, A. (2001). School library media specialists' perceptions of practice and importance of roles described in Information Power. *School Library Media Research, 4,* 2001. Retrieved April 14, 2010, from http://libproxy.uncg.edu:2072/hww/results/results_single_fulltext.jhtml;hwwilsonid=04ZOFLZVZS2YPQA3DILCFGOADUNGIIV0.

McGregor, J. (2006). Flexible scheduling: Implementing an innovation. *School Library Media Research, 9*, 1–27.

Michie, J., & Chaney, B. (2000). *Assessment of the role of school and public libraries in support of educational reform.* General Audience Report. Retrieved April 14, 2010, from http://www. eric.ed.gov/ERICDocs/data/ericdocs2sql/content_storage_01/0000019b/80/16/2f/f9.pdf.

Miller, M., & Shontz, M. (2003). The SLJ Spending survey: While funding takes a hit, libraries expand their services. *School Library Journal, 49*(10), 52–59.

Neuman, S. B., & Celano, D. (2001). Access to print in low-income and middle-income communities: An ecological study of four neighborhoods. *Reading Research Quarterly, 3*, 8–26.

Pribesh, S., & Gavigan, K. (2009, March/April). Association for Library and Information Science Education (ALISE)/Linworth 2009 Youth Services Paper Award: Equal opportunity? Poverty and characteristics of school library media centers. *Library Media Connection, 27*(5), 20–22.

Shannon, D. (1996). Tracking the transition to a flexible access library program in two Library Power elementary schools. *School Library Media Quarterly, 24*(3), 155–163.

Van Deusen, J. D. (1996). An analysis of the time use of elementary school library media specialists and factors that influence it. *School Library Media Quarterly, 24*(2), 85–92.

Van Deusen, J. D., & Tallman, J. (1994). The impact of scheduling on curriculum consultation and information skills instruction. Part one: The 1993–1994 AASL/Highsmith Research Award Study. *School Library Media Quarterly, 23*(1), 7–25.

Venturella, K. (1998). *Poor people and library services.* Jefferson, NC: McFarland & Company.

Zweizig, D. L. (1999). Access and use of library resources in Library Power. *School Libraries Worldwide, 5*(2), 16–28.

School Counselors and School Media Specialists: Innovative Leaders in Partnerships Promoting Student Mental Health with Online Resources

Kylie P. Dotson-Blake and Kaye B. Dotson

Bullying (Bond, Carlin, Thomas, Rubin, & Patton, 2001), depression and anxiety, nutrition and physical health, peer relationships (Jaycox et al., 2009), substance abuse (Cuellar, Markowitz, & Libby, 2004), pregnancy (Harden et al., 2007), sexual health (Kalmuss, Davidson, Cohall, Laraque, & Cassell, 2003), eating disorders and relational aggression (Crenshaw & Lee, 2010) provide just a brief overview of the issues impacting the mental health of teens and adolescents. As these young people enter middle and secondary schools, they are held to rigorous academic standards, often with little support for mental health issues which may impede their learning (U.S. Public Health Service, 2000). The professional charged with meeting the social/emotional mental health needs of students, the school counselor, is often overburdened with counseling-related and non-counseling tasks such as registration and testing. Consequently, the mental health needs of many students go unaddressed and students struggle to be academically successful (Dollarhide, Saginak, & Urofsky, 2008; Roeser, Eccles, & Freedman-Doan, 1999).

In a perfect world, school counselors would be able to forgo many of the non-counseling-related tasks associated with current school counseling practice and focus solely on the personal/social, academic, and career development of their students. Though as a profession, school counseling has made dramatic positive strides in this direction in recent years, the reality for many practicing school counselors is that they must struggle to balance a myriad of sometimes conflicting professional responsibilities and administrator expectations. Collaborative interdisciplinary partnerships provide a vehicle for harnessing resources readily available in the school counselor's

K.P. Dotson-Blake (✉)
Department of Higher, Adult and Counselor Education,
East Carolina University, ECU, 223-A Ragsdale Hall,
Greenville, NC 27858, USA
e-mail: blakek@ecu.edu

K.B. Dotson
Department of Library Science, East Carolina University, Greenville, NC, USA
e-mail: dotsonl@ecu.edu

M. Orey et al. (eds.), *Educational Media and Technology Yearbook: Volume 36, 2011*,
Educational Media and Technology Yearbook 36, DOI 10.1007/978-1-4614-1305-9_17,
© Springer Science+Business Media, LLC 2012

learning community to fulfill their most important professional responsibility, the responsibility to support and promote the academic success and mental health of students.

This chapter describes one such partnership between school library media specialists and school counselors. The digital age has transformed the work of school counselors and school library media specialists in ways responsive to the digital knowledge and competencies of today's youth. Thus, the partnership presented in this discussion will illuminate the process of developing an interdisciplinary partnership that fulfills the American Association of School Librarians (AASL) Standards for the 21st Century Learner (2007) and the American School Counselor Association (ASCA) National Model (2005) mandates and ultimately results in the development of a website to share resources to meet the social/emotional mental health needs of teens.

In the partnership described, the school counselor and school media specialist team together to work with high-school students to identify, evaluate, and compile resources to support and promote the mental health of teens. In the proposed partnership, the school media specialist's expertise in the areas of information literacy and media management and AASL's mandate to prepare students for twenty-first-century learning will serve as critical resources for the school counselor seeking to develop a school counseling program website including mental health components.

Bridging the Digital Divide

Though the counseling profession has forged ahead into the information age, many practicing school counselors still lack technological competencies necessary for creating and facilitating web-based services and resources for stakeholders. Conversely, contemporary students are highly competent with technology and most turn to the web to seek out needed information. Consequently, the digital divide existing between school counselors and their student stakeholders can serve as a barrier to students approaching the counselor for help with mental health concerns.

Fortunately, the school counselor has a valuable ally in the school, the school library media specialist. The school library media specialist is well-versed in technology (AASL, 2009) and works closely with students throughout their school careers to ensure that students are using technology and Internet resources safely, effectively, and appropriately (Dotson & Dotson-Blake, 2009). Additionally, information literacy and the process of identifying, locating and evaluating information and resources are key research and consumer skills that school media specialists impart to their students (Taylor, 2006). The combination of technology competency and information literacy renders the school library media specialist an expert in working with students and colleagues, like the school counselor, to identify and plan for the utilization of electronic media and resources. The school library media specialist can serve as a bridge to span to digital divide between technology-savvy teens and their less technology-competent counselors.

Interdisciplinary Collaboration for Healthy, Successful Students: Preparedness, Possibilities, Process

Interdisciplinary collaboration provides opportunities for partnering the resources and expertise of multiple professionals to provide comprehensive programming to address students' needs. To fully understand the impact of interdisciplinary collaboration, consider for a minute the effect of turning a kaleidoscope as one looks through the lens. As a kaleidoscope is turned the transparent colored objects inside shift and move together as light filters through, reflecting off of and passing through the transparent objects to mirrors which reflect the amazing patterns that are viewed by those lucky enough to look through the lens (Kaleidoscopes of America, 2006).

With each rotation of the kaleidoscope, the unique colored transparent objects fall and move together in dynamic ways creating rich and exciting patterns. Taken from the group, each individual object is unable to provide the rich, complex patterns that emerge when it is placed together with other unique objects in the kaleidoscope. Interdisciplinary collaboration is much the same. By oneself, each education professional is only able to contribute her or his particular expertise in a concentrated effort. However, when working in concert with other education professionals and their complementary expertise and resources, these professionals are able to provide results that are complex, comprehensive, and readily able to meet the multifaceted needs of students and stakeholders.

Preparedness

School library media specialists and school counselors are uniquely prepared to work in collaboration with other professionals. Professional consultation and collaboration are specific components of the national standards, which guide the education of pre-service school library media specialists and the practice of school library media specialists (AASL, 2007). In fact, AASL (2009) asserts that the school library media specialist's role as an instructional partner is essential to the future growth and progress of the profession. The ASCA National Model (2005), which guides the preparation and practice of school counselors, also includes specific mandates addressing the importance of collaboration and consultation with other educational professionals. Consequently, these professionals are professionally required to seek out and develop interdisciplinary partnerships to provide comprehensive services to students.

As a function of their training, as mandated by national standards, school library media specialists and school counselors have also been expertly prepared to design, implement, and facilitate collaborative partnerships with other professionals. The four top roles of school library media specialists are teacher, information specialist, instructional partner, and program administrator (AASL, 2009). These roles serve as the foundation for the development of the partnership described in this chapter and most importantly, the critical work of the school library media specialist with students under the umbrellas of each of these roles is supported and enhanced by the described partnership. The described partnership provides a way to fulfill many of the Standards for the 21st Century Learner put forth by AASL in intentional and strategic ways to not only improve the academic outcomes of students, but also to improve and strengthen the overall school learning community.

Possibilities

Though the professional training of school counselors and school library media specialists prepares them for collaborative partnerships, it may be difficult for on-the-job practitioners to conceptualize these partnerships. Some examples of possibilities for interdisciplinary collaborative partnerships include partnerships focused on curriculum development, partnerships focused on providing services to students and partnerships that seek to engage parents, families, and/or community members in the education of students. Other partnership opportunities certainly exist and a detailed exploration of as many partnership possibilities as possible would be helpful to practicing school library media specialists and school counselors seeking to develop collaborative partnerships in their schools. Though such a discussion is beyond the scope of this chapter, one example of a potential partnership between the school library media specialist and school counselor will be explored in depth. The intent of the authors is that by exploring this partnership possibility in detail, practicing school library media specialists and school counselors can use this chapter as a blueprint for implementing similar partnerships in their schools. As such, this chapter presents a case study exploring a dynamic partnership between a school library media specialist and school counselor to address the mental health needs of students.

Process

There are a few critical process components that must be included for an interdisciplinary partnership between the school library media specialist and school counselor to be successful. These components include open communication, flexibility, shared vision, common goals, respect, and trust. Muronago and Harada (1999) asserted that for interdisciplinary collaboration to be successful, the professionals involved must develop a shared vision for their collaboration and define goals for their work, while most importantly maintaining a context of respect and trust upon which to build their partnership. These are critically important building blocks for partnerships between school library media specialists and school counselors. Though turf-wars are prevalent in school communities (McKerrow, Dunn, & Killian, 2003), professionals seeking to engage in successful collaborative partnerships must be willing to set-aside territorial demarcations of responsibilities and roles and must embrace a process of leadership and effort that includes evolving and shifting roles and engagement. The case presented in this chapter has been developed with recognition of the importance of these foundational process-focused building blocks.

Case Example

School library media specialists in the twenty-first century seek to provide a diverse and supportive learning environment for all students and faculty, while school counselors offer supportive services from a similar, but different perspective. In their respective quests, both, appreciate and realize the significance of information seeking, the process by which one may gain valid information for meeting a range of needs effectively (Udoh, 1998).

Currently, though school counselors value the importance of information seeking and resource sharing, they often do not have sufficient time to devote to these tasks because of other responsibilities. On the other hand, school library media specialists devote much of their time to teaching students information seeking and how to gain knowledge through inquiry and critical thinking, as indicated by the AASL ranking the teaching role of these professionals first in their current roles in school settings (AASL, 2009).

Often school library media specialists seek to create assignments to encourage students to explore available resources, draw conclusions from the resources they uncover, and apply the knowledge they have gained in real-life scenarios, as encouraged by the common beliefs inherent in the Standards for 21st Century Learners (AASL, 2009). The elaborate real-life scenarios for assignments that school library media specialists create are quite helpful for student learners. However, consider the potential impact of using these assignments to encourage students to address real-life concerns of their particular school and stakeholder group. Each assignment the students complete could have direct, positive impacts on their learning community, promoting the students' understanding of the social context of learning (AASL) and the power of their personal engagement.

This case details a partnership that fulfills the vision of developing meaningful student assignments to address current needs of the students' school community. The partnership utilizes the school library media specialist's expertise in information seeking, technology competency and lessons with students to identify resources and compile this information into a counseling department website to share mental health and social/emotional support resources with students and stakeholders.

School Library Media Specialist Standards
Addressed by the Case

The Standards for 21st Century Learners (AASL, 2007) set forth by the AASL denoted four primary standards that school library media specialists must work to encourage their students to develop:

1. Inquire, think critically, and gain knowledge
2. Draw conclusions, make informed decisions, apply knowledge to new situations, and create new knowledge

3. Share knowledge and participate ethically and productively as members of our democratic society
4. Pursue personal and aesthetic growth

This case will include components that fulfill each of these standards and will include student outcomes that can be documented as support towards the school library media program's fulfillment of each of these standards.

Laying the Foundation

The first step in this collaborative partnership is to have the school counselor and school library media specialist meet to define the goals and objectives of this partnership. During this meeting, the school counselor shares information with the school library media specialist regarding the prevalent mental health issues facing students in their school. The school library media specialist articulates the process she/he will follow for working with the students to identify potentially useful resources and the two professionals develop a plan for meeting again to assess the progress of the students in identifying and compiling resource information.

Initiating Student Involvement

Following her/his meeting with the school counselor, the school library media specialist works with students to describe the project they will be embarking upon. She/he explains the purpose of the project and provides critical linkages to academic expectations for the students. Students are encouraged to ask questions about the project and their feedback is sought about the topics they will be researching. It is helpful to have the school counselor involved in this component of the discussion, in order to integrate the students' feedback into current programming addressing mental and social/emotional issues facing students. The inquiry component of this step in the partnership involves having the students consider thoughtfully the mental health issues presented by the school counselor and provide feedback about their perceptions of the importance of these issues for students in their school community. This inquiry can be documented by having the students submit a one-page reflection considering the topics that were presented to them. These reflections can provide powerful information for the school library media specialist and the school counselor to use in shaping the project to meet the developmental needs of the students.

Inquiry and Critical Evaluation of Print Resources

The next action step of this partnership is to review current media center resource holdings. The school media specialist will work with a group of students to review the school library media center's current collection and analyze needs to meet the shared mission of both the counseling department and the library. In this systematic approach to assist the school counselor, students under the direction of the school media specialist will begin the process by going through the media collection inventory to compile a list of resources currently held by media center related to the mental health and social/emotional issues identified.

The students will provide initial, brief reviews of the relevance of the material presented in the resources for their school's student population. Students must critically consider the materials and make informed decisions about the appropriateness of these materials for meeting the needs of their peers, fulfilling standards one and two of the Standards for 21st Century Learning (AASL, 2007). Following the student reviews, both the school counselor and school media specialist will review the materials for currency and appropriate content and use, utilizing the student reviews as an important piece of information to inform their decision-making process.

In this manner several purposes are met. The ongoing evaluation and weeding process so essential to the work of the school library media specialist is intertwined with the lessons being taught. Deficits in the print collection can be identified. Ultimately, the school counselor will have an updated, current list of available resources on specific topics. Another benefit for the school library media program is that the completed student reviews can serve as outcome evidence supporting the program's work towards the fulfillment of the Standards for 21st Century Learning (AASL, 2007). Most importantly, however, is that students become more familiar with the library collection, and learn valuable information-seeking skills in the process of completing the evaluation of print resources. As a community of learners, students, counselor and media specialist all benefit from this phase of the project (Kuhlthau, Maniotes, & Caspari, 2007).

Inquiry and Critical Evaluation of Electronic Resources

The next stage of the project development involves identifying and evaluating electronic resources related to the mental health issues specified. The possibilities are endless, but as students draw upon previously taught information evaluation skills, they will be able to select the most current and dependable resources from the enormous variety of materials available online. The school media specialist has a fertile opportunity here to readdress, and reaffirm, information literacy-searching techniques as students follow an inquiry-based process to connect academic learning with a real-life need. Students will identify, evaluate, and select appropriate web resources to address the issues provided by the school counselor. Accuracy, validity, and appropriateness are key concerns and are closely monitored by the school media specialist.

Together, students will compile a list of the electronic resources they have identified and create brief reviews of the appropriateness of the material for use with their peer group. The review step of this stage in the project and the previous stage are critical for student learning. The Standards for 21st Century Learners (AASL, 2007) stress the importance of inquiry, critical evaluation, and informed decision-making for contemporary students and the expectations for students at these two stages of the project seek to promote the development of these skills for students. Again, as in the previous stage of the project, the school library media specialist and school counselor will review the resources and the student reviews to critique each resource for appropriateness for meeting student and stakeholder needs. After this final professional critique, the school counselor and school library media specialist meet together to discuss the resources and choose the ones to include on the counseling department website. Once the professionals have decided which resources to include, students will begin the culmination of this project, the creation of the counseling department's website.

Creation of Website

Each student will use his/her skills to assist in the creation of a final product. This product should be a website designed to present the resources identified along with other basic information, including, but not limited to the counselor's contact information and a calendar that can be updated to include scholarship deadlines and other important dates, on the school counselor's website. Students can be allowed to work individually or in teams for this stage of the project. After each student (or group of students) completes a proposed website, students will present their website designs to their classmates and the school library media specialist. This presentation will encourage students to reflect on their work and participate collaboratively in the process of reviewing and critiquing each other's work. These presentations should be viewed as a time for sharing knowledge and celebrating learning, while working together to choose the most creative, professional elements of each web-design to incorporate into a final, comprehensive website. The development of the final, comprehensive website should draw from aspects of the presented websites and should encourage students to work together to develop a strong and effective final product. The shared interchange of ideas and skills will result in a creative, artistic, and informative tool the school counselor can use for the benefit of the greater school community.

The individual or team-created websites can serve as evidence of the fulfillment of the standard focused on applying knowledge and creating new knowledge (AASL, 2007). The final comprehensive website created collaboratively by the class provides a wonderful example of students working together to share knowledge and actively engage as members of a strong democratic society (AASL). Extending beyond the documentation of work towards achieving the standards, these websites serve as evidence of the students' ability to work together to address a pressing need in their school community. This achievement will, in turn, promote a sense of personal investment in learning for students, which may extend the benefits of this project for student learning far beyond the school library media center and school counseling program. This final benefit solidly assures the fulfillment of the final standard, the pursuit of growth in the areas of learning and motivation for learning (AASL).

Extensions of the Project

There are many ways to extend the proposed partnership to continue to develop technology-based resources for students and improve the information literacy of students. One potential extension is to have the school library media specialist lead students in the creation of open-access communication tools to allow students to pose mental health questions for the counselor and encourage student/faculty dialogue about difficult social/emotional student concerns. Students could use a range of available, accessible technology to design blogs or wikis appropriate for sharing information, promoting discourse among stakeholders, and eliciting feedback from students. These blogs or wikis could be used to elicit questions and provide feedback about current issues, allowing the school counselor to keep a finger on the pulse of the student population's mental health and level of awareness at all times.

Another potential extension of this partnership is to have students prepare presentations or wiki pages sharing brief information about different mental health concerns impacting students in their school. These wikis could provide students with limited, professionally screened information to increase student awareness of mental health concerns and share links to resources providing further information. The students could include presentations on their wikis that share a compilation of the information about the wiki topic that they gained through the use of their information literacy skills. Additionally, the wikis could include brief surveys to assess students' knowledge of the focused concern or perceptions of the importance and relevance of the information shared on the wiki to provide the school counselor with feedback to use in program planning and curriculum development.

Many more extensions of the partnership certainly exist. The developmental levels and abilities of students must be considered to effectively extend the partnership in ways appropriate for the reader's school and student population. These two are offered to spark readers' consideration of the possibilities for continued partnership work.

Conclusion

This comprehensive collaborative partnership addresses the professional mandate for school library media specialists to promote the development of twenty-first-century learning skills in students. In fulfilling this mandate through a partnership with the school counselor, the strategies for promoting the development of twenty-first-century skills can be used to also meet the mental health and social/emotional needs of students. Instead of working in isolation on similar goals, the collaborative partnership of the two programs results in meaningful learning with the creation of a positive product. The students who helped the website to become a reality can take pride in their service to the school community and rely on their skills gained in all future endeavors, knowing that they, individually, are able to make a significant contribution to the success of the larger community. It is hoped that through this partnership, students will realize the importance of identifying a need, devising a plan to meet that need, and most importantly, working together for a positive end result in an effective learning community.

References

American Association of School Librarians. (2007). *Standards for the 21st-century learner.* Chicago, IL: Author. Retrieved from http://www.ala.org/aasl/standards.

American Association of School Librarians. (2009). *Empowering learners: Guidelines for school library media programs.* Chicago, IL: Author.

American School Counselor Association. (2005). The ASCA national model: A framework for school counseling programs (2nd ed.). Alexandria, VA: Author.

Bond, L., Carlin, J. B., Thomas, L., Rubin, K., & Patton, G. (2001). Does bullying cause emotional problems: A prospective study of young teenagers. *British Medical Journal, 323*(1), 480–484. doi:10.1136/bmj.323.7311.480.

Crenshaw, D. A., & Lee, J. (2010). At-risk adolescents: Self-esteem, youth violence and teen pregnancy. In M. H. Guindon (Ed.), *Self-esteem across the life-span: Issues and interventions* (pp. 143–158). New York, NY: Routledge.

Cuellar, A. E., Markowitz, S., & Libby, A. M. (2004). Mental health and substance abuse treatment and juvenile crime. *Journal of Mental Health Policy and Economics, 7*(2), 59–68.

Dollarhide, C. T., Saginak, K. A., & Urofsky, R. I. (2008). Emerging issues for schools and students. In C. T. Dollarhide & K. A. Saginak (Eds.), *Comprehensive school counseling programs: K-12 delivery systems in action* (pp. 300–325). Boston: Pearson.

Dotson, K. B., & Dotson-Blake, K. P. (2009). Emerging trends in expanding the high school curriculum: Collaborative roles and responsibilities. In S. Jones & R. M. Branch (Eds.), *Educational media and technology yearbook* (Vol. 34, pp. 151–162). Littleton, CO: Springer.

Harden, K. P., Lynch, S. K., Turkheimer, E., Emery, R. E., D'Onofrio, B. M., Slutske, W. S., et al. (2007). A behavior genetic investigation of adolescent motherhood and offspring mental health problems. *Journal of Abnormal Psychology, 116*, 667–683. doi:10.1037/0021-843X.116.4.667.

Jaycox, L. H., Stein, B. D., Paddock, S., Miles, J. N. V., Chandra, A., Meredith, L. S., et al. (2009). Impact of teen depression on academic, social and physical functioning. *PEDIATRICS, 124*(4), e596–e605. doi:10.1542/peds.2008-3348.

Kaleidoscopes of America. (2006). F.A.Q.'s about kaleidoscopes. Retrieved from http://www.kaleido.com/faqs.htm.

Kalmuss, D., Davidson, A., Cohall, A., Laraque, D., & Cassell, C. (2003). Preventing sexual risk behaviors and pregnancy among teenagers: Linking research and programs. *Perspectives on Sexual and Reproductive Health, 35*, 87–93. doi:10.1363/3508703.

Kuhlthau, C. C., Maniotes, L. K., & Caspari, K. (2007). *Guided inquiry: Learning in the 21st century.* Westport, CT: Libraries Unlimited.

McKerrow, K., Dunn, R., & Killian, J. (2003). Beyond the turf wars: Collaboration in preparing school leaders. *Educational Leadership Review, 4*(1), 1–10.

Muronago, K., & Harada, V. (1999). Building teaching partnerships: The art of collaboration. *Teacher Librarian, 27*(1), 9–14.

Roeser, R. W., Eccles, J. S., & Freedman-Doan, C. (1999). Academic functioning and mental health in adolescence: Patterns, progressions and routes from childhood. *Journal of Adolescent Research, 14*(2), 135–174. doi:10.1177/0743558499142002.

Taylor, J. (2006). *Information Literacy and the School Library Media Center.* Westport, CT: Libraries Unlimited.

U.S. Public Health Service. (2000). *Report of the Surgeon General's Conference on Children's Mental Health: A National Action Agenda.* Washington, DC: Department of Health and Human Services.

Udoh, V. W. (1998). The perceived role of the teacher librarian in effective implementation of the educational programmed of the school counselor. In D. F. Elatureti (Ed.), *Nigerian school counselor librarianship: Yesterday, today and tomorrow* (pp. 15–28). Ibadan: NSLA.

Towards an Understanding of Professional Dispositions of Exemplary School Librarians

Jami L. Jones and Gail Bush

What Is Educator Effectiveness?

As former students ourselves, we know instinctively the qualities of exemplary educators even if we have difficulty naming them. We want our children, nieces, and nephews to be surrounded by teachers, counselors, school librarians, administrators, and others who emit these exemplary qualities because we recognize through experience that some educators *are* more effective than others (Collinson, 1996; Combs, 1972; Cushman, 2006).

Combs' (1972) research in the 1950s to identify differences between effective and ineffective helping professionals such as elementary school teachers, college teachers, nurses, counselors, and pastors revealed that effective helping professionals present clear differences based on sensitivity, the purposes they espouse, the personal fit of the methods they use, and their beliefs about people and themselves. Decades later, Usher (2002), a member of Combs' University of Florida research team, reformulated the latter's work to identify five dispositions of effective teachers: empathy; positive view of others; positive view of self; authenticity; and meaningful purpose and vision.

Collinson (1996) asked the most capable teachers she knew to describe the characteristics of exemplary teachers. Her inquiry reveals strengths in the following three areas: professional knowledge of the subject and pedagogy; interpersonal knowledge of students and their community; and intrapersonal knowledge such as reflection, ethics, and dispositions. Cushman (2006) employed a slightly different

J.L. Jones (✉)
Department of Library Science, East Carolina University, Greenville, NC 27858, USA
e-mail: jonesj@ecu.edu

G. Bush
Department of Reading and Language, National-Louis University, Skokie, IL 60077, USA
e-mail: gail.bush@nl.edu

M. Orey et al. (eds.), *Educational Media and Technology Yearbook: Volume 36, 2011*,   209
Educational Media and Technology Yearbook 36, DOI 10.1007/978-1-4614-1305-9_18,
© Springer Science+Business Media, LLC 2012

approach by asking 65 high-school students to describe the qualities they value in a teacher. Students want engaging classes that are taught by teachers who like and care about the material they teach. They want teachers who exhibit the dispositions of care, trustworthiness, and respect for them. These students responded that teachers must like their students, be trustworthy, and treat students as smart and capable of challenging work.

In addition to recognizing that teacher effectiveness is the foremost predictor of student learning, teachers and their actions have a lasting and profound impact on adult memories (Paul & Smith, 2000). Paul and Smith asked adults to recall the teacher they considered to be their best or favorite teacher and write a letter conveying their feelings to the person. Likewise, adults were asked to recall their least favorite teacher and to express their feelings through a letter. Adults clearly remember their favorite and least favorite teachers, which may produce strong emotions of appreciation or resentment (Paul and Smith).

A key to effective learning is identifying and understanding dispositions of exemplary educators and ensuring that these are exhibited. Knowledge and skills are not sufficient by themselves to prepare excellent teachers. The transformation of a person from one who merely possesses knowledge and technique into a superior teacher includes the development of characteristics such as a "capacity for active and creative communication, a tendency to probe, a willingness to explore topics from a variety of perspectives, and a desire to engage and encourage students who have a dizzying range of abilities, interests, and temperaments" (Teacher Preparation, 2007, para. 6).

Why Dispositions and Why Now?

Recent interest in dispositions arose from the 1980s standards movement to restructure America's schools that was largely the result of efforts by three professional groups: the National Council for the Accreditation of Teacher Education (NCATE), the Council of Chief State School Officers (CCSSO), and the National Board for Professional Teaching Standards (NBPTS). Their efforts culminated in the 1996 publication of *What Matters Most: Teaching for America's Future* by the National Commission on Teaching and America's Future (NCTAF), a 26-member panel that concluded that school improvement is heavily dependent on improving the quality of the teacher workforce.

The NCTAF set six goals in its report. The first one states, "All children will be taught by teachers who have knowledge, skills, and commitment [a term that precedes the usage of dispositions] to teach children well" (Darling-Hammond, 1996, p. 196). Authors of the report recognized that if this nation is to prepare all of its children for the challenges of the twenty-first century, teaching must be able to recruit and retain able, well-prepared teachers for all classrooms. These entrants must be equipped with the knowledge, skills, and dispositions that will enable them to succeed with all students (NCTAF, 1996).

As a result, the three participating professional groups developed standards to guide teacher education programs that stress the importance of performance-based assessments in evaluating teacher quality. The particularly robust Interstate New Teacher Assessment and Support Consortium (INTASC) standards of the aforementioned CCSSO are divided into the categories of knowledge, skills, and dispositions. The operating premise of INTASC is that an effective teacher must be able to integrate content knowledge with pedagogical understanding to ensure that all students learn at high levels. The professional dispositions that are implicit to the 10 INTASC (1992) principles are:

- Embracing reflection, being a lifelong learner and communicator.
- Understanding the diversity of students and recognizing and promoting growth in others.
- Promoting positive social interaction and developing healthy and helpful relationships with children and youth.
- Integrity and collaboration to advocate for children.
- Understanding and using a variety of instructional strategies, planning, organizing, and goal setting.

Other than fairness and a belief that all children can learn, NCATE (2007) leaves identification of additional dispositions to individual programs. NCATE (2008) defines professional dispositions as:

> Professional attitudes, values, and beliefs demonstrated through both verbal and non verbal behaviors as educators interact with students, families, colleagues, and communities. These positive behaviors support student learning and development. NCATE expects institutions to assess professional dispositions based on observable behaviors in educational settings. The two professional dispositions that NCATE expects institutions to assess are fairness and the belief that all students can learn. Based on their mission and conceptual framework, professional education units can identify, define, and operationalize additional professional dispositions. (pp. 89–90)

The National Board for Professional Teaching Standards (2002) does not define dispositions but expects that proficient teachers are able to employ the necessary "skills, capacities, and dispositions" in the interest of students (p. 2).

The AASL *Standards for the 21st-Century Learners* (ALA, 2007), which comprise four learning strands each consisting of skills, dispositions in action, responsibilities, and self-assessment strategies, moved dispositions to the forefront for school librarians. Although the AASL dispositions in action are intended for students, these can be considered the de facto dispositions of exemplary school librarians who must model these for students because, in the words of NBPTS, accomplished teachers are "models of educated persons, exemplifying the virtues they inspire in students" (NBPTS, 2002, p. 4). The pertinent dispositions cannot be successfully modeled for students until the educator possesses them. Development of dispositions, which is described in more detail later in the chapter, includes three steps:

- A sensitivity to pertinent dispositions.
- The inclination, tendency, and/or impulse to appropriately employ the dispositions identified in the previous step.
- The ability and willingness to apply the specific dispositional behavior (Tishman, Jay, & Perkins, 1994; Tishman & Perkins, 1997).

What Are Dispositions?

Dewey's (1933) observation of the poor thinking of well-educated persons led him to ponder why some people function at higher levels than others. He concludes that the ability to think well, which he describes as "habits of thought" does not result from repeated exercise, "as gymnastic exercises are supposed to develop the muscles" (p. 29). Rather, Dewey writes:

> Knowledge of methods alone will not suffice; there must be the desire, the will to employ them. This desire is an affair of personal disposition. But on the other hand the dispositions alone will not suffice. There must also be understanding of the forms and techniques that are the channels through which these attitudes operate to the best advantage. (p. 30)

According to Dewey (1922), it is dispositions, which he views as a "predisposition, readiness to act overtly in a specific fashion whenever opportunity is presented" that leads to the desire to employ knowledge (p. 41).

Arnstine was first to launch the philosophical discussion about dispositions into the educational field. Freeman (2007) writes, "So far as I can determine from searching the teacher education literature, Donald Arnstine was the first to discuss the concept of dispositions in education extensively and to suggest the importance of dispositions in teaching" (p. 7). Although infrequently cited in the educational literature, Arnstine's (1967) book, *Philosophy of Education: Learning and Schooling*, provides the philosophical foundation for understanding dispositions.

Arnstine (1967) examines effective learning, but recognizes that "the mere existence of schools does not guarantee that the learning we desire will take place" (p. 2). The purpose of school is to foster learning, which Ryle (1949) describes as a "coming to know" (p. 149). In addition to Ryle's knowing, Arnstine considers that learning is the acquisition of "behaviors, knowledge, skills, habits, and attitudes," the latter he defines as dispositions (p. 13). Therefore, learning based on knowledge is a continuing and lengthy process of acquiring and developing a great number of abilities and attitudes – or dispositions, or the changing of old ones.

Do Dispositions Predict Future Behaviors?

Arnstine (1967) writes that a disposition is

> not some sort of a thing or a mysterious unobservable property of a thing; rather, it is a concept that has its use in predictive statements. To ascribe a disposition to something or to someone is to say he has a tendency to behave in certain ways when certain conditions are realized. (p. 32)

A disposition can be verified "only after the occurrence of several relevant tests or observations…that is, the more and the more varied are the situations during which we observe an ascribed disposition being exercised, the more likely we are to assign credibility to the ascription" (Arnstine, 1967, p. 33). Dispositional actions based on past events predict future behaviors.

A dispositional statement (i.e., saying someone has a disposition) is a use of history for predicting the future. Therefore, assignment of dispositions, or making dispositional statements, is to observe a range of behavioral acts multiple times. One single act does not verify the disposition. Therefore, assessment of disposition is to be repeated over time and relates back to what has occurred in the past.

In making the distinction between the past and future, Arnstine (1967) writes that being disposed to do certain things is not the same as doing them. He cautions that to confuse the observation of the dispositional behavior with the disposition itself is to mistake a tendency to act a certain way for the act itself. Focus should not be on certain behavioral *acts* but on the development of a range of behaviors that are observable over time.

It is inaccurate to say that someone has the disposition of care (the reader may plug in other observable dispositional behaviors such as critical thinking, creativity, or flexibility). According to Arnstine's (1967) philosophical writings regarding dispositions, it is more accurate to say that one is disposed to act in a caring manner which may be observed as a range of caring behaviors, even if the observation of care is not observed in every instance. Therefore, the assessment of dispositions is longitudinal.

Although Arnstine (1967) laid the dispositional foundation, it was efforts by Katz and Raths (1985) to move the discussion about effectiveness and quality to the forefront of teacher education by proposing that "the goals of teacher education programs should include a class of outcomes we call professional *dispositions*" that focus "exclusively upon behaviors of teachers related to effective teaching in the classroom" (p. 302). Professional dispositions in teacher education are linked to the "salient question of what one is trying to foster in teacher education candidates" (Dottin, 2009, p. 84).

Katz (1993) defines dispositions as "a tendency to exhibit frequently, consciously, and voluntarily a pattern of behavior that is directed to a broad goal" (para. 4). Katz and Raths (1986) describe these as a "pattern of acts that were chosen by the teacher in particular contexts and at particular times" (p. 7); although

> we are not using the term dispositions to indicate a cause of behavior; the construct is descriptive rather than explanatory. For example, a teacher does not praise children because he has a disposition to be supportive. Rather, a teacher observed to make use of praise in a number of contexts and on frequent occasions, might be described as having a supportive disposition (1985, pp. 301–302).

Why Are Dispositions So Confusing?

Confusion regarding the concept of dispositions pertains to the usage of related terms such as skills, habits, and attitudes. In the 1990s, "without fanfare or much discussion, teacher educators began talking about 'dispositions'...and the traditional formulation of the domains of teacher education – knowledge, skills, and attitudes – was recast as knowledge, skills, and dispositions" (Freeman, 2007, p. 3).

Dewey (1922) recognizes the need for a word to describe the "internal motivator of a set of actions and responses to the world. Various alternatives come to mind: habits, dispositions, temperaments, passions, drives, desires, inclinations, and so on" (Ritchhart, 2002, p. 19). Dewey writes:

> But we need a word to express the kind of human activity which is influenced by prior activity and in that sense acquired; which contains within itself a certain ordering or systematization of minor elements of action; which is projective, dynamic in quality, ready for overt manifestation; and which is operative in some subdued subordinate form even when not obviously dominating activity. Habit even in its ordinary usage comes nearer to denoting these facts than any other word. If the facts are recognized, we may also use the words attitude and dispositions. (p. 41)

Dewey (1922) prefers the term habit to disposition; however, he links the two when he refers to "*habits, of active dispositions* which makes a man do what he does" (p 44). However, Arnstine (1967) distinguishes between habit and disposition, and writes that a "habit is seldom used synonymously with disposition" (p. 27). He views the owner of a habit as less discriminating than the owner of a disposition because "the owner of a habit can be expected to practice his habit whenever an occasion makes such practice possible, whether or not it is appropriate to that occasion" (Arnstine, p. 27).

Freeman (2007) writes that attitudes represent a "gap between intention and actual behavior that renders attitudes unsuitable as a domain of teacher education, particularly when attention moves from what one intends to do to actual performance" (Freeman, p. 6). Therefore, an attitude is not a reliable predictor of observable behavior because performance, not intention, is emphasized in recent standard setting, accreditation, and administration of state-level rules and regulations.

How Are Dispositions Developed?

Dispositions are developed through implicit and explicit instruction; however, a key component is modeling by teacher educators who "make students [pre-service teachers in an educational program] aware of the key dispositions, and then model them for the entire duration of the program" (Helm, 2006, p. 118). Dottin (2009) suggests that "pedagogical work should focus on enhancing a culture that fosters and nurtures dispositions" (p. 86) by providing:

- Examples of dispositions in action
- Examples in direct instruction
- Opportunities to practice a disposition
- Feedback (Tishman, Jay, & Perkins, 1992; Eisner, 1994; Dottin, 2009; Helm, 2006; Ritchhart, 2002)

Tishman et al. (1992) efforts to teach critical thinking dispositions utilize two approaches. The first is a transmission model to convey facts and skills whereby teachers "organize their teaching in terms of preparing and transmitting messages" (p. 150). The second is the enculturation model – a dispositional approach that consists of (1) providing exemplars of the disposition; (2) encouraging and orchestrating interactions involving the disposition; and (3) explicit teaching of the disposition (Tishman et al.). Ritchhart suggests that the development of dispositions is enhanced through "explicit instruction within a supportive cultural context over time," not solely through direct instruction (Ritchhart, 2002, p. 48).

Ritchhart (2002) suggests that dispositions can be developed by students when external triggers nurture the inclination, awareness, and motivation to demonstrate a disposition. Acquisition may occur when students observe dispositions that the teacher is modeling, the disposition is taught, and opportunities are provided to practice and demonstrate the disposition. However, Ritchhart warns that consistency must be maintained by the teacher during the acquisition process.

How Are Dispositions Assessed?

Clark (1995) writes that although many teacher education programs assess what students know and do, assessing dispositions is a new aspect of teacher quality that has not been examined before. The assessment of dispositions poses a problem for educators seeking clean, lean assessment measures for four reasons:

• Semantics: What is the meaning of dispositions? How do dispositions differ from similar concepts such as skills, traits, and attitudes?
• Identification and selection of dispositions: What is the process of identifying the most suitable professional dispositions?
• Acquisition of dispositions: How are dispositions best acquired?
• Assessment of dispositions: How are dispositions assessed? (Jones & Bush, 2009).

Lund, Wayda, Woodward, and Buck's (2007) research to identify dispositions of beginning physical education teachers indicates the difficulty of assessment. Even though dispositions such as trustworthiness, dedication, and taking initiative were indicated as important by 90% of the faculty interviewed, assessment occurred 50% of the time or less. The authors maintain that assessment of dispositions is especially complicated when the observable behaviors are difficult to define.

The first step in the assessment process is for teacher educators to define what beginning professionals need to know and be able to do. The second step is for faculty to create definitions of dispositions and place these on a continuum indicating strength of observable disposition (Bloom, Madaus, & Hastings, 1981). Only after defining the dispositions in observable terms can faculty discuss ways to teach and assess these behaviors (Lund et al. 2007, para. 24). Throughout this process, teacher candidates must be informed about and understand dispositional expectations that are subsequently taught and modeled. Even though some faculty might consider abandoning attempts to measure the less observable dispositions such as trustworthiness and taking the initiative, Lund et al. contend that opting out is not an option.

Why Does Assessment of Dispositions Matters?

Wasicsko (2007) writes that there are three reasons why dispositions should be applied to teacher preparation programs. First, dispositions should be part of the intentional and systematic effort to enhance candidates' performance as they progress through a program. This might be accomplished using assessment tools, frameworks, and so forth once dispositions are identified.

Second, dispositions information should be used as admission criteria. Wasicsko (2007) acknowledges that this causes debate among faculty especially with regard to ethical and legal considerations. Locke (as cited in Lund et al. 2007) writes that

> teacher educators must develop a system for screening out those students who display undesirable behaviors or behaviors that 'represent irremedial incompetence' because 'teacher educators have the responsibility to honor a public trust of not allowing incompetent individuals to become teachers and develop a system for ensuring that this will happen.' (para. 31)

Third, dispositions can be used to hire full- and part-time education faculty. Wasicsko (2007) writes that "it seems only reasonable that the faculty instructing future teachers should exhibit the dispositions that program completers are supposed to possess" (p. 69). Likewise, Jones and Bush (2009) use similar logic by arguing that school librarians must possess learning dispositions as an antecedent to modeling these for students.

Where Do We Go from Here?

The one aspect of clarity that has been documented historically regarding professional dispositions is the difficulty to achieve consensus and understand how these guide the development from novice to exemplary educator (Knopp & Smith, 2005). This irony is not lost on the authors. As so often happens in teacher education, this complex concept could be distilled into a simplistic checklist of behaviors – even though this runs counter to the developmental nature, definition, and intent of dispositions to identify and nurture behaviors that lead to increased teacher effectiveness and student learning. As professional dispositions become an integral part of school library education, it is imperative that thoughtful conversations and research focus on important questions about the future of this profession. Ongoing and fervent discussions about dispositions are necessary to provide school library educators the opportunity to move the purpose, role, and profession of school librarianship forward especially during tumultuous economic times that traditionally challenge the stability of the field. Understanding the philosophical underpinnings of dispositions helps educators reflect on the qualities of the educational environment that lead to student learning, which is the main goal of education. Without meeting this goal school libraries are not only susceptible to budget cuts, their very existence as a member of the school learning community is threatened.

A significant step toward recognizing the dynamic nature of dispositions would be to create assessments leading to the transformative development of the profession by nurturing and developing more effective school librarians. Thoughtfully developed performance-based assessments spring from conversations identified in the preceding paragraph. Assessments would indicate movement on a spectrum of developing professional dispositions rather than a static and stationary situation that is beyond improvement. Just as we continue our human development from children to adolescents to adults, we continue to develop throughout our professional lives.

References

American Library Association. (2007). *Standards for the 21st-century learner*. Retrieved from http://www.ala.org/aasl/standards.

Arnstine, D. (1967). *Philosophy of education: Learning and schooling*. New York, NY: Harper & Row.

Bloom, B. S., Madaus, G. F., & Hastings, J. T. (1981). *Evaluation to improve learning*. New York: McGraw-Hill.

Clark, K. B. (1995). A contemporary rationale for dispositions in education. In R. L. Smith, D. Skarbek, & J. Hurst (Eds.), *The passion of teaching: Dispositions in the schools* (pp. 15–26). Lanham, MD: Scarecrow education.

Collinson, V. (1996, July). *Becoming an exemplary teacher: Integrating professional, interpersonal, and intrapersonal knowledge*. Paper presented at the annual meeting of the Japan-United States Teacher Education Consortium, Naruto, Japan.

Combs, A. W. (1972). Some basic concepts for teacher education. *The Journal of Teacher Education, 23*(3), 286–290.

Cushman, K. (2006). Help us care enough to learn. *Educational Leadership, 63*(5), 34–37.

Darling-Hammond, L. (1996). What matters most a competent teacher for every child. *Phi Delta Kappan, 78*(3), 193–200.

Dewey, J. (1922). *Human nature and conduct*. New York, NY: Modern Library.

Dewey, J. (1933). *How we think: A restatement of the relation of reflective thinking to the educative process*. Boston: D.C. Heath.

Dottin, E. S. (2009). Professional judgment and dispositions in teacher education. *Teaching and Teacher Education, 25*(1), 83–88.

Eisner, E. W. (1994). *The educational imagination: On the design and evaluation of school programs* (3rd ed.). New York, NY: Macmillan.

Freeman, L. (2007). An overview of dispositions in teacher education. In M. E. Diez & J. Raths (Eds.), *Dispositions in teacher education* (pp. 3–29). Charlotte, NC: Information Age Publishing.

Helm, C. M. (2006). Teacher dispositions as predictors of good teaching. *The Clearing House, 79*(3), 117–118.

Interstate New Teacher Assessment & Support Consortium. (1992). *Model standards for beginning teacher licensure and development: A resource for state dialogue*. Washington, DC: Council of Chief State School Officers.

Jones, J. L., & Bush, G. (2009). What defines an exemplary school librarian? An exploration of professional dispositions. *Library Media Connection, 28*(6), 10–12.

Katz, L. (1993). *Dispositions as educational goals. ERIC Clearinghouse on Elementary and Early Childhood Education*. Retrieved from http://chiron.valdosta.edu/whuitt/files/edoutcomes.html.

Katz, L., & Raths, J. D. (1985). Dispositions as goals for teacher education. *Teaching and Teacher Education, 1*(4), 301–307.

Katz, L., & Raths, J. D. (1986, July). *Dispositional goals for teacher education: Problems of identification and assessment*. Paper presented at the World Assembly of the International Council on Education for Teaching, Kingston, Jamaica.

Knopp, T. Y., & Smith, R. L. (2005). A brief historical context for dispositions in teacher education. In R. L. Smith, D. Skarbek, & J. Hurst (Eds.), *The passion of teaching: Dispositions in the schools* (pp. 1–15). Lanham, MD: Rowman & Littlefield Publishing Group.

Lund, J., Wayda, V., Woodward, R., & Buck, M. (2007). Professional dispositions: What are we teaching prospective physical education teachers? *Physical Educator, 64*(1), 38–47.

National Board of Professional Teaching Standards. (2002). *What teachers should know and be able to do*. Arlington, VA: National Board for Professional Teaching Standards. Retrieved from http://www.nbpts.org/UserFiles/File/what_teachers.pdf.

National Commission on Teaching and America's Future. (1996). *What matters most: Teaching for America's future*. New York, NY: National Commission on Teaching & America's Future.

National Council for Accreditation of Teacher Education. (2008). *Professional Standards for the Accreditation of Teacher Preparation Institutions*. Retrieved from http://www.ncate.org/documents/standards/NCATE%20Standards%202008.pdf.

National Council for the Accreditation of Teacher Education. (2007). *NCATE issues call for action; Defines professional dispositions as used in teacher education*. Retrieved from http://www.ncate.org/public/102407.asp?ch=148.

Paul, J. L., & Smith, T. J. (2000). *Stories out of school: Memories and reflections on care and cruelty in the classroom*. Stamford, CT: Ablex.

Ritchhart, R. (2002). *Intellectual character: What it is, why it matters, and how to get it*. San Francisco, CA: Jossey-Bass.

Ryle, G. (1949). *A concept of mind*. New York, NY: Barnes and Noble.

Teacher preparation. (2007). Retrieved from http://www.aacte.org?programs/TEAMC/teacher_preparation_wsu.pdf.

Tishman, S., Jay, E., & Perkins, D. N. (1992). Teaching thinking skills: From transmission to enculturation. *Theory into Practice, 32*(3), 147–153.

Tishman, S., Jay, E., & Perkins, D. (1994). *The thinking classroom: Learning and teaching in a culture of thinking*. Boston: Allyn & Bacon.

Tishman, S., & Perkins, D. (1997). The language of thinking. *Kappan, 78*(5), 368–374.

Usher, D. (2002, November). *Arthur Combs' five dimensions of helper belief reformulated as five dispositions of teacher effectiveness*. Paper presented at the first annual symposium of educator dispositions: Effective teacher – Effective person. Richmond, Kentucky. Retrieved from http://coehs.nku.edu/educatordispositions/symposium_2002/day2/teacherrenewal.pdf.

Wasicsko, M. M. (2007). The perceptual approach to teacher dispositions: The effective teacher as an effective person. In M. E. Diez & J. Raths (Eds.), *Dispositions in teacher education* (pp. 31–52). Charlotte, NC: Information Age Publishing.

Revised *Library Media Standards* Adopted by the National Board for Professional Teaching Standards

Delia Neuman

On April 16, 2010, the Board of Directors of the National Board for Professional Teaching Standards (NBPTS) adopted the revised NBPTS *Library Media Standards,* which had been developed during the 2009–2010 academic year. These *Standards* describe what library media specialists need to know and be able to do in order to become National Board Certified as "accomplished" – the highest level of certification available to United States teachers. As of March 2010, over 2,300 library media specialists had earned certification under the original *Standards*, published in 2001. Across the country, over 82,000 teachers in various fields have earned National Board Certification.

Founded in 1987 and funded in part with grants from the US Department of Education and the National Science Foundation, "NBPTS is an independent, nonprofit, nonpartisan and nongovernmental organization" whose mission is "Maintaining high and rigorous standards for what accomplished teachers should know and be able to do; Providing a national voluntary system certifying teachers who meet these standards; Advocating related education reforms to integrate National Board Certification in American education and to capitalize on the expertise of National Board Certified Teachers" (http://nbpts.org). Governed by a 27-member board of directors, "the majority of whom are teachers, [the organization is] committed to basic reform in education [and recognizes] that the single most important action the nation can take to improve schools is to strengthen teaching" (NBPTS, 2001, p. v). NBPTS has worked systematically for over two decades to develop *Standards* for nearly 30 certificate areas, and all are reviewed and revised on a regular basis. The first revision of the NBPTS *Library Media Standards* since their debut in 2001, the *Standards* adopted in April reflect changes in the profession over the last decade and point the way to the future for the leading practitioners in the field. The final document – NBPTS *Library Media Standards*, 2nd edition – will be available in Spring 2012.

D. Neuman (✉)
College of Information Science and Technology, Drexel University, Philadelphia, PA, USA
e-mail: dneuman@drexel.edu

M. Orey et al. (eds.), *Educational Media and Technology Yearbook: Volume 36, 2011,*   219
Educational Media and Technology Yearbook 36, DOI 10.1007/978-1-4614-1305-9_19,

All NBPTS *Standards* documents reflect the "Five Core Propositions" of the Board, and the new NBPTS *Library Media Standards* are no exception. Like their analogs in other fields, these *Standards* are grounded in the propositions that:

- Teachers are committed to students and their learning.
- Teachers know the subjects they teach and how to teach those subjects to students.
- Teachers are responsible for managing and monitoring student learning.
- Teachers think systematically about their practice and learn from experience.
- Teachers are members of learning communities.

The Revised *NBPTS Library Media Standards*

The ten standards statements listed below were developed within the framework provided by these propositions. Each standard statement is also accompanied by a narrative elaboration that provides a detailed explanation and examples to clarify what is necessary to achieve the stated standard. Standards I, II, III, and V are essentially updates from the 2001 *Standards* document that reflect increased understanding of the needs and natures of students, of the evolution in the theories and practices of learning and teaching, of developments within the field of library and information studies, and of changes in administrative practice brought about largely by advances in technology. Standards IV and VI–X also include information updated from the earlier document but are substantially new in both content and emphases. These six "new" standards are discussed in detail after the list of the individual standards statements themselves.

NBPTS Library Media Standards

- Standard I: Knowledge of Students
    Accomplished library media specialists understand the academic, personal, and social characteristics of students and relate them to learning.
- Standard II: Teaching and Learning
    Accomplished library media specialists understand and apply principles and practices of effective teaching in support of student learning.
- Standard III: Knowledge of Library and Information Studies
    Accomplished library media specialists understand and apply the principles of library and information studies to support student learning and to create an effective, integrated library media program.
- Standard IV: Leadership
    Accomplished library media specialists are visionary leaders in their schools and in the profession.

- Standard V: Administration
   Accomplished library media specialists use a range of strategies and techniques to manage and administer effective library media programs.
- Standard VI: Integration of Technologies
   Accomplished library media specialists use technologies effectively to support student learning and library media program administration.
- Standard VII: Access, Equity, and Diversity
   Accomplished library media specialists provide access, ensure equity, and embrace diversity.
- Standard VII: Ethics
   Accomplished library media specialists uphold and promote professional ethics and ethical information behavior.
- Standard IX: Outreach and Advocacy
   Accomplished library media specialists promote the library media program through outreach and the development of advocates.
- Standard X: Reflective Practice
   Accomplished library media specialists engage in reflective practice to improve student learning. (National Board for Professional Teaching Standards 2010a, p. 2).

Major Changes in the Revised NBPTS *Library Media Standards*

Standard IV: Leadership – an outgrowth of 2001's Standard X: Leadership, Advocacy, and Community Partnerships – is now discussed immediately after the three standards describing the basic elements of effective library media performance: knowledge of students, knowledge of pedagogy, and knowledge of the key concepts of the discipline. The new standard statement and its elaboration reflect the critical importance of visionary leadership to today's accomplished library media specialist. The Committee agreed that a strong emphasis on instructional leadership, on administrative leadership, and on leadership in the profession is essential in today's educational environment.

Standard VI: Integration of Technologies represents an important refocusing of 2001's Standard V: Leading Innovation through the Library Media Program. The new standard recognizes the centrality of the accomplished library media specialist in understanding, introducing, and perfecting the use of the full range of technologies for teaching and learning and for administering a strong program. Now, the focus is no longer on using technology simply to provide access and support and basic data gathering but on fostering a deep understanding of how technologies can undergird twenty-first century learning and provide a means for effective program administration. The standard particularly addresses the use of technologies to support students' conduct of effective research and their creation of high-quality information products in a variety of formats.

Standard VII: Access, Equity, and Diversity adds an important ingredient to 2001's Standard IX, Ethics, Equity, and Diversity: a discussion of access as key to meeting the needs of all students. To thrive in today's world, students need access to a highly qualified library media specialist and to a strong and carefully focused library media program – not just to appropriate and well-targeted resources. The new standard emphasizes the key role of the accomplished library media specialist in being proactive in promoting equity and respect for diversity by actively seeking to anticipate and meet the needs of students at all levels and from all circumstances. The standard is grounded in the belief that the accomplished library media specialist has a role to play in helping all students develop into competent and well-informed citizens.

Standard VIII: Ethics is in part a response to the ethical issues that have emerged along with such advanced technological developments as the Internet and the World Wide Web. Pulled out from 2001's Standard IX noted above, the new standard deals specifically with contemporary issues of information ethics and underscores the importance of students, teachers, and administrators becoming good "digital citizens" and ethical users of information in all formats. Building on the field's traditional professional ethical stance regarding access to and use of information, this standard highlights the accomplished library media specialist's role as a model for understanding the principles of ethical information use and applying them in everyday life.

Standard IX: Outreach and Advocacy updates 2001's Standard X: Leadership, Advocacy, and Community Partnerships. With "leadership" now occupying a standard of its own, new Standard IX emphasizes activities that relate specifically to promoting the library media program within the school and creating relationships inside and outside the school that will lead to others' stepping up as program advocates. Recognizing that the most effective advocates are not library media specialists themselves but those whom they serve, the accomplished library media specialist is called upon to create partnerships with students, teachers, families, and members of the community so that they may speak from personal experience about the value of strong library media programs and call for strengthening and enhancing them, especially in times of need.

Standard X: Reflective Practice is similar to 2001's Standard VIII, Professional Growth, but the 2010 standard singles out the importance of reflection as a key to professional growth that is truly meaningful. Committee members who are themselves National Board Certified spoke strongly for including this specific standard in the document because they found that the reflection required to attain certification was critical to their own growth. Although each individual standard has its own "reflection" piece, this standard holds a special place – not only as indispensable in its own right but also as the summary and culmination of the process of becoming accomplished enough to gain National Board Certification by NBPTS.

The Development of the Revised *Standards*

The 2010 NBPTS *Library Media Standards* were developed by the Library Media Standards Committee, whose 12 members were selected by NBPTS from over 400 nominees. Committee members were demographically, geographically, and professionally diverse: they included nine women and three men from a range of races and ethnicities. They came from 12 states – from the Atlantic to the Pacific coasts and from the upper Midwest to the South. They included building-level practitioners from elementary through high school, supervisors and coordinators from both rural and urban districts of various sizes, and academics involved in programs that prepare library media specialists in universities. Five were National Board Certified Teachers – one in English Language Arts/Adolescence and four in Library Media. Two stakeholder organizations – the Association for Educational Communications and Technology and the American Association of School Librarians – were represented in the Committee.

The development process followed established NBPTS practice and was facilitated by three NBPTS staff with extensive experience in revising *Standards* documents. Based around four intensive face-to-face meetings held over extended weekends at sites near Washington, DC, the process also included WebEx discussions and other opportunities for Committee members to share their insights. Initially, the original standards statements and their accompanying elaborations were reviewed by all committee members, who also proposed new standards for consideration. Small groups took the responsibility for rewriting the existing elaborations as necessary and for drafting elaborations for proposed new standards. Ultimately, the committee as a whole determined which standards would go forward and finalized the elaboration for each. Over the course of the development process, all the elaborations were reviewed and discussed by changing small groups and by the group as a whole so that every committee member had full opportunity for input into each piece of the document. Toward the end of the process, the committee came to consensus on the standards' names, on the specific standards statements noted above, and on the final order of the standards and their elaborations in the *Standards* document.

NBPTS offered the draft document for public comment in January and February 2010. Stakeholder groups as well as a wide variety of other interested professionals were invited through listservs and personal contacts to access the NBPTS website in order to review the draft, to rate a series of statements about it, and to offer comments. National Board Certified Teachers (NBCTs) in related areas – specifically Library Media, English Language Arts, Early Childhood Generalists, and Middle Childhood Generalists – were directly invited, while other NBCTs across the country were also notified about the process. Ultimately, approximately 500 reviewers provided approximately 700 comments in response to the five statements offered for each standard:

- The standard as a whole describes a critical aspect of accomplished practice.
- The standard provides a complete and clear explanation of what accomplished library media specialists should know and be able to do.
- The elaboration includes varied examples that capture or describe accomplished practice.
- The standard reflects advanced-level practice of Library Media.
- The standard as a whole is forward-thinking in describing accomplished practice.

The data were compiled and analyzed extensively by NBPTS staff to determine the demographic characteristics of the respondents (gender, race/ethnicity, geographic representation, credentials, school characteristics, etc.) and to report the patterns as well as the details of their responses. For all ten standards statements, the overall rating for each of the five statements noted above was at least 90%:

- Critical aspects: 93%
- Clear elaboration: 91%
- Advanced-level teaching: 90%
- Varied examples: 93%
- Remain current into the future: 94%

For both the committee and the NBPTS staff, a major highlight of the analysis was the finding that "90% of respondents 'Agree' or '"Strongly Agree' with the following statement: 'The standards document as a whole describes all critical aspects of accomplished teaching'" (NBPTS, 2010b, slide 21).

Respondents' open-ended responses provided the material for the committee's final meeting in February, at which all the comments were reviewed. Suggestions and recommendations were weighed and discussed, the draft was revised accordingly, and the committee wrote and later finalized the introduction to the *Standards* document. Early in March, the document was approved by the NBPTS Certification Council – the governing body for the Standards, Assessment, and Operations division of the organization. In April, it was formally approved by the NBPTS Board of Directors. Upon publication, the revised *Standards* will become the basis for National Board Certification in Library Media.

Development of the Assessment

Committee members agreed that the National Board has created an exemplary process that resulted in the development of a comprehensive, thoughtful, and solid *Standards* document. The next part of the NBPTS process – the development of the revised assessment instruments that candidates will use to document their achievement of the revised NBPTS *Library Media Standards* – began in 2010. In that process, a committee member served as the liaison to the NBPTS assessment staff to design appropriate assessment exercises. Candidates for certification, who are required to have at least 3 years of experience in the profession, will complete these exercises as well as developing portfolio entries about their practice that provide performance-based evidence of their degree of mastery of each standard. They will

> prepare their portfolio [entries] by videotaping their teaching, gathering student learning products and other teaching artifacts, and providing detailed analyses of their practice... The portfolio is designed to capture teaching in real-time, real-life settings, thus allowing trained scorers... to examine how teachers translate knowledge and theory into practice. [The portfolio] also yields the most valued evidence NBPTS collects – videos of practice and samples of student work. (NBPTS, 2001, p. viii).

The portfolio entries also include the candidates' reflections on their practice and documentations of their effectiveness in various professional areas. Considered "a professional development vehicle of considerable power" (NBPTS, 2001, p. viii), the portfolio and the activities that lead to its development are the key to strengthening teaching – the ultimate goal of NBPTS.

References

National Board for Professional Teaching Standards. (2001). *NBPTS Library Media Standards*. Arlington, VA: National Board for Professional Teaching Standards.

National Board for Professional Teaching Standards. (2010a). *NBPTS Library Media Standards: Draft*. Arlington, VA: National Board for Professional Teaching Standards.

National Board for Professional Teaching Standards. (2010b). *NBPTS Library Media Standards: Public Comment Review*. Arlington, VA: National Board for Professional Teaching Standards.

Part III
Leadership Profiles

Introduction

Robert Maribe Branch

The purpose of this section is to profile individuals who have made significant contributions to the field of educational media and communication technology. Leaders profiled in the *Educational Media and Technology Yearbook* have typically held prominent offices, composed seminal works and made significant contributions that have influenced the contemporary vision of the field. The people profiled in this section have often been directly responsible for mentoring individuals, who have themselves become recognized for their own contributions to learning, design and technology.

There are special reasons to feature people of national and international reputation. This volume of the *Educational Media and Technology Yearbook* profiles individuals who continue to uphold the tradition of leadership in educational media and communication technology. The leaders profiled this year are:

Thomas C. Reeves
Ronald Zemke
Tillman (Tim) James Ragan
Glenn Snelbecker

R.M. Branch (✉)
Learning, Design, and Technology Program, University of Georgia, Athens, GA, USA
e-mail: rbranch@uga.edu

M. Orey et al. (eds.), *Educational Media and Technology Yearbook: Volume 36, 2011*,   229
Educational Media and Technology Yearbook 36, DOI 10.1007/978-1-4614-1305-9_20,
© Springer Science+Business Media, LLC 2012

The following people (listed alphabetically) were profiled in earlier volumes of the *Educational Media and Technology Yearbook*:

John C. Belland	Jean E. Lowrie
Robert K. Branson	Wesley Joseph McJulien
James W. Brown	M. David Merrill
Bob Casey	Michael Molenda
Betty Collis	David Michael Moore
Robert E. De Kieffer	Robert M. Morgan
Robert M. Diamond	Robert Morris
Walter Dick	James Okey
Frank Dwyer	Ronald Oliver
Donald P. Ely	Tjeerd Plomp
James D. Finn	W. Michael Reed
Robert Mills Gagné	Rita C. Richey
Castelle (Cass) G. Gentry	Paul Saettler
Thomas F. Gilbert	Wilbur Schramm
Kent Gustafson	Charles Francis Schuller
John Hedberg	Don Carl Smellie
Robert Heinich	Howard Sullivan
Stanley A. Huffman	William Travers
Harry Alleyn Johnson	Constance Dorothea Weinman
Roger Kaufman	Paul Welliver
Jerrold E. Kemp	Paul Robert Wendt
Addie Kinsinger	David R. Krathwohl

People profiled in this section are usually emeritus faculty who may or may not be active in the field. You are encouraged to nominate individuals to be featured in this section of the Yearbook. The editors of this Yearbook will carefully consider your nomination. Please direct comments, questions and suggestions about the selection process to the Editorial Office: *Educational Media and Technology Yearbook*, 604 Aderhold Hall, The University of Georgia, Athens, Georgia 30602 or mikeorey@uga.edu.

Tillman (Tim) James Ragan: Celebrating Four Decades of Excellent Scholarship

Diane Igoche

We always want to celebrate those who make contributions to our lives. Their many accomplishments, tireless efforts towards their callings, and selfless service to others are things that we praise them for but also acknowledge in a venue such as the Leadership Profile. Dr. Tillman James Ragan is one of such individuals who worked tirelessly and sometimes thanklessly for the betterment of those who worked with him, those who he mentored and those who would come after him. The Leadership profile would like to acknowledge an extraordinary scholar whose name and legacy will live on even as he is no longer with us. Dr. Tillman Ragan passed away on March 7th, 2010 after bravely facing multiple myeloma.

D. Igoche (✉)
Learning, Design, and Technology Program, The University of Georgia, Athens, GA, USA
e-mail: dai011@uga.edu

M. Orey et al. (eds.), *Educational Media and Technology Yearbook: Volume 36, 2011*,   231
Educational Media and Technology Yearbook 36, DOI 10.1007/978-1-4614-1305-9_21,
© Springer Science+Business Media, LLC 2012

An Extraordinary Colleague, Mentor and Scholar and Colleague

Dr. Tillman J. Ragan became a professor in the Instructional Psychology and Technology program at The University of Oklahoma in 1970. He received his Ph.D. in Instructional Technology from Syracuse University in 1970. His area of research and teaching was instructional technology, with specific interests in learner characteristics, visual literacy, and applications of computer technology to instruction. His research interests also focused around instructional design, the design, development, and evaluation of computer-based learning environments, interactive multimedia, and education and training systems. He also had extensive experience in curriculum development both within and outside the field of instructional technology.

Prior to beginning his doctoral degree program, Tillman served the country as an Air Force Officer. He was the Assistant Director of Student Operations at the Air University in Gunter Air Force Base in Alabama and then proceeded to work as an Instructor of Curriculum and Instructional Methods at the same institution. He did this while working as an Instructor of English Composition at Troy State College in Alabama. It is obvious that he was called to the field from the beginning. He continued to work in the field of Instructional Technology for more than 40 years.

Dr. Ragan is the author of five books and numerous articles on instructional technology, and he has been a columnist for the Educational Technology magazine. He was also on the editorial board of ETR&D. He has served on many committees and he has served as president of the Research and Theory Division and of the Division of Instructional Development of the American Educational Research Association (AERA), vice president of the International Visual Literacy Association (IVLA), and co-chair of the Professors of Instructional Design Technology conference (PIDT). He was also very active in the Association of Educational Communications and Technology (AECT).

Dr. Tillman Ragan's 1976 article on "A Multifactor Approach to Research in Instructional Technology" came at a time when the field was going through definitional changes. He used this piece to address the diversity of the field of Instructional Technology and explained how conceptual schemes and models are important in approaching the contributions that this field makes to other fields. Audiovisual instruction gained ground in the 1970s and Dr. Ragan's research at the time reflected this trend. He investigated the development and implementation of university courses that would start to embrace audiovisual learning techniques. He suggested that audiovisuals are intended to open-up or reawaken students' visual awareness and visual thinking processes to enhance learning. He continued to stay in the forefront of visual literacy in instructional technology and he thoroughly researched the field of visual imagery and visual literacy as it related to the brain. He also contributed immensely to the building of the knowledge base of visual literacy in instructional technology.

As audiovisuals evolved, so did Dr. Ragan's research in the area. A true instructional technologist, he expanded his research to other fields. He expanded his research to embrace mathematical concepts, neurolinguistic programming, motivation, and equipment manufacturing. As he expanded his research base, he also considered his home institution and the potential for merging of University of Oklahoma's Educational Psychology and Educational Technology programs. He believed that the merger would increase the research possibilities that existed between both fields. In 1989, the two programs were integrated; it was a golden opportunity to start his work on cognition and motivation.

The main research he conducted was very diverse; he was led by the interests of his students. One topic of interest was generative instruction versus discovery instruction. Dr. Ragan and Dr. Patricia Smith talk about this in their text; the text-book focused on a more cognitive view. In 1989, Dr. Tillman Ragan married Dr. Patricia Smith Ragan; they did not only embark on partnership as husband and wife, but they also joined forces as academic partners. Co-authoring books and articles together, they became a household name in the instructional technology field. Tim and Patricia worked together and collaborated even independently.

A testament to mentors everywhere, according to Dr. Ray Miller

> Dr Ragan's students loved him for a lack of better words. The turnout at his funeral was evident of the love that students had for him. His colleagues also held him dear to their hearts. He was energetic and fun to be around. Dr Ragan always had great ideas and was always interested in bettering of his home institution, and program area. I'd describe Tim's persona as what you see is what you get. He was very zealous about his work; he always had a little twinkle in his eye about it.

Dr. Tillman Ragan's life as a researcher, mentor, and colleague is one to be celebrated; his academic legacy will live on for many years to come.

Special thanks to Dr. Ray Miller for his contribution to this profile.

Thomas Reeves

Diane Igoche

Dr. Thomas C. Reeves is one of the most influential scholars in the field of Instructional Technology. Dr. Thomas C. Reeves began his educational journey as a doctoral student in the Division of Instructional Design, Development and Evaluation at Syracuse University. He earned his doctorate in 1979. Dr. Reeves has recently entered the ranks of Professor Emeritus, but as most of his colleagues and students have noted, he will probably not be slowing down in his contributions to the field.

Finding Instructional Technology at the Seminary

Long before he attained the title of "Dr.," Thomas C. Reeves served as a junior seminarian at St. Mary's Seminary in Pennsylvania. According to an interview he granted in Georgia State University, his first experience as an instructional technologist came about when he helped his Latin instructor prepare transparencies to

D. Igoche (✉)
Learning, Design, and Technology Program, The University of Georgia, Athens, GA, USA
e-mail: dai011@uga.edu

M. Orey et al. (eds.), *Educational Media and Technology Yearbook: Volume 36, 2011*, Educational Media and Technology Yearbook 36, DOI 10.1007/978-1-4614-1305-9_22, © Springer Science+Business Media, LLC 2012

illustrate lectures about Caesar's campaigns in Gaul. Thomas Reeves' service with the US Army produced another opportunity for him to begin the process of becoming an instructional technologist. In the US Army, he participated in an audiovisual program. Coupled with serving the United States of America, Thomas completed an Elementary Education degree at Georgia State University and taught Social Studies at the Junior High School level. Dr. Thomas C. Reeves finally made the decision to pursue a doctoral degree when he encountered frustrations with feeble attempts to motivate students via media clippings that he created. Not an individual to let a problem overtake him, he wanted to do more to solve his frustrations. With encouragement from his professor at Georgia State, he embarked on academic training as a graduate student at Syracuse University. At the end of his time at Syracuse, he became a Fulbright Lecturer in Peru from 1979 to 1980.

The University of Georgia recruited Dr. Thomas C. Reeves as a professor in the Department of Early Childhood Education, and he later joined the Instructional Technology program in 1985. Dr. Reeves settled into his position at The University of Georgia and continued his work as a phenomenal researcher, scholar, mentor, colleague and advisor to his students. Up until his retirement, he served as the Doctoral Program Coordinator. Current students at the University of Georgia's Learning, Design and Technology program listed his helpful nature as one of the things that captured their attention during their application process to the program. Dr. Reeves has been an inspiration to his colleagues at his program. Dr. Reeves taught multiple courses in the program; notable is the Instructional Product Evaluation course, a course that focuses on the evaluation of instructional products. Dr. Reeves designed the course to integrate real world problem solving as students had to evaluate instructional products of real clients. Some of his students have boasted making employment and internship connections via their participation in the course.

Dr. Thomas C. Reeves is a well sought after presenter and speaker in national and international presentations and workshops. Dr. Reeves has been an invited speaker in the United States of America, Australia, Europe, Asia, Africa and other parts of The Americas. He has served as editor of the *Journal of Interactive Learning Research* and the co-founder of the University of Georgia's Learning and Performance Support Lab. He has developed and evaluated numerous interactive multimedia programs for both education and training. He is a past president of the Association for the Development of Computer-based Instructional Systems (ADCIS). He has been a keynote speaker, invited speaker and frequent tutorial instructor at many AACE conferences, and he co-chaired the 1997 ED-MEDIA conference and the E-Learn conferences in 2002 and 2006. In 2003, he was the first person to receive the AACE Fellowship Award. Dr. Reeves was also selected as one the Top 100 people in multimedia by Multimedia Producer magazine.

Dr. Thomas C. Reeves studied with Dr. Edward F. Kelly as his Dissertation Advisor at Syracuse University. Dr. Kelly influenced and helped develop Dr. Reeves' passion for evaluation. Prior to being recruited by the University of Georgia, Dr. Reeves was an evaluator in places such as New York State of Mental Health and the University of Maryland. Dr. Reeves worked with Dr. John Hedberg, a former doctoral colleague who had continued his career as a multimedia designer and evaluator in Australia. Dr. Reeves joined forces with Dr. Hedberg to conduct workshops and develop evaluation tools, guidelines and templates that are used by evaluators today. Dr. Reeves and Dr. Hedberg co-authored the first book on evaluation that captured the evaluation process within the context of instructional design and technology.

Dr. Reeves' research agenda is one that is very diverse. He has conducted research on evaluation methods as they apply to products of instructional technology. His research agenda also expands to the development of electronic performance support systems for teachers and training developers, mental models that learners construct of interactive multimedia, applications of instructional technology in developing countries and educational design based research. Alongside articles and books that he has authored and co-authored, Dr. Reeves has also made contributions to technical publications for Apple Computer, Inc. He worked with Dr. Jim Laffey in producing an interactive videodisk course for Apple Computer, Inc which went on to become a Golden Cindy award winning course.

Dr. Reeves' portfolio is very strong because he has not only made academic contributions to the field of instructional technology but also gained practical work experience that strengthened his academic research giving him a wider understanding of the areas he researched and wrote about. Dr. Reeves has worked with MetaMedia Systems in Maryland and completed consultancies with Apple Computer, AT&T, Delta Airlines, IBM and the US Air Force Academy.

Dr. Thomas C. Reeves will transition into the position of Professor Emeritus of Learning, Design and Technology at The University of Georgia in the 2010–2011 school session. Dr. Reeves has undoubtedly become an international presence in various aspects of instructional technology. His contributions to the field will remain significant even as he enters the Emeritus status of his career.

Glenn Snelbecker

Diane Igoche

The diversity of the field of Instructional Technology requires individuals that are broad thinkers and that can understand the complexities of the human mind while engaging outside factors such as technology to stimulate a learner; Dr. Glenn E. Snelbecker portrays this. Dr. Snelbecker was an exemplary scholar who was a passionate advocate for his students while they were under his tutelage and onwards. He passed away on January 24th, 2010 after dedicating more than five decades to his career as an Instructional Technologist.

D. Igoche (✉)
Learning, Design, and Technology Program, The University of Georgia, Athens, GA, USA
e-mail: dai011@uga.edu

M. Orey et al. (eds.), *Educational Media and Technology Yearbook: Volume 36, 2011*,   239
Educational Media and Technology Yearbook 36, DOI 10.1007/978-1-4614-1305-9_23,
© Springer Science+Business Media, LLC 2012

In the Beginning

This extraordinary scholar began his career earning a Diploma and Bachelors of Science Degree in Business Education from Elizabethtown College in Pennsylvania. He proceeded to Bucknell University for a Master's Degree in Guidance and Counseling. Three years later, Cornell produced a dynamic academic that spearheaded research on Psychoeducational Design.

However, Dr. Snelbecker's career in academia did not begin until a number of years after his graduation from Cornell University. He secured a position at V.A. Hospital in Brockton, Massachusetts as a Clinical Psychologist and later became the Director of the Hospital's Behavior Research Laboratory. Dr. Snelbecker found a teaching position at an institution that he would make his home institution for the rest of his academic career. Temple University offered Dr. Snelbecker a faculty position in 1967; there he worked tirelessly contributing to the field of Educational Psychology and Technology.

Developing a Noteworthy Career

Dr. Glenn Snelbecker authored the book, *Learning Theory, Instructional Theory, and Psychoeducational Design* in 1974; it was reprinted by University of American Press in 1985. His book has been used in Europe (Eastern and Western Europe), Asia, Australia and New Zealand, North American, and South America. His research on Psychoeducational Design has been used as a framework for books focused on counseling theories implemented by counseling practitioners. Psychoeducational design has been discussed by various "knowledge producers" as well as by "knowledge users" in educational technology and media. In addition to other educational technology publications, he has contributed four chapters in three books edited by Professor Charles Reigeluth. He has published various journal papers, a textbook on learning theories and education and an ASTD book chapter on instructional technology, and has been directing or co-directing federally-, state- and foundation-funded projects on curricular and instructional applications of technology since the mid-1980s. He has been active in the development and implementation of "technology and education" ventures for the past four decades.

In 2004, he was the keynote speaker in two international meetings in the cities of Busan and Seoul in South Korea. He was interviewed by Professor Daniel F Oswald in a series of interviews of Educational Technology leaders. This interview was published in Educational Technology in the September–October 2002 issue. He has been listed in Marquis' "Who's Who in America" and "Who's Who in the World," multiple times as well as in several other "Who's Who" lists. One recent publication is a 2008 book chapter focusing on his concept of Functional Relevance as a means for clarifying how practitioners can be aided in selecting and using theories and research information to address practical problems when designing online learning.

Dr. Snelbecker was an American Psychological Association (APA) Fellow in Educational Psychology as well as an APA Fellow in Clinical Psychology. He was one of about 300 American Educational Research Association (AERA) members who were selected as "Inaugural Fellows" when AERA recently established the "Fellow" membership status. He made an indelible mark on our field and will be dearly missed.

Ron Zemke: A Leader on the Other Side of the Fence

The Educational Media and Technology Yearbook has continued to profile ground-breaking individuals that have made their mark in Academia. In this edition, EMTY will profile more leaders in the field of Instructional Technology; one of those leaders we will pay tribute to is an individual who made contributions to our field but from the business and industry realm. Ron Zemke was an Instructional Technologist who worked as a consultant, trainer, and an editor for *Training*: a professional development magazine that advocates training and workforce development as a business tool. The following tribute is dedicated to Mr. Ron Zemke who passed away on August 17th, 2004. His profile is an excerpt of a tribute written by Mr. Chris Lee, the former managing editor of Training Magazine and a colleague of Mr. Zemke.

The world became a little colder on August 17th because Ron had left us. He passed on from complications from non-Hodgkin's lymphoma. He was 62. He is

Adopted with permission from Training Magazine, written by Chris Lee

M. Orey et al. (eds.), *Educational Media and Technology Yearbook: Volume 36, 2011*, Educational Media and Technology Yearbook 36, DOI 10.1007/978-1-4614-1305-9_24, © Springer Science+Business Media, LLC 2012

survived by his wife Susan, mother, brothers, sister, nieces, and nephews. He gave a lot of himself during the three decades he contributed columns and articles to *Training Mag.* He told stories, shared lessons learned, passed along wisdom and taught valuable and sometimes unpleasant truths, mostly, with humor and insight that came from his real life and hard-earned experience.

Ron and I worked at *Training* and on other projects, for more than 20 years. I met him on my first day on the job. Ron was a mentor, teacher, colleague, and friend. I picture him, sitting in my office, leaning forward in his chair to listen before saying, "Try thinking about it this way". And then he will shift the prism just enough so that I could see the rainbow in living color. He specialized in creating that "aha!" experience we hear so much about. Jack Gordon, former editor of *Training* notes that "Ron was fiercely loyal to training professionals, but never pandered to them. Whatever the issue from the advantages and drawbacks of e-learning to the ethics of attempting to change personal belief systems in the name of job related training, he said what he thought, not just what he figured people wanted to hear".

Ron had the endless curiosity of a reporter and the born teacher's need to explain what he found in terms that were understandable and memorable. He did that explaining, both in print and in person, on a wide variety of topics and in venues around the globe. Ron was the senior editor of *Training;* he was also the President of Performance Research Associates, a Minneapolis consulting company he founded in 1972 to conduct organizational effectiveness and productivity improvement studies. He was a consultant to many Fortune 500 companies including Wachovia Bank and Trust, Citibank and American Express Financial Advisors. He was author or co-author of 38 books and a syndicated columnist with American Business journals. He served on the American Society for Training and Development's national board of directors, the Annenburg Corporation for Public Broadcasting's advisory committee, and the Journal of Applied Behavioral Analysis' editorial review board. In 1994, he received the Mobius award from the Society of Consumer Affairs Professionals, and was named one of America's "new quality gurus" by Quality Digest magazine. In 1999, he was given the Thomas F. Gilbert Distinguished Professional Achievement Award by the International Society of Performance and Instruction.

Ron's best selling 1985 book, *Service America! Doing Business in the New Economy,* co-authored with Karl Albretcht, started the American customer service revolution. His astute observations have earned him recognition throughout the business world. Though his wide-ranging interests and restless intellect led him all over the management map, he always returned to his instructional design roots; He was truly a trainer, first and last. His 1982 book, *Figuring Things Out*, co-authored with Tom Kramlinger, remains a classic needs assessment text. This book introduced him to Allison Rossett, Professor of Educational Technology at San Diego State University. When she later wrote her own textbook about needs assessment – citing him throughout it – he soon got in touch. She remembers "He told me he liked my book, he said he was interested in how my mind worked. I was interested in how my mind worked. I was interested in how his mind worked. Our Relationship for the next two and a half decades was based on mutual interest." Ron always kept tabs on what was going on with her and many others in the field of educational technology.

Part IV
Organizations and Associations
in North America

Introduction

Michael Orey

Part IV includes annotated entries for associations and organizations, most of which are headquartered in North America, whose interests are in some manner significant to the fields of learning, design and technology or library and information science. For the most part, these organizations consist of professionals in the field or agencies that offer services to the educational media community. In an effort to only list active organizations, I deleted all organizations that had not updated their information since 2006. Any readers are encouraged to contact the editors with names of unlisted media-related organizations for investigation and possible inclusion in the 2012 edition.

Information for this section was obtained through e-mails directing each organization to an individual web form through which the updated information could be submitted electronically into a database created by Michael Orey. Although the section editor made every effort to contact and follow up with organization representatives, responding to the annual request for an update was the responsibility of the organization representatives. The editing team would like to thank those respondents who helped assure the currency and accuracy of this section by responding to the request for an update. Figures quoted as dues refer to annual amounts unless stated otherwise. Where dues, membership, and meeting information are not applicable such information is omitted.

M. Orey (✉)
Learning, Design, and Technology Program, The University of Georgia, Athens, GA, USA
e-mail: mikeorey@uga.edu

M. Orey et al. (eds.), *Educational Media and Technology Yearbook: Volume 36, 2011*,   247
Educational Media and Technology Yearbook 36, DOI 10.1007/978-1-4614-1305-9_25,
© Springer Science+Business Media, LLC 2012

Organizations and Associations in the US and Canada

This information will be used solely to construct a directory of relevant organizations and associations within the *2011 Educational Media & Technology Yearbook*. The data supplied here will *not* be intentionally shared or publicized in any other form. Thank you for your assistance.

Name of Organization or Association – Adaptech Research Network

Acronym – n/a

Address:
Dawson College, 3040 Sherbrooke St. West
Montreal, QC
H3Z 1A4
Canada

Phone Number – 514-931-8731 #1546; **Fax Number** – 514-931-3567 Attn: Catherine Fichten

Email Contact – catherine.fichten@mcgill.ca; **URL** – http://www.adaptech.org

Leaders – Catherine Fichten, Ph.D., Co-director; Jennison V. Asuncion, M.A., Co-Director; Maria Barile, M.S.W., co-director.

Description – Based at Dawson College (Montreal), we are a Canada-wide, grant-funded team, conducting bilingual empirical research into the use of computer, learning, and adaptive technologies by postsecondary students with disabilities. One of our primary interests lies in issues around ensuring that newly emerging instructional technologies are accessible to learners with disabilities.

Membership – Our research team is composed of academics, practitioners, students, consumers, and others interested in the issues of access to technology by students with disabilities in higher education.

Dues – n/a

M. Orey et al. (eds.), *Educational Media and Technology Yearbook: Volume 36, 2011*, Educational Media and Technology Yearbook 36, DOI 10.1007/978-1-4614-1305-9_26, © Springer Science+Business Media, LLC 2012

Meetings – n/a

Publications – 2009 Fichten, C.S., Ferraro, V., Asuncion, J.V., Chwojka, C., Barile, M., Nguyen, M.N., Klomp, R., & Wolforth, J. (2009). Disabilities and e-learning problems and solutions: An exploratory study. Educational Technology and Society, 12 (4), 241–256. 2009 Fichten, C.S., Asuncion, J.V., Barile, M., Ferraro, & Wolforth, J. (2009). Accessibility of eLearning, computer and information technologies to students with visual impairments in postsecondary education. Journal of Visual Impairment and Blindness, 103(9), 543–557. 2009 Jorgensen, S., Fichten, C.S., & Havel, A. (2009). Academic success of graduates with and without disabilities – A comparative study of university entrance scores. Pédagogie Collégiale, 22(5) Special Issue, 26–29. 2009 Ferraro, V., Fichten, C.S., & Barile, M. (2009). Computer use by students with disabilities: Perceived advantages, problems and solutions. Pédagogie Collégiale, 22(5) Special Issue, 20–25. 2009 Nguyen, M.N., Fichten, C.S., & Barile, M. (2009). Les besoins technologiques des élèves handicapés du postsecondaire sont-ils satisfaits ? Résultats de l'utilisation de l'Échelle d'accessibilité des technologies informatiques adaptatives pour les élèves handicapés au postsecondaire (SAITAPSD) : version pour les élèves. Pédagogie Collégiale, 22(2), 6–11. 2007 Fichten, C.S., Nguyen, M.N., Barile, M., & Asuncion, J. (2007). Scale of Adaptive Information Technology Accessibility for Postsecondary Students with Disabilities (SAITAPSD): A preliminary investigation. Journal of Postsecondary Education and Disability, 20(1), 54–75. 2006 Barile, M., Fichten, C.S., Ferraro, V., & Judd, D. (2006). Ice storm experiences of persons with disabilities: Knowledge is safety. Review of Disability Studies, 2(3), 35–49. 2006 Nguyen, M.N., Fichten, C.S., Barile, M., & Lévesque, J.A. (2006). Facilitateurs et obstacles à la réussite des étudiants handicapés. Pédagogie Collégiale, 19(4), 20–26.

Name of Organization or Association – Agency for Instructional Technology

Acronym – AIT

Address:
Box A
Bloomington, IN
47402-0120
US

Phone Number – (812)339-2203; **Fax Number** – (812)333-4218

Email Contact – info@ait.net; **URL** – http://www.ait.net

Leaders – Charles E. Wilson, Executive Director

Description – The Agency for Instructional Technology has been a leader in educational technology since 1962. A nonprofit organization, AIT is one of the largest providers of instructional TV programs in North America. AIT is also a leading developer of other educational media, including online instruction, CDs, videodiscs, and instructional software. AIT learning resources are used on six continents and reach nearly 34 million students in North America each year. AIT products have received many national and international honors, including an Emmy and Peabody award. Since 1970, AIT has developed 39 major curriculum packages through the consortium process it pioneered. American state and Canadian provincial agencies have cooperatively funded and widely used these learning resources. Funding for other product development comes from state, provincial, and local departments of education; federal and private institutions; corporations and private sponsors; and AITs own resources.

Membership – None.

Dues – None.

Meetings – No regular public meetings.

Publications – None.

Name of Organization or Association – American Association of Colleges for Teacher Education

Acronym – AACTE

Address:
1307 New York Ave., N.W., Suite 300
Washington, DC
20005-4701
US

Phone Number – 202/293-2450 ; **Fax Number** – 202/457-8095

Email Contact – jmills@aacte.org; **URL** – http://www.aacte.org/

Leaders – Sharon P. Robinson, President and Chief Executive Officer

Description – The American Association of Colleges for Teacher Education is a national alliance of educator preparation programs dedicated to the highest quality professional development of teachers and school leaders in order to enhance PK-12 student learning. The 800 institutions holding AACTE membership represent public and private colleges and universities in every state, the District of Columbia, the Virgin Islands, Puerto Rico, and Guam. AACTE's reach and influence fuel its mission of serving learners by providing all school personnel with superior training and continuing education. AACTE employs three key strategies to achieve its goals: Advocacy: AACTE maintains a constant presence on Capitol Hill to expand its congressional network and provide members with up-to-the-minute analysis of education policy. Leadership: AACTE believes in consensus building through open and free-flowing dialogue on education matters, consistent support for diverse learners, and serving as a principal authority on issues pertaining to teacher quality. Service: AACTE provides members with vital communication regarding policy issues and events, publications targeting various areas of interest, and unique professional development opportunities.

Membership – Membership in AACTE is institutional with over 5,500 institutional representatives. There are two categories of membership: regular membership and affiliate membership. Regular membership is available to four-year degree-granting colleges and universities with significant commitment to the preparation of education personnel and that meet all the criteria for regular membership. Affiliate membership is also available. For more information please contact the membership department at membership@aacte.org or 202/293-2450.

Dues – None

Meetings – Annual Members Meeting, New Leadership Academy. State Leaders Institute, and more

Publications – None

Name of Organization or Association – American Association of Community Colleges

Acronym – AACC

Address:
One Dupont Circle, NW, Suite 410
Washington, DC
20036-1176
US

Phone Number – (202)728-0200; **Fax Number** – (202)833-9390

Email Contact – nkent@aacc.nche.edu; **URL** – http://www.aacc.nche.edu

Leaders – George R. Boggs, President and CEO

Description – AACC is a national organization representing the nations more than 1,195 community, junior, and technical colleges. Headquartered in Washington, D.C., AACC serves as a national voice for the colleges and provides key services in the areas of advocacy, research, information, and leadership development. The nations community colleges serve more than 11 million students annually, almost half (46%) of all U.S. undergraduates.

Membership – 1,195 institutions, 31 corporations, 15 international associates, 79 educational associates, 4 foundations.

Dues – vary by category

Meetings – Annual Convention, April of each year; 2009: April 4–7 Phoenix, AZ

Publications – Community College Journal (bi-mo.); Community College Times (biweekly newspaper); Community College Press (books, research and program briefs, and monographs).

Name of Organization or Association – American Association of School Librarians

Acronym – AASL

Address:
50 East Huron Street
Chicago, IL
60611-2795
US

Phone Number – (312) 280-4382 or (800) 545-2433, ext. 4382; **Fax Number** – (312) 280-5276

Email Contact – aasl@ala.org; **URL** – http://www.ala.org/aasl

Leaders – Julie A. Walker, Executive Director

Description – A division of the American Library Association, the mission of the American Association of School Librarians is to advocate excellence, facilitate change, and develop leaders in the school library media field.

Membership – 9,500

Dues – Personal membership in ALA (beginning FY 2009, 1st yr., $65; 2nd yr., $98; 3rd and subsequent yrs., $130) plus $50 for personal membership in AASL. Student, retired, organizational, and corporate memberships are available.

Meetings – National conference every two years; next national conference to be held in 2009.

Publications – School Library Media Research (electronic research journal at http://www.ala.org/aasl/SLMR), Knowledge Quest (print journal and online companion at http://www.ala.org/aasl/kqweb), AASL Hotlinks (e-mail newsletter), Nonserial publications (http://www.ala.org/ala/aasl/aaslpubsandjournals/aaslpublications.cfm)

Name of Organization or Association – American Educational Research Association

Acronym – AERA

Address:
1430 K Street, NW, Suite 1200
Washington, DC
20005
US

Phone Number – (202) 238-3200; **Fax Number** – (202) 238-3250

Email Contact – outreach@aera.net; **URL** – http://www.aera.net

Leaders – Lorraine M. McDonnell, President of the Council, 2008–2009

Description – The American Educational Research Association (AERA) is the national interdisciplinary research association for approximately 25,000 scholars who undertake research in education. Founded in 1916, AERA aims to advance knowledge about education, to encourage scholarly inquiry related to education, and to promote the use of research to improve education and serve the public good. AERA members include educators and administrators; directors of research, testing, or evaluation in federal, state, and local agencies; counselors; evaluators; graduate students; and behavioral scientists. The broad range of disciplines represented includes education, psychology, statistics, sociology, history, economics, philosophy, anthropology, and political science. AERA has more than 160 Special Interest Groups, including Advanced Technologies for Learning, NAEP Studies, Classroom Assessment, and Fiscal Issues, Policy, and Education Finance.

Membership – 25,000 Regular Members: Eligibility requires satisfactory evidence of active interest in educational research as well as professional training to at least the masters degree level or equivalent. Graduate Student Members: Any graduate student may be granted graduate student member status with the endorsement of a voting member who is a faculty member at the students university. Graduate Students who are employed full-time are not eligible. Graduate Student membership is limited to 5 years.

Dues – vary by category, ranging from $35 for graduate students to $120 for voting members, for one year. See AERA Web site for complete details: www.aera.net

Meetings – 2009 Annual Meeting, April 13–17, San Diego, California

Publications – Educational Researcher; American Educational Research Journal; Journal of Educational and Behavioral Statistics; Educational Evaluation and Policy Analysis; Review of Research in Education; Review of Educational Research. Books: Handbook of Research on Teaching, 2001. (revised, 4th edition) Ethical Standards of AERA, Cases and Commentary, 2002 Black Education: A Transformative Research and Action Agenda for the New Century, 2005 Studying Teacher Education: The Report of the AERA Panel on Research and Teacher Education, 2006 Standards for Educational and Psychological Testing (revised and expanded, 1999). Co-published by AERA, American Psychological Association, and the National Council on Measurement in Education

Name of Organization or Association – American Foundation for the Blind

Acronym – AFB

Address:
11 Penn Plaza, Suite 300
New York, NY
10001
US

Phone Number – (212)502-7600, (800)AFB-LINE (232-5463); **Fax Number** – (212)502-7777

Email Contact – afbinfo@afb.net; **URL** – http://www.afb.org

Leaders – Carl R. Augusto, Pres.; Kelly Parisi, Vice Pres. of Communications

Description – The American Foundation for the Blind (AFB) is a national nonprofit that expands possibilities for people with vision loss. AFB's priorities include broadening access to technology; elevating the quality of information and tools for the professionals who serve people with vision loss; and promoting independent and healthy living for people with vision loss by providing them and their families with relevant and timely resources. In addition, AFB's Web site serves as a gateway to a wealth of vision loss information and services. AFB is also proud to house the Helen Keller Archives and honor the over forty years that Helen Keller worked tirelessly with AFB. For more information visit us online at www.afb.org.

Membership – None

Dues – None

Meetings – None

Publications – AFB News (free); Journal of Visual Impairment & Blindness; AFB Press Catalog of Publications (free). AccessWorld™; Subscriptions Tel: (800) 232-3044 or (412) 741-1398

Name of Organization or Association – American Library Association

Acronym – ALA

Address:
50 E. Huron St.
Chicago, IL
60611
US

Phone Number – (800) 545-2433; **Fax Number** – (312) 440-9374

Email Contact – library@ala.org; **URL** – http://www.ala.org

Leaders – Keith Michael Fiels, Exec. Dir.

Description – The ALA is the oldest and largest national library association. Its 65,000 members represent all types of libraries: state, public, school, and academic, as well as special libraries serving persons in government, commerce, the armed services, hospitals, prisons, and other institutions. The ALA is the chief advocate of achievement and maintenance of high-quality library information services through protection of the right to read, educating librarians, improving services, and making information widely accessible. See separate entries for the following affiliated and subordinate organizations: American Association of School Librarians, Association of Library Trustees, Advocates, Friends and Foundations, Association for Library Collections and Technical Services, Association for Library Service to Children, Association of College and Research Libraries, Association of Specialized and

Cooperative Library Agencies, Library Leadership and Management Association, Library and Information Technology Association, Public Library Association, Reference and User Services Association, Young Adult Library Services Association, and the Learning Round Table of ALA (formerly the Continuing Library Education Network and Exchange Round Table).

Membership – 65,000 members at present; everyone who cares about libraries is allowed to join the American Library Association.

Dues – Professional rate: $65, first year; $98, second year; third year & renewing: $130 Library Support Staff: $46 Student members: $33 Retirees: $46 International librarians: $78 Trustees: $59 Associate members (those not in the library field): $59

Meetings – June 23–29, 2011-New Orleans, LA; June 21–26, 2012-Anaheim, CA; June 27–July 2, 2013-Chicago, IL//Midwinter Meeting: January 7–11, 2011 – San Diego, CA; January 20–24, 2012-Dallas, TX; January 25–29, 2013-Seattle, WA

Publications – American Libraries; Book Links; Booklist; BooklistOnline.com; Choice; Choice Reviews Online; Guide to Reference; Library Technology Reports; Newsletter on Intellectual Freedom; RDA Toolkit; Voice for Americas Libraries.

Name of Organization or Association – American Society for Training and Development

Acronym – ASTD

Address:
1640 King St., Box 1443
Alexandria, VA
22313
US

Phone Number – (703)683-8100; **Fax Number** – (703)683-1523

Email Contact – memberservices@astd.org; **URL** – http://www.astd.org

Leaders – Tony Bingham, President and CEO

Description – ASTD (American Society for Training & Development) is the world's largest professional association dedicated to the training and development field. In more than 100 countries, ASTD's members work in organizations of all sizes, in the private and public sectors, as independent consultants, and as suppliers. Members connect locally in 130 U.S. chapters and with 30 international partners. ASTD started in 1943 and in recent years has widened the profession's focus to align learning and performance to organizational results, and is a sought-after voice on critical public policy issues. For more information, visit www.astd.org.

Membership – 40,000 National and Chapter members.

Dues – The Classic Membership ($199.00) is the foundation of ASTD member benefits. Publications, newsletters, research reports, discounts, services, and much more are all designed to help you do your job better. There are also student memberships, joint chapter memberships, and special packages for international members. Here is what you have to look forward to when you join: T+ D magazine – Monthly publication of the Industry. Stay informed on trends, successful practices, public policy, ASTD news, case studies, and more. Links – bimonthly newsletter for and about members. The Buzz – a weekly compilation of news about the training profession. Learning Circuits – Monthly Webzine features articles, departments, and columns that examine new technologies and how they are being applied to workplace learning. Special Reports and Research – Research reports are published on topics that reflect important issues and trends in the industry. The State of the Industry report is published annually and analyzes spending, practices, and other important data related to learning and development. Research Assistance – ASTD provides a Knowledge Center that can provide you with the research you are looking for while you are on the phone. You can also use ASTDs Online Library, by EBSCO Host, to research thousands of publications. Career Navigator Tool – find out where you are in your career and what you need to do to develop professionally. Membership Directory – Online directory and searchable by a variety of criteria. Access to the Membership Directory is for Members Only and is being enhanced for future networking capabilities. Buyers Guide & Consultants Directory – A one-stop resource for information on over 600 suppliers of training and performance products and services.

Meetings – TechKnowledge Confernce: February 2–4, 2011, San Jose, CA; International Conference & Exposition, May 22–25, 2011, Orlando, FL and May 6–9, 2012, Denver, CO.

Publications – T+D (Training & Development) Magazine; InfoLine; Learning Circuits; Training and Development Handbook; State of the Industry Report; ASTD Press books; Research reports.

Name of Organization or Association – Association for Childhood Education International

Acronym – ACEI

Address:
17904 Georgia Ave., Suite 215
Olney, MD
20832
US

Phone Number – (301)570-2111; **Fax Number** – (301)570-2212

Email Contact – headquarters@acei.org; **URL** – http://www.acei.org

Leaders – Diane P. Whitehead, Acting Executive Director

Description – ACEI publications reflect careful research, broad-based views, and consideration of a wide range of issues affecting children from infancy through early adolescence. Many are media related in nature. The journal (Childhood Education) is essential for teachers, teachers-in-training, teacher educators, day care workers, administrators, and parents. Articles focus on child development and emphasize practical application. Regular departments include book reviews (child and adult); film reviews, pamphlets, software, research, and classroom idea-sparkers. Six issues are published yearly, including a theme issue devoted to critical concerns.

Membership – 10,000

Dues – $45, professional; $29, student; $23, retired; $85, institutional.

Meetings – 2009 Annual Conference, March 18–21, Chicago, IL USA

Publications – Childhood Education (official journal) with ACEI Exchange (insert newsletter); Journal of Research in Childhood Education; professional focus newsletters (Focus on Infants and Toddlers, Focus on Pre-K and K, Focus on Elementary, Focus on Middle School, Focus on Teacher Education, and Focus on Inclusive Education); various books.

Name of Organization or Association – Association for Computers and the Humanities

Acronym – ACH

Address:
[Address]
[City], ON
[Zip Code]
[Country]

Phone Number – [phone number; **Fax Number** – [fax number]

Email Contact – kretzsh@uga.edu; **URL** – http://www.ach.org/

Leaders – Executive Secretary, ACH

Description – The Association for Computers and the Humanities is an international professional organization. Since its establishment, it has been the major professional society for people working in computer-aided research in literature and language studies, history, philosophy, and other humanities disciplines, and especially research involving the manipulation and analysis of textual materials. The ACH is devoted to disseminating information among its members about work in the field of humanities computing, as well as encouraging the development and dissemination of significant textual and linguistic resources and software for scholarly research.

Membership – 300

Dues – Individual regular member, US $65 Student or Emeritus Faculty member, US $55 Joint membership (for couples), Add US $7

Meetings – Annual meetings held with the Association for Literary and Linguistic Computing.

Publications – ACH Publications: – Literary & Linguistic Computing – Humanist

Name of Organization or Association – Association for Continuing Higher Education

Acronym – ACHE

Address:
OCCE Admin Bldg Rm 233, 1700 Asp Ave
Norman, OK
73072
US

Phone Number – 800-807-2243; **Fax Number** – 405-325-4888

Email Contact – admin@acheinc.org; **URL** – http://www.acheinc.org/

Leaders – James P. Pappas, Ph.D., Executive Vice President

Description – ACHE is an institution-based organization of colleges, universities, and individuals dedicated to the promotion of lifelong learning and excellence in continuing higher education. ACHE encourages professional networks, research, and exchange of information for its members and advocates continuing higher education as a means of enhancing and improving society.

Membership – Approximately 1,600 individuals in approximately 650 institutions. Membership is open to institutions of higher learning, professionals, and organizations whose major commitment is in the area of continuing education.

Dues – $80, professional; $495, institutional

Meetings – For a list of Annual and Regional Meetings, see http://www.acheinc. org/annual_conference.html

Publications – Journal of Continuing Higher Education (3/yr.); Five Minutes with ACHE (newsletter, 9/yr.); Proceedings (annual).

Name of Organization or Association – Association for Educational Communications and Technology

Acronym – AECT

Address:
1800 N Stonelake Dr., Suite 2 P.O. Box 2447
Bloomington, IN
47404-2447
US

Phone Number – (812) 335-7675; **Fax Number** – (812) 335-7678

Email Contact – pharris@aect.org; **URL** – http://www.aect.org

Leaders – Phillip Harris, Executive Director; Michael Spector, Board President

Description – AECT is an international professional association concerned with the improvement of learning and instruction through media and technology. It serves as a central clearinghouse and communications center for its members, who include instructional technologists, library media specialists, religious educators, government media personnel, school administrators and specialists, and training media producers. AECT members also work in the armed forces, public libraries, museums, and other information agencies of many different kinds, including those related to the emerging fields of computer technology. Affiliated organizations include the International Visual Literacy Association (IVLA), Minorities in Media (MIM), New England Educational Media Association (NEEMA), SICET (the Society of International Chinese in Educational Technology), and KSET (the Korean Society for Educational Technology). The ECT Foundation is also related to AECT. Each of these affiliated organizations has its own listing in the Yearbook. AECT Divisions include: Instructional Design & Development, Information & , Training & Performance, Research & Theory, Systemic Change, Distance Learning, Media & Technology, Teacher Education, International, and Multimedia Productions.

Membership – 2500 members in good standing from K-12, college and university and private sector/government training. Anyone interested can join. There are different memberships available for students, retirees, corporations, and international parties. We also have a new option for electronic membership for international affiliates.

Dues – 125.00.00 standard membership discounts are available for students and retirees. Additional fees apply to corporate memberships or international memberships.

Meetings – Summer Leadership Institute held each July. In 2007 it will be in Chicago, IL. AECT holds an annual conference each year in October. In 2007, it will be held in Anaheim, CA.

Publications – TechTrends (6/yr., free with AECT membership; available by subscription through Springer at www.springeronline.com); Educational Technology Research and Development (6/yr. $46 members; available by subscription through Springer at www.springeronline.com); Quarterly Review of Distance Education (q., $55 to AECT members); many books.

Name of Organization or Association – Association for Experiential Education

Acronym – AEE

Address:
3775 Iris Avenue, Ste 4
Boulder, CO
80301-2043
US

Phone Number – (303)440-8844; **Fax Number** – (303)440-9581

Email Contact – executive@aee.org; **URL** – http://www.aee.org

Leaders – Paul Limoges, Executive Director

Description – AEE is a nonprofit, international, professional organization committed to the development, practice, and evaluation of experiential education in all settings. AEE's vision is to be a leading international organization for the development and application of experiential education principles and methodologies with the intent to create a just and compassionate world by transforming education.

Membership – Nearly 1,500 members in over 30 countries including individuals and organizations with affiliations in education, recreation, outdoor adventure programming, mental health, youth service, physical education, management development training, corrections, programming for people with disabilities, and environmental education.

Dues – $55–$115, individual; $145, family; $275–$500, organizational

Meetings – AEE Annual Conference in November. Regional Conferences in the Spring.

Publications – The Journal of Experiential Education (3/yr.); Experience and the Curriculum; Adventure Education; Adventure Therapy; Therapeutic Applications of Adventure Programming; Manual of Accreditation Standards for Adventure Programs; The Theory of Experiential Education, Third Edition; Experiential Learning in Schools and Higher Education; Ethical Issues in Experiential Education, Second Edition; The K.E.Y. (Keep Exploring Yourself) Group: An Experiential Personal Growth Group Manual; Book of Metaphors, Volume II; Women's Voices in Experiential Education; bibliographies, directories of programs, and membership directory. New publications since last year: Exploring the Boundaries of Adventure Therapy; A Guide to Women's Studies in the Outdoors; Administrative Practices of Accredited Adventure Programs; Fundamentals of Experience-Based Training; Wild Adventures: A Guidebook of Activities for Building Connections with Others and the Earth; Truth Zone: An Experimental Approach to Organizational Development; Exploring the Power of Solo, Silence, and Solitude.

Name of Organization or Association – Association for Library and Information Science Education

Acronym – ALISE

Address:
65 E. Wacker Place Suite 1900
Chicago, IL
60612
US

Phone Number – 312-795-0996; **Fax Number** – 312-419-8950

Email Contact – contact@alise.org; **URL** – http://www.alise.org

Leaders – Kathleen Combs Executive Director

Description – Seeks to advance education for library and information science and produces annual Library and Information Science Education Statistical Report. Open to professional schools offering graduate programs in library and information science; personal memberships open to educators employed in such institutions; other memberships available to interested individuals.

Membership – 500 individuals, 69 institutions

Dues – institutional, sliding scale, $350–2,500; $150 international; personal, $125 full-time; $75 part-time, $40 student, $60 retired

Meetings – Tuesday, January 20, through Friday, January 23, 2009 – Denver, Colorado

Publications – Journal of Education for Library and Information Science; ALISE Directory; Library and Information Science Education Statistical Report.

Name of Organization or Association – Association for Library Collections & Technical Services

Acronym – ALCTS

Address:
50 E. Huron St.
Chicago, IL
60611
US

Phone Number – (312)280-5037; **Fax Number** – (312)280-5033

Email Contact – alcts@ala.org; **URL** – www.ala.org/alcts

Leaders – Charles Wilt, Executive Director

Description – A division of the American Library Association, ALCTS is dedicated to acquisition, identification, cataloging, classification, and preservation of library materials; the development and coordination of the country's library resources; and aspects of selection and evaluation involved in acquiring and developing library materials and resources. Sections include Acquisitions, Cataloging and Classification, Collection Management and Development, Preservation and Reformatting, and Serials.

Membership – 4,800 membership is open to anyone who has an interest in areas covered by ALCTS.

Dues – $65 plus membership in ALA

Meetings – Annual Conference; Chicago, July 9–15, 2009, Washington, DC, June 24–30, 2010, New Orleans, June 23–29, 2011, Anaheim, June 21–27, 2012.

Publications – Library Resources & Technical Services (q.); ALCTS Newsletter Online (6/yr.)

Name of Organization or Association – Association for Library Service to Children

Acronym – ALSC

Address:
50 E. Huron St.
Chicago, IL
60611
US

Phone Number – (312)280-2163; **Fax Number** – (312)944-7671

Email Contact – alsc@ala.org; **URL** – http://www.ala.org/alsc

Leaders – Diane Foote

Description – Information about ALSC can be found at . Information on ALSCs various awards, including the nationally known Newbery Medal for authors and the Caldecott Medal for illustrators can be found at . The Association for Library Service to Children develops and supports the profession of children's librarianship by enabling and encouraging its practitioners to provide the best library service to our nations' children. The Association for Library Service to Children is interested in the improvement and extension of library services to children in all types of libraries. It is responsible for the evaluation and selection of book and nonbook library materials and for the improvement of techniques of library service to children from preschool through the eighth grade or junior high school age, when such materials and techniques are intended for use in more than one type of library. Committee membership is open to ALSC members. Full list of ALSC boards and committees can be found at.

Membership – Over 4,000 members

Dues – $45 plus membership in ALA; $18 plus membership in ALA for library school students; $25 plus membership in ALA for retirees

Meetings – National Institute, Fall.

Publications – Children and Libraries: The Journal of the Association for Library Service to Children (3x per year); ALSConnect (quarterly newsletter). ALSC Blog – .

Name of Organization or Association – Association of American Publishers

Acronym – AAP

Address:
50 F Street, NW, Suite 400
Washington, DC
20001
US

Phone Number – (202)347-3375; **Fax Number** – (202)347-3690

Email Contact – aoconnor@publishers.org; **URL** – http://www.publishers.org

Leaders – Tom Allen, Pres. and CEO (DC); Judith Platt, Dir. of Communications/ Public Affairs

Description – The Association of American Publishers is the national trade association of the U.S. book publishing industry. AAP was created in 1970 through the merger of the American Book Publishers Council, a trade publishing group, and the American Textbook Publishers Institute, a group of educational publishers. AAPs more than 300 members include most of the major commercial book publishers in the United States, as well as smaller and nonprofit publishers, university presses, and scholarly societies. AAP members publish hardcover and paperback books in every field and a range of educational materials for the elementary, secondary, post-secondary, and professional markets. Members of the Association also produce computer software and electronic products and services, such as online databases and CD-ROMs. AAPs primary concerns are the protection of intellectual property rights in all media, the defense of free expression and freedom to publish at home and abroad, the management of new technologies, development of education markets and funding for instructional materials, and the development of national and global markets for its member's products.

Membership – Regular Membership in the Association is open to all U.S. companies actively engaged in the publication of books, journals, looseleaf services, computer software, audiovisual materials, databases and other electronic products such as CD-ROM and CD-I, and similar products for educational, business, and personal use. This includes producers, packagers, and co-publishers who coordinate or manage most of the publishing process involved in creating copyrightable educational materials for distribution by another organization. "Actively engaged" means that the candidate must give evidence of conducting an ongoing publishing business with a significant investment in the business. Each Regular Member firm has one vote, which is cast by an official representative or alternate designated by the member company. Associate Membership (nonvoting) is available to U.S. not-for-profit organizations that otherwise meet the qualifications for regular membership. A special category of associate membership is open to nonprofit university presses. Affiliate Membership is a nonvoting membership open to paper manufacturers, suppliers, consultants, and other nonpublishers directly involved in the industry.

Dues – Dues are assessed on the basis of annual sales revenue from the print and electronic products listed above (under Regular Membership), but not from services or equipment. To maintain confidentiality, data is reported to an independent agent.

Meetings – Annual Meeting (February), Small and Independent Publishers Meeting (February), School Division Annual Meeting (January), PSP Annual Meeting (February)

Publications – AAP Monthly Report

Name of Organization or Association – Association of College and Research Libraries

Acronym – ACRL

Address:
50 E. Huron St.
Chicago, IL
60611-2795
US

Phone Number – (312)280-2523; **Fax Number** – (312)280-2520

Email Contact – acrl@ala.org; **URL** – http://www.ala.org/acrl

Leaders – Mary Ellen Davis, Executive Director

Description – The Association of College and Research Libraries (ACRL), the largest division of the American Library Association, is a professional association of academic librarians and other interested individuals. It is dedicated to enhancing the ability of academic library and information professionals to serve the information needs of the higher education community and to improve learning, teaching, and research. ACRL is the only individual membership organization in North America that develops programs, products, and services to meet the unique needs of academic and research librarians Information on ACRLs various committees, task forces, discussion groups, and sections can be found at . Information on ACRLs various awards can be found at.

Membership – With over 13,000 members, is a national organization of academic and research libraries and librarians working with all types of academic libraries – community and junior college, college, and university – as well as comprehensive and specialized research libraries and their professional staffs.

Dues – $55 plus membership in ALA; $35 plus membership in ALA for library school students and for retirees SECTIONS (two at no charge, additional sections $5 each): African American Studies Librarians (AFAS); Anthropology and Sociology Section (ANSS); Arts Section; Asian, African, and Middle Eastern Section (AAMES); College Libraries Section (CLS); Community and Junior College Libraries Section (CJCLS); Distance Learning Section (DLS); Education and Behavioral Sciences Section (EBSS); Instruction Section (IS); Law and Political Science Section (LPSS); Literatures in English (LES); Rare Books and Manuscripts Section (RBMS); Science and Technology Section (STS); Slavic and East European Section (SEES); University Libraries Section (ULS); Western European Studies Section (WESS); Womens Studies Section (WSS)

Meetings – ACRL 14th National Conference – March 12–15, 2009, Seattle, WA, Theme: Pushing the Edge: Explore, Engage, Extend

Publications – List of all print and electronic publications at ACRLog: Blogging for and by academic and research librarians – . ACRL Insider – The mission of the

ACRL Insider Weblog is to keep the world current and informed on the activities, services, and programs of the Association of College & Research Libraries, including publications, events, conferences, and eLearning opportunities. ACRL Podcasts – Academic Library Trends & Statistics (annually). Statistics data for all academic libraries reporting throughout the U.S. and Canada. Trends data examines a different subject each year. Available from ALA Order Fulfillment, P.O. Box 932501, Atlanta, GA 31193-2501 and from the ALA Online Store. Choice: Editor and Publisher, Irving E. Rockwood. ISSN 0009-4978. Published monthly. Only available by subscription: $315 per year for North America; $365 outside North America. CHOICE Reviews on Cards: $390 per year for North America – U.S., Canada, and Mexico); $440 outside North America. ChoiceReviews.online: See pricing for site licenses at . College & Research Libraries (6 bimonthly journal issues). Sent to all ACRL members. Subscriptions, $70 – US. $75 – Canada and other PUAS countries. $80 – other foreign countries. College & Research Libraries News (11 monthly issues, July–August combined). Sent to all ACRL members. Subscriptions: $46 – US. $52 – Canada and other PUAS countries. $57 – other foreign countries. RBM: A Journal of Rare Books, Manuscripts, and Cultural Heritage. (2 issues). Subscriptions, $42 – US. $47 – Canada and other PUAS countries. $58 – other foreign countries.

Name of Organization or Association – Association of Specialized and Cooperative Library Agencies

Acronym – ASCLA

Address:
50 E. Huron St.
Chicago, IL
60611
US

Phone Number – (800)545-2433, ext. 4398.; **Fax Number** – (312)944-8085

Email Contact – ascla@ala.org; **URL** – http://www.ala.org/ascla

Leaders – Executive Director

Description – A division of the American Library Association, ASCLA represents state library agencies, multitype library organizations, independent libraries, and libraries serving special populations to promote the development of coordinated library services with equal access to information and material for all persons.

Membership – 917

Dues – You must be a member of ALA to join ASCLA. See www.ala.org/membership for most current ALA dues rates. ASCLA individual membership: $40; organization membership: $50; State Library Agency dues: $500.

Meetings – ASCLA meets in conjunction with the American Library Association.

Publications – Interface, quarterly online newsletter; see Web site http://www.ala.org/ascla for a list of other publications.

Name of Organization or Association – Canadian Library Association/Association canadienne des bibliothèques

Acronym – CLA/ACB

Address:
328 Frank Street
Ottawa, ON
K2P 0X8
Canada

Phone Number – (613)232-9625; **Fax Number** – (613)563-9895

Email Contact – info@cla.ca; **URL** – http://www.cla.ca

Leaders – Linda Sawden Harris, Manager of Financial Services; Judy Green, Manager, Marketing & Communications; Don Butcher, Executive Director

Description – Our Mission CLA/ACB is my advocate and public voice, educator and network. We build the Canadian library and information community and advance its information professionals. Our Values: We believe that libraries and the principles of intellectual freedom and free universal access to information are key components of an open and democratic society. Diversity is a major strength of our Association. An informed and knowledgeable membership is central in achieving library and information policy goals. Effective advocacy is based upon understanding the social, cultural, political, and historical contexts in which libraries and information services function. Our Operating Principles: A large and active membership is crucial to our success. Our Association will have a governance structure that is reviewed regularly and ensures that all sectors of the membership are represented. Our Association will be efficiently run, fiscally responsible, and financially independent Technology will be used in efficient and effective ways to further our goals. Our Association places a high value on each of our members. Our Association will ensure that its staff are provided with tools and training necessary for them to excel at their jobs. Our Associations strategic plan will be continually reviewed and updated.

Membership – The Associations five constituent divisions are: Canadian Association for School Libraries (CASL), including the School Library Administrators (SLAS) section (approx. 200 members); Canadian Association of College and University Libraries (CACUL), including the Community and Technical College (CTCL) section (approx. 800 members); Canadian Association of Public Libraries (CAPL), including the Canadian Association of Childrens Librarians (CACL) section (approx. 650 members); Canadian Association of Special Libraries and Information Services (CASLIS), with chapters in Calgary, Edmonton, Manitoba, Ottawa, Toronto and Atlantic Canada (approx. 590 members); Canadian Library Trustees Association (approx. 180 members)

Dues – $ 25–$ 1000

Meetings – 2009 CLA/ACB National Conference 7 Tradeshow, Montreal, May 29–June 1

Publications – Feliciter (membership & subscription magazine, 6/yr.).

Name of Organization or Association – Canadian Museums Association/ Association des musées canadiens

Acronym – CMA/AMC

Address:
280 Metcalfe St., Suite 400
Ottawa, ON
K2P 1R7
Canada

Phone Number – (613)567-0099; **Fax Number** – (613)233-5438

Email Contact – info@museums.ca; **URL** – http://www.museums.ca

Leaders – John G. McAvity, Exec. Dir.

Description – The Canadian Museums Association is a nonprofit corporation and registered charity dedicated to advancing public museums and museum works in Canada, promoting the welfare and better administration of museums, and fostering a continuing improvement in the qualifications and practices of museum professionals.

Membership – 2,000 museums and individuals, including art galleries, zoos, aquariums, historic parks, etc.

Dues – Voting Categories Individual: For those who are, or have been, associated with a recognized museum in Canada. A $10 discount applies if you are associated with a CMA institutional member or if you are a member of a provincial museum association. $85 a year. Senior: For those who are retired and have been associated with a recognized museum in Canada. $50 a year. Institutional Association: For all recognized Canadian museums that are nonprofit, have a collection, and are open to the public. The fee is 0.001 (one tenth of one percent) of your operating budget (i.e., if your budget is $150,000, you would pay $150). The minimum fee payable is $100, and the maximum, $2,750. Nonvoting Categories Affiliate: For those outside of the museum community who wish to support the aims and programs of the CMA. $100 a year. International: For individuals and institutions outside of Canada. $100 a year. Corporate: For corporations wishing to support the aims and programs of the CMA while developing opportunities within the museum community. $250 a year. Student: For students in Canada. Please enclose a photocopy of your student ID. $50 a year. *Membership fees may be tax deductible. Check with your financial advisor for details

Meetings – CMA Annual Conference, spring

Publications – Muse (bimonthly magazine, color, Canadas only national, bilingual, magazine devoted to museums, it contains museum-based photography, feature articles, commentary, and practical information); The Official Directory of Canadian Museums and Related Institutions (online directory) lists all museums in Canada plus information on government departments, agencies, and provincial and regional museum associations.

Name of Organization or Association – Centre for Educational Technology, University of Cape Town

Acronym – CET

Address:
Hlanganani Building, Upper Campus University of Cape Town, Rondebosch
Cape Town, na
7700
South Africa

Phone Number – 27 21 650 3841; **Fax Number** – 27 21 650 5045

Email Contact – Laura.Czerniewicz@uct.ac.za; **URL** – http://www.cet.uct.ac.za

Leaders – Directors Laura Czerniewicz

Description – The Centre for Educational Technology (CET) enables and promotes and investigates the integration of learning technologies in teaching and learning at the University of Cape Town and in higher education. CET's areas of work are curriculum development, learning technologies, staff development and research.

Membership – We employ educational technology researchers, developers, staff developers, and learning designers with strong educational interests in diversity, redress, and access.

Dues – none

Meetings – none

Publications – See our Web site at http://www.cet.uct.ac.za. Recent research publications are listed at http://www.cet.uct.ac.za/ResearchOut.

Name of Organization or Association – Close Up Foundation

Acronym – CUF

Address:
44 Canal Center Plaza
Alexandria, VA
22314
US

Phone Number – (703)706-3300; **Fax Number** – (703)706-3329

Email Contact – cutv@closeup.org; **URL** – http://www.closeup.org

Leaders – Timothy S. Davis, President & CEO

Description – A nonprofit, nonpartisan civic engagement organization dedicated to providing individuals of all backgrounds with the knowledge, skills, and confidence to actively participate in democracy. Each year, Close Up brings 15,000 secondary and middle school students and teachers to Washington, D.C. for week-long government studies programs. In addition, Close Up produces an array of multimedia civic education resources for use in classrooms and households nationwide, including Close Up at the Newseum, a weekly youth-focused current affairs program C-SPAN.

Membership – Any motivated middle or high school student who wants to learn about government and American history is eligible to come on our programs. No dues or membership fees.

Dues – Tuition is required to participate on Close Up educational travel programs. A limited amount of tuition assistance is available to qualified students through the Close Up Fellowship program. With a designated number of students, teachers receive a fellowship that covers the adult tuition and transportation price. Please contact 1-800-CLOSE UP for more information.

Meetings – Meetings take place during weeklong educational programs in Washington, D.C.

Publications – Current Issues (new edition produced annually); The Bill of Rights: A Users Guide; Perspectives; International Relations; The American Economy; Face the Music: Copyright, Art & the Digital Age; documentaries on domestic and foreign policy issues.

Name of Organization or Association – Computer Assisted Language Instruction Consortium

Acronym – CALICO

Address:
214 Centennial Hall, Texas State University, 601 University Dr.
San Marcos, TX
78666
US

Phone Number – (512)245-1417; **Fax Number** – (512)245-9089

Email Contact – info@calico.org; **URL** – http://calico.org

Leaders – Robert Fischer, Exec. Dir.

Description – CALICO is devoted to the dissemination of information on the application of technology to language teaching and language learning.

Membership – 1,000 members from United States and 20 foreign countries. Anyone interested in the development and use of technology in the teaching/learning of foreign languages is invited to join.

Dues – $65 annual/individual

Meetings – 2011, University of Victoria, Canada; 2012, University of Notre Dame; 2013, University of Hawaii

Publications – CALICO Journal Online (three issues per year), CALICO Monograph Series (Monograph IX, 2010; Monograph V, second edition 2011).

Name of Organization or Association – Consortium of College and University Media Centers

Acronym – CCUMC

Address:
601 E. Kirkwood Ave. Franklin Hall 0009
Bloomington, IN
47405
US

Phone Number – (812)855-6049; **Fax Number** – (812)855-2103

Email Contact – ccumc@ccumc.org; **URL** – www.ccumc.org

Leaders – Aileen Scales, Executive Director

Description – CCUMC is a professional group whose mission is to provide leadership and a forum for information exchange to the providers of media content, academic technology, and support for quality teaching and learning at institutions of higher education. Fosters cooperative media/instructional technology-related support in higher education institutions and companies providing related products. Gathers and disseminates information on improved procedures and new developments in instructional technology and media center management.

Membership – 750 individuals at 325 institutions/corporations: Institutional Memberships – Individuals within an institution of higher education who are associated with the support to instruction and presentation technologies in a media center and/or technology support service. Corporate Memberships – Individuals within a corporation, firm, foundation, or other commercial or philanthropic enterprise whose business or activity is in support of the purposes and objectives of CCUMC. Associate Memberships – Individuals not eligible for an Institutional or Corporate membership; from a public library, religious, governmental, or other organization not otherwise eligible for other categories of membership. Student Memberships – Any student in an institution of higher education who is not eligible for an institutional membership.

Dues – Institutional or Corporate Membership: $325 for 1–2 persons, $545 for 3–4 persons, $795 for 5–6 persons, $130 each additional person beyond six Associate Membership: $325 per person Student Membership: $55 per person

Meetings – 2010 Conference, Buffalo New York (October 6–10, 2010); 2011 Conference South Padre Island Texas (October 5–9, 2011)

Publications – College & University Media Review (journal – annual) Leader (newsletter – 3 issues annually)

Name of Organization or Association – Council for Exceptional Children

Acronym – CEC

Address:
1110 N. Glebe Rd. #300
Arlington, VA
22201
US

Phone Number – (703)620-3660. TTY: (703)264-9446; **Fax Number** – (703)264-9494

Email Contact – cec@cec.sped.org.; **URL** – http://www.cec.sped.org

Leaders – Bruce Ramirez, Exec. Dir.

Description – CEC is the largest international organization dedicated to improving the educational success of students with disabilities and/or gifts and talents. CEC advocates for governmental policies supporting special education, sets professional standards, provides professional development, and helps professionals obtain conditions and resources necessary for high quality educational services for their students.

Membership – Teachers, administrators, professors, related services providers (occupational therapists, school psychologists, etc.), and parents. CEC has approximately 50,000 members

Dues – $111 a year

Meetings – Annual Convention & Expo attracting approximately 6,000 special educators

Publications – Journals, newsletters books, and videos with information on new research findings, classroom practices that work, and special education publications. (See also the ERIC Clearinghouse on Disabilities and Gifted Education.)

Name of Organization or Association – Delete

Acronym – NASTA

Address:
120 S. Federal Place, Room 206
Santa Fe, NM
87501
US

Phone Number – 505.827.1801; **Fax Number** – 505.827.1826

Email Contact – webmaster@nasta.org; **URL** – http://www.nasta.org

Leaders – David P. Martinez, President

Description – NASTAs purposes are to (1) foster a spirit of mutual helpfulness in adoption, purchase, and distribution of instructional materials; (2) arrange for study and review of textbook specifications; (3) authorize special surveys, tests, and studies; and (4) initiate action leading to better quality instructional materials. Services provided include a working knowledge of text construction, monitoring lowest prices, sharing adoption information, identifying trouble spots, and discussions in the industry. The members of NASTA meet to discuss the textbook adoption process and to improve the quality of the instructional materials used in the elementary, middle, and high schools. NASTA is not affiliated with any parent organization and has no permanent address.

Membership – Textbook administrators from each of the 21 states that adopt instructional material at the state level on an annual basis.

Dues – $25 annually per individual

Meetings – NASTA meets annually during the month of July

Publications – Manufacturing Standards and Specifications for Textbooks (MSST)

Name of Organization or Association – East–West Center

Acronym – none

Address:
1601 East-West Rd.
Honolulu, HI
96848-1601
US

Phone Number – (808)944-7111; **Fax Number** – (808)944-7376

Email Contact – ewcinfo@EastWestCenter.org; **URL** – http://www.eastwestcenter.org/

Leaders – Dr. Charles E. Morrison, Pres.

Description – The U.S. Congress established the East-West Center in 1960 with a mandate to foster mutual understanding and cooperation among the governments and peoples of Asia, the Pacific, and the United States. Officially known as the Center for Cultural and Technical Interchange Between East and West, it is a public, nonprofit institution with an international board of governors. Funding for the center comes from the U.S. government, with additional support provided by private agencies, individuals, and corporations, and several Asian and Pacific governments. The Center, through research, education, dialog, and outreach, provides a neutral meeting ground where people with a wide range of perspectives exchange views on topics of regional concern. Scholars, government and business leaders, educators, journalists, and other professionals from throughout the region annually work with Center staff to address issues of contemporary significance in such areas as international economics and politics, the environment, population, energy, the media, and Pacific islands development.

Membership – The East-West Center is not a membership-based institution. However, our alumni organization, The East-West Center Association (EWCA), is an international network of professionals who have a past affiliation with the East-West Center. Regardless of length of stay or type of participation, all are automatically members (associates) of the EWCA. There are no membership fees or other requirements to participate in the EWCA.

Dues – None

Meetings – Events are listed on our Web site, visit: eastwestcenter.org/events

Publications – East-West Center expertise and research findings are published by the East-West Center and by presses and collaborating organizations throughout the region and the world. Publications address a range of critical issues in the Asia Pacific region. The East-West Center sponsors or publishes several series, from short papers to books (see below). For more information about EWC publications, visit: http://www.eastwestcenter.org/publications/. The Asia Pacific Bulletin (APB), produced by the East-West Center in Washington, publishes summaries of Congressional Study Groups, conferences, seminars, and visitor roundtables, as well as short articles and opinion pieces. APB summaries are always two pages or less, designed for the busy professional or policymaker to capture the essence of dialogue and debate on issues of concern in US-Asia relations. East-West Dialogue, an online publication, is an interactive forum for discussion and debate of key issues in Asia-U.S. economic relations. The East-West Dialogue seeks to develop and promote innovative policy, business, and civic initiatives to enhance this critical partnership. Contemporary Issues in Asia and the Pacific is a book series that focuses on issues of contemporary significance in the Asia Pacific region, most notably political, social, cultural, and economic change. The series seeks books that focus on topics of regional importance, on problems that cross disciplinary boundaries, and that have the capacity to reach academic and other interested audiences. The Contemporary Issues in Asia and the Pacific book series is published by Stanford University Press. The Studies in Asian Security book series, published by Stanford University Press and sponsored by the East-West Center, promotes analysis, understanding, and explanation of the dynamics of domestic, transnational, and international security challenges in Asia. The peer-reviewed publications in the series analyze contemporary security issues and problems to clarify debates in the scholarly community, provide new insights and perspectives, and identify new research and policy directions. With a series committee comprising individuals from diverse theoretical persuasions who have undertaken extensive work on Asian security, books in the Studies in Asian Security series are designed to encourage original and rigorous scholarship, and seek to engage scholars, educators, and practitioners. Policy Studies presents scholarly analysis of key contemporary domestic and international political, economic, and strategic issues affecting Asia in a policy relevant manner. Written for the policy community, academics, journalists, and the informed public, the peer-reviewed publications in this series provide new policy insights and perspectives based on extensive fieldwork and rigorous scholarship. Pacific Islands Policy examines critical issues, problems, and opportunities that are relevant to the Pacific Islands region. The series is intended to influence the policy process, affect how people understand a range of contemporary Pacific issues, and help fashion solutions. A central aim of the series is to encourage scholarly analysis of economic, political, social, and cultural issues in a manner that will advance common understanding of current challenges and policy responses. East-West Center Special Reports present in-depth analysis and exposition that offer insights to specialists yet are accessible to readers outside the author's discipline. These peer-reviewed publications address diverse topics relevant to current and emerging policy debates in the Asia Pacific region and the United States. Papers in the AsiaPacific Issues series address topics of broad interest and significant impact relevant to current and emerging policy debates. These eight-page, peer-reviewed papers are accessible to readers outside the author's discipline.

Name of Organization or Association – Education Development Center, Inc.

Acronym – EDC

Address:
55 Chapel Street
Newton, MA
02458-1060
US

Phone Number – (617)969-7100; **Fax Number** – (617)969-5979

Email Contact – emarshall@edc.org; **URL** – http://www.edc.org

Leaders – Dr. Luther S. Luedtke, President and CEO

Description – EDC is a global nonprofit organization that designs, delivers, and evaluates innovative programs to address some of the world's most urgent challenges in education, health, and economic opportunity. Working with public-sector and private partners, we harness the power of people and systems to improve education, health promotion and care, workforce preparation, communications technologies, and civic engagement. EDC conducts 350 projects in 35 countries around the world.

Membership – Not applicable

Dues – Not applicable

Meetings – Not applicable

Publications – (1) Annual Report, (2) EDC Update, quarterly magazine, (3) EDC Online Report, quarterly enewsletter, (4) Detailed Web site with vast archive of publications, technical reports, and evaluation studies.

Name of Organization or Association – Education Northwest (Formerly Northwest Regional Educational Laboratory)

Acronym – N/A

Address:
101 SW Main St., Suite 500
Portland, OR
97204
US

Phone Number – (503)275-9500; **Fax Number** – 503-275-0448

Email Contact – info@educationnorthwest.org; **URL** – http://educationnorthwest.org

Leaders – Dr. Carol Thomas, Exec. Dir.

Description – Chartered in the Pacific Northwest in 1966 as Northwest Regional Educational Laboratory, Education Northwest now conducts more than 200 projects annually, working with schools, districts, and communities across the country on comprehensive, research-based solutions to the challenges they face. At Education Northwest, we are dedicated to and passionate about learning. Through our work, we strive to create vibrant learning environments where all youth and adults can succeed. Everything we do is evidence based, giving us a solid foundation upon which we stand with confidence. We work with teachers, administrators, policy-makers, and communities to identify needs, evaluate programs, and develop new solutions. The breadth of our work – ranging from training teachers, to developing curriculum, to restructuring schools, to evaluating programs – allows us to take a comprehensive look at education and to bring wide-ranging expertise and creativity to our clients' challenges. Our approach is highly customized to meet the needs of our clients, and our staff members take great pride in working closely with customers in the field to design the right approach for each situation. We are proud of our 40-year track record, but we do not rest on our laurels – instead, we strive constantly to identify and address emerging needs and trends in teaching and learning.

Membership – 856 organizations

Dues – None

Meetings – none

Publications – Education Northwest Magazine (quarterly journal)

Name of Organization or Association – Educational Communications, Inc., Environmental and Media Projects of

Acronym –

Address:
P.O. Box 351419
Los Angeles, CA
90035
US

Phone Number – (310)559-9160; **Fax Number** – (310)559-9160

Email Contact – ECNP@aol.com; **URL** – www.ecoprojects.org

Leaders – Nancy Pearlman, Executive Director and Producer

Description – Educational Communications is dedicated to enhancing the quality of life on this planet and provides radio and television programs about the environment. Serves as a clearinghouse on ecological issues. Programming is available on 100 stations in 25 states. These include: ECONEWS television series and ENVIRONMENTAL DIRECTIONS radio series. ECO-TRAVEL Television shows focus on ecotourism. Services provided include a speakers bureau, award-winning public service announcements, radio and television documentaries, volunteer and intern opportunities, and input into the decision-making process. Its mission is to educate the public about both the problems and the solutions in the environment. Other projects include the Ecology Center of Southern California (a regional conservation group), Project Ecotourism, Humanity and the Planet, Earth Cultures (providing ethnic dance performances), and more

Membership – $20.00 for yearly subscription to the Compendium Newsletter

Dues – $20 for regular. All donations accepted

Meetings – as needed

Publications – Compendium Newsletter (bimonthly newsletter) Environmental Directions radio audio cassettes, (1550 produced to date) ECONEWS and ECO-TRAVEL television series (over 550 shows in the catalog available on 3/4", VHS, and DVD)

Name of Organization or Association – Edvantia, Inc. (Formerly AEL, Inc.)

Acronym – Edvantia

Address:
P.O. Box 1348
Charleston, WV
25325-1348
US

Phone Number – (304)347-0400, (800)624-9120; **Fax Number** – (304)347-0487

Email Contact – carla.mcclure@edvantia.org; **URL** – http://www.edvantia.org

Leaders – Dr. Doris L. Redfield, President and CEO

Description – Edvantia is a nonprofit education research and development corporation, founded in 1966, that partners with practitioners, education agencies, publishers, and service providers to improve learning and advance student success. Edvantia provides clients with a range of services, including research, evaluation, professional development, and consulting.

Membership – None

Dues – None

Meetings – None

Publications – The Edvantia Electronic Library contains links to free online tools and information created by staff on a wide array of education-related topics. Visitors to the Edvantia Web site can also access archived webcasts and webinars and sign up for a free monthly newsletter.

Name of Organization or Association – ENC Learning Inc.

Acronym – ENC

Address:
1275 Kinnear Rd
Columbus, OH
43212
US

Phone Number – 800-471-1045; **Fax Number** – 877-656-0315

Email Contact – info@goenc.com; **URL** – www.goenc.com

Leaders – Dr. Len Simutis, Director

Description – ENC provides K–12 teachers and other educators with a central source of information on mathematics and science curriculum materials, particularly those that support education reform. Among ENCs products and services is ENC Focus, a free online magazine on topics of interest to math and science educators. Users include K–12 teachers, other educators, policymakers, and parents.

Membership – ENC is a subscription-based online resource for K–12 educators. Subscriptions are available for schools, school districts, college and universities, and individuals. Information for subscribers is available at www.goenc.com/subscribe

Dues – None

Meetings – None

Publications – ENC Focus is available as an online publication in two formats: ENC Focus on K–12 Mathematics, and ENC Focus on K–12 Science. Each is accessible via www.goenc.com/focus

Name of Organization or Association – Film Arts Foundation

Acronym – Film Arts

Address:
145 9th St. #101
San Francisco, CA
94103
US

Phone Number – (415)552-8760; **Fax Number** – (415)552-0882

Email Contact – info@filmarts.org; **URL** – http://www.filmarts.org

Leaders – K.C. Price – Interim Executive Director

Description – Service organization that supports the success of independent film and video makers. Some services are for members only and some open to the public. These include low-cost classes in all aspects of filmmaking; affordable equipment rental (including digital video, 16mm, Super-8, Final Cut Pro editing, ProTools mix room, optical printer, etc); Resource Library; free legal consultation; bimonthly magazine Release Print; grants program; year-round events and exhibitions; nonprofit sponsorship; regional and national advocacy on media issues, and significant discounts on film- and video-related products and services.

Membership – nearly 3,000

Dues – $45 for "Subscriber" level benefits including bimonthly magazine, discounts, and access to libraries and online databases. $65 for full "Filmmaker" benefits including above plus: significant discounts on classes and equipment rentals, eligibility for nonprofit fiscal sponsorship, free legal consultation, and filmmaking consultation.

Meetings – Annual membership meeting and regular networking events.

Publications – The award-winning bimonthly magazine Release Print

Name of Organization or Association – Great Plains National ITV Library

Acronym – GPN

Address:
P.O. Box 80669
Lincoln, NE
68501-0669
US

Phone Number – (402)472-2007, (800)228-4630; **Fax Number** – (800)306-2330

Email Contact – npba@umd.edu; **URL** – http://shopgpn.com/

Leaders – Stephen C. Lenzen, Executive Director

Description – Produces and distributes educational media, video, CD-ROMs and DVDs, prints and Internet courses. Available for purchase for audiovisual or lease for broadcast use.

Membership – Membership not required.

Dues – There are no dues required.

Meetings – There are no meetings. We do attend subject specific conventions to promote our products.

Publications – GPN Educational Video Catalogs by curriculum areas; periodic brochures. Complete listing of GPN's product line is available via the Internet along with online purchasing. Free previews available.

Name of Organization or Association – Health Sciences Communications Association

Acronym – HeSCA

Address:
One Wedgewood Dr., Suite 27
Jewett City, CT
06351-2428
US

Phone Number – (203)376-5915; **Fax Number** – (203)376-6621

Email Contact – hesca@hesca.org; **URL** – http://www.hesca.org/

Leaders – Ronald Sokolowski, Exec. Dir.

Description – An affiliate of AECT, HeSCA is a nonprofit organization dedicated to the sharing of ideas, skills, resources, and techniques to enhance communications and educational technology in the health sciences. It seeks to nurture the professional growth of its members; serve as a professional focal point for those engaged in health sciences communications; and convey the concerns, issues, and concepts of health sciences communications to other organizations which influence and are affected by the profession. International in scope and diverse in membership, HeSCA is supported by medical and veterinary schools, hospitals, medical associations, and businesses where media are used to create and disseminate health information.

Membership – 150.

Dues – $150, indiv.; $195, institutional ($150 additional institutional dues); $60, retiree; $75, student; $1,000, sustaining. All include subscriptions to the journal and newsletter.

Meetings – Annual meetings, May–June.

Publications – Journal of Biocommunications; Feedback (newsletter

Name of Organization or Association – Institute for the Future

Acronym – IFTF

Address:
124 University Avenue, 2nd Floor
Palo Alto, CA
94301
US

Phone Number – (650)854-6322; **Fax Number** – (650)854-7850

Email Contact – info@iftf.org; **URL** – http://www.iftf.org

Leaders – Dale Eldredge, COO

Description – The Institute for the Future (IFTF) is an independent nonprofit research group. We work with organizations of all kinds to help them make better, more informed decisions about the future. We provide the foresight to create insights that lead to action. We bring a combination of tools, methodologies, and a deep understanding of emerging trends and discontinuities to our work with companies, foundations, and government agencies. We take an explicitly global approach to strategic planning, linking macro trends to local issues in such areas as: * Work and daily life * Technology and society * Health and health care * Global business trends * Changing consumer society. The Institute is based in California's Silicon Valley, in a community at the crossroads of technological innovation, social experimentation, and global interchange. Founded in 1968 by a group of former RAND Corporation researchers with a grant from the Ford Foundation to take leading-edge research methodologies into the public and business sectors, the IFTF is committed to building the future by understanding it deeply.

Membership – Become a Member. To become a member of IFTF, companies and organizations can join one or more of our membership programs or contract with us for private work. Each membership program offers a distinct set of deliverables at different membership prices and enrollment terms. Please visit the individual program sites for more detailed information on a particular program. For more information on membership contact Sean Ness at sness@iftf.org or 650-854-6322. * Ten-Year Forecast Program * Technology Horizons Program * Health Horizons Program * Custom Private Work

Dues – Corporate-wide memberships are for one-year periods: * Ten-Year Forecast – $15,000/year * Technology Horizons – $65,000/year * Health Horizons – $65,000/year. At present, we do not have university, individual, or small-company programs set up. For those companies that support our research programs, we will often conduct custom research.

Meetings – Several a year, for supporting members.

Publications – IFTF blogs * Future Now – http://future.iftf.org – emerging technologies and their social implications * Virtual China – http://www.virtual-china.org – an exploration of virtual experiences and environments in and about China * Future of Marketing – http://fom.iftf.org – emerging technology, global change, and the future of consumers and marketing * Ten-Year Forecast (members only) – http://blogger.iftf.org/tyf – a broad scan of the leading edge of change in business, government, and the global community * Technology Horizons (members only) – http://blogger.iftf.org/tech – emerging technologies and their implications for business, society, and family life.

Name of Organization or Association – Instructional Technology Council

Acronym – ITC

Address:
One Dupont Cir., NW, Suite 360
Washington, DC
20036-1143
US

Phone Number – (202)293-3110; **Fax Number** – (202)822-5014

Email Contact – cmullins@itcnetwork.org; **URL** – http://www.itcnetwork.org

Leaders – Christine Mullins, Executive Director

Description – An affiliated council of the American Association of Community Colleges established in 1977, the Instructional Technology Council (ITC) provides leadership, information, and resources to expand access to, and enhance learning through, the effective use of technology. ITC represents higher education institutions in the United States and Canada that use distance learning technologies. ITC members receive a subscription to the ITC News and ITC list serv with information on what's happening in distance education, participation in ITCs professional development audioconference series, distance learning grants information, updates on distance learning legislation, discounts to attend the annual e-Learning Conference which features more than 80 workshops and seminars.

Membership – Members include single institutions and multicampus districts; regional and statewide systems of community, technical and two-year colleges; for-profit organizations; four-year institutions; and nonprofit organizations that are interested or involved in instructional telecommunications. Members use a vast array of ever-changing technologies for distance learning. They often combine different systems according to students needs. The technologies they use and methods of teaching include: audio and video conferences, cable television, compressed and full-motion video, computer networks, fiber optics, interactive videodisc, ITFS, microwave, multimedia, public television, satellites, teleclasses, and telecourses.

Dues – $450, Institutional; $750, Corporate

Meetings – Annual e-Learning Conference

Publications – Quality Enhancing Practices in Distance Education: Vol. 2 Student Services; Quality Enhancing Practices in Distance Education: Vol. 1 Teaching and Learning; New Connections: A Guide to Distance Education (2nd ed.); New Connections: A College President's Guide to Distance Education; Digital Video: A Handbook for Educators; Faculty Compensation and Support Issues in Distance Education; ITC News (monthly publication/newsletter); ITC Listserv.

Name of Organization or Association – International Association for Language Learning Technology

Acronym – IALLT

Address:
Instr. Media Svcs, Concordia Coll.
Moorhead, MN
56562
US

Phone Number – (218) 299-3464; **Fax Number** – (218) 299-3246

Email Contact – business@iallt.org; **URL** – http://iallt.org

Leaders – Mikle Ledgerwood, President; Ron Balko, Treasurer

Description – IALLT is a professional organization whose members provide leadership in the development, integration, evaluation, and management of instructional technology for the teaching and learning of language, literature, and culture.

Membership – 400 members Membership/Subscription Categories * Educational Member: for people working in an academic setting such as a school, college, or university. These members have voting rights. * Full-time Student Member: for full-time students interested in membership. Requires a signature of a voting member to verify student status. These members have voting rights. * Commercial Member: for those working for corporations interested in language learning and technology. This category includes, for example, language laboratory vendors, software and textbook companies. * Library Subscriber: receive our journals for placement in libraries.

Dues – 1 year: $50, voting member; $25, student; $60, library subscription; $200 commercial. 2 year: $90, voting member; $380 commercial.

Meetings – Biennial IALLT conferences treat the entire range of topics related to technology in language learning as well as management and planning. IALLT also sponsors sessions at conferences of organizations with related interests, including CALICO and ACTFL.

Publications – IALLT Journal of Language Learning Technologies (2 times annually); materials for language lab management and design, language teaching and technology. Visit our Web site for details. http://iallt.org

Name of Organization or Association – International Association of School Librarianship

Acronym – IASL

Address:
PO Box 83
Zillmere, QLD
4034
AUSTRALIA

Phone Number – 61 7 3216 5785; **Fax Number** – 61 7 3633 0570

Email Contact – iasl@kb.com.au; **URL** – www.iasl-slo.org/

Leaders – Peter Genco-President; Karen Bonanno-Executive Secretary

Description – Seeks to encourage development of school libraries and library programs throughout the world; promote professional preparation and continuing education of school librarians; achieve collaboration among school libraries of the world; foster relationships between school librarians and other professionals connected with children and youth and to coordinate activities, conferences, and other projects in the field of school librarianship.

Membership – 550 plus

Dues – $50 Zone A (e.g., United States, Canada, Western Europe, Japan), $35 Zone B (e.g., Eastern Europe, Latin America, Middle East), $20 Zone C (e.g., Angola, India, Bulgaria, China) based on GNP

Meetings – Annual Conference, Lisbon, Portugal, July 2006

Publications – IASL Newsletter (3/yr.); School Libraries Worldwide (semiannual); Conference Professionals and Research Papers (annual)

Name of Organization or Association – International Center of Photography

Acronym – ICP

Address:
1114 Avenue of the Americas at 43rd Street
New York, NY
10036
US

Phone Number – (212)857-0045; **Fax Number** – (212)857-0090

Email Contact – info@icp.org; **URL** – http://www.icp.org

Leaders – Willis Hartshorn, Dir.; Phyllis Levine, Dir. of Communications.

Description – Located on a dynamic two-part campus in midtown Manhattan, the International Center of Photography (ICP) stands amongst the nation's foremost museums dedicated to preserving the past and ensuring the future of the art of photography. One of the largest facilities of its kind, ICP presents changing exhibitions of the finest works of some of the most talented photographers in the world. With over 20 exhibitions each year, ICP presents an extensive array of historical and contemporary photographs, revealing the power and diversity of the medium from documentary photography to digital imaging. The School of the International Center of Photography fosters study of the history, techniques, aesthetics, and practices of photography in a wide range of programs: continuing education classes; two full-time certificate programs; a Master of Fine Arts program in collaboration with Bard

College, Master of Arts and Master of Fine Arts degree programs in conjunction with NYU; Digital Media Program; lectures; and symposia.

Membership – 4,430

Dues – Current levels available on request.

Meetings – The ICP Infinity Awards (annual – 2007 is the 23rd)

Publications – Martin Munkacsi; Ecotopia; Atta Kim: ON-AIR; Snap Judgments: New Positions in Contemporary African Photography; African American Vernacular Photography: Selections from the Daniel Cowin Collection; Modernist Photography: Selections from the Daniel Cowin Collection; Young America. The Daguerreotypes of Southworth and Hawes; and others!

Name of Organization or Association – International Council for Educational Media

Acronym – ICEM

Address:
Postfach 114
Vienna, n/a
A-1011
Austria

Phone Number – +43 660 5113241; **Fax Number** – n/a

Email Contact – lylt@a1.net; **URL** – www.icem-cime.org

Leaders – John Hedberg – President; Ray Laverty – Secretary General

Description – Welcome to ICEM. Our purposes are: * To provide a channel for the international exchange and evaluation of information, experience, and materials in the field of educational media as they apply to preschool, primary and secondary education, to technical and vocational, industrial and commercial training, teacher training, continuing and distance education. * To foster international liaison among individuals and organizations with professional responsibility in the field of educational media. * To cooperate with other international organizations in the development and application of educational technology for practice, research, production, and distribution in this field.

Membership – What are the main advantages of ICEM membership? IICEM membership enables those professionally involved in the production, distribution, and use of media in teaching and learning to establish a broad network of contacts with educators, researchers, managers, producers, and distributors of educational media from around the world. It also provides opportunities to discuss topics of mutual concern in an atmosphere of friendship and trust, to plan and carry out co-productions, to compare and exchange ideas and experiences, to keep abreast of the latest developments, and to work together towards the improvement of education on an international level. Membership in ICEM includes a subscription to the ICEM quarterly journal, Educational Media International, an entry in the Who's who on the ICEM Webpage, registration at ICEM events and activities either free of charge or at reduced rates, eligibility to engage in working groups or become a member of the Executive Committee, participate at the General Assembly and numerous other advantages. Our purposes are: * To provide a channel for the international exchange and evaluation of information, experience, and materials in the field of educational media as they apply to preschool, primary and secondary education, to technical and vocational, industrial and commercial training, teacher training, continuing and distance education. * To foster international liaison among individuals and organizations with professional responsibility in the field of educational media. * To cooperate with other international organizations in the development and application of educational technology for practice, research, production, and distribution in this field. Who can be a member of ICEM? Members are organizations and individuals who are involved in educational technology in any one of a variety of ways. There are several different types and categories of ICEM members: Individual Members, National Representatives, Deputy Representatives and Coordinators. Individual Members may join ICEM by paying individual membership fees. National Representatives are appointed by their Ministry of Education. National Coordinators are elected by other ICEM members in their country. Regional Representatives and Coordinators represent a group of several countries. ICEM Secretariat, c/o Ray Laverty SG Pf 114 1011 WIEN AUSTRIA E-mail: lylt-at-a1.net

Dues – N/A

Meetings – Annual General Assembly in Autumn; Executive Committee meeting in Spring; Locations vary.

Publications – Educational Media International (quarterly journal) http://www. icem-cime.org/emi/issues.asp. Aims & Scope: Educational media has made a considerable impact on schools, colleges, and providers of open and distance education. This journal provides an international forum for the exchange of information and views on new developments in educational and mass media. Contributions are drawn from academics and professionals whose ideas and experiences come from a number of countries and contexts. Abstracting & Indexing Educational Media International is covered by the British Education Index; Contents Pages in Education; Educational Research Abstracts online (ERA); Research into Higher Education Abstracts; ERIC; EBSCOhost; and Proquest Information and Learning.

Name of Organization or Association – International Recording Media Association

Acronym – IRMA

Address:
182 Nassau St., Suite 204
Princeton, NJ
08542-7005
US

Phone Number – (609)279-1700; **Fax Number** – (609)279-1999

Email Contact – info@recordingmedia.org; **URL** – http://www.recordingmedia.org

Leaders – Charles Van Horn, President; Guy Finley, Associate Exec. Director

Description – IRMA, the content delivery and storage association, is the worldwide forum on trends and innovation for the delivery and storage of entertainment and information. Founded in 1970, this global trade association encompasses organizations involved in every facet of content delivery. Beginning with the introduction of the audiocassette, through the home video revolution, and right up to today's digital delivery era, IRMA has always been the organization companies have turned to for news, networking, market research, information services, and leadership.

Membership – Over 400 corporations, IRMAs membership includes raw material providers, manufacturers, replicators, duplicators, packagers, copyright holders, logistics providers, and companies from many other related industries. Corporate membership includes benefits to all employees.

Dues – Corporate membership dues based on gross dollar volume in our industry.

Meetings – Annual Recording Media Forum (Palm Springs, CA); December Summit (New York, NY).

Publications – 9X annual Mediaware Magazine; Annual International Source Directory, Quarterly Market Intelligence

Name of Organization or Association – International Society for Performance Improvement

Acronym – ISPI

Address:
1400 Spring Street, Suite 260
Silver Spring, MD
20910
US

Phone Number – 301-587-8570; **Fax Number** – 301-587-8573

Email Contact – emember@ispi.org; **URL** – http://www.ispi.org

Leaders – Richard D. Battaglia, Exec. Dir.

Description – The International Society for Performance Improvement (ISPI) is dedicated to improving individual, organizational, and societal performance. Founded in 1962, ISPI is the leading international association dedicated to improving productivity and performance in the workplace. ISPI represents more than 10,000 international and chapter members throughout the United States, Canada, and 40 other countries. ISPI's mission is to develop and recognize the proficiency of our members and advocate the use of Human Performance Technology. This systematic approach to improving productivity and competence uses a set of methods and procedures and a strategy for solving problems for realizing opportunities related to the performance of people. It is a systematic combination of performance analysis, cause analysis, intervention design and development, implementation, and evaluation that can be applied to individuals, small groups, and large organizations.

Membership – 10,000 performance technologists, training directors, human resources managers, instructional technologists, human factors practitioners, and organizational consultants are members of ISPI. They work in a variety of settings including business, academia, government, health services, banking, and the armed forces.

Dues – Membership Categories Active Membership ($145 annually). This is an individual membership receiving full benefits and voting rights in the Society. Student Membership ($60 annually). This is a discounted individual full membership for full-time students. Proof of full-time enrollment must accompany the application. Retired Membership ($60 annually). This is a discounted individual full membership for individuals who are retired from full-time employment. Special Organizational Membership Categories These groups support the Society at the top level. Sustaining Membership ($950 annually). This is an organizational membership and includes five active memberships and several additional value-added services and discounts. Details available upon request. Patron Membership ($1400 annually). This is an organizational membership and includes five active memberships and several additional value-added services and discounts. Details available upon request.

Meetings – Annual International Performance Improvement Conference, Fall Symposiums, Professional Series Workshops, Human Performance Technology Institutes

Publications – Performance Improvement Journal (10/yr). The common theme is performance improvement practice or technique that is supported by research or germane theory. PerformanceXpress (12/yr). Monthly newsletter published online. Performance Improvement Quarterly PIQ is a peer-reviewed journal created to stimulate professional discussion in the field and to advance the discipline of HPT through publishing scholarly works. ISPI Bookstore. The ISPI online bookstore is hosted in partnership with John Wiley & Sons.

Name of Organization or Association – International Visual Literacy Association

Acronym – IVLA

Address:
Dr. Constance Cassity, IVLA Treasurer, Northeastern State University, 3100 E. New Orleans St.
Broken Arrow, OK
74014
US

Phone Number – 918-449-6511; **Fax Number** – 918-449-6146

Email Contact – IVLA_Treasurer@netzero.com; **URL** – www.ivla.org

Leaders – IVLA Treasurer, Constance Cassity

Description – IVLA provides a multidisciplinary forum for the exploration, presentation, and discussion of all aspects of visual learning, thinking, communication, and expression. It also serves as a communication link bonding professionals from many disciplines who are creating and sustaining the study of the nature of visual experiences and literacy. It promotes and evaluates research, programs, and projects intended to increase effective use of visual communication in education, business, the arts, and commerce. IVLA was founded in 1968 to promote the concept of visual literacy and is an affiliate of AECT.

Membership – Membership of 500 people, mostly from academia and from many disciplines. We are an international organization and have conferences abroad once every third year. Anyone interested in any visual-verbal area should try our organization: architecture, engineering, dance, the arts, computers, video, design, graphics, photography, visual languages, mathematics, acoustics, physics, chemistry, optometry, sciences, literature, library, training, education, etc.

Dues – $60 regular; $30 student and retired; $60 outside United States; $500 lifetime membership

Meetings – Yearly conference usually Oct./Nov. in selected locations.

Publications – The Journal of Visual Literacy (biannual – juried research papers) and Selected Readings from the Annual Conference.

Name of Organization or Association – Knowledge Alliance

Acronym – n/a

Address:
815 Connecticut Avenue, NW, Suite 220
Washington, DC
20006
US

Phone Number – 202-518-0847; **Fax Number** – n/a

Email Contact – waters@KnowledgeAll.net; **URL** – http://www.knowledgeall. net

Leaders – James W. Kohlmoos, Pres.

Description – Knowledge Alliance (formerly known as NEKIA) was founded in 1997 as a nonprofit, nonpartisan strategic alliance to address the increasingly urgent need to apply rigorous research to persistent educational challenges facing our country's schools. Composed of leading education organizations, Alliance members are involved in high-quality education research, development, dissemination, technical assistance, and evaluation at the federal, regional, state, tribal, and local levels. The Alliance works closely with the US Congress, US Department of Education, and other federal agencies in advocating knowledge-based policy for innovation and improvement in education. Our Mission Knowledge Alliances mission is to improve k-12 education by widely expanding the development and use of research-based knowledge in policy and practice. We believe that the effective use of research-based knowledge is essential to increasing student achievement and closing achievement gaps and should be a central organizing concept for the education reform efforts at all levels. We envision a new knowledge era in education policy and practice that focuses on the effective use of research-based knowledge to achieve successful and sustainable school improvement.

Membership – 28

Dues – Not available

Meetings – Board Meetings and Retreats; Invitational R&D Summit (2009); Hill Days; Communicators Institute

Publications – none

Name of Organization or Association – Learning Point Associates

Acronym – (none)

Address:
1120 E. Diehl Road Suite 200
Naperville, IL
60563-1486
US

Phone Number – (630)649-6500, (800)356-2735; **Fax Number** – (630)649-6700

Email Contact – info@learningpt.org; **URL** – www.learningpt.org

Leaders – Gina Burkhardt, Chief Executive Officer

Description – Learning Point Associates, with offices in Naperville, Illinois; Chicago; New York; and Washington, D.C., is a nonprofit educational organization with more than 20 years of direct experience working with and for educators and policymakers to transform educational systems and student learning. The national and international reputation of Learning Point Associates is built on a solid foundation of conducting rigorous and relevant education research and evaluation; analyzing and synthesizing education policy trends and practices; designing and conducting client-centered evaluations; delivering high-quality professional services; and developing and delivering tools, services, and resources targeted at pressing education issues. Learning Point Associates manages a diversified portfolio of work ranging from direct consulting assignments to major federal contracts and grants, including REL Midwest, the National Comprehensive Center for Teacher Quality, Great Lakes East Comprehensive Assistance Center, Great Lakes West

Comprehensive Assistance Center, The Center for Comprehensive School Reform and Improvement, and the NCLB Implementation Center.

Membership – Not applicable

Dues – None

Meetings – None

Publications – Visit the Publications section of our Web site.

Name of Organization or Association – Library Administration and Management Association

Acronym – LAMA

Address:
50 E. Huron St.
Chicago, IL
60611
US

Phone Number – (312)280-5032; **Fax Number** – (312)280-5033

Email Contact – lama@ala.org; **URL** – http://www.ala.org/lama

Leaders – Lorraine Olley, Executive Director; Catherine Murray-Rust, President.

Description – MISSION: The Library Administration and Management Association encourages and nurtures current and future library leaders, and develops and promotes outstanding leadership and management practices. VISION: LAMA will be the foremost organization developing present and future leaders in library and information services. IMAGE: LAMA is a welcoming community where aspiring and experienced leaders from all types of libraries, as well as those who support libraries, come together to gain skills in a quest for excellence in library management, administration, and leadership. Sections include: Buildings and Equipment Section (BES); Fundraising & Financial Development Section (FRFDS); Library Organization & Management Section (LOMS); Human Resources Section (HRS); Public Relation and Marketing Section (PRMS); Systems & Services Section (SASS); and Measurement, Assessment and Evaluation Section (MAES).

Membership – 4,800

Dues – $50 regular (in addition to ALA membership); $65 organizations and corporations; $15 library school students

Meetings – ALA Annual Conference 2006, New Orleans, June 22–27; Midwinter Meeting 2007, San Diego, Jan 9–14

Publications – Library Administration & Management (q); LEADS from LAMA (electronic newsletter, irregular).

Name of Organization or Association – Library and Information Technology Association

Acronym – LITA

Address:
50 E. Huron St
Chicago, IL
60611
US

Phone Number – (312)280-4270, (800)545-2433, ext. 4270; **Fax Number** – (312)280-3257

Email Contact – lita@ala.org; **URL** – http://www.lita.org

Leaders – Mary C. Taylor, Exec. Dir., mtaylor@ala.org

Description – A division of the American Library Association, LITA is concerned with library automation; the information sciences; and the design, development, and implementation of automated systems in those fields, including systems development, electronic data processing, mechanized information retrieval, operations research, standards development, telecommunications, video communications, networks and collaborative efforts, management techniques, information technology, optical technology, artificial intelligence and expert systems, and other related aspects of audiovisual activities and hardware applications.

Membership – LITA members come from all types of libraries and institutions focusing on information technology in libraries. They include library decision-makers, practitioners, information professionals, and vendors. Approximately 4,300 members.

Dues – $60 plus membership in ALA; $25 plus membership in ALA for library school students

Meetings – National Forum, fall.

Publications – LITA Blog – . Information Technology and Libraries (ITAL: Contains the table of contents, abstracts, and some full-text of ITAL, a refereed journal published quarterly by the Library and Information Technology Association. Technology Electronic Reviews (TER): TER is an irregular electronic serial publication that provides reviews and pointers to a variety of print and electronic resources about information technology. LITA Publications List: Check for information on LITA Guides and Monographs.

Name of Organization or Association – Lister Hill National Center for Biomedical Communications

Acronym – LHNCBC

Address:
National Library of Medicine, 8600 Rockville Pike
Bethesda, MD
20894
US

Phone Number – (301)496-4441; **Fax Number** – (301)402-0118

Email Contact – lhcques@lhc.nlm.nih.gov; **URL** – http://lhncbc.nlm.nih.gov/

Leaders – Clement J. McDonald, MD, Director, ClemMcDonald@mail.nih.gov

Description – The Lister Hill National Center for Biomedical Communications is a research and development division of the National Library of Medicine (NLM). The Center conducts and supports research and development in the dissemination of high quality imagery, medical language processing, high-speed access to biomedical information, intelligent database systems development, multimedia visualization, knowledge management, data mining, and machine-assisted indexing. The Lister Hill Center also conducts and supports research and development projects focusing on educational applications of state-of-the-art technologies including the use of microcomputer technology incorporating stereoscopic imagery and haptics, the Internet, and videoconferencing technologies for training health care professionals and disseminating consumer health information. The Centers Collaboratory for High Performance Computing and Communication serves as a focus for collaborative research and development in those areas, cooperating with faculties and staff of health sciences educational institutions. Health profession educators are assisted in the use and application of these technologies through periodic training, demonstrations, and consultations. High Definition (HD) video is a technology area that has been explored and developed within the Center, and is now used as the NLM standard for all motion imaging projects considered to be of archival value. Advanced three-dimensional animation and photorealistic rendering techniques have also become required tools for use in visual projects within the Center.

Membership – None

Dues – None

Meetings – None

Publications – Fact sheet (and helpful links to other publications) at: http://www.nlm.nih.gov/pubs/factsheets/lister_hill.html

Name of Organization or Association – Media Communications Association – International

Acronym – MCA-I

Address:
PO Box 5135
Madison WI 53705-0135, WI
53705-0135
US

Phone Number – Use Contact Form; **Fax Number** – Please Ask

Email Contact – info@mca-i.org; **URL** – http://www.mca-i.org

Leaders – Lois Weiland, Executive Director

Description – Formerly the International Television Association. Founded in 1968, MCA-Is mission is to provide media communications professionals opportunities for networking, forums for education, and resources for information. MCA-I also offers business services, such as low-cost insurance, buying programs, etc., to reduce operating costs. MCA-I also confers the highly acclaimed Media Festival awards (The Golden Reel is back!) on outstanding multimedia productions. Visit MCA-Is Web site for full details.

Membership – Over 3,000 individual and corporate members. Membership programs also are available to vendors for relationship and business development.

Dues – $160, individual; $455, organizational; PLATINUM – $5,000; GOLD – $4,000; SILVER – $2,500; BRONZE – $1,200.

Meetings – Various Partnerships with Association Conferences

Publications – MCA-I eNews (Monthly), LeaderLinks (Monthly), CONNECT (Quarterly), Find a Pro Directory (online)

Name of Organization or Association – Medical Library Association

Acronym – MLA

Address:
65 E. Wacker Pl., Ste. 1900
Chicago, IL
60601-7246
US

Phone Number – (312)419-9094; **Fax Number** – (312)419-8950

Email Contact – info@mlahq.org; **URL** – http://www.mlanet.org

Leaders – Carla J. Funk, MLS, MBA, CAE, Executive Director

Description – MLA, a nonprofit, educational organization, comprises health sciences information professionals with more than 4,500 members worldwide. Through its programs and services, MLA provides lifelong educational opportunities, supports a knowledgebase of health information research, and works with a global network of partners to promote the importance of quality information for improved health to the health care community and the public.

Membership – MLA, a nonprofit, educational organization, comprises health sciences information professionals with more than 4,500 members worldwide. Through its programs and services, MLA provides lifelong educational opportunities, supports a knowledgebase of health information research, and works with a global network of partners to promote the importance of quality information for improved health to the health care community and the public. Membership categories: Regular Membership, Institutional Membership, International Membership, Affiliate Membership, Student Membership

Dues – $165, regular; $110, introductory; $255–600, institutional, based on total library expenditures, including salaries, but excluding grants and contracts; $110, international; $100, affiliate; $40, student

Meetings – National annual meeting held every May; most chapter meetings are held in the fall.

Publications – MLA News (newsletter, 10/yr.); Journal of the Medical Library Association (quarterly scholarly publication); MLA DocKit series, collections of representative, unedited library documents from a variety of institutions that illustrate the range of approaches to health sciences library management topics); MLA BibKits, selective, annotated bibliographies of discrete subject areas in the health sciences literature; standards; surveys; and copublished monographs.

Name of Organization or Association – Mid-continent Research for Education and Learning

Acronym – McREL

Address:
4601 DTC Blvd., Suite 500
Denver, CO
80237
US

Phone Number – (303)337-0990; **Fax Number** – (303)337-3005

Email Contact – info@mcrel.org; **URL** – http://www.mcrel.org

Leaders – J. Timothy Waters, Exec. Dir.

Description – McREL is a private, nonprofit organization whose purpose is to improve education through applied research and development. McREL provides products and services, primarily for K-12 educators, to promote the best instructional practices in the classroom. McREL houses one of 10 regional educational laboratories funded by the U.S. Department of Education, Institute for Educational Science. The regional laboratory helps educators and policymakers work toward excellence in education for all students. It also serves at the North Central Comprehensive Center, providing school improvement support to the states of Iowa, Minnesota, Nebraska, North Dakota, and South Dakota. McREL has particular expertise in standards-based education systems, leadership for school improvement, effective instructional practices, teacher quality, mathematics and science education improvement, early literacy development, and education outreach programs.

Membership – not a membership organization

Dues – no dues

Meetings – NA

Publications – Changing Schools (q. newsletter); Noteworthy (irregular monograph on topics of current interest in education reform). Numerous technical reports and other publications. Check Web site for current listings.

Name of Organization or Association – Minorities in Media (An Affiliate of the Association for Educational Communications & Technology)

Acronym – MIM

Address:
P.O. Box 439147
Chicago, IL
60643-9147
US

Phone Number – (773) 841-3732; **Fax Number** – (773) 409-8583

Email Contact – pyoung@umbc.edu; **URL** – http://aectmim.ning.com/

Leaders – Patricia A. Young, President (2009–2011); Brandon C. Taylor, President Elect (2011–2013)

Description – MISSION STATEMENT: Minorities in Media's purpose is to encourage the effective utilization of educational media in the teaching learning process; provide leadership opportunities in advancing the use of technology as an integral part of the learning process; provide a vehicle through which minorities might influence the utilization of media in institutions; develop an information exchange network common to minorities in media; study, evaluate, and refine the educational technology process as it relates to the education of minorities and to encourage and improve the production of effective materials for the education of minorities.

Membership – Dr. Wesley Joseph McJulien founded Minorities In Media (MIM) around the late 1970s. In the April 1987 issue of Tech Trends, the article Black Contributors to Educational Technology chronicles the history of MIM. John W. Green & Wesley J. McJulien write: "In 1975, a group of Black technologists met in Dallas in an effort to band together and provide more opportunities for Blacks in the Association for Educational Communications and Technology. One of the assignments was to find the Black person who was the outstanding author in the field of educational technology and invite him to speak at the 1977 meeting of BUDDIES (an organization now called Minorities In Media). Dr. Greene was selected and his presentation, "The Role of Blacks in Instructional Technology," stressed that Black must participate in all areas of AECT and especially in research (p. 18)" This history is the foundation of who we are today as an organization. We celebrate our past and continue to spearhead our future. Membership is open to professionals and academics whose interests align with MIMs mission.

Dues – $10, student; $30 professional

Meetings – Annual meetings held during the Association for Educational Communications & Technology conference – www.aect.org.

Publications – MIM NING is free to sign up – http://aectmim.ning.com/

Name of Organization or Association – National Aeronautics and Space Administration

Acronym – NASA

Address:
NASA Headquarters, 300 E Street SW
Washington, DC
20546
US

Phone Number – (202)358-0103; **Fax Number** – (202)358-3032

Email Contact – education@nasa.gov; **URL** – http://education.nasa.gov

Leaders – Angela Phillips Diaz, Assistant Administrator for Education

Description – From elementary through postgraduate school, NASAs educational programs are designed to inspire the next generation of explorers by capturing students interest in science, mathematics, and technology at an early age; to channel more students into science, engineering, and technology career paths; and to enhance the knowledge, skills, and experiences of teachers and university faculty. NASAs educational programs include NASA Spacelink (an electronic information system); videoconferences (60-minute interactive staff development videoconferences to be delivered to schools via satellite); and NASA Television (informational and educational television programming). Additional information is available from the Office of Education at NASA Headquarters and counterpart offices at the nine NASA field centers. Further information may be obtained from the NASA Education Homepage and also accessible from the NASA Public Portal at See learning in a whole new light!

Membership – n/a

Dues – n/a

Meetings – n/a

Publications – Publications and Products can be searched and downloaded from the following URL – http://www.nasa.gov/audience/foreducators/5-8/learning/index.html

Name of Organization or Association – National Alliance for Media Arts and Culture

Acronym – NAMAC

Address:
145 Ninth Street, Suite 250
San Francisco, CA
94103
US

Phone Number – (415)431-1391; **Fax Number** – (415)431-1392

Email Contact – namac@namac.org; **URL** – http://www.namac.org

Leaders – Helen DeMichel, Co-Director

Description – NAMAC is a nonprofit organization dedicated to increasing public understanding of and support for the field of media arts in the United States. Members include media centers, cable access centers, universities, and media artists, as well as other individuals and organizations providing services for production, education, exhibition, distribution, and preservation of video, film, audio, and intermedia. NAMACs information services are available to the general public, arts and nonarts organizations, businesses, corporations, foundations, government agencies, schools, and universities.

Membership – 300 organizations, 75 individuals

Dues – $75-$450, institutional (depending on annual budget); $75, indiv.

Meetings – Biennial Conference

Publications – Media Arts Information Network; The National Media Education Directory, annual anthology of case-studies "A Closer Look," periodic White Paper reports, Digital Directions: Convergence Planning for the Media Arts

Name of Organization or Association – National Association for Visually Handicapped

Acronym – NAVH

Address:
22 West 21st St., 6th Floor
New York, NY
10010
US

Phone Number – (212) 889-3141; **Fax Number** – (212) 727-2931

Email Contact – navh@navh.org; **URL** – http://www.navh.org

Leaders – Dr. Lorraine H. Marchi, Founder/CEO; Cesar Gomez, Executive Director

Description – NAVH ensures that those with limited vision do not lead limited lives. We offer emotional support; training in the use of visual aids and special lighting; access to a wide variety of optical aids, electronic equipment, and lighting; a large print, nationwide, free-by-mail loan library; large print educational materials; free quarterly newsletter; referrals to eye care specialists and local low vision resources; self-help groups for seniors and working adults; and educational outreach to the public and professionals.

Membership – It is not mandatory to become a member in order to receive our services. However, your membership helps others retain their independence by allowing NAVH to provide low vision services to those who cannot afford to make a donation. In addition, members receive discounts on visual aids, educational materials, and our catalogs. Corporations and publishers may also join to help sponsor our services. Please contact us for more information.

Dues – Membership is $50 a year for individuals. Publishers and corporations interested in membership should contact NAVH.

Meetings – Seniors support group 2 times at month; seminar on low vision for ophthalmology residents; yearly showcase of the latest in low vision technology, literature, and services

Publications – Free quarterly newsletter distributed free throughout the English-speaking world; Visual Aids Catalog; Large Print Loan Library Catalog; informational pamphlets on vision, common eye diseases and living with limited vision; booklets for professionals who work with adults and children with limited vision

Name of Organization or Association – National Association of Media and Technology Centers

Acronym – NAMTC

Address:
NAMTC, 7105 First Ave. SW
Cedar Rapids, IA
52405
US

Phone Number – 319 654 0608; **Fax Number** – 319 654 0609

Email Contact – bettyge@mchsi.com; **URL** – www.namtc.org

Leaders – Betty Gorsegner Ehlinger, Executive Director

Description – NAMTC is committed to promoting leadership among its membership through networking, advocacy, and support activities that will enhance the equitable access to media, technology, and information services to educational communities. Membership is open to regional, K-12, and higher education media centers which serve K-12 students as well as commercial media and technology centers.

Membership – Institutional and corporate members numbering approximately 200.

Dues – $115 institutions; $325, corporations

Meetings – A national Leadership Summit is held in the winter.

Publications – Electronic NAMTC Newsletter is published 5 times per academic year.

Name of Organization or Association – National Commission on Libraries and Information Science

Acronym – NCLIS

Address:
1800 M Street, NW; Suite 350 North Tower
Washington, DC
20036-5841
US

Phone Number – (202)606-9200; **Fax Number** – (202)606-9203

Email Contact – info@nclis.gov.; **URL** – http://www.nclis.gov

Leaders – C. Beth Fitzsimmons, Chairman

Description – A permanent independent agency of the U.S. government charged with advising the executive and legislative branches on national library and information policies and plans. The Commission reports directly to the president and Congress on the implementation of national policy; conducts studies, surveys, and analyses of the nations library and information needs; appraises the inadequacies of current resources and services; promotes research and development activities; conducts hearings and issues publications as appropriate; and develops overall plans for meeting national library and information needs and for the coordination of activities at the federal, state, and local levels. The Commission provides general policy advice to the Institute of Museum and Library Services (IMLS) director relating to library services included in the Library Services and Technology Act (LSTA).

Membership – 16 commissioners (14 appointed by the president and confirmed by the Senate, the Librarian of Congress, and the Director of the IMLS).

Dues – none

Meetings – Average 2–3 meetings a year

Publications – N/A

Name of Organization or Association – National Communication Association

Acronym – NCA

Address:
1765 N Street, NW
Washington,, DC
22003
US

Phone Number – 202-464-4622; **Fax Number** – 202-464-4600

Email Contact – dwallick@natcom.org; **URL** – http://www.natcom.org

Leaders – Roger Smitter, Exec. Dir.

Description – A voluntary society organized to promote study, criticism, research, teaching, and application of principles of communication, particularly of speech communication. Founded in 1914, NCA is a nonprofit organization of researchers, educators, students, and practitioners, whose academic interests span all forms of human communication. NCA is the oldest and largest national organization serving the academic discipline of communication. Through its services, scholarly publications, resources, conferences, and conventions, NCA works with its members to strengthen the profession and contribute to the greater good of the educational enterprise and society. Research and instruction in the discipline focus on the study of how messages in various media are produced, used, and interpreted within and across different contexts, channels, and cultures.

Membership – 7,700

Dues – From $60 (Student) to $300 (Patron). Life membership also available.

Meetings – Four regional conferences (ECA, ESCA SSCA, WSCA) and one Annual National Conference.

Publications – Spectra Newsletter (mo.); Quarterly Journal of Speech; Communication Monographs; Communication Education; Critical Studies in Mass Communication; Journal of Applied Communication Research; Text and Performance Quarterly; Communication Teacher; Index to Journals in Communication Studies through 1995; National Communication Directory of NCA and the Regional Speech Communication Organizations (CSSA, ECA, SSCA, WSCA). For additional publications, request brochure.

Name of Organization or Association – National Council of Teachers of English: Commission on Media, Assembly on Media Arts

Acronym – NCTE

Address:
1111 W. Kenyon Rd.
Urbana, IL
61801-1096
US

Phone Number – (217)328-3870; **Fax Number** – (217)328-0977

Email Contact – public_info@ncte.org; **URL** – http://www.ncte.org

Leaders – Kent Williamson, NCTE Executive Director; David Bruce, Commission Director; Mary Christel, Assembly Chair

Description – The NCTE Commission on Media is a deliberative and advisory body which each year identifies and reports to the NCTE Executive Committee on key issues in the teaching of media; reviews what the Council has done concerning media during the year; recommends new projects and persons who might undertake them. The commission monitors current and projected NCTE publications (other than journals), suggests topics for future NCTE publications on media, and performs a similar role of review and recommendation for the NCTE Annual Convention program. Occasionally, the commission undertakes further tasks and projects as approved by the Executive Committee. The NCTE Assembly on Media Arts promotes communication and cooperation among all individuals who have a special interest in media in the English language arts; presents programs and special projects on this subject; encourages the development of research, experimentation, and investigation in the judicious uses of media in the teaching of English; promotes the extensive writing of articles and publications devoted to this subject; and integrates the efforts of those with an interest in this subject.

Membership – The National Council of Teachers of English, with 50,000 individual and institutional members worldwide, is dedicated to improving the teaching and learning of English and the language arts at all levels of education. Members include elementary, middle, and high school teachers; supervisors of English programs; college and university faculty; teacher educators; local and state agency English specialists; and professionals in related fields. The members of the NCTE Commission on Media are NCTE members appointed by the director of the group. Membership in the Assembly on Media Arts is open to members and nonmembers of NCTE.

Dues – Membership in NCTE is $40 a year; adding subscriptions to its various journals adds additional fees. Membership in the Assembly on Media Arts is $15 a year.

Meetings – http://www.ncte.org/conventions/ 96th NCTE Annual Convention, November 20–25, 2003, San Francisco, California; 94th NCTE Annual Convention, November 16–21, 2006, Nashville, Tennessee

Publications – NCTE publishes about 20 books a year. Visit http://www.ncte.org/pubs/books/ and http://www.ncte.org/store. NCTEs journals include Language Arts English Journal College English College Composition and Communication English Education Research in the Teaching of English Teaching English in the Two-Year College Voices from the Middle Primary Voices, K-6 Talking Points Classroom Notes Plus English Leadership Quarterly The Council Chronicle (included in NCTE membership) Journal information is available at http://www.ncte.org/pubs/journals/.

The Commission on Media doesn't have its own publication. The Assembly on Media Arts publishes Media Matters, a newsletter highlighting issues, viewpoints, materials, and events related to the study of media. Assembly members receive this publication.

Name of Organization or Association – National EBS Association

Acronym – NEBSA

Address:
PO Box 121475
Clermont, FL
34712-1475
US

Phone Number – (407) 401-4630; **Fax Number** – (321) 406-0520

Email Contact – execdirector@nebsa.org; **URL** – http://nebsa.org

Leaders – Lynn Rejniak, Chair, Bd. of Dirs.; Don MacCullough, Exec. Dir.

Description – Established in 1978, NEBSA is a nonprofit, professional organization of Educational Broadband Service (EBS) licensees, applicants, and others interested in EBS broadcasting. EBS is a very high frequency television broadcast service that is used to broadcast distance learning classes, two way internet service, wireless and data services to schools and other locations where education can take place. The goals of the association are to gather and exchange information about EBS, gather data on utilization of EBS, act as a conduit for those seeking EBS information, and assist migration from video broadcast to wireless, broadband Internet services using EBS channels. The NEBSA represents EBS interests to the FCC, technical consultants, and equipment manufacturers. The association uses its Web site and Listserv list to provide information to its members in areas such as technology, programming content, FCC regulations, excess capacity leasing and license and application data.

Membership – The current membership consists of educational Institutions and nonprofit organizations that hold licenses issued by the Federal Communications Commission for Educational Broadband Service (EBS). We also have members that have an interest in EBS and members such as manufacturers of EBS-related equipment and law firms that represent licensees.

Dues – We have two main types of memberships: Voting memberships for EBS licensees only, and nonvoting memberships for other educational institutions and sponsors. See the Web site http://www.nebsa.org for details.

Meetings – Annual Member Conference, February/March

Publications – http://www.nebsa.org

Name of Organization or Association – National Endowment for the Humanities

Acronym – NEH

Address:
Division of Public Programs, Media Program, 1100 Pennsylvania Ave., NW, Room 426
Washington, DC
20506
US

Phone Number – (202)606-8269; **Fax Number** – (202)606-8557

Email Contact – publicpgms@neh.gov; **URL** – http://www.neh.gov

Leaders – Tom Phelps, Director, Division of Public Programs

Description – The NEH is an independent federal grant-making agency that supports research, educational, and public programs grounded in the disciplines of the humanities. The Division of Public Programs Media Program supports film and radio programs in the humanities for public audiences, including children and adults. All programs in the Division of Public Program support various technologies, specifically Web sites both as stand-alone projects and as extensions of larger projects such as museum exhibitions.

Membership – Nonprofit institutions and organizations including public television and radio stations.

Dues – not applicable

Meetings – not applicable

Publications – Visit the Web site (http://www.neh.gov) for application forms and guidelines as well as the Media Log, a cumulative listing of projects funded through the Media Program.

Name of Organization or Association – National Federation of Community Broadcasters

Acronym – NFCB

Address:
1970 Broadway, Ste. 1000
Oakland, CA
94612
US

Phone Number – 510 451-8200; **Fax Number** – 510 451-8208

Email Contact – ginnyz@nfcb.org; **URL** – http://www.nfcb.org.

Leaders – Maxie C Jackson III, President and CEO

Description – NFCB represents noncommercial, community-based radio stations in public policy development at the national level and provides a wide range of practical services, including technical assistance.

Membership – 250. Noncommercial community radio stations, related organizations, and individuals.

Dues – range from $200 to $4000 for participant and associate members

Meetings – Annual Community Radio Conference; 2010 St. Paul; 2011 San Francisco

Publications – Public Radio Legal Handbook; Digital AudioCraft; Guide to Underwriting

Name of Organization or Association – National Film Board of Canada

Acronym – NFBC

Address:
1123 Broadway, STE 307
New York, NY
10010
US

Phone Number – (212)629-8890; **Fax Number** – (212)629-8502

Email Contact – NewYork@nfb.ca; **URL** – www.nfb.ca

Leaders – Dylan McGinty, US Sales Manager; Laure Parsons, US Sales and Marketing Associate

Description – Established in 1939, the NFBCs main objective is to produce and distribute high-quality audiovisual materials for educational, cultural, and social purposes.

Membership – none

Dues – none

Meetings – n/a

Publications – n/a

Name of Organization or Association – National Freedom of Information Coalition

Acronym – NFOIC

Address:
133 Neff Annex, University of Missouri
Columbia, MO
65211-0012
US

Phone Number – (573)882-4856; **Fax Number** – (573)884-6204

Email Contact – daviscn@missouri.edu; **URL** – http://www.nfoic.org

Leaders – Dr. Charles N. Davis, Executive Director

Description – The National Freedom of Information Coalition is a national membership organization devoted to protecting the public's right to oversee its government. NFOICs goals include helping start-up FOI organizations; strengthening existing FOI organizations; and developing FOI programs and publications appropriate to the membership.

Membership – The NFOIC offers active memberships to freestanding nonprofit state or regional Freedom of Information Coalitions, academic centers and First Amendment Centers, and associated memberships to individuals and entities supporting NFOICs mission. Membership information is available on the NFOIC Web page. Achieving and maintaining active membership in all 50 states is the primary goal of NFOIC.

Dues – Membership categories and levels of support are described on the NFOIC Web site.

Meetings – The National Freedom of Information Coalition host an annual meeting and a spring conference.

Publications – The FOI Advocate, an electronic newsletter available for free through email subscription. The FOI Report, a periodic White Paper, published electronically.

Name of Organization or Association – National Gallery of Art

Acronym – NGA

Address:
Department of Education Resources, 2000B South Club Drive
Landover, MD
20785
US

Phone Number – (202)842-6273; **Fax Number** – (202)842-6935

Email Contact – EdResources@nga.gov; **URL** – http://www.nga.gov/education/classroom/loanfinder/

Leaders – Leo J. Kasun Education Resources Supervisory Specialist

Description – This department of NGA is responsible for the production and distribution of 120+ educational audiovisual programs, including interactive technologies. Materials available (all loaned free to individuals, schools, colleges and universities, community organizations, and noncommercial television stations) range from videocassettes and color slide programs to CD-ROMs and DVDs. All videocassette and DVD programs are closed captioned. A free catalog of programs is available upon request. All CD-ROMs and DVDs utilizing digitized images on the gallery's collection are available for long-term loan.

Membership – Our free-loan lending program resembles that of a library and because we are a federally funded institution we have membership system. Last year we lent programs directly to over one million borrowers. Our programs are available to anyone who requests them which ranges from individuals to institutions.

Dues – None

Meetings – None

Publications – Extension Programs Catalogue.

Name of Organization or Association – National PTA

Acronym – National PTA

Address:
541 North Fairbanks Ct, Ste. 1300
Chicago, IL
60611
US

Phone Number – (312)670-6782; **Fax Number** – (312)670-6783

Email Contact – info@pta.org; **URL** – http://www.pta.org

Leaders – Warlene Gary, Chief Executive Officer

Description – Advocates the education, health, safety, and well-being of children and teens. Provides parenting education and leadership training to PTA volunteers. National PTA partners with the National Cable & Telecommunications Association on the "Taking Charge of Your TV" project by training PTA and cable representatives to present media literacy workshops. The workshops teach parents and educators how to evaluate programming so they can make informed decisions about what to allow their children to see. The National PTA in 1997 convinced the television industry to add content information to the TV rating system.

Membership – 6.2 million membership open to all interested in the health, welfare, and education of children and support the PTA mission – http://www.pta.org/aboutpta/mission_en.asp.

Dues – vary by local unit – national dues portion is $1.75 per member annually.

Meetings – National convention, held annually in June in different regions of the country, is open to PTA members; convention information available on the Web site

Publications – Our Children (magazine) plus electronic newsletters and other Web-based information for members and general public.

Name of Organization or Association – National Public Broadcasting Archives

Acronym – NPBA

Address:
Hornbake Library, University of Maryland
College Park, MD
20742
US

Phone Number – (301)405-9160; **Fax Number** – (301)314-2634

Email Contact – npba@umd.edu; **URL** – http://www.lib.umd.edu/NPBA

Leaders – Karen King, Acting Curator

Description – NPBA brings together the archival record of the major entities of noncommercial broadcasting in the United States. NPBAs collections include the archives of the Corporation for Public Broadcasting (CPB), the Public Broadcasting Service (PBS), and National Public Radio (NPR). Other organizations represented include the Midwest Program for Airborne Television Instruction (MPATI), the Public Service Satellite Consortium (PSSC), Americas Public Television Stations (APTS), Children's Television Workshop (CTW), and the Joint Council for Educational Telecommunications (JCET). NPBA also makes available the personal papers of many individuals who have made significant contributions to public broadcasting, and its reference library contains basic studies of the broadcasting industry, rare pamphlets, and journals on relevant topics. NPBA also collects and maintains a selected audio and video program record of public broadcastings national production and support centers and of local stations. Oral history tapes and transcripts from the NPR Oral History Project and the Televisionaries Nal History Project are also available at the archives. The archives are open to the public from 9 A.M. to 5 P.M., Monday through Friday. Research in NPBA collections should be arranged by prior appointment. For further information, call (301)405-9988.

Membership – NA

Dues – NA

Meetings – NA

Publications – NA

Name of Organization or Association – National Telemedia Council Inc.

Acronym – NTC

Address:
1922 University Ave.
Madison, WI
53726
USA

Phone Number – (608)218-1182; **Fax Number** – None

Email Contact – NTelemedia@aol.com; **URL** – http://www.nationaltelemedia-council.org , and www.journalofmedialiteracy.org

Leaders – Karen Ambrosh, President; Marieli Rowe, Exec. Dir.

Description – The National Telemedia Council is a national, nonprofit professional organization that has been promoting a media wise society for nearly six decades. Embracing a positive, nonjudgmental philosophy that values education, evaluation, and reflective judgment, NTC has a long history of a broad array of initiatives that have included annual conferences, workshops, major and innovative interactive forums, local, national, and international events for diverse participants (including children); and its major ongoing award, the "Jessie McCanse Award for Individual, Long-Term Contribution to the Field of Media Literacy." NTCs ongoing current activities continue to include its major publication, The Journal of Media Literacy, published up to three times per year (and a part of the organization since its inception in 1953 and earlier); the development of its archival Web site; and interactive collaborations to advance the field such as the "media literacy cafes" in connection with issues of the Journal of Media Literacy.

Membership – Member/subscribers to the Journal of Media Literacy, currently over 500, including individuals, organizations, schools, and university libraries across the globe including Asia, Australia, Europe, North and South America. Our membership is open to all those interested in media literacy.

Dues – Individuals: $35, basic; $50, contributing; $100, patron organizations/ library: $60 Corporate sponsorship: $500 (Additional Postage for Overseas)

Meetings – No major meetings scheduled this year

Publications – The Journal of Media Literacy

Name of Organization or Association – Native American Public Telecommunications

Acronym – NAPT

Address:
1800 North 33rd Street
Lincoln, NE
68503
US

Phone Number – (402)472-3522; **Fax Number** – (402)472-8675

Email Contact – rfauver1@unl.edu; **URL** – http://nativetelecom.org

Leaders – Shirley K. Sneve, Exec. Dir.

Description – Native American Public Telecommunications (NAPT) supports the creation, promotion, and distribution of native public media. We accomplish this mission by: • Producing and developing educational telecommunication programs for all media including public television and public radio. • Distributing and encouraging the broadest use of such educational telecommunications programs. • Providing training opportunities to encourage increasing numbers of American Indians and Alaska Natives to produce quality public broadcasting programs. • Promoting increased control and use of information technologies by American Indians and Alaska Natives. • Providing leadership in creating awareness of and developing telecommunications policies favorable to American Indians and Alaska Natives. • Building partnerships to develop and implement telecommunications projects with tribal nations, Indian organizations, and native communities.

Membership – No Membership

Dues – None

Meetings – None

Publications – The Vision Maker (e-newsletter).

Name of Organization or Association – Natural Science Collections Alliance

Acronym – NSC Alliance

Address:
P.O. Box 44095
Washington, DC
20026-4095
US

Phone Number – (202)633-2772; **Fax Number** – (202)633-2821

Email Contact – ddrupa@burkine.com; **URL** – http://www.nscalliance.org

Leaders – Executive Director

Description – Fosters the care, management, and improvement of biological collections and promotes their utilization. Institutional members include free-standing museums, botanical gardens, college and university museums, and public institutions, including state biological surveys and agricultural research centers. The NSC Alliance also represents affiliate societies and keeps members informed about funding and legislative issues.

Membership – 80 institutions, 30 affiliates, 120 individual and patron members.

Dues – Dues: depend on the size of collections.

Meetings – Annual Meeting (May or June)

Publications – Guidelines for Institutional Policies and Planning in Natural History Collections; Global Genetic Resources; A Guide to Museum Pest Control

Name of Organization or Association – New England School Library Association (formerly New England Educational Media Association)

Acronym – NESLA (formerly NEEMA)

Address:
c/o Merlyn Miller, President Burr & Burton Academy, 57 Seminary Avenue
Manchester, VT
05254
US

Phone Number – 802-362-1775; **Fax Number** – 802-362-0574

Email Contact – mmiller@burrburton.org; **URL** – www.neschoollibraries.org

Leaders – Merlyn Miller, President

Description – An affiliate of AECT, NESLA is a regional professional association dedicated to the improvement of instruction through the effective utilization of school library media services, media, and technology applications. For over 90 years, it has represented school library media professionals through activities and networking efforts to develop and polish the leadership skills, professional representation, and informational awareness of the membership. The Board of Directors consists of representatives from local affiliates within all six of the New England states, as well as professional leaders of the region. An annual leadership conference is offered.

Membership – NESLA focuses on school library media issues among the six New England states, consequently, membership is encouraged for school library media specialists in this region.

Dues – Regular membership $30. Student /retired membership $15.

Meetings – Annual Leadership Conference and Business Meeting

Publications – NESLA Views

Name of Organization or Association – New York Festivals

Acronym – NYF

Address:
260 West 39th Street, 10th Floor
New York, NY
10018
USA

Phone Number – 212-643-4800; **Fax Number** – 212-643-0170

Email Contact – info@newyorkfestivals.com; **URL** – http://www.newyorkfestivals.com

Leaders – Alisun Armstrong, Executive Director

Description – New York Festivals (NYF) is an international awards company founded in 1957. Recognizing The World's Best Work™ in advertising, programming, design, and marketing, NYF honors creativity and effectiveness in global communications through six different annual competitions. New York Festivals International Film & Video Awards is one of the oldest extant international festivals in the world. Known best for honoring informational, educational, and industrial film production, the New York Festivals Film & Video Awards is entering its 50th year of recognizing The Worlds Best Work™ in categories including Documentaries, Business Theatre, Short and Feature Length Films, Home Video Productions, Distance Learning, Slide Productions, and Multi-Screen Productions. Winners are honored in a black-tie event in Manhattan in January. The 2007 International Film & Video Awards will open for entry on July 5th. The Discount Deadline is August 23rd (enter online by that date and get a 10% discount off the entry total), and the final deadline will be September 22. For more information and fees, plus a full list of categories and the rules and regulations, please visit www.newyorkfestivals.com.

Membership – No membership feature. The competition is open to any nonbroadcast media production.

Dues – n/a

Meetings – n/a

Publications – Winners are posted on our Web site at www.newyorkfestivals.com

Name of Organization or Association – Northwest College and University Council for the Management of Educational Technology

Acronym – NW/MET

Address:
c/o WITS, Willamette University, 900 State St.
Salem, OR
97301
US

Phone Number – (503)370-6650; **Fax Number** – (503)375-5456

Email Contact – mmorandi@willamette.edu; **URL** – http://www.nwmet.org

Leaders – Doug McCartney, Director (effective April 14, 2007); Marti Morandi, Membership Chair.

Description – NW/MET is a group of media professionals responsible for campuswide media services. Founded in 1976, NW/MET is comprised of members from two provinces of Canada and four northwestern states.

Membership – The membership of NW/MET is composed of individuals who participate by giving time, energy, and resources to the support and advancement of the organization. Full Membership may be awarded to individuals whose primary professional role involves the facilitation of educational technology, who are employed by an institution of higher education located in the NW/MET membership region, and who submit a membership application in which they list their professional qualifications and responsibilities.

Dues – $35

Meetings – An annual conference and business meeting are held each year, rotating through the region.

Publications – An annual directory and Web site.

Name of Organization or Association – OCLC Online Computer Library Center, Inc.

Acronym – OCLC

Address:
6565 Kilgour Place
Dublin, OH
43017-3395
US

Phone Number – (614)764-6000; **Fax Number** – (614)764-6096

Email Contact – oclc@oclc.org; **URL** – http://www.oclc.org

Leaders – Jay Jordan, President and CEO

Description – Founded in 1967, OCLC is a nonprofit, membership, computer library service and research organization dedicated to the public purposes of furthering access to the world's information and reducing information costs. More than 60,000 libraries in 112 countries and territories around the world use OCLC services to locate, acquire, catalog, lend, and preserve library materials. Researchers, students, faculty, scholars, professional librarians, and other information seekers use OCLC services to obtain bibliographic, abstract, and full-text information. OCLC and its member libraries cooperatively produce and maintain WorldCat, the world's largest database for discovery of library materials. OCLC publishes the Dewey Decimal Classification. OCLC Digital Collection and Preservation Services provide digitization and archiving services worldwide. OCLCs NetLibrary provides libraries with eContent solutions that support Web-based research, reference, and learning.

Membership – OCLC welcomes information organizations around the world to be a part of our unique cooperative. A variety of participation levels are available to libraries, museums, archives, historical societies, other cultural heritage organizations, and professional associations. OCLC membership represents more than 60,000 libraries in 112 countries and territories around the world.

Dues – N/A

Meetings – OCLC Members Council (3/yr.) Held in Dublin, Ohio.

Publications – Annual Report (1/yr.; print and electronic); OCLC Newsletter (4/yr.; print and electronic); OCLC Abstracts (1/week, electronic only.)

Name of Organization or Association – Online Audiovisual Catalogers

Acronym – OLAC

Address:
n/a
n/a, n/a
n/a
US

Phone Number – n/a; **Fax Number** – n/a

Email Contact – neumeist@buffalo.edu; **URL** – http://www.olacinc.org/

Leaders – n/a

Description – In 1980, OLAC was founded to establish and maintain a group that could speak for catalogers of audiovisual materials. OLAC provides a means for exchange of information, continuing education, and communication among catalogers of audiovisual materials and with the Library of Congress. While maintaining a voice with the bibliographic utilities that speak for catalogers of audiovisual materials, OLAC works toward common understanding of AV cataloging practices and standards.

Membership – 500

Dues – United States and Canada Personal Memberships One year $20.00 Two years $38.00 Three years $55.00 Institutional Memberships One year $25.00 Two years $48.00 Three years $70.00 Other Countries All Memberships One year $25.00 Two years $48.00 Three years $70.00

Meetings – biannual

Publications – OLAC Newsletter

Name of Organization or Association – Ontario Film Association, Inc. (also known as the Association for the Advancement of Visual Media/Lassociation pour lavancement des médias visuels).

Acronym – OLA

Address:
50 Wellington St East Suite 201
Toronto, ON
M5E 1C8
Canada

Phone Number – (416)363-3388; **Fax Number** – 1-800-387-1181

Email Contact – info@accessola.com; **URL** – www.accessola.com

Leaders – Lawrence A. Moore, Exec. Dir.

Description – A membership organization of buyers and users of media whose objectives are to promote the sharing of ideas and information about visual media through education, publications, and advocacy.

Membership – 112

Dues – $120, personal membership; $215, associate membership.

Meetings – OFA Media Showcase, spring

Publications – Access

Name of Organization or Association – Pacific Film Archive

Acronym – PFA

Address:
University of California, Berkeley Art Museum, 2625 Durant Ave.
Berkeley, CA
94720-2250
US

Phone Number – (510)642-1437 (library); (510)642-1412 (general).; **Fax Number** – (510)642-4889

Email Contact – NLG@berkeley.edu; **URL** – http://www.bampfa.berkeley.edu

Leaders – Susan Oxtoby, Senior Curator of Film; Nancy Goldman, Head, PFA Library and Film Study Center

Description – Sponsors the exhibition, study, and preservation of classic, international, documentary, animated, and avant-garde films. Provides on-site research screenings of films in its collection of over 10,000 titles. Provides access to its collections of books, periodicals, stills, and posters (all materials are noncirculating). Offers BAM/PFA members and University of California, Berkeley, affiliates reference and research services to locate film and video distributors, credits, stock footage, etc. Library hours are 1 P.M.–5 P.M. Mon.–Thurs. Research screenings are by appointment only and must be scheduled at least two weeks in advance; other collections are available for consultation on a drop-in basis during library hours.

Membership – Membership is through our parent organization, the UC Berkeley Art Museum and Pacific Film Archive, and is open to anyone. The BAM/PFA currently has over 3,000 members. Members receive free admission to the Museum; reduced-price tickets to films showing at PFA; access to the PFA Library & Film Study Center; and many other benefits. Applications and more information is available at http://www.bampfa.berkeley.edu/join/

Dues – $50 individuals and nonprofit departments of institutions.

Meetings – none

Publications – BAM/PFA Calendar (6/yr.).

Name of Organization or Association – Pacific Resources for Education and Learning

Acronym – PREL

Address:
900 Fort Street Mall, Suite 1300
Honolulu, HI
96813
US

Phone Number – (808) 441-1300; **Fax Number** – (808) 441-1385

Email Contact – askprel@prel.org; **URL** – http://www.prel.org/

Leaders – Thomas W. Barlow, Ed.D., President and Chief Executive Officer

Description – Pacific Resources for Education and Learning (PREL) is an independent, nonprofit 501(c)(3) corporation that serves the educational community in the U.S.-affiliated Pacific islands, the continental United States, and countries throughout the world. PREL bridges the gap between research, theory, and practice in education and works collaboratively to provide services that range from curriculum development to assessment and evaluation. PREL serves the Pacific educational community with quality programs and products developed to promote educational excellence. We work throughout school systems, from classroom to administration, and collaborate routinely with governments, communities, and businesses. Above all, we specialize in multicultural and multilingual environments. From direct instruction to professional development to creation of quality educational materials, PREL is committed to ensuring that all students, regardless of circumstance or geographic location, have an equal opportunity to develop a strong academic foundation. PREL brings together in the Center for Information, Communications, and Technology (CICT) an experienced cadre of specialists in Web site development and design, educational technology, distance and online learning, multimedia production, interactive software development, writing and editing, graphics, and print production. By combining tested pedagogy with leading edge technology, PREL can create learning materials encompassing a wide variety of subject matter and delivery methods. PREL partners with researchers, schools, evaluators, publishers, and leaders in the learning technology industry to develop state-of-the-art learning tools and technology solutions. There are vast disparities across the Pacific when it comes to school resources, technology access, and bandwidth. PREL's goal is to work effectively in any type of setting in which an application is needed. With routine travel and a staff presence throughout the northern Pacific, PREL has resolved to reach underserved communities, determine their needs, and meet their requirements with the appropriate delivery and dissemination methods. Multimedia, Software, and Web site conception, design, and delivery have become critical components of many learning programs. Our projects include development of teacher and student resources and resource kits, learning games, software solutions, and complex interactive database design. Distance Learning Content and Delivery extend educational resources to audiences and individuals outside the classroom setting. Distance options both enhance and exponentially increase learning opportunities. The CICT is a premier provider of distance education, integrating curriculum and technology. High-Quality Publications are a PREL hallmark. PREL produces and distributes numerous high-quality publications for educators, including its research compendium, Research into Practice; Pacific Educator magazine; educational books and videos; and briefs and reports on research findings and current topics of interest.

Membership – PREL serves teachers and departments and ministries of education in American Samoa, Commonwealth of the Northern Mariana Islands, Federated States of Micronesia (Chuuk, Kosrae, Pohnpei, and Yap) Guam, Hawaii, the Republic of the Marshall Islands, and the Republic of Palau. In addition we work with the educational community on the continental United States and countries throughout the world. We are not a membership organization. We are grant funded with grants from the United States Departments of Education, Labor, Health and Human Services, and other federal funding agencies such as the Institute of Museum and Library Services and the National Endowment for the Arts. In addition, we have projects in partnership with regional educational institutions. Internationally we have worked with the International Labor Organization and the World Health Organization and are currently working with Save the Children on a US AID project in the Philippines.

Dues – N/A

Meetings – PREL supports the annual Pacific Educational Conference (PEC), held each July.

Publications – Publications are listed on the PREL Web site at http://ppo.prel.org/. Most are available in both PDF and HTML format. Some recent publications are described below: Focus on Professional Development, A (Research Based Practices in Early Reading Series) A Focus on Professional Development is the fourth in the Research-Based Practices in Early Reading Series published by the Regional Educational Laboratory (REL) at Pacific Resources for Education and Learning (PREL). Because reading proficiency is fundamental to student achievement across all subjects and grades, the preparation of the teachers and administrators who are responsible for providing early reading instruction is of special importance. This booklet examines what research tells us about professional development and about the role that effective professional development plays in improving both teacher performance and student achievement. http://www.prel.org/products/re_/prodevelopment.pdf (902K) Look and See: Using the Visual Environment as Access to Literacy (Research Brief) This paper describes how the visual environment – what we see when we look – can be used to develop both visual and verbal literacy, including aesthetic appreciation, comprehension, and vocabulary. http://www.prel. org/products/re_/look_see.pdf (1M) Measuring the Effectiveness of Professional Development in Early Literacy: Lessons Learned (Research Brief) This Research Brief focuses on the methodology used to measure professional development (PD) effectiveness. It examines the needs that generated this research, what PREL did to meet those needs, and lessons that have been learned as a result. In particular, it discusses the development of a new instrument designed to measure the quality of PD as it is being delivered. http://www.prel.org/products/re_/effect_of_pd.pdf (730K) Pacific Early Literacy Resource Kit CD-ROM (Early Literacy Learning Resources) The Pacific Early Literacy Resource Kit was developed from PRELs research-based work performed with early literacy teachers in US-affiliated Pacific islands. The contents of the Resource Kit represent information, products, and processes we found beneficial as we worked to support literacy teachers in their efforts to improve student literacy achievement. http://www.prel.org/toolkit/index.htm Research Into Practice 2006 (PREL Compendium) This 86-page volume of PRELs annual research compendium brings together articles detailing research conducted during 2005 by PREL. The six articles in this issue focus on putting research findings to work to improve education. http://www.prel.org/products/pr_/compendium06/tableofcontents.asp

Name of Organization or Association – Reference and User Services Association, a Division of the American Library Association

Acronym – RUSA

Address:
50 E. Huron St.
Chicago, IL
60611
US

Phone Number – (800)545-2433, ext. 4398.; **Fax Number** – Fax (312)280-5273

Email Contact – rusa@ala.org; **URL** – http://rusa.ala.org

Leaders – Barbara A. Macikas, Exec. Dir

Description – A division of the American Library Association, RUSA is responsible for stimulating and supporting in every type of library the delivery of reference information services to all groups and of general library services and materials to adults.

Membership – 5,200

Dues – Join ALA and RUSA $120; RUSA membership $60 (added to ALA membership); student member $55 ($30 for ALA and $25 for RUSA); retired, support staff or nonsalaried $72 ($42 for ALA and $30 for RUSA)

Meetings – Meetings are held in conjunction with the American Library Association.

Publications – RUSQ (q.), information provided on RUSA Web site at http://rusa.ala.org, RUSA Update, online membership newsletter, select publications.

Name of Organization or Association – Research for Better Schools, Inc.

Acronym – RBS

Address:
112 North Broad Street
Philadelphia, PA
19102-1510
US

Phone Number – (215)568-6150; **Fax Number** – (215)568-7260

Email Contact – info@rbs.org; **URL** – http://www.rbs.org/

Leaders – Keith M. Kershner Executive Director

Description – Research for Better Schools is a nonprofit education organization that has been providing services to teachers, administrators, and policy makers since 1966. Our mission is to help students achieve high learning standards by supporting improvement efforts in schools and other education environments. The staff are dedicated to and well experienced in providing the array of services that schools, districts, and states need to help their students reach proficient or higher learning standards: (1) technical assistance in improvement efforts; (2) professional development that is required for the successful implementation of more effective curricula, technologies, or instruction; (3) application of research in the design of specific improvement efforts; (4) evaluation of improvement efforts; (5) curriculum implementation and assessment; and (6) effective communication with all members of the school community. RBS has worked with a wide range of clients over the years, representing all levels of the education system, as well as business and community groups.

Membership – There is no membership in Research for Better Schools.

Dues – N/A

Meetings – N/A

Publications – RBS publishes a variety of books and other products designed for educators to use for schools improvement. The catalog for RBS Publications is online (visit our homepage at http://www.rbs.org).

Name of Organization or Association – SERVE Center @ UNCG

Acronym – We no longer use the acronym

Address:
5900 Summit Avenue, Dixon Building
Browns Summit, FL
27214
US

Phone Number – 800-755-3277, 336-315-7457; **Fax Number** – 336-315-7457

Email Contact – info@serve.org; **URL** – http://www.serve.org/

Leaders – Ludy van Broekhuizen, Executive Director

Description – The SERVE Center at the University of North Carolina at Greensboro, under the leadership of Dr. Ludwig David van Broekhuizen, is a university-based education organization with the mission to promote and support the continuous improvement of educational opportunities for all learners in the Southeast. The organization's commitment to continuous improvement is manifest in an applied research-to-practice model that drives all of its work. Building on research, professional wisdom, and craft knowledge, SERVE staff members develop tools, processes, and interventions designed to assist practitioners and policymakers with their work. SERVEs ultimate goal is to raise the level of student achievement in the region. Evaluation of the impact of these activities combined with input from stakeholders expands SERVEs knowledge base and informs future research. This rigorous and practical approach to research and development is supported by an experienced staff strategically located throughout the region. This staff is highly skilled in providing needs assessment services, conducting applied research in schools, and developing processes, products, and programs that support educational improvement and increase student achievement. In the last three years, in addition to its basic research and development work with over 170 southeastern schools, SERVE staff provided technical assistance and training to more than 18,000 teachers and administrators across the region. The SERVE Center is governed by a board of directors that includes the governors, chief state school officers, educators, legislators, and private sector leaders from Alabama, Florida, Georgia, Mississippi, North Carolina, and South Carolina. SERVEs operational core is the Regional Educational Laboratory. Funded by the U.S. Department of Educations Institute of Education Sciences, the Regional Educational Laboratory for the Southeast is one of ten Laboratories providing research-based information and services to all 50 states and territories. These Laboratories form a nationwide education knowledge network, building a bank of information and resources shared and disseminated nationally and regionally to improve student achievement. SERVEs National Leadership Area, Expanded Learning Opportunities, focuses on improving student outcomes through the use of exemplary pre–K and extended-day programs.

Membership – none

Dues – none

Meetings – none

Publications – Three titles available in the highlighted products area of Web site: A Review Of Methods and Instruments Used In State and Local School Readiness Evaluations Abstract: This report provides detailed information about the methods and instruments used to evaluate school readiness initiatives, discusses important considerations in selecting instruments, and provides resources and recommendations that may be helpful to those who are designing and implementing school readiness evaluations. Levers for Change: Southeast Region State Initiatives To Improve High Schools Abstract: This descriptive report aims to stimulate discussion about high school reform among Southeast Region states. The report groups recent state activities in high school reform into six "levers for change." To encourage critical reflection, the report places the reform discussion in the context of an evidence-based decision-making process and provides sample research on reform activities. Evidence-Based Decision making: Assessing Reading Across the Curriculum Intervention Abstract:: When selecting reading across the curriculum interventions, educators should consider the extent of the evidence base on intervention effectiveness and the fit with the school or district context, whether they are purchasing a product from vendors or developing it internally. This report provides guidance in the decision making.

Name of Organization or Association – Society for Photographic Education

Acronym – SPE

Address:
126 Peabody Hall, The School of Interdisciplinary Studies, Miami University
Oxford, OH
45056
US

Phone Number – (513) 529-8328; **Fax Number** – (513) 529-9301

Email Contact – speoffice@spenational.org; **URL** – www.spenational.org

Leaders – Richard Gray, Chairperson of SPE Board of Directors

Description – An association of college and university teachers of photography, museum photographic curators, writers, publishers, and students. Promotes discourse in photography education, culture, and art.

Membership – 1,800 membership dues are for the calendar year, January through December.

Dues – Membership Dues: $90 – Regular Membership $50 – Student Membership $600 – Corporate Member $380 – Collector Member (with print) $150 – Sustaining Member $65 – Senior Member

Meetings – Denver, CO, March 13–16, 2008

Publications – Exposure (Photographic Journal) – biannual – Quarterly Newsletter – Membership Directory – Conference Program Guide

Name of Organization or Association – Society of Cable Telecommunications Engineers

Acronym – SCTE

Address:
140 Philips Rd
Exton, PA
19341-1318
US

Phone Number – (610)363-6888; **Fax Number** – (610)363-5898

Email Contact – scte@scte.org; **URL** – http://www.scte.org

Leaders – Mark L, Dzuban, Pres. & CEO

Description – The Society of Cable Telecommunications Engineers (SCTE) is a nonprofit professional association that provides technical leadership for the telecommunications industry and serves its members through professional development, standards, certification, and information. SCTE currently has more than 14,000 members from the U.S. and 70 countries worldwide and offers a variety of programs and services for the industry's educational benefit. SCTE has 68 chapters and meeting groups and more than 3,000 employees of the cable telecommunications industry hold SCTE technical certifications. SCTE is an ANSI-accredited standards development organization. Visit SCTE online at www.scte.org.

Membership – SCTE is comprised of a global network of more than 14,000 broadband engineers, technology experts, industry analysts, technicians, corporate managers, and CEOs who work within the Cable Telecommunications industry. SCTE offers industry professionals a multitude of learning opportunities on the latest technological advances, industry news, and targeted resources to help keep members better informed, outperform their peers and advance in their careers at a pace that works best for them.

Dues – $68 Individual $350 Expo Partner $34 Full-time Student, Unemployed or Retired (one-year)

Meetings – SCTE Cable-Tec Expo®, Denver, CO, Oct. 28–30, 2009; SCTE Conference on Broadband Learning & Development, Denver, CO, Oct. 27, 2009; SCTE Conference on Emerging Technologies®;

Publications – SCTE Interval SCTE Monthly SCTE NewsBreak Credentials Standards Bulletin

Name of Organization or Association – Society of Photo Technologists

Acronym – SPT

Address:
11112 S. Spotted Rd.
Cheney, WA
99004
US

Phone Number – 800-624-9621 or (509)624-9621; **Fax Number** – (509)624-5320

Email Contact – cc5@earthlink.net; **URL** – http://www.spt.info/

Leaders – Chuck Bertone, Executive Director

Description – An organization of photographic equipment repair technicians, which improves and maintains communications between manufacturers and repair shops and technicians. We publish Repair Journals, Newsletters, Parts & Service Directory and Industry Newsletters. We also sponsor SPTNET (a technical email group), Remanufactured parts and residence workshops.

Membership – 1,000 shops and manufactures worldwide, eligible people or businesses are any who are involved full or part time in the camera repair field.

Dues – $97.50-$370. Membership depends on the size/volume of the business. Most one man shops are Class A/$170 dues. Those not involved full time in the field is $95.50/Associate Class.

Meetings – SPT Journal; SPT Parts and Services Directory; SPT Newsletter; SPT Manuals – Training and Manufacturer's Tours.

Publications – Journals & Newsletters

Name of Organization or Association – Southwest Educational Development Laboratory

Acronym – SEDL

Address:
211 East Seventh St.
Austin, TX
78701
US

Phone Number – (512) 476-6861; **Fax Number** – (512) 476-2286

Email Contact – info@sedl.org; **URL** – http://www.sedl.org

Leaders – Dr. Wesley A. Hoover, Pres. and CEO

Description – The Southwest Educational Development Laboratory (SEDL) is a private, not-for-profit education research and development corporation based in Austin, Texas. SEDL has worked in schools to investigate the conditions under which teachers can provide student-centered instruction supported by technology, particularly computers alone with other software. From that field-based research with teachers, SEDL has developed a professional development model and modules, which resulted in the production of Active Learning with Technology (ALT) portfolio. ALT is a multimedia training program for teachers to learn how to apply student-centered, problem-based learning theory to their instructional strategies that are supported by technologies. Copies of Active Learning with Technology Portfolio and other products used to integrate technology in the classroom can be viewed and ordered online at http://www.sedl.org/pubs/category_technology.html from SEDLs Office of Institutional Communications. SEDL operates the Southeast Comprehensive Center (SECC), funded by the U.S. Department of Education, which provides high-quality technical assistance in the states of Alabama, Georgia, Louisiana, Mississippi, and South Carolina. The goals of the SECC are to build the capacities of states in its region to implement the programs and goals of the No Child Left Behind Act of 2001 (NCLB) and to build states capacity to provide sustained support of high-needs districts and schools. SECC works closely with each state in its region to provide access and use of information, models, and materials that facilitate implementation of and compliance with NCLB. SEDLs Texas Comprehensive Center provides technical assistance and support to the Texas Education Agency to assure Texas has an education system with the capacity and commitment to eliminate achievement gaps and enable all students to achieve at high levels.

Membership – Not applicable.

Dues – Not applicable.

Meetings – Not applicable

Publications – SEDL LETTER and other newsletters and documents are available for free general distribution in print and online. Topic-specific publications related to educational change, education policy, mathematics, language arts, science, and disability research and a publications catalog are available at http://www.sedl.org/pubs on the SEDL Web site.

Name of Organization or Association – Special Libraries Association

Acronym – SLA

Address:
331 South Patrick Street
Alexandria, VA
22314
US

Phone Number – 703-647-4900; **Fax Number** – 703-647-4901

Email Contact – sla@sla.org; **URL** – http://www.sla.org

Leaders – The Honorable Janice R. Lachance, CEO

Description – The Special Libraries Association (SLA) is a nonprofit global organization for innovative information professionals and their strategic partners. SLA serves more than 11,000 members in 75 countries in the information profession, including corporate, academic, and government information specialists. SLA promotes and strengthens its members through learning, advocacy, and networking initiatives. For more information, visit us on the Web at www.sla.org.

Membership – 11,500

Dues – Full Membership: USD 160.00 (members earning greater than USD 35,000 in annual salary); USD 99.00 (members earning USD 35,000 or less in annual salary). Student/Retired Membership: USD 35.00

Meetings – 2006 Annual Conference and Exposition: 11–14 June, Baltimore; 2007 Annual Conference and Exposition: 3–6 June, Denver

Publications – Information Outlook (monthly glossy magazine that accepts advertising). SLA Connections (monthly electronic newsletter for members and stakeholders).

Name of Organization or Association – Teachers and Writers Collaborative

Acronym – T&W

Address:
520 Eighth Avenue, Suite 2020
New York, NY
10018
US

Phone Number – (212)691-6590, Toll-free (888)266-5789; **Fax Number** – (212)675-0171

Email Contact – bmorrow@twc.org; **URL** – http://www.twc.org and http://www.writenet.org

Leaders – Amy Swauger, Dir.

Description – T&W brings the joys and pleasures of reading and writing directly to children. As an advocate for the literary arts and arts education, we support writers and teachers in developing and implementing new teaching strategies; disseminate models for literary arts education to local, national, and international audiences; and showcase both new and established writers via publications and literary events held in our Center for Imaginative Writing. T&W was founded in 1967 by a group of writers and educators who believed that professional writers could make a unique contribution to the teaching of writing and literature. Over the past 40 years, 1,500 T&W writers have taught writing workshops in New York City's public schools.

Approximately 700,000 New York City students have participated in our workshops, and we have worked with more than 25,000 teachers. Our wealth of experience, which is reflected in T&W's 80 books about teaching writing, led the National Endowment for the Arts to single out T&W as the arts-in-education group "most familiar with creative writing/literature in primary and secondary schools." The American Book Review has written that T&W "has created a whole new pedagogy in the teaching of English."

Membership – T&W has over 1,000 members across the country. The basic membership is $35; patron membership is $75; and benefactor membership is $150 or more. Members receive a free book or T-shirt; discounts on publications; and a free one-year subscription to Teachers & Writers magazine. (Please see http://www.twc. org/member.htm.)

Dues – T&W is seeking general operating support for all of our programs and program support for specific projects, including: (1) T&W writing residencies in New York City area schools; (2) T&W publications, books and a quarterly magazine, which we distribute across the country; (3) T&W events, including readings for emerging writers and small presses; and (4) T&Ws Internet programs for teachers, writers, and students. Grants to T&Ws Endowment support the stability of the organization and help to guarantee the continuation of specific programs.

Meetings – T&W offers year-round public events in our Center for Imaginative Writing in New York City. For a list of events, please see http://www.twc.org/events. htm.

Publications – T&W has published over 80 books on the teaching of imaginative writing, including The T&W Handbook of Poetic Forms; The Dictionary of Wordplay; The Story in History; Personal Fiction Writing; Luna, Luna: Creative Writing from Spanish and Latino Literature; The Nearness of You: Students and Teachers Writing On-Line. To request a free publications catalog, please send email to info@twc.org or call 888-BOOKS-TW. (Please see http://www.twc.org/pubs)

Name of Organization or Association – The George Lucas Educational Foundation

Acronym – GLEF

Address:
P.O. Box 3494
San Rafael, CA
94912
US

Phone Number – (415)662-1600; **Fax Number** – (415)662-1619

Email Contact – edutopia@glef.org; **URL** – http://edutopia.org

Leaders – Milton Chen, PhD., Exec. Dir.

Description – Mission: The George Lucas Educational Foundation (GLEF) is a nonprofit operating foundation that documents and disseminates models of the most innovative practices in our nation's K-12 schools. We serve this mission through the creation of media – from films, books, and magazine to CD-ROMS and DVDs. GLEF works to provide its products as tools for discussion and action in conferences, workshops, and professional development settings. Audience: A successful educational system requires the collaborative efforts of many different stakeholders. Our audience includes teachers, administrators, school board members, parents, researchers, and business and community leaders who are actively working to improve teaching and learning. Vision: The Edutopian vision is thriving today in our country's best schools: places where students are engaged and achieving at the highest levels, where skillful educators are energized by the excitement of teaching, where technology brings outside resources and expertise into the classroom, and where parents and community members are partners in educating our youth.

Membership – All online content and the Edutopia magazine are offered free of charge to educators.

Dues – Free subscription to Edutopia magazine for those working in education.

Meetings – no public meetings; advisory council meets annually; board of directors meets quarterly

Publications – Edutopia Online: The Foundation's Web site, Edutopia (www.edutopia.org) celebrates the unsung heroes who are making Edutopia a reality. All of GLEF's multimedia content dating back to 1997 is available on its Web site. A special feature, the Video Gallery, is an archive of short documentaries and expert interviews that allow visitors to see these innovations in action and hear about them from teachers and students. Detailed articles, research summaries, and links to hundreds of relevant Web sites, books, organizations, and publications are also available to help schools and communities build on successes in education. Edutopia: Success Stories for Learning in the Digital Age: This book and CD-ROM include numerous stories of innovative educators who are using technology to connect with students, colleagues, the local community, and the world beyond. The CD-ROM contains more than an hour of video footage. Published by Jossey-Bass. Teaching in the Digital Age (TDA) Videocassettes This video series explores elements of successful teaching in the Digital Age. The project grows out of GLEFs belief that an expanded view is needed of all our roles in educating children and supporting teachers. The series explores School Leadership, Emotional Intelligence, Teacher Preparation, and Project-Based Learning and Assessment. Learn & Live This documentary film and 300-page companion resource book showcases innovative schools across the country. The film, hosted by Robin Williams, aired on public television stations nationwide in 1999 and 2000. The Learn & Live CD-ROM includes digital versions of the film and book in a portable, easy-to-use format. Edutopia Magazine A free magazine which shares powerful examples of innovative and exemplary learning and teaching. Edutopia Newsletter This free, semiannual print newsletter includes school profiles, summaries of recent research, and resources and tips for getting involved in public education. Instructional Modules Free teaching modules developed by education faculty and professional developers. They can be used as extension units in existing courses or can be used independently in workshops. Includes presenter notes, video segments, and discussion questions. Topics include project-based learning, technology integration, and multiple intelligences.

Name of Organization or Association – The NETWORK, Inc.

Acronym – NETWORK

Address:
136 Fenno Drive
Rowley, MA
01969-1004
USA

Phone Number – 800-877-5400, (978)948-7764; **Fax Number** – (978)948-7836

Email Contact – davidc@thenetworkinc.org; **URL** – www.thenetworkinc.org

Leaders – David Crandall, President

Description – A nonprofit research and service organization providing training, research and evaluation, technical assistance, and materials for a fee to schools, educational organizations, and private sector firms with educational interests. The NETWORK has been helping professionals manage and learn about change since 1969. Our Leadership Skills series of computer-based simulations extends the widely used board game versions of Making Change (tm) and Systems Thinking/Systems Changing(tm) with the addition of Improving Student Success: Teachers, Schools, and Parents to offer educators a range of proven professional development tools. Now available, Networking for Learning, originally developed for the British Department for Education and Skills, offers a contemporary leadership development resource for educators exploring the challenges of complex collaborations involving multiple organizations.

Membership – none required

Dues – no dues, fee for service

Meetings – call

Publications – Making Change: A Simulation Game [board and computer versions]; Systems Thinking/Systems Changing: A Simulation Game [board and computer versions]; Improving Student Success: Teachers, Schools and Parents [computer based simulation]; Systemic Thinking: Solving Complex Problems; Benchmarking: A Guide for Educators; Networking for Learning; Check Yourself into College: A quick and easy guide for high school students.

Name of Organization or Association – University Continuing Education Association

Acronym – UCEA

Address:
One Dupont Cir. NW, Suite 615
Washington, DC
20036
US

Phone Number – (202)659-3130; **Fax Number** – (202)785-0374

Email Contact – kjkohl@ucea.edu; **URL** – http://www.ucea.edu/

Leaders – Kay J. Kohl, Executive Director, kjkohl@ucea.edu

Description – UCEA is an association of public and private higher education institutions concerned with making continuing education available to all population segments and to promoting excellence in continuing higher education. Many institutional members offer university and college courses via electronic instruction.

Membership – 425 institutions, 2,000 professionals.

Dues – vary according to membership category; see: http://www.ucea.edu/membership.htm

Meetings – UCEA has an annual national conference and several professional development seminars throughout the year. See: http://www.ucea.edu/page02.htm

Publications – monthly newsletter; quarterly; occasional papers; scholarly journal, Continuing Higher Education Review; Independent Study Catalog. With Peterson's, The Guide to Distance Learning; Guide to Certificate Programs at American Colleges and Universities; UCEA-ACE/Oryx Continuing Higher Education book series; Lifelong Learning Trends (a statistical factbook on continuing higher education); organizational issues series; membership directory.

Name of Organization or Association – Young Adult Library Services Association

Acronym – YALSA

Address:
50 E. Huron St.
Chicago, IL
60611
US

Phone Number – (312)280-4390; **Fax Number** – (312)280-5276

Email Contact – yalsa@ala.org; **URL** – http://www.ala.org/yalsa

Leaders – Beth Yoke, Executive Director; Judy T. Nelson, President

Description – A division of the American Library Association (ALA), the Young Adult Library Services Association (YALSA) seeks to advocate, promote, and strengthen service to young adults as part of the continuum of total library services. Is responsible within the ALA to evaluate and select books and media and to interpret and make recommendations regarding their use with young adults. Selected List Committees include Best Books for Young Adults, Popular Paperbacks for Young Adults, Quick Picks for Reluctant Young Adult Readers, Outstanding Books for the College Bound, Selected Audiobooks for Young Adults, Great Graphic Novels for Teens and Selected Films for Young Adults. To learn more about our literary awards, such as the Odyssey Award for best audiobook production, and recommended reading, listening and viewing lists go to www.ala.org/yalsa/booklists. YALSA celebrates Teen Tech Week the first full week of March each year. To learn more go to www.ala.org/teentechweek.

Membership – 5,500. YALSA members may be young adult librarians, school librarians, library directors, graduate students, educators, publishers, or anyone for whom library service to young adults is important.

Dues – $50; $20 students; $20 retirees (in addition to ALA membership)

Meetings – 2 ALA conferences yearly, Midwinter (January) and Annual (June); one biennial Young Adult Literature Symposium (beginning in 2008)

Publications – Young Adult Library Services, a quarterly print journal YAttitudes, a quarterly electronic newsletter for members only
There are a total of 94 organizations in the database.

Part V
Graduate Programs

Introduction

Michael Orey

Part V includes annotated entries for graduate programs that offer degrees in the fields of learning, design and technology or library and information science. In an effort to only list active organizations, I deleted all programs that had not updated their information since 2006. All readers are encouraged to contact the institutions that are not listed for investigation and possible inclusion in the 2012 edition.

Information for this section was obtained through e-mail directing each program to an individual web form through which the updated information could be submitted electronically into a database created by Michael Orey. Although the section editor made every effort to contact and follow up with program representatives, responding to the annual request for an update was the responsibility of the program representatives. The editing team would like to thank those respondents who helped assure the currency and accuracy of this section by responding to the request for an update. In this year's edition, I asked for some data on the number of graduates, number of faculty, and amount of grants and contracts. These data were used as self-report top 20 lists in the preface to this book. Readers should be aware that these data are only as accurate as the person who filled the form for their program.

M. Orey (✉)
Learning, Design, and Technology Program, The University of Georgia, Athens, GA, USA
e-mail: mikeorey@uga.edu

M. Orey et al. (eds.), *Educational Media and Technology Yearbook: Volume 36, 2011*,
Educational Media and Technology Yearbook 36, DOI 10.1007/978-1-4614-1305-9_27,
© Springer Science+Business Media, LLC 2012

Organizations and Associations in the US and Canada

This information will be used solely to construct a directory of relevant organizations and associations within the *2011 Educational Media & Technology Yearbook*. The data supplied here will not be intentionally shared or publicized in any other form. Thank you for your assistance.

Name of Institution – Athabasca University

Name of Department or Program – Centre for Distance Education

Address:
1 University Drive
Athabasca, AB
T9S 3A3
Canada

Phone Number – 17806756406 **Fax Number** – 1-780-675-6170

Email Contact – mohameda@athabascau.ca **URL** – cde.athabascau.ca

Contact Person – Mohamed Ally

Specializations – Doctor of Education in Distance Education Master of Distance Education Graduate Diploma in Distance Education Technology Graduate Diploma in Instructional Design Graduate Certificate in Instructional Design

Features – Doctor of Education in Distance Education Master of Distance Education Graduate Diploma in Distance Education Technology Graduate Diploma in Instructional Design Graduate Certificate in Instructional Design

Admission Requirements – Doctorate of Education in Distance Education Admission requirements for the doctoral program include both academic and experiential elements. * Completion of a masters degree, preferably with a thesis or research project, in a relevant field or area of study (e.g., education or distance education, psychology or educational psychology, instructional technology, adult education, curriculum and

M. Orey et al. (eds.), *Educational Media and Technology Yearbook: Volume 36, 2011*, Educational Media and Technology Yearbook 36, DOI 10.1007/978-1-4614-1305-9_28, © Springer Science+Business Media, LLC 2012

instruction, and the like) from a recognized university, normally with a GPA of at least 3.7 or 85% (Graduate Grading Policy); * Significant experience in open or distance learning, which demonstrates that the student is capable of study at a distance, and of completing high quality original research with distance supervision only. Master of Distance Education Applicants to the MDE program must hold a baccalaureate degree from a recognized postsecondary education institution. If the potential applicant does not have a degree, but believes his or her education and experience is equivalent to an undergraduate degree, then it is the responsibility of the applicant to put forward this position in writing as part of the application process. Graduate Diploma in Distance Education Technology Applicants to the GDDET program must hold a baccalaureate degree from a recognized postsecondary education institution. If the potential applicant does not have a degree, but believes that his or her education and experience is equivalent to an undergraduate degree, then it is the responsibility of the applicant to put forward this position in writing as part of the application process. Graduate Diploma in Instructional Design Applicants to the GDID program must hold a baccalaureate degree from a recognized postsecondary education institution. If the potential applicant does not have a degree, but believes that his or her education and experience is equivalent to an undergraduate degree, then it is the responsibility of the applicant to put forward this position in writing as part of the application process. Graduate Certificate in Instructional Design Applicants to the GCID program must hold a baccalaureate degree from a recognized postsecondary education institution. If the potential applicant does not have a degree, but believes that his or her education and experience is equivalent to an undergraduate degree, then it is the responsibility of the applicant to put forward this position in writing as part of the application process.

Degree Requirements – Doctor of Education in Distance Education The Doctor of Education in Distance Education program will address the needs of a wide range of practitioners, scholars, and researchers who operate in the distance education arena. The doctorate will provide critical direction as distance education evolves and expands. The primary goal of the doctoral program is to provide students with a complete and rigorous preparation to assume senior responsibilities for planning, teaching, directing, designing, implementing, evaluating, researching, and managing distance education programs. Master of Distance Education Athabasca University's Master of Distance Education (MDE) program is designed to provide a common base of skills, knowledge, and values regarding distance education and training, independent of any special area of interest. Graduate Diploma in Distance Education Technology Athabasca University's Graduate Diploma in Distance Education Technology GDDET is a focused, 18-credit (six courses) program designed to provide a solid grounding in the current principles and practices of technology use in distance education and training. The program structure and course content emphasize the concepts and skills required of practitioners who are employed as instructors, teachers, trainers, decision makers, planners, managers, and administrators in distance education or "virtual" programs. The emphasis of the GDDET is on the user of technology for the preparation, delivery, and management of instruction. Graduate

Diploma in Instructional Design The Graduate Diploma in Instructional Design is an 18-credit program comprised of six (6) courses. For those who wish to pursue instructional design as a profession, this Diploma program provides more depth and breadth than the certificate. Graduate Certificate in Instructional Design The Graduate Certificate in Instructional Design is a 9-credit program, comprised of three (3) courses. For those wanting to enhance their instructional design expertise, the Certificate program is an expedient way to obtain the appropriate skills and knowledge.

Number of Full-Time Faculty – 11; **Number of Other Faculty** – 15

Degrees awarded in 2008–2009 Academic Year – Masters – 52; **PhD** – 0; **Other** – 12

Grant Monies awarded in 2008–2009 Academic Year – 0

Name of Institution – University of Calgary

Name of Department or Program – Office of Graduate Programs, Faculty of Education

Address:
Education Tower 940, 2500 University Drive NW, University of Calgary
Calgary, AB
T2N 1N4
Canada

Phone Number – 403-220-5675 **Fax Number** – 403-282-3005

Email Contact – dmjacobs@ucalgary.ca **URL** – http://educ.ucalgary.ca/gder/

Contact Person – Dr. Michele Jacobsen

Specializations – In a knowledge-based economy, the PhD, EDD, MA, and MEd programs in the Educational Technology specialization in GDER at the University of Calgary have proven valuable to public and private sector researchers, teachers, military/industrial trainers, health educators, instructional designers, managers, and leaders. A spectrum of entrepreneurs and public service experts have successfully completed our programs and are using their research, knowledge, and competencies in schools, in higher education, and a range of workplaces today. Our graduates have careers as practitioners and scholars in the top government, industry, K-12, and higher education institutions as professors, education and training leaders, teachers, and instructors – worldwide. Your academic and professional career growth is possible through our innovative, student-centered programs and supervision processes in this growing, vibrant area. Degree programs can be completed on campus, in blended formats or completely online.

Features – The Educational Technology Specialization is inter-disciplinary and is addressed to at least two audiences: (a) School Leaders and Teachers who are interested in the study and practice of educational technology in the classroom or who are interested in technology leadership positions or who are interested in academic careers in higher education; (b) those who are interested in instructional design and development in settings both within and outside elementary/secondary/tertiary schools, e.g., instructional developers and faculty developers in colleges, institutes of technology and universities, military/industrial trainers, health educators, and private training consultants. Students in this specialization have the opportunity to investigate a broad spectrum of instructional design and development theories and practices as they apply to current and emergent technologies and to explore new directions in instructional design and development and evaluation as they emerge in the literature and in practice.

Admission Requirements – The Master of Education (MEd) is a course-based professional degree. The MEd program is available in the on-campus and online formats. Admission requirements normally include a completed four-year bachelors degree and a 3.0 GPA. The Master of Arts (MA) is a thesis-based degree intended to prepare students for further research. Admission requirements normally include a completed four-year bachelors degree and a 3.3 GPA. The Doctor of Education (EdD) is a thesis-based degree intended to prepare scholars for careers in research, teaching, and leadership. The EDD program is available in the online format. Admission requirements normally include a completed Masters Degree and a 3.5 GPA. The Doctor of Philosophy (PhD) is a thesis-based degree intended to prepare scholars for careers in research and teaching. The PhD program is available in the on-campus format. Admission requirements normally include a completed Masters Thesis and a 3.5 GPA.

Degree Requirements – Program requirements for the Master of Education (MEd) program are completion of a minimum of six full-course equivalents (twelve half-courses). In Educational Technology, masters students complete 6 half-courses in the specialization of educational technology, 2 half-courses in research methodology, and 4 half-courses in elective areas (can also be in educational technology). Program requirements for the Master of Arts (MA) thesis program include: (a) One full-course equivalent (two half-courses) in research methods; (b) a minimum of one full-course equivalent (two half-courses) in the students area of specialization; (c) additional graduate courses or seminars are determined by the supervisor in consultation with the student; (d) a Masters thesis and an oral examination on the thesis. Program requirements for the Education Doctorate (EDD) program include: (a) EDER 700 (a full-course equivalent) is required of all doctoral students during their first year of program; (b) two half courses in research methodology; (c) 3–4 half courses in the specialization (EDER 779.01 required; EDER 779.02, EDER 779.03, and EDER 779.04). Additional graduate courses or seminars as determined by the supervisor in consultation with the student (normally, EdD students in Educational Technology complete four half-course equivalents in the specialization); (d) a candidacy examination demonstrating the students competence to undertake a thesis; (e) a Doctoral thesis and an oral examination on the thesis. Program requirements for the on campus Doctor of Philosophy (PhD) program include: (a) A minimum of one and one-half full-course equivalents, including EDER 700 (a full-course equivalent), is required of all doctoral students during their first year of program (the required half-course is normally a course in research methods suited to the students area of research); (b) Educational Technology: EDER 779.01 Advanced Doctoral Seminar in Educational Technology; (c) additional graduate courses or seminars are determined by the supervisor in consultation with the student; (d) a candidacy examination demonstrating the students competence to undertake a thesis; (e) a Doctoral thesis and an oral examination on the thesis.

Number of Full-Time Faculty – 8; **Number of Other Faculty** – 75

Degrees awarded in 2008–2009 Academic Year – Masters – 235; **PhD** – 11; **Other** – 15

Grant Monies awarded in 2008–2009 Academic Year – 20000000

Name of Institution – University of British Columbia

Name of Department or Program – Master of Educational Technology degree program

Address:
1304–2125 Main Mall
Vancouver, BC
V6T 1Z4
Canada

Phone Number – 1-888-492-1122 **Fax Number** – 1-604-822-2015

Email Contact – info@met.ubc.ca **URL** – http://met.ubc.ca

Contact Person – David Roy

Specializations – This innovative online program provides an excellent environment in which to learn the techniques of instructional design including the development and management of programs for international and intercultural populations. Attracting students from more than 30 countries, the program provides a unique opportunity to learn and collaborate with professionals and colleagues from around the world. The MET curriculum is designed for K-12 teachers, college and university faculty, course designers, adult and industry educators.

Features – MET fully online graduate degree. MET Graduate Certificate in Technology-Based Distributed Learning. MET Graduate Certificate in Technology-Based Learning for Schools.

Admission Requirements – Please see website.

Degree Requirements – Masters Program: 10 courses Graduate Certificates: 5 courses

Number of Full-Time Faculty – 9; **Number of Other Faculty** – 8

Degrees awarded in 2008–2009 Academic Year – Masters – 36; **PhD** – 0; **Other** – 0

Grant Monies awarded in 2008–2009 Academic Year – 0

Name of Institution – University of New Brunswick

Name of Department or Program – Faculty of Education

Address:
PO Box 4400
Fredericton, NB
E3B 5A3
Canada

Phone Number – 506-452-6125 **Fax Number** – 506-453-3569

Email Contact – erose@unb.ca **URL** – http://www.unbf.ca/education/

Contact Person – Dr. Ellen Rose

Specializations – Courses are offered in instructional design theories and processes, cultural studies in instructional design, instructional message design, needs assessment, and instructional design for online learning. In addition, students are expected to take other courses in the Faculty of Education or other applicable areas.

Features – Students can choose the course, project, or thesis stream. UNBs MEd in Instructional Design is very flexible, allowing students to customize their own learning experiences in order to meet their particular learning outcomes. While this is not an online program, several of the Instructional Design courses, and many other relevant courses in the Faculty of Education, are available online.

Admission Requirements – Applicants must have an undergraduate degree in Education or a relevant field, a grade point average of at least 3.0 (B, or its equivalent), and at least one year of teaching or related professional experience. Applicants whose first language is not English must submit evidence of their proficiency in the use of the English language. The minimum proficiency levels accepted by the Faculty of Education are scores of 650 on the TOEFL (280 computer-based) and 5.5 on the TWE.

Degree Requirements – Course route: 10 3-credit hour courses Project route: 8 3-credit hour courses and one project/report Thesis route: 5 3-credit hour courses and one thesis Required courses: ED 6221 Instructional Design Theories and ED 6902 Introduction to Research in Education

Number of Full-Time Faculty – 1; **Number of Other Faculty** – 2

Degrees awarded in 2008–2009 Academic Year – Masters – 10; **PhD** – 0; **Other** – 0

Grant Monies awarded in 2008–2009 Academic Year – 0

Name of Institution – Concordia University

Name of Department or Program – Education – MA in Educational Technology, Diploma in Instructional Technology and PhD (Education), Specialization, Educational Technology

Address:
1455 de Maisonneuve Blvd. West
Montreal, QC
H3G 1M8
Canada

Phone Number – (514) 848-2424 x2030 **Fax Number** – (514) 848-4520

Email Contact – anne@education.concordia.ca **URL** – education.concordia.ca

Contact Person – Ms. Anne Brown-MacDougall, Programs Coordinator

Specializations – Concordias Department of Education offers a 30-credit graduate Diploma in Instructional Technology, an MA in Educational Technology and our PhD in Education has a specialization in the area of Educational Technology as well. Main areas within the programs: Human Performance Technology – Distance Education – Interactive Multi-Media Applications – Cybernetics – Administration and Project Management Plus many other areas.

Features – Only graduate program in Quebec in this area.

Admission Requirements – For the MA Program: Applicants must have a GPA or 3.0 or higher from a variety of undergraduate disciplines. References, official transcripts, CV, and statement of purpose also required. For the Diploma program: Applicants must have a GPA of 2.7 or higher from a variety of undergraduate disciplines. References, official transcripts, CV, and statement of purpose also required. For students For the PhD (Education): Applicants must have a GPA of 3.0 in a masters degree, preferably in the field of educational technology, but related disciplines are also acceptable. References, official transcripts, CV, and statement of purpose

Degree Requirements – The PhD(Education) is 90-credit program, which includes required courses, tutorials, plus comprehensive examination, dissertation proposal and dissertation. The M.A. program is 60 credits which includes required courses, electives plus either an internship experience and a report or a small internship, thesis proposal and thesis. The Diploma consists of 30 credits of course work only.

Number of Full-Time Faculty – 9; **Number of Other Faculty** – 40

Degrees awarded in 2008–2009 Academic Year – Masters – 25; **PhD** – 5; **Other** – 5

Grant Monies awarded in 2008–2009 Academic Year – 100000

Name of Institution – University of Saskatchewan

Name of Department or Program – Educational Communications and Technology

Address:
28 Campus Drive, College of Education
Saskatoon, SK
S7N 0X1
Canada

Phone Number – 306-966-7558 **Fax Number** – 306-966-7658

Email Contact – richard.schwier@usask.ca **URL** – http://www.edct.ca

Contact Person – Richard A. Schwier

Specializations – We offer a general educational technology degree, but with a particular emphasis on instructional design.

Features – Most of our courses are delivered in flexible formats. Courses can be taken completely online or blended with classroom experiences. A few courses are only offered face to face, but an entire program can be taken online.

Admission Requirements – A professional Bachelors degree or the equivalent of a four-year Bachelor of Arts. Normally, we require a minimum of one year of practical experience in education or a related field. An average of 70% in your most recent 60 credit units of university coursework.

Degree Requirements – M.Ed (nonthesis) students need to undertake 24 credit units of graduate level coursework and the project seminar (ECMM 992.6) supervised by a faculty member in the programme. M.Ed (thesis) students need to complete 21 units of graduate level coursework and a thesis supervised by a faculty member in the programme and a committee.

Number of Full-Time Faculty – 4; **Number of Other Faculty** – 2

Degrees awarded in 2008–2009 Academic Year – **Masters** – 20; **PhD** – 0; **Other** – 0

Grant Monies awarded in 2008–2009 Academic Year – 200000

Name of Institution – The University of Hong Kong

Name of Department or Program – Faculty of Education

Address:
Pokfulam Road
Hong Kong, China

Phone Number – 852 2241 5856 **Fax Number** – 852 2517 0075

Email Contact – mite@cite.hku.hk **URL** – http://web.edu.hku.hk/programme/mite/

Contact Person – Dr Daniel Churchill

Specializations – The Master of Science in Information Technology in Education [MSc(ITE)] programme offers the following four specialist strands: – E-leadership – E-learning – Learning technology design

Features – The programme aims to provide – an investigation into Web2.0, mobile learning, and other emerging learning and teaching technology applications – an opportunity to apply technology in learning and teaching – an opportunity to work in technology-rich learning environment – an exploration of the cultural, administrative theoretical and practical implications of technology in education – an introduction to research in technology for education – an opportunity for those wishing to develop leadership capabilities in the use of technology in education

Admission Requirements – Applicants should normally hold a recognized Bachelor's Degree or qualifications of equivalent standard. Applicants may be required to sit for a qualifying examination.

Degree Requirements – To complete the following modules in one year full-time study or no more than four years of part-time studies: – 3 core modules – 2 modules from a specialist strand plus either of the following: o Independent project and 2 elective modules; or o Dissertation

Number of Full-Time Faculty – 12; **Number of Other Faculty** – 90

Degrees awarded in 2008–2009 Academic Year – **Masters** – 0; **PhD** – 0; **Other** – 0

Grant Monies awarded in 2008–2009 Academic Year – 0

Name of Institution – Université de Poitiers

Name of Department or Program – Ingénierie des médias pour léducation

Address:
95, avenue du Recteur Pineau
Poitiers, PC
86000
France

Phone Number – +33 5 49 36 62 06 **Fax Number** – +33 5 49 45 32 90

Email Contact – cerisier@univ-poitiers.fr **URL** – ll.univ-poitiers.fr/dime

Contact Person – Jean-François CERISIER

Specializations – – EUROMIME : European Master in Media Engineering for Education (Erasmus Mundus master) This Master's program trains high-quality specialists in the relatively new discipline of educational technology. Throughout the course, students will be required to develop projects relating to the conception, utilisation, and evaluation of various educational media. This work is applicable to the current development of distance teaching/learning. The course unifies several of the leading universities in this sector: the University of Poitiers (France), the National University for Distance Education at Madrid (Spain), and the Lisbon University of Technology (Portugal). For added regional contact, three universities from third countries also participate in this consortium: The National University of Brazil, the Catholic University of Peru, and the University of the Lakes, Chile. The consortium also utilises many other international links and networks. – MIME: national Master in Media Engineering for Education

Admission Requirements – application and interview

Degree Requirements – Bachelors degree

Number of Full-Time Faculty – 25; **Number of Other Faculty** – 25

Degrees awarded in 2008–2009 Academic Year – Masters – 23; **PhD** – 0; **Other** – 0

Grant Monies awarded in 2008–2009 Academic Year – 1000000

Name of Institution – Ewha Womans University

Name of Department or Program – Educational Technology Department

Address:
11-1 Daehyun-dong, Seodaemun-ku
Seoul, KO
120-750
Korea

Phone Number – 82-2-3277-2671 **Fax Number** – 82-2-3277-2728

Email Contact – et2670@hanmail.net **URL** – home.ewha.ac.kr/~et

Contact Person – Department Chair, Myunghee Kang

Specializations – Theory & Practice of Instructional Technology e-Leaning Design & Development, Quality Assurance HRD/HPT Program development

Features – Undergraduate Masters Program Ph.D Program Special Masters Program for In-Service Teachers

Admission Requirements – Portfolio Interview English Competency

Degree Requirements – 24 credit hours of coursework for Masters 60 credit hours of coursework for Ph.D and Qualifying Exam Dissertation

Number of Full-Time Faculty – 8; **Number of Other Faculty** – 2

Degrees awarded in 2008–2009 Academic Year – Masters – 6; **PhD** – 4; **Other** – 0

Grant Monies awarded in 2008–2009 Academic Year – 2000000

Name of Institution – Andong National University

Name of Department or Program – Department of Educational Technology, College of Education

Address:
388 Songchun-dong
Andong, Kyungbuk
760-749
Korea

Phone Number – +82-54-820-5580, 5585 **Fax Number** – +82-54-820-7653

Email Contact – ycyang@andong.ac.kr **URL** – http://edutech.andong.ac.kr/~try/2009-10/main1.html

Contact Person – Dr. Yong-Chil Yang

Specializations – Instruction Systems Design and e-HRD major for Master Degree Educational Technology major for Ph.D

Features – * Only Department supported by Ministry of Education in Korea * BA, MA, and Ph.D programs are offered * Established in 1996 * Inexpensive tuition and living expenses * Small class size

Admission Requirements – Fluent commanding English or Korean language

Degree Requirements – BA degree for Master MA degree in Education for Ph.D

Number of Full-Time Faculty – 5; **Number of Other Faculty** – 9

Degrees awarded in 2008–2009 Academic Year – Masters – 6; **PhD** – 1; **Other** – 5

Grant Monies awarded in 2008–2009 Academic Year – 12000

Name of Institution – Universiti Sains Malaysia

Name of Department or Program – Centre for Instructional Technology and Multimedia

Address:
Centre for Instructional Tech and Multimedia, Universiti Sains Malaysia
Minden, Pg
11800
Malaysia

Phone Number – 604-6533222 **Fax Number** – 604-6576749

Email Contact – Fauzy@usm.my **URL** – http://www.ptpm.usm.my

Contact Person – Assoc. Prof. Wan Mohd. Fauzy Wan Ismail Director,

Specializations – Instructional Design Web/Internet Instruction and Learning Educational Training/Resource Management Instructional Training Technology/ Evaluation Instructional System Development Design and Development of Multimedia/Video/Training materials Instructional and Training Technology Constructivism in Instructional Technology E-Learning Systems, Learning Management Systems

Features – Masters in Instructional Technology – entering its third academic year 2004–2005 – Full-time – 1–2 years, Part-time – 2–4 years. Teaching Programs – Post Graduate programs and research Consultancy – services on the application of educational/Instructional Design technology in teaching and learning Training and Diffusion, Continuing Education in support of Life Long Learning Academic Support Services – services to support research, teaching, and learning activities and centers within the university

Admission Requirements – Bachelors and Masters degree from accredited institution or relevant work experience

Degree Requirements – Part-time Full-time

Number of Full-Time Faculty – ; **Number of Other Faculty** –

Degrees awarded in 2008–2009 Academic Year – Masters – ; **PhD** – ; **Other** –

Grant Monies awarded in 2008–2009 Academic Year –

Name of Institution – Taganrog State Pedagogical Institute

Name of Department or Program – Media Education (Social Pedagogic Faculty)

Address:
Iniciativnaya, 48
Taganrog, –
347936
Russia

Phone Number – (8634)601753 **Fax Number** – (8634)605397

Email Contact – tgpi@mail.ru **URL** – http://www.tgpi.ru

Contact Person – Prof. Dr. Alexander Fedorov

Specializations – Media Education, Media Literacy, Media Competence

Admission Requirements – Various per year, please see http://www.tgpi.ru

Degree Requirements – admission after high school

Number of Full-Time Faculty – 10; **Number of Other Faculty** – 20

Degrees awarded in 2008–2009 Academic Year – Masters – 0; **PhD** – 1; **Other** – 25

Grant Monies awarded in 2008–2009 Academic Year – 150000

Name of Institution – Keimyung University

Name of Department or Program – Department of Education

Address:
2800 Dalgubeldaro
Dalseogu, Daegu
704-701
South Korea

Phone Number – 82-53-580-5962

Email Contact – weom@kmu.ac.kr

Contact Person – Wooyong Eom

Number of Full-Time Faculty – 9; **Number of Other Faculty** – 0

Degrees awarded in 2008–2009 Academic Year – Masters – 2; **PhD** – 1; **Other** – 0

Grant Monies awarded in 2008–2009 Academic Year – 0

Name of Institution – University of Balearic Islands

Name of Department or Program – Sciences of Education

Address:
Ctra. Valldemossa km 7,5
Palma de Mallorca, IB
07010
Spain

Phone Number – 34 071173000 **Fax Number** – 34 971173190

Email Contact – jesus.salinas@uib.es **URL** – http://www.uib.es

Contact Person – Dr. Jesus Salinas

Specializations – – Doctorado Interuniversitario de Tecnología Educativa [Interuniversity Doctorate of Educational Technology. University of Sevilla, University of Murcia, University of Balearic Islands and Rovira i Virgili Universitity – Master en Tecnología Educativa. E-learning y gestión del conocimiento . [Master in Educational Technology. E-learning and knowlegde management]. University of Balearic Islands and Universitat Rovira i Virgili. – Especialista Universitario en Tecnología Educativa. Diseño y elaboración de medios didácticos multimedia. [Specialist in Educational Technology. Design and development of didactic multimedia environments]. – "Curso de Dirección y gestión pedagógica de entornos virtuales." [Course of direction and pedagogical management of virtual environments]. University of Balearic Islands, Rovira I Virgili University, University of Sevilla, University Central of Venezuela, University of Panamá, Higher Institute Polytechnic Jose Antonio Echevarria.

Number of Full-Time Faculty – 6; **Number of Other Faculty** – 9

Degrees awarded in 2008–2009 Academic Year – **Masters** – 12; **PhD** – 6; **Other** – 28

Grant Monies awarded in 2008–2009 Academic Year – 0

Name of Institution – Università della Svizzera italiana

Name of Department or Program – New Media in Education Laboratory & red-ink doctoral school

Address:
via Buffi 13
Lugano, TI
6900
Switzerland

Phone Number – +41586664674 **Fax Number** – 41586664647

Email Contact – luca.botturi@lu.unisi.ch **URL** – www.newmine.org

Contact Person – Lorenzo Cantoni, Prof. & Luca Botturi, Ph.D.

Specializations – –

Features – red-ink is a doctoral school whose name stands for "Rethinking Education in the Knowledge Society." It strives to understand the complex issues related to the introduction, management, and impact of educational technologies and eLearning in the perspective of the new context of the knowledge society. To this purpose, RED-INK federates three Swiss universities in order to establish an outstanding multidisciplinary research team at National level, with expected international visibility and impact. The RED-INK doctoral school is funded by the pro*doc program of the Swiss National Research Fund, started in 2008 and will award its first doctoral degrees in 2010.

Admission Requirements – Completed masters degree in educational technology or related field

Number of Full-Time Faculty – 3; **Number of Other Faculty** – 0

Degrees awarded in 2008–2009 Academic Year – **Masters** – 0; **PhD** – 0; **Other** – 0

Grant Monies awarded in 2008–2009 Academic Year – 0

Name of Institution – University of Geneva

Name of Department or Program – Master of Science in Learning and Teaching Technologies

Address:
Pont darve 40
Geneva
1211
SWITZERLAND

Phone Number – 41 22 379 93 75 **Fax Number** – 41 22 379 93 79

Email Contact – Mireille.Betrancourt@unige.ch **URL** – http://tecfa.unige.ch/maltt

Contact Person – Prof. Dr. Mireille Bétrancourt

Specializations – User-centered design and ergonomy Design of computer-supported learning technology Mediated Communication and e-learning Information and communication technologies Research methods in educational technologies

Features – Blended education (face-to-face sessions alternately with tutored distance periods) 120 ECTS, two year program French language

Admission Requirements – Applicants should qualify to be admitted in master program at the University of Geneva. For more information, see http://tecfaetu.unige.ch/maltt/staf.php3?id_article=27

Degree Requirements – Bachelor degree training or experience in training, education, or psychology.

Number of Full-Time Faculty – 4; **Number of Other Faculty** – 1

Degrees awarded in 2008–2009 Academic Year – Masters – 10; **PhD** – 3; **Other** – 5

Grant Monies awarded in 2008–2009 Academic Year – 400000

Name of Institution – Utrecht University

Name of Department or Program – Educational Sciences Learning in Interaction

Address:
Heidelberglaan 1
Utrecht
3581RW
The Netherlands

Phone Number – +31302533910 **Fax Number** – +31302534300

Email Contact – t.wubbels@uu.nl **URL** – http://www.uu.nl/NL/Informatie/master/edsci/Pages/study.aspx

Contact Person – Theo Wubbels PhD

Specializations – The two-year (120 EC) programme concentrates on the theory, use and effects of innovative teaching and learning arrangements aimed at meaningful, enjoyable learning through the application of different theories, paradigms, and media. Research projects use both experimental and design-based approaches and combine qualitative and quantitative analyses of interaction processes and learning products in different teaching and/or learning environments.

Features – The programme combines high-level coursework with hands-on research skill and competence development. Students take courses on various theories of learning, instruction, and teaching, and are trained in advanced research techniques and statistical methods to study the design and effectiveness of innovative teaching and learning arrangements. Research seminars help students develop their academic skills. Participation in a senior faculty member's research project introduces each student to "hands-on" research. Throughout the programme, various electronic learning environments are used to support students in their collaborative study assignments, and to allow them to experiment with these innovative learning and instruction tools. The programme offers a systematic theoretical and empirical analysis of educational phenomena and problems. It emphasises three goals. Helping students develop: 1. A strong foundation in research and in theories of learning, instruction, and teaching 2. Competence in conducting high-quality educational research 3. Capacities and skills to apply basic knowledge and specific research methods from various domains to the study of learning in interaction in education. The programme concludes with writing a Master's thesis in the form of a draft research article for international publication.

Admission Requirements – Applicants should hold a BA or BSc in one of the relevant social or behavioural sciences (such as education, psychology, cognitive science, informatics, artificial intelligence) or in a domain relevant to teaching in schools (e.g., math, science, linguistics, history). It is required of applicants to have successfully completed several undergraduate courses on statistics in order to have a basic knowledge of multivariate analysis at the beginning of their first semester. There is a summer school for students who do not meet this requirement. Students meeting the above criteria who have a GPA of at least 2.85 (Dutch equivalent: 7.0) are encouraged to apply for admission. Students will be selected on the basis of their Grade Point Average (GPA), an essay on their motivation and their recommendations; in some cases, an intake interview will also be conducted. All courses are taught in English, therefore all students are required to provide proof of their English language proficiency. Examples of accepted minimum English language test scores: TOEFL paper: 580 TOEFL computer: 237 TOEFL internet: 93

Degree Requirements – Completion of all courses and thesis

Number of Full-Time Faculty – 12; **Number of Other Faculty** – 7

Degrees awarded in 2008–2009 Academic Year – Masters – 110; **PhD** – 5; **Other** – 0

Grant Monies awarded in 2008–2009 Academic Year – 2000000

Name of Institution – Middle East Technical University

Name of Department or Program – Computer Education & Instructional Technology

Address:
Inonu Bulvari
Ankara, Cankaya
06531
Turkey

Phone Number – +90-3122104193 **Fax Number** – +90-3122107986

Email Contact – myozden@metu.edu.tr **URL** – http://www.ceit.metu.edu.tr

Contact Person – M. Yasar OZDEN

Specializations – Computer education, instructional technology

Number of Full-Time Faculty – 20; **Number of Other Faculty** – 40

Degrees awarded in 2008–2009 Academic Year – Masters – 5; **PhD** – 10; **Other** – 0

Grant Monies awarded in 2008–2009 Academic Year – 0

Name of Institution – Hacettepe University

Name of Department or Program – Computer Education and Instructional Technology

Address:
Faculty of Education, Hacettepe University, Beytepe
Ankara, Turkey
06800
Turkey

Phone Number – +903122977176 **Fax Number** – +903122977176

Email Contact – altunar@hacettepe.edu.tr **URL** – http://www.ebit.hacettepe.edu.tr/

Contact Person – Arif Altun

Specializations – The CEIT department has been established in 1998. Innovations and improvements in technology have changed so many things in people's life. There have been huge improvements in terms of diffusion of information. Computers continue to make an ever increasing impact on all aspects of education from primary school to university and in the growing areas of open and distance learning. In addition, the knowledge and skills related to computers have become essential for everybody in the information age. However, at all levels in society there is a huge need for qualified personnel equipped with the skills that help them to be successful in their personal and professional life. The department aims to train students (prospective teachers) who would teach computer courses in K-12 institutions. It also provides individuals with professional skills in the development, organization, and application of resources for the solution of instructional problems within schools.

Features – The department has MS and Ph.D. programs. The research areas are: Learning objects and ontologies, diffusion of innovation, computerized testing, e-learning environments: design, development and assessment.

Admission Requirements – BS in education and computer related fields

Degree Requirements – BS

Number of Full-Time Faculty – 9; **Number of Other Faculty** – 10

Degrees awarded in 2008–2009 Academic Year – Masters – 15; **PhD** – 1; **Other** – 0

Grant Monies awarded in 2008–2009 Academic Year – 120

Name of Institution – Anadolu University

Name of Department or Program – Computer Education and Instructional Technology

Address:
Faculty of Education
Eskisehir
26470
Turkey

Phone Number – 00902223350580/3519 **Fax Number** – 00902223350579

Email Contact – fodabasi@anadolu.edu.tr **URL** – http://www.anadolu.edu.tr/ akademik/fak_egt/bilgveogrttekegt/eindex.htm

Contact Person – Ferhan Odabasi

Specializations – The basic aim of the department is to equip students, with up-to-date knowledge about computer and other information technologies, required for K12 computer teachers. Graduated students of the department can be employed in public or private schools of The Ministry of National Education, as teachers, instructional technologists, or academicians in the universities. The department offers Bachelor, Master, and Doctorate programs. Both department staff and students collaborate with international schools in terms of teaching and research through exchange programs. Some of the themes, having been studied by academic staff of the department, are: computer assisted instruction, computer assisted language instruction, educational technology, computer use in education and school systems, effects of technology on individuals, computer anxiety, industrial design, using Internet in education, educational design, educational software, statistic applications in computer, professional development.

Features – Computer Education and Instructional Technologies Department has 2 computer labs. Technical properties of the computers in both of the labs are up to date. In addition, students can use the main library which is around 100 meters to department building. Students may reach many books and journals about computers and instructional technologies, and have access to various databases and electronic journals. There is a nonsmoking cafeteria for students in the faculty building where they can find snacks, sandwiches, hot and cold drinks. There is also a small room for the smokers. There is a main student cafeteria for students on the campus. There are also fast food restaurants on the campus.

Admission Requirements – High School Diploma plus required scores from the Student Selection Examination administered by Student Selection and Placement Centre and successful completion of qualification examinations. For foreign students, High School Diploma plus required scores from the Foreign Student Examination and successful completion of qualification examinations. Associate Degree plus placement by Student Selection and Placement Centre according to the score obtained in the Student Selection Examination and the students preferences. In addition, may apply to masters or doctorate programmes in any field or proficiency in fine arts programmes. May apply to bachelors degree completion programmes in related fields of study in Distance Education System.

Degree Requirements – For bachelor degree, students are selected by Student Selection and Placement Center according to the students? scores in the Student Selection Exam. About 50 students are admitted to the department each year. The duration of the program is 4 years. Students must pass all courses and obtain a minimum GPA (Grade Point Average) of 2.00 before they can graduate. The official language of instruction is Turkish. Students who want to learn English can attend a one-year

English preparatory school before taking the department courses. The students are required to take courses and prepare and defend a thesis based on their research. It takes approximately two years to complete the Master degree. The doctorate degree requires course work and research. The students will conduct original research and prepare a dissertation, then make an oral defense of their completed research. Students require about four years beyond the Masters degree to complete a doctorate program.

Number of Full-Time Faculty – 12; **Number of Other Faculty** – 9

Degrees awarded in 2008–2009 Academic Year – Masters – 1; PhD – 1; Other – 0

Grant Monies awarded in 2008–2009 Academic Year – 0

Name of Institution – University of Manchester

Name of Department or Program – MA: Digital Technologies, Communication and Education

Address:
LTA, School of Education, Ellen Wilkinson Building, Oxford Road
Manchester, UK
M13 9PL
UK

Phone Number – +44 161 275 7843 **Fax Number** – +44 161 275 3484

Email Contact – andrew.whitworth@manchester.ac.uk **URL** – http://www. MAdigitaltechnologies.com

Contact Person – Dr. Andrew Whitworth

Specializations – Educators from any sector are catered for by the program: that is, primary, secondary (K-12), tertiary/higher education, adult education, corporate training, home educators, private tutors, and so on.

Features – The goals of this program are to promote the use of digital technologies, the broadcast media, and/or interpersonal, group or organizational communications techniques to enhance practice and the professional and academic development of educators in technology-rich environments. There is, therefore, a particular focus on professional development techniques, enquiry-based and problem-based learning, and transformations of practice as well as work with practical EMT techniques (such as web design, Flash, and video production). Students will study the history of educational media and technology, and its impact on the organization and management of education as well as on pedagogy. The course is available to study in both face-to-face and distance modes.

Admission Requirements – A first degree to at least a 2:2 (UK degree classification) or equivalent. IELTS score of at least 6.5 and preferably 7.0, or 600 in TOEFL. Teaching experience is desirable, though not mandatory.

Number of Full-Time Faculty – 2; **Number of Other Faculty** – 3

Degrees awarded in 2008–2009 Academic Year – Masters – 20; **PhD** – 0; **Other** – 0

Grant Monies awarded in 2008–2009 Academic Year – 0

Name of Institution – The Ohio State University

Name of Department or Program – Cultural Foundations, Technology, & Qualitative Inquiry

Address:
29 W. Woodruff Dr
Columbus, OH
43210
United States

Phone Number – (614)688-4007

Email Contact – voithofer.2@osu.edu **URL** – http://ehe.osu.edu/epl/academics/cftqi/technology.cfm

Contact Person – Rick Voithofer

Specializations – The Technology area in CFTQI offers both MA and PhD degrees. This interdisciplinary educational technology program focuses on intersections of learning, technology, and culture in formal and informal education and in society at large. Some of the settings addressed in the program include K-12 environments, distance education, e-learning, online education, higher education, urban education, private and nonprofit organizations, museums, and community-based organizations and programs. Students in the program are exposed to a variety of technologies and media including educational multimedia, computer-based instruction, pod/video casts, blogs and wikis, educational games, web-based instruction, video, and electronic portfolios. Recent areas of focus studied by faculty and students include: Educational technology, digital divides, and diverse populations Implications of Web 2.0 technologies for education Education and globalization Online educational research Education Policy and Technology Visual Culture and Visual Media Multiliteracies, learning, and technology Games and Simulations Technology, virtuality, and student identities Students in this area integrate theoretical and practical studies of technologies and media through pedagogical, social, cultural, economic, historical and political inquiry and critique, in addition to the production of educational media and cultural artifacts.

Admission Requirements – Please see: http://ehe.osu.edu/epl/academics/cftqi/downloads/cftqi-checklist.pdf

Degree Requirements – Please see: http://ehe.osu.edu/epl/academics/cftqi/degree-req.cfm

Number of Full-Time Faculty – 4; **Number of Other Faculty** – 2

Degrees awarded in 2008–2009 Academic Year – Masters – 10; **PhD** – 5; **Other** – 5

Grant Monies awarded in 2008–2009 Academic Year – 1200000

Name of Institution – WIDENER UNIVERSITY

Name of Department or Program – Instructional Technology

Address:
One UNIVERSITY PLACE
Media, pa
19013
United States

Phone Number – 610-499-4256

Email Contact – kabowes@Widener.Edu **URL** – http;//www.educator.widener.edu

Contact Person – Dr. Kathleen A. Bowes

Specializations – Instructional Technology, Educational Leadership

Features – Wideners Instructional Technology program has three branches: 1. Masters of Education in Instructional Technology 2. Instructional Technology Specialist Certification (PA nonteaching certificate) 3. Doctor of School Administration with an Instructional Technology Tract Most courses are hybrids.

Admission Requirements – 3.0 undergraduate, MATs three letters of recommendation, writing sample

Degree Requirements – undergraduate degree

Number of Full-Time Faculty – 1; **Number of Other Faculty** – 4

Degrees awarded in 2008–2009 Academic Year – **Masters** – 0; **PhD** – 0; **Other** – 2

Grant Monies awarded in 2008–2009 Academic Year – 150000

Name of Institution – University of Alabama

Name of Department or Program – School of Library and Information Studies

Address:
Box 870252
Tuscaloosa, AL
35487-0252
US

Phone Number – (205)348-4610 **Fax Number** – (205)348-3746

Email Contact – vwright@bamaed.ua.edu **URL** – http://www.slis.ua.edu

Contact Person – Joan Atkinson, Director; Gordy Coleman, Coordinator of School Media Program

Specializations – M.L.I.S. degrees in a varied program including school, public, academic, and special libraries. Ph.D. in the larger College of Communication and Information Sciences; flexibility in creating individual programs of study. Also a Master of Fine Arts Program in Book Arts (including history of the book).

Features – M.L.I.S. is one of 56 accredited programs in the United States and Canada

Admission Requirements – M.L.I.S.: 3.0 GPA; 50 MAT or 1000 GRE and an acceptable score on Analytical Writing. Doctoral: 3.0 GPA; 60 MAT or 1200 GRE and acceptable score on Analytical Writing.

Degree Requirements – Master's: 36 semester hours. Doctoral: 48–60 semester hours plus 24 hours dissertation research.

Number of Full-Time Faculty – 0; **Number of Other Faculty** – 0

Degrees awarded in 2008–2009 Academic Year – Masters – 0; **PhD** – 0; **Other** – 0

Grant Monies awarded in 2008–2009 Academic Year – 0

Name of Institution – University of Central Arkansas

Name of Department or Program – Leadership Studies

Address:
201 Donaghey
Conway, AR
72035
US

Phone Number – (501)450-5430 **Fax Number** – (501)852-2826

Email Contact – steph@uca.edu **URL** – http://www.coe.uca.edu/

Contact Person – Stephanie Huffman, Program Director of the Library Media and Information Technologies Program

Specializations – M.S. in Library Media and Information Technologies is School Library Media program.

Features – Specialization in school library media.

Admission Requirements – transcripts, GRE scores, and a copy of the candidates teaching certificate.

Degree Requirements – 36 semester hours, practicum (for School Library Media), and a professional portfolio.

Number of Full-Time Faculty – 4; **Number of Other Faculty** – 2

Degrees awarded in 2008–2009 Academic Year – Masters – 40; **PhD** – 0; **Other** – 20

Grant Monies awarded in 2008–2009 Academic Year – 0

Name of Institution – Arizona State University; Educational Technology program

Name of Department or Program – Division of Psychology in Education

Address:
Box 870611
Tempe, AZ
85287-0611
US

Phone Number – (480)965-3384 **Fax Number** – (480)965-0300

Email Contact – dpe@asu.edu **URL** – http://coe.asu.edu/psyched

Contact Person – Dr. Willi Savenye, Associate Professor; Nancy Archer, Admissions Secretary

Specializations – The Educational Technology program at Arizona State University offers an M.Ed. degree and a Ph.D. degree which focus on the design, development, and evaluation of instructional systems and educational technology applications to support learning.

Features – The program offers courses in a variety of areas such as instructional design technology, media development, technology integration, performance improvement, evaluation, and distance education. The doctoral program emphasizes research using educational technology in applied settings.

Admission Requirements – Requirements for admission to the M.Ed. program include a 4-year undergraduate GPA of 3.0 or above and a score of either 500 or above on verbal section of the GRE or a scaled score of 400 on the MAT. A score of 550 or above on the paper-based TOEFL (or 213 on the computer-based test or 80 internet-based test) is also required for students who do not speak English as their first language. Requirements for admission to the Ph.D. program include a 4-year undergraduate GPA of 3.20 or above and a combined score of 1200 or above on the verbal and quantitative sections of the GRE. A score of 600 or above on the paper-based TOEFL (or 250 on the computer-based testor 100 internet-based test) is also required for students who do not speak English as their first language.

Degree Requirements – The M.Ed. degree requires completion of a minimum of 30 credit hours including 18 credit hours of required course work and a minimum of 12 credit hours of electives. M.Ed. students also must complete an internship and a comprehensive examination. The Ph.D. degree requires a minimum of 84 semester hours beyond the bachelors degree. At least 54 of these hours must be taken at ASU after admission to the program. Ph.D. students must fulfill a residence requirement and are required to be continuously enrolled in the program. Students also take a comprehensive examination and must satisfy a publication requirement prior to beginning work on their dissertation.

Number of Full-Time Faculty – 5; **Number of Other Faculty** – 5

Degrees awarded in 2008–2009 Academic Year – Masters – 10; **PhD** – 5; **Other** – 0

Grant Monies awarded in 2008–2009 Academic Year – 2000000

Name of Institution – California State University at East Bay

Name of Department or Program – Educational Technology Leadership

Address:
25800 Carlos Bee Blvd.
Hayward, CA
94542
US

Phone Number – 510-885-2509 **Fax Number** – 510-8854632

Email Contact – bijan.gillani@csueastbay.edu **URL** – http://edtech.csueastbay.edu

Contact Person – Dr. Bijan Gillani

Specializations – Advances in the field of technology and the explosive growth of the Internet in recent years have revolutionized the way instruction is delivered to students. In parallel with these technological advances, the field of Learning Sciences has made phenomenal contributions to how people learn. For the most part, the advances in these two fields (technology and learning sciences) have gone their separate ways. A synergy of these two fields would enable educators and instructional designers to design and develop more effective educational materials to be transmitted over the Internet. To provide a solution for this synergy we the Institute of Learning Sciences and Technology focuses on providing a systematic and more intelligent approach to the design of e-learning environments by applying the research findings in the field of Learning Sciences to the design and development of technological environments.

Features – * How do people learn? What are learning theories? What are the instructional principles that we can derive from learning theories? How can we apply these instructional principles to the design of meaningful learning with existing and emerging technology? How do we make these principles accessible to faculty who wish to use technology more effectively? How do we develop pedagogically sound learning environments that prepare students to pursue meaningful lifework that has local and global contribution?

Admission Requirements – A completed University Graduate Application (Online Only) Two official copies of each transcript (Mail to the Enrollment Office) Statement of residency (Mail to the Department) A Department Application Form (Mail to the Department) Two letter of recommendations (Mail to the Department). GPA 3.0.

Degree Requirements – * Completion of required 24 Units of Core Courses. * Completion of 16 units of Elective Courses. * Completion of Master Degree Project or Thesis Project. * Completion of graduate check list (Online and Forms)

Number of Full-Time Faculty – 3; **Number of Other Faculty** – 3

Degrees awarded in 2008–2009 Academic Year – **Masters** – 20; **PhD** – 0; **Other** – 20

Grant Monies awarded in 2008–2009 Academic Year – 90

Name of Institution – California State University-San Bernardino

Name of Department or Program – Dept. of Science, Mathematics, and Technology Education

Address:
5500 University Parkway
San Bernardino, CA
92407
US

Phone Number – (909)537-5692 **Fax Number** – (909)537-7040

Email Contact – aleh@csusb.edu **URL** – http://www.csusb.edu/coe/programs/inst_tech/index.htm

Contact Person – Dr. Amy Leh

Specializations – Technology integration, online instruction, instructional design, STEM education

Features – Preparing educators in K-12, corporate, and higher education

Admission Requirements – Bachelors degree, 3.0 GPA, completion of university writing requirement

Degree Requirements – 48 units including a Master's project (33 units completed in residence); 3.0 GPA; grades of "C" or better in all courses.

Number of Full-Time Faculty – 4; **Number of Other Faculty** – 2

Degrees awarded in 2008–2009 Academic Year – Masters – 9; **PhD** – 0; **Other** – 0

Grant Monies awarded in 2008–2009 Academic Year – 100000

Name of Institution – San Diego State University

Name of Department or Program – Educational Technology

Address:
5500 Campanile Dr.
San Diego, CA
92182-1182
US

Phone Number – (619)594-6718 **Fax Number** – (619)594-6376

Email Contact – bober@mail.sdsu.edu **URL** – http://edtec.sdsu.edu/

Contact Person – Dr. Marcie Bober, Assoc. Prof., Chair.

Specializations – Certificate in Instructional Technology. Advanced Certificate in Distance Learning, and Software Design. Masters degree in Education with an emphasis in Educational Technology. Doctorate in Education with an emphasis in Educational Technology (a joint program with the University of San Diego).

Features – Focus in design of intervention to improve human performance via strategies that combine theory and practice in relevant, real-world experiences. Offer both campus and online programs.

Admission Requirements – Please refer to SDSU Graduate bulletin at http://libweb.sdsu.edu/bulletin/. Requirements include a minimum score of 950 on the GRE (verbal + quantitative), and 4.5 on the analytical. See our website at http://edtec.sdsu.edu for more information.

Degree Requirements – 36 semester hours for the masters (including 6 prerequisite hours). 15 to 18 semester hours for the certificates.

Number of Full-Time Faculty – ; **Number of Other Faculty** –

Degrees awarded in 2008–2009 Academic Year – Masters – 40; **PhD** – ; **Other** –

Grant Monies awarded in 2008–2009 Academic Year –

Name of Institution – San Jose State University

Name of Department or Program – Instructional Technology

Address:
One Washington Square
San Jose, CA
95192-0076
US

Phone Number – (408) 924-3620 **Fax Number** – (408) 924-3713

Email Contact – rbarba@email.sjsu.edu **URL** – http://sweeneyhall.sjsu.edu/depts/it

Contact Person – Dr. Robertta Barba, Program Chair

Specializations – Master's degree.

Features – MA in Education with an emphasis on Instructional Technology.

Admission Requirements – Baccalaureate degree from approved university, appropriate work experience, minimum GPA of 2.5, and minimum score of 550 on TOEFL (Test of English as a Foreign Language). 36 semester hours (which includes 6 prerequisite hours).

Degree Requirements – 30 units of approved graduate studies

Number of Full-Time Faculty – ; **Number of Other Faculty** –

Degrees awarded in 2008–2009 Academic Year – Masters – 42; **PhD** – ; **Other** –

Grant Monies awarded in 2008–2009 Academic Year –

Name of Institution – University of Southern California, Rossier School of Education

Name of Department or Program – Educational Psychology & Instructional Technology

Address:
3470 Trousdale Parkway
Los Angeles, CA
90089-4036
US

Phone Number – (213)740-3465 **Fax Number** – (213)740-2367

Email Contact – rsoemast@usc.edu **URL** – http://www.usc.edu/dept/education/academic/masters/index.htm

Contact Person – For Admissions Info (soeinfo@usc.edu), For general program info (rsoemast@usc.edu), For specific program info (rueda@usc.edu)

Specializations – The Educational Psychology/Instructional Technology program focuses on learning and motivation, emphasizing the study of new information and performance technologies used to improve instruction among diverse student populations. To understand human learning, educational psychologists study areas such as motivation; developmental and individual differences; social, cultural, and group processes; instructional technology; and the evaluation of instruction. Students will be prepared to apply a wide range of computer and telecommunications technologies in achieving educational goals within school, community, corporate and public settings.

Features – Distinctive Features: – Focus on learning and motivation with a strong emphasis on technology and a major concern with urban education settings. – Major objective is to learn how to diagnose and solve learning and motivation problems, especially those characteristic of urban learning settings. – Faculty are well known in the field and are active researchers. Special emphasis upon instructional design, human performance at work, systems analysis, and computer-based training.

Admission Requirements – Bachelor's degree, 1000 GRE.

Degree Requirements – Program of Study: 28 Units 7 core courses and 2 elective courses. Core Courses: EDPT 576 Technology in Contemporary Education and Training EDPT 550 Statistical Inference EDPT 502 Learning and Individual Differences EDPT 510 Human Learning EDPT 540 Introduction to Educational Measurement and Evaluation EDPT 571 Instructional Design CTSE 593A & B Master's Seminar Electives (2 classes): EDPT 511 Human Motivation in Education EDPT 520 Human Lifespan Development EDPT 570 Language and Cultural Diversity in Learning CTSE 573 Management of Instructional Resources EDPA 671 The Computer and Data Processing Education

Number of Full-Time Faculty – ; **Number of Other Faculty** –

Degrees awarded in 2008–2009 Academic Year – **Masters** – 15; **PhD** – ; **Other** –

Grant Monies awarded in 2008–2009 Academic Year –

Name of Institution – Azusa Pacific University

Name of Department or Program – EDUCABS – Advanced Studies

Address:
901 E. Alosta
Azusa, California
91702
US

Phone Number – (626)815-5355 **Fax Number** – (626)815-5416

Email Contact – kbacer@apu.edu **URL** – http://www.apu.edu

Contact Person – Kathleen Bacer- Online Master of Arts in Educational Technology

Specializations – Educational Technology, online learning, Infusing technology in teaching/learning environments, digital learning for the 21st century learner

Features – 100% Online Master of Arts in Educational Technology program designed for the K-12 educator

Admission Requirements – undergraduate degree from accredited institution with at least 12 units in education, 3.0 GPA

Degree Requirements – 36 unit program

Number of Full-Time Faculty – 2; **Number of Other Faculty** – 8

Degrees awarded in 2008–2009 Academic Year – **Masters** – 90; **PhD** – 0; **Other** – 0

Grant Monies awarded in 2008–2009 Academic Year – 10000

Name of Institution – San Francisco State University

Name of Department or Program – College of Education, Department of Instructional Technology

Address:
1600 Holloway Ave.
San Francisco, California
94132
US

Phone Number – (415)338-1509 **Fax Number** – (415)338-0510

Email Contact – kforeman@sfsu.edu **URL** – www.itec.sfsu.edu

Contact Person – Dr. Kim Foreman, Chair; Anna Kozubek, Office Coord.

Specializations – Masters degree with emphasis on Instructional Multimedia Design, Training and Designing Development, and Instructional Computing. The school also offers an 18-unit Graduate Certificate in Training Systems Development, which can be incorporated into the Master's degree.

Features – This program emphasizes the instructional systems approach to train teachers, trainers, and e-learning professionals by providing practical design experience in the field. Most of our courses are delivered both face to face and online.

Admission Requirements – Bachelors degree, appropriate work experience, 2.5 GPA, purpose statement, 2 letters of recommendation, interview with the department chair.

Degree Requirements – 30 semester hours, field study project, or thesis. Three to nine units of prerequisites, assessed at entrance to the program

Number of Full-Time Faculty – 3; **Number of Other Faculty** – 9

Degrees awarded in 2008–2009 Academic Year – Masters – 50; **PhD** – 0; **Other** – 0

Grant Monies awarded in 2008–2009 Academic Year – 0

Name of Institution – University of Colorado Denver

Name of Department or Program – School of Education and Human Development

Address:
Campus Box 106, P.O. Box 173364
Denver, CO
80217-3364
US

Phone Number – (303)315-4963 **Fax Number** – (303)315-6311

Email Contact – brent.wilson@cudenver.edu **URL** – http://www.ucdenver.edu/ academics/colleges/SchoolOfEducation/Academics/MASTERS/ILT/Pages/ eLearning.aspx

Contact Person – Brent Wilson, Program Coordinator, Information and Learning Technologies

Specializations – M.A. in Information & Learning Technologies (ILT) – includes options for eLearning, K12 Teaching, Instructional Design/Adult Learning, and School Librarianship. Graduate Certificates are available in eLearning Design and Implementation (15 graduate credits), and Digital Storytelling (9 graduate credits). The EdD in Educational Equity is available with concentration in adult education and professional learning, where students can focus on learning technologies. A PhD program option is also available for those choosing careers in higher education and research.

Features – The ILT program focuses on design and use of digital learning resources and social support for online learning. Masters students prepare a professional portfolio, published online, that showcases their skills and accomplishments. The doctoral program is cross-disciplinary, drawing on expertise in technology, adult learning, professional development, social justice, systemic change, research methods, reflective practice, and cultural studies.

Admission Requirements – MA and PhD: satisfactory GPA, GRE, writing sample, letters of recommendation, transcripts. See website for more detail.

Degree Requirements – MA: 30 semester hours including 27 hours of core coursework; professional portfolio; field experience. EdD: 50 semester hours of coursework and labs, plus 20 dissertation hours; dissertation.

Number of Full-Time Faculty – 3; **Number of Other Faculty** – 8

Degrees awarded in 2008–2009 Academic Year – Masters – 84; **PhD** – 1; **Other** – 0

Grant Monies awarded in 2008–2009 Academic Year – 5600

Name of Institution – University of Northern Colorado

Name of Department or Program – Educational Technology

Address:
College of Education and Behavioral Sciences
Greeley, CO
80639
US

Phone Number – (970)351-2816 **Fax Number** – (970)351-1622

Email Contact – james.gall@unco.edu **URL** – http://www.unco.edu/cebs/edtech

Contact Person – James Gall, Associate Professor, Program Coordinator, Educational Technology

Specializations – M.A. in Educational Technology; M.A. in School Library Educational; Nondegree endorsement for school library media specialists; Ph.D. in Educational Technology.

Features – Graduates are prepared for careers as instructional technologists, course designers, trainers, instructional developers, media specialists, and human resource managers. Graduates typically follow employment paths into K-12 education, higher education, business, industry, and occasionally the military.

Admission Requirements – M.A.: Bachelors degree, 3.0 undergraduate GPA, 3 letters of recommendation, statement of career goals. Endorsement: Same as MA. Ph.D.: 3.2 GPA in last 60 hours of coursework, three letters of recommendation, congruency between applicants statement of career goals and program goals, GRE, interview with faculty.

Degree Requirements – MA-Ed Tech: 33 semester hours (min) MA-School Library Education: 32 semester hours (min) School Library Endorsement (K-12 Added Endorsement): 26 semester hours (min) PhD: 67 semester hours (min)

Number of Full-Time Faculty – 4; **Number of Other Faculty** – 2

Degrees awarded in 2008–2009 Academic Year – **Masters** – 16; **PhD** – 4; **Other** – 0

Grant Monies awarded in 2008–2009 Academic Year – 0

Name of Institution – Fairfield University

Name of Department or Program – Educational Technology

Address:
N. Benson Road
Fairfield, Connecticut
06824
US

Phone Number – (203)254-4000 **Fax Number** – (203)254-4047

Email Contact – ihefzallah@mail.fairfield.edu **URL** – http://www.fairfield.edu

Contact Person – Dr. Ibrahim M. Hefzallah, Prof., Chair., Educational Technology Department; Dr. Justin Ahn, Assistant Professor of Educational Technology

Specializations – M.A. and a certificate of Advanced Studies in Educational Technology in one of five areas of concentrations: Computers-in-Education, Instructional Development, School Media Specialist, Applied Educational Technology in Content Areas, and Television Production; customized course of study also available

Features – emphasis on theory, practice, and new instructional developments in computers in education, multimedia, school/media, and applied technology in education

Admission Requirements – Bachelors degree from accredited institution with 2.67 GPA.

Degree Requirements – 33 credits

Number of Full-Time Faculty – 0; **Number of Other Faculty** – 0

Degrees awarded in 2008–2009 Academic Year – **Masters** – 12; **PhD** – 0; **Other** – 0

Grant Monies awarded in 2008–2009 Academic Year – 0

Name of Institution – University of Connecticut

Name of Department or Program – Educational Psychology

Address:
249 Glenbrook Rd, Unit-2064
Storrs, CT
06269-2064
US

Phone Number – (860)486-0182 **Fax Number** – (860)486-0180

Email Contact – myoung@UConn.edu **URL** – http://www.epsy.uconn.edu/

Contact Person – Michael Young, program coordinator

Specializations – M.A. in Educational Technology (portfolio or thesis options), 1-year partially online Masters (summer, fall, spring, summer), 6th Year certificate in Educational Technology and Ph.D. in Learning Technology

Features – MA can be on-campus or 2 Summers (on campus) and Fall-Spring (Online) that can be completed in a year. The PhD. emphasis in Learning Technology is a unique program at UConn. It strongly emphasizes Cognitive Science and how technology can be used to enhance the way people think and learn. The Program seeks to provide students with knowledge of theory and applications regarding the use of advanced technology to enhance learning and thinking. Campus facilities include $2 billion 21st Century UConn enhancement to campus infrastructure, including a new wing to the Neag School of Education. Faculty research interests include interactive video for anchored instruction and situated learning, telecommunications for cognitive apprenticeship, technology-mediated interactivity for learning by design activities, and in cooperation with the National Research Center for Gifted and Talented, research on the use of technology to enhance cooperative learning and the development of gifted performance in all students.

Admission Requirements – admission to the graduate school at UConn, GRE scores (or other evidence of success at the graduate level). Previous experience in a related area of technology, education, or experience in education or training.

Degree Requirements – completion of plan of study coursework, comprehensive exam (portfolio-based with multiple requirements), and completion of an approved dissertation.

Number of Full-Time Faculty – 0; **Number of Other Faculty** – 0

Degrees awarded in 2008–2009 Academic Year – Masters – 0; **PhD** – 0; **Other** – 0

Grant Monies awarded in 2008–2009 Academic Year – 0

Name of Institution – George Washington University

Name of Department or Program – School of Education and Human Development

Address:
2134 G Street NW Suite 103
Washington, District of Columbia
20052
US

Phone Number – (202)994-1701 **Fax Number** – (202)994-2145

Email Contact – etladmin@gwu.edu **URL** – http://www.gwu.edu/~etl

Contact Person – Dr. Michael Corry, Educational Technology Leadership Program. Contact student advisors at toll free (866) 498-3382/email etlinfo@gwu.edu.

Specializations – M.A. in Education and Human Development with a major in Educational Technology Leadership as well as the following Graduate Certificates: Instructional Design, Multimedia Development, Leadership in Educational Technology, E-Learning, Training and Educational Technology, Integrating Technology into Education.

Features – 0

Admission Requirements – application fee, transcripts, GRE or MAT scores (50th percentile), two letters of recommendation from academic professionals, computer access, undergraduate degree with 2.75 GPA. No GRE or MAT is required for entry into the Graduate Certificate programs.

Degree Requirements – MASTERS PROGRAM: 36 credit hours (including 27 required hours and 9 elective credit hours). Required courses include computer application management, media and technology application, software implementation and design, public education policy, and quantitative research methods. GRADUATE CERTIFICATE PROGRAMS: 15 credit hours

Number of Full-Time Faculty – 0; **Number of Other Faculty** – 0

Degrees awarded in 2008–2009 Academic Year – **Masters** – 0; **PhD** – 0; **Other** – 0

Grant Monies awarded in 2008–2009 Academic Year – 0

Name of Institution – Florida Institute of Technology

Name of Department or Program – Science and Mathematics Education Department

Address:
150 University Blvd.
Melbourne, FL
32901-6975
US

Phone Number – (321)674-8126 **Fax Number** – (321)674-7598

Email Contact – dcook@fit.edu **URL** – http://www.fit.edu/catalog/sci-lib/comp-edu.html#master-info

Contact Person – Dr. David Cook, Dept. Head.

Specializations – Master's degree in Computer Education Ph.D. degree in Science Education with options for research and major technical area concentrations in Computer Science, Computer Education and Instructional Technology.

Features – Flexible program depending on student experience.

Admission Requirements – Masters: 3.0 GPA for regular admission Ph.D.: Masters degree and 3.2 GPA

Degree Requirements – Masters: 33 semester hours (15 in computer or and technology education, 9 in education, 9 electives); practicum; no thesis or internship required or 30 semester hrs. for thesis option. Ph.D.: 42 semester hours (Includes dissertation and research. Also requires 21 graduate hours in computer science/computer information systems 6 of which may be applicable to the required 42 hours.)

Number of Full-Time Faculty – 2; **Number of Other Faculty** – 4

Degrees awarded in 2008–2009 Academic Year – **Masters** – 0; **PhD** – 0; **Other** – 0

Grant Monies awarded in 2008–2009 Academic Year – 0

Name of Institution – Nova Southeastern University – Fischler Graduate School of Education and Human Services

Name of Department or Program – Programs in Instructional Technology and Distance Education (ITDE)

Address:
1750 NE 167th Street
North Miami Beach, FL
33162
US

Phone Number – 954-262-8572. (800)986-3223, ext. 8572 **Fax Number** – (954)262-3905

Email Contact – itdeinfo@nova.edu;scisinfo@nova.edu **URL** – itde.nova.edu

Contact Person – Marsha L. Burmeister, Recruitment Coordinator & Program Professor ITDE

Specializations – M.S. and Ed.D in Instructional Technology and Distance Education.

Features – M.S. 21 months (M.S. ITDE program graduates may continue with the Ed.D. program as second year students) Ed.D. 36 months M.S. and Ed.D. combined: 4+ years Blended/hybrid delivery model with limited face-to-face and via instruction at-a-distance using Web-based technologies.

Admission Requirements – • Active employment in the field of instructional technology/distance education • Completion of bachelor's degree for M.S. program (2.5 minimum GPA); master's degree required for admission to Ed.D. program (3.0 minimum GPA). • Miller Analogies Test (MAT) score (test taken within last 5 years) • Submission of application/supplementary materials • Approval of Skills Checklist (application) • Three letters of recommendation • Official copies of transcripts for all graduate work • Resume • Oral interview (via telephone) • Demonstrated potential for successful completion of the program via acceptance of application • Internet Service Provider; Laptop computer

Degree Requirements – 21 months and 30 semester credits. Ed.D. 3 years and 65 semester credits. M.S. Program: 3 "extended weekends:" One extended weekend in the fall (5 days), one extended weekend in the spring (4 days), one summer instructional session (4–5 days; July), final term online delivery. Ed.D. program: same as above, continues throughout the 3 years (3 sessions in first year, 2 sessions in the second year, and one instructional session in the third year for a total of six (6) face-to-face sessions)

Number of Full-Time Faculty – 0; **Number of Other Faculty** – 0

Degrees awarded in 2008–2009 Academic Year – Masters – 100; **PhD** – 0; **Other** – 0

Grant Monies awarded in 2008–2009 Academic Year – 0

Name of Institution – Barry University

Name of Department or Program – Department of Educational Computing and Technology, School of Education

Address:
11300 N.E. Second Ave.
Miami Shores, Florida
33161
US

Phone Number – (305)899-3608 **Fax Number** – (305)899-3718

Email Contact – dlenaghan@bu4090.barry.edu **URL** – http://www.barry.edu/ed/programs/masters/ect/default.htm

Contact Person – Donna Lenaghan, Dir.

Specializations – M.S. and Ed.S. in Educational Technology Applications and Ph.D. degree in Educational Technology Leadership.

Features – These programs and courses prepare educators to integrate computer/ technologies in their disciplines and/or train individuals to use computers/technologies. The focus is on improving the teaching and learning process through integration of technologies into curricula and learning activities.

Admission Requirements – GRE scores, letters of recommendation, GPA, interview, achievements.

Degree Requirements – M.S. or Ed. S.: 36 semester credit hours. Ph.D.: 54 credits beyond the Masters including dissertation credits.

Number of Full-Time Faculty – 0; **Number of Other Faculty** – 0

Degrees awarded in 2008–2009 Academic Year – Masters – 75; **PhD** – 0; **Other** – 0

Grant Monies awarded in 2008–2009 Academic Year – 0

Name of Institution – Florida State University

Name of Department or Program – Educational Psychology and Learning Systems

Address:
3210 Stone Building
Tallahassee, Florida
32306-4453
US

Phone Number – (850)644-4592 **Fax Number** – (850)644-8776

Email Contact – mmckee@oddl.fsu.edu **URL** – http://insys.fsu.edu

Contact Person – Mary Kate McKee, Program Coordinator

Specializations – M.S. and Ph.D. in Instructional Systems with specializations for persons planning to work in academia, business, industry, government, or military, both in the United States and in International settings.

Features – Core courses include systems and materials development, performance improvement, online learning, development of multimedia, project management, psychological foundations, current trends in instructional design, and research and statistics. Internships are recommended. Strong alumni network. M.S. courses available both on campus and online.

Admission Requirements – M.S.: 3.0 GPA in last two years of undergraduate program, 1000 GRE (verbal plus quantitative), 550 TOEFL (for international applicants). Ph.D.: 1100 GRE (V+Q), 3.5 GPA in last two years; international students, 550 TOEFL.

Degree Requirements – M.S.: 36 semester hours, 2–4 hour internship, comprehensive exam preparation of professional portfolio

Number of Full-Time Faculty – 5; **Number of Other Faculty** – 4

Degrees awarded in 2008–2009 Academic Year – Masters – 30; PhD – 10; **Other** – 0

Grant Monies awarded in 2008–2009 Academic Year – 0

Name of Institution – University of Central Florida

Name of Department or Program – College of Education – ERTL

Address:
4000 Central Florida Blvd.
Orlando, Florida
32816-1250
US

Phone Number – (407)823-4835 **Fax Number** – (407)823-4880

Email Contact – hirumi@mail.ucf.edu;ggunter@mail.ucf.edu **URL** – http://www.education.ucf.edu/insttech/#

Contact Person – Drs. Glenda A. Gunter, Educational Technology and eLearning
2c Hirumi, Instructional Systems
Tom Atkinson, Instructional Systems

Specializations – M.A. in Instructional Technology/Instructional Systems, http://pegasus.cc.ucf.edu/~instsys/; M.Ed. in Instructional Technology/Educational Media – entirely web-based, Ph.D. and Ed.D. with specialization in Instructional Technology. http://www.graduate.ucf.edu There are approximately 18 Ed.D. students and 22 Ph.D. students in the doctoral programs. Program Web site: http://www.education.ucf.edu/insttech/#

Features – All programs rely heavily on understanding of fundamental competencies as reflected by NCATE, ASTD, AECT, AASL, and ISTE. There is an emphasis on the practical application of theory through intensive hands-on experiences. Orlando and the surrounding area is home to a plethora of high-tech companies, military training and simulation organizations, and tourist attractions. UCF, established in 1963, now has in excess of 36,000 students, representing more than 90 countries. It has been ranked as one of the leading "most-wired" universities in North America.

Admission Requirements – Interviews (either in person or via e-mail); GRE score of 840 if last 60 hours of undergraduate degree is 3.0 or above, 1000 if less; TOEFL of 550 (270 computer-based version) if English is not first language; three letters of recommendation; resume, statement of goals; residency statement, and health record. Financial statement if coming from overseas.

Degree Requirements – M.A. in Instructional Technology/Instructional Systems, 39 semester hours; M.A. in Instructional Technology/Educational Technology, 39 semester hours, M.A. in Instructional Technology/eLearning, 39 semester hours. Practicum required in all three programs: thesis, research project, or substitute additional course work. Ph.D. and Ed.D. require between 58 and 69 hours beyond the masters for completion.

Number of Full-Time Faculty – 3; **Number of Other Faculty** – 5

Degrees awarded in 2008–2009 Academic Year – Masters – 65; PhD – 12; Other – 7

Grant Monies awarded in 2008–2009 Academic Year – 0

Name of Institution – University of South Florida

Name of Department or Program – Instructional Technology Program, Secondary Education Department, College of Education

Address:
4202 E. Fowler Avenue, EDU162,
Tampa, Florida
33620-5650
US

Phone Number – (813)974-3533 **Fax Number** – (813)974-3837

Email Contact – IT@coedu.usf.edu **URL** – http://www.coedu.usf.edu/it

Contact Person – Dr. William Kealy, Graduate Certificates; Dr. Frank Breit, Master's program; Dr. Ann Barron, Education Specialist program; Dr. James White, Doctoral program.

Specializations – Graduate Certificates in Web Design, Instructional Design, Multimedia Design, School Networks, and Distance Education M.Ed., Ed.S., and Ph.D. in Curriculum and Instruction with emphasis in Instructional Technology

Features – Many student gain practical experience in the Florida Center for Instructional Technology (FCIT), which provides services to the Department of Education and other grants and contracts; the Virtual Instructional Team for the Advancement of Learning (VITAL), which provides USF faculty with course development services; and Educational Outreach. The College of Education is one of the largest in the US in terms of enrollment and facilities. As of Fall 1997, a new, technically state-of-the-art building was put into service. The University of South Florida has been classified by the Carnegie Foundation as a Doctoral/Research University – Extensive.

Admission Requirements – See http://www.coedu.usf.edu/it

Degree Requirements – See http://www.coedu.usf.edu/it

Number of Full-Time Faculty – 0; **Number of Other Faculty** – 0

Degrees awarded in 2008–2009 Academic Year – Masters – 60; **PhD** – 0; **Other** – 0

Grant Monies awarded in 2008–2009 Academic Year – 0

Name of Institution – Georgia Southern University

Name of Department or Program – College of Education

Address:
Box 8131
Statesboro, GA
30460-8131
US

Phone Number – (912)478-5307 **Fax Number** – (912)478-7104.

Email Contact – JRepman@georgiasouthern.edu **URL** – http://coe.georgiasouthern.edu/eltr/tech/inst_tech/index.htm

Contact Person – Judi Repman. Professor, Dept. of Leadership, Technology, and Human Development.

Specializations – Online M.Ed. and GA certification for School Library Media Specialist. An Instructional Technology strand is available in the Ed.S. in Teaching and Learning Program and in the Ed.D. program in Curriculum Studies.

Features – Completely online program. GA Special Technology Certification course available strong emphasis on technology

Admission Requirements – BS (teacher certification NOT required) GRE or MAT not required for applicants who are certified teachers with a 2.5 undergraduate grade point average

Degree Requirements – 36 semester hour

Number of Full-Time Faculty – 7; **Number of Other Faculty** – 1

Degrees awarded in 2008–2009 Academic Year – Masters – 40; **PhD** – 0; **Other** – 0

Grant Monies awarded in 2008–2009 Academic Year – 0

Name of Institution – Georgia State University

Name of Department or Program – Middle-Secondary Education and Instructional Technology

Address:
Box 3976
Atlanta, GA
30302-3976
US

Phone Number – (404)413-8060 **Fax Number** – (404)413-8063

Email Contact – swharmon@gsu.edu. **URL** – http://edtech.gsu.edu

Contact Person – Dr. Stephen W. Harmon, contact person.

Specializations – M.S. and Ph.D. in Instructional Design and Technology or Library Media Technology. Ed.S. in Library Media Technology. Endorsement in Online Teaching and Learning.

Features – Focus on research and practical application of instructional technology in educational and corporate settings. Online MS in Instructional Design and Technology available.

Admission Requirements – M.S.: Bachelors degree, 2.5 undergraduate GPA, 800 GRE, 550 TOEFL. Ed.S.: Master's degree, teaching certificate, 3.25 graduate GPA, 900 GRE. Ph.D.: Master's degree, 3.30 graduate GPA, 500 verbal plus 500 quantitative GRE or 500 analytical GRE.

Degree Requirements – M.S.: 36 sem. hours, internship, portfolio, comprehensive examination. LMT Ed.S.: 30 sem. hours, internship, and scholarly project. Ph.D.: 66 sem. hours, internship, comprehensive examination, dissertation.

Number of Full-Time Faculty – 6; **Number of Other Faculty** – 2

Degrees awarded in 2008–2009 Academic Year – **Masters** – 18; **PhD** – 3; **Other** – 2

Grant Monies awarded in 2008–2009 Academic Year – 1600000

Name of Institution – University of Georgia

Name of Department or Program – Department of Educational Psychology and Instructional Technology, College of Education

Address:
604 Aderhold Hall
Athens, GA
30602-7144
US

Phone Number – (706)542-3810 **Fax Number** – (706)542-4032

Email Contact – mikeorey@uga.edu **URL** – http://www.coe.uga.edu/epit/

Contact Person – Dr. Michael Orey, LDT Program Chair

Specializations – M.Ed. and Ed.S. in Learning, Design and Technology with two emphasis areas: Instructional Design & Development and School Library Media; Ph.D. for leadership positions as specialists in instructional design and development and university faculty. The program offers advanced study for individuals with previous preparation in instructional media and technology, as well as a preparation for personnel in other professional fields requiring a specialty in instructional systems or instructional technology. Representative career fields for graduates include designing new courses, educational multimedia (especially web based), tutorial programs, and instructional materials in state and local school systems, higher education, business and industry, research and nonprofit settings, and in instructional products development.

Features – Minor areas of study available in a variety of other departments. Personalized programs are planned around a common core of courses and include practice, internships, or clinical experiences. Research activities include grant-related activities and applied projects, as well as dissertation studies.

Admission Requirements – All degrees: application to graduate school, satisfactory GRE score, other criteria as outlined in Graduate School Bulletin and on the program Web site.

Degree Requirements – M.Ed.: 36 semester hours with 3.0 GPA, portfolio with oral exam. Ed.S.: 30 semester hours with 3.0 GPA and project exam. Ph.D.: three full years of study beyond the Master's degree, two consecutive semesters full-time residency, comprehensive exam with oral defense, internship, dissertation with oral defense.

Number of Full-Time Faculty – 11; **Number of Other Faculty** – 0

Degrees awarded in 2008–2009 Academic Year – Masters – 40; **PhD** – 3; **Other** – 10

Grant Monies awarded in 2008–2009 Academic Year – 400000

Name of Institution – University of West Georgia

Name of Department or Program – Department of Media and Instructional Technology

Address:
138 Education Annex
Carrollton, GA
30118
US

Phone Number – 678-839-6558 **Fax Number** – 678-839-6153

Email Contact – ebennett@westga.edu **URL** – http://coe.westga.edu/mit

Contact Person – Dr. Elizabeth Bennett, Professor and Chair

Specializations – M.Ed. with specializations in School Library Media or Instructional Technology and Add-On certification in School Library Media for students with Master's degrees in other disciplines. The Department also offers an Ed.S. program in Media with two options, Media Specialist or Instructional Technology. The program strongly emphasizes technology integration in the schools and online and blended learning environments in P-12 school settings.

Features – School library media and certification students complete field experiences as part of each school library media course they take. All courses range from 85% to 100% online.

Admission Requirements – M.Ed.: 800 GRE, 396 MAT, 2.7 undergraduate GPA. Ed.S.: 900 GRE, 400 MAT, and 3.00 graduate GPA.

Degree Requirements – 36 semester hours for M.Ed 27 semester hours for Ed.S

Number of Full-Time Faculty – 10; **Number of Other Faculty** – 4

Degrees awarded in 2008–2009 Academic Year – Masters – 40; **PhD** – 0; **Other** – 45

Grant Monies awarded in 2008–2009 Academic Year – 50000

Name of Institution – Valdosta State University

Name of Department or Program – Curriculum, Leadership, & Technology

Address:
1500 N. Patterson St.
Valdosta, GA
31698
US

Phone Number – (229)333-5633 **Fax Number** – (229)259-5094

Email Contact – ewiley@valdosta.edu **URL** – http://www.valdosta.edu/coe/clt/

Contact Person – Ellen Wiley

Specializations – M.Ed. in Instructional Technology with two tracks: Library/Media or Technology Applications; Online Ed.S. in Instructional Technology with two tracks: Library/Media or Technology Applications; Ed.D. in Curriculum and Instruction.

Features – The program has a strong emphasis on systematic design and technology in M.Ed., Ed.S., and Ed.D. Strong emphasis on change leadership, reflective practice, applied research in Ed.S and Ed.D.

Admission Requirements – M.Ed.: 2.5 GPA, 800 GRE. Ed.S.: Master's degree, 3 years of experience, 3.0 GPA, 850 GRE, MAT 390 and less than 5 years old. Ed.D.: Masters degree, 3 years of experience, 3.50 GPA, 1000 GRE.

Degree Requirements – M.Ed.: 33 semester hours. Ed.S.: 27 semester hours. Ed.D.: 54 semester hours.

Number of Full-Time Faculty – 20; **Number of Other Faculty** – 10

Degrees awarded in 2008–2009 Academic Year – Masters – 14; **PhD** – 0; **Other** – 34

Grant Monies awarded in 2008–2009 Academic Year – 0

Name of Institution – University of Hawaii-Manoa

Name of Department or Program – Department of Educational Technology

Address:
1776 University Ave
Honolulu, Hawaii
96822-2463
US

Phone Number – (808) 956-7671 **Fax Number** – (808)956-3905

Email Contact – edtech-dept@hawaii.edu **URL** – http://etec.hawaii.edu

Contact Person – Catherine P. Fulford, Phd, Chair

Specializations – M.Ed. in Educational Technology

Features – This nationally accredited program prepares students to create resources for teaching and learning through diverse media as well as integrate technology into educational environments. Educational Technology (ETEC) provides theoretical knowledge and scientific principles that can be applied to problems that arise in a social context; prepares individuals to devise effective messages, teams, materials, devices, techniques, and settings; and involves the study of theory and practice of design, development, utilization, management, and evaluation of processes and resources for learning. Practitioners in educational technology, whether they are teachers, trainers, developers, administrators, or support personnel, seek innovative and effective ways of organizing the teaching and learning process through the best possible application of technological developments. The program places emphasis on applications of technology in educational settings rather than simple technical skills. Individuals from diverse backgrounds can immediately apply what they learn to their particular context. Upon graduation, these new professionals will have a clearer vision of how they can prepare learners for the future. ETEC graduates are found in many learning environments including K-12 and higher education, government, business, industry, and health occupations.

Admission Requirements – A baccalaureate degree from an accredited institution in any field of study is acceptable to the Department, provided the student's undergraduate scholastic record is acceptable to the Graduate Division. A "B" average (i.e., 3.0 on a 4-point scale) in the last 60 semester hours of the undergraduate program is required for regular admission. Students from foreign countries must submit the results of the Test of English as a Foreign Language (TOEFL). The minimum score is 600, representing approximately the 77th percentile rank. Students must submit: an "Intent to Apply for Admission Form," a "Graduate Program Supplemental Information Form," and a "Statement of Objectives Form." These are available on the ETEC website. Three letters of recommendation, to be submitted with the application for admission, should evaluate the applicant's potential in the field of educational technology, not only his or her academic abilities to do graduate work. All applicants should submit a resume, and additional materials, documentation, or samples of work relevant to the evaluation and selection process.

Degree Requirements – The ETEC M.Ed. program requires a minimum of 36 semester credit hours, with seven required and five elective ETEC courses. All required and most elective courses are 3 credits each. Full-time students usually complete their coursework in two academic years. Students attending part-time may take three or more years to finish program requirements. Of the seven (7) required courses, four comprise the core of the Educational Technology program. Students are required to complete the core courses in sequence during the first year. The program is designed as a cohort system in which students admitted at the same time take initial courses together to build a sense of support and professional community. In the final year of the program the students will complete an electronic portfolio and final masters project.

Number of Full-Time Faculty – 7; **Number of Other Faculty** – 7

Degrees awarded in 2008–2009 Academic Year – Masters – 21; **PhD** – 0; **Other** – 0

Grant Monies awarded in 2008–2009 Academic Year – 1097246

Name of Institution – University of Northern Iowa

Name of Department or Program – Educational Technology Program

Address:
618 Schinder Education Center
Cedar Falls, IA
50614-0606
US

Phone Number – (319)273-3250 **Fax Number** – (319)273-5886

Email Contact – mary.herring@uni.edu **URL** – http://ci.coe.uni.edu/edtech/index.html

Contact Person – Sharon E. Smaldino

Specializations – M.A. in Curriculum & Instruction: Educational Technology, M.A. in Performance and Training Technology.

Features – The masters degrees are designed to meet the AECT/ECIT standards and are focused on addressing specific career choices. The Educational Technology masters is designed to prepare educators for a variety of professional positions in educational settings, including: school building level, school district level, vocational-technical school, community college, and university. The Performance and Training Technology masters is designed for persons planning to work in nonschool settings. Majors in this area will complete a basic core of course work applicable to all preparing for work as media specialists, trainers in industry and business, or communications designers. Specific areas of interest will determine the supporting electives. Licensure as a teacher is not required for admission to either masters in Iowa. The bachelors degree may be in any field.

Admission Requirements – Bachelors degree, 3.0 undergraduate GPA, 500 TOEFL

Degree Requirements – 38 semester credits, optional thesis worth 6 credits or alternative research paper of project, comprehensive exam

Number of Full-Time Faculty – 0; **Number of Other Faculty** – 0

Degrees awarded in 2008–2009 Academic Year – **Masters** – 32; **PhD** – 0; **Other** – 0

Grant Monies awarded in 2008–2009 Academic Year – 0

Name of Institution – Boise State University

Name of Department or Program – Instructional & Performance Technology

Address:
1910 University Drive, ET-327
Boise, Idaho
83725
US

Phone Number – (208)424-5135;(800)824-7017 ext. 61312 **Fax Number** – (208)426-1970

Email Contact – jfenner@boisestate.edu **URL** – http://ipt.boisestate.edu/

Contact Person – Dr. Don Stepich, IPT Program Chair.; Jo Ann Fenner, IPT Program Developer and distance program contact person.

Specializations – The Master of Science in Instructional & Performance Technology (IPT) degree is intended to prepare students for careers in the areas of instructional technology, performance technology, instructional design, performance improvement, training, education and training management, e-learning, human resources, organizational development, and human performance consulting.

Features – Leading experts in learning styles, evaluation, e-learning, performance improvement, and leadership principles serve as adjunct faculty in the program via computer and modem from their various remote locations. For details, visit our faculty web page at http://ipt.boisestate.edu/faculty.htm

Admission Requirements – undergraduate degree with 3.0 GPA, one-to-two page essay describing why you want to pursue this program and how it will contribute to your personal and professional development, and a resume of personal qualifications and work experience. For more information, visit http://ipt.boisestate.edu/application_admission.htm

Degree Requirements – 36 semester hours in instructional and performance technology and related course work; and four options for a culminating activity; project, thesis, portfolio, or oral comprehensive exam (included in 36 credit hours).

Number of Full-Time Faculty – 0; **Number of Other Faculty** – 0

Degrees awarded in 2008–2009 Academic Year – **Masters** – 45; **PhD** – 0; **Other** – 0

Grant Monies awarded in 2008–2009 Academic Year – 0

Name of Institution – Governors State University

Name of Department or Program – College of Arts and Sciences

Address:
1 University Parkway
University Park, IL
60466
US

Phone Number – (708)534-4051 **Fax Number** – (708)534-7895

Email Contact – m-lanigan@govst.edu **URL** – http://faculty.govst.edu/users/glanigan/homepage.htm

Contact Person – Mary Lanigan, Associate Prof., Human Performance and Training

Specializations – M.A. in Communication and Training with HP&T major – Program concentrates on building instructional design skills. Most classes are delivered in a hybrid format of online and face to face. Some classes are almost all online.

Features – Instructional Design overview; front-end analysis including both needs and task; design and delivery using various platforms; evaluation skills and how to predict behavior transfer; various technologies; consulting; project management; systems thinking; principles of message design; and more.

Admission Requirements – Undergraduate degree in any field.

Degree Requirements – 36 credit hours (trimester), All in instructional and performance technology; internship or advanced field project required. Metropolitan Chicago area based

Number of Full-Time Faculty – 1; **Number of Other Faculty** – 3

Degrees awarded in 2008–2009 Academic Year – **Masters** – 10; **PhD** – 0; **Other** – 0

Grant Monies awarded in 2008–2009 Academic Year – 0

Name of Institution – Southern Illinois University at Carbondale

Name of Department or Program – Department of Curriculum and Instruction

Address:
625 Wham Drive, Mailcode 4610
Carbondale, IL
62901
US

Phone Number – (618) 4534218 **Fax Number** – (618) 4534244

Email Contact – sashrock@siu.edu. **URL** – http://idt.siu.edu/

Contact Person – Sharon Shrock, Coord., Instructional Design/Instructional Technology

Specializations – M.S.Ed. in Curriculum & Instruction (with specializations in Instructional Design and Instructional Technology)
Ph.D. in Education (with concentration in Instructional Technology)

Features – All specializations are oriented to multiple education settings.

The ID program emphasizes nonschool (primarily corporate) learning environments, human performance technology, and criterion-referenced performance assessment.

The IT program covers many essential skills and tools leading to the production of e-Learning and performance assessment using digital games and other virtual learning environments.

Admission Requirements – M.S.: Bachelors degree, 2.7 undergraduate GPA, transcripts.

Ph.D.: Masters degree, 3.25 GPA, GRE scores, 3 letters of recommendation, transcripts, writing sample.

International students without a degree from a US institution must submit TOEFL score.

Degree Requirements – M.S., 32 credit hours with thesis; 36 credit hours without thesis;

Ph.D. , 40 credit hours beyond the masters degree in courses, 24 credit hours for the dissertation.

Number of Full-Time Faculty – 3; **Number of Other Faculty** – 1

Degrees awarded in 2008–2009 Academic Year – **Masters** – 5; **PhD** – 0; **Other** – 0

Grant Monies awarded in 2008–2009 Academic Year – 71000

Name of Institution – University of Illinois at Urbana-Champaign

Name of Department or Program – Curriculum, Technology, and Education Reform (CTER) Program, Department of Educational Psychology

Address:
226 Education Bldg.1310 S. 6th St.
Champaign, IL
61820
US

Phone Number – (217)244-3315 **Fax Number** – (217)244-7620

Email Contact – cter-info-L@listserv.illinois.edu **URL** – http://cter.ed.uiuc.edu

Contact Person – Doe-Hyung Kim, Visiting Project Coordinator, Dept. of Educational Psychology

Specializations – Ed.M. in Educational Psychology with emphasis in Curriculum, Technology, and Education Reform

Features – This Master of Education program is geared toward teachers and trainers interested in learning more about the integration of computer-based technology in the classroom. This online set of project-based courses offers an opportunity to earn a coherent, high-quality masters degree online, with most interactions through personal computers and Internet connections at home or workplace.

Admission Requirements – Application to the Graduate College, three letters of recommendation, personal statement. For more information go to: http://cterport. ed.uiuc.edu/admissions_folder/application_procedures_html

Degree Requirements – Eight courses (5 requirements + 3 electives) required for Ed.M.

Number of Full-Time Faculty – 4; **Number of Other Faculty** – 2

Degrees awarded in 2008–2009 Academic Year – Masters – 28; **PhD** – 0; **Other** – 0

Grant Monies awarded in 2008–2009 Academic Year – 0

Name of Institution – Northern Illinois University

Name of Department or Program – Educational Technology, Research and Assessment

Address:
208 Gabel Hall
DeKalb, Illinois
60115
US

Phone Number – (815) 753-9339 **Fax Number** – (815) 753-9388

Email Contact – edtech@niu.edu **URL** – http://www.cedu.niu.edu/etra

Contact Person – Dr. Jeffrey B. Hecht, Department Chair

Specializations – M.S.Ed. in Instructional Technology with concentrations in Instructional Design, Distance Education, Educational Computing, and Media Administration; Ed.D. in Instructional Technology, emphasizing instructional design and development, computer education, media administration, and preparation for careers in business, industry, and higher education. In addition, Illinois state certification in school library media is offered in conjunction with either degree or alone.

Features – Program is highly individualized. All facilities remodeled and modernized in 2002–2003 featuring five smart classrooms and over 110 student use desktop and laptop computers. Specialized equipment for digital audio and video editing, web site and CD creation, and presentations. All students are encouraged to create portfolios highlighting personal accomplishments and works (required at Masters). Masters program started in 1968, doctorate in 1970.

Admission Requirements – M.S.Ed.: 2.75 undergraduate GPA, GRE verbal and quantitative scores, two references. Ed.D.: 3.25 M.S. GPA, writing sample, three references, interview.

Degree Requirements – M.S.Ed.: 39 hours, including 30 in instructional technology; portfolio. Ed.D.: 63 hours beyond Master's, including 15 hours for dissertation.

Number of Full-Time Faculty – 0; **Number of Other Faculty** – 0

Degrees awarded in 2008–2009 Academic Year – Masters – 0; **PhD** – 0; **Other** – 0

Grant Monies awarded in 2008–2009 Academic Year – 0

Name of Institution – Southern Illinois University Edwardsville

Name of Department or Program – Instructional Technology Program

Address:
School of Education
Edwardsville, Illinois
62026-1125
US

Phone Number – (618) 650-3277 **Fax Number** – (618) 650-3808

Email Contact – yliu@siue.edu **URL** – http://www.siue.edu/education/edld/it/index.shtml

Contact Person – Dr. Yuliang Liu, Dir., Dept. of Educational Leadership

Specializations – The Educational Technologies option enables teachers and other school personnel to learn how to plan, implement, and evaluate technology-based instruction and learning activities in p-12 settings. Students pursuing this option will become knowledgeable users of technology as well as designers of curriculum and instruction that effectively utilize and integrate technology to improve student learning. Students interested in leadership roles in educational technology, such as those wishing to become technology coordinators in schools or school districts, can work toward meeting the standards for the Illinois State Board of Education's (ISBE) Technology Specialist endorsement through this program. The Library Information Specialist option enables teachers and other school personnel to learn how to plan, implement, and evaluate library information-based activities in P-12 settings. Students pursuing this option will become knowledgeable users of library information as well as designers of curriculum and instruction that effectively utilize and integrate library information to improve student learning. Students interested in Library Information Specialist endorsement can work towards meeting the standards for the Illinois State Board of Education's Library Information Specialist endorsement through this program. The Instructional Design & Performance Improvement option focuses on skills necessary for careers in the areas of instructional technology, performance technology, instructional design, training, and performance consulting.

Emphasis is placed on systematic instructional design and on the use of various media and technologies for learning and instruction. Students in this option may also focus on the design and development of online learning and other performance improvement strategies. The Interactive Multimedia Technologies option is appropriate for people wishing to pursue the design and development of various interactive multimedia and web-based learning experiences. This option prepares students for careers with publishing and production companies, consulting firms, and other businesses that produce engaging multimedia applications for learning and other opportunities. Course work focuses on theories and methods for designing compelling user experiences, developing skills with tools for web and other delivery media, and project management strategies.

Features – Several unique features of the program provide students with opportunities for important practical experiences that complement course work. Juried presentations provide students with an opportunity to share their work with a jury of professors and peers, and defend their work in light of their own goals and the content of their degree program. Design Studios provide students with opportunities to work on real-world projects for a variety of real clients in order to develop skills in collaboration, design, development tools and techniques, and project management.

Admission Requirements – The requirements for admission are a bachelor's degree and a GPA of 3.0 or above during their last two years of undergraduate work.

Degree Requirements – 36 semester hours; Thesis or Final Project options.

Number of Full-Time Faculty – 4; **Number of Other Faculty** – 4

Degrees awarded in 2008–2009 Academic Year – **Masters** – 16; **PhD** – 0; **Other** – 0

Grant Monies awarded in 2008–2009 Academic Year – 0

Name of Institution – Western Illinois University

Name of Department or Program – Instructional Technology and Telecommunications

Address:
47 Harrabin Hall
Macomb, Illinois
61455
US

Phone Number – (309)298-1952 **Fax Number** – (309)298-2978

Email Contact – hh-hemphill@wiu.edu **URL** – http://www.wiu.edu/idt

Contact Person – Hoyet H. Hemphill, Ph.D., Chair. Ph.D. in Instructional Technology

Specializations – Undergraduate programs B.S options in: – Instructional Multimedia and Web-Based Development – Instructional Simulation and Games – Instructional Methods and Training Undergraduate Minors in: – Web Design – Digital Media – Photographic Media Graduate Program M.S. in Instructional Design and Technology (available online) Six Post-Baccalaureate Certificates (PBC) – two completely online (K-12 Technology Specialist option for M.S. or PBC)

Features – M.S. program approved by Illinois Board of Higher Education in January 1996 with emphases in Instructional Design and Technology, Web-Design, Interactive Multimedia, and Distance Education. M.S. can be completed entirely online. B.S. in Instructional Design and Technology approved in 1997. Three options for B.S. Courses are lab-based, hands-on. Undergraduate Minors in: – Web Design – Digital Media – Photographic Media

Admission Requirements – M.S.: Bachelor's degree with minimum 2.75 GPA overall or 3.0 for last two years. English proficiency (TOEFL) for international students.

Degree Requirements – M.S.: 32 semester hours, thesis or applied project, or 35 semester hours with portfolio. Certificate Program in Instructional Technology Specialization. Graphic applications, training development, video production. Each track option is made of 5 courses or a total of 15 semester hours, except for Technology Specialist, which is 24 semester hours. B.S.: 120 hour program

Number of Full-Time Faculty – 8; **Number of Other Faculty** – 3

Degrees awarded in 2008–2009 Academic Year – Masters – 24; PhD – 0; Other – 11

Grant Monies awarded in 2008–2009 Academic Year – 0

Name of Institution – Indiana State University

Name of Department or Program – Dept. of Curriculum, Instruction, and Media Technology

Address:
n/a
Terre Haute, Indiana
47809
US

Phone Number – (812)237-2937 **Fax Number** – (812)237-4348

Email Contact – espowers@isugw.indstate.edu **URL** – 0

Contact Person – Dr. James E. Thompson, Program Coord.

Specializations – Master's degree in Instructional Technology with education focus or with noneducation focus; Specialist Degree program in Instructional Technology; Ph.D. in Curriculum, Instruction with specialization in Media Technology

Features – 0

Admission Requirements – 0

Degree Requirements – Master's: 32 semester hours, including 18 in media; thesis optional; Ed.S.: 60 semester hours beyond bachelor's degree; Ph.D., approximately 100 hours beyond bachelor's degree.

Number of Full-Time Faculty – 0; **Number of Other Faculty** – 0

Degrees awarded in 2008–2009 Academic Year – **Masters** – 0; **PhD** – 0; **Other** – 0

Grant Monies awarded in 2008–2009 Academic Year – 0

Name of Institution – Clarke College

Name of Department or Program – Graduate Studies

Address:
1550 Clarke Drive
Dubuque, Iowa
52001
US

Phone Number – (563)588-8180 **Fax Number** – (563)584-8604

Email Contact – llester@clarke.edu **URL** – http://www.clarke.edu

Contact Person – Margaret Lynn Lester

Specializations – M.A.E. (Two tracks: Instructional Leadership & Literacy)

Features – The "Instructional Leadership track of this program offers hybrid courses in educational technology. Courses are offered through WEB-ST and face to face. Outcomes are aligned with the National Educational Technology Standards for Educators.

Admission Requirements – Completed graduate application, official transcripts, photocopy of all teaching certificates and licenses, 2.75 GPA (4 point scale), two letters of reference, interview, statement of goals, and $25 application fee. (Minimum TOEFL score of 550 if English is not first language).

Degree Requirements – 9 hours in Research Core; 9 hour in Instructional Core; and 18 hours in Instructional Leadership Track.

Number of Full-Time Faculty – ; **Number of Other Faculty** –

Degrees awarded in 2008–2009 Academic Year – **Masters** – ; **PhD** – ; **Other** –

Grant Monies awarded in 2008–2009 Academic Year –

Name of Institution – Iowa State University

Name of Department or Program – College of Education

Address:
E262 Lagomarcino Hall
Ames, Iowa
50011
US

Phone Number – (515)294-7021 **Fax Number** – (515)294-6260

Email Contact – pkendall@iastate.edu **URL** – http://www.educ.iastate.edu/

Contact Person – Niki Davis, Director, Center for Technology in Learning and Teaching

Specializations – M.Ed., M.S., and Ph.D. in Curriculum and Instructional Technology. Features: Prepares candidates as practitioners and researchers in the field of curriculum and instructional technology. All areas of specialization emphasize appropriate and effective applications of technology in teacher education. M.Ed. program also offered at a distance (online and face-to-face learning experiences).

Features – practicum experiences related to professional objectives, supervised study and research projects tied to long-term studies within the program, development and implementation of new techniques, teaching strategies, and operational procedures in instructional resources centers and computer labs, program emphasis on technologies for teachers.

Admission Requirements – Admission Requirements: M.Ed. and M.S.: Bachelors degree, top half of undergraduate class, official transcripts, three letters, autobiography. Ph.D.: top half of undergraduate class, official transcripts, three letters, autobiography, GRE scores, scholarly writing sample.

Degree Requirements – Degree Requirements: M.Ed. 32 credit hours (7 research, 12 foundations, 13 applications and leadership in instructional technology); and action research project. M.S. 36 credit hours (16 research, 12 foundations, 8 applications and leadership in instructional technology); and thesis. Ph.D. 78 credit hours (minimum of 12 research, minimum of 15 foundations, additional core credits in conceptual, technical, and advanced specialization areas, minimum of 12 dissertation); portfolio, and dissertation.

Number of Full-Time Faculty – 0; **Number of Other Faculty** – 0

Degrees awarded in 2008–2009 Academic Year – Masters – 0; **PhD** – 0; **Other** – 0

Grant Monies awarded in 2008–2009 Academic Year – 0

Name of Institution – Emporia State University

Name of Department or Program – School of Library and Information Management

Address:
1200 Commercial, P.O. Box 4025
Emporia, Kansas
66801
US

Phone Number – 800/552-4770 **Fax Number** – 620/341-5233

Email Contact – idt@emporia.edu **URL** – http://slim.emporia.edu

Contact Person – Daniel Roland, Director of Communications

Specializations – Masters of Library Science (ALA accredited program); Masters in Legal Information Management – in partnership with the University of Kansas School of Law – 50 semester hours or 15 hour certificate. School Library Certification program, which includes 27 hours of the M.L.S. program; Ph.D. in Library and Information Management B.S. in Information Resource Studies Information Management Certificate – 18 hours of MLS curriculum Library Services Certificates – 6 separate 12-hour programs of undergraduate work available for credit or non-credit. Areas include Information Sources and Services; Collection Management; Technology; Administration; Youth Services; and Generalist.

Features – The Master of Library Science program is also delivered to satellite campus sites in Denver, Salt Lake City, Portland, Oregon. New programs tend to start every three years in each location. New programs include Denver – Summer 2004, Portland – Spring 2005, Salt Lake City – Fall 2005.

Admission Requirements – Undergrad GPA of 3.0 or better for masters degrees, 3.5 or better for PhD. GRE score of 1,000 points combined in Verbal and Analytical sections for masters degrees, 1,100 for PhD. GRE can be waived for students already holding a graduate degree in which they earned a 3.75 GPA or better. Admission interview.

Degree Requirements – M.L.S.: 42 semester hours. Ph.D.: total of 55–59 semester hours beyond the masters.

Number of Full-Time Faculty – 0; **Number of Other Faculty** – 0

Degrees awarded in 2008–2009 Academic Year – Masters – 0; PhD – 0; Other – 0

Grant Monies awarded in 2008–2009 Academic Year – 0

Name of Institution – Kansas State University

Name of Department or Program – Curriculum & Instruction

Address:
364 Bluemont Hall
Manhattan, KS
66506
US

Phone Number – 785-532-5716 **Fax Number** – (785)532-7304

Email Contact – talab@ksu.edu **URL** – http://coe.ksu.edu/ecdol

Contact Person – Dr. Rosemary Talab

Specializations – The Educational Computing, Design, and Online Learning Program has these specializations: I. M.S. in Curriculum & Instruction with specialties in (1) Educational Computing, Design, and Online Learning (online option) (2) Digital Teaching and Learning (online) II. Ph.D. in Curriculum & Instruction with specialty in Educational Computing, Design, and Online Learning (online) III. KSU Graduate School Certificate in Digital Teaching and Learning Masters program started in 1982; doctoral in 1987; Certificate in 1999

Features – All coursework for the Certificate, M.A., and Ph.D. can be taken online. ECDOL is an online program that focuses on research, theory, practice, ethics, and the design of learning environments, with an emphasis on emerging technologies. Coursework includes instructional design, virtual learning environments, digital video, the design and evaluation of e-learning and blended learning coursework, wireless and mobile learning, etc., as classes are offered on a rotating basis. A cohort group is taken each fall for the Professional Seminar 1 and 2 academic year via videoconferencing. E-portfolios are required at the Certificate and Masters degree levels. The Ph.D. program allows the student to tailor the classes to individual needs. At the Certificate and masters level the DTL program offers classroom teachers leadership opportunities as technology facilitators and lead teachers, with coursework available in integrating emerging technologies into instruction to improve student achievement through a blend of practical technology skills with research and theory. The masters level ECDOL program is offered to those who have B.A.s in other fields who wish to pursue a specialty in instructional design or prepare for the Ph.D. in ECDOL or who wish to design technology-enhanced, online, and virtual learning environments. The KSU Graduate School Certificate in DTL is a 15-hour completely online program for the classroom teacher with uniform exit outcomes and an e-portfolio requirement. The emphasis is on skills

Admission Requirements – M.S. in ECDOL: B average in undergraduate work, mid-range scores on TOEFL. M.S./Certificate in DTL: B average in undergraduate work and teaching experience. Ph.D.: B average in undergraduate and graduate work, GRE, three letters of recommendation, experience or basic courses in educational computing.

Degree Requirements – Certificate is 15 hours and requires an e-portfolio and technology project DTL is a 15-hour KSU Graduate School Certificate program; e-portfolio and project are required M.S.: 31 semester hours (minimum of 15 in specialty); thesis, internship, or practicum not required, but all three are possible; e-portfolio and project are required. The Ph.D. degree is 36–42 hours, with 30 hours of research, for a total of 60 hours, minimum. Certificate: 15 hours M.S. 31 hours Ph.D.: 60 hours semester hours are required and 30 hours are taken from the students masters program. There is a minimum of 21 hours in Educational Computing, Design, and Online Learning or related area approved by committee and 30 hours for dissertation research.

Number of Full-Time Faculty – 1; **Number of Other Faculty** – 6

Degrees awarded in 2008–2009 Academic Year – Masters – 2; **PhD** – 0; **Other** – 3

Grant Monies awarded in 2008–2009 Academic Year – 0

Name of Institution – University of Louisville

Name of Department or Program – College of Education and Human Development

Address:
Belknap Campus
Louisville, KY
40292
US

Phone Number – (502)852-6667 **Fax Number** – (502)852-4563

Email Contact – rod.githens@louisville.edu **URL** – http://www.louisville.edu/edu

Contact Person – Rod Githens

Specializations – M.S. in Human Resource Education Ph.D. in Educational Leadership and Organizational Development

Features – Our program is Relevant, Rigorous, and Conceptually Sound: – Relevant. The program has a strong emphasis on hands-on, applied projects that provide direct application to the field. Our instructors have practitioner experience in the field and many currently work in HR-related positions in Louisville and around the country. – Rigorous. Expect to work hard and complete challenging assignments. Our goal is to help you develop the skills to think unconventionally about conventional problems. – Conceptually Sound. The program is designed around research-based competencies from the American Society for Training and Development, International Society for Performance Improvement, and the Society for Human Resource Management. Faculty members have strong theoretical and conceptual backgrounds that guide both their teaching and their practical approach to the field.

Admission Requirements – 3.0 GPA, 800 GRE, 2 letters of recommendation, goal statement, resume, application fee

Degree Requirements – 30 semester hours, internship/fieldwork

Number of Full-Time Faculty – 11; **Number of Other Faculty** – 14

Degrees awarded in 2008–2009 Academic Year – Masters – 25; **PhD** – 5; **Other** – 0

Grant Monies awarded in 2008–2009 Academic Year – 0

Name of Institution – Louisiana State University

Name of Department or Program – School of Library and Information Science

Address:
267 Coates Hall
Baton Rouge, LA
70803
US

Phone Number – (225)578-3158 **Fax Number** – (225)578-4581

Email Contact – bpaskoff@lsu.edu **URL** – http://slis.lsu.edu

Contact Person – Beth Paskoff, Dean, School of Library and Information Science

Specializations – Archives, academic libraries, information technology, medical libraries, public libraries, special libraries, youth services, Louisiana School Library Certification. Dual degrees are available in Systems Science and in History

Features – Distance education courses available at 7 locations in Louisiana.

Admission Requirements – Bachelors degree, prefer 3.00 gpa GRE scores: prefer 500+ on verbal

Degree Requirements – M.L.I.S.: 40 hours, comprehensive exam, completion of degree program in five years

Number of Full-Time Faculty – 11; **Number of Other Faculty** – 0

Degrees awarded in 2008–2009 Academic Year – Masters – 60; **PhD** – 0; **Other** – 2

Grant Monies awarded in 2008–2009 Academic Year – 111841

Name of Institution – Boston University

Name of Department or Program – School of Education

Address:
Two Siber Way
Boston, MA
02215-1605
US

Phone Number – (617)353-3181 **Fax Number** – (617)353-3924

Email Contact – whittier@bu.edu **URL** – http://web.bu.edu/EDUCATION

Contact Person – David B. Whittier, Asst. Professor and Coord., Program in Educational Media and Technology.

Specializations – Ed.M., CAGS (Certificate of Advanced Graduate Study) in Educational Media and Technology; Ed.D. in Curriculum and Teaching, Specializing in Educational Media and Technology; preparation for Massachusetts public school License as Instructional Technology Specialist

Features – The Masters Program prepares graduates for professional careers as educators, instructional designers, developers of educational materials, and managers of the human and technology-based resources necessary to support education and training with technology. Graduates are employed in pK-12 schools, higher education, industry, medicine, public health, government, publishing, and a range of services such as finance and insurance. Students come to the program from many different backgrounds and with a wide range of professional goals. The doctoral program sets the study of Educational Media & Technology within the context of education and educational research in general, and curriculum and teaching in particular. In addition to advanced work in the field of Educational Media and Technology, students examine and conduct research and study the history of educational thought and practice. Graduates make careers in education as professors and researchers, technology directors and managers, and as developers of technology-based materials and systems. Graduates who work in both educational and noneducational organizations are often responsible for managing the human and technological resources required to create learning experiences that include the development and delivery of technology-based resources and distance education.

Admission Requirements – All degree programs require either the GRE or MAT test score completed within past five years and recommendations. Specific programs also include: Ed.M.: undergraduate degree and GPA. For CAGS, in addition to above, an earned Ed.M is required. For Ed.D. 3 letters of recommendation, test scores, transcripts, earned masters degree, and two writing samples: a statement of goals and qualifications and an analytical essay are required. Contact Graduate Admissions office.

Degree Requirements – Ed.M.: 36 credit hours (including 26 hours from required core curriculum, 10 from electives). CAGs: 32 credits beyond Ed.M., one of which must be a curriculum and teaching course and a comprehensive exam. Ed.D.: 60 credit hours of courses selected from Educational Media and Technology, curriculum and teaching, and educational thought and practice with comprehensive exams; course work and apprenticeship in research; dissertation

Number of Full-Time Faculty – 1; **Number of Other Faculty** – 10

Degrees awarded in 2008–2009 Academic Year – Masters – 12; **PhD** – 0; **Other** – 0

Grant Monies awarded in 2008–2009 Academic Year – 20000

Name of Institution – Fitchburg State College

Name of Department or Program – Division of Graduate and Continuing Education

Address:
160 Pearl Street
Fitchburg, MA
01420
US

Phone Number – (978) 665-3544 **Fax Number** – (978) 665-3055

Email Contact – rhowe@fsc.edu **URL** – http://www.fsc.edu

Contact Person – Dr. Randy Howe, Chair

Specializations – M.S. in Applied Communication with specializations in Applied Communication and Library Media. M.Ed in Educational Leadership and Management with specialization in Technology Leadership.

Features – Collaborating with professionals working in the field both for organizations and as independent producers, Fitchburg offers unique M.S. and MEd programs. The objectives are to develop in candidates the knowledge and skills for the effective implementation of communication within business, industry, government, not-for-profit agencies, health services, and education.

Admission Requirements – MAT or GRE scores, official transcript(s) of a baccalaureate degree, two or more years of experience in communications or media or education, three letters of recommendation.

Degree Requirements – 39 semester credit hours.

Number of Full-Time Faculty – 5; **Number of Other Faculty** – 7

Degrees awarded in 2008–2009 Academic Year – Masters – 10; PhD – 0; **Other** – 0

Grant Monies awarded in 2008–2009 Academic Year – 0

Name of Institution – Lesley University

Name of Department or Program – Technology In Education

Address:
29 Everett St.
Cambridge, MA
02138-2790
US

Phone Number – (617)349-8419 **Fax Number** – (617)349-8169

Email Contact – gblakesl@lesley.edu **URL** – http://www.lesley.edu/soe/111tech.html

Contact Person – Dr. George Blakeslee, Division Director

Specializations – M.Ed. in Technology in Education CAGS / Ed.S. in Technology in Education PhD in Educational Studies with specialization in Technology in Education

Features – M.Ed. program is offered off-campus at 70+ sites in 21 states; contact 617-349-8311 for information. The degree is also offered completely online. Contact Maureen Yoder, myoder@lesley.edu, or (617)348-8421 for information. Or check our website: url above.

Admission Requirements – Completed bachelors Teaching certificate

Degree Requirements – M.Ed.: 33 semester hours in technology, integrative final project in lieu of thesis, no internship or practicum. C.A.G.S.: 36 semester hours. Ph.D. requirements available on request.

Number of Full-Time Faculty – ; **Number of Other Faculty** –

Degrees awarded in 2008–2009 Academic Year – Masters – ; **PhD** – ; **Other** –

Grant Monies awarded in 2008–2009 Academic Year –

Name of Institution – Harvard University

Name of Department or Program – Graduate School of Education

Address:
Appian Way
Cambridge, Massachusetts
02138
US

Phone Number – (617)495-3543 **Fax Number** – (617)495-9268

Email Contact – pakir@gse.harvard.edu **URL** – http://www.gse.harvard.edu/tie

Contact Person – Joseph Blatt, director, Technology, Innovation, and Education Program; Irene Pak, program coordinator, Technology, Innovation, and Education Program

Specializations – The Technology, Innovation, and Education Program (TIE) at Harvard prepares students to contribute to the thoughtful design, implementation, and assessment of educational media and technology initiatives. Graduates of the program fill leadership positions in a wide range of fields, including design and production, policy development and analysis, technology integration and administration, research and evaluation, and teaching with new technologies. Some distinctive features of studying educational technology in TIE include: * Focus on learning and teaching: Our approach puts learning and teaching at the center, with technology as the means, not the mission. Our courses examine cutting-edge technologies that bridge distance and time, the research behind them and the design that goes into them – but we always center on the cognitive, affective, and social dimensions of learning, not on hardware or fashion. * A world-class faculty: Our faculty combines internationally recognized researchers with leading professionals in design and evaluation. We are all committed teachers and learners, dedicated to supporting you as a student and helping you craft a course of study that meets your goals. * A curriculum that builds leaders: Our curriculum bridges three broad strands of design, implementation, and research. Design courses apply learning principles to creating software, networks, digital video and television, handheld applications, and multiuser virtual environments. Implementation courses focus on using new technologies to bring about transformative changes in educational practice. Courses on research emphasize formulating evaluation designs that are both rigorous and practical. To deepen connections between theory and practice, TIE students often undertake an internship in one of the many research projects, educational technology firms, or media production organizations in the Boston area. * A diverse community of learners: Our community includes students of all ages, from all parts of the globe, with varied professional backgrounds and experience in technology. The upshot is that students have endless opportunities to learn from one another, exchanging insights about the potential role for learning technologies in different settings and cultures. More information about the program, our faculty, and the student experience is available on our Web site, http://www.gse.harvard.edu/tie.

Features – Courses in design, technology policy and leadership, research and evaluation, leading to the Ed.M. degree in Technology, Innovation, and Education. The program offers access to other courses throughout Harvard University, and at MIT, as well as many internship opportunities in the Greater Boston media and technology community.

Admission Requirements – GRE scores, 600 TOEFL, academic transcripts, 3 letters of recommendation, and a statement of purpose. Students interested in further information about the TIE Program should visit our Web site, http://www.gse.harvard.edu/tie, which includes a link to the Harvard Graduate School of Education online application.

Degree Requirements – 32 semester credits

Number of Full-Time Faculty – 5; **Number of Other Faculty** – 6

Degrees awarded in 2008–2009 Academic Year – Masters – 40; **PhD** – 0; **Other** – 0

Grant Monies awarded in 2008–2009 Academic Year – 3000000

Name of Institution – Simmons College

Address:
300 The Fenway
Boston, Massachusetts
02115-5898
US

Phone Number – (617)521-2800 **Fax Number** – (617)521-3192

Email Contact – michele.cloonan@simmons.edu **URL** – http://www.simmons.edu/gslis/

Contact Person – Michèle V. Cloonan

Specializations – M.S. Dual degrees: M.L.S./M.A. in Education (for School Library Media Specialists); M.L.S./M.A. in History (Archives Management Program). A Doctor of Arts in Administration is also offered.

Features – The program prepares individuals for a variety of careers, media technology emphasis being only one. There are special programs for School Library Media Specialist and Archives Management with strengths in Information Science/Systems, Media Management.

Admission Requirements – B.A. or B.S. degree with 3.0 GPA, statement, three letters of reference.

Degree Requirements – 36 semester hours.

Number of Full-Time Faculty – 0; **Number of Other Faculty** – 0

Degrees awarded in 2008–2009 Academic Year – **Masters** – 0; **PhD** – 0; **Other** – 0

Grant Monies awarded in 2008–2009 Academic Year – 0

Name of Institution – McDaniel College (formerly Western Maryland College)

Name of Department or Program – Graduate and Professional Studies

Address:
2 College Hill
Westminster, MD
21157
US

Phone Number – (410)857-2507 **Fax Number** – (410)857-2515

Email Contact – rkerby@mcdaniel.edu **URL** – http://www.mcdaniel.edu

Contact Person – Dr. Ramona N.Kerby, Coord., School Library Media Program, Graduate Studies

Specializations – M.S. in Education with an emphasis in School Library Media

Features – School librarianship

Admission Requirements – 3.0 Undergraduate GPA, 3 reference checklist forms from principal and other school personnel, acceptable application essay, acceptable Praxis test scores

Degree Requirements – 37 credit hours, including professional digital portfolio.

Number of Full-Time Faculty – 1; **Number of Other Faculty** – 5

Degrees awarded in 2008–2009 Academic Year – **Masters** – 15; **PhD** – 0; **Other** – 0

Grant Monies awarded in 2008–2009 Academic Year – 0

Name of Institution – Towson University

Name of Department or Program – College of Education

Address:
Hawkins Hall
Towson, Md
21252
US

Phone Number – (410)704-4226 **Fax Number** – (410)704-4227

Email Contact – jkenton@towson.edu **URL** – http://wwwnew.towson.edu/coe/rset/insttech/

Contact Person – Dr. Jeffrey M. Kenton, Assistant Professor. Dept.: Educational Technology and Literacy

Specializations – M.S. degrees in Instructional Development, and Educational Technology (Contact Jeff Kenton, kkenton@towosn.edu) and School Library Media (Contact, David Robinson: derobins@towson.edu). Ed. D. degrees in Instructional Technology (Contact, William Sadera, bsadera@towson.edu).

Features – Excellent labs. Strong practical hands-on classes. Focus of MS program – Students produce useful multimedia projects for use in their teaching and training. Many group activities within courses. School library media degree confers with Maryland State Department of Education certification as a Prek-12 Library Media Specialist. Innovative Ed. D. program with online hybrid courses and strong mix of theory and practical discussions.

Admission Requirements – Bachelor's degree from accredited institution with 3.0 GPA. (Conditional admission granted for many applicants with a GPA over 2.75).

Degree Requirements – MS degree is 36 graduate semester hours without thesis. Ed. D. is 63 hours beyond the MS degree.

Number of Full-Time Faculty – 17; **Number of Other Faculty** – 5

Degrees awarded in 2008–2009 Academic Year – **Masters** – 157; **PhD** – 0; **Other** – 4

Grant Monies awarded in 2008–2009 Academic Year – 0

Name of Institution – Eastern Michigan University

Name of Department or Program – Teacher Education

Address:
313 John W. Porter Building
Ypsilanti, MI
48197
US

Phone Number – (734)487-3260 **Fax Number** – (734)487-2101

Email Contact – ncopeland@emich.edu **URL** – http://www.emich.edu

Contact Person – Jon Margerum-Leys, Ph.D. – Associate Professor/Graduate Coordinator

Specializations – M.A. and Graduate Certificate in Educational Media and Technology. The mission of this program is to prepare professionals who are capable of facilitating student learning in a variety of settings. The program is designed to provide students with both the knowledge base and the application skills that are required to use technology effectively in education. Focusing on the design, development, utilization, management, and evaluation of instructional systems moves us toward achieving this mission. Students who complete the educational technology concentration will be able to: (a) provide a rationale for using technology in the educational process; (b) identify contributions of major leaders in the field of educational media technology and instructional theory, and the impact that each leader has had on the field; (c) assess current trends in the area of educational media technology and relate the trends to past events and future implications; (d) integrate technology into instructional programs; (e) teach the operation and various uses of educational technology in instruction; (f) act as consultants/facilitators in educational media technology; (g) design and develop instructional products to meet specified needs; and (h) evaluate the effectiveness of instructional materials and systems.

Features – Courses in our 30 credit hour Educational Media & Technology (EDMT) program include technology and the reflective teacher, technology and student-centered learning, technology enhanced learning environments, issues and emerging technologies, instructional design, development of online materials, psychology of the adult learner, principles of classroom learning, curriculum foundations, research seminar and seminar in educational technology. Since Spring 2003, all of the EDMT courses have been taught online. The program can be completed online. Students who do not want to receive a masters degree can apply for admission to our 20 credit hour Educational Media and Technology certificate. The EDMT courses for the certificate are also offered online.

Admission Requirements – Individuals seeking admission to this program must: 1-Comply with the Graduates School admission requirements. 2-Score 550 or better on the TOEFL and 5 or better on TWE, if a nonnative speaker of English. 3-Have a 2.75 undergraduate grade point average, or a 3.30 grade point average in 12 hours or more of work in a masters program. 4-Solicit three letters of reference. 5-Submit a statement of professional goals.

Degree Requirements – In order to graduate, each student is expected to: 1-Complete all work on an approved program of study. (30 semester hours) 2-Maintain a "B" (3.0 GPA) average or better on course work taken within the program. 3-Get a recommendation from the faculty adviser. 4-Fill out an application for graduation and obtain the advisers recommendation. 5-Meet all other requirements for a masters degree adopted by the Graduate School of Eastern Michigan University. 6-Complete a culminating experience (research, instructional development or evaluation project) as determined by the student and faculty adviser.

Number of Full-Time Faculty – 5; **Number of Other Faculty** – 0

Degrees awarded in 2008–2009 Academic Year – **Masters** – 10; **PhD** – 0; **Other** – 0

Grant Monies awarded in 2008–2009 Academic Year – 0

Name of Institution – Michigan State University

Name of Department or Program – College of Education

Address:
509D Erickson Hall
East Lansing, MI
48824
US

Phone Number – 517-432-7195 **Fax Number** – 517-353-6393

Email Contact – msumaet@msu.edu **URL** – http://edutech.msu.edu

Contact Person – Leigh Wolf

Specializations – M.A. in Educational Technology with Learning, Design and Technology specialization.

Features – Extensive opportunities to work with faculty in designing online courses and online learning environments.

Admission Requirements – Please visit: http://edutech.msu.edu/apply_masters. html

Degree Requirements – 30 semester hours, Web-based portfolio.

Number of Full-Time Faculty – 6; **Number of Other Faculty** – 6

Degrees awarded in 2008–2009 Academic Year – **Masters** – 40; **PhD** – 0; **Other** – 0

Grant Monies awarded in 2008–2009 Academic Year – 0

Name of Institution – Wayne State University

Name of Department or Program – Instructional Technology

Address:
381 Education
Detroit, MI
48202
US

Phone Number – (313)577-1728 **Fax Number** – (313)577-1693

Email Contact – tspannaus@wayne.edu **URL** – http://www2.coe.wayne.edu/aos/it

Contact Person – Timothy W. Spannaus, PhD, Program Coord., Instructional Technology Programs, Div. of Administrative and Organizational Studies, College of Education.

Specializations – M.Ed. degrees in Instructional Design, Performance Improvement and Training, K-12 Technology Integration, and Interactive Technologies. Ed.D. and Ph.D. programs to prepare individuals for leadership in academic, business, industry, health care, and the K-12 school setting as professor, researcher, instructional design and development specialists; media or learning resources managers or consultants; specialists in instructional video; and web-based instruction and multimedia specialists. The school also offers a six-year specialist degree program in Instructional Technology. The IT program offers certificates in Online Learning, Educational Technology, and University Teaching.

Features – Guided experiences in instructional design and development activities in business and industry are available. M.Ed. programs are available face to face and online.

Admission Requirements – Ph.D.: Masters degree, 3.5 GPA, GRE, strong academic recommendations, interview.

Degree Requirements – Ph.D. 113 Cr. Hrs, including IT core and electives, research courses, graduate seminars, 30 cr. dissertation. M.Ed.: 36 semester hours, including required project; internship recommended.

Number of Full-Time Faculty – 6; **Number of Other Faculty** – 10

Degrees awarded in 2008–2009 Academic Year – **Masters** – 48; **PhD** – 11; **Other** – 8

Grant Monies awarded in 2008–2009 Academic Year – 750000

Name of Institution – Walden University

Address:
155 5th Avenue South
Minneapolis, Minnesota
55401
US

Phone Number – (800)444-6795

Email Contact – info@waldenu.edu. **URL** – http://www.waldenu.edu; http://www.waldenu.edu/ecti/ecti.html.

Contact Person – Dr. Gwen Hillesheim, Chair

Specializations – M.S. in Educational Change and Technology Innovation. Ph.D. in Education in Learning and Teaching with specialization in Educational Technology. In 1998 a specialization in Distance Learning will be added. In addition, there is a generalist Ph.D. in Education in which students may choose and design their own areas of specialization.

Features – delivered primarily online.

Admission Requirements – accredited Bachelor's. Ph.D.: accredited Master's, goal statement, letters of recommendation

Degree Requirements – Master's: 45 credit curriculum, 2 brief residencies, Master's project.

Number of Full-Time Faculty – 0; **Number of Other Faculty** – 0

Degrees awarded in 2008–2009 Academic Year – Masters – 0; **PhD** – 0; **Other** – 0

Grant Monies awarded in 2008–2009 Academic Year – 0

Name of Institution – Northwest Missouri State University

Name of Department or Program – Department of Computer Science/Information Systems

Address:
800 University Ave.
Maryville, Missouri
64468
US

Phone Number – (660)562-1600. **Fax Number** – 660-562-1963

Email Contact – nzeliff@nwmissouri.edu **URL** – http://www.nwmissouri.edu/csis

Contact Person – Dr. Nancy Zeliff

Specializations – M.S.Ed. in Instructional Technology. Certificate Program in Instructional Technology.

Features – These degrees are designed for industry trainers and computer educators at the elementary, middle school, high school, and junior college level.

Admission Requirements – 3.0 undergraduate GPA, 700 GRE (V+Q).

Degree Requirements – 32 semester hours of graduate courses in computer science, education and instructional technology courses. Fifteen hours of computer education and instructional technology courses for the certificate.

Number of Full-Time Faculty – 5; **Number of Other Faculty** – 7

Degrees awarded in 2008–2009 Academic Year – Masters – 10; **PhD** – 0; **Other** – 0

Grant Monies awarded in 2008–2009 Academic Year – 0

Name of Institution – St. Cloud State University

Name of Department or Program – College of Education

Address:
720 Fourth Avenue South
St. Cloud, MN
56301-4498
US

Phone Number – (308)255-2062 **Fax Number** – (308)255-4778

Email Contact – cim@stcloudstate.edu **URL** – http://www.stcloudstate.edu/cim

Contact Person – Merton E. Thompson Coordinator, Center for Information Media.

Specializations – Undergraduate major and minor in Information Media. Undergraduate certificate in Instructional Technology. Masters degrees in Information Technologies, Educational Media, and Instructional Design & Training. Graduate certificates in Instructional Technology, Design for E-learning, and School Library Media.

Features – Most courses are available online as well as face to face.

Admission Requirements – acceptance to Graduate School, written and oral preliminary examination

Degree Requirements – Master's: 42 semester credits with thesis; 39 semester credits with starred paper or portfolio; 200-hour practicum is required for library media licensure. Course work for licensure may be applied to Educational Media Master's program.

Number of Full-Time Faculty – 5; **Number of Other Faculty** – 21

Degrees awarded in 2008–2009 Academic Year – **Masters** – 15; **PhD** – 0; **Other** – 0

Grant Monies awarded in 2008–2009 Academic Year – 0

Name of Institution – University of Missouri-Columbia

Name of Department or Program – School of Information Science & Learning Technologies

Address:
303 Townsend Hall
Columbia, MO
65211
US

Phone Number – (573)884-2670 **Fax Number** – (573)884-2917

Email Contact – wedmanj@missouri.edu **URL** – http://sislt.missouri.edu

Contact Person – John Wedman

Specializations – The Educational Technology program takes a theory-based approach to designing, developing, implementing, and researching computer-mediated environments to support human activity. We seek individuals who are committed to life-long learning and who aspire to use advanced technology to improve human learning and performance. Graduates of the program will find opportunities to use their knowledge and competencies as classroom teachers, media specialists, district technology specialists and coordinators, designers and developers of technology-based learning and information systems, training specialists for businesses, medical settings, and public institutions, as well as other creative positions. The curriculum at the Masters and Specialist levels has two focus areas: Technology in Schools and Learning Systems Design and Development; with coursework tailored to each focus area. For information regarding our PhD, see http://education. missouri.edu/SISLT/PhD/index.php

Features – Both focus areas are available online via the Internet or on the MU campus. The Technology in Schools focus area is based on the ISTE competencies and culminates in an online portfolio based on these competencies. Several courses are augmented by technical resources developed at MU, including a technology integration knowledge repository and online collaboration tools. The Learning Systems Design and Development focus area links to business, military, and government contexts. This focus area offers a challenging balance of design and development coursework, in addition to coursework dealing with needs assessment and evaluation. For information regarding our PhD, see http://sislt.missouri.edu/phd

Admission Requirements – Master: Bachelors degree, GRE (V>500; A>500; W>3.5) EdS: Masters degree, GRE (V>500; A>500; W>3.5) Ph.D.: 3.5 graduate GPA, GRE (V>500; A>500; W>3.5) See website for details

Degree Requirements – Masters and EdS: Minimum of 30 graduate credit hours required for the degree; 15 hours of upper division coursework. Maximum of 6 hours of transfer credit. PhD. See website for details

Number of Full-Time Faculty – 10; **Number of Other Faculty** – 8

Degrees awarded in 2008–2009 Academic Year – Masters – 59; **PhD** – 10; **Other** – 18

Grant Monies awarded in 2008–2009 Academic Year – 1585885

Name of Institution – The University of Southern Mississippi

Name of Department or Program – Instructional Technnology and Design

Address:
118 College Drive #5036
Hattiesburg, MS
39406-0001
US

Phone Number – 601-266-4446 **Fax Number** – 601-266-5957

Email Contact – Taralynn.Hartsell@usm.edu **URL** – http://dragon.ep.usm.edu/~it

Contact Person – Dr. Taralynn Hartsell

Specializations – The Department of Technology Education at the University of Southern Mississippi has two graduate programs relating to Instructional Technology and Design. The Masters of Science in Instructional Technology is a 33–36 hour program, and the Ph.D. of Instructional Technology and Design is a 60–75 hour program.

Features – The Masters of Science concentrates more on the technology application and integration aspect that helps students learn both hands-on application of technology, as well as theoretical and historical aspects related to the field of study. A majority of the coursework in the program can be completed online (about 70%), and the remaining coursework are hybrid or blended in nature (about 60% online and 40% traditional). The Ph.D. program is a new advanced study program for those wishing to pursue their education in the application of technology and design, research, and leadership (begins in Fall 2009). The Ph.D. program also has two emphasis areas that meet student's needs: instructional technology or instructional design. A majority of the coursework in the program can be completed online (between 60 and 80% depending upon emphasis area selected), and the remaining coursework are hybrid or blended in form (about 60% online and 40% traditional).

Admission Requirements – Please review the IT Web site for more information on the application procedures for each program: http://dragon.ep.usm.edu/~it. The GRE is mandatory for graduate programs.

Degree Requirements – Please review the IT Web site for more information on degree requirements for each program: http://dragon.ep.usm.edu/~it

Number of Full-Time Faculty – 4; **Number of Other Faculty** – 2

Degrees awarded in 2008–2009 Academic Year – Masters – 7; **PhD** – 0; **Other** – 0

Grant Monies awarded in 2008–2009 Academic Year – 0

Name of Institution – University of Montana

Name of Department or Program – School of Education

Address:
32 Campus Drive
Missoula, MT
59812
US

Phone Number – (406)243-2563 **Fax Number** – (406)243-4908

Email Contact – sally.brewer@mso.umt.edu **URL** – http://www.umt.edu

Contact Person – Dr. Sally Brewer, Associate Professor of Library/Media

Specializations – M.Ed. and Specialist degrees; K-12 School Library Media specialization with Library Media endorsement Not represented in the rest of this is that we also have a Masters in Curricular Studies with an option in Instructional Design for Technology. Dr. Martin Horejsi is the coordinator of this program. His phone is 406.243.5785. His email is martin.horejsi@umontana.edu This program is 37 credits and can be taken totally online. There are 3 full-time faculty members in this program.

Features – Combined online program with University of Montana-Western in Dillon, MT. 25 credits.

Admission Requirements – (both degrees): GRE, letters of recommendation, 2.75 GPA

Degree Requirements – M.Ed.: 37 semester credit hours (18 overlap with library media endorsement). Specialist: 28 semester hours (18 overlap).

Number of Full-Time Faculty – 3; **Number of Other Faculty** – 1

Degrees awarded in 2008–2009 Academic Year – Masters – 2; PhD – 0; **Other** – 19

Grant Monies awarded in 2008–2009 Academic Year – 0

Name of Institution – East Carolina University

Name of Department or Program – Department of Mathematics, Science, and Instructional Technology Education

Address:
MSITE Department, Mail Stop 566 East Carolina University
Greenville, NC
27858-4353
US

Phone Number – (252)328-9353 **Fax Number** – (252)328-4368

Email Contact – browncar@mail.ecu.edu **URL** – http://www.ecu.edu/educ/msite/it/maed/index.cfm

Contact Person – Dr. Carol Brown, MAEd Program Coordinator

Specializations – Master of Arts in Education (North Carolina Instructional Technology Specialist licensure); Master of Science in Instructional Technology; Certificate in Distance Education; Certificate in Virtual Reality in Education and Training; Certificate in Performance Improvement; Certificate for Special Endorsement in Computer Education.

Features – M.A.Ed. graduates are eligible for North Carolina Instructional Technology certification; Cert. for Special Endorsement in Computer Education for North Carolina Licensure as Technology Facilitator. ALL programs available 100% online. The program is housed in the Department of Mathematics, Science, and

Instructional Technology Education. An important mission for this program is the emphasis on STEM in K12 schools including support of math and science teachers who are teacher leaders in their school systems.

Admission Requirements – Bachelor's degree; Admission to East Carolina University Graduate School. GRE [or Millers Analogy Test], references, and writing sample.

Degree Requirements – M.A.Ed.: 39 semester hours;

Number of Full-Time Faculty – 7; **Number of Other Faculty** – 2

Degrees awarded in 2008–2009 Academic Year – Masters – 48; **PhD** – 0; **Other** – 0

Grant Monies awarded in 2008–2009 Academic Year – 0

Name of Institution – North Carolina State University

Name of Department or Program – Department of Curriculum and Instruction, Instructional Technology Program

Address:
602 Poe Hall, Campus Box 7801
Raleigh, NC
27695-7801
US

Phone Number – (919) 515-6229 **Fax Number** – (919) 515-6978

Email Contact – kevin_oliver@ncsu.edu **URL** – http://ced.ncsu.edu/ci/it/index.php

Contact Person – Dr. Kevin Oliver, Assistant Professor

Specializations – Certificate in E-Learning. M.Ed. and M.S. in Instructional Technology. Ph.D. in Curriculum and Instruction with a concentration in Instructional Technology.

Features – Fully online E-Learning Certificate and Masters programs with flexibility for residents near the Raleigh-Durham area to take some on-campus courses if they wish. Doctoral program is not online. A limited number of assistantships are available for students who live near Raleigh, go to school full-time (9 hours/semester), and can work on campus 20 hours per week. Pays $15k per semester with health benefits and tuition remission.

Admission Requirements – Master's: undergraduate degree from an accredited institution, 3.0 GPA in major or in latest graduate degree program; transcripts; GRE or MAT scores; 3 references; goal statement. Ph.D.: undergraduate degree from accredited institution, 3.0 GPA in major or latest graduate program; transcripts; recent GRE scores, writing sample, three references, vita, research and professional goals statement (see http://ced.ncsu.edu/ci/admissions.php).

Degree Requirements – Masters: 36 semester hours, internship, thesis optional (note, the number of hours required for the Masters may reduce from 36 to 30 in Fall 2009). Ph.D.: 72 hours beyond Bachelors (minimum 33 in Curriculum and Instruction core, 27 in Research). Up to 12 hours of graduate-level transfer credits may be applied to any Masters or Ph.D. program. The transfer credits should be in Instructional Technology or similar to another required course in a program area.

Number of Full-Time Faculty – 3; **Number of Other Faculty** – 3

Degrees awarded in 2008–2009 Academic Year – Masters – 2; **PhD** – 1; **Other** – 0

Grant Monies awarded in 2008–2009 Academic Year – 300000

Name of Institution – University of North Carolina

Name of Department or Program – School of Information and Library Science

Address:
100 Manning Hall, CB#3360
Chapel Hill, NC
27599-3360
US

Phone Number – (919)843-5276 **Fax Number** – (919)962-8071

Email Contact – smhughes@email.unc.edu **URL** – http://www.ils.unc.edu/

Contact Person – Sandra Hughes-Hassell, Associate Professor, Coord., School Media Program

Specializations – Master of Science Degree in Library Science (M.S.L.S.) with specialization in school library media. Post-Masters certification program

Features – Rigorous academic program plus field experience requirement; excellent placement record.

Admission Requirements – Competitive admission based on all three GRE components (quantitative, qualitative, analytical), undergraduate GPA (plus graduate work if any), letters of recommendation, and student statement of career interest and school choice.

Degree Requirements – 48 semester hours, field experience, comprehensive exam, Master's paper

Number of Full-Time Faculty – 31; **Number of Other Faculty** – 1

Degrees awarded in 2008–2009 Academic Year – Masters – 111; **PhD** – 3; **Other** – 22

Grant Monies awarded in 2008–2009 Academic Year – 6843136

Name of Institution – University of Nebraska at Kearney

Name of Department or Program – Teacher Education

Address:
905 West 25th Street
Kearney, NE
68849-5540
US

Phone Number – (308)865-8833 **Fax Number** – (308)865-8097

Email Contact – fredricksons@unk.edu **URL** – http://www.unk.edu/academics/ecampus.aspx?id=6217

Contact Person – Dr. Scott Fredrickson, Professor and Chair of the Instructional Technology Graduate Program

Specializations – M.S.ED in Instructional Technology, M.S.ED in Library Media.

Features – Two main emphasis areas – Instructional Technology and Library Media;

Admission Requirements – M.S. GRE (or electronic portfolio meeting dept. requirements), acceptance into graduate school, approval of Instructional Technology Committee

Degree Requirements – M.S.: 36 credit hours, Instructional technology project or field study.

Number of Full-Time Faculty – 5; **Number of Other Faculty** – 24

Degrees awarded in 2008–2009 Academic Year – Masters – 40; **PhD** – 0; **Other** – 0

Grant Monies awarded in 2008–2009 Academic Year – 0

Name of Institution – University of Nebraska-Omaha

Name of Department or Program – Department of Teacher Education

Address:
College of Education, Kayser Hall 514G
Omaha, NE
68182
US

Phone Number – (402)554-2119 **Fax Number** – (402)554-2125

Email Contact – rpasco@unomaha.edu **URL** – http://www.unomaha.edu/libraryed/

Contact Person – Dr. R. J. Pasco

Specializations – Undergraduate Library Science Program public, academic and special libraries) School Library Media Endorsement (undergraduate and Graduate) M.S. in Secondary Education with School Library Media concentration M.S. in Elementary Education with School Library Media concentration M.S. in Reading with School Library Media concentration Masters in Library Science Program (Cooperative program with University of Missouri)

Features – Web-assisted format (combination of online and on-campus) for both undergraduate and graduate programs. School Library programs nationally recognized by American Association of School Librarians (AASL) Public, Academic and Special Libraries programs Cooperative UNO/University of Missouri MLS program is ALA accredited

Admission Requirements – As per University of Nebraska at Omaha undergraduate and graduate admissions requirements

Degree Requirements – School Library Media Endorsement (Undergraduate and Graduate) – 33 hours M.S. in Secondary and Elementary Education, M.A. in Secondary and Elementary Education, both with School Library Media concentration – 36 hours M.S. in Reading with School Library Media concentration – 36 hours Masters in Library Science Program (Cooperative program with University of Missouri at Columbia) – 42 hours

Number of Full-Time Faculty – 1; **Number of Other Faculty** – 10

Degrees awarded in 2008–2009 Academic Year – **Masters** – 41; **PhD** – 0; **Other** – 13

Grant Monies awarded in 2008–2009 Academic Year – 10000

Name of Institution – Rutgers-The State University of New Jersey

Name of Department or Program – School of Communication and Information

Address:
4 Huntington Street New Brunswick NJ USA
New Brunswick, NJ
08901-1071
US

Phone Number – (732)932-7500 Ext 8264 **Fax Number** – (732)932-2644

Email Contact – kcassell@rutgers.edu **URL** – http://www.comminfo.rutgers.edu/

Contact Person – Dr. Kay Cassell, Director, Master of Library and Information Science, Dept. of Library and Information Studies, School of Communication, Information and Library Studies. (732)932-7500 Ext 8955. Fax (732)932-2644. Dr. Michael Lesk, Chair.

Specializations – The Master of Library and Information Science (M.L.I.S.) program provides professional education for a wide variety of service and management careers in libraries, information agencies, the information industry, and in business, industry, government, research, and similar environments where information is a vital resource. Specializations include: school library media; services for children and youth; digital libraries; information retrieval/information systems; knowledge management (http://comminfo.rutgers.edu/master-of-library-and-information-science/curriculum-overview.html)

Features – The M.L.I.S. program, available both oncampus and online, is organized around six themes in the field of library and information science: human–information interaction; information access; information and society; information systems; management; and organization of information. Six lead courses, one in each area, form the foundation of the curriculum and offer general knowledge of the major principles and issues of the field. Two or more central courses in each theme offer basic understanding and competencies in important components of the field. Specialization courses in each theme allow students to develop expertise in preparation for specific career objectives. The specialization in School Librarianship is certified with the NJ Department of Education. All students on campus in the New Brunswick M.L.I.S. program work with an advisor to plan a course of study appropriate for their interests and career objectives.

Admission Requirements – A bachelors degree or its equivalent from a recognized institution of higher education with a B average or better; GRE scores; Personal statement which presents a view of the library and information science profession and applicants aspirations and goals in the library and information science professions; 3 Letters of recommendation which focus on the applicants academic capacity to undertake a rigorous program of graduate study.

Degree Requirements – A minimum of thirty-six credits, or twelve courses, is required to earn the M.L.I.S. degree. All students are required to enroll in two non-credit classes, 501 – Introduction to Library and Information Professions in their first semester, and 502 – Colloquium in a later semester. There are no language requirements for the M.L.I.S. degree, and there is no thesis or comprehensive examination.

Number of Full-Time Faculty – 22; **Number of Other Faculty** – 15

Degrees awarded in 2008–2009 Academic Year – Masters – 144; **PhD** – 3; **Other** – 0

Grant Monies awarded in 2008–2009 Academic Year – 500000

Name of Institution – Appalachian State University

Name of Department or Program – Department of Curriculum and Instruction

Address:
College of Education
Boone, North Carolina
28608
US

Phone Number – 828-262-2277 **Fax Number** – 828-262-2686

Email Contact – muffoletto@appstate.edu;riedlre@appstate.edu **URL** – http://edtech.ced.appstate.edu

Contact Person – Robert Muffoletto

Specializations – M.A. in Educational Media and Technology with three areas of concentration: Computers, Media Literacy, and Media Production. A plan of study in internet distance teaching is offered online. Two certificate programs: (1) Distance Learning – Internet delivered; (2) Media Literacy

Features – Business, university, community college, and public school partnership offers unusual opportunities for learning. The programs are focused on developing learning environments over instructional environments.

Admission Requirements – Undergraduate degree

Degree Requirements – 36 graduate semester hours. We also have certificates in (1) Distance Learning and (2) Media Literacy

Number of Full-Time Faculty – 0; **Number of Other Faculty** – 0

Degrees awarded in 2008–2009 Academic Year – **Masters** – 5; **PhD** – 0; **Other** – 0

Grant Monies awarded in 2008–2009 Academic Year – 0

Name of Institution – Buffalo State College

Name of Department or Program – Computer Information Systems Department

Address:
1300 Elmwood Avenue, Chase Hall 201
Buffalo, NY
14222-1095
US

Phone Number – (716) 878-5528 **Fax Number** – (716) 878-6677

Email Contact – gareause@buffalostate.edu **URL** – http://www.buffalostate.edu/cis/x471.xml

Contact Person – Dr. Stephen E. Gareau, Program Coordinator

Specializations – M.S. in Education in Educational Technology

Features – This program is designed for K-12 and higher education educators, as well as trainers from business and industry, who wish to develop and expand their knowledge and skills in the development and application of various educational technologies. A wide range of media and tools are covered in the program, including text, graphics, audio, video, animation, models, simulations, games, and Web tools.

Admission Requirements – Bachelor's degree from accredited institution, under-graduate 3.0 GPA, 3 letters of recommendation, one letter from applicant.

Degree Requirements – 36 semester hours. See http://www.buffalostate.edu/cis/x471.xml for full details.

Number of Full-Time Faculty – 3; **Number of Other Faculty** – 2

Degrees awarded in 2008–2009 Academic Year – **Masters** – 50; **PhD** – 0; **Other** – 0

Grant Monies awarded in 2008–2009 Academic Year – 25000

Name of Institution – Fordham University

Name of Department or Program – MA Program in Public Communications in the Department of Communication and Media Studies

Address:
Rose Hill Campus, 441 E. Fordham Rd.
Bronx, NY
10458
US

Phone Number – (718)817-4860 **Fax Number** – (718)817-4868

Email Contact – andersen@fordham.edu **URL** – http://www.fordham.edu

Contact Person – James VanOosting, Department Chair, Robin Andersen, Director of Graduate Studies

Specializations – The MA in Public Communications has three concentrations, (1) Media Analysis and Criticism, (2) Industries, Publics and Policy, (3) Screen Arts and Culture.

Features – Extensive Internship program: full-time students can complete program in twelve months, but many students take eighteen months to complete the program.

Admission Requirements – 3.0 undergraduate GPA. Fellowship Applicants must take the GREs.

Degree Requirements – 10 courses (30) credits and either a media project, or a research paper or an MA Thesis to complete the degree.

Number of Full-Time Faculty – 12; **Number of Other Faculty** – 4

Degrees awarded in 2008–2009 Academic Year – **Masters** – 19; **PhD** – 0; **Other** – 0

Grant Monies awarded in 2008–2009 Academic Year – 150000

Name of Institution – Ithaca College

Name of Department or Program – School of Communications

Address:
Park Hall
Ithaca, NY
14850
US

Phone Number – (607)274-1025 **Fax Number** – (607)274-7076

Email Contact – hkalman@ithaca.edu **URL** – http://www.ithaca.edu/gps/gradprograms/comm/

Contact Person – Howard K. Kalman, Associate Professor, Chair, Graduate Program in Communications; Roy H. Park, School of Communications.

Specializations – M.S. in Communications. Students in this program find employment in such areas as instructional design/training, web development, corporate/community/public relations and marketing, and employee communication. The program can be tailored to individual career goals.

Features – Program is interdisciplinary, incorporating organizational communication, instructional design, management, and technology.

Admission Requirements – 3.0 GPA, recommendations, statement of purpose, resume, application forms and transcripts, TOEFL 550 (or 213 computer-scored; 80 on the iBT version) where applicable.

Degree Requirements – 36 semester hours including capstone seminar.

Number of Full-Time Faculty – 6; **Number of Other Faculty** – 0

Degrees awarded in 2008–2009 Academic Year – Masters – 15; **PhD** – 0; **Other** – 0

Grant Monies awarded in 2008–2009 Academic Year – 0

Name of Institution – State University College of Arts and Science at Potsdam

Name of Department or Program – Information and Communication Technology

Address:
392 Dunn Hall
Potsdam, NY
13676
US

Phone Number – (315)267-2670 **Fax Number** – (315)267-3189

Email Contact – betrusak@potsdam.edu **URL** – http://www.potsdam.edu/ict

Contact Person – Dr. Anthony Betrus, Chair, Information and Communications Technology

Specializations – M.S. in Education in Instructional Technology with concentrations in: Educational Technology Specialist, K-12 Track Educational Technology Specialist, Non-K-12 Track Organizational Performance, Leadership, and Technology.

Features – A progressive, forward looking program with a balance of theoretical and hands-on practical coursework.

Admission Requirements – 1. Submission of an official transcript of an earned baccalaureate degree from an accredited institution. 2. A minimum GPA of 2.75 (4.0 scale) in the most recent 60 credit hours of coursework. 3. Submission of the Application for Graduate Study (w/$50 nonrefundable fee). 4. For students seeking the Educational Technology Specialist Certification, a valid NYS Teaching Certificate is required.

Degree Requirements – 36 semester hours, including internship or practicum; culminating project required

Number of Full-Time Faculty – 3; **Number of Other Faculty** – 3

Degrees awarded in 2008–2009 Academic Year – Masters – 32; **PhD** – 0; **Other** – 0

Grant Monies awarded in 2008–2009 Academic Year – 0

Name of Institution – Wright State University

Name of Department or Program – College of Education and Human Services, Dept. of Educational Leadership

Address:
421 Allyn Hall, 3640 Colonel Glenn Highway
Dayton, OH
45435
US

Phone Number – (937)775-2509 or (937)775-4148 **Fax Number** – (937)775-2405

Email Contact – susan.berg@wright.edu **URL** – http://www.cehs.wright.edu/academic/educational_leadership/lib-media/index.php

Contact Person – Dr. Susan Berg, Library Media Program Advisor

Specializations – M.Ed. or M.A. in Computer/Technology or Library Media

Features – Ohio licensure available in Multi-age library media (ages 3–21) Computer/technology endorsement Above licensure only available on a graduate basis. Multi-age library media licensure available in two tracks: initial (no previous teaching license) and advanced (with current teaching license in another field). The computer/technology endorsement must be added to a current teaching license.

Admission Requirements – Completed application with nonrefundable application fee, Bachelor's degree from accredited institution, official transcripts, 2.7 overall GPA for regular status (conditional acceptance possible), statement of purpose, satisfactory scores on MAT or GRE.

Degree Requirements – M.Ed. requires a comprehensive portfolio; M.A. requires a 6-hour thesis

Number of Full-Time Faculty – 3; **Number of Other Faculty** – 5

Degrees awarded in 2008–2009 Academic Year – Masters – 10; **PhD** – 0; **Other** – 0

Grant Monies awarded in 2008–2009 Academic Year – 0

Name of Institution – Kent State University

Name of Department or Program – Instructional Technology

Address:
405 White Hall
Kent, Ohio
44242
US

Phone Number – (330) 672-2294 **Fax Number** – (330) 672-2512

Email Contact – dtiene@kent.edu **URL** – http://www.ehhs.kent.edu/itec/

Contact Person – Dr. Drew Tiene, Coord., Instructional Technology Program

Specializations – M.Ed. or M.A. in Instructional Technology, and licensure programs in Computing/Technology and Library/Media; Ph.D. in Educational Psychology with specialization in Instructional Technology.

Features – Programs are planned with advisors to prepare students for careers in elementary, secondary, or higher education, business, industry, government agencies, or health facilities. Students may take advantage of independent research, individual study, practica, and internships. Most courses and programs can be taken online.

Admission Requirements – Master's: Bachelors degree with 3.00 undergraduate GPA

Degree Requirements – Master's: 37–42 semester hours; portfolio Doctoral: 45 postmasters semester hours; comprehensive exam; dissertation

Number of Full-Time Faculty – 4; **Number of Other Faculty** – 0

Degrees awarded in 2008–2009 Academic Year – Masters – 20; **PhD** – 3; **Other** – 0

Grant Monies awarded in 2008–2009 Academic Year – 0

Name of Institution – Ohio University

Name of Department or Program – Instructional Technology

Address:
250 McCracken Hall
Athens, Ohio
45701-2979
US

Phone Number – (740)597-1322 **Fax Number** – (740)593-0477

Email Contact – moored3@ohio.edu **URL** – http://www.ohio.edu/education/dept/
es/it/index.cfm

Contact Person – David Richard Moore, Instructional Technology Program
Coordinator

Specializations – M.Ed. in Computer Education and Technology. Ph.D. in
Curriculum and Instruction with a specialization in Instructional Technology also
available; call for details (740-593-4561) or visit the website: http://www.ohio.edu/
education/dept/es/it/index.cfm

Features – Masters program is a blended online delivery.

Admission Requirements – Bachelors degree, 3.0 undergraduate GPA, 35 MAT,
500 GRE (verbal), 400 GRE (quantitative), 550 TOEFL, three letters of recommendation, Paper describing future goals and career expectations from completing a
degree in our program.

Degree Requirements – Masters – 54 qtr. credits, electronic portfolio or optional
thesis worth 2–10 credits or alternative seminar research paper. Students may earn
two graduate degrees simultaneously in education and in any other field. PhD – 109
hours with 15 hours being dissertation work

Number of Full-Time Faculty – 4; **Number of Other Faculty** – 0

Degrees awarded in 2008–2009 Academic Year – Masters – 18; **PhD** – 10;
Other – 0

Grant Monies awarded in 2008–2009 Academic Year – 500000

Name of Institution – University of Cincinnati

Name of Department or Program – College of Education

Address:
401 Teachers College, ML002
Cincinnati, Ohio
45221-0002
US

Phone Number – (513)556-3579 **Fax Number** – (513)556-1001

Email Contact – richard.kretschmer@uc.edu **URL** – http://www.uc.edu/

Contact Person – Richard Kretschmer

Specializations – M.Ed. or Ed.D. in Curriculum and Instruction with an emphasis on Instructional Design and Technology; Educational Technology degree programs for current professional, technical, critical, and personal knowledge.

Features – Contact division for features

Admission Requirements – Bachelor's degree from accredited institution, 2.8 undergraduate GPA; GRE 1500 or better

Degree Requirements – 54 qtr. hours, written exam, thesis or research project (12–15 credit hours college core; 12–15 C&I; 18–27 credit hours specialization; 3–6 credit hours thesis or project).

Number of Full-Time Faculty – ; **Number of Other Faculty** –

Degrees awarded in 2008–2009 Academic Year – Masters – ; **PhD** – ; **Other** –

Grant Monies awarded in 2008–2009 Academic Year –

Name of Institution – University of Toledo

Name of Department or Program – Curriculum & Instruction

Address:
2801 W. Bancroft Street, Mail Stop 924
Toledo, Ohio
43606
US

Phone Number – (419)530-7979 **Fax Number** – (419)530-2466

Email Contact – Berhane.Teclehaimanot@utoledo.edu **URL** – http://tipt3.utoledo.edu

Contact Person – Berhane Teclehaimanot, Ph.D.

Specializations – Technology Using Educator/Technology Coordinator, Instructional Designer, and Performance Technologist

Features – Graduate students may concentrate in one of the three primary "roles," or may choose a blended program of study. Program was completely redesigned in 2004.

Admission Requirements – Master's: 3.0 undergrad. GPA, GRE (if undergrad. GPA < 2.7), recommendations; Doctorate: Master's degree, GRE, TOEFL (as necessary), recommendations, entrance writing samples, and interview.

Degree Requirements – Computer Technology Endorsement: 36 semester hours; Master's: 30 semester hours, culminating project; Doctorate: 60 semester hours (after Ms), major exams, dissertation.

Number of Full-Time Faculty – 3; **Number of Other Faculty** – 4

Degrees awarded in 2008–2009 Academic Year – Masters – 21; **PhD** – 4; **Other** – 1

Grant Monies awarded in 2008–2009 Academic Year – 0

Name of Institution – The University of Oklahoma

Name of Department or Program – Instructional Psychology and Technology, Department of Educational Psychology

Address:
321 Collings Hall
**Norman, OK
73019
US

Phone Number – (405)325-5974 **Fax Number** – (405)325-6655

Email Contact – bradshaw@ou.edu **URL** – http://education.ou.edu/ipt/

Contact Person – Dr. Amy Bradshaw, Program Area Coordinator

Specializations – Master's degree with emphases in Instructional Design & Technology (includes tracks: Instructional Design; and Interactive Learning Technologies), and Instructional Psychology & Technology (includes tracks: Instructional Psychology & Technology; Teaching & Assessment; Teaching & Learning; and Integrating Technology in Teaching). Doctoral degree in Instructional Psychology and Technology.

Features – Strong interweaving of principles of instructional psychology with instructional design and development. Application of IP&T in K-12, vocational education, higher education, business and industry, and governmental agencies.

Admission Requirements – Master's: acceptance by IPT program and Graduate College based on minimum 3.00 GPA for last 60 hours of undergraduate work or last 12 hours of graduate work; written statement that indicates goals and interests compatible with program goals. Doctoral: minimum 3.25 GPA, GRE scores, written statement that indicates goals and interests compatible with program goals, writing sample, and letters of recommendation.

Degree Requirements – Master's: 36 hours course work with 3.0 GPA; successful completion of thesis or comprehensive exam. Doctorate: see program description from institution or http://education.ou.edu/ipt/

Number of Full-Time Faculty – 11; **Number of Other Faculty** – 0

Degrees awarded in 2008–2009 Academic Year – Masters – 3; **PhD** – 2; **Other** – 0

Grant Monies awarded in 2008–2009 Academic Year – 0

Name of Institution – Bloomsburg University

Name of Department or Program – Instructional Technology & Institute for Interactive Technologies

Address:
2221 McCormick Bldg.
Bloomsburg, PA
17815
US

Phone Number – (717)389-48875 **Fax Number** – (717)389-4943

Email Contact – tphillip@bloomu.edu **URL** – http://iit.bloomu.edu

Contact Person – Dr. Timothy L. Phillips, contact person

Specializations – M.S. in Instructional Technology – Corporate Concentration M.S. in Instructional Technology – Instructional Technology Specialist Concentration (education M.S. Instructional Technology – Instructional Game and Interactive Environments Concentration (currently under development) eLearning Developer Certificate

Features – M.S. in Instructional Technology with emphasis on preparing for careers as Instructional Technologist in corporate, government, healthcare, higher education and K-12 educational settings. The program is highly applied and provides opportunities for students to work on real-world projects as part of their coursework. Our program offers a corporate concentration and an Instructional Technology Specialist Concentration for educators. The program offers a complete masters degree online as well as on campus. Graduate assistantships are available for full-time students. The program is closely associated with the nationally known Institute for Interactive Technologies.

Admission Requirements – Bachelors degree

Degree Requirements – 33 semester credits (27 credits + 6 credit thesis, or 30 credits + three credit internship).

Number of Full-Time Faculty – 5; **Number of Other Faculty** – 3

Degrees awarded in 2008–2009 Academic Year – Masters – 40; **PhD** – 0; **Other** – 5

Grant Monies awarded in 2008–2009 Academic Year – 400000

Name of Institution – Drexel University

Name of Department or Program – The iSchool at Drexel, College of Information Science and Technology

Address:
3141 Chestnut Street
Philadelphia, PA
19104-2875
US

Phone Number – (215) 895-2474 **Fax Number** – (215) 895-2494

Email Contact – info@ischool.drexel.edu **URL** – http://www.ischool.drexel.edu

Contact Person – Dr. David E. Fenske, Dean

Specializations – The ALA-accredited Master of Science (MS) in Library and Information Science curriculum prepares professionals for information-providing organizations. In April 2009, the MS was ranked 9th among library science programs in the nation, according to U.S. News & World Report's "America's Best Graduate Schools." The MS degree qualifies students for a wide variety of positions, including school library media specialist. Students may formally declare a concentration in School Library Media, Youth Services, Competitive Intelligence and Knowledge Management, Digital Libraries, or Information and Library Services. The School Library Media concentration is for students who wish to work in K-12 school library programs in both public and private schools. Designed to prepare graduates to be eligible for certification as school librarians by the Pennsylvania Department of Education (PDE), the program meets the requirements of the State of Pennsylvania and provides a strong basis for seeking certification in other states as well. Three course sequences are available within the concentration: one for students who have no prior teaching certification from PDE; one for students who have prior teaching certification from PDE and who wish to add school librarian certification to their credentials; and one for students with ALA-accredited master's degrees who wish to seek school librarian certification from PDE. In addition to the concentrations outlined above, students may choose to specialize in Healthcare Informatics or Archival Management. In keeping with the flexibility and personal planning emphasis of the College's MS, students may also select a "no concentration" option. The College also offers a Master of Science in Information Systems (MSIS), a Master of Science in Software Engineering (MSSE), and a Ph.D. There is an Advanced Certificate in Information Studies and Technology which is a nondegree program providing specialized training beyond the masters degree, and an online Certificate in Healthcare Informatics providing knowledge and skills in the application of information technology (IT) in the provision of healthcare.

Features – The MS degree (as well as the MSIS and MSSE) is offered on campus and online. Students may take the degree completely on campus, completely online, or as a mixture of the two. Currently, all courses in the School Library Media Concentration except the Field Study (INFO 891) are offered online. INFO 891 must be completed in approved sites and is augmented with an online seminar.

Admission Requirements – Admission Requirements for the masters program: Official Graduate Record Exam (GRE) Scores (may be waived with a 3.2 GPA CUM or in the last half (credits) of a completed undergraduate or graduate degree; department decision). For a full list of admission requirements, visit the website at www.ischool.drexel.edu

Degree Requirements – 15 courses. Additional coursework is required for those seeking teaching certification in Pennsylvania.

Number of Full-Time Faculty – 38; **Number of Other Faculty** – 73

Degrees awarded in 2008–2009 Academic Year – Masters – 332; **PhD** – 9; **Other** – 91

Grant Monies awarded in 2008–2009 Academic Year – 2000000

Name of Institution – Lehigh University

Name of Department or Program – Teaching, Learning, and Technology

Address:
111 Research Drive
Bethlehem, PA
18015
US

Phone Number – (610)758-3249 **Fax Number** – (610)758-6223

Email Contact – TLTProgram@Lehigh.edu **URL** – http://www.lehigh.edu/education/tlt/

Contact Person – MJ Bishop, Associate Professor and Teaching, Learning, and Technology Program Coordinator

Specializations – M.S. in Instructional Technology: Emphasizes implementation, integration, and evaluation of technology in school settings. The degree is well suited to both classroom teachers and technology specialists. Graduate certificate in Technology Use in the Schools: This twelve-credit grad certificate focuses on integrating technology into daily practice in the schools. Ph.D. in Learning Sciences and Technology: Emphasizes cognitive processes and their implications for the design, implementation, and evaluation of technology-based teaching and learning products in a variety of settings. Involves university-wide coursework in departments in all four colleges of the university.

Features – High level of integration with teacher education and certification, leading to a practical and quickly applicable program of study. Our Integrated Professional Development School approach offers further opportunities to get into the schools and work on solving meaningful teaching and learning problems, not just "tech support." Both masters and doctoral students collaborate with faculty on projects and studies (including national presentation and publication).

Admission Requirements – M.S. (competitive): 3.0 undergraduate GPA or 3.0 graduate GPA, GREs recommended, transcripts, at least 2 letters of recommendation, statement of personal and professional goals, application fee. Application deadlines: July 15 for fall admission, Dec 1 for spring admission, Apr 30 for summer admission. Ph.D. (highly competitive): 3.5 graduate GPA, GREs required. Copy of two extended pieces of writing (or publications); statement of future professional goals; statement of why Lehigh best place to meet those goals; identification of which presentations, publications, or research by Lehigh faculty attracted applicant to Lehigh. Application deadline: February 1 (admission only once per year from competitive pool)

Degree Requirements – M.S.: 30 credits; thesis option. Ph.D.: 72 credits past bachelors or 48 credits past masters (including dissertation). Qualifying Research Project (publication quality) + Comprehensive Exams (written and oral) + dissertation.

Number of Full-Time Faculty – 6; **Number of Other Faculty** – 7

Degrees awarded in 2008–2009 Academic Year – **Masters** – 40; **PhD** – 2; **Other** – 0

Grant Monies awarded in 2008–2009 Academic Year – 1000000

Name of Institution – Pennsylvania State University

Name of Department or Program – Instructional Systems

Address:
314 Keller Bldg.
University Park, PA
16802
US

Phone Number – (814)865-0473 **Fax Number** – (814)865-0128

Email Contact – nxc1@psu.edu **URL** – http://www.ed.psu.edu/insys/

Contact Person – Priya Sharma, Associate Professor of Education, Professor in Charge of Instructional Systems

Specializations – M.Ed., M.S., D.Ed, and Ph.D. in Instructional Systems. Current teaching emphases are on Learning Technology Design, Educational Systems Design, Learning Sciences, and Corporate Training. Research interests include multimedia, visual learning, educational reform, emerging technologies, constructivist learning, open-ended learning environments, scaffolding, technology integration in classrooms, technology in higher education, change and diffusion of innovations.

Features – A common thread throughout all programs is that candidates have basic competencies in the understanding of human learning; instructional design, development, and evaluation; and research procedures. Practical experience is available in mediated independent learning, research, instructional development, computer-based education, and dissemination projects. Exceptional opportunities for collaboration with faculty (30%+ of publications and presentations are collaborative between faculty and students).

Admission Requirements – D.Ed., Ph.D.: GRE (including written GRE), TOEFL, transcript, three letters of recommendation, writing sample, vita or resume, and letter of application detailing rationale for interest in the degree, match with interests of faculty.

Degree Requirements – M.Ed.: 33 semester hours; M.S.: 36 hours, including either a thesis or project paper; doctoral: candidacy exam, courses, residency, comprehensives, dissertation

Number of Full-Time Faculty – 7; **Number of Other Faculty** – 5

Degrees awarded in 2008–2009 Academic Year – Masters – 28; **PhD** – 10; **Other** – 0

Grant Monies awarded in 2008–2009 Academic Year – 373028

Name of Institution – The University of Rhode Island

Name of Department or Program – Graduate School of Library and Information Studies

Address:
Rodman Hall, 94 W. Alumni Ave.
Kingston, RI
02881-0815
US

Phone Number – (401)874-2947 **Fax Number** – (401)874-4964

Email Contact – geaton@mail.uri.edu **URL** – http://www.uri.edu/artsci/lsc

Contact Person – E. Gale Eaton, Director

Specializations – M.L.I.S. degree with specialties in School Library Media Services, Information Literacy Instruction, Youth Services Librarianship, Public Librarianship, Academic Librarianship, and Special Library Services.

Features – Fifteen-credit Post-Baccalaureate Certificate in Information Literacy Instruction

Admission Requirements – undergraduate GPA of 3.0, score in 50th percentile or higher on SAT or MAT, statement of purpose, current resume, letters of reference

Degree Requirements – 42 semester-credit program offered in Rhode Island and regionally in Worcester, MA and Durham, NH

Number of Full-Time Faculty – 7; **Number of Other Faculty** – 36

Degrees awarded in 2008–2009 Academic Year – Masters – 80; **PhD** – 0; **Other** – 0

Grant Monies awarded in 2008–2009 Academic Year – 0

Name of Institution – University of South Carolina Aiken and University of South Carolina Columbia

Name of Department or Program – Aiken: School of Education; Columbia: Department of Educational Psychology

Address:
471 University Parkway
Aiken, SC
29801
US

Phone Number – 803.641.3489 **Fax Number** – 803.641.3720

Email Contact – smyth@usca.edu **URL** – http://edtech.usca.edu

Contact Person – Dr. Thomas Smyth, Professor, Program Director

Specializations – Master of Education in Educational Technology (A Joint Program of The University of South Carolina Aiken and Columbia)

Features – The Masters Degree in Educational Technology is designed to provide advanced professional studies in graduate level coursework to develop capabilities essential to the effective design, evaluation, and delivery of technology-based instruction and training (e.g., software development, multimedia development, assistive technology modifications, web-based development, and distance learning). The program is intended (1) to prepare educators to assume leadership roles in the integration of educational technology into the school curriculum, and (2) to provide graduate-level instructional opportunities for several populations (e.g., classroom teachers, corporate trainers, educational software developers) that need to acquire both technological competencies and understanding of sound instructional design principles and techniques. The program is offered entirely online as high-quality, interactive, web-based courses. There are occasional optional meetings on the Columbia or Aiken campuses.

Admission Requirements – Application to the Educational Technology Program can be made after completion of at least the bachelor's degree from a college or university accredited by a regional accrediting agency. The standard for admission will be based on a total profile for the applicant. The successful applicant should have an undergraduate grade point average of at least 3.0, a score of 45 on the Miller's Analogies Test or scores of 450 on both the verbal and quantitative portions of the Graduate Record Exam, a well-written letter of intent that matches the objectives of the program and includes a description of previous technology experience, and positive letters of recommendation from individuals who know the professional characteristics of the applicant. Any exceptions for students failing to meet these standards shall be referred to the Admissions Committee for review and final decision.

Degree Requirements – 36 semester hours, including instructional theory, computer design, and integrated media

Number of Full-Time Faculty – 3; **Number of Other Faculty** – 3

Degrees awarded in 2008–2009 Academic Year – **Masters** – 11; **PhD** – 0; **Other** – 0

Grant Monies awarded in 2008–2009 Academic Year – 0

Name of Institution – Dakota State University

Name of Department or Program – Educational Technology

Address:
820 North Washington Ave.
Madison, SD
57042
US

Phone Number – 1-888-DSU-9988 **Fax Number** – (605) 256-5093

Email Contact – mark.hawkes@dsu.edu **URL** – http://www.dsu.edu/mset/index. aspx

Contact Person – Mark Hawkes

Specializations – The MSET program offers two specializations: Distance Education and Technology Systems. These specializations are indicated on the official transcript. Students who wish to choose one of these specializations or the technology endorsement must take designated electives as follows: Distance Education: CET 747 Web & ITV Based Applications of Dist Ed (3 credit hours) CET 749 Policy and Management of Distance Education (3 credit hours) CET 769 Adult Learning for Distance Education (3 credit hours) Technology Systems CET 747 Web & ITV Based Applications of Dist Ed (3 credit hours) CET 750 Multimedia II (2 credit hours) CET 753 Network Management in Educational Institutions (3 credit hours) CET 758 Advanced Instructional Programming (2 credit hours) K-12 Educational Technology Endorsement Individuals who hold or are eligible for teaching certification may earn the K-12 Educational Technology Endorsement by completing specified courses within the MSET program.

Features – The Master of Science in Educational Technology (MSET) is an instructional technology program designed to meet the rapidly increasing demand for educators who are trained to integrate computer technologies into the curriculum and instruction. As computers and technology have become a significant part of the teaching and learning process, addressing the information needs of teachers has become the key to integrating technology into the classroom and increasing student learning. The primary emphasis of the masters program is to prepare educators who can create learning environments that integrate computing technology into the teaching and learning process. The MSET degree is an advanced degree designed to equip educators to be: leaders in educational technology current in teaching and learning processes and practices current in research technologies and designs knowledgeable of technologies and programming skills knowledgeable of current, technology-based educational tools and products. Specifically by the end of the program, MSET students will understand the capabilities of the computer and its impact upon education. They will be proficient in the use and application of computer software and will be able to demonstrate proficiency in using computers and related technologies to improve their own and their students learning needs. The program integrates a highly technological environment with a project-based curriculum. Its focus is supported by an institutionally systemic belief that there is a substantial role for technology in teaching and learning in all educational environments.

Admission Requirements – Baccalaureate degree from an institution of higher education with full regional accreditation for that degree. Satisfactory scores on the GRE. The test must have been taken within the last five years. The GRE test can be waived if one of the following conditions is met: A cumulative grade point average of 3.25 or higher on a 4.0 scale for a baccalaureate degree from a regionally accredited college or university in the U.S. Official admission into and demonstrated success in a regionally accredited graduate program in the U.S. Demonstrated success is defined as grades of A or B in at least 12 hours of graduate work. OR Graduation from a regionally accredited college/university in the U.S. at least 15 years ago or more. Other factors (such as student maturity, references, or special expertise) also may be used to determine admission to the program. Also see program specific admission requirements for additional requirements. Demonstrated basic knowledge of computers and their applications for educational purposes. Basic knowledge can be demonstrated in one of the following ways: Technology endorsement from an accredited university; or in-service position as full- or part-time technology coordinator in a public school. A personal statement of technological competency. The statement should not exceed 2 pages and should be accompanied by supporting documentation or electronic references, e.g., URL.

Degree Requirements – The program requires a total of 36 credits beyond the baccalaureate degree. All students must take the following: 25 hours of required courses. 11 hours of electives. It is possible to specialize in either Distance Education or Technology Systems by selecting the designated electives for that specialization. You can also get a K-12 Educational Technology Endorsement. It is also possible to select the thesis option from among the electives. MSET courses are offered using a variety of distance delivery methods. At this time, one required course and one elective course has a limited length hands-on campus requirement. These courses are offered in summer and the residency requirement is limited to one week per course. Alternatives may be available for the distance student.

Number of Full-Time Faculty – 3; **Number of Other Faculty** – 5

Degrees awarded in 2008–2009 Academic Year – Masters – 30; **PhD** – 0; **Other** – 0

Grant Monies awarded in 2008–2009 Academic Year – 0

Name of Institution – Texas A&M University

Name of Department or Program – Educational Technology Program, Dept. of Educational psychology

Address:
College of Education & Human Development
College Station, Texas
77843-4225
US

Phone Number – (979)845-7276 **Fax Number** – (979)862-1256

Email Contact – zellner@tamu.edu **URL** – http://educ.coe.tamu.edu/~edtc

Contact Person – Ronald D. Zellner, Assoc. Prof., Coord. Program information/ Carol Wagner for admissions materials

Specializations – M.Ed. in Educational Technology; EDCI Ph.D. program with specializations in Educational Technology and in Distance Education; Ph.D. in Educational Psychology Foundations: Learning & Technology. The purpose of the Educational Technology Program is to prepare educators with the competencies required to improve the quality and effectiveness of instructional programs at all levels. A major emphasis is placed on multimedia instructional materials development and techniques for effective distance education and communication. Teacher preparation with a focus on field-based instruction and school to university collaboration is also a major component. The program goal is to prepare graduates with a wide range of skills to work as professionals and leaders in a variety of settings, including education, business, industry, and the military.

Features – Program facilities include laboratories for teaching, resource development, and production. Computer, video, and multimedia development are supported in a number of facilities. The college and university also maintain facilities for distance education materials development and fully equipped classrooms for course delivery to nearby collaborative school districts and sites throughout the state.

Admission Requirements – M.Ed.: Bachelors degree, (range of scores, no specific cut-offs) 400 GRE Verbal, 550 (213 computer version) TOEFL; Ph.D.: 3.0 GPA, 450 GRE Verbal. Composite score from GRE verbal & Quantitative and GPA, letters of recommendation, general background, and student goal statement.

Degree Requirements – M.Ed.: 39 semester credits, oral exam; Ph.D.: course work varies with student goals – degree is a Ph.D. in Educational Psychology Foundations with specialization in educational technology.

Number of Full-Time Faculty – 3; **Number of Other Faculty** – 0

Degrees awarded in 2008–2009 Academic Year – Masters – 8; **PhD** – 4; **Other** – 0

Grant Monies awarded in 2008–2009 Academic Year – 876000

Name of Institution – The University of Texas at Austin

Name of Department or Program – Curriculum & Instruction

Address:
406 Sanchez Building
Austin, Texas
78712-1294
US

Phone Number – (512)471-5942 **Fax Number** – (512)471-8460

Email Contact – Mliu@mail.utexas.edu **URL** – http://www.edb.utexas.edu/education/departments/ci/programs/it/

Contact Person – Min Liu, Ed.D., Professor and IT Program Area Coordinator/ Graduate Advisor

Specializations – The Instructional Technology (IT) Program at the University of Texas at Austin is a graduate program and offers degrees at the master and doctoral levels. Masters degrees in IT provide students with knowledge and skills of cutting-edge new media technologies, learning theories, instructional systems design, human–computer interaction, and evaluation. They prepare students to be practitioners in various educational settings, such as K-12, higher education, and training in business and industry. Ph.D. program provides knowledge and skills in areas such as instructional systems design, learning and instructional theories, instructional materials development, and design of learning environments using various emerging technology-based systems and tools. Graduates assume academic, administrative, and other leadership positions such as professors, instructional technologists at school district level, managers and researchers of instructional design and instructional evaluators.

Features – The program is interdisciplinary in nature, although certain competencies are required of all students. Programs of study and dissertation research are based on individual needs and career goals. Learning resources include state-of-art labs in the Learning Technology Center in the College of Education, and university-wide computer labs. Students can take courses offered by other departments and colleges as relevant to their interests. Students, applying to the program, have diverse backgrounds and pursue careers of their interests. The program caters students with both K-12 as well as corporate backgrounds.

Admission Requirements – Instructional Technology program considers only applications for Fall admission, with the deadline of December 15. November 15 – Deadline for consideration of financial award Admission decisions are rendered based on consideration of the entire applicant file, including GPA, test scores, references, experience, and stated goals. No single component carries any more significance than another. However, priority may be given to applicants who meet the following preferred criteria: GPA 3.0 or above GRE 1100 or above (verbal + quantitative, with at least 400 verbal) TOEFL 213 or above (computer)/550 or above (paper-based)/79 or 80 (Internet-based) TOEFL

Degree Requirements – see http://www.edb.utexas.edu/education/departments/ci/ programs/it/studentinfo/cstudents/grad/degrees/for details

Number of Full-Time Faculty – 4; **Number of Other Faculty** – 40

Degrees awarded in 2008–2009 Academic Year – Masters – 4; **PhD** – 5; **Other** – 0

Grant Monies awarded in 2008–2009 Academic Year – 133020

Name of Institution – East Tennessee State University

Name of Department or Program – College of Education, Dept. of Curriculum and Instruction

Address:
Box 70684
Johnson City, Tn
37614-0684
US

Phone Number – (423)439-7843 **Fax Number** – (423)439-8362

Email Contact – danielsh@etsu.edu **URL** – http://www.etsu.edu/coe/cuai/emet-ma.asp

Contact Person – Harold Lee Daniels

Specializations – (1) M. Ed. in School Library Media (2) M.Ed. in Educational Technology (3) School Library Media Specialist add on certification for those with current teaching license and a masters degree. (4) M.Ed. in Classroom Technology for those with teaching license.

Features – Two (MAC &PC) dedicated computer labs (45+ computers) Online and evening course offerings for part-time, commuter, and employed students. Student pricing/campus licensing on popular software (MS, Adobe, Macromedia, etc.) Off-site cohort programs for classroom teachers Extensive software library (900 + titles) with review/checkout privileges

Admission Requirements – Bachelor's degree from accredited institution with undergraduate GPA of 3.0 or higher, transcripts, personal application essay, interview, in some cases GRE may be required.

Degree Requirements – 36 semester hours, including 12 hours in common core of instructional technology and media, 18 professional content hours, and 5 credit hour practicum (200 field experience hours)

Number of Full-Time Faculty – 4; **Number of Other Faculty** – 4

Degrees awarded in 2008–2009 Academic Year – Masters – 18; **PhD** – 0; **Other** – 2

Grant Monies awarded in 2008–2009 Academic Year – 32000

Name of Institution – University of Tennessee-Knoxville

Name of Department or Program – Instructional Technology and Educational Studies, College of Education

Address:
A535 Claxton Addition
Knoxville, TN
37996-3456
US

***Phone Number – 865- 974-5037 **Fax Number** – .

Email Contact – ecounts1@utk.edu **URL** – http://ites.tennessee.edu/

Contact Person – Jay Pfaffman

Specializations – M.S. Ed.S. and Ph.D. in Ed. Concentrations in Curriculum/ Evaluation/Research and Instructional Technology; M.S. and Ph.D. in Ed. Concentration in Cultural Studies in Education

Features – course work in media production and management, advanced software production, utilization, research, theory, instructional computing, and instructional development.

Admission Requirements – See Graduate Catalog for current program requirements.

Degree Requirements – See Graduate Catalog for current program requirements.

Number of Full-Time Faculty – 0; **Number of Other Faculty** – 0

Degrees awarded in 2008–2009 Academic Year – **Masters** – 0; **PhD** – 0; **Other** – 0

Grant Monies awarded in 2008–2009 Academic Year – 0

Name of Institution – Texas Tech University

Name of Department or Program – Instructional Technology

Address:
Box 41071,TTU
Lubbock, TX
79409
US

Phone Number – (806)742-1998, ext. 433 **Fax Number** – (806)742-2179

Email Contact – Steven.Crooks@ttu.edu **URL** – http://www.educ.ttu.edu/edit

Contact Person – Dr. Steven Crooks, Program Coordinator, Instructional Technology

Specializations – M.Ed. in Instructional Technology; completely online M.Ed. in Instructional Technology; Ed.D. in Instructional Technology

Features – Program is NCATE accredited and follows ISTE and AECT guidelines.

Admission Requirements – Holistic evaluation based on GRE scores (Doctorate only), GPA, student goals and writing samples

Degree Requirements – M.Ed.: 39 hours (30 hours in educational technology, 6 hours in education, 3 hours electives). Ed.D.: 93 hours (60 hours in educational technology, 21 hours in education or resource area, 12 hours dissertation.

Number of Full-Time Faculty – 4; **Number of Other Faculty** – 2

Degrees awarded in 2008–2009 Academic Year – Masters – 11; PhD – 10; **Other** – 0

Grant Monies awarded in 2008–2009 Academic Year – 6000000

Name of Institution – University of Houston

Name of Department or Program – Curriculum & Instruction

Address:
256 Farish
Houston, TX
77204-5027
US

Phone Number – 713-743-4975 **Fax Number** – 713-743-4990

Email Contact – brobin@uh.edu **URL** – http://www.it.coe.uh.edu/

Contact Person – Bernard Robin

Specializations – Instructional design Urban community partnerships enhanced by technology Integration of technology in teacher education Visual representation of information Linking instructional technology with content area instruction Educational uses of digital media (including digital photography, digital video, and digital storytelling) Collaborative Design of Multimedia Uses of instructional technology in health science education

Features – The IT Program at the University of Houston can be distinguished from other IT programs at other institutions through our unique philosophy based on a strong commitment to the broad representations of community, the individual, and the collaboration that strengthens the two. We broadly perceive community to include our college, the university, and the local Houston environment. The community is a rich context and resource from which we can solicit authentic learning tasks and clients, and to which we can contribute new perspectives and meaningful products. Our students graduate with real-world experience that can only be gained by experience with extended and coordinated community-based projects, not by contrived course requirements. Our program actively seeks outside funding to promote and continue such authentic projects because we so strongly believe it is the best context in which our students can develop expertise in the field. We recognize that each student brings to our program a range of formal training, career experience, and future goals. Thus, no longer can we be satisfied with presenting a single, static curriculum and still effectively prepare students for a competitive marketplace. Our beliefs have led us to develop a program that recognizes and celebrates student individuality and diversity. Students work with advisors to develop a degree plan that begins from their existing knowledge and strives toward intended career goals. We aim to teach not specific software or hardware operations, but instead focus on transferable technical skills couched in solid problem-solving experiences, theoretical discussions, and a team-oriented atmosphere. Students work throughout the program to critically evaluate their own work for the purpose of compiling a performance portfolio that will accurately and comprehensively portray their individual abilities to themselves, faculty, and future employers. Completing our philosophical foundation is a continuous goal of collaboration. Our faculty operates from a broad collaborative understanding that recognizes how everyone involved in any process brings unique and valuable experiences and perspectives. Within the IT program, faculty, staff, and students rely on each other to contribute relevant expertise. Faculty members regularly seek collaboration with other faculty in the College of Education, especially those involved with teacher education, as well as with faculty in other schools across campus. Collaboration is a focus that has been infused through the design of our courses and our relationships with students.

Admission Requirements – Admission information for graduate programs: http://www.it.coe.uh.edu/ Masters program: 3.0 grade point average (GPA) for unconditional admission or a 2.6 GPA or above for conditional admission over the last 60 hours of coursework attempted Graduate Record Exam: The GRE must have been taken within five (5) years of the date of application for admission to any Graduate program in the College of Education. Doctoral program: Each applicant must normally have earned a masters degree or have completed 36 semester hours of appropriate graduate work with a minimum GPA of 3.0 (A = 4.0). Graduate Record Exam: The GRE must have been taken within five (5) years of the date of application for admission to any Graduate program in the College of Education.

Degree Requirements – Masters: Students with backgrounds in educational technology can complete the Masters program with 36 hours of coursework. For the typical student, the M.Ed. in Instructional Technology consists of 9 semester hours of core courses required by the College of Education, and an additional 18 hour core in Instructional Technology as well as 9 hours that are determined by the students career goals (K-12, higher education, business and industry). Students take a written comprehensive examination over the program, coursework, and experiences. Doctoral: The minimum hours required in the doctoral program is 66. More details about the courses and requirements can be found online at: http://coe.uh.edu/IT/doctorate.cfm

Number of Full-Time Faculty – 6; **Number of Other Faculty** – 0

Degrees awarded in 2008–2009 Academic Year – **Masters** – 15; **PhD** – 10; **Other** – 0

Grant Monies awarded in 2008–2009 Academic Year – 2000000

Name of Institution – University of North Texas

Name of Department or Program – Technology & Cognition (College of Education)

Address:
Box 311337
Denton, TX
76203-1337
US

Phone Number – (940)565-2057 **Fax Number** – (940)565-2185

Email Contact – iyoung@unt.edu **URL** – http://www.cecs.unt.edu

Contact Person – Dr. Mark Mortensen & Mrs. Donna Walton, Computer Education and Cognitive Systems. Dr. Jon Young, Chair, Dept. of Technology and Cognition.

Specializations – M.S. in Computer Education and Cognitive Systems – two emphasis areas: Instructional Systems Technology & Teaching & Learning with Technology. Ph.D. in Educational Computing. See www.cecs.unt.edu.

Features – Unique applications of theory through research and practice in curriculum integration of technology, digital media production, and web development. See www.cecs.unt.edu.

Admission Requirements – Toulouse Graduate School Requirements, 18 hours in education, acceptable GRE: 405 V,489 A, 3 Analytical Writing for M.S. Degree. Increased requirements for Ph.D. program.

Degree Requirements – 36 semester hours (12 hour core, 12 hour program course requirement based on M.S. track, 12 hour electives). see www.cecs.unt.edu.

Number of Full-Time Faculty – 0; **Number of Other Faculty** – 0

Degrees awarded in 2008–2009 Academic Year – Masters – 0; **PhD** – 0; **Other** – 0

Grant Monies awarded in 2008–2009 Academic Year – 0

Name of Institution – Brigham Young University

Name of Department or Program – Department of Instructional Psychology and Technology

Address:
150 MCKB, BYU
Provo, Utah
84602
US

Phone Number – (801)422-5097 **Fax Number** – (801)422-0314

Email Contact – andy-gibbons@byu.edu **URL** – http://www.byu.edu/ipt

Contact Person – Russell Osguthorpe, Prof., Chair.

Specializations – M.S. degrees in Instructional Design, Research and Evaluation, and Multimedia Production. Ph.D. degrees in Instructional Design, and Research and Evaluation

Features – Course offerings include principles of learning, instructional design, assessing learning outcomes, evaluation in education, empirical inquiry in education, project management, quantitative reasoning, microcomputer materials production, multimedia production, naturalistic inquiry, and more. Students participate in internships and projects related to development, evaluation, measurement, and research.

Admission Requirements – both degrees: transcript, 3 letters of recommendation, letter of intent, GRE scores. Apply by Feb 1. Students agree to live by the BYU Honor Code as a condition for admission

Degree Requirements – Master's: 38 semester hours, including prerequisite (3 hours), core courses (14 hours), specialization (12 hours), internship (3 hours), thesis or project (6 hours) with oral defense. Ph.D.: 94 semester hours beyond the Bachelor's degree, including: prerequisite and skill requirements (21 hours), core course (16 hours), specialization (18 hours), internship (12 hours), projects (9 hours), and dissertation (18 hours). The dissertation must be orally defended. Also, at least two consecutive 6-hour semesters must be completed in residence.

Number of Full-Time Faculty – 10; **Number of Other Faculty** – 0

Degrees awarded in 2008–2009 Academic Year – Masters – 15; **PhD** – 10; **Other** – 0

Grant Monies awarded in 2008–2009 Academic Year – 250000

Name of Institution – Utah State University

Name of Department or Program – Department of Instructional Technology & Learning Sciences, Emma Eccles Jones College of Education and Human Services

Address:
2830 Old Main Hill
Logan, Utah
84322-2830
US

Phone Number – (435)797-2694 **Fax Number** – (435)797-2693

Email Contact – mimi.recker@usu.edu **URL** – http://itls.usu.edu

Contact Person – Dr. Mimi Recker, Prof., Chair.

Specializations – M.S. and M.Ed. with concentrations in the areas of Instructional Technology, Learning Sciences, Multimedia, Educational Technology, and Information Technology/School Library Media Administration. Ph.D. in Instructional Technology & Learning Sciences is offered for individuals seeking to become professionally involved in instructional/learning sciences research and development in higher education, corporate education, public schools, community colleges, and government.

Features – M.Ed. programs in Instructional Technology/School Library Media Administration and Educational Technology are also available completely online. The doctoral program is built on a strong Master's and Specialists program in Instructional Technology. All doctoral students complete a core with the remainder of the course selection individualized, based upon career goals.

Admission Requirements – M.S. and Ed.S.: 3.0 GPA, a verbal and quantitative score at the 40th percentile on the GRE or 43 MAT, three written recommendations. Ph.D.: relevant Master's degree, 3.0 GPA, verbal and quantitative score at the 40th percentile on the GRE, three written recommendations, essay on research interests.

Degree Requirements – M.S.: 39 sem. hours; thesis or project option. Ed.S.: 30 sem. hours if M.S. is in the field, 40 hours if not. Ph.D.: 60 total hours, dissertation, 3-sem. residency, and comprehensive examination.

Number of Full-Time Faculty – 10; **Number of Other Faculty** – 1

Degrees awarded in 2008–2009 Academic Year – Masters – 48; **PhD** – 9; **Other** – 0

Grant Monies awarded in 2008–2009 Academic Year – 500000

Name of Institution – George Mason University

Name of Department or Program – Instructional Technology Programs

Address:
Mail Stop 5D6, 4400 University Dr.
Fairfax, VA
22030-4444
US

Phone Number – (703)993-3798 **Fax Number** – (703)993-2722

Email Contact – pnorton@gmu.edu **URL** – http://it.gse.gmu.edu/

Contact Person – Dr. Priscilla Norton, Coord. of Instructional Technology Academic Programs

Specializations – Learning Technologies Design Research PhD Program Masters Degrees Curriculum and Instruction with emphasis in Instructional Technology Track I – Instructional Design & Development Track II – Integration of Technology in Schools Track III – Assistive Technology Graduate Certificates eLearning Integration of Technology in Schools Teaching Secondary Students in Virtual Environments Assistive Technology

Features – The Instructional Technology program promotes the theory-based design of learning opportunities that maximize the teaching and learning process using a range of technology applications. Program efforts span a range of audiences, meeting the needs of diverse learners – school-aged, adult learners, and learners with disabilities – in public and private settings. Within this framework, the program emphasizes research, reflection, collaboration, leadership, and implementation and delivery models. The Instructional Technology (IT) program provides professionals with the specialized knowledge and skills needed to apply today's computer and telecommunications technologies to educational goals within school, community, and corporate settings. The IT program serves professional educators as well as those involved in instructional design, development, and training in government and private sectors. Master degrees and certificates can be earned in each of three program tracks. Refer to the IT website (http://it.gse.gmu.edu/) for detailed information on admissions, Track 1 – Instructional Design and Development (IDD) – Students are prepared to craft effective solutions within public, private, and educational contexts to instructional challenges by using the latest information technologies in the design and development of instructional materials. Track II – Integration of Technology in Schools (ITS) – Students are prepared to effectively integrate technology in the K-12 learning environment. Graduates frequently become the local expert and change agent for technology in schools. Track III – Assistive/ Special Education Technology (A/SET) – Graduates will use technology to assist individuals to function more effectively in school, home, work, and community environments. Graduates are prepared to incorporate technology into the roles of educators, related service providers, Assistive Technology consultants, hardware/ software designers, and school-based technology coordinators.

Admission Requirements – Teaching or training experience, undergrad GPA of 3.0, TOEFL of 575 (written)/230 (computer), three letters of recommendation, goal statement.

Degree Requirements – M.Ed. in Curriculum and Instruction Track I and III: 30 hours; practicum, internship, or project. M.Ed. in Curriculum and Instruction Track II: 36 hours; practicum M.Ed. in Special Education: 30 hours. Ph.D.: 56–62 hours beyond Master's degree for either specialization. Certificate programs: 15 hours

Number of Full-Time Faculty – 7; **Number of Other Faculty** – 5

Degrees awarded in 2008–2009 Academic Year – **Masters** – 130; **PhD** – 15; **Other** – 0

Grant Monies awarded in 2008–2009 Academic Year – 2500000

Name of Institution – Virginia Tech

Name of Department or Program – College of Liberal Arts and Human Sciences

Address:
144 J Smyth Hall
Blacksburg, VA
24061-0488
US

Phone Number – (540)231-5587 **Fax Number** – (540)231-9075

Email Contact – jburton@vt.edu **URL** – http://www.soe.vt.edu/idt/

Contact Person – John Burton, Program Area Leader, Instructional Design & Technology, Dept. of Learning Sciences & Technologies

Specializations – M.A., Ed.S. Ed.D., and Ph.D. in Instructional Design and Technology. Graduates of our Masters and Educational Specialist programs find themselves applying their expertise in a variety of rewarding, professional venues; for example, as instructional designers, trainers, or performance consultants in industrial settings and as teachers or technology coordinators in preK-12. Graduates of our Doctoral program typically assume exciting roles as faculty in higher education, advancing research in the field and preparing the next generation of instructional technologists for the profession.

Features – Areas of emphasis are Instructional Design, Distance Education, and Multimedia Development. Facilities include two computer labs, extensive digital video and audio equipment, distance education classroom, and computer graphics production areas.

Admission Requirements – Ed.D. and Ph.D.: 3.3 GPA from Masters degree, GRE scores, writing sample, three letters of recommendation, transcripts. MA.: 3.0 GPA Undergraduate.

Degree Requirements – Ph.D.: 96 hrs above B.S., 2 year residency, 12 hrs. research classes, 30 hrs. dissertation; Ed.D.: 90 hrs. above B.S., 1 year residency, 12 hrs. research classes; MA.: 30 hrs. above B.S.

Number of Full-Time Faculty – 6; **Number of Other Faculty** – 5

Degrees awarded in 2008–2009 Academic Year – Masters – 15; **PhD** – 7; **Other** – 3

Grant Monies awarded in 2008–2009 Academic Year – 1800000

Name of Institution – University of Virginia

Name of Department or Program – Department of Curriculum, Instruction and Special Education, Curry School of Education

Address:
Ruffner Hall
Charlottesville, Virginia
22903
US

Phone Number – (434)924-7471 **Fax Number** – (434)924-1387

Email Contact – jbb2s@virginia.edu **URL** – http://curry.edschool.virginia.edu/curry/dept/edlf/instrtech/

Contact Person – John B. Bunch, Assoc. Prof., Coord., Instructional Technology Program, Dept. of Leadership, Foundations and Policy Studies.

Specializations – M.Ed., Ed.S., Ed.D, and Ph.D. degrees with focal areas in Media Production, Interactive Multimedia, e-Learning/Distance learning and K-12 Educational Technologies

Features – The IT program is situated in a major research university with linkages to multiple disciplines. Graduate Students have the opportunity to work with faculty across the Curry School and the University.

Admission Requirements – Undergraduate degree from accredited institution in any field, undergraduate GPA 3.0,1000 GRE (V+Q), 600 TOEFL. Highly competitive and fully funded small 4 year mentored PhD research program.

Degree Requirements – M.Ed.: 36 semester hours, comprehensive examination. Ed.S.: 60 semester hours beyond undergraduate degree. Ed.D.: 54 semester hours, dissertation, at least one conference presentation or juried publication, comprehensive examination, residency; Ph.D.: same as Ed.S. with the addition of 18 semester hours. For specific degree requirements, see Web site, write to the address above, or refer to the UVA

Number of Full-Time Faculty – 3; **Number of Other Faculty** – 5

Degrees awarded in 2008–2009 Academic Year – Masters – 2; **PhD** – 3; **Other** – 0

Grant Monies awarded in 2008–2009 Academic Year – 500000

Name of Institution – University of Washington

Name of Department or Program – College of Education

Address:
115 Miller Hall, Box 353600
Seattle, WA
98195-3600
US

Phone Number – (206)543-1847 **Fax Number** – (206)543-1237

Email Contact – billwinn@u.washington.edu **URL** – http://www.educ.washington.edu/COE/c-and-i/c_and_i_med_ed_tech.htm

Contact Person – William Winn, Prof. of Education

Specializations – M.Ed., Ed.D, and Ph.D. for individuals in business, industry, higher education, public schools, and organizations concerned with education or communication (broadly defined)

Features – Emphasis on design of materials and programs to encourage learning and development in school and nonschool settings; research and related activity in such areas as interactive instruction, web-based learning, virtual environments, use of video as a tool for design and development. Close collaboration with program in Cognitive Studies.

Admission Requirements – M.Ed.: goal statement (2–3 pp.), writing sample, 1000 GRE (verbal plus quantitative), undergraduate GPA indicating potential to successfully accomplish graduate work. Doctoral: GRE scores, letters of reference, transcripts, personal statement, Master's degree or equivalent in field appropriate to the specialization with 3.5 GPA, two years of successful professional experience and/or experience related to program goals desirable.

Degree Requirements – M.Ed.: 45 qtr. hours (including 24 in technology); thesis or project recommended, exam optional. Ed.D.: see http://www.educ.washington.edu/COEWebSite/programs/ci/EdD.html Ph.D.: http://www.educ.washington.edu/COEWebSite/students/prospective/phdDescrip.html

Number of Full-Time Faculty – ; **Number of Other Faculty** –

Degrees awarded in 2008–2009 Academic Year – Masters – 5; **PhD** – ; **Other** –

Grant Monies awarded in 2008–2009 Academic Year –

Name of Institution – Western Washington University

Address:
MS 9087
Bellingham, Washington
98225-9087
US

Phone Number – 360)650-3387 **Fax Number** – (360)650-6526

Email Contact – Tony.Jongejan@wwu.edu **URL** – http://www.wce.wwu.edu/depts/IT

Contact Person – Tony Jongejan

Specializations – M.Ed. with emphasis in Instructional Technology in Adult Education, Special Education, Elementary Education, and Secondary Education

Admission Requirements – 3.0 GPA in last 45 qtr. credit hours, GRE or MAT scores, 3 letters of recommendation, and, in some cases, 3 years of teaching experience

Degree Requirements – 48–52 qtr. hours (24–28 hours in instructional technology; 24 hours in education-related courses, thesis required; internship and practicum possible).

Number of Full-Time Faculty – 0; **Number of Other Faculty** – 0

Degrees awarded in 2008–2009 Academic Year – **Masters** – 0; **PhD** – 0; **Other** – 0

Grant Monies awarded in 2008–2009 Academic Year – 0

Name of Institution – University of Alaska Southeast

Name of Department or Program – Educational Technology Program

Address:
11120 Glacier Hwy, HA1
Juneau, AK
99801
USA

Phone Number – 907-796-6050 **Fax Number** – 907-796-6059

Email Contact – marsha.gladhart@uas.alaska.edu **URL** – http://uas.alaska.edu/education/experienced

Contact Person – Marsha Gladhart

Specializations – Educational Technology

Features – * distance program * standards-based learning * integration of the most current technologies * collaboration with other teachers * instructors with k-12 teaching experience * focus on improving student learning * use of technology as a tool to assist learning

Admission Requirements – # A completed graduate application and $60 processing fee. # Official academic transcript indicating baccalaureate degree and a GPA of 3.0 # Two (2) general recommendations written by former or current professors, employers, or supervisors who are familiar with your work and performance. Each recommendation must be submitted using the Letter of Recommendation for Graduate Programs form. # A recommendation documenting your ability to meet the educational technology standards required for entry to the program. This recommendation should be completed by an administrator, supervisor, or technology leader. # Statement of Professional Objectives. # A copy of a current teaching or administrative certificate.

Degree Requirements – Official academic transcript indicating baccalaureate degree and a GPA of 3.0

Number of Full-Time Faculty – 2; **Number of Other Faculty** – 5

Degrees awarded in 2008–2009 Academic Year – **Masters** – 11; **PhD** – 0; **Other** – 0

Grant Monies awarded in 2008–2009 Academic Year – 0

Name of Institution – University of South Alabama

Name of Department or Program – Department of Behavioral Studies and Educational Technology, College of Education

Address:
University Commons 3700
Mobile, AL
36688
USA

Phone Number – (251)380-2861 **Fax Number** – (251)380-2713

Email Contact – jdempsey@usouthal.edu **URL** – http://www.southalabama.edu/coe/bset/

Contact Person – Daniel W. Surry, IDD Program Coor.; Mary Ann Robinson, Ed Media Program Coor

Specializations – M.S. and Ph.D. in Instructional Design and Development. M.Ed. in Educational Media (Ed Media). Online masters degrees in ED Media and IDD are available for qualified students. For information about online masters degree programs, http://usaonline.southalabama.edu

Features – The IDD masters and doctoral programs emphasize extensive education and training in the instructional design process, human performance technology and multimedia – and online-based training. The IDD doctoral program has an additional emphasis in research design and statistical analysis. The Ed Media masters program prepares students in planning, designing, and administering library/media centers at most levels of education, including higher education.

Admission Requirements – For the ED Media & IDD Masters: undergraduate degree in appropriate academic field from an accredited university or college; admission to Graduate School; satisfactory score on the GRE. ED Media students must have completed requirements for a certificate at the baccalaureate or masters level in a teaching field. For IDD Ph.D.: Masters degree, all undergraduate & graduate transcripts, 3 letters of recommendations, written statement of purpose for pursuing Ph.D. in IDD, satisfactory score on GRE.

Degree Requirements – Ed Media masters: satisfactorily complete program requirements (minimum 33 semester hours), 3.0 or better GPA, satisfactory score on comprehensive exam. IDD masters: satisfactorily complete program requirements (minimum 40 semester hours), 3.0 or better GPA; satisfactory complete comprehensive exam. Ph.D.: satisfactory complete program requirements (minimum 82 semester hours of approved graduate courses), one-year residency, satisfactory score on examinations (research and statistical exam and comprehensive exam), approved dissertation completed. Any additional requirements will be determined by students doctoral advisory committee.

Number of Full-Time Faculty – 0; **Number of Other Faculty** – 0

Degrees awarded in 2008–2009 Academic Year – Masters – 0; **PhD** – 0; **Other** – 0

Grant Monies awarded in 2008–2009 Academic Year – 0

Name of Institution – University of Arkansas

Name of Department or Program – Educational Technology

Address:
255 Graduate Education Building
Fayetteville, AR
72701
USA

Phone Number – 479-575-5111 **Fax Number** – 479-575-2493

Email Contact – cmurphy@uark.edu **URL** – http://etec.uark.edu

Contact Person – Dr. Cheryl Murphy

Specializations – The program prepares students for a variety of work environments by offering core courses that are applicable to a multitude of professional venues. The program also allows for specific emphasis area studies via open-ended assignments and course electives that include courses particularly relevant to business/industry or K-12 environments. The primary focus of the program is on the processes involved in instructional design, training and development, media production, teacher education, and utilization of instructional technologies. Because technology is continually changing, the program emphasizes acquisition of a process over the creation of a product. Although skills necessary in making Educational Technology products are taught, technology changes rapidly; therefore, a primary emphasis on making technological products would lead to the acquisition of skills that are quickly outdated. However, learning the principles and mental tools critical to producing successful training and education will endure long after "new" technologies have become obsolete. That is why the University of Arkansas ETEC program focuses on the processes as opposed to specific technologies.

Features – The Educational Technology Program is a 33-hour nonthesis online masters program that prepares students for professional positions as educational technologists of education, business, government, and the health professions. Because the program is offered online, there are no on-campus requirements for the completion of this degree.

Admission Requirements – The Educational Technology online masters program admits students in the fall, spring, and summer. Applications and all accompanying documents must be submitted within three months of the desired starting semester to ensure adequate processing time. To qualify for admission applicants must have an earned bachelors degree and an undergraduate GPA of 3.0 within the last 60 hours of coursework. Specific application materials can be found at http://etec.uark.

edu/1069.htm Applicants for the M.Ed. degree must have met all requirements of Graduate School admission, completed a bachelors degree and earned a 3.0 GPA in all undergraduate coursework or obtain an acceptable score on the Graduate Record Examinations or Miller Analogies Test. A Graduate School application, ETEC Program Application, writing sample, autobiographical sketch, and letters of recommendation are required for admission consideration.

Degree Requirements – In addition to general admission requirements, students must complete a minimum of 33 hours to include 18 semester hours of educational technology courses; six semester hours of educational technology electives; and nine semester hours from the College of Education and Health Professions common core. Additionally, a Culminating Student Portfolio must be successfully completed during the last three hours of coursework. There are no on-campus requirements for the completion of this degree, although approved courses that meet the college core requirements may be taken on campus if desired.

Number of Full-Time Faculty – 2; **Number of Other Faculty** – 3

Degrees awarded in 2008–2009 Academic Year – Masters – 11; **PhD** – 0; **Other** – 0

Grant Monies awarded in 2008–2009 Academic Year – 0

Name of Institution – University of Arkansas at Little Rock

Name of Department or Program – Learning Systems Technology

Address:
2801 S. University
Little Rock , AR
72204
USA

Phone Number – 501-569-3269 **Fax Number** – (501) 569-3547

Email Contact – dsspillers@ualr.edu **URL** – http://ualr.edu/med/LSTE/

Contact Person – David S. Spillers

Specializations – The Learning Systems Technology master's degree prepares you for the design, production, and application of these new methods, including creating and designing the following learning products: * documents and electronic displays * interactive tutorials for web-based delivery * instructional blogs * useful web pages * complete instructional packages using digital images and film clips * courses using a variety of online course management systems * learning resource centers

Features – This program is offered entirely online.

Admission Requirements – Admission to the LSTE master's program requires: * a baccalaureate degree from a regionally accredited institution with substantially the same undergraduate programs as the University of Arkansas at Little Rock * a

3.0 GPA on the last 60 hours (including postbaccalaureate hours or a 2.7 GPA on all undergraduate hours taken for the baccalaureate degree) * successful application to the UALR graduate school * academic evaluation by the LSTE program coordinator After you have completed your online application to the Graduate School, your folder with all of your transcripts will be sent to the program coordinator for evaluation. The program coordinator will then send you a letter with your status in the process. Once you get your letter of acceptance you will be able to start the program in any semester: Fall, Spring, or Summer. If you have any questions, please contact the program coordinator.

Degree Requirements – The 36 graduate credit hours include: * 9 Educational Foundations hours * 18 Learning Technologies hours * up to 3 elective courses (Foundations, English writing, Learning Technologies or other content area approved by the adviser) or a 3 to 6 hour field experience No more than six hours of workshop credit will be accepted in the program. No more than six hours earned within the last 3 years of transfer credit will be accepted in the program.

Number of Full-Time Faculty – 1; **Number of Other Faculty** – 5

Degrees awarded in 2008–2009 Academic Year – Masters – 7; **PhD** – 0; **Other** – 0

Grant Monies awarded in 2008–2009 Academic Year – 0

Name of Institution – California State Polytechnic University

Name of Department or Program – Educational Multimedia Design

Address:
3801 West Temple Ave
Pomona, CA
91768
USA

Phone Number – 909-869-2255 **Fax Number** – 909-869-5206

Email Contact – slotfipour@csupomona.edu **URL** – www.csupomona.edu/emm

Contact Person – Dr. Shahnaz Lotfipour

Specializations – Design and production of eLearning materials and educational multimedia software (including audio, video, animation, web programming, graphics, etc.) for educational and corporate training environments using the sound instructional principles and strategies.

Features – Hands-on training, project-based, combination of online and hybrid courses, internship possibilities in educational and corporate settings

Admission Requirements – Undergraduate GPA of 3.0, three strong letters of recommendations, satisfying graduate writing test

Degree Requirements – BA or BS

Number of Full-Time Faculty – 3; **Number of Other Faculty** – 5

Degrees awarded in 2008–2009 Academic Year – Masters – 26; PhD – 2; **Other** – 0

Grant Monies awarded in 2008–2009 Academic Year – 0

Name of Institution – California State University Monterey Bay (CSUMB)

Name of Department or Program – Interdisciplinary Master in Instructional Science and Technology (MIST)

Address:
100 Campus Center
Seaside, CA
93955
USA

Phone Number – 831-582-3621 **Fax Number** – 831-582-4484

Email Contact – mist@csumb.edu **URL** – http://itcd.csumb.edu/mist

Contact Person – Eric Tao, Ph.D.

Features – Interdisciplinary collaboration that integrates instructional science and information technology is the hallmark of the IST graduate program and a CSUMB core value. Recognizing that the use of technology is critical to the design, development, and delivery of instruction in the 21st century, IST integrates modern learning technology and pedagogy to create educational experiences adequate for the contemporary world. This technology infusion models best practices to learners. Rather than setting aside one course that deals solely with ethics and social responsibility, our curriculum integrates ethical reflection and practice throughout the program. All required courses incorporate the basic concepts and concerns of ethics into their design, development, and delivery. Multiculturalism and globalism are infused into the IST curriculum, including discussion of diversity in the conduct of instructional design and diversity in the understanding of ethics. Applied learning is critical to the IST program, and we use an integrated pedagogy that builds on each semesters outcome.

Admission Requirements – 1. Complete and submit an application form at CSUMENTOR.org and $55.00 application fee payable to CSUMB. A. Select Summer 2009 as the application term. B. On line 10a, insert "INTD" as the objective, "49993" as the program code, and indicate "IDMA/IST" as the emphasis. On line 10b, enter "5" signifying that the degree is a Master of Arts degree. 2. Submit all required supporting documents. All supporting documents should be submitted to: School of Information Technology and Communication Design Attention: IDMA/IST Program, Building 18, Room 150 100 Campus Center Seaside, CA 93955 A. Submit two (2) official copies of each of the following: (1) Transcripts of all college coursework taken * Have two (2) official transcripts from all colleges and universities you have attended mailed directly to the IDMA/IST Program at the address listed above. (We recommend that you request that an additional copy be mailed directly to you at home and that you leave that envelope unopened until you have confirmation that we have received our copies.) * A GPA of 3.0 is expected for the most recent 60 units of college-level work attempted. GPA between 2.5 and 3.0 may be considered with substantial alternative demonstration of ability to succeed in the program. (2) Test scores (TOEFL, GRE, etc.), (if applicable) * We recommend that you take the GRE test to improve your competitive standing but it is not required. CSUMBs school code for ETS is 1945. * For those students required to demonstrate English proficiency: the IDMA/IST program requires a TOEFL score of 575 for admission. Selected applicants with TOEFL scores between 525 and 574 and applicants demonstrating English proficiency with test scores other than TOEFL must pass a writing workshop offered by ITCD before the first day of classes as a condition of admission. Applicants with TOEFL scores below 525 will not be considered. * CSUMB minimum requirements for English proficiency for applicants with degrees from foreign universities are listed on the Admissions & Recruitment website at: http://ar.csumb.edu/site/x5362.xml#requirements (3) Foreign Credential Evaluation (if applicable) * All transcripts from schools outside the United States must be sent, at the applicants expense, to a foreign credential evaluation service. A detailed "course-by-course" report is required for all programs. Three credential evaluation services accepted by CSU Monterey Bay are: 1. World Education Services WES http://www.wes.org/ 2. American Association of Collegiate Registrars and Admissions Offices AACRAO http://www.aacrao.org/credential/ 3. International Education Research Foundation IERF http://www.ierf.org/ * CSUMB minimum requirements for foreign credential evaluation for applicants with degrees from foreign universities are listed on the Admissions & Recruitment website at: http://ar.csumb.edu/site/x5362.xml#requirements B. Submit an original "Statement of Purpose" (one copy is sufficient). * Include a 1000–2000 word Statement of Purpose (statement of educational and professional goals) that demonstrates your writing ability. C. Submit two (2) or three (3) letters of reference (one copy of each is sufficient). * Include two or three letters of recommendation from individuals familiar with your professional and academic work. D. Technology Screening Assessment * Upon receipt of your application, we will email you a technology screening assessment that you must complete and submit prior to your document deadline. The results of the technology assessment will be considered in the selection process

Degree Requirements – Outcomes, Courses, and Assessment The Interdisciplinary Master of Arts with Instructional Science and Technology Emphasis (IST) degree requires 24 semester hours of core courses, four semester hours of an elective, and four semester hours for the culminating Capstone experience or thesis. [Learn more at CSUMB.EDU/capstone]. As the title signifies, the core courses are a cluster of instructional design, instructional systems, and best educational practices that represent the core of the collaborative program. By guiding you toward the Learning Outcomes (LOs) listed below, these courses provide you with the skills necessary to become an effective instructional designer and e-learning developer in today's high-tech, global marketplace. Given the complexities that emanate from strong and growing global forces and conflicting values, we discuss international and ethical issues in all courses. The IST program consists of four terms that must be taken sequentially covering the following courses and outcomes. Term I Courses: IST 522 Instructional Design IST 524 Instructional Technology Outcomes: LO 1 Learning Theories LO 2 Instructional Design Students generate a detailed instructional design document that applies learning theories appropriate to the target audience. Students are encouraged to incorporate projects from their current employment into the class assignments. Term II Courses: IST 520 Learning Theory IST 526 Interactive Multimedia for Instruction Outcomes: LO 3 Instructional Technology LO 4 Interactive Multimedia Students use the design document generated in the previous term to collaboratively construct a functioning learning module using interactive multimedia software, information technology, and media. Term III Courses: IST 622 Assessment and Evaluation IST 624 Research Methods for Instructional Sciences Outcomes: LO 5 Assessment and Evaluation LO 6 Research Methods Students apply the learning objectives produced in the previous term and develop an assessment and research plan that uses academic research methods to evaluate the efficacy of their learning objectives. Term IV Courses: IST 630 Graduate Capstone in Instructional Sciences and Technology Minimum of four elective upper-division or graduate-level credits, approved by program coordinator and faculty advisor, related to the field of instructional science and technology. For example: CST 336, CST 451, CST 610, CST 655, CST 551, CST 404, CST 424, etc. Outcomes: LO 7 Breadth of Knowledge LO 8 Instructional Sciences and Technology Capstone Project or Thesis Students finish a Capstone project or thesis that connects with their career as the culminating experience.

Number of Full-Time Faculty – 10; **Number of Other Faculty** – 12

Degrees awarded in 2008–2009 Academic Year – **Masters** – 30; **PhD** – 0; **Other** – 50

Grant Monies awarded in 2008–2009 Academic Year – 1000000

Name of Institution – California State University, Fresno

Name of Department or Program – Certificate of Advanced Study in Educational Technology

Address:
None
Fresno, CA
93740
USA

Phone Number – 559-278-0245 **Fax Number** – 559-278-0107

Email Contact – royb@csufresno.edu **URL** – http://education.csufresno.edu/departments/ci/ci_aset.htm

Contact Person – Dr. Roy M. Bohlin

Specializations – None

Features – None

Admission Requirements – None

Degree Requirements – Bachelors degree

Number of Full-Time Faculty – 3; **Number of Other Faculty** – 2

Degrees awarded in 2008–2009 Academic Year – Masters – 7; **PhD** – 0; **Other** – 0

Grant Monies awarded in 2008–2009 Academic Year – 0

Name of Institution – Metropolitan State College of Denver

Name of Department or Program – Department of Special Education, Early Childhood Education, Reading, and Educational Technology

Address:
Teacher Education, Campus Box 21 P.O Box 173362
Denver, CO
80217
USA

Phone Number – (303)556-3322 **Fax Number** – (303) 556-5353

Email Contact – mchung3@mscd.edu **URL** – http://www.mscd.edu/~ted

Contact Person – Dr. Miri Chung

Number of Full-Time Faculty – 3; **Number of Other Faculty** – 3

Degrees awarded in 2008–2009 Academic Year – Masters – 0; **PhD** – 0; **Other** – 0

Grant Monies awarded in 2008–2009 Academic Year – 0

Name of Institution – Regis University

Name of Department or Program – School of Education and Counseling

Address:
3333 Regis Boulevard
Denver, CO
80221
USA

Phone Number – 800-388-2366 **Fax Number** – 303-964-5053

Email Contact – chruskoc@regis.edu **URL** – www.regis.edu

Contact Person – Dr. Carole Hruskocy

Specializations – Instructional Technology Curriculum, Instruction, and Assessment Professional Leadership Adult Learning, Training, and Development Self-Designed Reading Space Studies

Features – The majority of our programs are offered in the online format.

Admission Requirements – Essay Letters of Recommendation Minimum GPA of 2.75

Number of Full-Time Faculty – 15; **Number of Other Faculty** – 150

Degrees awarded in 2008–2009 Academic Year – Masters – 200; **PhD** – 0; **Other** – 0

Grant Monies awarded in 2008–2009 Academic Year – 0

Name of Institution – University of Bridgeport

Name of Department or Program – Instructional Technology

Address:
126 Park Avenue
Bridgeport, CT
06604
USA

Phone Number – 2035764217 **Fax Number** – 2035764633

Email Contact – jcole@bridgeport.edu **URL** – http://www.bridgeport.edu/imsit

Contact Person – Jerald D. Cole

Specializations – Masters and Professional Diploma (6th Year) Instructional Technology Tracks: 1. Teacher 2. Trainer 3. Developer 4. Technology Education 5. Technology Leadership

Features – 1. Open Source Curriculum and Software Model. 2. Cross Platform Mobil Tablet Computing Initiative. 3. Social Constructionist Pedagogy. 4. Hybrid and online courses. 5. Cohort-based. 6. Tuition-free internships for Teacher track.

Admission Requirements – Online Application Essay on experience and objectives for study Two letters of reference Praxis 1 for teacher track TOEFL for nonnative English speakers Transcripts Phone interview

Degree Requirements – 4 core courses, 2 distribution requirements, 1 research, 1 practicum, 4 electives

Number of Full-Time Faculty – 14; **Number of Other Faculty** – 21

Degrees awarded in 2008–2009 Academic Year – Masters – 294; **PhD** – 15; **Other** – 117

Grant Monies awarded in 2008–2009 Academic Year – 350000

Name of Institution – University of Florida

Name of Department or Program – School of Teaching and Learning

Address:
2403 Norman Hall
Gainesville, FL
32611-7048
USA

Phone Number – 352-392-9191 X261 **Fax Number** – 352-392-9193

Email Contact – kdawson@coe.ufl.edu **URL** – http://www.coe.ufl.edu/school/edtech/index.htm (Hybrid programs); http://www.coe.ufl.edu/online/edtech/index.html (Online programs)

Contact Person – Kara Dawson

Specializations – Hybrid Program: Educational technology students may earn M.Ed., Ed.S., Ed.D., or Ph.D. degrees and have an opportunity to specialize in one of two tracks: (1) Teaching and teacher education or (2) Design and Production of educational materials. Many students merge these tracks. Teacher education students and students in other degree programs may also elect to specialize in Educational Technology. Online Programs: We offer an online Masters, Ed.S., and Ed.D. degrees in "Teaching, learning & facilitating change with educational technology" http://www.coe.ufl.edu/online/edtech/index.html

Features – Students take core courses listed on our Educational Technology website and then select an area of specialization. Opportunities to collaborative research, write and design with faculty members. Strong community of graduate students.

Admission Requirements – Please see the Educational Technology website for the most up-to-date information.

Degree Requirements – Please see the Educational Technology website for the most up-to-date information. Program and college requirements must be met but there is considerable flexibility for doctoral students to plan an appropriate program with their advisors.

Number of Full-Time Faculty – 5; **Number of Other Faculty** – 3

Degrees awarded in 2008–2009 Academic Year – Masters – 20; **PhD** – 5; **Other** – 15

Grant Monies awarded in 2008–2009 Academic Year – 1000000

Name of Institution – University of West Florida

Name of Department or Program – Instructional and Performance Technology

Address:
11000 University Parkway
Pensacola , FL
32514
USA

Phone Number – 850-474-2300 **Fax Number** – 850-474-2804

Email Contact – krasmuss@uwf.edu **URL** – http://uwf.edu/ect/graduate.cfm#IPT

Contact Person – Karen Rasmussen

Specializations – M.Ed., Instructional Technology: Curriculum and Technology Telecommunications and Distance Learning Technology Leadership Human Performance Technology M.S.A., H.P.T.: Human Performance Technology Ed.S., Instructional Technology Performance Technology Distance Learning Ed.D., Curriculum and Instruction, Instructional Technology Specialization: Performance Technology Distance Learning

Features – Fully online programs Small classes Recognized nationally as a "Best Buy" in Online Degree Programs in Human Performance Technology based on quality and affordability.

Admission Requirements – GRE or MAT Score Official Transcripts Letter of Intent See Department Website for additional information.

Degree Requirements – M.Ed., 36 credit hours M.S.A., 33 credit hours Ed.S., 36 credit hours Ed.D., 66 credit hours

Number of Full-Time Faculty – 3; **Number of Other Faculty** – 1

Degrees awarded in 2008–2009 Academic Year – **Masters** – 25; **PhD** – 0; **Other** – 22

Grant Monies awarded in 2008–2009 Academic Year – 350700

Name of Institution – Ball State University

Name of Department or Program – Masters of Arts in Curriculum and Educational Technology

Address:
Teachers College
Muncie, IN
47306
USA

Phone Number – (765) 285-5461 **Fax Number** – (765) 285-5489

Email Contact – jmclaus@bsu.edu **URL** – http://www.bsu.edu/edstudies/edtech/

Contact Person – Jon M. Clausen

Specializations – Specialization tracks in curriculum or educational technology

Features – The Masters of Arts in Curriculum and Educational Technology is a 30-hour program designed for educators seeking to integrate technology into K12 curriculum and other instructional contexts where teaching and learning occur. Graduates are prepared to become leaders within their instructional contexts by coursework and experiences that focus on development of a conceptual framework in which technology is an embedded aspect of the teaching and learning process. The program prepares graduates to utilize technology to meet learning needs of students and to critically examine technology's ever-changing presence within schools and society.

Admission Requirements – Prospective students should apply to the Graduate College and provide official transcripts from all universities/colleges attended. A student seeking admittance for a Masters degree must meet the following minimum criteria: – Hold an earned bachelors degree from a college or university that is accredited by its regional accrediting association. – Have one of the following: – An undergraduate cumulative GPA of at least 2.75 on a scale of 4.0 – A cumulative GPA of at least 3.0 on a 4.0 scale in the latter half of the baccalaureate. Additional information regarding application and admission to the graduate college can be found at the following website. http://www.bsu.edu/gradschool

Degree Requirements – Successful completion of 30 graduate hours.

Number of Full-Time Faculty – 8; **Number of Other Faculty** – 4

Degrees awarded in 2008–2009 Academic Year – Masters – 15; **PhD** – 0; **Other** – 0

Grant Monies awarded in 2008–2009 Academic Year – 0

Name of Institution – Indiana University

Name of Department or Program – School of Education

Address:
W. W. Wright Education Bldg., Rm. 2276, 201 N. Rose Ave.
Bloomington, IN
47405-1006
USA

Phone Number – (812)856-8451 **Fax Number** – (812)856-8239

Email Contact – istdept@indiana.edu **URL** – http://education.indiana.edu/~ist/

Contact Person – Elizabeth Boling, Chair, Dept. of Instructional Systems Technology

Specializations – The M.S. and Ed.S. degrees are designed for individuals seeking to be practitioners in the field of Instructional Technology. The M.S. degree is also offered in a web-based format with instructional product and portfolio requirements, with specializations in Workplace Learning and Performance Improvement; Instructional Systems Design Practice; and Learning Technologies. A Studio specialization is available to residential students. Online certificate and licensure programs are also available.

The Ph.D. degree features a heavy research emphasis via faculty-mentored research groups and student dossiers for assessing research, teaching, and service competencies. An online Ed.D. is in the approval process.

Features – Requires computer skills as a prerequisite and makes technology utilization an integral part of the curriculum; eliminates separation of various media formats; and establishes a series of courses of increasing complexity integrating production and development. The latest in technical capabilities have been incorporated, including teaching, computer, and laptop-ready laboratories, a multimedia laboratory, and video and audio production studios.

Ph.D. students participate in faculty-mentored research groups throughout their program. Students construct dossiers with evidence of research, teaching, and service that are evaluated by faculty on three occasions during the program. The second and third dossier reviews replace the traditional written and oral examinations.

Admission Requirements – M.S.: Bachelor's degree from an accredited institution, 1350 GRE (3 tests required) or 900 plus 3.5 analytical writing (new format), 2.75 undergraduate GPA. Ed.S. and Ph.D.: 1650 GRE (3 tests required) or 1100 plus 4.5 analytical writing (new format), 3.5 graduate GPA.

Degree Requirements – M.S.: 36 credit hours (including 15 credits in required courses); colloquia; an instructional product; and 9 credits in outside electives, and portfolio. Ed.S.: 65 hours, capstone project with written report and a portfolio. Ph.D.: 90 hours, dossier reviews, and thesis

Number of Full-Time Faculty – 10; **Number of Other Faculty** – 4

Degrees awarded in 2008–2009 Academic Year – **Masters** – 16; **PhD** – 7; **Other** – 3

Grant Monies awarded in 2008–2009 Academic Year – 93188

Name of Institution – Purdue University

Name of Department or Program – College of Education, Department of Curriculum and Instruction

Address:
100 N. University St.
West Lafayette, IN
47907-2098
USA

Phone Number – (765)494-5669 **Fax Number** – (765)496-1622

Email Contact – edtech@soe.purdue.edu **URL** – http://www.edci.purdue.edu/et/

Contact Person – Dr. Tim Newby, Prof. of Educational Technology.

Specializations – Master's degree and Ph.D. in Educational Technology. Master's program started in 1982; Ph.D. in 1985

Features – Vision Statement The Educational Technology Program at Purdue University nurtures graduates who are effective designers of learning experiences and environments that incorporate technology to engage learners and improve learning.

Admission Requirements – Master's and Ph.D: 3.0 GPA, three letters of recommendation, statement of personal goals. A score of 550 (paper-based) or 213 (computer-based) or above on the Test of English as a Foreign Language (TOEFL) for individuals whose first language is not English. Ph.D. Additional Requirement: 1000 GRE (V+Q); Verbal score of at least 500 preferred.

Degree Requirements – Masters: minimum of 32 semester hours (17 in educational technology, 6–9 in research, development, and exit requirements, 6–9 electives); thesis optional. Ph.D: 60 semester hours beyond the Masters degree (15–18 in educational technology, 27–30 in education and supporting areas; 15 dissertation research hours)

Number of Full-Time Faculty – 0; **Number of Other Faculty** – 0

Degrees awarded in 2008–2009 Academic Year – Masters – 3; **PhD** – 0; **Other** – 0

Grant Monies awarded in 2008–2009 Academic Year – 0

Name of Institution – Purdue University Calumet

Name of Department or Program – Instructional Technology

Address:
2200 169th Street
Hammond, IN
46323
USA

Phone Number – 219-989-2692 **Fax Number** – 219-983215

Email Contact – buckenme@calumet.purdue.edu **URL** – http://www.calumet.purdue.edu/education/grad/it.html

Contact Person – Janet Buckenmeyer

Specializations – Instructional Technology and Instructional Design

Features – The Instructional Technology program at Purdue University Calumet is a practitioner-based program. Students entering the program may be teachers but do not need a teaching license to enroll. The program does not lead to licensure.

Admission Requirements – 3.0 GPA; Three (3) letters of recommendation; Essay; Two (2) official copies of all transcripts; Interview

Number of Full-Time Faculty – 3; **Number of Other Faculty** – 1

Degrees awarded in 2008–2009 Academic Year – Masters – 10; **PhD** – 0; **Other** – 0

Grant Monies awarded in 2008–2009 Academic Year – 125000

Name of Institution – Emporia State University

Name of Department or Program – Instructional Design and Technology

Address:
1200 Commercial St. – Campus Box 4037
Emporia, KS
66801
USA

Phone Number – 620-341-5829 **Fax Number** – 620-341-5785

Email Contact – mchildre@emporia.edu **URL** – http://idt.emporia.edu

Contact Person – Dr. Marcus D. Childress, Chair

Specializations – Distance learning, online learning, corporate education, P-12 technology integration

Features – All program courses are offered online. The online Master of Science in Instructional Design and Technology program prepares individuals for leadership in the systematic design, development, implementation, evaluation, and management of technology-rich learning in a variety of settings. Individuals obtaining the IDT degree serve as instructional designers/trainers in business, industry, health professions, and the military and are charged with training, development, and eLearning programs within their organizations. Other graduates hold leadership positions in P-12 and postsecondary institutions. In addition to positions in the workplace, graduates regularly choose to pursue their Ph.D. degrees in IDT at top-ranked universities. IDT faculty members hold leadership positions on the Association for Educational Communications and Technology (AECT) board of directors, executive committee, and research and theory division. Forms and application materials available at the website, http://idt.emporia.edu Other social media contacts, Ning – http://idtesu.ning.com/ Twitter – http://twitter.com/idtesu Blogspot – http://idtesu.blogspot.com/ YouTube – http://www.youtube.com/idtesu

Admission Requirements – Graduate application, official transcripts, GPA of 2.75 or more based on a 4-point scale in the last 60 semester hours of undergraduate study, resume, two current recommendations, writing competency. The program admits on a rolling basis. The departmental admission committee reviews and decides on applications as they are received, until there are no remaining openings.

Degree Requirements – 36 credit hours: 21 cr. core, 6 cr. research, 9 cr. electives.

Number of Full-Time Faculty – 6; **Number of Other Faculty** – 4

Degrees awarded in 2008–2009 Academic Year – Masters – 48; **PhD** – 0; **Other** – 0

Grant Monies awarded in 2008–2009 Academic Year – 10000

Name of Institution – Pittsburg State University

Name of Department or Program – Masters Degree in Educational Technology

Address:
1701 S. Broadway
Pittsburg, KS
66762
USA

Phone Number – 620 235 4484

Email Contact – jstidham@pittstate.edu **URL** – http://www.pittstate.edu

Contact Person – Dr. Sue Stidham

Specializations – Library Media licensure

Number of Full-Time Faculty – 3; **Number of Other Faculty** – 0

Degrees awarded in 2008–2009 Academic Year – **Masters** – 0; **PhD** – 0; **Other** – 0

Grant Monies awarded in 2008–2009 Academic Year – 0

Name of Institution – Morehead State University

Name of Department or Program – Educational Technology Program

Address:
Ginger Hall
Morehead, KY
40351
USA

Phone Number – 606-783-2040

Email Contact – c.miller@morehead-st.edu **URL** – www.moreheadstate.edu/education

Contact Person – Christopher T. Miller

Specializations – Focus on technology integration and instructional design.

Features – Fully online

Admission Requirements – Standard or Provisional Teaching Certificate, a statement of eligibility for teaching, or documentation stating role of educational support. Those students seeking to develop expertise in the area of educational support will be able to obtain the Master's Degree, but it cannot be used for initial teacher certification. Minimum composite GRE score of 750 on the verbal and quantitative section. Demonstration of basic writing proficiency by scoring at least 2.5 on the analytic writing subtest of the GRE. Minimum 2.75 undergraduate GPA

Degree Requirements – Satisfy general degree requirements. Students are required to apply for the exit exam at least two weeks prior to the exam date and must have advisor permission to take the exam. Additional written and/or oral examinations may be required as part of the comprehensive examination. The student must submit a professional portfolio demonstrating work completed within the program. The student must apply for graduation in the Graduate Office, 701 Ginger Hall. Maintain a 3.0 GPA in all courses taken after completing the Bachelor's degree. Must be unconditionally admitted. If a student has not been unconditionally admitted after completing twelve graduate hours, he/she will not be allowed to register for additional hours.

Number of Full-Time Faculty – 2; **Number of Other Faculty** – 0

Degrees awarded in 2008–2009 Academic Year – Masters – 6; **PhD** – 0; **Other** – 0

Grant Monies awarded in 2008–2009 Academic Year – 0

Name of Institution – University of Massachusetts, Amherst

Name of Department or Program – Learning, Media and Technology Masters Program/Math Science and Learning Technology Doctoral Program

Address:
813 N. Pleasant St.
Amherst, MA
01003
USA

Phone Number – 413-545-0246 **Fax Number** – 413-545-2879

Email Contact – fsullivan@educ.umass.edu **URL** – http://www.umass.edu/education/academics/tecs/ed_tech.shtml

Contact Person – Florence R. Sullivan

Specializations – The Master of Education concentration in Learning, Media and Technology prepares students to understand, critique, and improve technology- and media-based learning and teaching. The program is structured such that students construct solid knowledge of theories of learning and instruction, as well as theories of the design and use of educational technologies and media. Just as importantly, we offer a number of courses and research experiences through which students develop facility with applied aspects of technology-centered educational practices (e.g., authoring software systems, utilizing tools such as Director and Flash). By encountering multiple opportunities for the analysis, design, and testing of educational technology/media, students develop a principled approach to technology- and media-based instruction and learning. The overall mission of the Mathematics, Science and Learning Technologies doctoral program of study is to use new research findings to improve the learning and teaching of mathematics and science – from preschool to higher education, in schools and in nonformal settings – by preparing professional mathematics/science educators, scholars, and researchers.

Features – In the masters program, we consider media and technology both as tools in learning and teaching specific disciplines (e.g., mathematics and science) and as objects of study in and of themselves. With regard to the former, and in line with the affiliated faculty's expertise, students explore the educational uses of a variety of technological forms (e.g., robotics systems for learning engineering, physics, programming, and the arts) and computer-based environments (e.g., software systems for learning scientific image processing). As for the latter, students actively engage in designing and using various learning technologies and media, including Web-based environments, computer-mediated communications systems, computer-based virtual worlds, and new media for new literacies. The features of the doctoral program of study are: * provide an interconnected locus of intellectual activity for graduate students and faculty; * increase equity (in gender, ethnicity, and opportunities) in recruitment, admission, and retention of students and faculty and pursue issues of equity in science education; * teach relevant courses, seminars, and independent studies in mathematics and science education; * conduct pertinent research studies in mathematics and science learning, teaching, curriculum development, and assessment; * build a base of scholarship, disseminate new knowledge, and apply it actively in education; * provide apprenticeship opportunities for graduate students; * understand and support effective practice in mathematics and science education; * coordinate outreach efforts with K-12 schools and related projects; * collaborate with faculty in the Department, School, and University as well as in the wider profession throughout the Commonwealth of Massachusetts, nationally, and internationally.

Admission Requirements – For the masters program – GPA of 2.75 or higher, TESOL test score of 80 points or higher, excellent letters of recommendation, clear statement of purpose. For the doctoral program – earned masters degree in math, natural sciences, learning technology or education, GPA of 2.75 or higher, TESOL test score of 80 points or higher, excellent letters of recommendation, clear statement of purpose.

Degree Requirements – Masters degree – 33 credit hours and thesis. Doctoral degree – 36 credit hours beyond the masters degree, 18 dissertation credit hours, successful completion of comprehensive exams, successful completion of doctoral dissertation.

Number of Full-Time Faculty – 7; **Number of Other Faculty** – 1

Degrees awarded in 2008–2009 Academic Year – Masters – 6; **PhD** – 2; **Other** – 0

Grant Monies awarded in 2008–2009 Academic Year – 2300000

Name of Institution – Oakland University

Name of Department or Program – Master of Training and Development Program

Address:
2200 North Squirrel Road
Rochester, MI
48309-4494
USA

Phone Number – 248 370-4171 **Fax Number** – 248 370-4095

Email Contact – ouhrdmtd@gmail.com **URL** – www2.oakland.edu/sehs/hrd/

Contact Person – Dr. Chaunda L. Scott – Graduate Coordinator

Specializations – The Master of Training and Development Program at Oakland University provides a unique blend of knowledge and skills in all aspects of training and development. Students can choose between two area of emphasis: * Instructional Design and Technology * Organizational Development and Leadership

Features – The Master of Training and Development Program develops practitioners with the knowledge and skills required to enhance individual performance. Graduates of the program will be able to lead interventions associated with diagnosing performance problems and opportunities. Graduates will also be able to design and implement individual and organizational solutions and evaluate results. All courses are taught by outstanding faculty who have diverse backgrounds and experience in business and academia. The Master of Training and Development Program can be completed in two and one half years. Graduates of the program will be qualified to work as human resource development professionals, including directors of training centers, organizational development consultants, instructional designers, and performance technologists.

Admission Requirements – Official transcripts for undergraduate and graduate coursework showing a bachelors degree from a regionally accredited institution and a cumulative GPA of 3.0 or higher. A formal statement, between 100 and 1500 words, highlighting work and life experience – preferably one year or longer that have led to desire to pursue the Master of Training and Development Degree. Three letters of recommendations to attest to the quality and scope of the applicants academic and professional ability and a interview will be required.

Degree Requirements – The completion of 36 credits approved credits with an overall GPA of 3.0 or better and a grade of 2.8 or above in each additional course. The completion of five core courses is also required; HRD 530 Instructional Design, HRD 506 Theoretical Foundations of Training and Development, HRD 507 Needs Assessment, HRD 605 Program Evaluation, and HRD 611 Program Administration

Number of Full-Time Faculty – 7; **Number of Other Faculty** – 4

Degrees awarded in 2008–2009 Academic Year – **Masters** – 15; **PhD** – 0; **Other** – 0

Grant Monies awarded in 2008–2009 Academic Year – 0

Name of Institution – University of Michigan

Name of Department or Program – Department of Educational Studies

Address:
610 East University
Ann Arbor, MI
48109-1259
USA

Phone Number – (734) 763-7500 **Fax Number** – (734) 615-1290

Email Contact – fishman@umich.edu **URL** – http://www.soe.umich.edu/learningtechnologies/

Contact Person – Barry J. Fishman

Specializations – Ph.D. in Learning Technologies M.A. in Educational Studies with a focus on Digital Media & Education

Features – The Learning Technologies Program at the University of Michigan integrates the study of technology with a focus in a substantive content area. A unique aspect of the program is that your learning and research will engage you in real-world educational contexts. You will find that understanding issues related to a specific content area provides an essential context for meaningful research in learning. Your understanding of technology, school contexts, and a content area will place you among the leaders who design and conduct research on advanced technological systems that change education and schooling. The Doctoral specialization in Learning Technologies must be taken in conjunction with a substantive concentration designed in consultation with your advisor. Current active concentrations include: Science, Literacy, Culture and Gender, Teacher Education, Design and Human-Computer Interaction, Policy, and Social Studies. Other areas are possible. The Master's Degree in Educational Studies with a focus on Digital Media & Education at the University of Michigan prepares professionals for leadership roles in the design, development, implementation, and research of powerful technologies to enhance learning. Our approach to design links current knowledge and research about how people learn with technological tools that enable new means of organizing and evaluating learning environments. Course and project work reflects the latest knowledge and practice in learning, teaching, and technology. Core courses prepare students to use current understandings about learning theory, design principles, research methodologies, and evaluation strategies in educational settings ranging from classrooms to web-based and distributed learning environments. Faculty work with students to shape programs that meet individual interests. Practical experience is offered through internships with area institutions.

Admission Requirements – GRE, B.A. for M.A., or Ph.D.; TOEFL (minimum score of 84) for students from countries where English is not the primary language

Degree Requirements – M.A.: 30 hours beyond B.A. Ph.D.: 60 hours beyond B.A. or 30 hours beyond Masters plus research paper/qualifying examination, and dissertation.

Number of Full-Time Faculty – 3; **Number of Other Faculty** – 5

Degrees awarded in 2008–2009 Academic Year – Masters – 4; **PhD** – 2; **Other** – 0

Grant Monies awarded in 2008–2009 Academic Year – 0

Name of Institution – Bemidji State University

Name of Department or Program – Professional Education

Address:
1500 Birchmont Drive NE
Bemidji, MN
56601
USA

Phone Number – 218-755-3734

Email Contact – solson@bemidjistate.edu **URL** – http://www.bemidjistate.edu

Contact Person – Shari Olson

Number of Full-Time Faculty – 0; **Number of Other Faculty** – 0

Degrees awarded in 2008–2009 Academic Year – Masters – 0; **PhD** – 0; **Other** – 0

Grant Monies awarded in 2008–2009 Academic Year – 0

Name of Institution – University of Missouri – Columbia

Name of Department or Program – School of Information Science & Learning Technologies

Address:
303 Townsend Hall
Columbia, MO
65211
USA

Phone Number – 573-882-4546 **Fax Number** – 573-884-2917

Email Contact – sislt@missouri.edu **URL** – www.coe.missouri.edu/~sislt

Contact Person – John Wedman

Specializations – The Educational Technology emphasis area prepares educators and technologists for excellence and leadership in the design, development, and implementation of technology in education, training, and performance support. The program offers three focus areas: Technology In Schools Networked Learning Systems Training Design and Development Each focus area has its own set of competencies, coursework, and processes.

Features – All three focus areas are available online via the Internet or on the MU campus. The Technology in Schools focus area is based on the ISTE competencies and culminates in an online portfolio based on these competencies. Several courses are augmented by technical resources developed at MU, including a technology integration knowledge repository and online collaboration tools. The Networked Learning Systems focus area offers a truly challenging and innovative set of technical learning experiences. Students have opportunities to work on large-scale software development projects, acquiring valuable experience and broadening their skill set. The Digital Media ZONE supports anytime/anywhere technical skill development. The Training and Development focus area links to business, military, and government contexts. The curriculum is offered by faculty with extensive experience in these contexts and is grounded in the problems and processes of today's workplace. EdS and PhD programs are also available.

Admission Requirements – Bachelors degree with 3.0 in last 60 credit hours of course work. GRE (V>500; A>500; W>3.5) TOEFL of 540 (207 computer-based test) (if native language is not English) Letters of reference

Degree Requirements – Masters: 30–34 credit credit hours; 15 hours at 400 level. Specific course requirements vary by focus area.

Number of Full-Time Faculty – 0; **Number of Other Faculty** – 0

Degrees awarded in 2008–2009 Academic Year – Masters – 72; **PhD** – 0; **Other** – 0

Grant Monies awarded in 2008–2009 Academic Year – 0

Name of Institution – University of Missouri-Kansas City

Name of Department or Program – Curriculum and Instructional Leadership

Address:
4100 Oak Street
Kansas City, MO
64101
USA

Phone Number – 314.210.6996 **Fax Number** – 816.235.5270

Email Contact – russelldl@umkc.edu **URL** – http://r.web.umkc.edu/russelldl/

Contact Person – Donna Russell

Specializations – 3D Virtual Learning Environments

Number of Full-Time Faculty – 30; **Number of Other Faculty** – 15

Degrees awarded in 2008–2009 Academic Year – Masters – 60; **PhD** – 3; **Other** – 0

Grant Monies awarded in 2008–2009 Academic Year – 700000

Name of Institution – East Carolina University

Name of Department or Program – Mathematics, Science, and Instructional Technology Education

Address:
342 Flanagan
Greenville, NC
27858
USA

Phone Number – 252-328-9353 **Fax Number** – 252-328-9371

Email Contact – sugarw@coe.ecu.edu **URL** – http://www.ecu.edu/educ/msite/it/

Contact Person – William Sugar

Specializations – MS in Instructional Technology MAEd in Instructional Technology (see corresponding Educational Media & Technology Yearbook entry) Certificates in Computer-based Instruction, Distance Learning and Administration; Performance Improvement and Virtual Reality

Features – All required and elective courses are offered online. Courses include innovative approaches to online instruction.

Admission Requirements – MAT or GRE exam score

Degree Requirements – Bachelors degree

Number of Full-Time Faculty – 7; **Number of Other Faculty** – 3

Degrees awarded in 2008–2009 Academic Year – **Masters** – 20; **PhD** – 0; **Other** – 0

Grant Monies awarded in 2008–2009 Academic Year – 0

Name of Institution – University of North Carolina at Wilmington

Name of Department or Program – Master of Science in Instructional Technology– Dept. of Instructional Technology, Foundations & Secondary Education

Address:
601 South College Rd.
Wilmington, NC
28403
USA

Phone Number – 910-962-4183 **Fax Number** – 910-962-3609

Email Contact – moallemm@uncw.edu **URL** – http://www.uncw.edu/ed/mit

Contact Person – Mahnaz Moallem

Specializations – The Master of Science degree in Instructional Technology (MIT) program provides advanced professional training for teachers and school technology coordinators; business and industry personnel such as executives, trainers, and human resource development employees; persons in the health care field; and community college instructors. The program focuses on the theory and practice of design and development, utilization, management, and evaluation of processes and resources for learning. It emphasizes product development and utilization of advanced technology and provides applied training in the total design, development, implementation, and evaluation of educational and training programs.

Features – As an exciting and innovative program, MIT provides students the opportunity to gain skills and knowledge from educational and applied psychology, instructional systems design, computer science, systems theory, and communication theory, allowing for considerable flexibility to tailor individual needs across other academic disciplines. Students from diverse fields can plan programs which are consistent with their long-range academic and professional goals. MIT courses are offered both on campus and online, allowing professionals to earn their degrees and/or certificates by taking MIT on-campus courses, or MIT online courses, or a combination of both types. In addition, the MIT program is directed toward preparing students to function in a variety of roles to be performed in a broad range of settings, including business and industry, human services, health institutions, higher education, government, military, and public and private K-12 education.

Admission Requirements – Students desiring admission into the graduate program in instructional technology must present the following: A bachelors degree from an accredited college or university or its equivalent from a foreign institution of higher education based on a four-year program. A strong academic record (an average GPA of 3.0 or better is expected) in the basic courses required in the area of the proposed graduate study. Academic potential as indicated by satisfactory performance on standardized test scores (e.g., Miller Analogy Test or Graduate Record Examination). The MAT or GRE must have been taken within the last five years. Three recommendations from individuals who are in a position to evaluate the student's professional competence as well as potential for graduate study. A statement of career goals and degree objectives. A letter describing educational and professional experiences, their reasons for pursuing graduate study, and the contributions that the student hopes to make after completing the degree. North Carolina essential and advanced technology competencies. Individuals who fall below a specified criterion may be admitted if other factors indicate potential for success. Individuals with identified deficiencies may be accepted provisionally with specified plans and goals for the remediation of those deficiencies. Such remediation may include a requirement of additional hours beyond those normally required for the degree.

Number of Full-Time Faculty – 5; **Number of Other Faculty** – 5

Degrees awarded in 2008–2009 Academic Year – Masters – 10; **PhD** – 0; **Other** – 0

Grant Monies awarded in 2008–2009 Academic Year – 0

Name of Institution – University of North Dakota

Name of Department or Program – Instructional Design & Technology

Address:
231 Centennial Drive, Stop 7189
Grand Forks, ND
58202
USA

Phone Number – 701-777-3574 **Fax Number** – 701-777-3246

Email Contact – richard.vaneck@und.edu **URL** – idt.und.edu

Contact Person – Richard Van Eck

Specializations – Serious Games, Game-Based Learning K-12 Technology Integration Human Performance Technology eLearning Problem-Based Learning

Features – Online Hybrid with synchronous and asynchronous learning Masters and Certificates fully available at a distance Three graduate certificates (K-12 Technology Integration; Corporate Training & Performance; eLearning) M.S. and M.Ed. Ph.D. Interdisciplinary studies Research Opportunities: Northern Plains Center for Behavioral Research Odegard School of Aerospace Sciences (Aviation & Radar simulators; Unmanned Aerial Systems Training)

Admission Requirements – See idt.und.edu

Degree Requirements – See idt.und.edu

Number of Full-Time Faculty – 3; **Number of Other Faculty** – 1

Degrees awarded in 2008–2009 Academic Year – **Masters** – 5; **PhD** – 0; **Other** – 2

Grant Monies awarded in 2008–2009 Academic Year – 50000

Name of Institution – Valley City State University

Name of Department or Program – School of Education and Graduate Studies

Address:
101 College St
Valley City, ND
58072
USA

Phone Number – 701-845-7303 **Fax Number** – 701-845-7305

Email Contact – terry.corwin@vcsu.edu **URL** – www.vcsu.edu/graduate

Contact Person – Terry Corwin

Specializations – The Master of Education program has four concentrations that focus on technology and the learner Teaching and Technology concentration Technology Education concentration Library and Information Technologies concentration Teaching English Language Learners concentration

Features – This is a completely online program which focuses on how technology can be used in a school setting to enhance student learning.

Admission Requirements – 1. Baccalaureate degree with a 3.0 undergraduate GPA or a test is required. 2. Three letters of recommendation 3. Written goals statement

Degree Requirements – Completion of 32–37 credits depending on concentration. Action Research report. Final portfolio demonstrating program core values.

Number of Full-Time Faculty – 12; **Number of Other Faculty** – 5

Degrees awarded in 2008–2009 Academic Year – Masters – 23; **PhD** – 0; **Other** – 168

Grant Monies awarded in 2008–2009 Academic Year – 450000

Name of Institution – New York Institute of Technology

Name of Department or Program – Dept. of Instructional Technology and Educational Leadership

Address:
Tower House/ 16 61st Street
Old Westbury/New York City, New York
11568/10023
USA

Phone Number – (516)686-7777/(212)261-1529 **Fax Number** – (516)686-7655

Email Contact – smcphers@nyit.edu **URL** – http://www.nyit.edu/education

Contact Person – Sarah McPherson, Chair, Dept. of Instructional Technology and Educational Leadership

Specializations – M.S. in Instructional Technology for Educators for Educational Technology Specialist Certification, and for Professional Trainers; Certificates in Computers in Education, Teaching 21st Century Skills, Science Technology Engineering Mathematics (STEM); Advanced Diploma Educational Leadership and Technology for School Building and Advanced Certificate for District Leader; M.S. in Childhood Education.

Features – Courses offered in Long Island, New York City and upstate New York in partnership with Teacher Centers, School Districts and related to special grant funding graduate courses. Program is offered 100% online statewide, national and internationally. Technology integration in content areas for K-12 teachers; Leadership and Technology for school building and district administrators;

Professional Trainer for corporate training, government and nonprofit agencies. All courses are hand-on instruction in technology labs; online courses; hybrid courses; evening, weekend, and summer courses.

Admission Requirements – Bachelors degree from accredited college with 3.0 cumulative average; Advanced Diploma and Advanced Certificate require Masters for admission.

Degree Requirements – 36 credits with 3.0 GPA for Master of Science, 18 credits with 3.0 GPA for Certificates; Advanced Diploma 33 credits and Advanced Certificate, 15 credits.

Number of Full-Time Faculty – 6; **Number of Other Faculty** – 50

Degrees awarded in 2008–2009 Academic Year – Masters – 130; **PhD** – 0; **Other** – 0

Grant Monies awarded in 2008–2009 Academic Year – 0

Name of Institution – Montclair State University

Name of Department or Program – Department of Curriculum & Teaching

Address:
1 College Avenue
Montclair, NJ
07043
USA

Phone Number – (973)655-5187 **Fax Number** – (973)655-7084

Email Contact – dominev@mail.montclair.edu **URL** – http://cehs.montclair.edu

Contact Person – Dr. Vanessa Domine, Professor of Educational Technology

Specializations – MSU offers 1) an M.Ed. degree program in Educational Technology (EDTC); 2) a post-bac certification program for Associate School Library Media Specialists (ALMS); and 3) an advanced certification program for School Library Media Specialists (SLMS).

Features – All three programs draw from the same pool of educational technology courses and can be completed together in a carefully assembled program of approximately 46 graduate credits. Three areas comprise coursework: Philosophical foundations, Pedagogical design and integration, and Practical design and application. In the M.Ed. program, students can choose to emphasize in one of three areas: (A) Administration, Policy, and Leadership; (B) Organizational Planning and Development; and (C) Curriculum and Technology Integration.

Admission Requirements – Students can apply in person or online to the Graduate School (http://www.montclair.edu/graduate). The M.Ed. program requires submission of GRE scores, letters of recommendation, and a project sample. The ALMS program requires a bachelors degree and standard NJ teaching license. The SLMS program requires a masters degree, a standard NJ teaching license, and at least one year of successful teaching as an associate school library media specialist.

Degree Requirements – The M.Ed. program requires 33 credits of coursework and field experience. The ALMS program requires 18–21 credits of coursework and field experience. The SLMS program requires 36 credits of coursework and field experience.

Number of Full-Time Faculty – ; **Number of Other Faculty** –

Degrees awarded in 2008–2009 Academic Year – Masters – ; **PhD** – ; **Other** –

Grant Monies awarded in 2008–2009 Academic Year –

Name of Institution – Richard Stockton College of New Jersey

Name of Department or Program – Master of Arts in Instructional Technology (MAIT)

Address:
Jimmie Leeds
Pomona, NJ
08240
USA

Phone Number – 609-652-4688 **Fax Number** – 609-626-5528

Email Contact – leej@stockton.edu **URL** – http://intraweb.stockton.edu/eyos/page.cfm?siteID=73&pageID=47

Contact Person – Jung Lee

Specializations – The Master of Arts in Instructional Technology offered by The Richard Stockton College of New Jersey is designed to bring the best instructional technologies into both public and corporate curricula. With a strong theoretical foundation, the degree enables graduates to use technology as a tool to enhance learning and training.

Features – The program serves (1) students who seek or will continue employment in the P-12 schools; (2) students who wish to pursue coordinator or supervisor positions in P-12 schools and districts; and (3) students seeking or holding careers in business, industry, or nonprofit organizations.

Admission Requirements – Minimum 3.0 GPA, relevant experience, reference letters and GRE General Exam scores or MAT (Miller Analogies Test scores).

Degree Requirements – 11 graduate courses (33 credits) including capstone project course

Number of Full-Time Faculty – 3; **Number of Other Faculty** – 5

Degrees awarded in 2008–2009 Academic Year – Masters – 22; **PhD** – 0; **Other** – 0

Grant Monies awarded in 2008–2009 Academic Year – 0

Name of Institution – New York University

Name of Department or Program – Educational Communication and Technology Program, Steinhardt School of Education

Address:
239 Greene St., Suite 300
New York, NY
10003
USA

Phone Number – (212)998-5520 **Fax Number** – (212)995-4041

Email Contact – jan.plass@nyu.edu **URL** – http://www.nyu.edu/education/alt/ectprogram

Contact Person – Francine Shuchat-Shaw, Assoc. Prof. (MA Advisor), Dir.; W. Michael Reed, Prof., (Doctoral Advisor)

Specializations – M.A., Ed.D., and Ph.D. in Education – for the preparation of individuals as instructional media designers, developers, media producers, and/or researchers in education, business and industry, health and medicine, community services, government, museums and other cultural institutions; and to teach or become involved in administration in educational communications and instructional technology programs in higher education, including instructional television, micro-computers, multimedia, Internet and telecommunications. The program also offers a post-M.A. 30-point Certificate of Advanced Study in Education.

Features – emphasizes theoretical foundations, especially a cognitive science perspective of learning and instruction, and their implications for designing media-based learning environments and materials. All efforts focus on video, multimedia, instructional television, web-based technology and telecommunications; participation in special research and production projects and field internships. CREATE – Consortium for Research and Evaluation of Advanced Technologies in Education – uses an apprenticeship model to provide doctoral students and advanced MA students with research opportunities in collaboration with faculty.

Admission Requirements – M.A.: 3.0 undergraduate GPA, responses to essay questions, interview related to academic and professional goals. Ph.D.: 3.0 GPA, 1000 GRE, responses to essay questions, interview related to academic or professional preparation and career goals. For international students, 600 TOEFL and TWE.

Degree Requirements – M.A.: 36 semester hours including specialization, elective courses, thesis, English Essay Examination. Ph.D.: 57 semester hours beyond MA, including specialization, foundations, research, content seminar, and elective course work; candidacy papers; dissertation; English Essay Examination.

Number of Full-Time Faculty – 0; **Number of Other Faculty** – 0

Degrees awarded in 2008–2009 Academic Year – **Masters** – 0; **PhD** – 0; **Other** – 0

Grant Monies awarded in 2008–2009 Academic Year – 0

Name of Institution – Syracuse University

Name of Department or Program – Instructional Design, Development, and Evaluation Program, School of Education

Address:
330 Huntington Hall
Syracuse, NY
13244-2340
USA

Phone Number – (315)443-3703 **Fax Number** – (315)443-1218

Email Contact – nlsmith@syr.edu **URL** – http://idde.syr.edu

Contact Person – Nick Smith, Professor and Department Chair

Specializations – Certificates in Educational Technology and Adult Lifelong Learning, M.S., M.S. in Instructional Technology, C.A.S., and Ph.D. degree programs in Instructional Design, Educational Evaluation, Human Issues in Instructional Development, Technology Integration, and Educational Research and Theory (learning theory, application of theory, and educational media research). Graduates are prepared to serve as curriculum developers, instructional designers, program and project evaluators, researchers, resource center administrators, technology coordinators, educational technology specialist, distance learning design and delivery specialists, trainers and training managers, and higher education faculty.

Features – The courses and programs are typically project-centered. Collaborative project experience, field work and internships are emphasized throughout. There are special issue seminars, as well as student- and faculty-initiated mini-courses, seminars and guest lecturers, faculty–student formulation of department policies, and multiple international perspectives. International collaborations are an ongoing feature of the program. The graduate student population is highly diverse.

Admission Requirements – Certificates and M.S.: undergraduate transcripts, recommendations, personal statement, interview recommended; TOEFL for international applicants; GRE recommended. Certificate of Advanced Study: Relevant Masters degree from accredited institution or equivalent, GRE scores, recommendations, personal statement, TOEFL for international applicants; interview recommended.

Doctoral: Relevant Masters degree from accredited institution or equivalent, GRE scores, recommendations, personal statement, TOEFL for international applicants; interview strongly encouraged.

Degree Requirements – Certificates: 15 and 24 semester hours. M.S.: 36 semester hours, portfolio required. M.S. in Instructional Technology: 37 semester hours, practicum and portfolio required. C.A.S.: 60 semester hours, exam and project required. Ph.D.: 90 semester hours, research apprenticeship, portfolio, qualifying exams and dissertation required.

Number of Full-Time Faculty – 4; **Number of Other Faculty** – 5

Degrees awarded in 2008–2009 Academic Year – Masters – 9; **PhD** – 2; **Other** – 1

Grant Monies awarded in 2008–2009 Academic Year – 92228

Name of Institution – East Stroudsburg University

Name of Department or Program – Instructional Technology, Media Communication and Technology Department

Address:
200 Prospect Street
East Stroudsburg, PA
18301
USA

Phone Number – 470 422 3621 **Fax Number** – (570) 422-3876

Email Contact – bsockman@po-box.esu.edu **URL** – www.esu.edu/gradmcom

Contact Person – Beth Rajan Sockman

Specializations – The graduate programs are designed to develop the technology literacy of educators, prepare specialists to work in K-12 schools, school districts, or instructional technology personnel in education, business, or industry. Students can obtain a Masters of Education degree in Instructional Technology and/or a Pennsylvania Instructional Technologist Specialist Certificate. Students interested in PK-12 education may choose to concentrate in Technology Integration.

Features – The program provides students with an opportunity to take courses from ESU and Kutztown University. Students who successfully complete the program become proficient in using technology in teaching. Students can choose courses that explore that following areas: * Desktop publishing * Interactive web design (Including Web 2.0 applications) * Graphics * Video * New and emerging technologies * Instructional design * Learning theories * Research in Instructional Technology

Admission Requirements – For M.Ed. degree: * Two letters of recommendation * Portfolio or interview (Interview is granted after the application is received) * For full admission a minimum overall undergraduate 2.5 QPA * Rolling deadline

For certification: * Contact the graduate coordinator for additional admission information to comply with Pennsylvania Department of Education requirements. * Minimum overall undergraduate QPA 3.0 (Pennsylvania Act 354) * If not 3.0 QPA, then completion of nine credits of Media Communication and Technology Department courses with prior written approval of department faculty adviser * Two letters of recommendation * Rolling deadline

Degree Requirements – Total = 33 credits # Take courses and learn – Take 30 credits of courses for the masters and learn based on your needs. You will learn to use and implement technologies outside average persons experience. # Create, Submit and Present your Portfolio – This is the time to display your learning in a professional manner. In the portfolio you articulate your goals and may identify learning goals for your internship. Click here for the Portfolio Guidelines. # Complete an Internship – You complete a 90-hour internship that extends your knowledge base – 3 credits. # Complete Portfolio and Graduate

Number of Full-Time Faculty – 7; **Number of Other Faculty** – 3

Degrees awarded in 2008–2009 Academic Year – Masters – 6; **PhD** – 0; **Other** – 0

Grant Monies awarded in 2008–2009 Academic Year – 3400

Name of Institution – Penn State Great Valley School of Graduate Professional Studies

Name of Department or Program – Education Division/Instructional Systems Program

Address:
30 E. Swedesfordd Road
Malvern, PA
19355
usa

Phone Number – 610-725-5250 **Fax Number** – 610-725-5232

Email Contact – ydl1@psu.edu **URL** – http://www.sgps.psu.edu

Contact Person – Doris Lee

Specializations – Instructional Systems/Designs

Admission Requirements – online application, MAT/GRE scores, 2 letters of recommendations,

Degree Requirements – 36 cr.

Number of Full-Time Faculty – 10; **Number of Other Faculty** – 15

Degrees awarded in 2008–2009 Academic Year – Masters – 45; **PhD** – 0; **Other** – 0

Grant Monies awarded in 2008–2009 Academic Year – 0

Name of Institution – Temple University

Name of Department or Program – Department of Psychological Studies in Education

Address:
1301 Cecil B. Moore Avenue
Philadelphia, PA
19122
USA

Phone Number – (215) 204-4497 **Fax Number** – (215) 204-6013

Email Contact – susan.miller@temple.edu **URL** – http://www.temple.edu/education/

Contact Person – Susan Miller, Ph.D.

Specializations – Instructional and Learning Technology (ILT) is a new masters program within the Educational Psychology Program in the Department of Psychological Studies in Education. As such, ILT is designed to address conceptual as well as technical issues in using technology for teaching and learning. Program areas include (a)instructional theory and design issues, (b) application of technology, and (c) management issues.

Features – Instructional Theory and Design topics includes psychology of the learner, cognitive processes, instructional theories, human development, and individual differences as well as psychological and educational characteristics of technology resources, and identification of strengths and weaknesses of instructional technology resources. The Application of Technology area focuses on clarification of instructional objectives, identification of resources to facilitate learning, operation and application of current and emergent technologies, facility using graphic design, multimedia, video, distributed learning resources, WWW, and print publishing. Management and Consultation is structured around defining instructional needs, monitoring progress, and evaluating outcomes, designing technology delivery systems, preparing policy statements, budgets, and facility design criteria, managing skill assessment and training, understanding legal and ethical issues, and managing and maintaining facilities.

Admission Requirements – Bachelors Degree from an accredited institution, GRE(MAT) scores, 3 letters of recommendation, transcripts from each institution of higher learning attended (undergraduate and graduate), goal statement

Degree Requirements – Coursework (33 hours: 5 core courses, 3 technology electives, 3 cognate area courses) Practicum in students area of interest Comprehensive Exam Portfolio of Certification Competencies (for students interested in PA Dept. of Ed Certification as Instructional Technology Specialist)

Number of Full-Time Faculty – ; **Number of Other Faculty** –

Degrees awarded in 2008–2009 Academic Year – Masters – ; **PhD** – ; **Other** –

Grant Monies awarded in 2008–2009 Academic Year –

Name of Institution – University of Memphis

Name of Department or Program – Instruction and Curriculum Leadership/ Instructional Design & Technology

Address:
406 Ball Hall
Memphis, TN
38152
USA

Phone Number – 901-678-5672 **Fax Number** – 901-678-3881

Email Contact – clifmims@memphis.edu **URL** – http://idt.memphis.edu

Contact Person – Dr. Clif MIms

Specializations – Instructional Design, Web-based instruction, Computer-based instruction, Digital Video, K-12 NTeQ technology integration model, Instructional Games, Pedagogical Agents

Features – The Advanced Instructional Media (AIM) lab, staffed and run by IDT faculty and students, serves as an R&D space for coursework and research involving technologies such as digital media, WBT/CBT (Dreamweaver, Flash, Authorware, WebCT, DV cameras, DV editing, DVD authoring, etc.), pedagogical agents, gaming and simulation. The AIM lab and IDT program is connected to the Center for Multimedia Arts in the FedEx Institute of Technology. The AIM Lab brings in outside contract work from corporate partners to provide real-world experience to students. We have also partnered with the Institute for Intelligent Systems and the Tutoring Research Group (www.autotutor.org) to work on intelligent agent development and research.

Admission Requirements – Minimum standards which identify a pool of masters level applicants from which each department selects students to be admitted: An official transcript showing a bachelors degree awarded by an accredited college or university with a minimum GPA of 2.0 on a 4.0 scale, competitive MAT or GRE scores, GRE writing test, two letters of recommendation, graduate school and departmental application. Doctoral students must also be interviewed by at least two members of the program.

Degree Requirements – M.S.: 36 hours, internship, masters project or thesis, 3.0 GPA. Ed.D: 54 hours, 45 in major, 9 in research; residency project; comprehensive exams; dissertation.

Number of Full-Time Faculty – 6; **Number of Other Faculty** – 0

Degrees awarded in 2008–2009 Academic Year – **Masters** – 0; **PhD** – 0; **Other** – 0

Grant Monies awarded in 2008–2009 Academic Year – 0

Name of Institution – Texas A&M University-Commerce

Name of Department or Program – Department of Educational Leadership

Address:
PO Box 3011
Commerce, TX
75429-3011
USA

Phone Number – (903)886-5607 **Fax Number** – (903)886-5507

Email Contact – Sue_Espinoza@tamu-commerce.edu **URL** – http://www.tamu-commerce.edu/

Contact Person – Dr. Sue Espinoza, Professor, Program Coordinator

Specializations – M.S. or M.Ed. degrees in Educational Technology-Leadership and in Educational Technology-Library Science Certification programs – School Librarian, and Technology Applications, both approved by the Texas State Board for Educator Certification.

Features – Programs may be completed totally online, although some courses may also be offered in web-enhanced formats, and one or more electives may be offered only face to face.

Admission Requirements – Apply to the Graduate School at Texas A&M University-Commerce. For school library certification, must also apply to the professional certification program.

Degree Requirements – 36 hours for each Masters Degree; each program contains core courses, and specialization area courses are selected in consultation with advisor, who is assigned when each student is admitted to the program

Number of Full-Time Faculty – 3; **Number of Other Faculty** – 6

Degrees awarded in 2008–2009 Academic Year – **Masters** – 19; **PhD** – 0; **Other** – 0

Grant Monies awarded in 2008–2009 Academic Year – 0

Name of Institution – Old Dominion University

Name of Department or Program – Instructional Design & Technology

Address:
Education 228
Norfolk, VA
23529
USA

Phone Number – 757-683-6275 **Fax Number** – 757-683-5862

Email Contact – gmorriso@odu.edu **URL** – http://education.odu.edu/eci/idt/

Contact Person – Gary R. Morrison

Specializations – Our faculty engages students in a rigorous course of study tailored to meet individual educational and career interests. Research opportunities and course work ensures that all students receive a solid foundation in Instructional Design Instructional Design Theory Human Performance Technology Gaming and Simulation Distance Education Evaluation & Assessment Trends and Issues in Instructional Technology Quantitative and Qualitative Research

Features – All of our courses are offered via distance using a hybrid format. Classroom instruction uses a virtual classroom that allows all students to participate in a face-to-face classroom. A reduced tuition rate is available for students living outside of Virginia who are accepted into the program.

Admission Requirements – MS degree: GRE scores or MAT scores; transcripts for undergraduate and graduate courses Ph.D.: GRE scores, transcripts for undergraduate and graduate courses, letters of recommendation, and an essay describing professional goals.

Degree Requirements – MS program is 30–36 hours PhD program is a postmaster degree consisting of 60 hours

Number of Full-Time Faculty – 5; **Number of Other Faculty** – 0

Degrees awarded in 2008–2009 Academic Year – **Masters** – 2; **PhD** – 2; **Other** – 0

Grant Monies awarded in 2008–2009 Academic Year – 0

Name of Institution – Concordia University Wisconsin

Name of Department or Program – Educational Technology

Address:
12800 N Lakeshore Drive
Mequon, WI
53092
USA

Phone Number – 262-243-4595 **Fax Number** – 262-243-3595

Email Contact – bernard.bull@cuw.edu **URL** – http://www.cuw.edu/go/edtech

Contact Person – Dr. Bernard Bull

Specializations – Digital culture, designing digital age learning experiences, and social/spiritual/ethical implications of technology.

Features – Courses are available via e-learning or face to face. Some cohorts are also offered at off-campus sites in Wisconsin and beyond. In addition, we run occasional thematic cohorts where a group of students work through the program together over an 18–24 month period, all agreeing to focus their thesis or culminating project upon the cohort theme (e.g., new literacies, bridging the digital divide, global education, discipleship in the digital age).

Admission Requirements – To be considered for admission, a student must: Have a bachelors degree from an accredited college or university. Have a minimum GPA of 3.00 in the undergraduate program.

Degree Requirements – Required Courses EDT 970 – Integrating Technology in the Classroom (3) EDT 889 – Applying Technology in the Content Areas (3) EDT 908 – Critical Issues in Educational Technology (3) EDT 892 – Instructional Design (3) EDT 893 – Theories of Learning and Design (3) EDT 815 – Research in Educational Technology (3) EDT 927, 928, 929 – Portfolio I, II, and III (0) EDT 895 – Capstone Project (3) OR EDT 890 – Thesis Completion Seminar (3) Electives EDT 805 – Online Teaching and Learning (3) EDT 814 – Educational Ministry in the Digital World (3) EDT 894 – Digital Literacy (3) EDT 907 – Multimedia for the Classroom (3) EDT 939 – School Leadership in Technology (3) EDT 940 – Networking, Support, and Delivery Systems for Schools (3) EDT 957 – Building Online Learning Communities (Web 2.0 / Learning 2.0) (3) EDT 971 – Grants and Funding for Educational Technology Initiatives (3) EDT 804 – Strategies for Teaching and Learning with Interactive Whiteboards (1) Other electives as approved by the program director.

Number of Full-Time Faculty – 3; **Number of Other Faculty** – 6

Degrees awarded in 2008–2009 Academic Year – **Masters** – 0; **PhD** – 0; **Other** – 0

Grant Monies awarded in 2008–2009 Academic Year – 0

Name of Institution – University of Wisconsin-Madison

Name of Department or Program – Curriculum and Instruction, School of Education

Address:
225 North Mills Street
Madison, WI
53706
USA

Phone Number – 608) 263-4670 **Fax Number** – (608) 263-9992

Email Contact – kdsquire@wisc.edu **URL** – http://www.education.wisc.edu/ci/

Contact Person – Kurt D. Squire

Specializations – M.S. and Ph.D. degree programs to prepare Educational Technology faculty and professionals. On-going research includes: – studying the impact of contemporary gaming practices on learning, schooling, and society – understanding ways in which online play spaces align (or fail to align) with practices valued outside the game (i.e., informal scientific reasoning, collaborative problem-solving, and media literacy) – interrogating the implementation of technology-rich innovations in local and international schools as well as the role of culture in the design of instruction – using photography as a research method in education.

Features – Educational Technology courses are processed through social, cultural, historical, and design-based frames of reference. Current curriculum emphasizes new media theories, critical cultural and visual culture theories, and constructivist theories of instructional design and development. Many courses offered in the evening.

Admission Requirements – Master's and Ph.D.: previous experience in Instructional Technology preferred, previous teaching experience, 3.0 GPA on last 60 undergraduate credits, acceptable scores on GRE, 3.0 GPA on all graduate work.

Degree Requirements – M.S.: 24 credits plus thesis and exam (an additional 12 credits of Educational Foundations if no previous educational background); Ph.D.: 1 year of residency beyond the Bachelor's, major, minor, and research requirements, preliminary exam, dissertation, and oral exam.

Number of Full-Time Faculty – 4; **Number of Other Faculty** – 0

Degrees awarded in 2008–2009 Academic Year – Masters – 1; **PhD** – 1; **Other** – 0

Grant Monies awarded in 2008–2009 Academic Year – 1000000

Name of Institution – Texas A&M University-Texarkana

Name of Department or Program – College of Education and Liberal Arts

Address:
2600 N. Robinson Road
Texarkana, TX
75505-5518
USA

Phone Number – 903-223-3166 **Fax Number** – 903-223-3120

Email Contact – bosede.aworuwa@tamut.edu **URL** – http://www.tamut.edu/ited

Contact Person – Dr. Bosede Aworuwa

Specializations – Master of Science in Instructional Technology; Master of Science in Instructional Technology with combined Master Technology Teacher Certification (EC-12)

Features – Approval for totally online version of the MSIT program is pending. May become available fall 2009.

Admission Requirements – Bachelor degree, 3.0 GPA in the last 60 hours of undergraduate coursework, GRE score, TOEFL score for international candidates

Number of Full-Time Faculty – 2; **Number of Other Faculty** – 2

Degrees awarded in 2008–2009 Academic Year – Masters – 13; **PhD** – 0; **Other** – 0

Grant Monies awarded in 2008–2009 Academic Year – 0
There are a total of 162 graduate programs in the database.

Part VI
Mediagraphy

Print and Non-print Resources

Introduction

Jinn-Wei Tsao

Contents

This resource lists journals and other resources of interest to practitioners, researchers, students, and others concerned with educational technology and educational media. The primary goal of this section is to list current publications in the field. The majority of materials cited here were published in 2009 or mid-2010. Media-related journals include those listed in the past issues of EMTY, as well as new entries in the field. A thorough list of journals in the educational technology field has been updated for the 2010 edition using Ulrich's Periodical Index Online and journal websites. This chapter is not intended to serve as a specific resource location tool, although it may be used for that purpose in the absence of database access. Rather, readers are encouraged to peruse the categories of interest in this chapter to gain an idea of recent developments within the field. For archival purposes, this chapter serves as a snapshot of the field of instructional technology publications in 2009. Readers must bear in mind that technological developments occur well in advance of publication and should take that fact into consideration when judging the timeliness of resources listed in this chapter.

J.-W. Tsao (✉)
Learning, Design, and Technology Program, The University of Georgia, Athens, GA, USA
e-mail: miketsao@uga.edu

M. Orey et al. (eds.), *Educational Media and Technology Yearbook: Volume 36, 2011*,
Educational Media and Technology Yearbook 36, DOI 10.1007/978-1-4614-1305-9_29,
© Springer Science+Business Media, LLC 2012

Selection

Items were selected for the Mediagraphy in several ways. The EBSCO Host
Databases were used to locate most of the journal citations. Others were taken from
the journal listings of large publishing companies. Items were chosen for this list
when they met one or more of the following criteria: reputable publisher, broad
circulation, coverage by indexing services, peer review, and coverage of a gap in the
literature. The author chose items on subjects that seem to reflect the instructional
technology field as it is today. Because of the increasing tendency for media producers to package their products in more than one format and for single titles to contain
mixed media, titles are no longer separated by media type. The author makes no
claims as to the comprehensiveness of this list. It is, instead, intended to be
representative.

Obtaining Resources

Media-related periodicals: The author has attempted to provide various ways to
obtain the resources listed in this Mediagraphy, including telephone and fax numbers, Web and postal addresses, as well as email contacts. Prices are also included
for individual and institutional subscriptions. The information presented reflects the
most current information available at the time of publication.

ERIC Documents: As of December 31, 2003, ERIC was no longer funded. However,
ERIC documents can still be read and copied from their microfiche form at any
library holding an ERIC microfiche collection. The identification number beginning
with ED (for example, ED 332 677) locates the document in the collection.
Document delivery services and copies of most ERIC documents can also continue
to be available from the ERIC Document Reproduction Service. Prices charged
depend on the format chosen (microfiche or paper copy), length of the document,
and method of shipping. Online orders, fax orders, and expedited delivery are
available.

To find the closest library with an ERIC microfiche collection, contact: ACCESS
ERIC, 1600 Research Blvd, Rockville, METHOD 20850-3172; (800) LET-ERIC
(538-3742); email: acceric@inet.ed.gov.

To order ERIC documents, contact:

ERIC Document Reproduction Services (EDRS)
7420 Fullerton Rd, Suite 110, Springfield, VA 22153-2852
(800) 433-ERIC (433-3742); (703) 440-1400
Fax: (703) 440-1408
Email: service@edrs.com.

Journal articles: Photocopies of journal articles can be obtained in one of the following ways: (1) from a library subscribing to the title, (2) through interlibrary loan, (3) through the purchase of a back issue from the journal publisher, or (4) from an article reprint service such as UMI:

UMI Information Store, 500 Sansome St, Suite 400
San Francisco, CA 94111
(800) 248-0360 (toll-free in U.S. and Canada); (415) 433-5500 (outside U.S. and Canada)
Email: orders@infostore.com.

Journal articles can also be obtained through the Institute for Scientific Information (ISI):

ISI Document Solution
P.O. Box 7649
Philadelphia, PA 19104-3389
(215) 386-4399
Fax: (215) 222-0840 or (215) 386-4343
Email: ids@isinet.com.

Arrangement

Mediagraphy entries are classified according to major subject emphasis under the following headings:

- Artificial Intelligence, Robotics, and Electronic Performance Support Systems
- Computer-Assisted Instruction
- Distance Education
- Educational Research
- Educational Technology
- Information Science and Technology
- Instructional Design and Development
- Learning Sciences
- Libraries and Media Centers
- Media Technologies
- Professional Development
- Simulation, Gaming, and Virtual Reality
- Special Education and Disabilities
- Telecommunications and Networking

Mediagraphy

Artificial Intelligence, Robotics, and Electronic Performance Support Systems

Artificial Intelligence Review. Springer Science+Business Media, PO Box 2485, Secaucus, NJ 07096-2485. www.springer.com/journal/10462, tel: 800-777-4643, fax: 201-348-4505, service-ny@springer.com [8/yr; $840 inst (print/online), $1088 inst (print + online, content through 1997)] Publishes commentary on issues and development in artificial intelligence foundations and current research.

AI Magazine. Association for the Advancement of Artificial Intelligence, 445 Burgess Dr, Suite 100, Menlo Park, CA 94025. www.aaai.org/Magazine/magazine. php, tel: 650-328-3123, fax: 650-321-4457, info08@aaai.org [4/yr; $55 student, $125 indiv, $250 inst] Proclaimed "journal of record for the AI community," this magazine provides full-length articles on research and new literature, but is written to allow access to those reading outside their area of expertise.

International Journal of Robotics Research. Sage Publications, 2455 Teller Rd, Thousand Oaks, CA 91320. ijr.sagepub.com, tel: 800-818-7243, fax: 800-583-2665, journals@sagepub.com [14/yr; $1725 inst (online, content through 1999), $1917 inst (online + backfile, content through Volume 1, Issue 1), $1879 inst (print), $1917 inst (print + online), $2109 inst (print + online + backfile)] Interdisciplinary approach to the study of robotics for researchers, scientists, and students. The first scholarly publication on robotics research.

M. Orey et al. (eds.), *Educational Media and Technology Yearbook: Volume 36, 2011*, Educational Media and Technology Yearbook 36, DOI 10.1007/978-1-4614-1305-9_30, © Springer Science+Business Media, LLC 2012

Journal of Intelligent and Robotic Systems. Springer Science+Business Media, PO Box 2485, Secaucus, NJ 07096-2485. www.springer.com/journal/10846, tel: 800-777-4643, fax: 201-348-4505, service-ny@springer.com [16/yr; $2095 inst (print/online), $2514 inst (print + online, content through 1997)] Main objective is to provide a forum for the fruitful interaction of ideas and techniques that combine systems and control science with artificial intelligence and other related computer science concepts. It bridges the gap between theory and practice.

Journal of Interactive Learning Research. Association for the Advancement of Computing in Education, PO Box 1545, Chesapeake, VA 23327-1545. www.aace. org/pubs/jilr, tel: 757-366-5606, fax: 703-997-8760, info@aace.org [4/yr; $35 for AACE student members, $115 AACE members (discount available for ordering multiple AACE journals), $195 inst] Publishes articles on how intelligent computer technologies can be used in education to enhance learning and teaching. Reports on research and developments, integration, and applications of artificial intelligence in education.

Knowledge-Based Systems. Elsevier, Inc., Journals Customer Service, 3251 Riverport Lane, Maryland Heights, MO 63043. www.elsevier.com/locate/knosys, tel: 877-839-7126, fax: 314-447-8077, journalcustomerservice-usa@elsevier.com [8/yr; $202 indiv, $1319 inst] Interdisciplinary applications-oriented journal on fifth-generation computing, expert systems, and knowledge-based methods in system design.

Minds and Machines. Springer Science+Business Media, PO Box 2485, Secaucus, NJ 07096-2485. www.springer.com/journal/11023, tel: 800-777-4643, fax: 201-348-4505, service-ny@springer.com [4/yr; $760 inst (print/online), $912 inst (print + online, content through 1997)] Discusses issues concerning machines and mentality, artificial intelligence, epistemology, simulation, and modeling.

Computer-Assisted Instruction

AACE Journal. Association for the Advancement of Computing in Education, PO Box 1545, Chesapeake, VA 23327-1545. www.aace.org/pubs/aacej, tel: 757-366-5606, fax: 703-997-8760, info@aace.org [4/yr; $35 for AACE student members, $115 AACE members (discount available for ordering multiple AACE journals), $195 inst] Publishes articles dealing with issues in instructional technology.

CALICO Journal. Computer Assisted Language Instruction Consortium, 214 Centennial Hall, Texas State Univ, San Marcos, TX 78666. calico.org, tel: 512-245-1417, fax: 512-245-9089, info@calico.org [3/yr; $50 indiv, $35 K-12 or community college teacher, $30 students or senior citizen, $85 inst] Provides information on the applications of technology in teaching and learning languages.

Children's Technology Review. Active Learning Associates, 120 Main St, Flemington, NJ 08822. childrenstech.com, tel: 800-993-9499, fax: 908-284-0405, lisa@childrenssoftware.com [12/yr; $24 online, $108 print+online] Provides reviews and other information about software to help parents and educators more effectively use computers with children.

Computers and Composition. Elsevier, Inc., Journals Customer Service, 3251 Riverport Lane, Maryland Heights, MO 63043. www.elsevier.com/locate/comp-com, tel: 877-839-7126, fax: 314-447-8077, journalcustomerservice-usa@elsevier.com [4/yr; $75 indiv, $400 inst] International journal for teachers of writing that focuses on the use of computers in writing instruction and related research.

Computers & Education. Elsevier, Inc., Journals Customer Service, 3251 Riverport Lane, Maryland Heights, MO 63043. www.elsevier.com/locate/compedu, tel: 877-839-7126, fax: 314-447-8077, journalcustomerservice-usa@elsevier.com [8/yr; $370 indiv, $1942 inst] Presents technical papers covering a broad range of subjects for users of analog, digital, and hybrid computers in all aspects of higher education.

Computers in Education Journal. American Society for Engineering Education, Computers in Education Division, Port Royal Square, PO Box 68, Port Royal, VA 22535. www.asee.org/publications/divisions/coed.cfm, tel: 804-742-5611, fax: 804-742-5030, ed-pub@crosslink.net [4/yr; $20 student, $69 indiv, inst prices vary] Covers transactions, scholarly research papers, application notes, and teaching methods.

Computers in Human Behavior. Elsevier, Inc., Journals Customer Service, 3251 Riverport Lane, Maryland Heights, MO 63043. www.elsevier.com/locate/com-phumbeh, tel: 877-839-7126, fax: 314-447-8077, journalcustomerservice-usa@elsevier.com [6/yr; $290 indiv, $1535 inst] Scholarly journal dedicated to examining the use of computers from a psychological perspective.

Computers in the Schools. Taylor & Francis Group, Customer Service Dept, 325 Chestnut Street, Suite 800, Philadelphia, PA 19106. www.tandf.co.uk/journals/titles/07380569, tel: 800-354-1420, fax: 215-625-2940, subscriptions@tandf.co.uk [4/yr; $124 indiv, $659 inst (online), $694 inst (print+online)] Features articles that combine theory and practical applications of small computers in schools for educators and school administrators.

Converge. e.Republic, Inc., 100 Blue Ravine Rd, Folsom, CA 95630. www.convergemag.com, tel: 800-940-6039, fax: 916-932-1470, subscriptions@convergemag.com [4/yr; free] Explores the revolution of technology in education.

Dr. Dobb's Journal. United Business Media LLC, PO Box 1093, Skokie, IL 60076. www.ddj.com, tel: 888-847-6188, fax: 902-563-4807, drdobbsjournal@halldata. com [12/yr; free to qualified applicants] Articles on the latest in operating systems, programming languages, algorithms, hardware design and architecture, data structures, and telecommunications; in-depth hardware and software reviews.

eWEEK. Ziff Davis Media Inc., PO Box 3402, Northbrook, IL 60065-3402. www. eweek.com, tel: 888-663-8438, fax: 847-564-9453, eweek@ziffdavis.com [36/yr; $125 (print), $85 (online), free to qualified applicants] Provides current information on the IBM PC, including hardware, software, industry news, business strategies, and reviews of hardware and software.

Instructor. Scholastic Inc., PO Box 420235, Palm Coast, FL 32142-0235. teacher. scholastic.com/products/instructor, tel: 866-436-2455, fax: 212-343-4799, instructor@ emailcustomerservice.com [8/yr; $8)] Features articles on applications and advances of technology in education for K-12 and college educators and administrators.

Interactive Learning Environments. Taylor & Francis Group, Customer Services Dept, 325 Chestnut St, Suite 800, Philadelphia, PA 19106. www.tandf.co.uk/journals/titles/10494820, tel: 800-354-1420, fax: 215-625-2940, subscriptions@tandf. co.uk [4/yr; $175 indiv, $519 inst (online), $545 inst (print + online)] Explores the implications of the Internet and multimedia presentation software in education and training environments.

Journal of Computer Assisted Learning. John Wiley & Sons, Inc., Journal Customer Services, 350 Main St, Malden, MA 02148. www.blackwellpublishing. com/journals/JCA, tel: 800-835-6770, fax: 781-388-8232, cs-agency@wiley.com [6/yr; $216 individual (print + online), $1249 inst (print/online), $1374 inst (print + online)] Articles and research on the use of computer-assisted learning.

Journal of Educational Computing Research. Baywood Publishing Co., Inc., 26 Austin Ave, Box 337, Amityville, NY 11701-0337. www.baywood.com/journals/ previewjournals.asp?id=0735-6331, tel: 800-638-7819, fax: 631-691-1770, info@ baywood.com [8/yr; $209 indiv (online), $220 indiv (print + online), $527 inst (online), $555 inst (print + online)] Presents original research papers, critical analyses, reports on research in progress, design and development studies, article reviews, and grant award listings.

Journal of Educational Multimedia and Hypermedia. Association for the Advancement of Computing in Education, PO Box 1545, Chesapeake, VA 23327-1545. www.aace.org/pubs/jemh, tel: 757-366-5606, fax: 703-997-8760, info@aace. org [4/yr; $35 for AACE student members, $115 AACE members (discount available for ordering multiple AACE journals), $195 inst] A multidisciplinary information source presenting research about and applications for multimedia and hypermedia tools.

Journal of Research on Technology in Education. International Society for Technology in Education, 180 West 8th Ave., Suite 300, Eugene, OR 97401-2916. www.iste.org/jrte, tel: 800-336-5191, fax: 541-434-8948, iste@iste.org [4/yr; $54 member, $155 non-member] Contains articles reporting on the latest research findings related to classroom and administrative uses of technology, including system and project evaluations.

Language Resources and Evaluation. Springer Science+Business Media, PO Box 2485, Secaucus, NJ 07096-2485. www.springer.com/journal/10579, tel: 800-777-4643, fax: 201-348-4505, service-ny@springer.com [4/yr; $747 inst (print/online), $896.40 inst (print + online, content through 1997)] Contains papers on computer-aided studies, applications, automation, and computer-assisted instruction.

Learning and Leading with Technology. International Society for Technology in Education, 180 West 8th Ave., Suite 300, Eugene, OR 97401-2916. www.iste.org/LL, tel: 800-336-5191, fax: 541-302-3778, iste@iste.org [8/yr; $100] Focuses on the use of technology, coordination, and leadership; written by educators for educators. Appropriate for classroom teachers, lab teachers, technology coordinators, and teacher educators.

MacWorld. Mac Publishing, Macworld Subscription Services, PO Box 37781, Boone, IA 50037. www.macworld.com/magazine, tel: 800-288-6848, fax: 515-432-6994, subhelp@macworld.com [12/yr; $19.97] Describes hardware, software, tutorials, and applications for users of the Macintosh microcomputer.

OnCUE. Computer-Using Educators, Inc., 877 Ygnacio Valley Road, Suite 104, Walnut Creek, CA 94596. www.cue.org/oncue, tel: 925-478-3460, fax: 925-934-6799, cueinc@cue.org [4/yr; $30 student, $40 indiv] Contains articles, news items, and trade advertisements addressing computer-based education.

PC Magazine. Ziff Davis Media Inc., 28 E 28th St, New York, NY 10016-7930. www.pcmag.com, tel: 212-503-3500, fax: 212-503-4399, pcmag@ziffdavis.com [12/yr; $12] Comparative reviews of computer hardware and general business software programs.

Social Science Computer Review. Sage Publications, 2455 Teller Rd, Thousand Oaks, CA 91320. ssc.sagepub.com, tel: 800-818-7243, fax: 800-583-2665, journals@sagepub.com [4/yr; $604 inst (online, content through 1999), $671 inst (online + backfile, content through Volume 1, Issue 1), $658 inst (print), $671 inst (print + online), $738 inst (print + online + backfile)] Interdisciplinary peer-reviewed scholarly publication covering social science research and instructional applications in computing and telecommunications; also covers societal impacts of information technology.

Wireless Networks. Springer Science+Business Media, PO Box 2485, Secaucus, NJ 07096-2485. www.springer.com/journal/11276, tel: 800-777-4643, fax: 201-348-4505, service-ny@springer.com [8/yr; $801 inst (print/online), $961.20 inst (print+online, content through 1997)] Devoted to the technological innovations that result from the mobility allowed by wireless technology.

Distance Education

American Journal of Distance Education. Taylor & Francis Group, Customer Services Dept, 325 Chestnut St, Suite 800, Philadelphia, PA 19106. www.tandf. co.uk/journals/titles/08923647, tel: 800-354-1420, fax: 215-625-2940, subscriptions@tandf.co.uk [4/yr; $70 indiv, $258 inst (online), $271 inst (print+online)] Created to disseminate information and act as a forum for criticism and debate about research on and practice of systems, management, and administration of distance education.

Journal of Distance Education. Canadian Network for Innovation in Education, BCIT Learning & Teaching Centre, British Columbia Institute of Technology, 3700 Willingdon Ave, Burnaby, BC, V5G 3 H2, Canada. www.jofde.ca, tel: 604-454-2280, fax: 604-431-7267, journalofde@gmail.com [at least 2/yr; $40 (print); free online] Aims to promote and encourage scholarly work of empirical and theoretical nature relating to distance education in Canada and throughout the world.

Journal of Library & Information Services in Distance Learning. Taylor & Francis Group, Customer Service Dept, 325 Chestnut Street, Suite 800, Philadelphia, PA 19106. www.tandf.co.uk/journals/titles/1533290X, tel: 800-354-1420, fax: 215-625-2940, subscriptions@tandf.co.uk [4/yr; $75 indiv, $187 inst (online), $197 inst (print+online)] Contains peer-reviewed articles, essays, narratives, current events, and letters from distance learning and information science experts.

Journal of Research on Technology in Education. International Society for Technology in Education, 180 West 8th Ave., Suite 300, Eugene, OR 97401-2916. www.iste.org/jrte, tel: 800-336-5191, fax: 541-434-8948, iste@iste.org [4/yr; $54 member, $155 non-member] Contains articles reporting on the latest research findings related to classroom and administrative uses of technology, including system and project evaluations.

Open Learning. Taylor & Francis Group, Customer Services Dept, 325 Chestnut St, Suite 800, Philadelphia, PA 19106. www.tandf.co.uk/journals/titles/02680513, tel: 800-354-1420, fax: 215-625-2940, subscriptions@tandf.co.uk [3/yr; $108 indiv, $324 inst (online), $341 inst (print+online)] Academic, scholarly publication on aspects of open and distance learning anywhere in the world. Includes issues for debate and research notes.

Educational Research

American Educational Research Journal. Sage Publications, 2455 Teller Rd, Thousand Oaks, CA 91320. aer.sagepub.com, tel: 800-818-7243, fax: 800-583-2665, journals@sagepub.com [4/yr; $289 inst (online, content through 1999), $321 inst (online + backfile, content through Volume 1, Issue 1), $315 inst (print), $321 inst (print + online), $353 inst (print + online + backfile)] Reports original research, both empirical and theoretical, and brief synopses of research.

Educational Research. Taylor & Francis Group, Customer Services Dept, 325 Chestnut St, Suite 800, Philadelphia, PA 19106. www.tandf.co.uk/journals/titles/00131881, tel: 800-354-1420, fax: 215-625-2940, subscriptions@tandf.co.uk [4/yr; $182 indiv, $511 inst (online), $538 inst (print + online)] Reports on current educational research, evaluation, and applications.

Educational Researcher. Sage Publications, 2455 Teller Rd, Thousand Oaks, CA 91320. edr.sagepub.com, tel: 800-818-7243, fax: 800-583-2665, journals@sagepub.com [9/yr; $310 inst (online, content through 1999), $344 inst (online + backfile, content through Volume 1, Issue 1), $337 inst (print), $344 inst (print + online), $378 inst (print + online + backfile)] Contains news and features of general significance in educational research.

Journal of Interactive Learning Research. Association for the Advancement of Computing in Education, PO Box 1545, Chesapeake, VA 23327-1545. www.aace.org/pubs/jilr, tel: 757-366-5606, fax: 703-997-8760, info@aace.org [4/yr; $35 for AACE student members, $115 AACE members (discount available for ordering multiple AACE journals), $195 inst] Publishes articles on how intelligent computer technologies can be used in education to enhance learning and teaching. Reports on research and developments, integration, and applications of artificial intelligence in education.

Learning Technology. IEEE Computer Society, Technical Committee on Learning Technology, 150 Androutsou Street, Piraeus GR-18352, GREECE. lttf.ieee.org/learn_tech, tel: (+30) 210-4142766, fax: (+30) 210-4142767, sampson@unipi.gr [4/yr; free] Online publication that reports developments, projects, conferences, and findings of the Learning Technology Task Force.

Meridian. North Carolina State University, College of Education, Poe Hall, Box 7801, Raleigh, NC 27695-7801. www.ncsu.edu/meridian, meridian_mail@ncsu.edu [2/yr; free] Online journal dedicated to research in middle-school educational technology use.

Research in Science & Technological Education. Taylor & Francis Group, Customer Services Dept, 325 Chestnut St, Suite 800, Philadelphia, PA 19106. www. tandf.co.uk/journals/titles/02635143, tel: 800-354-1420, fax: 215-625-2940, subscriptions@tandf.co.uk [3/yr; $345 indiv, $1664 inst (online), $1752 inst (print+online)] Publication of original research in the science and technological fields. Includes articles on psychological, sociological, economic, and organizational aspects of technological education.

Educational Technology

Appropriate Technology. Research Information Ltd., Grenville Court, Britwell Rd, Burnham, Bucks, SL1 8DF, United Kingdom. www.researchinformation.co.uk/apte.php, tel: +44 (0) 1628 600499, fax: +44 (0) 1628 600488, info@researchinformation.co.uk [4/yr; $316] Articles on less technologically advanced, but more environmentally sustainable, solutions to problems in developing countries.

British Journal of Educational Technology. John Wiley & Sons, Inc., Journal Customer Services, 350 Main St, Malden, MA 02148. www.blackwellpublishing. com/journals/BJET, tel: 800-835-6770, fax: 781-388-8232, cs-agency@wiley.com [6/yr; $200 indiv (print+online), $1188 inst (print/online), $1309 inst (print+online)] Published by the National Council for Educational Technology, this journal includes articles on education and training, especially theory, applications, and development of educational technology and communications.

Canadian Journal of Learning and Technology. Canadian Network for Innovation in Education (CNIE), 260 Dalhousie St., Suite 204, Ottawa, ON, K1N 7E4, Canada. www.cjlt.ca, tel: 613-241-0018, fax: 613-241-0019, cjlt@ucalgary.ca [3/yr; free] Concerned with all aspects of educational systems and technology.

Educational Technology. Educational Technology Publications, Inc., 700 Palisade Ave, Englewood Cliffs, NJ 07632-0564. www.bookstoread.com/etp, tel: 800-952-2665, fax: 201-871-4009, edtecpubs@aol.com [6/yr; $199] Covers telecommunications, computer-aided instruction, information retrieval, educational television, and electronic media in the classroom.

Educational Technology Abstracts. Taylor & Francis Group, Customer Services Dept, 325 Chestnut St, Suite 800, Philadelphia, PA 19106. www.tandf.co.uk/journals/titles/02663368, tel: 800-354-1420, fax: 215-625-2940, subscriptions@tandf. co.uk [1/yr; $621 indiv, $1595 inst (online), $1679 inst (print+online)] An international publication of abstracts of recently published material in the field of educational and training technology.

Educational Technology Research & Development. Springer Science+Business Media, PO Box 2485, Secaucus, NJ 07096-2485. www.springer.com/journal/11423, tel: 800-777-4643, fax: 201-348-4505, service-ny@springer.com [6/yr; $338 inst (print/online), $405.60 inst (print+online, content through 1997)] Focuses on research, instructional development, and applied theory in the field of educational technology.

International Journal of Technology and Design Education. Springer Science+Business Media, PO Box 2485, Secaucus, NJ 07096-2485. www.springer. com/journal/10798, tel: 800-777-4643, fax: 201-348-4505, service-ny@springer. com [4/yr; $397 inst (print/online), $476.40 inst (print+online, content through 1997)] Publishes research reports and scholarly writing about aspects of technology and design education.

Journal of Computing in Higher Education. Springer Science+Business Media, PO Box 2485, Secaucus, NJ 07096-2485. www.springer.com/journal/12528, tel: 800-777-4643, fax: 201-348-4505, service-ny@springer.com [3/yr; $137 inst (print/online), $164.40 inst (print+online, content through 1997)] Publishes scholarly essays, case studies, and research that discuss instructional technologies.

Journal of Educational Technology Systems. Baywood Publishing Co., Inc., 26 Austin Ave, Box 337, Amityville, NY 11701-0337. www.baywood.com/journals/previewjournals.asp?id=0047-2395, tel: 800-638-7819, fax: 631-691-1770, info@baywood.com [4/yr; $359 inst (online), $379 (print+online)] Deals with systems in which technology and education interface; designed to inform educators who are interested in making optimum use of technology.

Journal of Interactive Media in Education. Open University, Knowledge Media Institute, Milton Keynes, MK7 6AA, United Kingdom. www-jime.open.ac.uk, tel: +44 (0) 1908 653800, fax: +44 (0) 1908 653169, jime@open.ac.uk [Irregular; free] A multidisciplinary forum for debate and idea sharing concerning the practical aspects of interactive media and instructional technology.

Journal of Science Education and Technology. Springer Science+Business Media, PO Box 2485, Secaucus, NJ 07096-2485. www.springer.com/journal/10956, tel: 800-777-4643, fax: 201-348-4505, service-ny@springer.com [6/yr; $1022 inst (print/online), $1226.40 inst (print+online, content through 1997)] Publishes studies aimed at improving science education at all levels in the U.S.

MultiMedia & Internet@Schools. Information Today, Inc., 143 Old Marlton Pike, Medford, NJ 08055-8750. www.mmischools.com, tel: 609-654-6266, fax: 609-654-4309, custserv@infotoday.com [6/yr; $19.95] Reviews and evaluates hardware and software. Presents information pertaining to basic troubleshooting skills.

Science Communication. Sage Publications, 2455 Teller Rd, Thousand Oaks, CA 91320. scx.sagepub.com, tel: 800-818-7243, fax: 800-583-2665, journals@sagepub.com [4/yr; $710 inst (online, content through 1999), $789 inst (online + backfile, content through Volume 1, Issue 1), $773 inst (print), $789 inst (print + online), $868 inst (print + online + backfile)] An international, interdisciplinary journal examining the nature of expertise and the translation of knowledge into practice and policy.

Social Science Computer Review. Sage Publications, 2455 Teller Rd, Thousand Oaks, CA 91320. ssc.sagepub.com, tel: 800-818-7243, fax: 800-583-2665, journals@sagepub.com [4/yr; $604 inst (online, content through 1999), $671 inst (online + backfile, content through Volume 1, Issue 1), $658 inst (print), $671 inst (print + online), $738 inst (print + online + backfile)] Interdisciplinary peer-reviewed scholarly publication covering social science research and instructional applications in computing and telecommunications; also covers societal impacts of information technology.

TechTrends. Springer Science+Business Media, PO Box 2485, Secaucus, NJ 07096-2485. www.springer.com/journal/11528, tel: 800-777-4643, fax: 201-348-4505, service-ny@springer.com [6/yr; $120 inst (print/online), $144 inst (print + online, content through 1997)] Targeted at leaders in education and training; features authoritative, practical articles about technology and its integration into the learning environment.

T.H.E. Journal. 1105 Media, 9201 Oakdale Ave. Suite 101, Chatsworth, CA 91311. www.thejournal.com, tel: 818-734-1520, fax: 818-734-1522, subscriptions@thejournal.com [12/yr; $29, free to those in K-12, free online] For educators of all levels; focuses on a specific topic for each issue, as well as technological innovations as they apply to education.

Information Science and Technology

Canadian Journal of Information and Library Science. University of Toronto Press, Journals Division, 5201 Dufferin St, Toronto, ON, M3H 5 T8, Canada. www.utpjournals.com/cjils/cjils.html, tel: 416-667-7777, fax: 800-221-9985, journals@utpress.utoronto.ca [4/yr; $75 indiv, $109 inst] Published by the Canadian Association for Information Science to contribute to the advancement of library and information science in Canada.

EContent. Information Today, Inc., 143 Old Marlton Pike, Medford, NJ 08055-8750. www.econtentmag.com, tel: 609-654-6266, fax: 609-654-4309, custserv@infotoday.com [10/yr; $119] Features articles on topics of interest to online database users; includes database search aids.

Information Processing & Management. Elsevier, Inc., Journals Customer Service, 3251 Riverport Lane, Maryland Heights, MO 63043. www.elsevier.com/locate/infoproman, tel: 877-839-7126, fax: 314-447-8077, journalcustomerservice-usa@elsevier.com [6/yr; $338 indiv, $1962 inst] International journal covering data processing, database building, and retrieval.

Information Services & Use. IOS Press, Nieuwe Hemweg 6B, 1013 BG Amsterdam, The Netherlands. www.iospress.nl/html/01675265.php, tel: +31 20 688 3355, fax: +31 20 687 0039, info@iospress.nl [4/yr; $135 indiv (online), $530 inst (online), $585 inst (print + online)] An international journal for those in the information management field. Includes online and offline systems, library automation, micrographics, videotex, and telecommunications.

The Information Society. Taylor & Francis Group, Customer Services Dept, 325 Chestnut St, Suite 800, Philadelphia, PA 19106. www.tandf.co.uk/journals/titles/01972243, tel: 800-354-1420, fax: 215-625-2940, subscriptions@tandf.co.uk [5/yr; $171 indiv, $442 inst (online), $465 inst (print + online)] Provides a forum for discussion of the world of information, including transborder data flow, regulatory issues, and the impact of the information industry.

Information Technology and Libraries. American Library Association, Subscriptions, 50 E Huron St, Chicago, IL 60611-2795. www.lita.org/ala/mgrps/divs/lita/ital/italinformation.cfm, tel: 800-545-2433, fax: 312-944-2641, subscription@ala.org [4/yr; $65] Articles on library automation, communication technology, cable systems, computerized information processing, and video technologies.

Information Today. Information Today, Inc., 143 Old Marlton Pike, Medford, NJ 08055-8750. www.infotoday.com/it, tel: 609-654-6266, fax: 609-654-4309, custserv@infotoday.com [11/yr; $87.50] Newspaper for users and producers of electronic information services. Includes articles and news about the industry, calendar of events, and product information.

Information Technology Management. IGI Global, 701 E Chocolate Ave, Suite 200, Hershey, PA 17033-1240. www.igi-pub.com/journals/details.asp?id=200, tel: 866-342-6657, fax: 717-533-8661, cust@igi-global.com [2/yr; $70 indiv, $90 inst] Designed for library information specialists, this bi-annual newsletter presents current issues and trends in information technology presented by and for specialists in the field.

Internet Reference Service Quarterly. Taylor & Francis Group, Customer Services Dept, 325 Chestnut St, Suite 800, Philadelphia, PA 19106. www.tandf.co.uk/journals/WIRS, tel: 800-354-1420, fax: 215-625-2940, subscriptions@tandf.co.uk [4/yr; $84 indiv, $206 inst (online), $216 inst (print + online)] Discusses multidisciplinary aspects of incorporating the Internet as a tool for reference service.

Journal of Access Services. Taylor & Francis Group, Customer Services Dept, 325 Chestnut St, Suite 800, Philadelphia, PA 19106. www.tandf.co.uk/journals/WJAS, tel: 800-354-1420, fax: 215-625-2940, subscriptions@tandf.co.uk [4/yr; $79 indiv, $206 inst (online), $216 inst (print + online)] Explores topics and issues surrounding the organization, administration, and development of information technology on access services and resources.

Journal of the American Society for Information Science and Technology. John Wiley & Sons, Inc., Journal Customer Services, 350 Main St, Malden, MA 02148. www3.interscience.wiley.com/journal/117946195/grouphome/home.html, tel: 800-835-6770, fax: 781-388-8232, cs-agency@wiley.com [12/yr; $2331 inst (print), $2565 inst (print + online)] Provides an overall forum for new research in information transfer and communication processes, with particular attention paid to the context of recorded knowledge.

Journal of Database Management. IGI Global, 701 E Chocolate Ave, Suite 200, Hershey, PA 17033-1240. www.idea-group.com/journals/details.asp?id=198, tel: 866-342-6657, fax: 717-533-8661, cust@igi-global.com [4/yr; $195 indiv, $545 inst (print/online), $795 inst (print + online)] Provides state-of-the-art research to those who design, develop, and administer DBMS-based information systems.

Journal of Documentation. Emerald Group Publishing Limited, One Mifflin Place Suite 400 Harvard Square, Cambridge, MA 02138. www.emeraldinsight.com/jd.htm, tel: 888-622-0075, fax: 617-354-6875, america@emeraldinsight.com [6/yr; $1019] Focuses on theories, concepts, models, frameworks, and philosophies in the information sciences.

Journal of Interlibrary Loan, Document Delivery & Electronic Reserve. Taylor & Francis Group, Customer Services Dept, 325 Chestnut St, Suite 800, Philadelphia, PA 19106. www.tandf.co.uk/journals/titles/1072303X, tel: 800-354-1420, fax: 215-625-2940, subscriptions@tandf.co.uk [4/yr; $104 indiv, $388 inst (online), $408 inst (print + online)] A forum for ideas on the basic theoretical and practical problems regarding all aspects of library resource sharing faced by planners, practitioners, and users of network services.

Journal of Library Metadata. Taylor & Francis Group, Customer Services Dept, 325 Chestnut St, Suite 800, Philadelphia, PA 19106. www.tandf.co.uk/journals/titles/19386389, tel: 800-354-1420, fax: 215-625-2940, subscriptions@tandf.co.uk [4/yr; $82 indiv, $244 inst (online), $248 inst (print + online)] A forum for the latest research, innovations, news, and expert views about all aspects of metadata applications and information retrieval in libraries.

Instructional Design and Development

Human-Computer Interaction. Taylor & Francis Group, Customer Services Dept, 325 Chestnut St, Suite 800, Philadelphia, PA 19106. www.tandf.co.uk/journals/ titles/07370024, tel: 800-354-1420, fax: 215-625-2940, subscriptions@tandf.co.uk [4/yr; $76 indiv, $648 inst (online), $682 institution (print + online)] A journal of theoretical, empirical, and methodological issues of user science and of system design.

Instructional Science. Springer Science+Business Media, PO Box 2485, Secaucus, NJ 07096-2485. www.springer.com/journal/11251, tel: 800-777-4643, fax: 201-348-4505, service-ny@springer.com [6/yr; $814 inst (print/online), $976.80 inst (print + online, content through 1997)] Promotes a deeper understanding of the nature, theory, and practice of the instructional process and the learning resulting from this process.

International Journal of Human-Computer Interaction. Taylor & Francis Group, Customer Services Dept, 325 Chestnut St, Suite 800, Philadelphia, PA 19106. www.tandf.co.uk/journals/titles/10447318, tel: 800-354-1420, fax: 215-625-2940, subscriptions@tandf.co.uk [12/yr; $176 indiv, $1427 inst (online), $1502 inst (print + online)] Addresses the cognitive, social, health, and ergonomic aspects of work with computers. It also emphasizes both the human and computer science aspects of the effective design and use of computer interactive systems.

Journal of Educational Technology Systems. Baywood Publishing Co., Inc., 26 Austin Ave, Box 337, Amityville, NY 11701-0337. www.baywood.com/journals/ previewjournals.asp?id=0047-2395, tel: 800-638-7819, fax: 631-691-1770, info@ baywood.com [4/yr; $359 inst (online), $379 inst (print + online)] Deals with systems in which technology and education interface; designed to inform educators who are interested in making optimum use of technology.

Journal of Instructional Delivery Systems. Learning Technology Institute, 50 Culpeper St, Warrenton, VA 20186. www.salt.org/salt.asp?ss=l&pn=jids, tel: 540-347-0055, fax: 540-349-3169, info@lti.org [4/yr; $30 member, $45 non-member, $40 lib] Devoted to the issues, problems, and applications of instructional delivery systems in education, training, and job performance.

Journal of Interactive Instruction Development. Learning Technology Institute, 50 Culpeper St, Warrenton, VA 20186. www.salt.org/salt.asp?ss=l&pn=jiid, tel: 540-347-0055, fax: 540-349-3169, jiid@lti.org [4/yr; $30 member, $45 non-member, $40 lib] A showcase of successful programs that will heighten awareness of innovative, creative, and effective approaches to courseware development for interactive technology.

Journal of Technical Writing and Communication. Baywood Publishing Co., Inc., 26 Austin Ave, Box 337, Amityville, NY 11701-0337. www.baywood.com/journals/previewjournals.asp?id=0047-2816, tel: 800-638-7819, fax: 631-691-1770, info@baywood.com [4/yr; $97 indiv (online), $102 indiv (print+online), $359 inst (online), $379 inst (print+online)] Essays on oral and written communication, for purposes ranging from pure research to needs of business and industry.

Journal of Visual Literacy. International Visual Literacy Association, Dr. David R. Moore, IVLA Executive Treasurer, Ohio University, 250 McCracken Hall, Athens, OH 45701. www.ohio.edu/visualliteracy, tel: 740-597-1322, jvleditor@ohio.edu [2/yr; $30 student, $60 indiv] Explores empirical, theoretical, practical, and applied aspects of visual literacy and communication.

Performance Improvement. John Wiley & Sons, Inc., Journal Customer Services, 350 Main St, Malden, MA 02148. www3.interscience.wiley.com/journal/112729556/home, tel: 800-835-6770, fax: 781-388-8232, cs-agency@wiley.com [10/yr; $80 indiv, $317 inst (print), $349 inst (print+online)] Promotes performance science and technology. Contains articles, research, and case studies relating to improving human performance.

Performance Improvement Quarterly. John Wiley & Sons, Inc., Journal Customer Services, 350 Main St, Malden, MA 02148. www3.interscience.wiley.com/journal/117865970/home, tel: 800-835-6770, fax: 781-388-8232, cs-agency@wiley.com [4/yr; $65 indiv, $164 inst (print), $181 inst (print+online)] Presents the cutting edge in research and theory in performance technology.

Training. Nielsen Business Media, Customer Service, PO Box 3601, Northbrook, IL 60065-3601. www.trainingmag.com, tel: 847-763-9050, fax: 847-647-0226, iv@halldata.com [12/yr; $79] Covers all aspects of training, management, and organizational development, motivation, and performance improvement.

Learning Sciences

International Journal of Computer-Supported Collaborative Learning. Springer Science+Business Media, PO Box 2485, Secaucus, NJ 07096-2485. www.springer.com/journal/11412, tel: 800-777-4643, fax: 201-348-4505, service-ny@springer.com [6/yr; $424 inst (print/online), $508 inst (print+online, content through 1997)] Promote a deeper understanding of the nature, theory, and practice of the uses of computer-supported collaborative learning.

Journal of the Learning Sciences. Taylor & Francis Group, Customer Services Dept, 325 Chestnut St, Suite 800, Philadelphia, PA 19106. www.tandf.co.uk/journals/titles/10508406, tel: 800-354-1420, fax: 215-625-2940, subscriptions@tandf.co.uk [4/yr; $70 indiv, $676 inst (online), $711 inst (print+online)] Provides a forum for the discussion of research on education and learning, with emphasis on the idea of changing one's understanding of learning and the practice of education.

Libraries and Media Centers

Collection Building. Emerald Group Publishing Limited, One Mifflin Place Suite 400 Harvard Square, Cambridge, MA 02138. www.emeraldinsight.com/cb.htm, tel: 888-622-0075, fax: 617-354-6875, america@emeraldinsight.com [4/yr; $1639] Provides well-researched and authoritative information on collection maintenance and development for librarians in all sectors.

Computers in Libraries. Information Today, Inc., 143 Old Marlton Pike, Medford, NJ 08055-8750. www.infotoday.com/cilmag/default.shtml, tel: 609-654-6266, fax: 609-654-4309, custserv@infotoday.com [10/yr; $99.95] Covers practical applications of microcomputers to library situations and recent news items.

The Electronic Library. Emerald Group Publishing Limited, One Mifflin Place Suite 400 Harvard Square, Cambridge, MA 02138. info.emeraldinsight.com/products/journals/journals.htm?id=el, tel: 888-622-0075, fax: 617-354-6875, america@emeraldinsight.com [6/yr; $739] International journal for minicomputer, microcomputer, and software applications in libraries; independently assesses current and forthcoming information technologies.

Government Information Quarterly. Elsevier, Inc., Journals Customer Service, 3251 Riverport Lane, Maryland Heights, MO 63043. www.elsevier.com/locate/govinf, tel: 877-839-7126, fax: 314-447-8077, journalcustomerservice-usa@elsevier.com [4/yr; $179 indiv, $584 inst] International journal of resources, services, policies, and practices.

Information Outlook. Special Libraries Association, Information Outlook Subscriptions, 1700 Eighteenth Street, NW, Washington, DC 20009-2514. www.sla.org/pubs/serial/io, tel: 703-647-4900, fax: 1-202-234-2442, magazine@sla.org [12/yr; $125] Discusses administration, organization, and operations. Includes reports on research, technology, and professional standards.

The Journal of Academic Librarianship. Elsevier, Inc., Journals Customer Service, 3251 Riverport Lane, Maryland Heights, MO 63043. www.elsevier.com/locate/jacalib, tel: 877-839-7126, fax: 314-447-8077, journalcustomerservice-usa@elsevier.com [6/yr; $128 indiv, $358 inst] Results of significant research, issues, and problems facing academic libraries, book reviews, and innovations in academic libraries.

Journal of Librarianship and Information Science. Sage Publications, 2455 Teller Rd, Thousand Oaks, CA 91320. lis.sagepub.com, tel: 800-818-7243, fax: 800-583-2665, journals@sagepub.com [4/yr; $599 inst (online, content through 1999), $666 inst (online + backfile, content through Volume 1, Issue 1), $653 inst (print), $666 inst (print + online), $733 inst (print + online + backfile)] Deals with all aspects of library and information work in the United Kingdom and reviews literature from international sources.

Journal of Library Administration. Taylor & Francis Group, Customer Services Dept, 325 Chestnut St, Suite 800, Philadelphia, PA 19106. www.tandf.co.uk/journals/titles/01930826, tel: 800-354-1420, fax: 215-625-2940, subscriptions@tandf.co.uk [8/yr; $209 indiv, $763 inst (online), $803 inst (print + online)] Provides information on all aspects of effective library management, with emphasis on practical applications.

Library & Information Science Research. Elsevier, Inc., Journals Customer Service, 3251 Riverport Lane, Maryland Heights, MO 63043. www.elsevier.com/locate/lisres, tel: 877-839-7126, fax: 314-447-8077, journalcustomerservice-usa@elsevier.com [4/yr; $151 indiv, $447 inst] Research articles, dissertation reviews, and book reviews on issues concerning information resources management.

Library Hi Tech. Emerald Group Publishing Limited, One Mifflin Place Suite 400 Harvard Square, Cambridge, MA 02138. www.emeraldinsight.com/lht.htm, tel: 888-622-0075, fax: 617-354-6875, america@emeraldinsight.com [4/yr; $469] Concentrates on reporting on the selection, installation, maintenance, and integration of systems and hardware.

Library Hi Tech News. Emerald Group Publishing Limited, One Mifflin Place Suite 400 Harvard Square, Cambridge, MA 02138. www.emeraldinsight.com/lhtn.htm, tel: 888-622-0075, fax: 617-354-6875, america@emeraldinsight.com [10/yr; $599] Supplements Library Hi Tech and updates many of the issues addressed in-depth in the journal; keeps the reader fully informed of the latest developments in library automation, new products, network news, new software and hardware, and people in technology.

Library Journal. Media Source, Inc., 160 Varick Street, 11th Floor, New York, NY 10013. www.libraryjournal.com, tel: 800-588-1030, fax: 712-733-8019, LJLcustserv@cds-global.com [23/yr; $157.99] A professional periodical for librarians, with current issues and news, professional reading, a lengthy book review section, and classified advertisements.

Library Media Connection. Linworth Publishing, Inc., PO Box 204, Vandalia, Ohio 45377. www.linworth.com/lmc, tel: 800-607-4410, fax: 937-890-0221, linworth@linworthpublishing.com [6/yr; $69] Journal for junior and senior high-school librarians; provides articles, tips, and ideas for day-to-day school library management, as well as reviews of audiovisuals and software, all written by school librarians.

The Library Quarterly. University of Chicago Press, Journals Division, Journals Division, PO Box 37005, Chicago, IL 60637. www.journals.uchicago.edu/LQ, tel: 877-705-1878, fax: 877-705-1879, subscriptions@press.uchicago.edu [$25 students (online), $46 indiv (print), $45 indiv (online), $50 indiv (print+online), inst prices vary] Scholarly articles of interest to librarians.

Library Resources & Technical Services. American Library Association, Subscriptions, 50 E Huron St, Chicago, IL 60611-2795. www.ala.org/ala/mgrps/divs/alcts/resources/lrts/index.cfm, tel: 800-545-2433, fax: 312-944-2641, subscription@ala.org [4/yr; $75] Scholarly papers on bibliographic access and control, preservation, conservation, and reproduction of library materials.

Library Trends. Johns Hopkins University Press, PO Box 19966, Baltimore, MD 21211-0966. www.press.jhu.edu/journals/library_trends, tel: 800-548-1784, fax: 410-516-3866, jrnlcirc@press.jhu.edu [4/yr; $80 indiv (print/online), $140 inst (print)] Each issue is concerned with one aspect of library and information science, analyzing current thought and practice, and examining ideas that hold the greatest potential for the field.

Public Libraries. American Library Association, Subscriptions, 50 E Huron St, Chicago, IL 60611-2795. www.ala.org/ala/mgrps/divs/pla/plapublications/publiclibraries/index.cfm, tel: 800-545-2433, fax: 312-944-2641, subscription@ala.org [6/yr; $65] News and articles of interest to public librarians.

Public Library Quarterly. Taylor & Francis Group, Customer Services Dept, 325 Chestnut St, Suite 800, Philadelphia, PA 19106. www.tandf.co.uk/journals/WPLQ, tel: 800-354-1420, fax: 215-625-2940, subscriptions@tandf.co.uk [4/yr; $113 indiv, $352 inst (online), $371 inst (print+online)] Addresses the major administrative challenges and opportunities that face the nation's public libraries.

Reference and User Services Quarterly. American Library Association, Subscriptions, 50 E Huron St, Chicago, IL 60611-2795. rusq.org, tel: 800-545-2433, fax: 312-944-2641, subscription@ala.org [4/yr; $25 student, $60 indiv] Disseminates information of interest to reference librarians, bibliographers, adult services librarians, those in collection development and selection, and others interested in public services.

The Reference Librarian. Taylor & Francis Group, Customer Services Dept, 325 Chestnut St, Suite 800, Philadelphia, PA 19106. www.tandf.co.uk/journals/WREF, tel: 800-354-1420, fax: 215-625-2940, subscriptions@tandf.co.uk [4/yr; $248 indiv, $1016 inst (online), $1070 inst (print + online)] Each issue focuses on a topic of current concern, interest, or practical value to reference librarians.

Reference Services Review. Emerald Group Publishing Limited, One Mifflin Place Suite 400 Harvard Square, Cambridge, MA 02138. www.emeraldinsight.com/rsr. htm, tel: 888-622-0075, fax: 617-354-6875, america@emeraldinsight.com [4/yr; $499] Dedicated to the enrichment of reference knowledge and the advancement of reference services. It prepares its readers to understand and embrace current and emerging technologies affecting reference functions and information needs of library users.

School Library Journal. Media Source, Inc., 160 Varick Street, 11th Floor, New York, NY 10013. www.slj.com, tel: 800-595-1066, fax: 712-733-8019, sljcustserv@cds-global.com [23/yr; $157.99] For school and youth service librarians. Reviews about 4,000 children's books and 1,000 educational media titles annually.

School Library Media Activities Monthly. Libraries Unlimited, Inc., PO Box 291846, Kettering OH 45429. www.schoollibrarymedia.com, tel: 800-771-5579, fax: 937-890-0221, schoollibrarymonthly@sfsdayton.com [8/yr; $55] A vehicle for distributing ideas for teaching library media skills and for the development and implementation of library media skills programs.

School Library Media Research. American Library Association and American Association of School Librarians, Subscriptions, 50 E Huron St, Chicago, IL 60611-2795. www.ala.org/ala/aasl/aaslpubsandjournals/slmrb/schoollibrary.cfm, tel: 800-545-2433, fax: 312-944-2641, subscription@ala.org [annual compilation; free online] For library media specialists, district supervisors, and others concerned with the selection and purchase of print and non-print media and with the development of programs and services for preschool through high-school libraries.

Teacher Librarian. The Scarecrow Press, Inc., 4501 Forbes Blvd, Suite 200, Lanham, MD 20706. www.teacherlibrarian.com, tel: 800-462-6420, fax: 800-338-4550, admin@teacherlibrarian.com [5/yr; $56 prepaid, $61 billed] "The journal for school library professionals"; previously known as Emergency Librarian. Articles, review columns, and critical analyses of management and programming issues.

Media Technologies

Broadcasting & Cable. NewBay Media, LLC., 28 E. 28th St. 12th Floor, New York, NY 10016. www.broadcastingcable.com, tel: 800-554-5729, fax: 712-733-8019, bcbcustserv@cdsfulfillment.com [47/yr; $199] All-inclusive newsweekly for radio, television, cable, and allied business.

Communication Abstracts. Sage Publications, 2455 Teller Rd, Thousand Oaks, CA 91320. atgstg01.sagepub.com/journalsProdDesc.nav?prodId=Journal200918, tel: 800-818-7243, fax: 800-583-2665, journals@sagepub.com [6/yr; $353 indiv (print), $1749 inst (print)] Abstracts communication-related articles, reports, and books. Cumulated annually.

Educational Media International. Taylor & Francis Group, Customer Services Dept, 325 Chestnut St, Suite 800, Philadelphia, PA 19106. www.tandf.co.uk/journals/titles/09523987, tel: 800-354-1420, fax: 215-625-2940, subscriptions@tandf.co.uk [4/yr; $134 indiv, $500 inst (online), $526 inst (print+online)] The official journal of the International Council for Educational Media.

Historical Journal of Film, Radio and Television. Taylor & Francis Group, Customer Services Dept, 325 Chestnut St, Suite 800, Philadelphia, PA 19106. www.tandf.co.uk/journals/titles/01439685, tel: 800-354-1420, fax: 215-625-2940, subscriptions@tandf.co.uk [4/yr; $392 indiv, $1071 inst (online), $1127 inst (print+online)] Articles by international experts in the field, news and notices, and book reviews concerning the impact of mass communications on political and social history of the 20th century.

International Journal of Instructional Media. Westwood Press, Inc., 118 5 Mile River Rd, Darien, CT 06820-6237. www.adprima.com/ijim.htm, tel: 203-656-8680, fax: 212-353-8291, PLSleeman@aol.com [4/yr; $181.20] Focuses on quality research on ongoing programs in instructional media for education, distance learning, computer technology, instructional media and technology, telecommunications, interactive video, management, media research and evaluation, and utilization.

Journal of Educational Multimedia and Hypermedia. Association for the Advancement of Computing in Education, PO Box 1545, Chesapeake, VA 23327-1545. www.aace.org/pubs/jemh, tel: 757-366-5606, fax: 703-997-8760, info@aace.org [4/yr; $35 for AACE student members, $115 AACE members (discount available for ordering multiple AACE journals), $195 inst] A multidisciplinary information source presenting research about and applications for multimedia and hypermedia tools.

Journal of Popular Film and Television. Heldref Publications, PO Box 830350, Birmingham, AL 35283-0350. www.heldref.org/pubs/jpft/about.html, tel: 866-802-7059, fax: 205-995-1588, heldref@subscriptionoffice.com [4/yr; $58 indiv (online), $61 (print+online), $167 inst (online), $175 (print+online)] Articles on film and television, book reviews, and theory. Dedicated to popular film and television in the broadest sense. Concentrates on commercial cinema and television, film and television theory or criticism, filmographies, and bibliographies. Edited at the College of Arts and Sciences of Northern Michigan University and the Department of Popular Culture, Bowling Green State University.

Learning, Media & Technology. Taylor & Francis Group, Customer Services Dept, 325 Chestnut St, Suite 800, Philadelphia, PA 19106. www.tandf.co.uk/journals/titles/17439884, tel: 800-354-1420, fax: 215-625-2940, subscriptions@tandf.co.uk [4/yr; $439 indiv, $1562 inst (online), $1644 inst (print + online)] This journal of the Educational Television Association serves as an international forum for discussions and reports on developments in the field of television and related media in teaching, learning, and training.

Media & Methods. American Society of Educators, 1429 Walnut St, Philadelphia, PA 19102. www.media-methods.com, tel: 215-563-6005, fax: 215-587-9706, info@media-methods.com [5/yr; $35] The only magazine published for the elementary school library media and technology specialist. A forum for K-12 educators who use technology as an educational resource, this journal includes information on what works and what does not, new product reviews, tips and pointers, and emerging technologies.

Multichannel News. NewBay Media, LLC., 28 E. 28th St. 12th Floor, New York, NY 10016. www.multichannel.com, tel: 888-343-5563, fax: 712-733-8019, mulcustserv@cdsfulfillment.com [47/yr; $199] A newsmagazine for the cable television industry. Covers programming, marketing, advertising, business, and other topics.

MultiMedia & Internet@Schools. Information Today, Inc., 143 Old Marlton Pike, Medford, NJ 08055-8750. www.mmischools.com, tel: 609-654-6266, fax: 609-654-4309, custserv@infotoday.com [6/yr; $19.95] Reviews and evaluates hardware and software. Presents information pertaining to basic troubleshooting skills.

Multimedia Systems. Springer Science+Business Media, PO Box 2485, Secaucus, NJ 07096-2485. www.springer.com/journal/00530, tel: 800-777-4643, fax: 201-348-4505, service-ny@springer.com [6/yr; $634 inst (print/online), $760.80 inst (print + online, content through 1997)] Publishes original research articles and serves as a forum for stimulating and disseminating innovative research ideas, emerging technologies, state-of-the-art methods and tools in all aspects of multimedia computing, communication, storage, and applications among researchers, engineers, and practitioners.

Telematics and Informatics. Elsevier, Inc., Journals Customer Service, 3251 Riverport Lane, Maryland Heights, MO 63043. www.elsevier.com/locate/tele, tel: 877-839-7126, fax: 314-447-8077, journalcustomerservice-usa@elsevier.com [4/yr; $141 indiv, $1271 inst] Publishes research and review articles in applied telecommunications and information sciences in business, industry, government, and educational establishments. Focuses on important current technologies, including microelectronics, computer graphics, speech synthesis and voice recognition, database management, data encryption, satellite television, artificial intelligence, and the ongoing computer revolution.

Professional Development

Journal of Digital Learning in Teacher Education. International Society for Technology in Education, Special Interest Group for Teacher Educators, 180 West 8th Ave., Suite 300, Eugene, OR 97401. www.iste.org/jdlte, tel: 800-336-5191, fax: 541-302-3778, iste@iste.org [4/yr; $32 member, $122 non-member] Contains refereed articles on preservice and inservice training, research in computer education and certification issues, and reviews of training materials and texts.

Journal of Technology and Teacher Education. Association for the Advancement of Computing in Education, PO Box 1545, Chesapeake, VA 23327-1545. www.aace.org/pubs/jtate, tel: 757-366-5606, fax: 703-997-8760, info@aace.org [4/yr; $35 for AACE student members, $115 AACE members (discount available for ordering multiple AACE journals), $195 inst] Serves as an international forum to report research and applications of technology in preservice, inservice, and graduate teacher education.

Simulation, Gaming, and Virtual Reality

Simulation & Gaming. Sage Publications, 2455 Teller Rd, Thousand Oaks, CA 91320. sag.sagepub.com, tel: 800-818-7243, fax: 800-583-2665, journals@sagepub.com [4/yr; $941 inst (online, content through 1999), $1035 inst (online + backfile, content through Volume 1, Issue 1)] An international journal of theory, design, and research focusing on issues in simulation, gaming, modeling, role-playing, and experiential learning.

Special Education and Disabilities

Journal of Special Education Technology. Technology and Media Division, JSET, P.O. Box 3853, Reston, VA 20195. www.tamcec.org/jset, tel: 703-709-0136, fax: 405-325-7661, info@exinn.net [4/yr; $79 indiv, $189 inst] Provides information, research, and reports of innovative practices regarding the application of educational technology toward the education of exceptional children.

Telecommunications and Networking

Canadian Journal of Learning and Technology. Canadian Network for Innovation in Education (CNIE), 260 Dalhousie St., Suite 204, Ottawa, ON, K1N 7E4, Canada. www.cjlt.ca, tel: 613-241-0018, fax: 613-241-0019, cjlt@ucalgary.ca [3/yr; free] Concerned with all aspects of educational systems and technology.

Computer Communications. Elsevier, Inc., Journals Customer Service, 3251 Riverport Lane, Maryland Heights, MO 63043. www.elsevier.com/locate/comcom, tel: 877-839-7126, fax: 314-447-8077, journalcustomerservice-usa@elsevier.com [18/yr; $2089 inst] Focuses on networking and distributed computing techniques, communications hardware and software, and standardization.

EDUCAUSE Review. EDUCAUSE, 4772 Walnut St, Suite 206, Boulder, CO 80301-2536. www.educause.edu/er, tel: 303-449-4430, fax: 303-440-0461, er-subs @educause.edu [6/yr; $35] Features articles on current issues and applications of computing and communications technology in higher education. Reports on EDUCAUSE consortium activities.

International Journal on E-Learning. Association for the Advancement of Computing in Education, PO Box 1545, Chesapeake, VA 23327-1545. www.aace. org/pubs/ijel, tel: 757-366-5606, fax: 703-997-8760, info@aace.org [4/yr; $35 for AACE student members, $115 AACE members (discount available for ordering multiple AACE journals), $195 inst] Reports on current theory, research, development, and practice of telecommunications in education at all levels.

The Internet and Higher Education. Elsevier, Inc., Journals Customer Service, 3251 Riverport Lane, Maryland Heights, MO 63043. www.elsevier.com/locate/iheduc, tel: 877-839-7126, fax: 314-447-8077, journalcustomerservice-usa@elsevier. com [4/yr; $73 indiv, $388 inst] Designed to reach faculty, staff, and administrators responsible for enhancing instructional practices and productivity via the use of information technology and the Internet in their institutions.

Internet Reference Services Quarterly. Taylor & Francis Group, Customer Services Dept, 325 Chestnut St, Suite 800, Philadelphia, PA 19106. www.tandf. co.uk/journals/titles/10875301, tel: 800-354-1420, fax: 215-625-2940, subscriptions@tandf.co.uk [4/yr; $84 indiv, $206 inst (online), $216 inst (print+online)] Describes innovative information practice, technologies, and practice. For librarians of all kinds.

Internet Research. Emerald Group Publishing Limited, One Mifflin Place Suite 400 Harvard Square, Cambridge, MA 02138. www.emeraldinsight.com/intr.htm, tel: 888-622-0075, fax: 617-354-6875, america@emeraldinsight.com [5/yr; $2929] A cross-disciplinary journal presenting research findings related to electronic networks, analyses of policy issues related to networking, and descriptions of current and potential applications of electronic networking for communication, computation, and provision of information services.

Online. Information Today, Inc., 143 Old Marlton Pike, Medford, NJ 08055-8750. www.infotoday.com/online, tel: 609-654-6266, fax: 609-654-4309, custserv@infotoday.com [6/yr; $124.50] For online information system users. Articles cover a variety of online applications for general and business use.

Index

A

AASL. *See* American Association of School
 Librarians
Access issues, school library media centers
 AASL documents, 187
 description, 187–188
 literature's review, 188–189
 methodology
  NCSLMA and VEMA, 190
  purpose, 189–190
 poverty, 193–195
 school library
  closures, 191–193
  schedules, 190–191
Achterman, D., 92
Adams, C., 139–152
Adams, J., 107
Adequate yearly progress (AYP), 58
AECT. *See* Association for Educational
 Communications and
 Technology
AERA. *See* American Educational Research
 Association
Akarasriworn, C., 99–110
Alien Rescue environment
 data-richness, 117
 description, 115, 116
 goals and multimedia technology,
  114
 hypothesis testing, 117
 screen shots, 117, 118
 share cognitive load, 115
 six alien species, 114–115
 and Solar System Database, 117
 student-centered learning, 114
 support cognitive processes, 116

 technology-enriched problem-based-
  learning, 114
 TEKS, 115
Allen, I.A., 70, 72
American Association of School Librarians
 (AASL), 157, 200
American Educational Research Association
 (AERA), 241, 253–254
American Psychological Association (APA),
 24–25, 241
American School Counselor Association
 (ASCA), 200
American Society for Training and
 Development (ASTD), 68, 69,
 99–100
Anderson, T., 43
APA. *See* American Psychological Association
Apperson, J.M., 141
Arnstine, D., 212–214
Arroway, P., 71, 72
ASCA. *See* American School Counselor
 Association
Asessment
 game design (*see* Instructional game
  design and assessment)
 non-cognitive variables, 168
 situating, authentic contexts
  aspirations, 135
  CyGaMEs, 132–133
  data analysis, 133–135
 student, 57, 73
 teacher librarians, 168
 technological barriers, learning, 158
Association for Educational Communications
 and Technology (AECT)
 collaborative process, 83

Association for Educational Communications
        and Technology (AECT) (*cont.*)
    educational technology, 85
    ISTE, 157
    K-12 context, 83–84
ASTD. *See* American Society for Training
        and Development
AYP. *See* Adequate yearly progress

B
Bednar, A.K., 81–88
Bekerman, Z., 10, 11, 18
Bembenutty, H., 26
Benchmarking Forum (BMF), 68
Benefield, P., 10
Bereiter, C., 42
Biggs, J., 162, 163
BMF. *See* Benchmarking Forum
Borgmann, A., 150
Branch, R.M., 23–34, 229–230
Broadband connectivity
    administrators' responses, 174–175
    Americans, 174
    bandwidth leverage techniques, 175
    ISPs, 174
    NTIA, 174
Brown, A., 67–79
Brush, T., 122
Buck, M., 215
Buckner, E., 7–20
Bueschel, A.C., 100, 108
Burt, M.T., 37
Bush, G., 209–217

C
Caffarella, E.P., 100
Carmen, A.D., 107
Caruso, J.B., 71
CCS. *See* Curriculum Customization Service
CCSSO. *See* Council of Chief State School
        Officers
Celano, D., 189
Chang. M., 122
Chen, P.P., 27
Cheong, M.C., 38
Cheung, W.S., 37–46
Circulation
    book, 190
    estimated means, book, 191
    vs. schedule, 191
Clark, K.B., 215
CMS. *See* Course management systems

Cognition
    analogical reasoning, 127
    fostering, CSCL (*see* Computer supported
        collaborative learning)
    metacognition, 25–26
Cognitive tools, media-rich
    Alien Rescue (*see Alien Rescue*
        environment)
    audio signal, 124
    description, 113
    design effective, 113
    framework, 113–114
    higher-level thinking skills, 123
    problem solution, student
        chi-square analyses, 120
        cluster analysis, 119–120
        MANOVA, 120, 121
        scaffolding and support, 119
        sixth-graders, 119
    real-time 3D graphics, 123–124
    students' and teachers' motivation
        authentic and "adult world", 122
        dynamic and just-in-time guidance, 122
        interview, 121
        intrinsic motivation, 122
Collaboration
    CSCL (*see* Computer supported
        collaborative learning)
    edu-techKNOWiki, 82–85
    interdisciplinary collaboration, students,
        201–202
Collinson, V., 209
Combs, A.W., 209
Computer supported collaborative learning
        (CSCL)
    asynchronous discussions, 37
    in-depth critical thinking
        facilitation techniques, 40–41
        guidelines, 38–40
    knowledge building
        characteristics, 42–43
        data analysis, 43–44
        intervention, 43
        participants, 43
        results, 44–45
    surface-level and critical thinking,
        37–38
Concierge, 92–93
Conflict
    borders, Israel and Palestine, 8–9
    effects, 17–18
    students, regions, 17
Connectivity
    assistance program, 173

broadband (*see* Broadband connectivity)
network, 183
Copeland, N.L., 81–88
Council of Chief State School Officers
    (CCSSO), 210, 211
Course/instructional design
    game design and assessment (*see*
        Instructional game design
        and assessment)
    improvement approaches, 84
Course management systems (CMS), 71
Cress, U., 82
Critical-thinking
    building, 37
    devices manipulate, students, 16
    dispositions, 214–215
    in-depth
        discussion guidelines, 38–40
        facilitation techniques, 40–41
Cruise director, 94–95
CSCL. *See* Computer supported collaborative
    learning
Culturally sensitive learning practices
    assessment issues, 168
    benchmarks, 162
    Biggs' model, 163
    collective societies, 163
    description, 161
    implications, 162
    instructional design factors
        description, 165
        discussion topics, 166
        learner participation, 167
        learning activities, 167
        resource choice, 166–167
        student-teacher relations, 166
    learner examination, 163
    learning, larger environment, 163–164
    solutions, language problems, 164–165
    technology issues, 169–170
Curriculum Customization Service (CCS)
    curricular materials, DPS Earth science,
        57–58
    curricular unit home screen, 56–57
    Denver Public Schools Earth Science, 55
    digital library, 54
    DLS, 55–56
    evaluating teachers technology adoption
        criteria, 50
        description, 49–50
        integration stage, 51
        qualitative and quantitative educational
            researchers, 51
        reorientation, 51–52

stage models, 52
theorists, 50–51
method
    data analysis, 60–61
    sample and data collection, 58–60
    setting, 58
NDSL and DLESE, 54–55
qualitative findings, 62–63
quantitative findings, 61–62
technology adoption (*see* Technology
    adoption)
Cushman, K., 209–210
CyGaMEs
    alignment, 128
    application
        game goals, 129
        structure mapping theory, 128
    assessment aspirations
        eight-channel flow model and
            cumulative timed report trace, 134,
            135
        pre-learning boredom to post-learning
            anxiety, 135
    authentic intellectual work, 132
    data analysis, 133, 135
    embedded assessment
        gesture reports, 132–133
        timed report and flowometer, 133
    embodied prior knowledge, 129
    gameplay type and functions, 129
    LOGO turtle programming, 129
    lunar construction
        selene classic, 130
        selene II instructional videogame 2010,
            130, 131
    methods, 131
    performance-based assessment, 131–132
    reform-based K-12 education scholars, 132
    Valve's steam digital delivery system, 132

D
Daniels, L., 141
Davidson-Shiver, G.V., 100
Deem, R., 23
Deering, T.E., 108
DeFleur, M.H., 107
Dewey, J., 212, 214
Dickinson, G., 157, 187–195
Digital learning
    media and application, 180
    teacher education, 505
    technologies, 175
Digital Learning Sciences (DLS), 55–56

Digital Library for Earth System Education
    (DLESE)
  digital resources, 63
  and NDSL, 54–55
Digital media. *See* PowerPoint
Dispositions, exemplary school librarians
  AASL, 211
  assessment, 215
  confusion, 213–214
  development, 214–215
  education goal, 216
  educator effectiveness, 209–210
  effective learning, 212
  future behavior prediction
    disposition, 213
    Katz and Raths, 213
  INTASC, 210–211
  NCATE, 211
  NCTAF, 210
  static and stationary situation, 217
  usage, 216
Distance education, mediagraphy
  American Journal of Distance Education, 490
  Journal of Distance Education, 490
  Journal of Library & Information Services
      in Distance Learning, 490
  Journal of Research on Technology in
      Education, 490
  Open Learning, 490
Diteeyont, W., 99–110
DLESE. *See* Digital Library for Earth System
    Education
DLS. *See* Digital Learning Sciences
Dobbs, R.R., 107
Doctoral programs, US
  ASTD and AECT, 99–100
  campus-based programs *vs.* online doctoral
      degrees, 107
  competency framework, 100
  data analysis
    campus-based and online programs, 103
    three-quarter hours, 104
  data sources
    The College Blue Book, 102
    media and technology yearbook, 101
    self-reported curricula data, 101–102
  definition and IDT, 99
  degree requirements, Ed.D. *vs.* Ph.D., 106
  dissertation hours, 105–106
  future employment and in-depth, 101
  growth, 104
  institutions, 104
  instructional technology, 107
  interpretations, 100–101

ISPI and IBSTPI, 99–100
  lifestyles and second-career college, 107
  parallels development, 106
  Ph.D./Ed.D. degree, 108–109
  procedures
    course *vs.* curriculum requirements, 103
    cross-checking, 102
    paired three groups, 102
    triangulate program data, 102
  research address, 101
  skills, 107
  total credit hours, 105
  variation and frequency, 105
Domer, D., 165
Dotson-Blake, K.P., 199–208
Dotson, K.B., 199–208
Dottin, E.S., 214
Dousay, T.A., 23–34
Dreyfus, H.L., 149

E
Education
  higher education (*see* Higher education)
  K-12 (*see* K-12 education)
Educational data mining, 293
Educational media and technology, Israeli and
      Palestinian children
  borders and conflict, 8–9
  children's mental and physical health, 17
  data collection and analysis, student
      stories, 17–18
  global and mobile stories, 11–15
  mobile devices, use, 18–19
  and peace education, 9–10
  project implementation, students, 15–17
  social problems, 7–8
Educational Media and Technology Yearbook
    (EMTY), 243
Educational reform
  K-12 education scholars, 132
  National Board Certification in American
      education, 219
Educational research, mediagraphy
  American Educational Research Journal, 491
  Journal of Interactive Learning Research, 491
  Learning Technology, 491
  Meridian, 491
  Research in Science & Technological
      Education, 492
Educational technology
  edu-techKNOWiki project (*see*
      edu-techKNOWiki project)K-12
      education, 72–73

mediagraphy
    abstracts, 492
    Appropriate Technology, 492
    British Journal of Educational
        Technology, 492
    Canadian Journal of Learning and
        Technology, 492
    Educational Technology Research &
        Development, 493
    International Journal of Technology
        and Design Education, 493
    Journal of Computing in Higher
        Education, 493
    Journal of Educational Technology
        Systems, 493
    Journal of Interactive Media in
        Education, 493
    Journal of Science Education and
        Technology, 493
    MultiMedia & Internet@Schools, 493
    Science Communication, 494
    Social Science Computer Review,
        494
    TechTrends, 494
    T.H.E., 494
    qualitative approaches, 51
edu-techKNOWiki project
    approaches, builts, 82–83
    communities of practice, 85
    contradictions, types, 84
    contributors, 85–86
    educational technology, 83–84
    elements of activity, 84
    goals, 81
    graphic representation, 83
    information, 82
    K-12 educators, 84
    knowledge management, 82
    sociogram, 83
    sustainability, 88
    technical elements, 86–88
    use, 86
Ee, J., 25
EMTY. See Educational Media and
        Technology Yearbook
Evans, C., 170
Everhart, N., 173–184

F
Farmer, L.S.J., 161–171
Feuerverger, G., 10
Figuring Things Out, 244
Firer, R., 10

Fixed scheduling, 188
Flexible scheduling, 187, 189
Foehr, U.G., 77
Free and reduced price lunch (FRPL)
    eligibility, 194
    percentage, 193
    student, 158–159
Freeman, L., 212, 214
FRPL. See Free and reduced price lunch

G
Game design. See Instructional game design
        and assessment
Gavigan, K., 187–195
Gentry, C.G., 100
Geurtz, R., 122
Gibson, J.J., 140
Global mobile stories
    and global identities, 11–12
    mobile learning devices, 12–13
    model, 13–15
Golde, C.M., 100, 108
Gorman, G., 165
Grabedian, K.J., 100, 108
Graduate programs, 333
Grady, M., 37
Greaves, T.W., 174
Green, T., 67–79
Guha, S., 107
Gunawardena, C., 43

H
Harada, V., 202
Hara, N., 57
Harry, B., 162
Hastings, N., 141
Hayes, J., 174
Hayles, N.K., 151
Heidegger, M., 143, 144, 145
Hew, K., 57
Hew, K.F., 37–46, 38
Higher education
    information technology (IT), 70–71
    student computing, 72
    technology support
        campus, 71
        faculty, 71–72
Hoaas, D.J., 141
Hofstede, J., 162, 165
Hooper, S., 51, 52, 53
Horton, L., 113–124
Hosler, K., 99–110

Howells, K., 149
Hubbard, J., 94

I
IAM. *See* Interaction Analysis Model
IBSTPI. *See* International Board of Standards
    for Training, Performance and
    Instruction
IDT. *See* Instructional design and technology
IES. *See* Investigating Earth Systems
Igoche, D, 239–241
Igoche, D., 23–34, 231–233, 235–237
Ihde, D., 146
Illich, I., 143
Information science and technology,
        mediagraphy
    Canadian Journal of Information
        and Library Science, 494
    EContent, 494
    Information Processing & Management, 495
    Information Services & Use, 495
    The Information Society, 495
    Information Technology and Libraries, 495
    Information Technology Management, 495
    Information Today, 495
    Internet Reference Service Quarterly, 495
    Journal of Access Services, 496
    Journal of Database Management, 496
    Journal of Documentation, 496
    Journal of Interlibrary Loan, Document
        Delivery & Electronic Reserve, 496
    Journal of Library Metadata, 496
    Journal of the American Society for
        Information Science and
        Technology, 496
Instructional design and development,
        mediagraphy
    Instructional Science, 497
    International Journal of Human-Computer
        Interaction, 497
    Journal of Educational Technology
        Systems, 497
    Journal of Instructional Delivery Systems,
        497
    Journal of Interactive Instruction
        Development, 497
    Journal of Technical Writing and
        Communication, 498
    Journal of Visual Literacy, 498
    Performance Improvement, 498
    Performance Improvement Quarterly, 498
    Training, 498
Instructional design and technology (IDT),
        99, 100

Instructional game design and assessment
    alignment, 128
    conceptual knowledge, 127
    CyGaMEs (*see* CyGaMEs)
        description, 127
    game-based entertainment to game-based
        instruction, 130
    knowledge acquisition, 129
Instructional technology, mobile devices
    corporate training and development
        ASTDs, 68
        expenditure for learning, 68–69
        instructional content, 69
        surprising emphasis, face-to-face
            instruction, 69–70
    developments
        mobile computing devices, 68
        online learning, 68
        roles, 67
    higher education
        campus technology support, 71
        information technology (IT), 70–71
        student computing, 72
        technology support, faculty, 71–72
    K-12 education
        certification, 75–76
        funding, 74
        innovative, emerging technologies and
            practices, 78
        issues, 73
        professional development, 75–76
        reports, 72–73
        student use and ownership, 76–77
        teacher technology availability and use,
            74–75
        training, teacher technology,
            75–76
INTASC. *See* Interstate NewTeacher
        Assessment and Support
        Consortium
Interaction Analysis Model (IAM)
    level, 44
    phases, 44
Interdisciplinary partnerships
    possibilities, 202
    preparedness
        ASCA national model, 201
        school library media specialists and
            counselors, 201–202
    process, 202
International Board of Standards for Training,
        Performance and Instruction
        (IBSTPI), 99–100
International Society for Performance
        Improvement (ISPI), 99–100

International Society for Technology in
        Education (ISTE)
    AECT, 157
    K-12 education, 83–84
Internet service providers (ISPs), 174
Interstate New Teacher Assessment and
        Support Consortium (INTASC),
        210–211
Investigating Earth Systems (IES), 54, 55, 56
ISPI. *See* International Society for
        Performance Improvement
ISPs. *See* Internet service providers
Israel. *See* Educational media and technology,
        Israeli and Palestinian children
ISTE. *See* International Society for
        Technology in Education

J
Jay, E., 214
Jonassen, D.H., 114
Jones, J.L., 209–217
Jones, S.A., 157–160

K
Kalyanpur, M., 162
Kask, S., 141
Katz, L., 213
K-12 education
    certification, 75–76
    funding, 74
    innovative, emerging technologies
        and practices, 78
    issues, 73
    professional development, 75–76
    reports, 72–73
    student use and ownership, 76–77
    teacher technology
        availability and use, 74–75
        training, 75–76
    technology, 73
Kember, D., 163
Khine, M.S., 37
Kimmerle, J., 82
Kim, P., 7–20
Kirshner, B.R., 49–64
Klopfer, E., 130
Knapp, N.F., 91–96
Knowledge building, 42–43
Knowledge management
    edu-techKNOWiki (*see* edu-techKNOWiki
        project)
    technical requirements, 87
    tools, 82

Koh, C., 25
Krashen, S., 193, 195
Ku, H.-Y., 99–110

L
Lajoie, S.P., 115
Laws, E.L., 141
Leadership profiles
    description, 229
    Educational Media and Technology
        Yearbook, 229–230
*Learning Theory, Instructional Theory, and
        Psychoeducational Design*, 240
Lee, S.T., 122
Leonard, J., 107
Leung, D., 163
Levasseur, D.G., 141
Lewin, K., 140
Library closures
    ANCOVA, school type, 193
    full and partial days school, 191–192
    Library media. *See also* Access issues,
        school library media centers
    revised NBPTS standards (*see* Revised
        NBPTS library media standards)
    specialist standards, 203–204
Library schedules
    book circulation, 191
    factors, 191
    flexible scheduling, 190
Lin, T.-Y., 99–110
Literacy. *See* School librarians, literacy
        learning
Liu, M., 113–124
Liu, W.C., 25
Livingstone, D., 24
Lok, A.T.C., 37
Lowe, C., 43
Lowenthal, P., 100
Lowry, R.B., 141
Lucas, L., 23
Lundahl, B., 23, 28
Lund, J., 215
Lynch, K., 24

M
MANOVA, 120, 121
Mantei, E.J., 141
Maor, D., 38
Mardis, M., 173–184
Martin, T., 131
Maull, K.E., 49–64
May, L., 3–6

McMann, G., 37
Mead, G.H., 140
Mediagraphy
    classification, 483
    computer-assisted instruction
        AACE Journal, 486
        CALICO Journal, 486
        Children's Technology Review, 487
        Computers and Composition, 487
        Computers & Education, 487
        Computers in Education Journal, 487
        Computers in Human Behavior, 487
        Computers in the Schools, 487
        Converge, 487
        Dr. Dobb's Journal, 488
        eWEEK, 488
        Instructor, 488
        Interactive Learning Environments, 488
        Journal of Computer Assisted Learning,
            488
        Journal of Educational Computing
            Research, 488
        Journal of Educational Multimedia and
            Hypermedia, 488
        Journal of Research on Technology in
            Education, 489
        Language Resources and Evaluation, 489
        Learning and Leading with Technology,
            489
        MacWorld, 489
        OnCUE, 489
        PC Magazine, 489
        Social Science Computer Review, 489
        Wireless Networks, 490
    distance education, 490
    EBSCO host databases, 482
    educational research, 491–492
    educational technology, 492–494
    ERIC documents, 482
    information science and technology, 494–496
    instructional design and development,
        497–498
    journal articles, 483
    learning sciences
        International Journal of Computer-
            Supported Collaborative Learning,
            498
        Journal of the Learning Sciences., 499
    libraries and media centers
        Collection Building, 499
        Computers in Libraries, 499
        The Electronic Library, 499
        Government Information Quarterly, 499
        Information Outlook, 499

    The Journal of Academic Librarianshi,
        500
    Journal of Librarianship and
        Information Science, 500
    Journal of Library Administration, 500
    Library Hi Tech, 500
    Library Hi Tech News, 500
    Library & Information Science
        Research, 500
    Library Journal, 500
    Library Media Connection, 501
    The Library Quarterly, 501
    Library Resources & Technical
        Services, 501
    Library Trends, 501
    Public Libraries, 501
    Public Library Quarterly, 501
    Reference and User Services Quarterly,
        501
    The Reference Librarian, 502
    Reference Services Review, 502
    School Library Journal, 502
    School Library Media Activities
        Monthly, 502
    School Library Media Research, 502
    Teacher Librarian, 502
media-related periodicals, 482
media technologies
    Broadcasting & Cable, 502
    Communication Abstracts, 503
    Educational Media International, 503
    Historical Journal of Film, Radio and
        Television, 503
    International Journal of Instructional
        Media, 503
    Journal of Educational Multimedia and
        Hypermedia, 503
    Journal of Popular Film and Television,
        503
    Learning, Media & Technology, 504
    Media & Methods, 504
    Multichannel News, 504
    MultiMedia & Internet@Schools, 504
    Multimedia Systems, 504
    Telematics and Informatics, 504
professional development
    Journal of Digital Learning in Teacher
        Education, 505
    Journal of Technology and Teacher
        Education, 505
publications, 481
simulation, gaming and virtual reality,
    505
special education and disabilities, 505

systems
  AI Magazine, 485
  Artificial Intelligence Review, 485
  International Journal of Robotics
    Research, 485
  Journal of Intelligent and Robotic
    Systems, 486
  Journal of Interactive Learning
    Research, 486
  Knowledge-Based Systems, 486
  Minds and Machines, 486
  telecommunications and networking,
    505–506
Mobile technology
  global-mobile stories, 13
  innovative peace education, 19
  Israeli and Palestinian students, 15
  strategizing process, 13
Moore, G., 50
Multimedia
  design, 124
  enhanced PBL, 114
  environment, 122
  learning, 117
Muronago, K., 202
My Stuff, 56, 57

N
National board for professional teaching
    standards (NBPTS), 219
National Commission on Teaching and
    America's Future (NCTAF), 210
National Council for the Accreditation of
    Teacher Education (NCATE), 210
National Science Digital Library (NSDL),
    54–55
National Telecommunications and Information
    Administration (NTIA), 174
NBPTS. *See* National board for professional
    teaching standards
NCATE. *See* National Council for the
    Accreditation of Teacher Education
NCSLMA. *See* North Carolina School Library
    Media Association
NCTAF. *See* National Commission on
    Teaching and America's Future
Nerad, M., 108
Neuman, 159–160
Neuman, S.B., 159–160, 189
Neuman, D., 219–225
NGOs. *See* Non-governmental organizations
Non-governmental organizations (NGOs), 16
Norman, J., 12

North Carolina School Library Media
    Association (NCSLMA), 190
NSDL. *See* National Science Digital Library
NTIA. *See* National Telecommunications and
    Information Administration

O
Oatman, E., 94
O'Neil, J., 141
Online discussions
  asynchronous, 37, 38
  BlackBoard forums, 40
  in-depth critical thinking, 40
Open educational resource, 14
Orey, M., 3–6, 247, 333, 374
Organizations and associations, North
    America, 247
Organizations and associations, US
    and Canada
  Adaptech Research Network, 249–250
  Agency for Instructional Technology
    (AIT), 250–251
  American Association of Colleges for
    Teacher Education (AACTE),
    251–252
  American Association of Community
    Colleges (AACC), 252
  American Association of School Librarians
    (AASL), 253
  American Educational Research
    Association (AERA), 253–254
  American Foundation for the Blind (AFB),
    254–255
  American Library Association (ALA),
    255–256
  American Society for Training and
    Development (ASTD), 256–257
  Anadolu University, 351–353
  Andong National University, 344–345
  Appalachian State University, 410–411
  Arizona State University; Educational
    Technology program, 356–357
  Association for Childhood Education
    International (ACEI), 257–258
  Association for Computers and the
    Humanities (ACH), 258–259
  Association for Continuing Higher
    Education (ACHE), 259
  Association for Educational
    Communications and Technology
    (AECT), 259–260
  Association for Experiential Education
    (AEE), 260–261

Organizations and associations, US
     and Canada (*cont.*)
  Association for Library and Information
       Science Education (ALISE), 261–262
  Association for Library Collections and
       Technical Services (ALCTS),
       262–263
  Association for Library Service to Children
       (ALSC), 263
  Association of American Publishers
       (AAP), 263–264
  Association of Specialized and Cooperative
       Library Agencies (ASCLA), 266
  Association of College and Research
       Libraries (ACRL), 265–266
  Athabasca University, 335–337
  Azusa Pacific University, 362
  Ball State University, 451–452
  Barry University, 369–370
  Bemidji State University, 461
  Bloomsburg University, 419
  Boise State University, 379
  Boston University, 391–392
  Brigham Young University, 433–434
  Buffalo State College, 411–412
  California State Polytechnic University,
       444–445
  California State University at East Bay, 358
  California State University, Fresno, 447–448
  California State University Monterey Bay
       (CSUMB), 445–447
  California State University-San
       Bernardino, 359
  Canadian Library Association/Association
       canadienne des bibliothèques (CLA/
       ACB), 267
  Canadian Museums Association/
       Association des musées canadiens
       (CMA/AMC), 268
  Centre for Educational Technology,
       University of Cape Town (CET), 269
  Clarke College, 386
  Close Up Foundation (CUF), 269–270
  Computer Assisted Language Instruction
       Consortium (CALICO), 270
  Concordia University, 340–341
  Concordia University Wisconsin, 476–477
  Consortium of College and University
       Media Centers (CCUMC), 271
  Council for Exceptional Children (CEC), 272
  Dakota State University, 425–426
  Delete (NASTA), 272–273
  Drexel University, 419–421
  East Carolina University, 405–406, 463

Eastern Michigan University, 397–399
East Stroudsburg University, 471–472
East Tennessee State University, 429
East–West Center, 273–275
Educational Communications, Inc.,
     Environmental and Media Projects
     of, 276–277
Education Development Center, Inc.
     (EDC), 275
Education Northwest (Formerly Northwest
     Regional Educational Laboratory),
     276
Edvantia, Inc. (Formerly AEL, Inc.)
     (Edvantia), 277–278
Emporia State University, 388, 454–455
ENC Learning Inc. (ENC), 278
Ewha Womans University, 344
Fairfield University, 365
Film Arts Foundation (Film Arts), 278–279
Fitchburg State College, 393
Florida Institute of Technology, 367–368
Florida State University, 370–371
Fordham University, 412
The George Lucas Educational Foundation
     (GLEF), 326–328
George Mason University, 435–436
George Washington University, 366–367
Georgia Southern University, 373
Georgia State University, 373–374
Governors State University, 380
Great Plains National ITV Library (GPN),
     279–280
Hacettepe University, 350–351
Harvard University, 394–395
Health Sciences Communications
     Association (HeSCA), 280
Indiana State University, 385–386
Indiana University, 452–453
Institute for the Future (IFTF), 280–281
Instructional Technology Council (ITC), 282
International Association for Language
     Learning Technology (IALLT), 283
International Association of School
     Librarianship (IASL), 283–284
International Center of Photography (ICP),
     284–285
International Council for Educational
     Media (ICEM), 285–286
International Recording Media Association
     (IRMA), 286–287
International Society for Performance
     Improvement (ISPI), 287–288
International Visual Literacy Association
     (IVLA), 288–289

Iowa State University, 387
Ithaca College, 413
Kansas State University, 388–390
Keimyung University, 346
Kent State University, 415
Knowledge Alliance, 289–290
Learning Point Associates, 290–291
Lehigh University, 421–422
Lesley University, 393–394
Library Administration and Management
    Association (LAMA), 291
Library and Information Technology
    Association (LITA), 292
Lister Hill National Center for Biomedical
    Communications (HNCBC), 292–293
Louisiana State University, 391
McDaniel College (formerly Western
    Maryland College), 396
Media Communications Association–
    International (MCA-I), 293–294
Medical Library Association (MLA),
    294–295
Metropolitan State College of Denver, 448
Michigan State University, 399
Mid-continent Research for Education and
    Learning (McREL), 295–296
Middle East Technical University, 350
Minorities in Media (An Affiliate of the
    Association for Educational
    Communications & Technology)
    (MIM), 296–297
Montclair State University, 467–468
Morehead State University, 456–457
National Aeronautics and Space
    Administration (NASA), 297
National Alliance for Media Arts and
    Culture (NAMAC), 298
National Association for Visually
    Handicapped (NAVH), 298–299
National Association of Media and
    Technology Centers (NAMTC),
    299–300
National Commission on Libraries and
    Information Science (NCLIS), 300
National Communication Association
    (NCA), 301
National Council of Teachers of English:
    Commission on Media, Assembly
    on Media Arts (NCTE), 301–303
National EBS Association (NEBSA), 303
National Endowment for the Humanities
    (NEH), 304
National Federation of Community
    Broadcasters (NFCB), 304–305

National Film Board of Canada (NFBC), 305
National Freedom of Information Coalition
    (NFOIC), 305–306
National Gallery of Art (NGA), 306–307
National PTA (National PTA), 307
National Public Broadcasting Archives
    (NPBA), 308
National Telemedia Council Inc.(NTC),
    308–309
Native American Public Telecommunications
    (NAPT), 309–310
Natural Science Collections Alliance (NSC
    Alliance), 310
The NETWORK, Inc. (NETWORK), 328
New England School Library Association
    (formerly New England Educational
    Media Association) (NESLA
    (formerly NEEMA)), 311
New York Festivals (NYF), 311–312
New York Institute of Technology, 466–467
New York University, 469–470
North Carolina State University, 406–407
Northern Illinois University, 382–383
Northwest College and University Council
    for the Management of Educational
    Technology (NW/MET), 312–313
Northwest Missouri State University, 401
Nova Southeastern University–Fischler
    Graduate School of Education and
    Human Services, 368–369
Oakland University, 458–459
OCLC Online Computer Library Center,
    Inc. (OCLC), 313–314
The Ohio State University, 354
Ohio University, 416
Old Dominion University, 475–476
Online Audiovisual Catalogers (OLAC), 314
Ontario Film Association, Inc.
    (Association for the Advancement
    of Visual Media/Lassociation pour
    lavancement des médias visuels)
    (OLA), 314–315
Pacific Film Archive (PFA), 315–316
Pacific Resources for Education and
    Learning (PREL), 316–318
Penn State Great Valley School of
    Graduate Professional Studies, 472
Pennsylvania State University, 422–423
Pittsburg State University, 455–456
Purdue University, 453–454
Purdue University Calumet, 454
Reference and User Services Association,
    a Division of the American Library
    Association (RUSA), 318–319

Organizations and associations, US and
     Canada (*cont.*)
  Regis University, 448–449
  Research for Better Schools, Inc. (RBS), 319
  Richard Stockton College of New Jersey,
     468–469
  Rutgers-The State University of New
     Jersey, 409–410
  San Diego State University, 359–360
  San Francisco State University, 362–363
  San Jose State University, 360
  SERVE Center @ UNCG, 320–321
  Simmons College, 395–396
  Society for Photographic Education (SPE),
     321–322
  Society of Cable Telecommunications
     Engineers (SCTE), 322
  Society of Photo Technologists (SPT), 323
  Southern Illinois University at Carbondale,
     380–381
  Southern Illinois University Edwardsville,
     383–384
  Southwest Educational Development
     Laboratory (SEDL), 323–324
  Special Libraries Association (SLA),
     324–325
  State University College of Arts and
     Science at Potsdam, 413–414
  St. Cloud State University, 402
  Syracuse University, 470–471
  Taganrog State Pedagogical Institute, 346
  Teachers and Writers Collaborative
     (T&W), 325–326
  Temple University, 473
  Texas A&M University, 427
  Texas A&M University-Commerce, 475
  Texas A&M University-Texarkana, 478
  Texas Tech University, 430–431
  Towson University, 397
  Università della Svizzera italiana, 347–348
  Université de Poitiers, 343–344
  Universiti Sains Malaysia, 345–346
  University Continuing Education
     Association (UCEA), 329
  University of Alabama, 355–356
  University of Alaska Southeast, 440
  University of Arkansas, 442–443
  University of Arkansas at Little Rock,
     443–444
  University of Balearic Islands, 347
  University of Bridgeport, 449
  University of British Columbia, 339
  University of Calgary, 337–339
  University of Central Arkansas, 356

University of Central Florida, 371–372
University of Cincinnati, 416–417
University of Colorado Denver, 363–364
University of Connecticut, 365–366
University of Florida, 449–450
University of Geneva, 348–349
University of Georgia, 374–375
University of Hawaii-Manoa, 377–378
The University of Hong Kong, 342–343
University of Houston, 431–432
University of Illinois at Urbana-
     Champaign, 381–382
University of Louisville, 390–391
University of Manchester, 353–354
University of Massachusetts, Amherst,
     457–458
University of Memphis, 474
University of Michigan, 459–461
University of Missouri-Columbia, 402–403
University of Missouri–Columbia, 461–462
University of Missouri-Kansas City, 462
University of Montana, 404–405
University of Nebraska at Kearney, 408
University of Nebraska-Omaha, 408–409
University of New Brunswick, 340
University of North Carolina, 407
University of North Carolina at
     Wilmington, 463–464
University of North Dakota, 465
University of Northern Colorado, 364–365
University of Northern Iowa, 378–379
University of North Texas, 433
The University of Oklahoma, 418–419
The University of Rhode Island, 423
University of Saskatchewan, 341–342
University of South Alabama, 441–442
University of South Carolina Aiken and
     University of South Carolina
     Columbia, 424–425
University of Southern California, Rossier
     School of Education, 361–362
The University of Southern Mississippi,
     403–404
University of South Florida, 372–373
University of Tennessee-Knoxville, 430
The University of Texas at Austin, 428–429
University of Toledo, 417–418
University of Virginia, 437–438
University of Washington, 438–439
University of West Florida, 450–451
University of West Georgia, 375–376
University of Wisconsin-Madison, 477–478
Utah State University, 434–435
Utrecht University, 349–350

Valdosta State University, 376
Valley City State University, 465–466
Virginia Tech, 436–437
Walden University, 400–401
Wayne State University, 399–400
Western Illinois University, 384–385
Western Washington University, 439–440
WIDENER UNIVERSITY, 355
Wright State University, 414–415
Young Adult Library Services Association
    (YALSA), 329–330
Osterweil, S., 130

P

Palestine. *See also* Educational media and
    technology, Israeli and Palestinian
    childrenborders and conflict, 8–9
cross-border storytelling project, 13
peace education (*see* Peace education,
    Israelis and Palestinians)
Paradise, A., 69
Parker, I., 146
Patel, L., 69
Peace education, Israelis and Palestinians
global-mobile stories, model, 13–15
global stories and identities, 11–12
humanism, 11
mobile learning devices, 12–13
national identities, 11
and technology
    definition, 9
    encounter programs, 10
    human ills, 9–10
    media, 10
    re-conceptualization, 10
    Virtual Peace Education, 10
Perkins, D.N., 214
Persichitte, K.A., 99, 101
Plantz-Masters, S., 99–110
Popper, K.R., 42
Poverty
    Power of Reading, 193, 195
    school FRPL eligibility, 193, 194
    school library accessibility, 193–195
Power of Reading, 193–195
PowerPoint
    analytical thinking and understanding, 141
    click to add title and click to add text, 144
    cognitive end point, 148
    cognitive tool, 141
    critical artworks, groupthink, 142
    digital technologies, 139–140
    framework, 143

fresh instrument, 140
handy encounter, 145
human–technology dialogue, 147–148
increased levels, academic performance, 141
inhuman impact, 151
keyboard, 145
line force, 140
managed indeterminacy/invocation, 146
maximal efficiency, 149
method
    hermeneutic phenomenology, 142
    LEDs, 143
    objective/subjective phenomena, 142
mimetic interventions, 152
mimetic vehicles, 151
paratextual machines, 151
pedagogic relations, 150
"powerful" solutions, 149
practical exemplars, 140–141
punctum/evocative capacity, 150
relational esthetics, theory, 141
self-competence, synchrony and slide, 147
sensuous and mimetic, 152
shortening the circuit, 150–151
software tools, education setting, 139
stick and plan, 148
students attitude and orientation, 147
technicity, current mode, 149
visible proof, preparation and organization,
    148–149
windows open, 144–145
work-object/focal project, 145
Pribesh, S., 187–195
Problem-based learning (PBL). *See* Cognitive
    tools, media-rich
Professional development, 222

Q

Qualitative data, CCS
    classroom observation cycles, 60
    surveys, 59
    technology adoption, 60
Quantitative data, CCS, 58–59

R

Ragan, T.J.
    "A Multifactor Approach to Research in
        Instructional Technology", 232
    description, 231
    instructional technology, 232
    and Patricia, 233
    research, 232–233

Rankin, E.L., 141
Rasmussen, K.L., 100
Raths, J.D., 213
Reading
    adults, 95
    apprenticeship (RA) program, 95
    recreational, 93
    schools, 92
Redden, E., 108
Reese, D.D., 127–136
Reeves, T.
    description, 235
    instructional technology, seminary
        career, 236–237
        education, 235–236
        portfolio, 237
        research agenda, 237
        University of Georgia, 236
Reiser, R.A., 99, 100, 107
Research method selection, 29
Revised NBPTS library media standards
    assessment development, 224–225
    changes
        community partnerships, 222
        ethical information, 222
        leadership, 221
        specialist, 221–222
        technologies integration, 221
    description, 219–220
    development
        description, 222–223
        draft document, public comment, 223
        process, 223
        suggestions and recommendations, 224
    statements, 220–221
Rideout, V.J., 77
Rieber, L.P., 51–53
Ritchhart, R., 215
Roberts, D.F., 77
Rogers, E.M., 50, 52
Roles of counselors and librarians, 202
Ryle, G., 212

S
Sachs, J., 32
Salaway, G., 71
Saldivar, M.G., 49–64, 58
Salen, K., 130
Sarkodie-Manash, K., 165
Sawyer, J.K., 141
Saye, J.W., 122
Scaffolding, 149, 151, 152
Scardamalia, M., 42

Scepansky, J.A., 141
School counselors and media specialists
    AASL and ASCA, 200
    assignments, creation, 203
    counseling, 199–200
    electronic resources, 205–206
    foundation, laying, 204
    initiating student involvement, 204
    interdisciplinary collaboration, 201–202
    mental health, 199
    partnership, 200
    print resources, 204–205
    standards, 203–204
    website creation, 206
School librarians, literacy learning
    basals, 91
    courses, 96
    importants, 92
    literacy research, 91–92
    roles
        concierge, 92–93
        cruise director, 94–95
        Sherpa, 94
School libraries
    access issues, media centers (see Access
        issues, school library media centers)
    broadband connectivity, 174–175
    internet use, 173–174
    learning environments, broadband impacts
        administrators, 179–180
        description, 175
        innovative learning technologies, 177
        students, 176
        teachers, 178–179
        technology tools, 178
        web-based applications, 177–178
    librarian roles, 180–182
    thoughts and recommendations
        actors and actions, broadband issues,
            183–184
        broadband integration, 183
        educators and students, 181, 183
Schunk, D.H., 32
Schwartz, D.L., 131
Seaman, J., 70, 72
Self-regulated learning (SRL)
    learning goals, 27
    and SPS, 26
Senese, D.J., 106
Sentence period spacing (SPS)
    and cognitive learning processes
        APA, 24–25
        data collection and analysis, 28
        motivation and metacognition, 25–26

rationale, 27–28
research design, 28–29
self-efficacy, 32–33
self-regulated learning, 26–27
student-led research teams, 25
student perception, 33
team members, 25
team members and initiator project, 33
participation
conducting research, 29–30
graduate student, 30–31
new faculty member, 31
Serious games, 465
*Service America! Doing Business in the New
Economy*, 244
Shared Stuff, 57
Sharma, B., 71, 72
Sherpa, 94
Shulman, L.S., 100, 108
Smith, S.D., 71
Snelbecker, G.
APA and AERA, 241
career, 240
description, 239
educational technology leaders interviews,
240
*Learning Theory, Instructional Theory, and
Psychoeducational Design*, 240
Spinosa, C., 149
SRL. *See* Self-regulated learning
Standards
revised NBPTS library media (*see* Revised
NBPTS library media standards)
*Standards for the 21st Century
Student Learner*, 181
Stanford University School of Education
(SUSE), 14
Storytelling
Alien Rescue program, 5
class discussions, 4
collaborative learning tool, 4
CyGaMEs, 5–6
Educational Technology Related Doctoral
Programs, US, 5
edu-teKNOWiki, 4–5
issues and trends in instructional
technology, 4
onsite librarians, importance, 5
self-regulated learning, 3–4
TeacherMate, 3
Sumner, T.R., 49–64
Surface-and in-depth level critical thinking, 39
SUSE. *See* Stanford University School of
Education

Susskind, J.E., 141
Szabo, A., 141

T
Tan, O.S., 25
Tan, S.C., 37–46
Teacher effectiveness
capability, student, 209–210
characteristics development, 210
description, 209
helping professionals, 209
predictor, student learning, 210
Teacher professional development, 75–76
Teaching educational research methods, students
description, 23
participation, SPS
conducting research, 29–30
graduate student, 30–31
new faculty member, 31
skills and techniques, 23–24
SPS and cognitive learning processes
APA, 24–25
data collection and analysis, 28
motivation and metacognition, 25–26
rationale, 27–28
research design, 28–29
self-efficacy, 32–33
self-regulated learning, 26–27
student-led research teams, 25
student perception, 33
team members, 25
team members and initiator project, 33
team-based learning, 24
Technology adoption
evaluating teachers
criteria, 50
description, 49–50
integration stage, 51
qualitative and quantitative educational
researchers, 51
qualitative stage models, 52
reorientation, 51–52
technology adoption theorists,
50–51
qualitative and quantitative description, 53
Technology leadership, 180, 337
TEKS. *See* Texas essential knowledge and skills
Telecommunications and networking,
mediagraphy
Canadian Journal of Learning and
Technology, 505
Computer Communications, 506
EDUCAUSE Review, 506

Telecommunications and networking,
        mediagraphy (*cont.*)
    International Journal on E-Learning, 506
    The Internet and Higher Education,
        506
    Internet Reference Services Quarterly,
        506
    Internet Research, 506
    Online, 506
Texas essential knowledge and skills (TEKS),
        115
Tishman, S., 214
Tomlinson, K., 10
Toprac, P., 113–124
Training
    data from education week, 76
    and development, ASTDs, 68
Tsao, J.-W, 481
Tufte, E.R., 141
Turkle, S., 141, 142

U
UN Relief and Works Agency (UNRWA), 16
UNRWA. *See* UN Relief and Works Agency
Usher, D., 209

V
VEMA. *See* Virginia Educational Media
        Association
Virginia Educational Media Association
        (VEMA), 190

W
Waid, C.A., 107
Wang, C.J., 25
Wasicsko, M.M., 216
Wayda, V., 215
Wellman, J., 108
Wenger, E., 85
Wheeler, D., 82
Wheeler, S., 82
Wiki
    definition, 82
    edu-techKNOWiki (*see* edu-techKNOWiki
        project)
Wilson, B.G., 100
Wivagg, J., 122
Woodward, R., 215

Y
Yeap, L.L., 37
Yeomans, P., 82
Yuen, T.T., 113–124

Z
Zemke, R.
    EMTY, 243
    Figuring Things Out, 244
    *Service America! Doing Business in the
        New Economy*, 244
    Training, 243–244
Zhang, L.F., 168
Zimmerman, B.J., 26